THE SHADOW OF THE EMPRESS

The Shadow of the Empress

FAIRY-TALE OPERA
AND THE END OF
THE HABSBURG MONARCHY

Larry Wolff

STANFORD UNIVERSITY PRESS
Stanford, California

STANFORD UNIVERSITY PRESS
Stanford, California

© 2023 by Larry Wolff. All rights reserved.

No part of this book may be reproduced or transmitted in any form or by any means, electronic or mechanical, including photocopying and recording, or in any information storage or retrieval system, without the prior written permission of Stanford University Press. Printed in the United States of America on acid-free, archival-quality paper

Library of Congress Cataloging-in-Publication Data

Names: Wolff, Larry, author.
Title: The shadow of the empress : fairy-tale opera and the end of the Habsburg monarchy / Larry Wolff.
Description: Stanford, California : Stanford University Press, 2023. | Includes bibliographical references and index.
Identifiers: LCCN 2022046132 (print) | LCCN 2022046133 (ebook) | ISBN 9781503634589 (cloth) | ISBN 9781503635647 (paperback) | ISBN 9781503635654 (epub)
Subjects: LCSH: Opera—Political aspects—Austria—History—20th century. | Strauss, Richard, 1864-1949. Frau ohne Schatten. | Zita, Empress, consort of Charles I, Emperor of Austria, 1892-1989. | Charles I, Emperor of Austria, 1887-1922. | Habsburg, House of. | Kings and rulers in opera. | World War, 1914-1918—Austria—Music and the war. | Austria—History—1918-1938.
Classification: LCC ML3918.O64 W65 2023 (print) | LCC ML3918.O64 (ebook) | DDC 782.109436/130904—dc23/eng/20221004
LC record available at https://lccn.loc.gov/2022046132
LC ebook record available at https://lccn.loc.gov/2022046133

Cover art: Alfred Roller's 1919 design for the opening scene of *Die Frau ohne Schatten*, set on the roof terrace of the imperial palace (background). KHM-Museumsverband, Theatermuseum, Vienna. Roller's costume design for the Empress in her nightgown, intended for her first appearance on the roof terrace (inset). Lebrecht Music Arts / Bridgeman Images.

Text design: Elliott Beard

Typeset by Newgen North America in 10/14.75 Adobe Caslon Pro

For Josephine, my amazing daughter!
with love and admiration

Rien n'est plus difficile, et donc plus précieux, que de pouvoir décider.
NAPOLÉON BONAPARTE

N'interrompez jamais un ennemi qui est en train de faire une erreur.
NAPOLÉON BONAPARTE

La gloire est éphémère, mais l'obscurité est pour toujours.
NAPOLÉON BONAPARTE

The people came to the Queen about all sorts of family quarrels and neighbourly misunderstandings—from a fight between brothers over the division of an inheritance, to the dishonest and unfriendly conduct of a woman who had borrowed a cooking-pot at the last New Year's festival, and not returned it yet.

And the Queen decided everything, very, very decidedly indeed. At last she clapped her hands quite suddenly and with extreme loudness, and said—"The audience is over for today."

Everyone said, "May the Queen live forever!" and went out.
E. NESBIT, *The Story of the Amulet*

The non-sectarian girls' schools of good standing looked askance at would-be entrants whose parentage was as socially questionable, not to say bizarre, as that represented by Ravenal mère and père. The daughter of a professional gambler and an ex-show-boat actress would have received short shrift at the hands of the head mistress of Miss Dignam's School for Girls at Somethingorother-on-the Hudson.
EDNA FERBER, *Show Boat*

Just speak very loudly and quickly, and state your position with utter conviction, as the French do, and you'll have a marvelous time!
JULIA CHILD

Contents

Acknowledgments   xi

Introduction   1

PART I
Prewar
FAIRY-TALE EMPIRE

1 **Hofmannsthal's Viennese Celebrity**   13
   and Princess Zita's Habsburg Marriage

2 **Emblems of Imperial Marriage**   25
   The Golden Apple, the Silver Rose, the Human
   Shadow, the Dirigible Balloon

3 **Descent from the Imperial Heights**   40
   Karl, Zita, and Hofmannsthal in Galicia

4 **Marriage and Childbirth in the Imperial Dynasty**   54
   and the Fairy-Tale Opera
   Subterranean Development and Artistic
   Collaboration

5 **"A Traitor Wind"**   71
   Treachery in the Opera and in the Empire

6 *Hexentanz* — 89
   The Renunciation of Motherhood and the
   Assassination at Sarajevo

PART II
Wartime
HABSBURG CATASTROPHE, OPERATIC TRANSFIGURATION

7 *Menschenblut* — 109
   The Sons of Adam and the Outbreak of War

8 "**The Shadow Hovering in the Air**" — 128
   Wartime Propaganda, Musical Patriotism, and
   Operatic Collaboration

9 "**Spirit of the Carpathians**" — 144
   Military Service, the Preoccupations of Wartime,
   and the Trials of Separation

10 **The Empress at the Threshold** — 161
   The Imminence of Catastrophe and the Last
   Romantic Opera

11 **Empress Zita** — 180
   Imperial Motherhood and the Pursuit of Peace

12 **Departure from Schönbrunn** — 207
   The End of the Habsburg Monarchy and the
   Rebirth of Austrian Culture

PART III
Postwar
THE AFTERLIVES OF EMPRESSES

13 **The Emperor and the Empress** — 227
   In Exile in Switzerland and on Stage in Vienna

14 **Premiere 1919** — 247
   Die Frau ohne Schatten, the *Märchenkaiser*, and the
   Viennese Critics

15 **Imperial Afterlife** 266
The Politics of Hungarian Habsburg Restoration
and Austrian Operatic Repertory

16 **"The Thread of Past Time"** 290
Postimperial Perspectives in the 1920s

17 **Nazi Germany and Austrian Anschluss** 305
Political and Operatic Prospects in the 1930s

18 **The Empress in America** 331
Escape from Nazi Europe

19 **The Empress Returns** 347
Zita and *Die Frau ohne Schatten* after
World War II

Notes 367

Index 417

Acknowledgments

This was my pandemic book. I wrote it during the scariest and most insecure time of my life, and it became somehow essential to me to wake up every morning in 2020 to Hugo von Hofmannsthal and Richard Strauss and their collaboration, more than a hundred years earlier, on *Die Frau ohne Schatten*. The creation of opera through a time of catastrophe—World War I—was for me a reminder that scholarship could also continue even under frightening and unprecedented circumstances.

Die Frau ohne Schatten is an opera about the trials, the complications, and ultimately the marvelous entwinement to be found in marriage, and Perri Klass, my wife, my beloved companion, my closest friend, the only person who knows me, has helped me through these difficult years and made it imaginable for me to write this book. We have been locked down together, in different degrees of rigor, over the course of these years, and, even losing so much of the normal world, I have loved the world that we have made together.

Die Frau ohne Schatten is also an opera that sings passionately of the importance of childbirth and children, and though the pandemic has sometimes kept me apart from my children—no longer children—in complicated and unexpected ways, I have thought about them every day and lamented the ways that their lives have been touched by such unexpected circumstances. I have deeply admired the courage and spirit of Orlando, who has worked through this pandemic in the psychiatric emergency rooms of New York City; I have thoroughly appreciated the endeavor of Anatol as he took off for Taiwan to undertake strenuous quarantine, archival research, opera excursions, and the pursuit of dumplings in a global pandemic; and I have taken heart and found renewed resolve in watching Josephine complete her own pandemic book, which has already been published before mine. My book is dedicated to her, as she has always had an affinity for empresses.

I could not have written this book without the lifeline of my daily phone calls with my parents, even during the long months when we could not see each other during the pandemic. It was my father who told me the story of *Die Frau ohne Schatten*, many years ago when I was a child, and instilled in me a love of opera that has marvelously enriched my life and my scholarship. From my mother, born in Vienna, I received my sense of connection to the Habsburg world, and her family odyssey, her departure from Vienna at the age of four with her parents in 1938, has been a point of reference for me as I wrote this book about Vienna in the twentieth century. I was lucky to be working on this project at a time when I was regularly in touch with my brother, David Wolff, on a long visit from Japan; he so very well appreciates what opera means in our family and at the same time the pleasures and challenges of historical research. All of our grandparents were born as subjects of Habsburg Emperor Franz Joseph, and all lived as subjects of Emperor Karl and Empress Zita from 1916 to 1918. I have thought about my Habsburg grandparents constantly as I wrote this book.

My reflections on Hofmannsthal go back a very long way to a freshman seminar in the Harvard German Department with Professor Jack Stein in the fall of 1974, a seminar on the Strauss-Hofmannsthal collaboration and *Ariadne auf Naxos*. My junior tutorial in History and Literature at Harvard with Professor Dorrit Cohn focused on Viennese literature, with Hofmannsthal absolutely central, and my junior essay, written for her, was on the subject of Hofmannsthal and World War I, involving material that I have revisited in the writing of this book. It would be impossible for me to do justice to the ways that Dorrit Cohn shaped my scholarly interest in Vienna by helping me begin to appreciate the subtleties of Viennese literature and thought. As a graduate student at Stanford, also cross-registering at Berkeley, it was my great privilege to work on and think about the Habsburg monarchy with my professors Wayne Vucinich, Gordon Craig, and William Slottman.

Good friends have shaped my approach to writing this book, starting with Maria Tatar, whose brilliant studies of fairy-tale culture have been important to me over many years, and Philipp Ther, my great longtime friend at the University of Vienna, who has led the way in thinking about opera in relation to politics and society. At the height of the pandemic I found great pleasure in piano-saxophone duets with Philipp on Zoom, including the "Zita-Walzer".... I'm so lucky to have, as my inspirational friend and colleague, Mike Beckerman in the Music Department at New York University; his encouragement has helped me to take on the musical subjects that have become central to my work as a historian.

I'm immensely grateful to the readers for Stanford University Press, revealed as Pieter Judson and Alison Frank Johnson, who know so much more about so many aspects of this book than I do myself, who read the manuscript with such spectacular attention and generosity, and who have helped me immeasurably to make this a better book.

I have during this pandemic cherished my connections with friends and colleagues who care about opera, including Tamara Mitchel, Ke-Chin Hsia, Francesco Izzo, Gaia Varon, and Mauro Campus. It is immensely rewarding for me to work again with my wonderful editor at Stanford University Press, Margo Irvin.

Through the course of the pandemic different friends have given me great encouragement in and around New York City: let me mention Peter Baldwin and Lisbet Rausing on a rainy night on Waverly Place, Katy Fleming at the intersection of Christopher and Gay, and Pierre Saint-Amand in Madison Square Park.

At NYU Florence I've benefited from all kinds of support from my colleagues Lisa Cesarani, Lorenzo Ricci, Francesca Baldry, Elisabetta Clementi, Barbara Bonciani, and Alexa Farah. I was lucky to have the chance to discuss this project with the marvelous Gaia Servadio at Villa La Pietra shortly before her death. In the final stages of writing I've been hugely grateful for the assistance of the ideal research assistant, Paul Csillag of the European University Institute.

I've written this book through a long pandemic in Manhattan, in Cambridge, Massachusetts, in Wellfleet, Cape Cod, and at Villa La Pietra in Florence.

THE SHADOW OF THE EMPRESS

INTRODUCTION

"Something Big"

On January 26, 1911, the Semper Opera House in Dresden presented the premiere of *Der Rosenkavalier*, with music by the Bavarian composer Richard Strauss set to a libretto by the Viennese poet Hugo von Hofmannsthal. The opera was an instant hit—necessitating special trains to Dresden for another fifty performances that year, even as the opera was also being staged in Munich, Vienna, and Berlin. Hofmannsthal had been a celebrated lyric poet in the 1890s, already as a high school student at the age of seventeen, and had then given up poetry for drama in his twenties; he now found new celebrity with a broad musical public by collaborating with Strauss. For Strauss, ten years older, initially famous as a composer of orchestral tone poems (like *Don Juan*, *Don Quixote*, *Death and Transfiguration*, and *Thus Spoke Zarathustra*), opera offered a whole new musical vocation, and he found in Hofmannsthal a literary and dramatic sensibility that would bring out his own best musical work.

On February 26, 1911, exactly one month after the *Rosenkavalier* premiere, Hofmannsthal made some brief notes on an idea for a new project: "*Die Frau ohne Schatten* [*The Woman without a Shadow*], a fantastic drama. The Empress, a fairy daughter, is childless."[1] This project would preoccupy both Hofmannsthal and Strauss for the rest of the decade, conceived and begun before World War I, completed during the catastrophic war itself, but not actually performed till the war was over in 1919. The opera would tell the story of a mythological emperor married to a magical empress who could not bear children because she cast no shadow. Like Prince Tamino in Mozart's *Die Zauberflöte (The Magic Flute)*—which Hofmannsthal took as a point of reference from the beginning—the Empress would have to undergo trials in order to discover her own humanity and thus to win her shadow.[2]

On October 21, 1911, Archduke Karl, grandnephew of the reigning Habsburg Emperor Franz Joseph, married Princess Zita of Bourbon-Parma at Schwarzau Castle, fifty miles south of Vienna; Karl and Zita were to become, five years later, the last Habsburg emperor and empress. Zita, born in 1892, was a direct descendent of the Bourbon French King Louis XIV; her father was the deposed duke of Parma and her mother was the daughter of the deposed king of Portugal. She thus belonged to the very small and select set of families that were permitted to marry into the Habsburg dynasty. Growing up as part of a family of displaced royalty (a club that she would eventually join in her own right after the abolition of the Habsburg monarchy), she was married at nineteen in ivory satin and a diamond tiara, her wedding gift from Franz Joseph. The eighty-one-year-old emperor arrived at the wedding in an automobile which made a very modern impression.

The wedding band played a Viennese-style "Zita Waltz," specially composed by the military bandleader Hermann Dostal: a sweeping waltz melody in G major gave way to a second waltz melody in F, followed by a spirited and syncopated interlude in B-flat.[3] It was very much an occasional composition, one thoroughly in the nineteenth-century waltzing spirit of Johann Strauss II. The waltz both welcomed the Bourbon princess to the Viennese imperial family and also assimilated her foreign grandeur into a Viennese popular style. Five years later, on the occasion of Zita's accession as empress in 1916, the Viennese prodigy Erich Korngold would compose the "Empress Zita Hymn," imbued with the spirit of wartime patriotism.

In 1911 the Habsburg Emperor Franz Joseph in Vienna, the Hohenzollern Emperor Wilhelm II of Germany in Berlin, the Romanov Tsar Nicholas II in St. Petersburg, and the Ottoman Sultan Mehmed V in Constantinople all reigned imperially, and no one imagined that their dynasties and empires would all be swept away during and after World War I. Europe in 1911 was

Figure 1. The "Zita-Walzer" or "Zita Waltz" was composed in honor of Zita's wedding to Karl in 1911 by military bandleader Hermann Dostal. Written in the spirit of Johann Strauss II, the "Zita Waltz" welcomed the Bourbon princess into the Viennese imperial family by making use of a popular Viennese musical form. (Reproduced with the kind permission of the Bibliothèque Nationale de France)

a continent of imperial palaces and courts, imperial rituals and occasions, imperial alliances and rivalries, from Schönbrunn to Topkapi to the Winter Palace. With the death of Edward VII in 1910, George V became king of England, and in 1911 he traveled with Queen Mary to New Delhi where they were acclaimed at the Delhi Durbar as Emperor and Empress of India. A new imperial crown was created for the occasion with more than six thousand diamonds topped with a 32-carat emerald, an expression of confidence in the survival of the Indian empire, which itself then lasted only another generation, until Indian independence in 1947.

Dating back to the ancient Roman Empire, and followed by the Holy Roman Empire of the Middle Ages, an emperor was understood to hold the highest of sovereign rankings, making him politically the overlord even of kings. An emperor might rule over a diversity of lands and peoples rather than a single nation, and the Habsburg Empire attempted to sustain this model of imperial transnational government into the early twentieth century. In 1911 the only signal that dynastic empires were nearing the conclusion of their historical epoch came from China, where the last emperor of the Qing dynasty, five-year-old Puyi, faced the outbreak of the Xinhai Chinese Revolution, which led to the establishment of a republic. Krishan Kumar has noted the seeming viability of empires, even in the early twentieth century, in adapting to the circumstances of modern politics and society.[4]

At the time of his wedding in 1911, Archduke Karl was not the direct heir to the Habsburg Empire but stood just behind his cousin Archduke Franz Ferdinand, who would be assassinated at Sarajevo in 1914. Karl and Zita thus became the Emperor and Empress of Austria (and King and Queen of Hungary) in 1916 following Franz Joseph's death, but they had to surrender their thrones following World War I, when Austria became a republic. Without ever formally abdicating, they left the country in 1919, the same year that Strauss and Hofmannsthal placed the fairytale Emperor and Empress on the operatic stage in *Die Frau ohne Schatten*. Karl died young, in exile on Madeira in 1922, but Zita lived deep into the twentieth century, until 1989. Conceived in 1911 in the age of the late Habsburg Empire, and addressing allegorically the question of what made emperors and empresses human and humane, *Die Frau ohne Schatten* was produced only after the war when European empires had been abolished, when emperors and empresses had indeed become fairy-tale figures in postimperial culture.

Die Frau ohne Schatten *and* Die Zauberflöte

"Don't forget: I've still no work for the summer," wrote Strauss on March 17, 1911, from his villa in Garmisch in the Bavarian Alps. "Writing symphonies does not make me happy anymore."[5] Hofmannsthal took the hint and replied on March 20 from Rodaun on the outskirts of Vienna, proposing his new idea for *Die Frau ohne Schatten*.

> If we wanted once again to work on something big [*etwas Grosses*] it would have to have strong and colorful action. . . . I have something quite definite in mind which fascinates me very much. . . . It is a magic fairy tale [*Zaubermärchen*] in which two men and two women encounter one another.[6]

The two couples would be the Emperor (*der Kaiser*) and the Empress (*die Kaiserin*), dwelling in their imperial palace, and Barak the Dyer (*der Färber*) and the Dyer's Wife (*die Färberin*), living in a world of urban poverty. The Empress, who had no shadow and therefore could not have children, would seek to obtain the shadow and the fertility of the Dyer's Wife. Fairy-tale rivals for the same single shadow, the two women would eventually be brought to life by sopranos with rival claims upon the operatic audience; in Vienna in 1919 the sopranos would be Maria Jeritza as the Empress and Lotte Lehmann as the Dyer's Wife, both legendary figures in operatic history.

Strauss had established himself as an opera composer in Dresden in 1905, with *Salome*, taking the libretto from Oscar Wilde and offering a role of almost unprecedented drama to sopranos as the biblical princess, singing her final scene ecstatically to the severed head of John the Baptist. The work was musically daring in its dissonances, but it was the blasphemous dramatic content that made it impossible to produce in many European opera houses, including Vienna. Strauss's next opera, *Elektra*, performed in Dresden in 1909, was similarly violent and dissonant in its expressiveness, with another heroine who insisted upon bloody murder. Strauss took his libretto from the verse translation of Sophocles made by Hofmannsthal in 1903. This led to the collaboration of Strauss and Hofmannsthal on *Der Rosenkavalier*—which would, in turn, be followed by intricate collaborations, fully documented in the Strauss-Hofmannsthal correspondence, on *Ariadne auf Naxos* and *Die Frau ohne Schatten* before and during World War I, and then *Die ägyptische Helena* and *Arabella* after the war.[7]

The fairy-tale quality of *Die Frau ohne Schatten* was essential to Hofmannsthal from the beginning: "the whole thing colorful, with palace and hut, priests, ships, torches, rock tunnels, choruses, children." Hofmannsthal envisioned it in a modern Mozartean spirit, "in the same relation to *Die Zauberflöte* as *Rosenkavalier* to *Figaro*—that is, in neither case an imitation, but a definite analogy."[8] *Die Frau ohne Schatten* would echo the solemn Masonic fantasy of *Die Zauberflöte*, an enchanted and magical world in which princes sought to prove themselves worthy of enlightenment.

While *Der Rosenkavalier* was very explicitly an opera of Viennese society and manners, set in the reign of Empress Maria Theresa, *Die Frau ohne Schatten*, as a fairy-tale opera, had no precisely recognizable setting, though the libretto noted that the Emperor and the Empress ruled over the "Southeastern Islands"—which might suggest somewhere in Polynesia. Yet, though fairy tales could be conceived in the spirit of implicit orientalism, the figures of an emperor and empress would have been not the least fantastic or fabulous for European politics in the early twentieth century. In 1911 Strauss and Hofmannsthal lived as the subjects of the German and Austrian emperors.

"Problem Child"

Die Frau ohne Schatten, conceived in 1911, first performed in 1919, was a cultural project that bridged the prewar and postwar worlds, actually composed and completed during the war as a fairy-tale fantasy. Strauss later explained that this opera was a "problem child [*Schmerzenskind*] . . . completed in grief and worries during the war."[9] Its composition offers insight into the transformations of cultural modernism in the crucible of war, and the particular impact of World War I on European culture.[10] Both Hofmannsthal and Strauss were committed to the Austrian and German national causes, with the poet actually dedicating himself to writing wartime propaganda even as he completed the libretto for *Die Frau ohne Schatten*. They agreed that the opera should be held back in wartime, so that it might inaugurate the postwar era, which it finally did at the Vienna Opera in 1919. The opera's resonance would have been very different if it had been published in the aftermath of a German-Austrian victory, as the creators certainly intended, and this book will consider how its meaning in performance was transformed by changing cultural and political contexts across the twentieth century.

As a wartime work, the opera addressed what was to become one of the paramount issues of the postwar moment, the question of the relevance of emperors and empresses after four years of horrendous war perpetrated partly by imperial governments. The Russian tsar and tsarina were murdered by the Bolsheviks in July 1918, while the German kaiser abdicated as the war was ending and went into Dutch exile. In Austria-Hungary, Karl and Zita, after reigning for only two years, withdrew from political life in November 1918 without formally abdicating and went into Swiss exile in 1919—just as Strauss and Hofmannsthal were about to stage their fairy-tale opera about an emperor and an empress who must undergo trials in order to learn lessons of humanity.[11]

Die Frau ohne Schatten thus illuminates the moment when emperors and empresses gave up their political roles. In the case of Zita, her survival until 1989 meant that she had a long imperial afterlife across the bulk of the twentieth century. Many details of her life were assembled by the Austrian monarchist journalist Erich Feigl, and the recent movement for Zita's possible beatification has led to further scrutiny.[12] She never ceased to see herself as the Empress of Austria and Queen of Hungary, and her life would seem increasingly like a fairy tale as the period of her actual reign receded into the ever more remote past.

The prewar culture of Habsburg Vienna became a well-defined subject of historical study some sixty years ago when Carl Schorske published in the *American Historical Review* his pioneering article, "Politics and the Psyche in Fin-de-siècle Vienna: Schnitzler and Hofmannsthal." The cultural history of Austria after World War I has also prominently featured Hofmannsthal, as in the work of Michael Steinberg, *The Meaning of the Salzburg Festival: Austria as Theater and Ideology*, and Steinberg has translated and edited Hermann Broch's brilliant Austrian essay, *Hofmannsthal and His Time*.[13] Hofmannsthal, whose full intellectual career has been treated in an important Austrian study by Ulrich Weinzierl, remains a crucial figure for understanding the wartime evolution of culture and ideas from the prewar empire to the postwar Austrian republic.[14] The creation of *Die Frau ohne Schatten* occurred in the context of that historical evolution.

The view of *Die Frau ohne Schatten* as a "problem child" meant that Strauss continued to worry over its reception in the years following the premiere, but even when he was composing the work in 1916 he declared that he wanted it to be the "last Romantic opera"—both a culmination and a turning point in his operatic endeavors. He lived until 1949, witnessing the ongoing performance of the Strauss-Hofmannsthal operas, including *Die Frau ohne Schatten*, in the age of Nazi Germany and Austria.[15]

The original soprano stars of *Die Frau ohne Schatten* lived even longer, embodying and preserving the cultural legacy of Strauss and Hofmannsthal. Maria Jeritza, the Moravian soprano who created the role of the Empress in *Die Frau ohne Schatten*, was born in Brno, a subject of Franz Joseph who supposedly helped to advance her career, while Karl, as emperor, would make her an official court opera singer before the abolition of the court itself. Jeritza's brilliant artistic career evolved within the context of imperial and postimperial Habsburg culture; she brought a part of that legacy to America, and she died in New Jersey in 1982. German soprano Lotte Lehmann, who created the role of the Dyer's Wife in *Die Frau ohne Schatten*, left Europe in the 1930s and died in California in 1976.[16] These two sopranos who sang together on the stage in Vienna in 1919 had European and transatlantic careers in which their repertory roles became icons of postimperial culture, preserving rituals of performance that would register differently for new generations of singers and audiences. They lived to witness the rediscovery of *Die Frau ohne Schatten* after World War II, as an opera about the renewal of humane political leadership after a period of supreme brutality.

Though emperors and empresses came to seem increasingly remote, and even anachronistic, in the twentieth century, the premise of this book is that for the generation born at midcentury (including myself), the Habsburg Empire was the world of our grandparents. All four of my grandparents, whom I knew well, were born in the late 1890s as subjects of Franz Joseph and lived for two years as subjects of Karl and Zita. The lives of my grandparents belonged to the same epochal transition from imperial to postimperial society and culture, and they will play a part on the margins of this history. By a curious coincidence my own academic life has also intersected with the posthumous story of Empress Zita, in relation to the historical research undertaken as part of the (still ongoing) efforts toward her beatification and eventual sainthood. It was this unexpected involvement that started me thinking about the ways in which the afterlife of an empress might be considered supernaturally in relation to both the sanctity of religion and the magic of fairy tales. The particular trajectories of Strauss and Hofmannsthal, the specific passage from the prewar to the postwar worlds, and the distinctive characters of the Emperor and the Empress in *Die Frau ohne Schatten*—juxtaposed with the real-life Emperor and Empress Karl and Zita—suggest a modern connection between the lingering political implications of imperial charisma and the ideological intimations of European operatic culture.

Prewar

FAIRY-TALE EMPIRE

I

Hofmannsthal's Viennese Celebrity and Princess Zita's Habsburg Marriage

"The Miracle of Hofmannsthal"

In the late nineteenth century Franz Joseph was Emperor of Austria and, simultaneously, King of Hungary, ruling two separate realms jointly under two different titles according to the unique political form of the Austro-Hungarian compromise (*Ausgleich*) of 1867. His wife—Empress Elisabeth, a Bavarian princess by birth, known as Sisi—was Empress of Austria and Queen of Hungary, roles which she filled with a dramatically romantic mystique that drew upon her celebrated beauty and nervous temperament; she was often away from the Viennese court, with a particular affinity for the Greek island of Corfu where she established an alternative imperial residence of neo-Hellenic fantasy: the Achilleion.

In 1898 Empress Elisabeth was stabbed to death in Geneva, along the lakeside, by an Italian anarchist. Mark Twain, who was then in Austria, reported that the "consternation was stupefying," and predicted that the assassination "will still be talked of and described and painted a thousand years from now."[1] Adopting a peculiarly royalist tone, uninflected by his trademark irony, Twain paid lavish tribute to Elisabeth: "She was so blameless, the Empress; and so beautiful, in mind and heart, in person and spirit; and whether with a crown upon her head or without it and nameless, a grace to the human race, and almost a justification of its creation." (Twain almost seemed to echo

Edmund Burke writing about Marie Antoinette in *Reflections on the Revolution in France*.)[2] Rather less reverent, though still sympathetic to Elisabeth, was the reaction in the Viennese diary of nineteen-year-old Alma Schindler (four years before she became Alma Mahler): "The Empress is dead . . . a woman who never harmed a soul, who never got involved in politics, who never got anything out of life but pain and anxiety, which had caused her to grow depressive. Fancy stabbing such a poor broken woman!"[3] The Italian poet of decadence (and precursor of fascism) Gabriele D'Annunzio wrote a tribute of adulation to Elisabeth in 1898, viewing her assassination as a transfiguration: "With the violence of this unerringly aimed death blow there was suddenly revealed to our eyes the secret beauty of this imperial life." Her story was "like a myth," or like a fairy tale: "Is it not as if we had read about it years ago in an old book?"[4]

The D'Annunzio tribute, written in Italian, was then translated into German—by Hugo von Hofmannsthal. For Elisabeth had been the Empress of Hofmannsthal's childhood, a figure already quasi-mythological in her own lifetime and all the more so after her assassination. A marble monument of Elisabeth was unveiled in the Vienna Volksgarten in 1907. Even today Elisabeth's face, along with the face of Mozart, is one of the two most likely to be found on any souvenir Viennese box of chocolates.

While the imperial mystique and tragic assassination of Elisabeth exercised a fin de siècle fascination in the 1890s, the most politically important Habsburg empress reigned in the eighteenth-century: Maria Theresa, who initiated the crucial transformation of the Habsburg dynastic possessions into a modern administrative state. In *Der Rosenkavalier* Hofmannsthal conjured the rococo age of Vienna under Maria Theresa, and the leading soprano role, the exquisitely aristocratic Marschallin, allusively bore the same name as the empress: Marie Thérèse von Werdenberg.

The governess, teacher, and close companion of Empress Maria Theresa, dating back to her girlhood, was Countess Marie Karoline von Fuchs-Mollard, who received a little palace as a token of appreciation from the Empress and, eventually, even a burial place in the Habsburg imperial crypt, the Kapuzinergruft. The palace of Countess Fuchs—the "Fuchs-Schlössl"—was located in Rodaun and acquired by Hofmannsthal in 1901. He lived in the palace of Empress Maria Theresa's governess for the rest of his life.

On March 18, 1911, the Austrian legal scholar Joseph Redlich wrote to Hofmannsthal to congratulate him on the success of *Der Rosenkavalier*. For Redlich, the opera's success was also a matter of patriotic interest, something that "nourishes my pride as an Austrian and as your old and loyally admiring friend." He was particularly satisfied to see that "the age of the great Empress of Austria, who so strongly and happily incarnated the fame of Vienna and our innermost essence a century and a half ago, was magically conjured back to life."[5] Redlich regarded *Der Rosenkavalier* as an occasion to reflect upon the importance of Empress Maria Theresa in Austrian history and politics:

> The great Empress forged our state, and even today everything alive in it goes back to her, just as, I believe, everything cultural in our life is rooted in that epoch. Only when we will again have a strong Austrian state—indeed on other principles than those of Maria Theresa—will we also experience a powerful Renaissance of Austrian culture.[6]

This letter would have reached Hofmannsthal just as he was writing to Strauss to propose the new operatic project. In *Die Frau ohne Schatten* Hofmannsthal would actually place an empress on stage, and Strauss would make her sing with stunning beauty. She would eventually come to life in Vienna, the city of Maria Theresa, the city of Elisabeth, but she remained a fairy-tale empress, an empress without a name—"Die Kaiserin" in the opera program—capable of evoking a fantasy empire of the past or the future.

In 1697 the French writer Charles Perrault created the genre of the European literary fairy tale with a collection that included stories of fairy-tale royalty like "Cinderella" and "Sleeping Beauty." In 1704 Antoine Galland published in French the first translations from the Arabic collection of tales, the *Thousand and One Nights*, with stories often set in the medieval Baghdad caliphate of Harun al-Rashid. The Brothers Grimm, collecting oral folk narratives, published their landmark volume of German fairy tales—*Märchen*—in 1812. The Romantic writer E. T. A. Hoffmann composed his own literary fairy tales, such as "The Nutcracker and the Mouse King" in 1816, which was to become one of the most famous fairy tales in modern culture, especially after Tchaikovsky made it the basis of his ballet *The Nutcracker* in 1892. Writing within this literary tradition, in 1895 Hofmannsthal published a fairy tale called "Tale of the

672nd Night"—self-consciously inspired by the *Thousand and One Nights*—relating the story of a merchant's son and his four servants in a splendidly furnished mansion that stood in stark contrast to the harrowing world of the city outside.[7]

Hofmannsthal wrote to his German friend Count Harry Kessler in June 1911 about his idea for *Die Frau ohne Schatten*: "I have a wonderfully beautiful fantastic subject, made for music. . . . The atmosphere for the subject is the *Thousand and One Nights*, but to be quite bizarrely transposed as if seen through the eyes of the eighteenth century."[8] Mozart's *Die Zauberflöte* was the principal eighteenth-century point of reference, but Hofmannsthal also considered the possibility that the work might be "comical fantastic" in the style of Carlo Gozzi, the eighteenth-century Venetian writer who dramatized fairy-tale scenarios.[9] In the 1920s Puccini would look to Gozzi for the story of *Turandot*.

Vienna itself could appear as a fairy-tale city out of the *Thousand and One Nights*, and one young art student, who came to Vienna from the provinces in 1908, always remembered the magnificent buildings on the Ringstraße: "For hours I could stand in front of the Opera, for hours I could gaze at the Parliament; the whole Ring Boulevard seemed to me like an enchantment out of the *Thousand and One Nights*."[10] Those were the impressions of the young Adolf Hitler, who was actually in Vienna in 1911 when Hofmannsthal conceived of *Die Frau ohne Schatten*. Hitler saw himself as a struggling outsider in the art world of Vienna, whereas Hofmannsthal was the consummately privileged Viennese insider.

Hofmannsthal certainly identified himself with the merchant's son in the "Tale of the 672nd Night." The poet's Jewish great-grandfather Isaak Löw Hofmann, born in Bohemia in 1759 during the reign of Empress Maria Theresa, became an important silk merchant in Vienna and was ennobled by the Habsburg emperor in 1835. The poet's grandfather converted to Catholicism—as Hofmannsthal explained it, "in accord with a perfectly natural trend, perhaps the only possible one at the beginning of the nineteenth century, to step out of an isolation that no longer made any sense, and to enter what was generally considered the cultivated sphere."[11] In 1873, the year before the poet's birth, the Viennese stock market crash badly damaged the Hofmannsthal family fortune, but they preserved their title and prestige.

By the beginning of the twentieth century the family was so thoroughly assimilated into Austrian Roman Catholic aristocratic culture that when Hofmannsthal married the daughter of a Viennese Jewish banker in 1901, she converted to Catholicism for him.

His own family nobility—coming from silk—provided the background for what Austrian writer Hermann Broch regarded as Hofmannsthal's fairy-tale life.

> Every child is a fairy-tale figure to himself, but whereas other children's experiences of reality cause them to . . . become princes and princesses in their fantasies, young Hofmannsthal was already in reality—in any case his reality—a thorough fairy-tale prince, singled out by beauty and spirit and triumph, singled out by his own seclusion, singled out by the Emperor himself as a "nobleman," to the point where he felt a closer identification with the Emperor, that ornately costumed figure gazing down at him from the portrait on the classroom wall, than he did with his teachers and peers. . . . The vision of the Emperor would never quit Hofmannsthal's imagination. It remained a dream within a dream, a fairy tale within a fairy tale . . .[12]

For Hofmannsthal to envision a fairy-tale opera with an emperor and empress, tenor and soprano, as leading protagonists, was, in part, the dramatic projection of his own fairy-tale life.

The crucial episode of his personal fairy tale was the transformative moment, at the age of seventeen, when he became a famous poet. He had been writing under a pseudonym but now unmasked himself, and the leading figures of Viennese literary life learned that the dazzling lyric poetry by "Loris" had been written by a teenager in high school. Stefan Zweig, in his memoir of Vienna, *The World of Yesterday*, recounted the story of the discovery, when Viennese critic Hermann Bahr received a writing sample from the unidentified Loris:

> Bahr wrote at once to the unknown and arranged for a meeting in a coffee house—the famous Café Griensteidl, the chief meeting place of the young literati. One day a slender beardless Gymnasium [high school] student in short trousers approached his table with quick light steps, bowed, and, in a high voice which had not yet broken, said briefly and to the point, "Hofmannsthal! I am Loris."[13]

For Broch this was the fairy tale of Hofmannsthal as *Wunderkind*—comparable in Austrian artistic history to the story of Mozart as *Wunderkind* in the eighteenth century. Hofmannsthal was the miraculous poet-prince, descended from the Jewish silk merchant.

Following Bahr's discovery of Hofmannsthal, the leading Viennese writer of drama and fiction, Arthur Schnitzler—also a neurologist whom Freud once described as his own *Doppelgänger*—invited the teenage poet to come read his work. Zweig related the story as told to him later by Schnitzler:

> Hofmannsthal appeared in his short trousers, somewhat nervous and ill at ease, and began to read. "After a few minutes," Schnitzler told me, "we riveted our attention on him, and exchanged astonished, almost frightened, glances. We had never heard verses of such perfection, such faultless plasticity, such musical feeling, from any living being."[14]

Hofmannsthal's precocious genius was considered to be somehow magical within the literary world of fin de siècle Vienna. He instantly became the center of the flourishing Viennese cult of aestheticism: "His language glowed darkly with purple and gold, shimmered with world-weary mother of pearl," according to historian Carl Schorske. "Small wonder too that he became the idol of Vienna's culture-ravenous intelligentsia."[15] Hofmannsthal would later have to wrestle with the implications of this hothouse aestheticism of which he became the emblem.

Stefan Zweig, seven years younger than Hofmannsthal, belonged to the cohort of schoolboys who were most starstruck by the teenage poet, and they too began avidly to write poetry of their own as teenagers.

> Without hoping that any of us could ever repeat the miracle of Hofmannsthal, we were none the less strengthened by his mere physical existence. It proved tangibly that a poet was possible in our time, in our city, in our midst. For after all, his father, a banker, came from the same Jewish middle class as the rest of us; this genius had grown up in a house similar to our own.[16]

A generation of artistically inclined schoolboys dreamed of becoming Hofmannsthal and participated in his cult. The fairy tale of his discovery offered space to the fantasy of other boys, the possibility of miraculous artistic flowering in the unexpected context of quotidian Viennese childhood.

The flavor of Hofmannsthal's teenage poetry may be taken from a poem of 1892, when he was eighteen, written as a poetic prologue to Schnitzler's drama of Viennese libertinism, *Anatol*. The poem conjured a magnificent eighteenth-century Viennese garden where plays could be staged in the open air, and Hofmannsthal explored the idea that life itself was theatrical:

Also spielen wir Theater,	So we play theater
Spielen unsre eignen Stücke,	Play our own pieces,
Frühgereift und zart und traurig,	Precociously ripe and tender and sad,
Die Komödie unsrer Seele,	The comedy of our soul,
Unsres Fühlens Heut und Gestern,	Our feelings of today and yesterday,
Böser Dinge hübsche Formel,	Unpleasant things in pretty forms,
Glatte Worte, bunte Bilder,	Smooth words, colorful pictures,
Halbes, heimliches Empfinden,	Secret semi-sensations,
Agonien, Episoden . . .	Agonies, episodes . . .
Manche hören zu, nicht alle . . .	Some are listening, but not all . . .
Manche träumen, manche lachen,	Some are dreaming, some laughing,
Manche essen Eis . . . und manche	Some eating ice cream . . . and some
Sprechen sehr galante Dinge. . . .	Are saying very gallant things. . . .[17]

The gently hypnotic rhythms of "glatte Worte, bunte Bilder," the cryptic punctuation with dreamy ellipses, suggest the mesmerizing effect that Hofmannsthal had on his public, even as he alerted them to the tender and perhaps painful secrets and sensitivities that lay just beneath the social surfaces of charming conversation and cold ice cream.

Habsburgs and Bourbons

The future Empress Zita was born in 1892, the same year that Hofmannsthal wrote his prologue to Schnitzler's *Anatol*. Although the poet evoked the dusty elegance of the *ancien régime* in the spirit of cultural nostalgia, the princess would actually grow up in the surviving social structures of that world. "I had in my family an unusually merry and happy childhood," recalled Zita. "We were, all together, twenty-four brothers and sisters."[18] All of them were princes and princesses by title (three died in infancy), all to be addressed as "Your Royal Highness." They were the children of Duke Robert of Bourbon-Parma, who was a reigning sovereign only from the age of six to eleven, deposed in 1859 when the duchy of Parma was about to be incorporated into the kingdom of Italy. He later married twice, fathering two large sets of half-siblings, rivals for their father's substantial riches and empty claims. The children were also eligible for royal marriages—or marriages to royal pretenders—though some of the daughters ended up in extremely well-endowed convents. Zita, the seventeenth of the twenty-four children, was rewarded with the most splendid fairy-tale outcome of all her siblings when she became the Empress of Austria.

She spent her childhood moving back and forth—with the whole clan of siblings—between two particular palaces, Villa Pianore near Lucca in Italy (where Zita was born) and Schloss Schwarzau near Vienna. Her father also inherited from his uncle the spectacular French Renaissance Château de Chambord in the Loire Valley. Schloss Schwarzau was established as an Austrian home for the Bourbon-Parma family in part because of its close proximity to Schloss Frohsdorf, legendary for its associations with deposed and exiled royalty: first, the daughter of Louis XVI and Marie Antoinette, Marie Thérèse, who survived the French Revolution and lived at Frohsdorf until her death in 1851, and then her cousin the Count de Chambord, the Bourbon pretender to the throne of France as Henry V, who died at Frohsdorf in 1883. Zita's whole Bourbon-Parma family life took place in the shadow of interconnected histories of deposed dynasties.

Already as a child she became aware of her future husband as the friend of her brother Prince Sixtus. "I don't know anymore when I first saw Archduke Karl," recalled Zita. "He came to us and lived with us at Schwarzau . . . we made mischief together, hunted, and swam . . . we were children in the same family circle." She even remembered the future emperor's childhood initiation as a hunter: "With us in Schwarzau he killed his first rabbit and was mightily proud of it."[19] The Emperor in *Die Frau ohne Schatten* would be a fiercely dedicated hunter, a characteristic Habsburg passion. Hofmannsthal imagined the Emperor falling in love while hunting, when he pursued a gazelle who turned out to be a supernatural being in animal form: the Empress.

Zita learned to play the piano as a child and even played the organ in the family chapel at Schwarzau. Music continued to play a part in her education when she was sent away for a year to study at the Benedictine convent on the Isle of Wight, St. Cecilia's, where her German grandmother Princess Adelaide of Braganza lived as a nun, the widow of the Portuguese pretender.[20] Zita herself would have a lifelong sense of affiliation with the Benedictines and would later spend long retreats at the convent at Solesmes in France. After her grandmother died in 1909, the seventeen-year-old Zita left her convent school to spend some time at the Habsburg Bohemian spa at Franzensbad (Františkovy Lázně) with her cousin Habsburg Archduchess Maria Annunziata. There they were visited by Archduke Karl, who as a young Habsburg officer was stationed not too far away at his Bohemian garrison.[21]

"I would never have thought that Austria was foreign for me," she commented—though Austrians would sometimes think of her as a foreign empress when Austria was fighting against France and Italy during World War I. It was easy for her to embrace the Habsburg mission based on a "transnational universal imperial idea"—for as the child of a deposed dynasty she was herself fundamentally transnational.[22] "Parma was once a dreamland for artists," she reflected, mentioning the Renaissance painters Correggio and Parmigianino. The idea of Parma as a dreamland and of her own dreamy relation to its cultural legacy allowed her, as a princess in exile, to feel at home everywhere.

Marcel Proust (precisely of Hofmannsthal's literary generation) invented a fictional Princess of Parma as one of the titled luminaries in the Paris circle of the Guermantes family. Proust's fictional princess would have come from the same deposed dynasty as Zita, but Zita's mystique was dramatically enhanced by her marriage into an actually sovereign dynasty, her translation from a Bourbon-Parma princess into a Habsburg archduchess. Hofmannsthal too, the magically inspired *Wunderkind* and poet-prince, knew what it was like to experience life as a fairy tale. His personal and family history shaped his conception of the fairy-tale opera and helped him to imagine a fairy-tale empress on the operatic stage.

The Awakening of the Empress

"I want a palace with columned halls and hanging gardens [*mit Säulenhallen und hängenden Gärten*]," Empress Elisabeth is supposed to have fantasized in the 1880s as she envisioned the Achilleion on Corfu. The palace was to shelter her from all intruding eyes—"like a fairy tale, proud, and holy [*märchenhaft, hochmütig, heilig*]," worthy of Achilles who despised all mortal men.[23]

Her words could have described the opening scene of *Die Frau ohne Schatten*, for the opera begins on the roof terrace of the imperial palace, overlooking the imperial gardens. The Empress herself does not step on stage for the first ten minutes, but Strauss and Hofmannsthal made those ten minutes all about her, even in her absence.

The Messenger of the Empress's father, Keikobad, has come to ask whether she, the spirit daughter of a spirit king, has become human enough to cast a shadow after a full year of marriage to a mortal emperor. Her companion, the Nurse, replies that the Empress does not cast a shadow: "light passes through her body as if she were made of glass." The Nurse's words instantly evoke the Empress, the notes sensuously leaping to a sustained high F-sharp along with a solo violin and solo cello, while the shimmering F-sharp chords of two celestas ring delicately as if to suggest the tinkling of glass.[24] The leaping theme—up a fourth and then another full octave—is closely associated with the empress throughout the opera. Immediately, it is clear that the Nurse is enraptured with the Empress whom she serves, even as the composer and librettist lure the audience into the spirit of that rapture.

The Messenger harshly condemns the Nurse for having failed to keep the Empress in custody, for allowing the Emperor to carry her off. The Nurse defends herself with further revelations of the Empress's nature: she had been given the power of metamorphosis, so that she could always elude custody, could become a bird or a gazelle.[25] The Messenger asks if he can see the Empress, to confirm that she is shadowless, but the Nurse replies that the Empress is not alone. She is always with the Emperor all night long, for he always desires her. "He is a hunter and a lover—and nothing else," says the Nurse, disdainfully, but not without sensual relish. The Messenger, however, declares that, if the Empress still cannot cast a shadow in three days, the Emperor will be turned to stone, and the marriage between human emperor and spirit empress will be over.

And still the Empress does not appear. It is the Emperor who comes on stage, directly from their marital bed, sexually invigorated in tenorial exuberance. There is a hint of dawn in the sky, and it is time for him to go hunting. "Die Herrin schläft" (the mistress sleeps), he explains to the nurse, singing the Empress's own ascending theme, jumping the octave to a tenor's high F-sharp, sustained across the bar. He recalls, along with the clarinet, his first

Figure 2. In the opening scene Strauss introduced his most expansive melody, the theme of the Emperor's passionate love for the Empress, "Denn meiner Seele und meinen Augen" (for of my soul and of my eyes). Singing in the heroic key of E-flat, his tenor voice is warmly and vigorously accompanied by the strings but also ornamented by the harps that hint at the delicacy of the Empress, the object of his passion. He is the hunter, and "she is the prize of all prizes." (*Die Frau ohne Schatten*, 1919)

encounter with the Empress when he hunted her in the form of a white gazelle, and then the retransformation by which she became, in his arms, a woman. Strauss's full orchestra sounds the long melodic line of his romantic passion, which the tenor himself sings out at the conclusion of the scene in the heroic key of E-flat: "Denn meiner Seele und meinen Augen und meinen Händen und meinem Herzen ist sie die Beute aller Beuten" (Of my soul and my eyes, my hands, my heart, she is the prize of all prizes). The word for prize is a hunting term, "Beute"—more prey than prize—as the Emperor hurls his tenorial masculinity into a high B-flat and exits the scene, which is finally prepared for the entrance of the Empress.[26]

Dawn has now arrived, with birdsong in the flutes, harps, and tremolo strings, and the key gradually shifts from the Emperor in sonorous E-flat to the Empress in the transcendent dimension of F-sharp. She sings in intimate dialogue with the solo violin, as if with her inner self, and accompanied by harps, like an angel. She longs to go back to sleep and to dream herself back into the form of a bird, as Strauss ornaments her vocal line with runs and trills. She touches the top notes of the musical staff, returning to high F-sharp and G-sharp, but sometimes reaching up to B and even to high D.[27] Hofmannsthal introduces her as a fairy-tale spirit and Strauss immediately establishes her musical mystique. The Emperor's falcon, however, appears from the sky and warns her that if she cannot cast a human shadow within three days the Emperor will be turned to stone. So she prepares to descend—as fairy-tale empresses must do—from the heights of the imperial palace to the depths of the human city, in search of a human shadow.[28]

2

Emblems of Imperial Marriage

THE GOLDEN APPLE, THE SILVER ROSE, THE HUMAN SHADOW, THE DIRIGIBLE BALLOON

Habsburg Baroque

In his letter of March 20, 1911, Hofmannsthal imagined *Die Frau ohne Schatten* from the very beginning in an elaborate staging that involved torches and tunnels, ships and palaces. It was to be opera on the grandest and most imposing scale: "The whole thing really hovers before my eyes with real force and even disturbs me at work."[1] Vienna was once the city of magnificent baroque spectacles, dating back to the age of Habsburg Emperor Leopold I (the direct ancestor of Karl, nine generations back), cultural rival and military enemy of the Bourbon French King Louis XIV. Leopold, himself a talented composer, was a great patron of baroque opera—including all the kinds of spectacular stage effects and lavish scenery that Hofmannsthal later envisioned for *Die Frau ohne Schatten*. Leopold presented in Vienna an epic performance of Antonio Cesti's opera *Il pomo d'oro* (*The Golden Apple*), originally scheduled to celebrate the Emperor's wedding to his cousin, the fifteen-year-old Spanish Infanta Margarita Teresa in 1666. The production, however, was so challenging, with more than twenty changes of scenery, that it had to be postponed for her seventeenth birthday in 1668, when she was already reigning as empress. Margarita Teresa was no stranger to artistic attention: when she was only five, the Spanish artist Diego Velázquez painted her at the dead center of his masterpiece *Las Meninas* of 1656, the self-conscious child star of the Spanish Habsburg court in Madrid.

The production of *Il pomo d'oro* in 1668 required baroque machines to create the effects of storms, earthquakes, and dragons, and a huge cast of singers and ballet dancers performed five very long acts over the course of two days in a specially constructed theater. In the end, the golden apple would be awarded not to Juno, not to Venus, not to Pallas Athena, but to Empress Margarita Teresa herself, in the audience with Leopold.

> To the most exalted princess the world has ever seen, or will see; the daughter and wife of the greatest monarch of the world; the most beautiful, most powerful, wisest of all . . . in that she unites the fame of Venus through her beauty, the excellence of Pallas through her intellect, and the glory of Juno through her bravery, each of these goddesses may congratulate herself that she has received the golden apple.[2]

The designer of the spectacle was Ludovico Burnacini, and his concluding *coup de théâtre* showed the Emperor and the Empress appearing in the clouds among their Habsburg ancestors and descendants.[3] Historian R. J. W. Evans has observed that, in the absence of a coherent early modern central government, the Habsburg enterprise rested crucially upon the baroque court and Habsburg patronage of the arts, including "the dramatic extravagance of opera."[4] Evans has argued further that baroque art, including opera, contributed to the ideological legitimacy of Habsburg rule, and, in fact, *Il pomo d'oro* featured an allegorical figure of Austrian Glory (*La Gloria Austriaca*) singing in a soprano voice.

When Margarita Teresa married Emperor Leopold in 1666, she acquired the venerable title of Empress of the Holy Roman Empire, an imperial role that dated back to the ninth century with Empress Ermengarde, wife of Louis the Pious, the son of Charlemagne. Margarita Teresa died in 1673 at the age of twenty-one, but in *Il pomo d'oro* she had been already deified in operatic form. Hofmannsthal, when he proposed to Strauss in 1911 an opera with tunnels and torches, was certainly imagining something like the baroque spectacles of the seventeenth-century, with lavish changes of scene and an emperor and empress who would occupy an elevated sphere that mediated between gods and humans. *Die Frau ohne Schatten* would also feature a sort of earthquake—as in *Il pomo d'oro*—and the neobaroque staging would even require a golden fountain at the threshold of the spirit world. At the moment of its eventual premiere in 1919, *Die Frau ohne Schatten* was recognized in the Viennese press as a "festival opera, like the old baroque operas, suitable for elevating the audience above its daily human world."[5] Baroque operas, like *Il pomo d'oro*, could present scenarios of power and magnificence relevant to the ideological legitimation of early modern Habsburg rule, and *Die Frau ohne Schatten*, with its operatic presentation of imperial rulers, was similarly implicated in the modern cultural construction of dynastic political legitimacy, though that significance was transformed by the collapse of the dynasty itself in 1918.

For *Der Rosenkavalier* Hofmannsthal scripted the presentation of a silver rose, not a golden apple, and the recipient was not a seventeen-year-old empress but Sophie von Faninal, the fifteen-year-old daughter of an ennobled bourgeois merchant, representing a parvenu family with some resemblance to Hofmannsthal's own eighteenth-century ancestry. It was Sophie who received the ultimate prize in the opera's happy ending, marrying Count Octavian, a nobleman of impeccable descent inscribed in the Almanach de Gotha. In *Die Frau ohne Schatten* the fairy-tale empress would be seeking not a silver rose, and not a golden apple, but a human shadow with the promise of a human family.

The wedding of Leopold and Margarita Teresa in 1666 was an ongoing baroque spectacle, from the fireworks that welcomed the infanta to Vienna in 1666 to the great equestrian ballet of carnival season in January 1667, with giant machines to represent Habsburg supremacy over the elements: the clouds of the air, the mountains of the earth, and the ship of state at sea. The actual operatic performance of *Il pomo d'oro* in 1668 for the Empress's birthday was therefore the culmination of the nuptial festivities that had been already in spectacular progress for two years. The twentieth-century wedding of Karl and Zita at Schloss Schwarzau in October 1911, the year that Hofmannsthal first envisioned *Die Frau ohne Schatten*, presented a very different sort of spectacle. Royalty was present: Emperor Franz Joseph, the heir apparent Archduke Franz Ferdinand, and the royal family of Saxony (as Karl's

Figure 3. The wedding of Karl and Zita in October 1911 at Schloss Schwarzau was attended by Emperor Franz Joseph, eighty-one years old. He presented Zita with her diamond tiara as a wedding gift. In this photograph he is accompanied by Karl's mother, Princess Maria Josepha of Saxony (who was also a cousin of Zita's within the Portuguese royal family). At this traditional dynastic ceremonial union there were some very modern elements: for instance, airplanes flew overhead in tribute to the young couple who were aviation enthusiasts. (Reproduced with the kind permission of the Österreichische Nationalbibliothek)

mother was a Saxon princess). The wedding entertainment was provided by a military band, and the program might have served for a far less elevated wedding. In addition to the "Zita Waltz," composed for the occasion, there were waltzes by Johann Strauss II and Franz Lehár, and arrangements from Strauss's operetta *The Gypsy Baron* and Leo Fall's *The Dollar Princess*.[6] These latter works were middle-class fantasies of aristocracy and princessdom, the former about a gypsy girl who turns out to be a princess, the latter about an American heiress or "dollar princess"—oddly incongruous allusions at the wedding of a real European princess of undisputed royal descent. Zita's ivory satin dress had a Bourbon pattern of fleurs-de-lis while Karl wore his military uniform with the Habsburg Order of the Golden Fleece.[7]

There were some strikingly neobaroque elements to the wedding celebration in 1911. Burnacini, who staged the supremacy of the Habsburgs in the clouds, would have been thrilled to witness the arrival of a dirigible balloon, which did occur at the wedding of Zita and Karl. The airship appeared over Schloss Schwarzau at an elevation of 200 meters, attracted the awestruck attention of the guests down below, and sent down a shower of bouquets and little flags in the Habsburg colors of black and gold. Austrian pilots, furthermore, flew early airplanes overhead to offer homage and tribute: like the "machines" that operated in the spectacular idiom of baroque theater.[8] Just as Galileo, in baroque dynastic tribute, named the moons of Jupiter as "Medici stars" in the seventeenth century, one of the asteroids discovered by Austrian astronomer Johann Palisa in the early twentieth century was named in the bride's honor: 689 Zita, still orbiting the sun every three and a half years.[9]

The first zeppelin dirigible airship dated from 1900 at Lake Constance, and the Wright brothers made their famous first flights in 1903 at Kitty Hawk. In 1909 Louis Blériot flew across the English Channel, and by 1911 the growing number of Austrian flight enthusiasts included both Karl and Zita. By chance, their wedding took place just at the time of the First Austrian Flight Week (*Flugwoche*) at Wiener Neustadt, very close to Schloss Schwarzau.

A few days before their wedding Karl and Zita had been present at Wiener Neustadt for a flight demonstration. Karl was the chairman of an association for the advancement of Austrian aviation, and Zita turned out to be unexpectedly knowledgeable about flight, discussing issues of turbulence with the pilots at Wiener Neustadt in 1911. It was reported in the press that, after a small airplane accident, "the archduke drove in his automobile to the site of the accident, picked up a large piece of the smashed propeller, and drove back to present it to his bride."[10] His gallantry made aviation into a part of their royal romance, and the presence of the dirigible airship added to their wedding an element of spectacle worthy of Karl's Habsburg ancestors. Ten years later, in October 1921—in fact, on the day before their tenth wedding anniversary—Karl and Zita would go by plane to Hungary in an unsuccessful coup attempt to regain the Hungarian crown.

"Beyond the Threshold of Consciousness"

The waltzes at the wedding do not seem to have included Richard Strauss's *Rosenkavalier* waltzes, though 1911 was the year of *Der Rosenkavalier*, with the January premiere in Dresden followed by productions all over Germany and Austria-Hungary and across the Alps to Milan and Rome.[11] The opera, however, was a historical tribute to Hofmannsthal's own native city, and the Vienna premiere on April 8 was supposed to be a triumphant homecoming for *Der Rosenkavalier*. The production featured the sets and stagings of Austrian favorites Alfred Roller and Max Reinhardt, with the orchestra led by Viennese conductor Franz Schalk and the Vienna Opera star bass-baritone Richard Mayr taking on what would become one of his most famous roles as Baron Ochs. Yet it was observed from even as far away as New York that *Der Rosenkavalier* in Vienna "did not arouse the enthusiasm it has called forth everywhere in Germany."[12] The leading newspaper of Vienna, the *Neue Freie Presse*, offered a notably critical review by its principal critic, Julius Korngold, father of the teenage composer Erich Korngold, whose ballet *The Snowman* had been performed at the Vienna Opera in 1910, when the boy was only thirteen.[13]

The review of *Der Rosenkavalier* by Julius Korngold was not very enthusiastic about Strauss's score—"what is new in *Rosenkavalier* is not all that rich in significance; and what is beautiful is not all that new"—but the critic was even more hostile to the libretto. Hofmannsthal was faulted especially for his alleged failure to give the opera a convincing Viennese scenario: "He invents for himself an individual language, an Esperanto of Maria Theresa-Viennese rococo that occasionally modulates into *Tristan* German or Viennese-operetta German."[14] The first World Esperanto Congress had convened only six years before in 1905, and Korngold was already using Esperanto as a bludgeon for ridiculing as inauthentic the Viennese libretto of *Der Rosenkavalier*.

Korngold reserved his most extreme contempt for Strauss's lavish musical attention to the characteristically Viennese waltz form. The critic pedantically pointed out that the waltz was an anachronism in Maria Theresa's eighteenth-century, for it had only been created as a musical dance form in the nineteenth century, and he disapproved of Strauss's excessive reliance on "unimaginably shallow waltzes," making *Der Rosenkavalier* into a Viennese musical caricature:

> If Vienna is really the city of waltzes, it is by no means the city of the expressionless, paper-cutout, banal operetta waltzes that are popular at the moment. Waltzes of this type really do not stand up under the social elevation that Richard Strauss has in mind for them—in profound misapprehension, on top of everything else, of the art of Johann Strauss.[15]

That Viennese waltzes were indeed susceptible to "social elevation" at that moment was perfectly evident from their prominence—Johann Strauss II, Franz Lehár—in the musical entertainment at the wedding of Karl and Zita at Schloss Schwarzau, including even the "Zita Waltz" composed expressly for the elevated occasion.

Hofmannsthal's ideas in 1911 for new operas evaded the historical Viennese specificity of *Der Rosenkavalier* and looked to the mythological subject of *Ariadne auf Naxos* and the fairy-tale scenario of *Die Frau ohne Schatten*. Strauss and Hofmannsthal would work on both these projects over the course of the decade. *Ariadne*—conceived by Hofmannsthal for "heroic mythological figures in eighteenth-century costume with hoop skirts and ostrich feathers, the heroic element continually interwoven with figures from the *commedia dell'arte*"—was always intended to be a much lighter work than *Die Frau ohne Schatten*. His plan was to insert the short opera of *Ariadne* into Molière's comedy *Le bourgeois gentilhomme*, in place of the original Turkish *divertissement* composed by the French baroque court composer Jean-Baptiste Lully. Since *Le bourgeois gentilhomme* was first presented in 1670 at the court of Louis XIV, it belonged to the baroque moment of *Il pomo d'oro*. *Ariadne*, with its ostrich feathers, *commedia dell'arte*, and comic Molière frame, was to prepare the way—as an interim work (*Zwischenarbeit*)—for the weightier work, *Die Frau ohne Schatten*.[16]

In his earliest notes for *Die Frau ohne Schatten* from February 1911 Hofmannsthal had specified: "The second pair (after the Emperor and the Empress) are Harlequin and Smeraldina." As in *Ariadne auf Naxos*, *Die Frau ohne Schatten*, in its first conception, was supposed to combine mythical figures with *commedia dell'arte* characters in the spirit of Carlo Gozzi. The frivolous

Smeraldina (also sometimes known as Columbina) would give away her child and her shadow to the Empress, who would ultimately feel compelled to return the child to its proper mother.[17]

The Emperor and the Empress would remain fundamental to the project from beginning to end, but the *commedia dell'arte* couple were quickly reimagined. "For Harlequin and Smeraldina," noted Hofmannsthal, "there soon entered into my fantasy two Viennese folk figures." He imagined "two worlds confronting one another"—the Emperor and the Empress ruling over an imperial upper sphere, while the ordinary Viennese folk pair inhabited "the lower sphere" and spoke in Viennese dialect. The two women would be summoned to a scene of "Solomon's judgment," rivals in motherhood.[18]

By the time Hofmannsthal proposed the project to Strauss on March 20, the character of the Dyer's Wife had been endowed with some resemblance to Strauss's own wife, Pauline, a former opera diva: "Your wife might well, in all discretion, be taken as a model." Hofmannsthal now saw the Dyer's Wife as "a *bizarre* woman with a fundamentally very good soul; incomprehensible, moody, domineering, and yet sympathetic; she would in fact be the principal character."[19] Thus, the second female figure (who would never quite displace the Empress as the "principal character") had begun as a puppetlike *commedia dell'arte* role, evolved into a prototypical "Viennese folk figure" speaking in dialect—and then, over the course of just a month of creative reflection, become a complex human being, the Dyer's Wife, partly modeled on Pauline Strauss. She would be endowed by Hofmannsthal—and then by Strauss—with human traits and human weaknesses, though she would never receive a name. Strauss was immediately enthusiastic, writing to Pauline on April 4 (when he met with Hofmannsthal in Vienna for *Der Rosenkavalier*) that the poet's new operatic subject was "the most beautiful of the beautiful."[20]

"Dear Poet, I want to inquire how *Die Frau ohne Schatten* is doing," wrote Strauss importunately from Garmisch on May 15. "Can't I get a finished draft or maybe even a first act to look at some time soon?"[21] He was reading Wagner's autobiography *Mein Leben*, which received its first general publication in 1911, almost forty years after the composer's death. Strauss was eager to be composing an opera, but Hofmannsthal replied immediately from Rodaun in a spirit of deferral, evasion, and even obfuscation. He was not working on the opera:

With such a beautiful subject as *Die Frau ohne Schatten* . . . with a subject so fit to become the vehicle of beautiful poetry and beautiful music, with such a subject as this all haste and hurry and forcing of oneself would be a crime. Every detail must be present in the imagination clear-cut and definite, succinct and precise and true. In silence, beyond the threshold of consciousness [*unter der Schwelle des Bewusstseins*], the relation of the characters to one another must take on shape and realize itself naturally in the colorful action of an effortless symbolism; the profound must be brought to the surface . . .[22]

The message was clearly intended as a rebuff, with Strauss cast as the too-pushy petitioner, implicitly guilty of "haste, hurry, and forcing of oneself [*sich forcieren*]"—as if he were Baron Ochs—while Hofmannsthal himself understood the importance of patience and creative self-restraint, in the interest of intellectual clarity and artistic truth. The poet proposed a creative framework that seemed to be borrowed from the Freudian dynamics of psychoanalysis, recently articulated in Vienna when Freud published the *Interpretation of Dreams* in 1899. The artistic truth of *Die Frau ohne Schatten* had to be discovered "beyond the threshold of consciousness" and then brought from the depths "to the surface."

At the turn of the century, just as Freud was publishing the *Interpretation of Dreams*, Hofmannsthal experienced an artistic crisis that he described in the "Chandos Letter" of 1902. A fictive epistolary document from a young English Renaissance nobleman at the court of Queen Elizabeth I, the letter of Lord Chandos described a condition of depression that prevented him from writing—though he had once been celebrated as a teenage Elizabethan poet. The letter declared itself to be his very last letter, announcing that "I have completely lost the capacity to think or to speak coherently about anything at all." The disjuncture between the experience of the world and the descriptive function of language belonged to a general crisis of language and meaning in turn-of-the-century Vienna, which—as suggested by scholars Allan Janik and Stephen Toulmin in their book *Wittgenstein's Vienna*—would eventually exercise an influence on the *Tractatus Logico-Philosophicus* of Ludwig Wittgenstein, born in Vienna in 1889.[23] For Hofmannsthal, his personal crisis of language led him away from the lyric poetry that had made him famous in his youth and toward a new vocation as a dramatist and librettist looking to the stage for a more direct connection between words and experience, between author and public. The collaboration with Strauss was one way to make this connection—with another artist and with another public—but, in the aftermath of his Chandos crisis, Hofmannsthal also acknowledged the power of his own inner reticence. He would not offer up a libretto for *Die Frau ohne Schatten* until the subject had ripened within him, until he received, beyond the threshold of consciousness, real poetic inspiration.

On May 18, 1911, Gustav Mahler died in Vienna, and Strauss wrote to Hofmannsthal on May 20: "Mahler's death has moved me greatly: now he'll also become the great man in Vienna."[24] He was probably Strauss's most significant contemporary rival among German and Austrian composers who straddled the stylistic threshold between opulent late Romanticism and nervous discordant modernism. Mahler was young, only fifty when he died, with his Tenth Symphony unfinished, while Strauss, four years younger, was confiding in Hofmannsthal that "writing symphonies does not make me happy anymore."[25] In 1911, perhaps especially with the success of *Der Rosenkavalier*, Strauss was the more celebrated composer, famous for his tone poems and operas, while Mahler's symphonies remained daunting and controversial. For Mahler to be fully accepted as a great man in Vienna would wait much longer, for his posthumous "return"—half a century after his death—when Leonard Bernstein conducted his symphonies with the Vienna Philharmonic in the 1960s and 1970s.

As the musical director of the Vienna Opera and conductor of the Vienna Philharmonic orchestra, Mahler had dominated the musical life of Vienna for ten years, from 1897 to 1907. Born into a Jewish family in Habsburg Bohemia, he converted to Roman Catholicism in 1897 as the Habsburg Emperor's court conductor, conforming to dynastic tradition. The combination of fierce musical politics and a scurrilous anti-Semitic campaign pushed Mahler to resign in 1907 and accept a position in New York, where he conducted the New York Philharmonic for several seasons. His medical collapse took place in New York in February 1911; diagnosed with a serious infection aggravating a weak heart, he sailed for Europe, went into the Loew Sanatorium in Vienna, and died on May 18.

One of Mahler's most important collaborators at the Vienna Opera had been the stage designer Alfred Roller, who had been one of the founders, along with Gustav Klimt, of the Viennese artistic Sezession. Mahler and Roller together created an acclaimed production of Wagner's *Tristan und Isolde* in 1903, followed by Beethoven's *Fidelio* in 1904. At the time of Mahler's death in the spring of 1911, Roller was just presenting, together with Strauss and Hofmannsthal, the Viennese production of *Der Rosenkavalier*, applying the modernist spirit of art nouveau to the rococo style of the eighteenth century. Roller would also eventually work with Strauss and Hofmannsthal to design the sets for *Die Frau ohne Schatten*.

If Strauss and Mahler were rival titans of modern music in 1911, their modernism—with its chromatic harmonies, discordant developments, and crashing orchestral climaxes—were about to be contested by a whole new school of modernist music. Like Mahler's symphonies, Strauss's operas often required gigantic orchestras: Mahler's Eighth Symphony was called the "Symphony of a Thousand," first performed in 1910, and *Die Frau ohne Schatten* would require one of the largest orchestras in the operatic repertory with 164 instruments, including eight horns, six trumpets, six trombones, and five Chinese gongs. In 1911 Arnold Schoenberg composed "six little piano pieces" in which he turned his back on the epic ambitions of late Romanticism and offered instead tiny atonal masterpieces of extreme concision and mysterious irresolution. The sixth little piece was composed following Mahler's funeral in Grinzing just outside Vienna, marked *sehr langsam* (very slow) and *pianississimo* (*ppp*). Schoenberg's six little pieces eschewed the principles of classical harmony, adumbrating his later codification of twelve-tone atonal music which would become doctrinally fundamental for many modernist composers in the later twentieth century. This was a modernism that completely rejected the late Romanticism of Strauss and Mahler. In his search for a new musical language, Schoenberg also participated in the crisis of language and expression that beset the young Hofmannsthal in the "Chandos Letter."

Imperial Premonitions

At Wiener Neustadt, at the airshow of the First Austrian Flight Week and just before their wedding in October 1911, Zita experienced with Karl what she claimed was "the first and last serious discord in our life together." They were greeted on the aviation field by ovations from the flight enthusiasts, but Zita felt strangely uncomfortable.

> That's what I said when we reached the small pavilion on the edge of the airfield, and yet Archduke Karl, who was naturally very gladdened by the cheering of the crowd, did not understand right away what I meant. So I spoke very openly about the experiences of my own family at Parma, about the similar experiences of the relations of our imperial house in Modena and Florence, of the overthrow [of the throne] in Portugal, about the uncertainty of all power.
>
> "Please say more," said Archduke Karl.
>
> So I spoke my thoughts about the circumstances of the empire, about the infinite "reverence" that all circles, according to their perspectives, brought to the old Emperor. And they were saying: As long as he lives . . . and what then? I spoke only about how we had to behave soberly. How "fragile" our lives were, and power so insecure.[26]

It was a prophetic prenuptial conversation, situated unusually on the edge of an airfield and therefore, technologically as well as chronologically, on the threshold of the twentieth century. Such a conversation could really only take place in that rarified realm of royal marriages in which the scion of a reigning dynasty joined himself to the daughter of a deposed dynasty.

Zita's remembrances of her life were recorded much later, and her supposed premonitions of the future therefore benefited from the advantage of historical hindsight. Her long interviews with the Austrian journalist Erich Feigl took place in 1972, the year of her eightieth birthday, and allowed her to shape the presentation of her life in retrospect, constructing a narrative of imperial afterlife. Looking back to the scene on the airfield in 1911, she told the story as if it were a fairy tale, in which the prince was sadly unable to learn from the premonitions of the princess. Karl simply closed the subject:

> "I believe I understand what you wanted to say, but in Austria it's different. I pray you—let us speak no more about this!" So for years we spoke no more about it. I often wanted to know what Emperor Karl was thinking in all the difficult years that followed. But he was silent.
>
> It was on March 24, 1919, immediately after we crossed over the border and entered into the inferno of exile, that Emperor Karl seemingly

quite randomly said to me: "You were right." Eight years lay between that moment and our debate on the edge of the airfield of Wiener Neustadt. But I knew immediately what Emperor Karl was referring to.

"What wouldn't I give to have been wrong," I said gently.[27]

The forebodings of the Empress, as in a fairy tale, had come to pass, and the Emperor's overthrow proved her unhappy vindication. After the long years of silence they now, with just one cryptic utterance, understood each other perfectly, for his dynasty had joined hers in political misfortune. Six months later, in October 1919, *Die Frau ohne Schatten* had its premiere in Vienna, and the fairy-tale Empress took the stage, seeking to ward off a different catastrophe that hung over her husband the Emperor.

The Empress and the Falcon

Die Frau ohne Schatten, first conceived in the year of the First Austrian Flight Week, has an aerial dimension of its own. It's not just that the palace of the Emperor and Empress lies vertically above the human world, though that is clearly the case: "Hinab!" the Empress sings, as she goes down into the world in search of a shadow. There is also a falcon who appears in the skies overhead, and who sings with the voice of a soprano in the first scene of the opera. Before the Empress even sees the falcon, the bird appears in the music, at the very top of the score, with the piccolo first sounding the phrase that will always accompany the bird. Oddly, it's not a melody or an ornamental phrase of birdsong; the falcon's presence is signaled by repeated monotone, preceded by a grace note that gives the monotone an even stronger emphasis, two long soundings and then a series of three, as the tempo increases. The note is a high C-sharp, dominant to the empress's lovely F-sharp identity.[28]

The empress looks up and sees the falcon: *Da droben, sieh!* Look, up there! She recognizes it as the Emperor's red falcon, the falcon who once hunted her in the form of a gazelle and enabled him to capture her and marry her. *Sei mir gegrüßt, schöner Vogel.* Greetings, beautiful bird, she sings, soaring herself up to high A-flat, then high B-flat. The tempo still increasing (*noch rascher*), the falcon tries to communicate with her, the piccolo sounding its reiterated C-sharp, now reinforced by clarinet and oboe and emphasized by the throbbing grace note, creating an oddly insistent, almost mechanical

Figure 4. The falcon intones "Die Frau wirft keinen Schatten, der Kaiser muss versteinen" (the woman casts no shadow, the Emperor must turn to stone), singing on a monotone C-sharp with a plangent grace note, accompanied by oboe and clarinet. The Empress harmonizes with the soprano falcon in a brief and haunting duet. (*Die Frau ohne Schatten*, 1919)

effect, *fortissimo*. The falcon alights on a branch and continues to call to the Empress, who recognizes the plaintive sound as the sound of weeping. She seems to echo the mechanical two-note descent as she addresses the bird, "Falke, Falke," and asks, "Why are you crying?" The piccolo, clarinet, and oboe become ever more insistent, and the falcon finds its voice, principally on the note of C-sharp, sometimes rising to D in order to descend again to C-sharp: "Why should I not weep? The woman casts no shadow, the Emperor must turn to stone."29

The Empress now reveals herself to be a woman with a presentiment, like Zita in 1911, for the falcon has reminded the Empress of a magic talisman that she somehow lost in the ecstasy of her first sexual communion with the Emperor. With the harps magically accompanying her, she suddenly remembers that the talisman was engraved with a curse, foretelling the terrible fate of the woman without a shadow, the woman she now recognizes as herself. She therefore understands that the Emperor is doomed, and that she herself is the cause.

The scene culminates in a brief but uncanny passage of duet for the two sopranos, the falcon and the Empress, both lamenting that the Emperor must turn to stone (*Der Kaiser muss versteinen*): the falcon holding to its characteristic C-sharp at the top of the staff, and the Empress, capable earlier of beautiful flights of birdsong, now singing in a monotone, harmonizing with the falcon vocally from below, while the falcon is perched above her.[30] Like Zita in 1911 with her presentiment of imperial doom, the fairy-tale Empress of Hofmannsthal and Strauss receives from the magical singing falcon a glimpse of the terrible fate in store for the empire. In Zita's story she can only wait, like Cassandra, for her prophecy of the end of empire to come true. The fairy-tale Empress, however, sets out to find a shadow, to counter the curse, to save the Emperor and avert the tragic destiny of their mythological empire.

3

Descent from the Imperial Heights

KARL, ZITA, AND HOFMANNSTHAL IN GALICIA

Habsburg Honeymoon

"Now Archduke Karl wanted me to learn to know my new homeland very thoroughly," observed Zita, recalling the very beginning of her marriage, "not just between Wiener Neustadt and Semmering where we rode around diligently on our bicycles, but all the way down to Kotor and all the way up to Galicia." This turned into a honeymoon on the Habsburg Adriatic coast with Archduke Karl showing her his family realm: "He remained my travel leader and guide, even into my dreams, knew a thousand stories, showed, explained. We spent hours and hours in the excavations of Aquileia, Salona, and Spalato."[1] The last of these Adriatic locations, Spalato or Split, was the most imperial of destinations, site of the palace of Roman Emperor Diocletian with the whole town built into the palatial remains. Split was a site for reflecting upon the decline and fall of empires, and the Dalmatian coast was also a region of flammable contemporary tensions between Italian and Slavic nationalists within the Habsburg monarchy. The newlyweds traveled by ship along that coast, all the way to the triple bay of Kotor in contemporary Montenegro, then the southernmost outpost of Habsburg power in Europe. The bay of Kotor, at the foot of Mount Lovćen, was the site of a Habsburg naval base and later the location of fierce fighting during World War I. This would shadow Zita's memories of her own honeymoon: she and Karl could not suspect "what terrible battles would so soon be raging there, what a sacrifice of peoples would occur there for the preservation of the empire."² Zita's recollections were narrated in the overlapping dimensions of multiple chronologies: her intimations of the empire's fragility, her retrospective knowledge of its demise in the aftermath of war. The future Empress would remember 1911 as a year of foreboding, with intimations of a massive empire moving toward its end, even as Hofmannsthal began to sketch the mythological dimensions of the fairy-tale Empress on the operatic stage.

From the Adriatic coast there was then a triumphal honeymoon procession by train, heading inland through Bosnia and culminating in a visit to Sarajevo. Karl and Zita were greeted with cheers and ovations everywhere but, supposedly, with greatest enthusiasm in Sarajevo, just three years before the assassination of Archduke Franz Ferdinand and his wife in June 1914.³ The Ottoman Pashaluk of Bosnia and Herzegovina was occupied by the Habsburgs in 1878, following a Christian South Slavic uprising against the sultan in Constantinople, and the province was then annexed by Austria-Hungary in 1908, causing a diplomatic crisis that risked war with Russia. For Emperor Franz Joseph the occupation and annexation constituted his singular venture in augmenting the Habsburg dynastic possessions, his single colonial achievement as other European powers carved out overseas empires in Africa and Asia. Austria-Hungary promptly assumed a civilizing and modernizing mission in Bosnia, laying railroad tracks to Sarajevo, encouraging agriculture and industry in tobacco and in steel. At the same time Bosnia remained a site of orientalist fantasy for Vienna, and the illustrated account of the province in "word and image" (*Wort und Bild*), published in 1901, showed Bosnians in baggy pants and turbans, with architectural images of the mosque, the medrese, and the Turkish bath in Sarajevo.⁴ It was the world of Austria's fairy-tale Arabian nights. Emperor Franz Joseph, turning eighty in 1910, made a ceremonial tour of the newly annexed province and strode across the sixteenth-century Ottoman bridge at Mostar in Herzegovina.

When Franz Joseph married in 1854, his bride Elisabeth was sixteen, and Crown Prince Rudolf was born in 1858. In the shadow of his father's conservatism, the prince would grow up as the focus of liberal hopes for the future of the Habsburg Empire; his empress would have been Princess Stephanie of Belgium, who married him when she was still sixteen. They would never become emperor and empress, however, because in January 1889 Rudolf, then thirty, killed himself and his seventeen-year-old girlfriend, Baroness Mary Vetsera, at the imperial hunting lodge at Mayerling, causing one of the great scandals of the nineteenth century which the Habsburg court sought vainly to suppress. Princess Stephanie published her memoirs half a century later in 1935, under the title *Ich sollte Kaiserin werden* (*I Was Supposed to Become Empress*).

Since Rudolf and Stephanie had only a daughter, the succession to the Habsburg throne then passed to Franz Joseph's brother Archduke Karl Ludwig and then, after his death in 1896 (from typhoid after drinking from the Jordan River on a pilgrimage to the Holy Land), to Karl Ludwig's son Franz Ferdinand. The new heir was a world traveler (had been to Australia, had crossed the Pacific, had visited America), an intensely dedicated hunter (like the Emperor in *Die Frau ohne Schatten*), and a political reformer who envisioned new kinds of political autonomy for the Slavic peoples of the Habsburg monarchy. His political views were disagreeable to Franz Joseph, but perhaps even more offensive was the archduke's marriage in 1900 to the Bohemian Countess Sophie Chotek. Because she was merely noble but not actually the member of a reigning dynasty (or a formerly reigning dynasty, like Zita), the countess was considered unfit to marry the Habsburg heir. The marriage was therefore deemed morganatic—so she could never become the Habsburg empress, and her sons could never become Habsburg emperors. She was assassinated alongside Franz Ferdinand in Sarajevo in 1914.

Karl was Emperor Franz Joseph's grandnephew and Archduke Franz Ferdinand's nephew. Karl's own father, Archduke Otto "der Schöne" (Otto the Handsome), died in 1906 in the tertiary stage of syphilis, involving the collapse of his nose. Therefore, by the time Karl married Zita in 1911, he was second in the line of succession right behind Franz Ferdinand, whose own death was only three years away. Oddly, since Franz Ferdinand's wife could never be crowned as empress, Zita was next in line to be empress, even while Karl was only second in line to be emperor. Following her betrothal to Karl, Zita traveled to Rome for an audience with Pope Pius X, who was later canonized as a saint. The pope congratulated Zita on her coming marriage to the Habsburg successor, to which she replied: "Your Holiness, my intended husband is not the Archduke-Successor. My intended husband is Archduke

Karl." But the pope supposedly insisted that Karl would be the next emperor, and Zita could hardly contradict the pope. Later she made a joke out of it with her mother, the Portuguese infanta, saying "Thank God, the pope is not also infallible in political questions." Three years later, after the assassination at Sarajevo, Zita recalled the pope's prediction, and her mother explained, "I understood the Holy Father very well at the time. . . . I am happy though that you did not understand. . . . I thought that this not-knowing would give you a few more happy years."[5] Zita's sense of her own story—as she carefully recalled it in retrospect—was one of mystical predestination, of premonitions and prophesies, of foreordained futures in fairy-tale narratives.

In 1911 while Zita and Karl were in Sarajevo, Gavrilo Princip was also there, the future assassin of Franz Ferdinand. Princip was seventeen, just two years younger than Zita; he was in high school, and in 1911 he joined the political movement "Young Bosnia" (*Mlada Bosna*) which was committed to breaking away from Habsburg rule and joining with Serbia.[6] Also in 1911, a group of militants in Serbia constituted the secret terrorist society called Unification or Death (Уједињење или смрт), also known as the Black Hand. They were determined to bring about the unification with Serbia of all the lands that they considered Serbian, including Bosnia. Aiming high, they first contemplated the assassination of Emperor Franz Joseph in 1911, and they would ultimately drive the conspiracy that led to the assassination of Franz Ferdinand in 1914.

"My Alter Ego"

Unification or Death was founded in May 1911, while Strauss and Hofmannsthal busily corresponded about *Ariadne auf Naxos*. "Ariadne may turn out very pretty [*sehr hübsch*]," wrote Strauss on May 22 with some reserve, while Hofmannsthal, on June 15, suggested, tantalizingly, that "*Die Frau ohne Schatten* could, I sometimes think, become the most beautiful of all existing operas."[7] The opera was still inchoate in his imagination, but very beautiful, beyond the threshold of consciousness.

At the end of June Hofmannsthal was working on *Ariadne* at Rodaun and nervous about his collaboration with Strauss: "My dear Dr. Strauss, What is the matter with you? I am quite uneasy when I do not hear from my alter ego [*von meinem zweiten Ich*] for so long."⁸ Strauss replied from Garmisch, "Dear Poet, You are funny [*komisch*]. You want to hear something from me! But I want to read something from you, and only then will you be able to 'hear' something from me."⁹ For Strauss the collaboration was very much a working relationship, and it fed upon the real materials of text and music.

For Hofmannsthal, however, the element of psychological entwinement, even dependency, was fundamental, and his epistolary anxieties suggested some of the ways that the collaboration was, for him, as sensitive as a love affair.

> Was I really so funny? Couldn't you understand that I wanted from you some sign of life, just a simple word that you were back at Garmisch and at leisure? That I did not want to send my manuscript into the void? . . . The whole thing was conceived only for you, only for your music!¹⁰

It was notable that the poet who insisted on bringing the *commedia dell'arte* into the heroic mythology of *Ariadne*, the author of the famously farcical cross-dressing third act of *Der Rosenkavalier*, himself took umbrage when accused of behaving comically. His collaboration with Strauss touched him too closely for him to be able to find humor in their incompatibilities. At the same time, it was striking that even as he identified Strauss as his own most intimate alter ego, they both continued to pursue their correspondence in the formal second-person: *Sie* instead of *Du*. The *Ariadne* project was only for you, wrote Hofmannsthal, only for your music: "nur für Sie, nur für Ihre Musik."

In July Hofmannsthal himself was at leisure for the summer in his Alpine retreat at Bad Aussee and wrote to explain the two contrasting female leads of *Ariadne auf Naxos*: the fundamentally faithful Ariadne, abandoned by Theseus, and the frivolously promiscuous Zerbinetta, the coquette of the *commedia dell'arte*. "These two spiritual worlds," according to Hofmannsthal, "are in the end ironically brought together in the only way in which they can be brought together: in noncomprehension [*das Nichtverstehen*]."¹¹ Strauss, however, worried that audiences and critics might also fail to understand Hofmannsthal's ironies and complexities.¹²

"The pure poetic content of a work of art, the real meaning it contains is never understood at first," wrote Hofmannsthal to Strauss, rather severely, on July 23. "What is understood is only that which needs no understanding, the anecdotal story: *Tosca, Madama Butterfly*, and such like."[13] The poet's condescension toward Puccini's recent masterpieces underlined his sense of his own sophistication and perhaps his anxiety that Strauss might like to compose popular triumphs of Puccinian accessibility.

Hofmannsthal wanted Strauss to be willing to collaborate on challenging works that were difficult to understand at first encounter, and the poet's letter of July 23 went on to propose as a further complication for *Ariadne* the addition of a dramatic prologue (that Strauss would eventually set to music).[14] The prologue would feature the character of the Composer—so that *Ariadne auf Naxos* could be intricately conceived as an opera within an opera. Strauss replied the next day, approving of the prologue and commenting humorously, "Zerbinetta might have an affair with the Composer, so long as he is not too close a portrait of me."[15] Actually, Hofmannsthal would create the Composer rather more as a portrait of his younger self—the precocious genius—even satirizing his own sensitivity, volatility, and presumption of artistic refinement.[16]

"A Tunnel through the Darkness"

After their wedding Karl and Zita resided in the imperial villa Schloss Wartholz, located in the near vicinity of Zita's family home at Schloss Schwarzau. The Viennese architect of Schloss Wartholz, Heinrich von Ferstel, was closely associated with the historicist architecture of the Ringstraße style that characterized the development of Vienna in the later nineteenth century. Ferstel designed Vienna's Votivkirche in the neo-Gothic style and the University of Vienna in the neo-Renaissance style.[17] In 1911, however, the urban landscape of Vienna was already being transformed by frankly modernist works of architecture that made Ferstel seem hopelessly old-fashioned. Adolf Loos completed in 1911 the austerely unadorned Looshaus on the Michaelerplatz, supposedly causing distress to Emperor Franz Joseph who could see it across the square from his own residence in the baroque Hofburg palace.

In late November 1911, after his honeymoon, Karl, as an officer in the Habsburg army, had to rejoin his regiment in Bohemia, at Brandys on the

Elbe River. Karl and Zita made a triumphal procession through town upon their arrival in Brandys; there were arches adorned with flags and coats of arms to greet the newlywed couple.[18] The music of the patriotic Habsburg "Radetzky March," by Johann Strauss (the father), is still played today in Brandys at an annual occasion that commemorates the presence of Karl and celebrates his beatification in 2004. The town website notes that "we also remember his wife Empress Zita who, together with Karl, spent several happy years of their life together in Brandys."[19]

In November 1911, Hofmannsthal wrote to Strauss declining to attend the Berlin premiere of *Der Rosenkavalier*, pleading the need to remain focused on *Die Frau ohne Schatten*: "Sometimes a happy thought drills a tunnel through the darkness of the very difficult middle act."[20] After refusing for the whole year to be pressured by Strauss even to speak about *Die Frau ohne Schatten*, now as the year drew to a close Hofmannsthal felt that he was making creative progress. In fact, he had had his moment of epiphany on Sunday, October 29, when he went to hear Wagner, not Strauss, at the opera in Vienna. Afterward he wrote on November 1 to his close friend, the young widow Countess Ottonie Degenfeld, the live model for Ariadne and the object of his romantic devotion. He confided in her now about his experience in the opera house: "I had a corner seat in the back of the orchestra level (they performed *The Flying Dutchman*) and I paid little attention to anyone or anything, and suddenly I was able to spin out beautifully the plot to *Die Frau ohne Schatten* . . . and I found some intimacy with the characters that had been lacking for me till then." Hofmannsthal was now prepared, on November 4, to promise Strauss some text in the coming year: "If you wish, I'll write you the first act of *Die Frau ohne Schatten* for next summer."[21]

On December 18, Hofmannsthal felt the need to affirm his own importance within the collaboration: "I know the worth of my work, and I know that for generations past no poet of the first rank . . . has worked with joy and devotion for a musician." He was distressed that Strauss was hesitating over entrusting the premiere of *Ariadne auf Naxos* to the direction of Austrian impresario Max Reinhardt, then working in Berlin. Like the Composer in the prologue of *Ariadne* who feared to see his opera desecrated, Hofmannsthal now reacted with outrage at the anticipated "debasement" (*Erniedrigung*) of his work: "How am I to develop within myself with love another project

Figure 5. Strauss (right) and Hofmannsthal in 1912, looking comfortable with each other at Hofmannsthal's home in Rodaun. "I wish you a good year in 1912 with health and happiness and steady progress and a beautiful *Frau ohne Schatten*," wrote Strauss at the beginning of the year. (Album/Alamy Stock Photo)

of a similar kind? How am I to write a single line of *Die Frau ohne Schatten*?"[22] His wounded sense of *amour propre* launched him into an aria of denunciation against Strauss and also triggered inner anxieties about debasing himself within the collaboration. Those anxieties led him back to his artistic insecurity about *Die Frau ohne Schatten*, about whether it was too difficult to write and too subtle to realize on stage—and, once again, he threatened to withhold the libretto, but now as a sort of punishment for Strauss's lack of appreciation. By the day after Christmas Strauss had conceded the indispensability of Reinhardt, and on January 2 he wrote to Hofmannsthal, "I wish you a good year in 1912 with health and happiness and steady progress and a beautiful *Frau ohne Schatten*."[23]

The Misery of Galicia

On February 7, 1912, Hofmannsthal added a postscript to a letter to Strauss: "Last night beautiful ideas for *Die Frau ohne Schatten*. This could really become a beautiful beautiful thing, let us hope!" On February 10 he was hoping for a meeting with Strauss in Vienna and worrying over the fact that their travel schedules did not intersect.[24] On February 12 Archduchess Zita made a public appearance at the Hofburg imperial palace in Vienna, receiving the members of the diplomatic corps, including the accredited envoys, and impressing them with her many languages.[25] Her ceremonial appearance at the center of Habsburg power preceded the military posting of Karl and Zita to the empire's frontier province of Galicia.

This was a very dramatic displacement, from the imperial palace in Vienna to the remote, impoverished, provincial frontier, a region of violent ethnic and religious tensions among Poles, Ukrainians, and Jews—Galicia, where the Habsburg viceroy Polish Count Andrzej Potocki had been assassinated by a young Ukrainian nationalist four years earlier in 1908.[26] In 1888, Polish entrepreneur Stanisław Szczepanowski had published his account *Nędza Galicji w cyfrach* (*The Misery of Galicia in Statistics*), which revealed with numerical evidence that the province was one of the poorest and least economically productive regions in Europe. From that moment on "Galician misery" became proverbial.[27]

In the 1890s Hofmannsthal—already a famous poet—was sent to Galicia to fulfill his Austrian military service, and, as a young aesthete, he was shocked by the Galician misery. In 1896 he wrote from Tłumach, near Stanislaviv, to a friend in Vienna: "Everything around me is more ugly than you can imagine. Everything is ugly, miserable, and dirty [*hässlich, elend und schmutzig*], the people, the horses, the dogs, even the children. I am very low and dispirited. Yesterday, in the evening twilight, an old beggar crawled into my room on all fours and kissed my feet."[28] Two years later Hofmannsthal returned to Galicia for further military service, and in 1898 he reported from Chortkiv in a letter to his father: "In the evenings I walk up and down the only road where there is no deep shit . . . here stand the Ruthenian peasants with their miserable horses, the size of dogs, and let themselves be cheated by the Jews . . . for hours I walk up and down amidst this swarm [*Gewimmel*] as if I were alone upon a silent mountain peak."[29] His Viennese aestheticism was confronted with the human "swarm," the ugliness of mundane reality, here represented by the experience of Galicia. "I am correcting my conception of life," noted Hofmannsthal. "What life is for most people is much more joyless and low than one would like to think."[30] This sense of the contrast between life in the imperial metropolis and human existence in the empire's poorest province—its ugliness and misery—would contribute to Hofmannsthal's conception of the human world in *Die Frau ohne Schatten*.

For Zita, raised as a princess of Bourbon-Parma, now a Habsburg archduchess, the misery of Galicia must have been all the more striking. For her too there could have been prostrations, more appropriate for an archduchess on a dynastic visit than for a poet doing his military service. Having arrived in Galicia by train, the archducal procession across Galicia then took place on horseback, on the road to the eastern garrison town of Kolomyia. Karl and Zita were saluted all along the way with Joseph Haydn's Habsburg imperial anthem, "Gott erhalte," sung variously by Galician Poles, Jews, and Ukrainians, and in Kolomyia they were greeted by a torch procession.[31]

Kolomyia was a small town and roughly half the population was Jewish; it was just thirty miles south of Tlumach where Hofmannsthal had done his military service in 1896 and found everything "ugly, miserable, and dirty." Another eighty miles northwest of Tlumach was the town of Boryslav, which boomed in the late nineteenth century as the center of Galicia's important oil industry.[32] Lucy Erber was born into a Jewish family in Boryslav in 1899— with the Jewish name of Hencze Erber—and she later moved with her family to Vienna. On February 12, 1912, the day that Zita received the diplomatic corps in the Hofburg, Lucy celebrated her thirteenth birthday. Born a subject of Emperor Franz Joseph, she would later, during the war, live as the subject of Emperor Karl and Empress Zita. Lucy would leave Vienna in 1938, after the Austrian Anschluss with Nazi Germany, bringing her young daughter, Renee, who would grow up to be my mother.

Zita, who was pregnant in Galicia in 1912, had to create some sort of home for herself in Kolomiya, remote from the palaces of her childhood. She had put together a small menagerie of pets as she traveled through the province, and she established herself in Kolomiya with birds, cats, dogs, and even a tame deer.[33] To be sure, a special relation to the animal world was an aspect of magical fairy-tale empresses, like the Empress in *Die Frau ohne Schatten*, whose talisman allowed her to become a gazelle, and who was hunted by the Emperor in her antelopian form.

In August Karl and Zita visited the Galician provincial capital of Lemberg—Lwów in Polish, Lviv today in Ukraine—for the Habsburg summer military maneuvers, particularly significant because of the close proximity to the Russian border. Eastern Galicia would become the crucial military front between Russia and Austria-Hungary when World War I began two years later. As recently as 1908 Emperor Franz Joseph himself had traveled to Galicia for the summer maneuvers in the year of his sixtieth jubilee. In 1912 the emperor turned eighty-two, and it was Karl at twenty-five who participated in the maneuvers, including a simulated cavalry attack. The simulation, however, was so forceful that the archduke's horse collapsed, and Karl fell unconscious with a concussion and a hoofmark on his helmet. There was no question of trusting his health to the hospitals of eastern Galicia, and he was sent, by way of the Austrian train system, as quickly as possible back to Vienna. He recovered in time to participate devoutly in the International Eucharistic Congress that was held in Vienna in early September. Karl and Zita could now return home to Schloss Wartholz where their son, Otto, was born in November.[34]

Over the course of 1911 and 1912 Zita, the former princess, now archduchess and future empress, had the opportunity to emerge from the royal palaces that were her customary abodes and learn something about rougher frontiers, less developed lands, more impoverished peoples, and more alien populations—such as the Muslim Bosnians and Galician Jews who would not have attended the International Eucharistic Congress in Vienna. Like the Empress whom Hofmannsthal was imagining for the operatic stage at that very same time, Zita descended from her imperial heights to discover the peoples whose needs and aspirations would eventually become her imperial responsibility.

"Among Humans!"

The descent from the imperial palace to the world of human misery occurs in the middle of act 1 of *Die Frau ohne Schatten*, as the Empress and the Nurse undertake their mission to obtain a human shadow from the impoverished Dyer's Wife. The Empress asks the Nurse where to find a shadow, and the Nurse replies, "Among humans! Aren't you afraid?" (*Bei den Menschen! Graust's dich nicht?*) The frightening darkness of the human world is suggested by the bass clarinet and contrabassoon.[35] In an almost waltzing 6/8 rhythm, the Nurse now warns the Empress that they will have to leave behind the imperial palace. Harps and flutes perform ascending runs as the Nurse describes the fountains of the palace which suggest "the purity of heavenly empires." The Nurse then simulates the descent to the human world, with the phrase "noch tiefer hinab" (still deeper down), descending from a high G to a low C-sharp, and warning the Empress that it will be dreadful to mix with, live with, deal with ordinary humans (*hausen mit ihnen, handeln mit ihnen*). Aren't you afraid? she asks one more time, diving all the way down to a sustained low G, joined by trombones, contrabassoon, and bass clarinet.[36]

The Empress is undaunted, and sings, almost ecstatically, "Ein Tag bricht an"—a day is dawning—as she soars over the full orchestra, rising from F-sharp, to G, to high A. The Nurse now echoes that phrase, while adding the crucial qualification: "A day is dawning, a human day [*ein Menschentag*]." Hofmannsthal's verse style made use of brief and emphatic phrases, as the Nurse conjured the chaotic intensity of the human world:

ein wildes Getümmel,	a wild turmoil,
gierig, sinnlos—	greedy, senseless—
ein ewiges Trachten ohne Freude!	eternal striving without joy![37]

It was a verse that seemed almost to have been taken from Hofmannsthal's letters from Galicia, *Getümmel* as the rhyming replacement for *Gewimmel*,

52   Chapter 3

and then the same reflection on Galician lives without joy: "What life is for most people is much more joyless and low than one would like to think." Hofmannsthal's military service in Galicia in the 1890s would have shaped his sense of what it meant for a mythological empress to descend to the world of ordinary humans, and while he was working on the libretto for the first act in 1912 he would also, very likely, have been aware—from the Viennese press—that the Habsburg archducal couple was actually present in Galicia for a large part of that year.

The descent of the Empress and the Nurse to the human world was one of the challenging scenic transformations for which Strauss would write an orchestral interlude. According to the libretto, as "they descend into the abyss [*Abgrund*] of the human world [*Menschenwelt*], the orchestra takes up their flight to earth [*Erdenflug*]."[38] The curtain goes down, but there is no pause in the music for the scene change, only Strauss's brassy music of flight at a moment of Austrian fascination with early aviation. In two minutes of orchestral music the scene undergoes a transformation, and the audience experiences the disorientation of an empress who is coming down from the splendid refinement of a heavenly palace to the joyless turmoil of ordinary people living in poverty: her very own subjects, whose world was completely unfamiliar to her.

The curtain rises again on the one-room house of a working man, the Dyer Barak who works with colors and fabrics. The room is both home and workshop for the Dyer and could be described in one hyphenated expression as "oriental-poor" (*orientalisch-dürftig*). It might have been the fairy-tale

Figure 6. After the Empress and the Nurse descend to the human world, the scene changes to Barak's "oriental-poor" dwelling, introduced by cacophony in the percussion: kettledrums, rods, castanets, the wind machine, the tam-tam, and two great Chinese gongs. (*Die Frau ohne Schatten*, 1919)

Orient of the *Thousand and One Nights*, but within Austria-Hungary Galicia was also described as oriental, the far eastern frontier of the empire; a famous series of stories about Galicia, published by Galician writer Karl Emil Franzos in 1876, was titled *Halb-Asien* (Half-Asia).[39]

The transition to the Dyer's "oriental-poor" dwelling was signaled by the entry of a whole new percussion section: kettledrums, xylophone, rods, castanets, Chinese gongs, tam-tam, and a cylinder wind machine, all contributing to a hammering cacophony.[40] Barak's three brothers are on stage in the room, not only poor men but also disabled: the one-eyed brother, the one-armed brother, the hunchback. They sing thirteen measures of discordant trio, the high notes of the tenor hunchback grating on the ear; the brothers musically represent the ugly world of poverty and conflict, the "wildes Getümmel" that the Nurse has already described to the Empress. The Dyer's Wife now denounces Barak's brothers as dogs, threatening to throw them out of the house, and they turn on her, reminding her that in their father's home there were thirteen children, but there was always food for a poor stranger.[41] She, however, is a woman of anger, resentment, and frustration, living in the lower world of human misery. The Empress and the Nurse have descended from the "purity of heavenly empires" to seek her out, to persuade her to give up her human shadow.

4

Marriage and Childbirth in the Imperial Dynasty and the Fairy-Tale Opera

SUBTERRANEAN DEVELOPMENT AND ARTISTIC COLLABORATION

"Constantly Cloudy Here"

In February 1912, while Archduchess Zita was receiving the diplomatic corps in the Hofburg in Vienna, Gavrilo Princip participated, along with the group Young Bosnia, in a Sarajevo demonstration against the government of Austria-Hungary, and he ended up being expelled from high school. He was seventeen. In May he traveled to Belgrade in Serbia and it was there in 1912 that he made his first contacts with the secret society Unification or Death.

On April 15 the *Titanic* sank after striking an iceberg in the North Atlantic, and fifteen hundred people died at sea, including all eight of the ship's musicians (a trio and a quintet), who played for the passengers as the ship went down. Their repertory is supposed to have included Austro-Hungarian operetta melodies by Johann Strauss II and Franz Lehár. On April 22, when Hofmannsthal wrote to Strauss, there was no mention of the *Titanic*, but the poet was sleeping poorly and felt that he desperately needed a vacation in Italy. "My head is miserable, the nights are bad, my fantasy completely dead," he wrote. "For two months, I have not had a single idea, neither for *Die Frau ohne Schatten* nor for any of my subjects."[1] He well knew what Strauss would find most disappointing.

On April 30 Hofmannsthal sent a letter to his German friend art historian Eberhard von Bodenhausen, revealing that the spiritual malaise was also political: "Constantly cloudy here, cloudy for our old Austria. I ask myself sometimes with fear: in what sort of decades are my two boys growing up.... The South Slavs inside the monarchy, not only the Serbs but also the Croats, are in half-revolt.... The Bohemians treacherously lurking with bared teeth—Galicia, the Ruthenian part, undermined by Russian agents—Italy as much an enemy as an ally."[2] He saw the situation as Gordian—perhaps impossible to resolve and, in spite of his ambivalence about Italy, he was determined to go south to escape from his own spiritual troubles. He had in mind a trip to Umbria and Tuscany where he just missed intersecting with Strauss in Siena: "Arrived here a few hours after your departure," wrote the poet on May 18.[3]

Hofmannsthal was on his way to Paris to meet with Sergei Diaghilev and Vaslav Nijinsky to discuss a dance project with the Ballets Russes. The poet happened to be in Paris for one of the most sensational events in the history of ballet, Nijinsky's performance to his own choreography of Debussy's *Afternoon of a Faun*, which concluded with the dancer sensuously simulating masturbation on stage.[4] Hofmannsthal, together with Harry Kessler, discussed with Diaghilev and Nijinsky the idea for a ballet based on the biblical story of Joseph and Potiphar's wife—eventually produced as *Josephslegende*, with music, of course, by Richard Strauss.[5] It was yet another assignment that further deferred work on *Die Frau ohne Schatten*, but Strauss would allow himself some exotic Egyptian percussive coloring—xylophone, celesta, wind machine, castanets, and four harps—that later contributed to the oriental spirit of the fairy-tale opera.

On July 9 Hofmannsthal, preparing for his summer stay at Bad Aussee in the Alps, wrote to Strauss, "I am sincerely grateful to you for your delicacy (*Zartgefühl*) in not pressing me to work on *Die Frau ohne Schatten*, and indeed only rarely and gently reminding me of it." Now the poet promised to focus his "inner eye" on the fairy-tale characters "for as long as they require this illumination for their subterranean growth [*zu ihrem unterirdischen Wachstum*]."[6] Hofmannsthal here sketched a topography of literary creativity for *Die Frau ohne Schatten*, with its materials and resources still subterranean, presumably buried within his own unconscious mind and capable of being unearthed only by the steadiness of his own inner eye.

On September 8, Hofmannsthal wrote exultantly to Strauss over his breakthrough with the opera:

> Because I know it will give you joy I write to tell you that *Die Frau ohne Schatten* has forcefully come before my soul, so that now, for the first time, I really possess this subject, link by link, scene by scene, every transition, every intensification, the overall shape of the whole work.[7]

Hofmannsthal finally felt that he could apply himself to writing the libretto for the first act in the coming autumn. Strauss replied immediately on September 11: "Congratulations on *Die Frau ohne Schatten*."[8]

The composer was, however, querulous about the ballet on Joseph and Potiphar's wife: "The chaste Joseph is not right for me," wrote Strauss.[9] Hofmannsthal, however, saw Joseph not as some "pious seminarist" but rather as "this shepherd boy, the brilliant child of a mountain tribe," someone whose search for God was actually balletic: "in wild upward swinging . . . wild leaping toward the high-hanging fruit of inspiration . . . thrusting himself upward in a pure solitary orgy."[10] This was indeed Joseph as orgiastically conceived for Nijinsky (who would break with his lover and impresario Diaghilev in 1913 and never dance the role). The figure of Potiphar's wife lusting after Joseph in her own home would recur in *Die Frau ohne Schatten*, when the Dyer's Wife was sexually tempted by the apparition of a seductive youth, conjured to encourage her to surrender her shadow to the Empress.

On October 9, with the Stuttgart premiere of *Ariadne* a few weeks away, Hofmannsthal was focused on *Die Frau ohne Schatten*—"which will, I hope, establish me once and for all as your house court poet."[11] It was epistolary banter which seemed to play with the idea that the two collaborators could have occupied baroque roles at the imperial Habsburg court in past centuries, as poet and composer in the service of an emperor and an empress. The model for Hofmannsthal might perhaps have been the Italian Pietro Metastasio, court poet, or *Hofdichter*, in the age of Maria Theresa in eighteenth-century Habsburg Vienna, writing libretti for baroque operas. The allusion reinforced the idea that *Die Frau ohne Schatten* was intended as an imperial spectacle, even as it placed an emperor and empress on the operatic stage rather than in the privileged imperial box among the audience.

That same day, October 9, Hofmannsthal wrote to Strauss furiously about a public banquet being planned in Stuttgart following the premiere of *Ariadne*, his snobbism outraged at the thought of "intimacy with newspaper hacks and Stuttgart philistines who will call you and me '*Du*' while drinking champagne."[12] Strauss and Hofmannsthal did not even call each other *Du*— the intimate second-person pronoun in German—and the very thought of such exchanges with strangers was distressing to the fastidious poet. Hofmannsthal made no mention of what must have seemed like a small item of international news from the previous day, October 8, when Montenegro, one of the smallest countries in Europe, declared war against the Ottoman Empire. It would become the signal for a broader war, the First Balkan War of 1912, to be followed by the Second Balkan War of 1913, which would set the stage for the assassination at Sarajevo and the coming of World War I in 1914.[13]

On October 17, 1912, Bulgaria, Serbia, and Greece, forming a Balkan League, joined Montenegro in the war against the Ottomans, with the intention of seizing what remained of the Ottoman Empire in Europe, principally Thrace and Macedonia. Austria-Hungary was hostile to the Balkan League, both for fear that it would amplify Russian influence in the region and from suspicion of Serbia, which was so clearly opposed to Habsburg rule in Bosnia. Gavrilo Princip, in Serbia in 1912, wanted to enlist in an irregular fighting force with the Balkan League but was supposedly rejected for service because he was too short.

On October 25 *Ariadne auf Naxos* had its premiere in Stuttgart, with Reinhardt directing Molière's *Le bourgeois gentilhomme* in Hofmannsthal's German version and concluding with the opera itself. The joining of the two works was not a success with the public because, according to Strauss, "the public that goes to the drama theater does not want to hear an opera, and vice versa."[14] The grandly conceived role of Ariadne was performed by the little-known twenty-five-year-old Czech soprano from Brno, Maria Jeritza. She had already attracted the attention of Emperor Franz Joseph, who had heard her sing in Johann Strauss's *Die Fledermaus* at Bad Ischl during the summer of 1910. He wanted to see her at the Hofoper in Vienna, supposedly commenting, "Must our singers always be old and ugly?"[15] Richard Strauss was also impressed by Jeritza, who would go on to become one of the greatest Straussian sopranos of the twentieth century. In 1919 Jeritza would create the role of the Empress in *Die Frau ohne Schatten*.

Habsburg Childbirth

On November 5, 1912, Woodrow Wilson, the man who would eventually preside over the formal dissolution of the Habsburg Empire at the Paris Peace Conference in 1919, was elected president of the United States.[16] In November 1912, Zita and Karl—having returned from Galicia—were living south of Vienna in Schloss Wartholz where, on November 25, Zita gave birth to a son, Otto, the first of their eight children. The attending obstetrician, Heinrich Peham, had trained at the University of Vienna and was chief of gynecology at the Allgemeine Poliklinik.[17] This same clinic was probably the setting for Arthur Schnitzler's 1912 drama *Professor Bernhardi*, about anti-Semitism and elite medical practice at a fictional hospital named for a Habsburg empress, the "Elisabethinum." Schnitzler's play, which began with an abortion, had its premiere in Berlin on November 28 but was banned for performance in Austria. Schnitzler himself had trained as a neurologist at the Allgemeine Poliklinik.

In addition to Dr. Peham, there were also present at Schloss Wartholz for Otto's birth Zita's mother, the Portuguese infanta, and Karl's mother, the Saxon princess, so there was no lack of royalty on the scene. The birth took place at three in the morning, and Peham reported the birth of a "healthy, strong boy," with Zita herself in "excellent condition."[18] Peham would attend several of Zita's childbirths and would eventually be ennobled by Emperor Karl in 1918. Otto would live until 2011 but never reign as emperor.

The christening of Otto took place on November 25, and though the godfather was designated as Emperor Franz Joseph, he himself remained in Vienna and was represented by Archduke Franz Ferdinand. Schloss Wartholz had been built by Ferstel for Archduke Karl Ludwig, the father of Franz Ferdinand, who therefore knew the castle from his childhood and returned now with his morganatic wife, Sophie, who had been given the title Duchess of Hohenberg. That title was just distinguished enough to guarantee her the lowest-ranked precedence within the imperial family; on ceremonial occasions she would have been expected to defer to Zita. Furthermore, Sophie's children with Franz Ferdinand, Maximilian born in 1902 and Ernst born in 1904, were specifically excluded from the imperial succession. While Zita, of course, had not actually stolen Sophie's shadow, Zita's newborn son Otto was endowed with all the dynastic prerogatives that were denied to the other woman's children. Otto's christening in November 1912 brought together the two Habsburg wives and mothers.

Franz Ferdinand came to Schloss Wartholz for the christening immediately after a visit with German Kaiser Wilhelm II in Berlin; they had gone hunting together and discussed the new Balkan War. According to Franz Ferdinand, "Emperor William was especially gracious and declared he was willing to support us in everything"—that is, to support Austria-Hungary against Russian ambitions in southeastern Europe, even if it came to open war, as it finally did in 1914.[19] The Balkan War was thus a looming presence even at the christening of Otto.

Cardinal Franz Xaver Nagl, archbishop of Vienna, officiated at the baptism in the chapel at Schloss Wartholz, and the infant received a grand total of seventeen baptismal names, of which Otto was only the first. Franz Ferdinand presented Zita with a diamond necklace as the baptismal gift of Franz Joseph. On the evening of the christening, there were celebratory fires in the Alpine mountains and illuminations in the town near the castle, showing Karl and Zita's initials and the Habsburg double-headed eagle. There were individual light displays at the post office, the butcher's shop, and the veterinarian's clinic. At seven that evening, the mayor led a torch procession through the town to Schloss Wartholz, where the townspeople were greeted by Archduke Karl. The local band performed Hermann Dostal's "Zita Waltz" in honor of the new mother.[20] In 1912 Dostal composed a zeppelin dirigible operetta, *Der fliegende Rittmeister* (*The Flying Cavalry Captain*), with a "Fliegermarsch" ("Aviator's March") that became very well known—and would certainly have interested patrons of aviation like Karl and Zita.

"The Enormous Richness of Humanity"

The year 1913 would be important for defining musical modernism, beginning with Arnold Schoenberg's "Skandalkonzert" in Vienna in March, presenting the work of what was to become the second Vienna school—himself, Alban Berg, and Anton Webern—the composers whose atonality would define, for many, the meaning of modernist composition.[21] The concert caused a commotion in the audience, and even fighting, which ended the evening early—before the scheduled performance of Mahler's *Kindertotenlieder*. In May there would be even more of a commotion in Paris at the first performance of Igor Stravinsky's *Rite of Spring*, with its fierce dissonances and violent syncopations, along with the corresponding ferocity and violence of Nijinsky's choreography.[22]

Strauss had created a scandal of his own with the unsettling dissonance and blasphemous eroticism of *Salome* in 1905, but by 1913 he was very much the established master. In that year he approved the awarding of a stipend for Arnold Schoenberg with the casual reservation that he would be better off shoveling snow than scribbling notes on staff paper. When Schoenberg learned of the comment, he wrote to Alma Mahler, "I have had many moments when I felt inclined to take not the snow shovel, but rather the dung fork, to search critically through Strauss's intellect and artistry."[23] Strauss had had enormous success, ever since the 1880s, and such success naturally inspired enmity, reinforced in Schoenberg's case by his ideological commitment to an atonal musical revolution. Both Hofmannsthal and Strauss had become celebrated modernists in the late nineteenth century, but as they contemplated *Die Frau ohne Schatten*, they found themselves working in a cultural climate with shifting and contested models of twentieth-century modernism.

As the new year 1913 began, Hofmannsthal noted for Strauss their mutual good fortune in finding each other at the right moment in their respective trajectories. The poet commented on Goethe's attempts to write an opera libretto, attempts which foundered on his failure to find the right composer. Writing on January 20, Hofmannsthal announced that he had achieved a breakthrough on the fairy-tale opera:

> In the past eight days *Die Frau ohne Schatten* has made decisive progress. The most important scenes are now organized in every detail, including all the twists and turns of the dialogue; the transitions, seven times, from one world to the other, arouse in me a kind of envy for the composer who

Marriage and Childbirth in the Imperial Dynasty and the Fairy-Tale Opera 61

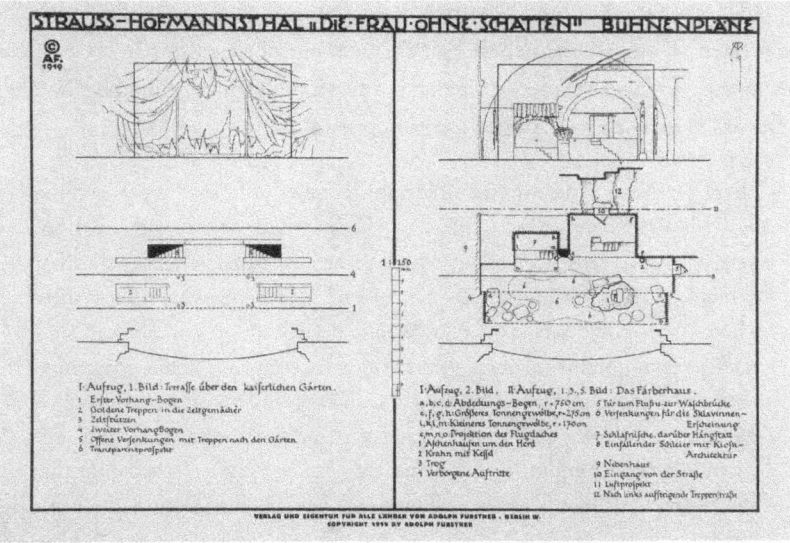

Figure 7. Alfred Roller prepared the stage designs for *Die Frau ohne Schatten* in 1919. This sheet shows (on the left) the design for the opening scene, the terrace (*Terrasse*) over the imperial gardens where the Empress awakens and is visited by the falcon. Elaborate curtaining indicates the tented imperial pavilion with golden stairs and a backdrop view suggesting the heights from which the Empress will have to descend when she seeks out the human world. That world is staged (on the right) as the Dyer's house (*Färberhaus*), a darkly vaulted space with descending stairs; there is a door to the street, a door to the river, and spaces for the conjuring of supernatural apparitions, like the slaves who will be summoned to appeal to the fantasies of the Dyer's Wife. Roller with his stage designs, like Strauss with his music, attempted to convey Hofmannsthal's sense of the dramatic difference between the upper and lower worlds. (Reproduced with the kind permission of the KHM-Museumsverband, Theatermuseum Vienna)

will have the chance of filling out with music what I must leave empty.... The profound content of the subject, the effortless symbolism of all the situations, the enormous richness of humanity [*der ungeheuere Reichtum des Menschlichen*] never fail to fill me with joyous astonishment.[24]

It was the topography of the scenario, the moving between two worlds, upper and lower, that seemed most exciting to the poet.

Hofmannsthal quoted Goethe's conception of opera as "bedeutende Situationen in einer künstlichen Folge" (meaningful situations in an artificial sequence)—which seemed relevant to the scenic structure of the *Die Frau ohne Schatten*, with its juxtaposition of upper and lower worlds.

> There are eleven meaningful situations, concise almost like pantomime, but it is their connection [*Verbindung*]—by which two worlds, two human pairs, two related conflicts which resolve by turns, reflect each other, enhance each other and finally cancel each other—producing a unified whole, which in itself, as a play, would be already remarkable and attractive enough, but through the music will receive its final consummation and consecration [*Vollendung und Weihe*], the music that entwines everything, mirrors everything, can even transform one thing into another, like an alchemist with the elements. It is certainly no accident that two individuals like us have encountered one another within the same epoch . . .[25]

In *Die Frau ohne Schatten* the musical and dramatic correspondences were the whole point: the mergings and mirrorings, the multidimensional geometry, even the Einsteinian relativity of two worlds in dramatic motion with respect to one another. In 1911, the year that Hofmannsthal first envisioned the opera in Habsburg Vienna, Albert Einstein, working in Habsburg Prague, was studying gravitational fields and the hypothetical bending of starlight as he moved from special relativity to the curvature of space-time in general relativity.[26]

The relations between higher and lower worlds had been of interest to Hofmannsthal dating back to his earliest lyric poetry from the 1890s:

Manche freilich müssen drunten sterben	Many must die down below
wo die schweren Ruder der Schiffe streifen,	where the ship's heavy oars move,
andere wohnen bei dem Steuer droben,	others dwell above by the helm,
kennen Vogelflug und die Länder der Sterne . . .	know bird flight and the lands of the stars . . .
Doch ein Schatten fällt von jenen Leben	But a shadow falls from those
in die anderen Leben hinüber,	upon the other lives,
und die leichten sind an die schweren	the light bound to the heavy,
wie an Luft und Erde gebunden . . .	as to air and earth.[27]

The connections of upper and lower worlds also posed for Hofmannsthal the ongoing question of his own relation as an aristocratic poet of refined sensibility to a wider world that lay beyond the narrowly defined boundaries of his own artistic refinement, between aesthetes and galley slaves. The 1890s were already a decade of mass politics in the Habsburg monarchy, further intensified by the advent of universal male suffrage in 1907.[28] *Die Frau ohne Schatten* would explore a possible musical reconciliation between the imperial palace and the homes of impoverished working people like Barak the Dyer and the Dyer's Wife.

Voyage to Italy

Strauss was scheduled to conduct in Rome in April 1913, and, as he planned his journey, he issued an invitation to Hofmannsthal:

> [I am] driving alone in my car via Verona, Mantua, Bologna, Florence, Arezzo, Orvieto to Rome. . . . Would you like to come along? . . . when we feel like it we'll chat [*plaudern*]—but silence and contemplative enjoyment also very welcome. It would be very nice, and especially at this stage it would be a good thing to be together for a somewhat longer period, undisturbed, and work out *Die Frau ohne Schatten*. Perhaps you could reach a stage by then with your work where an exchange of thoughts [*Gedankenaustausch*] would be useful . . .[29]

Strauss had begun his career as a composer with the tone poem "Aus Italien" in the 1880s, and Hofmannsthal also had an affinity for Italy, for his Habsburg noble pedigree appropriately included a grandmother from Milan, Petronilla von Rhò, his father's mother. Traveling together Strauss and Hofmannsthal might recover the spirit of Italian spectacle from the Habsburg baroque court of Leopold I and *Il pomo d'oro* or retrace the cultural course of Goethe's eighteenth-century *Italienische Reise*.

Hofmannsthal expressed cautious enthusiasm for the proposed trip to Italy, regretting the short notice:

> But I should very much like to say "yes" on this occasion, for as a matter of fact the scenario for *Die Frau ohne Schatten* is so well worked out and definite in my mind, that we could certainly talk about it; and this

personal contact (which we have never had over anything we have done before) might greatly benefit this our common principal work (for as such it appears to me).³⁰

For Hofmannsthal the opera, with the libretto barely begun, was already their masterpiece, hovering before him, drawing them together into closer collaboration and urging them onward into the Italian peninsula.

Hofmannsthal would be visiting a friend in Lucca, close to Zita's birthplace at Villa Pianore, and he proposed to meet Strauss in Verona.³¹ In fact, Verona had been a nineteenth-century Habsburg city up until 1866 when it became part of the kingdom of Italy. Milan, Venice, and Florence all had Habsburg histories. Wherever Hofmannsthal and Strauss traveled in northern Italy, they would encounter the shadows and associations of a former Habsburg presence, reminders of the transience of the power of emperors and empresses.

In March 1913, while Strauss and Hofmannsthal planned their trip to Italy, Russia celebrated the three hundredth anniversary of the Romanov imperial dynasty. Tsar Nicholas and Tsarina Alexandra, the unpopular empress of German origin (at this time under the hypnotic sway of Rasputin), presided over the celebration of the dynasty that would be swept away four years later by the Russian Revolution. St. Petersburg marked the anniversary with illuminations, fireworks, and opera: Glinka's *A Life for the Tsar*, composed in the 1830s on the historical subject of the founding of the dynasty. It was performed all over the empire in 1913, its final chorus and peeling bells echoing the live acclamations of the tricentennial year.³²

Hofmannsthal and Strauss traveled together through Italy from March 30 until the first week in April, focusing on a fairy-tale empire. They planned to arrive in Rome on April 3, taking rooms at the Hotel de Russie, located on Via Babuino between the Spanish Steps and Piazza del Popolo. It was a favored lodging for Diaghilev and Nijinsky when traveling with the Ballets Russes in the early twentieth century. "Hofmannsthal and I worked together beautifully," wrote Strauss to his wife Pauline on April 4. He promised her she would be pleased with *Die Frau ohne Schatten*: "Regarding the portrait of yourself, you need have no worry. He [Hofmannsthal] has adopted a few very general features. . . . No one will recognize you in this, have no fear."³³

Hofmannsthal, when he first mentioned the project to Strauss in 1911, had suggested that the Dyer's Wife might be modeled on Pauline.

Writing to Pauline from Rome again on April 5, Strauss reported on the success of the voyage to Italy.

> I have something most gratifying to report to you, that Hofmannsthal this afternoon at length narrated to me the whole complete design of *Die Frau ohne Schatten*: unbelievably noble, magnificent, mature and interesting, with splendid dramatic moral problems, noble scenic operations. If I preserve my health and strength to complete this work, it will become our most beautiful and sublime effort. I am really fortunate to have found such a collaborator, full of dramatic talent, moral maturity, and the most moving and brilliant ideas.[34]

Only now in April 1913, two years after Hofmannsthal first proposed the project in March 1911, did Strauss feel he knew enough about it to appreciate its qualities. Without having composed a single note, he agreed with Hofmannsthal that this would be the pinnacle of their collaboration.

Pauline Strauss had been a talented soprano (singing originally as Pauline de Ahna), and she always preserved the volatile temperament of a diva.[35] Strauss would eventually, in the 1920s, create a whole opera about her, *Intermezzo*, but already in *Die Frau ohne Schatten* the Dyer's Wife was endowed with Pauline's moodiness and sensitivity. Pauline sang the starring role of Elisabeth in *Tannhäuser* in Bayreuth in 1894, with Strauss conducting; she married him that year, and gave birth to their only child Franz in 1897. After his birth she no longer sang in opera, though she continued to give song recitals, with Strauss at the piano, until 1905 when she fully retired as a singer. Hofmannsthal's idea that her character was "incomprehensible, moody, domineering, and yet sympathetic" corresponded in some fashion to Strauss's own characterization of her as "very complex, a little perverse, a little flirtatious, never the same, changing from minute to minute."[36] Changeable moods, unpredictable reactions, this was part of how Strauss and Hofmannsthal conceived the character of the Dyer's Wife.

Pauline Strauss was also capable of making a very negative impression, and Hofmannsthal was present in Berlin in 1905 for a gathering at which Ida Dehmel, the wife of the poet Richard Dehmel, reported on Pauline: "She managed to utter so many ignorant, tactless, and crude indiscretions that it was the absolute lowest anyone could have experienced from a woman. 'Yes, men,' she said. 'The main thing is to keep a tight rein on them.' At the same time she made a gesture of reining in a horse, while making whipping motions."[37] The soprano Lotte Lehmann, who would create both of the roles supposedly based on Pauline Strauss, first the Dyer's Wife in 1919, then the role of Christine Storch in *Intermezzo* in 1924, took a more indulgent view of the marriage. "I often caught a glance or a smile passing between her and her husband, touching in its love and happiness, and I began to sense something of the profound affection between these two human beings, a tie so elemental in strength that none of Pauline's shrewish truculence could ever trouble it seriously."[38] As the Dyer's Wife, Lehmann would have to convey the intermingling of extreme discontent and real affection within her troubled onstage marriage.

In October 1897, six months after the birth of their son Franz, Strauss wrote to Pauline following some sort of explosion between them.

> Thank you once again for your adorable contrition: but you really ought not make so much of these things. Since I know you so very well and also know for certain that you are very fond of me, "scenes" like this are never going to be able to shake my trust in you. The only thing is that I'm often distressed for you, because your nerves are not strong enough to help you stand up to these bursts of feeling as you should. . . . So calm down, my sweet darling, because all the dear, good things I have from you, not least our splendid, glorious baby, always make me forget these little "incidents" very quickly, and my love for you is always the same. So there's nothing to forgive.[39]

In *Die Frau ohne Schatten*, the Dyer's Wife was very much a woman who made scenes and created incidents, a woman of weak nerves and bursts of extreme feeling, and the whole drama of the opera concerned the dynamics of reconciliation between her and her husband.

"The Blessing of Revocability"

After the Dyer's Wife throws the one-armed, one-eyed, and hunchbacked brothers out of the house, she mocks contemptuously their family narrative

Figure 8. Richard Mayr as Barak. Austrian bass-baritone Richard Mayr, after achieving huge success in Vienna in the role of the boorish aristocrat Baron Ochs in *Der Rosenkavalier*, went on to perform the very different role of Barak the Dyer, a humble craftsman, in *Die Frau ohne Schatten*. His lyrical and melodic part was intended to make him particularly sympathetic to the public as a Viennese man of the people. (Tully Potter/Bridgeman Images)

Figure 9. Feeling joy in his heart (*Freude im Herzen*) as he imagines his wife pregnant, Barak reaches up to an enraptured high D on the first syllable of *Freude*, and the strings play *pianissimo* to launch the D-major orchestral interlude that conveys Barak's tender feelings for his wife. The basic phrase consists of a rising interval, a falling interval, and a poignant turn of sixteenth notes. (*Die Frau ohne Schatten*, 1919)

of thirteen children and food for everyone. In jagged phrases, accompanied by shrill flutes and plucked strings, she makes abrupt octave leaps, imitating the brothers, so that her irritability is reflected in the musical language. As soon as Barak begins to sing, however, the tempo slows down (*etwas langsamer*) and the music becomes melodic. He too would gladly provide food for thirteen children, and he sings, with aching lyricism, "Ich will preisen ihre Begierde" (I want to cherish their appetite), with the first syllable of *preisen* on a sustained baritone high C. The music becomes even calmer (*immer ruhiger*) as he reaches out and touches his wife, asking gently, "When will you give me children?" But then the tempo immediately picks up (*viel lebhafter*) and the strings race through descending chromatic scales in staccato thirty-second notes, reflecting her fiercely nervous reaction as she pulls back from his sexual advance.[40]

Together in a reflective duet they recall the local wise women who have prepared spells for them to make Barak sexually fertile and to make his wife pregnant. Imagining her pregnant, Barak feels "Freude im Herzen" (joy in the heart), reaching up to a high D on the beautiful first syllable of *Freude* and down to a low D on the final syllable of *Herzen*, as the strings begin *pianissimo* on the gorgeous D-major orchestral interlude that characterizes Barak's tenderness toward his difficult wife. The basic phrase consists of a rising interval, a falling interval, and a movingly elegant turn of sixteenth notes. The flutes and oboes join, then the clarinets; the oboes and horns are a harmonizing presence as the strings build *crescendo*, returning more intensely to the ornamental turn in measure after measure as they reach a climax, *forte*, and then diminish to conclude *pianissimo*.⁴¹ Strauss's music affirms the power of human love to overcome the difficulties of human character, conveys the tenderness that a loving husband might feel for a troubled wife.

The Dyer's Wife, however, remains unpersuaded, and the tempo slows even further as she lays out her harsh resolution. After two and half years of failing to become pregnant she is determined to give up the humiliating effort, resolved to stop sleeping with her husband. She no longer wants to have children. When Barak replies—"with unforced solemnity and piety of heart"—he receives "tenderly expressive" accompaniment from the orchestra, especially the horns.⁴² They were always particularly important in the Straussian orchestra, for Strauss was the son of a horn player.

Now the horns support Barak as he sings Hofmannsthal's text, which could almost have been taken from Strauss's letter of reconciliation to Pauline back in 1897. Strauss provided a melodic setting to convey the text with maximal baritone clarity:

Aus einem jungen Mund	From a young mouth
Gehen harte Worte	come hard words
Und trotzige Reden,	and defiant speeches,
Aber sie sind gesegnet	but they are blessed
Mit dem Segen der Widerruflichkeit.	with the blessing of revocability.⁴³

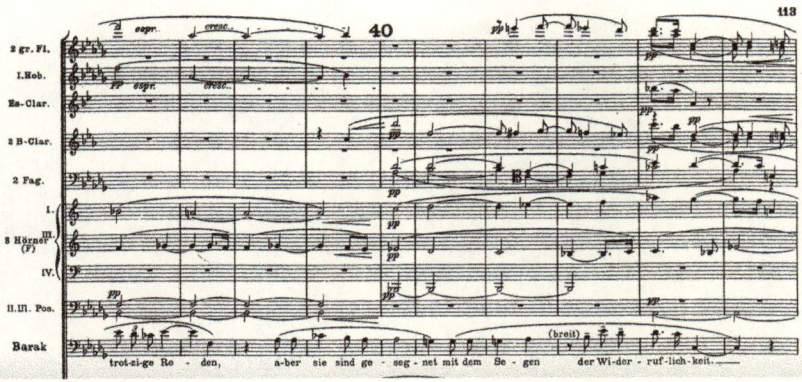

Figure 10. When the Dyer's Wife, under the malign influence of the Nurse, announces that she no longer wants to have children, Barak responds gently by commenting that her harsh words are "blessed with the blessing of revocability" (*Widerruflichkeit*). He is supported, as so often, by the horns, and gives beautiful baritone pathos to the five syllables of *Widerruflichkeit*. (*Die Frau ohne Schatten*, 1919)

The five syllables of the German word *Widerruflichkeit* were cushioned by the winds and the horns, playing *pianissimo*, offering the gentle hope of reconciliation.[44] Barak could not know that as soon as he left the house, his unhappy wife would receive a visit from an empress who coveted her shadow and her fertility, a fairy empress who wished to have human children and save her husband from being turned to stone.

5

"A Traitor Wind"

TREACHERY IN THE OPERA AND IN THE EMPIRE

Two Orchestras

After their several days in Rome together at the Hotel de Russie in April 1913, Hofmannsthal left Strauss to his conducting obligations and himself returned to Lucca, where they would meet again in a week and travel part of the way back to Austria and Bavaria together. On June 1 Strauss, back in Garmisch, was irate about the poor production of *Ariadne* in Munich, especially the Molière dramatic frame, and he inquired only very obliquely about *Die Frau ohne Schatten*: "When may I soon hear something beautiful from you?"[1] Hofmannsthal replied accordingly on June 3:

> For all the world just don't become impatient now for *Die Frau ohne Schatten*—and not your dear wife either!—or else you will endanger not only my nerves but, above all, the work itself. It is a fearfully delicate [*furchtbar heikle*], infinitely difficult thing, and more than once I have deeply despaired. I have now rewritten the first half of Act I three times, from the first word to the last, and it's not yet definitive.[2]

The poet pleaded not only the conditions of his submerged unconscious creativity but also his own psychological health: his frayed nerves and the possibility of a breakdown in deep despair. The terrible "delicacy" of the work was expressed as *heikel*, a word that hinted with its suggestion of trickiness, sensitivity, difficulty, and discomfort at the state of Hofmannsthal's aggravated nerves. The whole literary world knew, from the "Chandos Letter," that Hofmannsthal's nervous sensitivity was capable of silencing him altogether.

The first week in June 1913 was a week of heightened nerves throughout Austria-Hungary. On May 25 Colonel Alfred Redl, born in Galicia, committed suicide in Vienna; he had been discovered selling Austrian military secrets to Russia, possibly compelled by blackmail over his secret homosexual life. Probably the Russians received some account of Habsburg military defenses and mobilization plans along the Galician border, where Karl and Zita attended maneuvers in 1912. During the first week of June 1913 details of the case began to be publicized, the minister of war was questioned in the Reichsrat, and the army was criticized for having encouraged Redl to shoot himself instead of allowing a full investigation.[3] Hofmannsthal, however, was entirely preoccupied with *Die Frau ohne Schatten* during that first week in June, as he labored over the scenario:

> I am always delighted again and again by the richness within each individual scene, at the tremendous opportunities for the composer offered in the lyrical passages and in transitions requiring music. But the difficulties of compression, of wording and style, were enormous. . . . Since the end of April I have lived only for this work, have completely interrupted my correspondence, refused to have visitors, receive almost no one; but still you must have patience![4]

Just as *Die Frau ohne Schatten*, like *Die Zauberflöte*, was to be an opera of fairy-tale tasks, probationary trials, and ritual purification, so the creation of the opera became itself a set of challenges for Hofmannsthal, culminating in the trial of solitude. He then made it into an analogous challenge for Strauss, beginning with the trial of patience. "Sei standhaft, duldsam, und verschwiegen," sing the three spirit boys to Prince Tamino in *Die Zauberflöte*: "Be steady, patient, and discreet."

For Hofmannsthal, the crucial work that remained to be done was to plot the precise and intricate relation between the higher domain of the Emperor and Empress and the human world of the Dyer and Dyer's Wife. Hofmannsthal felt he could not complete the libretto for the first act until he had plotted particular scenes of the second act: "namely IIb and IId, the 'upper' scenes." These second and fourth scenes of act 2, involving the Emperor and the Empress respectively, would punctuate an act that moved back and forth between the human and imperial spheres, requiring careful dramatic planning and four changes of scene within a single act. Therefore, it was important for the opening of act 1, in the imperial palace, "to present the spiritual state [*Seelenzustand*] of the Emperor and of the Empress, so that IIb and IId may offer just lyrical effusions (as points of repose within the steadily progressing action on earth IIa, IIc, IIe)."[5] Hofmannsthal undertook a numerical, almost numerological, calculation of structure, with the juxtaposition and alternation of higher and lower spheres.

It was during the Italian trip that the composer and librettist had hit upon a plan for musically characterizing these two different dimensions with two different sets of orchestral forces. The moment of insight did not occur in Rome but afterward, as Hofmannsthal recalled, when they were traveling back across the Alps, on the road to Bolzano (Bozen) in South Tyrol.

> Splendid, your idea in the moonlight (between San Michele and Bozen), of accompanying the upper world with the *Ariadne* orchestra, and the denser, more colorful earth atmosphere with the full orchestra. . . . Wonderful transitions from one orchestra to the other occur naturally, as in [scene] Ia: as soon as the Empress has decided to descend to the human world.[6]

They had just composed *Ariadne* for an orchestra with thirty-seven players, while *Die Frau ohne Schatten* would have 164 instrumental parts. The awakening and entrance of the Empress in the upper sphere is accompanied by solo violin, harp, woodwinds, and celesta, while her decision to descend—"Ein Tag bricht an"—marks the moment for the full orchestra, with brass and percussion, to signal the coming change of scene to another world.[7] The Empress in her palace breathes a different air with the crystalline elegance of the celesta and the empyrean rippling of the harp, in a sphere where the voices of solo instruments like those of solo singers can be clearly heard and understood. The Dyer's Wife struggles with her poverty, with her husband's brothers, with her own rages and resentments, but she must also labor to make herself heard above the full intensity of the Straussian orchestra.

While he wrote to Strauss, Hofmannsthal suddenly found himself actually writing his libretto into the correspondence. The character who first sang out within that letter was not the Empress but the Nurse, the servant who would unscrupulously mastermind the plan to acquire for her imperial mistress a shadow from a human woman. Hofmannsthal set the scene for Strauss with all its colors:

Green early morning sky, then pale violet, gradually becoming the most intense fiery red of sunrise.

AMME: Wahnwitziges Kind,	NURSE: Crazy child,
Zu herrschen gewohnt!	Accustomed to rule!
Ein Tag bricht an,	Day is breaking,
Ein Menschentag!	A human day![8]

Strauss's orchestral tone poems had excelled in their creative expression of musical color, and Hofmannsthal confidently called upon him to paint the colors of the dawn. The libretto would set the style for the higher diction of the upper world and the ordinary speech of the lower world, but the distinctive recitations of the Nurse particularly required that Strauss follow the emphatic rhythms of her speech: "Wahnwitziges Kind!"[9]

The Nurse warned the Empress against the harshness of the dawning day in the human world, a world "without joy" (*ohne Freude*), but also observed that the human world was a treacherous world:

Ein Verräter Wind	A traitor wind
schleicht sich heran . . .	sneaks up on you . . .[10]

Hofmannsthal noted for Strauss that with the Nurse's quoted lines, "the musical atmosphere thickens uncannily [*verdichtet sich unheimlich*]."[11] In the context of June 1913, the spirit of treason creeping around the human world might have offered an implicit allusion to the Redl scandal of the moment: Redl, the ultimate traitor, who had betrayed his country's secrets to a foreign power. In *Die Frau ohne Schatten* the Nurse herself would emerge as a treasonous double agent, pretending to serve the Empress in her quest for a shadow but also serving the hidden world of the spirits—where it was hoped that the Empress would fail in her quest and then return to the realm of her father. The double dealing of the Nurse emerged at precisely the moment that the Redl affair revealed how thoroughly the Habsburg Empire was compromised by hidden treason.

Hofmannsthal worried that fairy-tale characters like the Empress and the Nurse might seem either overdrawn or too allegorical, that "the figures would lose their charm (which lies in their psychologically broken contours), become schematic and the whole thing trivially operatic."[12] This was an opera in which, ultimately, only one of the principal characters would even have a name, Barak the Dyer. Yet Hofmannsthal did not want them to appear as mere archetypes; he wanted the public to respond to them as recognizable humans and believable sovereigns. His fear that the characters might seem "trivially operatic" was certainly based on a misplaced condescension toward traditional opera, as was evident in his jaundiced perspective on Puccini.

Hofmannsthal, however, was also determined not to take Wagner as a model: "If I were to think of the libretto being composed in Wagner's ever-dragging [*ewig-schleppend*] solemn Andante, I would find it impossible, for the opera would last seven hours." Hofmannsthal was rightly concerned that an opera full of fairy-tale symbolism was at risk of feeling ponderous, and his blasphemous slur on Wagner—*ewig-schleppend*—was meant as an admonishment to Strauss in advance. "It is terrifying [*erschreckend*] how short the libretto for *Tristan* is, for instance, and how long it takes to perform," observed Hofmannsthal.[13] In the end *Die Frau ohne Schatten* would have about three and a half hours of music in three acts.

On June 12 Hofmannsthal sent Strauss the new libretto for the prologue to *Ariadne auf Naxos*, which was now to be set to music. The prologue would permit them to renounce the unsuccessful experiment of combining the *Ariadne* opera with the Molière play. At the same time, Hofmannsthal was finding *Die Frau ohne Schatten* "hellishly difficult" and declared that he could not deliver the libretto for the first act ("even if it were finished"), because he needed to think about the work as a whole in order to map out the second and third acts more fully. *Die Frau ohne Schatten* had to be conceived as "a world of deepest connection and most inexorable unity" (*eine Welt der tiefsten Bindung und unerbittlichster Einheit*)—such that all three acts had to be fully correlated before any part of the whole could be entrusted to the composer.[14]

"When are you going to Aussee?" inquired Strauss on June 15, with summer approaching. "Maybe I'll come with the car one day to visit you." Though adjusting comfortably to the age of the automobile, Strauss was probably not thinking only of the pleasure of the drive. The postscript to his letter made very clear what was on his mind: "The little hors d'oeuvre of verses from *Die Frau ohne Schatten* is most promising."[15] Strauss was intrigued by the Nurse's dark reflections on the degradation of the human world.

By July Hofmannsthal was at Aussee and Strauss was in the Dolomites, working on the ballet score for *Josephslegende* but also making general inquiries whose focus was pointedly clear: "Are you working hard? Is the work progressing to your satisfaction?"[16] In September Hofmannsthal was in Venice and writing to apologize for his failure to produce the libretto that Strauss was waiting for: "The serious blocks [*Stockungen*] I have suffered in writing *Die Frau ohne Schatten* must have amazed you, because in Rome it seemed that I already saw it all so clearly before me." The problem was that, having conceived of the work in terms of two different worlds, the verse itself had to reflect those contrasting spheres. The verse for the spirit world had to be rendered "simple, transparent, like a fairy tale [*märchenhaft*]" rather than "heavy in tone, too dark, too symbolic." Recalling perhaps his own lyric poem, "Manche freilich," about the privileged passengers on deck and the suffering oarsmen down below, he tried to find in his libretto the balance and contrast "between the lighter upper world and the somber human world" (*zwischen der leichteren oberen und der trüben Menschenwelt*).[17] Hofmannsthal himself claimed to suffer from "a sort of spiritual depression" (*eine Art geistiger Trübung*). Weighed down by his own depression the poet had to struggle to achieve the appropriate "lightness" (*Leichtigkeit*) of spirit for suggesting the opera's upper sphere, "in the fairy opera style."[18]

"To Sacrifice the Blood of Our Children"

In September 1913 Hofmannsthal was writing from the supremely elevated touristic level of the Grand Hotel Britannia in Venice, where he was meeting with Diaghilev to discuss *Josephslegende*.[19] From the northern shore of the Adriatic Sea, Hofmannsthal did not register in his letters any of the weightier human struggles taking place on the other side of the sea in southeastern Europe. The outbreak of the Second Balkan War in early June saw Serbia and

Greece now at war against Bulgaria (their recent ally against the Ottomans in the First Balkan War), with fierce fighting over the territory of Macedonia. In Habsburg Bosnia the Serbian population especially—including Gavrilo Princip, now back in Sarajevo—was so agitated by the Balkan Wars that for much of 1913 the Habsburg administration governed by emergency decree without reference to the provincial assembly. Bosnian-Serbian cultural and political organizations were suppressed, and the government held numerous treason trials. All this had the effect of radicalizing Serbian discontent in Bosnia, thus motivating the future assassins of Franz Ferdinand.[20]

While Hofmannsthal's correspondence with Strauss remained largely free from political concerns, on August 24 the poet wrote about Viennese politics to his friend Leopold von Andrian, writer and diplomat, serving in 1913 as Habsburg consul general in Russian-ruled Warsaw. "They are destroying Vienna," wrote Hofmannsthal from Aussee. "Vienna has been delivered over to the rule of the mob [*Pöbelherrschaft*], the worst there is, that of the malicious, stupid, wicked petty bourgeoisie [*Kleinbürgertum*]."[21] He meant the Viennese lower middle classes who had been mobilized to support the demagogically anti-Semitic Christian Socialist party, the party of Karl Lueger, mayor of Vienna from 1897 until his death in 1910. Carl Schorske has written about Lueger as one of the creators of "politics in a new key"—thwarting an older generation of liberals by drawing on the volatile forces of mass politics.[22] "I decide who is a Jew," remarked Lueger, expressing the opportunistic spirit of his political anti-Semitism. Hitler lived in Vienna from 1908 until 1913 and admired Lueger's political style.

In 1913 the mayor of Vienna was Lueger's close associate Richard Weiskirchner, representing the *Pöbelherrschaft* that Hofmannsthal so detested. The masses recognized no authority but their own, Hofmannsthal lamented, not the church, the nobility, or public opinion, "which they, with some justification, denounce as Jewish opinion."[23] Hofmannsthal was himself not immune to some anti-Semitic sentiments, assuming the persona of the Austrian aristocrat and erasing his own remote Jewish origins, while writing to Andrian who was himself the half-Jewish grandson of composer Giacomo Meyerbeer.

Hofmannsthal supposed that the only person who might be able to stand up to the mob would be the heir to the throne, Archduke Franz Ferdinand, but doubted that he possessed any of the necessary qualities of character:

"persistent dedication to a goal, substance, skill with people of all classes, a great and flexible understanding of the world connected to the firmest possible character." The poet had his vision of an ideal emperor and the necessary qualities to rule in an age of modern mass politics, but he did not believe in either the Habsburg heir or the Austrian aristocracy. "I have completely lost that confidence in the upper class, the high nobility, that I used to have," he confided, "the conviction that it could mean something and contribute something here in Austria."[24] It was a moment in some ways analogous to his Chandos crisis at the turn of the century, for the loss of faith in words and meaning was echoed here in his loss of faith in society and politics. This was, certainly, part of the spiritual depression that he referenced in his correspondence with Strauss; the inability to find the right balance for the libretto of *Die Frau ohne Schatten*, a libretto about the connection between upper and lower social spheres, was surely related to Hofmannsthal's personal distress over the political role of the popular classes in Vienna. The libretto, ultimately, would present a mythological imperial regime that surmounted its crisis and regained political faith in itself.

Because 1913 was also a year of anxiety about war, when the government contemplated involvement in the Balkan Wars, Hofmannsthal further confessed to Andrian anxieties about Austria and the imminent possibility of military mobilization.

> We must admit to each other, Poldy, that we have a homeland, but no fatherland—in place of which we have only a ghost [*Gespenst*]. It is bitter to think that we may at some point have to sacrifice the blood of our children for this ghost. Not that it would be desirable or bearable for me to contemplate the falling apart of this old empire. But for a mere existence, without any idea, without any direction beyond today and the next day . . . In contrast the Metternich epoch had a soul, because, reactionary or not, it served an idea. What about us?[25]

The summer of 1913, when Hofmannsthal struggled with the libretto of *Die Frau ohne Schatten*, trying to breathe life into a fairy-tale emperor and empress, was also the summer that he admitted his crisis of faith in the contemporary Habsburg Empire, and his libretto became the challenging literary space for fantasies about the regeneration of social and political life.

Many years earlier Hofmannsthal, only eighteen in 1892, had written a short verse play about Renaissance Venice called *The Death of Titian*, set at the moment of the artist's death in 1576. Titian's followers gaze upon Venice from a distance, fearing the supposed horrors of urban misery: "Da wohnt die Hässlichkeit und die Gemeinheit" (there dwells ugliness and commonness).[26] Hofmannsthal's Renaissance artists, like the young artists of Vienna in the 1890s, prefer to live in a walled-off world of aesthetic refinement. The conception of two worlds—an elevated sphere of beauty and light, a lower urban sphere of ugliness and misery—was something that Hofmannsthal first envisioned as a teenage poet in Vienna and imagined in the literary setting of Renaissance Venice. Now in 1913 he stayed at the Grand Hotel Britannia in Venice while contemplating the upper and lower spheres of *Die Frau ohne Schatten*.

Totem and Taboo

On September 30, Hofmannsthal wrote to Strauss once more to justify his slow progress on the libretto. "It is a matter of proportions," he explained, a matter of balancing the opera's multiple scenes and themes. On October 25, though the libretto for act 1 was still incomplete, the poet's imagination was preoccupied with the hypothetical music for the later acts: the conclusion of act 2 in the lower world, impossible to imagine "without horror" (*ohne Grausen*), but then the conclusion of act 3 in the upper sphere, "ascending by degrees to the heaven of music."[27] By December Hofmannsthal was not even working on the libretto but was now writing *Die Frau ohne Schatten* as a prose fairy tale, to be published separately.[28] This prose version would eventually arrive at the disproportionate length of 35,000 words, a very weighty fairy tale, even as the poet claimed to be looking for "lightness" in the libretto.

On December 26, Hofmannsthal wrote to Strauss, "I had intended sending you a Christmas present, but now you will not get it until New Year's Eve. It is the first, shorter half of the first act of *Die Frau ohne Schatten*, a section which I feel entitled to consider final and which, I believe, lends itself even more readily to music than anything I have previously done for you." On December 28 he posted the scene: "Here is my little New Year's gift. I want you to have it with you, and to give your imagination [*Phantasie*] now and then something to play with."²⁹ Finally Strauss had a part of the libretto to compose.

Hofmannsthal proposed mathematical specifications of proportion as a framework for the composer's creativity: "Since the complete first act must not last longer than sixty to seventy minutes . . . and since the second part of act 1 is far weightier [*gewichtiger*] than the first part and half as long again, this first half-act ought not to run to more than twenty or twenty-five minutes." Hofmannsthal wanted music that would be "light, flowing, ethereal" (*Leichtes, Fliessendes, Gehauchtes*), with the opening episodes joined by "a common spirit quality" (*ein gemeinsames Geisterhaftes*), an unearthliness.³⁰ The balance between two spheres, light and heavy, spirit and human, was to be reflected meticulously in the music. The opening scene, which actually encompassed four subsidiary episodes—Nurse and Spirit Messenger, Emperor's Departure, Empress and Falcon, Nurse and Empress—remained principally in the spirit world, overlapping with the imperial world, right up until the descent into the human city.

This opening scene introduced three of the principal characters—the Nurse, the Emperor, and the Empress—and Hofmannsthal's New Year's letter addressed each of these three figures who inhabited the upper sphere. He began with the Emperor:

> Of the five main characters in the piece, the Emperor is the least prominent; his fairy-tale fate of being turned to stone and redeemed again is his most striking feature. His traits are typical rather than individual; he is the hunter and lover. What the music will have to give him is not so much pronounced characterization as a more truly musical element; his is to be the sweet and well-tempered voice [*eine süsse, schöngeführte Stimme*] throughout.³¹

Hofmannsthal imagined a musically youthful emperor, sweet in voice, the hunter and lover who Franz Joseph might have been half a century earlier in the 1850s—or else the youthful emperor of the next generation. Strauss would not quite follow the poet's guidance here, for the musical character of the Emperor would be ardent and heroic, rather than sweet and light, a vocal part suitable for the heavy voice of a Wagnerian *Heldentenor*.

Hofmannsthal was particularly keen to have Strauss understand how to present the figure of the Empress in her first scene, inasmuch as her character was exceptionally complex:

> Of the threefold nature of the Empress, part animal, part human, and part spirit, only the animal and spirit aspects are apparent in this scene; these two together make her the strange being she is. In between there is a vacuum: the humanity is missing. To acquire this humanity—that is the meaning of the whole work, even in the music. Not until the third act will the voice of the Empress gain its full human ring; then the animal and spirit aspects will appear fused in a new being [*zu einer neuen Wesenheit verschmolzen*] on a higher plane.[32]

The Empress's voice in this opening scene was to be oddly characterized by an absence, the smaller ethereal orchestra accompanying a voice with inhuman or superhuman qualities but without fully human amplitude, warmth, or feeling. Those human qualities would come along with her quest for the shadow, with her potential fertility, her imminent motherhood.

The Empress's relation to the animal world was made vividly clear in the opening scene. The Emperor recalls their first encounter—"she had the body of a white gazelle and cast no shadow"—and then the Empress, awakening, thinks that "perhaps I might dream myself back into the light body of a bird or of a young white gazelle."[33] In 1913, as Hofmannsthal worked on the libretto, Sigmund Freud in Vienna published *Totem and Taboo*, a study of the intimate spiritual relation between "primitive" peoples and their totem animals. Drawing upon anthropological ideas concerning tribal peoples of the South Pacific—that is, the same domain as the operatic Emperor of the Southeastern Islands—Freud considered how institutions of marriage and reproduction were embedded in the social context of tribal taboos and a universe of spirits conceived according to animist beliefs. Following James Frazer in *The Golden Bough*, Freud stressed the sacred nature of the totem animal which could be hunted, killed, or eaten: "A member of a clan seeks to emphasize his relationship to the totem in various significant ways; he imitates an exterior similarity by dressing himself in the skin of the totem animal, by having the picture of it tattooed upon himself." While observing the special intimacy between humans and animals through the totem, Freud noted that knowledge about such totem beliefs came not only from anthropologists but also as revealed in "legends, myths, and fairy tales."[34] Hofmannsthal's Empress—who had once been able to transform herself into a gazelle, who was still marvelously able to hold conversation with a falcon—came from a totemist world of intimate relations among humans, animals, and spirits. Hers was also the fairy-tale world of the precious collection of Japanese *netsuke*—including the hare with amber eyes—belonging to the great Jewish banking family of the Ephrussi and treasured during these years in the Ephrussi Palace on the Ringstraße in Vienna.[35]

Nursing

As Hofmannsthal offered Strauss his auspicious New Year's gift for 1914, introducing the figure of the Empress in her threefold nature, Archduchess Zita was about to give birth to her second child on January 3. Adelheid was born at Schloss Hetzendorf, the creation of the great baroque architect Johann Lucas von Hildebrandt, on the outskirts of the imperial capital in the vicinity of Schönbrunn. This time Emperor Franz Joseph was present for the baptism, though the godfather was Prince Sixtus of Bourbon-Parma, Zita's brother. The doctor, again Heinrich Peham, reported that medically everything was in order, which was particularly important since the Fasching carnival ball season was approaching at the end of the month, and Zita was to be the particular patroness of the *Industriellenball* in the concert hall of the Musikverein.[36] According to Wilhelm Franz Exner, a distinguished engineer and the honorary president of the *Industriellenball* committee at that time, "The special character of the *Industriellenball* that was never achieved by any other ball was its fusion [*Verschmelzung*] of the otherwise so exclusive court society and middle-class circles."[37] As an occasion that connected industrialists and businessmen to court society, the *Industriellenball* dated back to the 1860s and would be held for the very last time in 1914, under Zita's patronage, for it would not continue during or after the war.

Zita remembered this as the moment of settling into family life with her husband and children after the more itinerant beginning of her marriage:

First we wandered as vagabonds through the garrisons of the monarchy, and then in Vienna Karl had General Staff instruction at home every evening, but I had the children. I remember an indescribably beautiful *Lohengrin* performance at the Hofoper, and a Caruso evening, and a series of charity events.[38]

Enrico Caruso's last performance at the Vienna Opera took place on September 18, 1913, singing Rodolfo in *La Bohème*, probably the performance that Zita was remembering. There were a half-dozen performances of *Lohengrin* during the 1913–14 season, and three of them featured Maria Jeritza in one of her famous roles as Elsa; she had now joined the Hofoper at the special request of Emperor Franz Joseph. If it was Jeritza who sang in *Lohengrin* for Zita, Strauss's future operatic Empress would have been singing for the actual future Empress.

With Otto born in November 1912 and Adelheid born in January 1914, Zita already had a small family before the outbreak of war. Zita, as one of her father's twenty-four children, must have grown up in a household of attendant servants who cared for the young princes and princesses. Even with only two children of her own, she certainly would have had assistance with child care. Throughout the nineteenth century European royalty made use of wet nurses for nursing their children, rather than maternal breastfeeding. A lactating woman in the role of wet nurse would provide milk from her own breasts for the newborn child of the royal family. Queen Victoria had wet nurses for all of her children. Franz Joseph and Empress Elisabeth had the infant Crown Prince Rudolf nursed by a Moravian peasant wet nurse named Marianka in the 1850s.[39] Though maternal rituals were changing in the early twentieth century, and cow's milk was also safer following the invention of pasteurization, the role of the wet nurse persisted: Hofmannsthal and his wife Gerty had a wet nurse for their son Franz, born in 1903.[40] It is very possible that Zita, with her busy schedule of charity activities and musical evenings, also had a wet nurse for Otto and then another for Adelheid: the Nurse, *die Amme*.

Concerning the three principal characters introduced in act 1, scene 1, Hofmannsthal's letter of December 28 offered a paragraph on the Emperor

Figure 11. *Die Amme*, the Nurse, is the Empress's treacherous companion—"between the demonic and the grotesque," according to Hofmannsthal. He wanted Strauss to compose a *Hexentanz*, a witch's dance, for the Nurse, and Roller clearly conceived her as a witch, represented here in sinister profile. In popular culture the figure of the wet nurse was often regarded with suspicion, but in *Die Frau ohne Schatten* she actually takes on Mephistophelean dimensions in pursuit of the desired shadow. (Wikimedia Commons)

and another on the Empress, but just a brief comment to characterize the third character: "the dual face [*das Doppelgesicht*] of the Nurse, who vacillates between the demonic and the grotesque."[41] That she was called the Nurse—*die Amme*—rather than simply the Servant of the Empress signified that she knew the Empress from infancy, nursed her at the breast like a mother, and had accompanied her ever since.

The demonic side of the Nurse also reflected suspicions about wet nurses that lay very deep in European society and culture; for centuries wet nurses, entrusted intimately with the family's most precious good, were also regarded with apprehension about hidden traits and secret habits that could be harmful to the infant. When an infant died—which was very common before the twentieth century—the wet nurse might be suspected of concealed malice or merely negligence. In the early modern centuries, wet nurses, like midwives, might be accused of witchcraft. Alfred Roller's costume design for the premiere of *Die Frau ohne Schatten* showed the Nurse in profile, with a prominent nose and dark brows, holding around herself a black shawl that covered her head, moving stealthily forward as if confronting a hostile world with frank hostility and some anxiety.[42]

As her intimate confidante, the Nurse guides the Empress through the human world in pursuit of a shadow like Mephistopheles accompanying Faust, and certainly Hofmannsthal had Goethe on his mind while thinking about *Die Frau ohne Schatten*. Another model, however, might have been Brangäne from Wagner's *Tristan*, for she was Isolde's intimate confidante—sometimes even referred to as her nurse. It was Brangäne who betrayed Isolde, not quite unintentionally, by giving her, in act 1, the wrong magic potion. For certain, Hofmannsthal was studying the libretto of *Tristan* in 1913, when he noted how short the libretto was in proportion to the length of the opera. Strauss perhaps also intuited the connection, for the roles of Brangäne and the Nurse are often within the repertory of the same mezzo-sopranos.

Sigmund Freud, when he carried out his pioneering self-analysis in Vienna in 1897, attached great importance to memories and dreams of a childhood nurse or nanny (the term he used was *Kinderfrau*) whom he remembered as "an ugly, older, but clever woman who told me a lot about dear God and Hell." She took him treacherously to church as a child (though he was Jewish), and he later wondered whether she might have sexually abused him—though his mother explained that the nurse had actually been dismissed for stealing.[43] In Freud's life too the Nurse played a sinister role, many years later still haunting his Viennese dreams.

The Nurse in Waltz Time

The Nurse's appearance in act 1, scene 2, in Barak's dwelling, shows her fully in command of the whole drama and reveals her Mephisthelean dimensions. After the Dyer's Wife has told Barak that she no longer wants to have sex with him, and when he has gently replied that he can wait with patience for her to revoke her harsh resolve, he departs for the market. As soon as he is gone the harps begin running up and down the scale, *glissando*, joined by the flute, and muted strings are bowed *sul ponticello*, close to the bridge, for a ghostly sound—all to suggest that there is imminent magic in the air. The Nurse and the Empress then appear—"as if they had not entered by the door"—with the Empress disguised in the humble clothes of a servant, the Nurse's servant, a strange reversal of roles.[44]

The Nurse also takes over the vocal score, leaving the Empress almost silent in the scene that follows. In a deceitfully gay 6/8 waltz-like rhythm, the Nurse launches into a gushing burst of false flattery addressed to the dumbfounded Dyer's Wife: "Ach! Schönheit ohnegleichen!"—O peerless beauty!—sings the Nurse. "Who is this princess? Where is her retinue?" The flattery, however, is so extreme that the Dyer's Wife realizes that she is being mocked by Mephistopheles: "You winking one [*Du Zwinkernde*] whom I have never seen before, and don't know how you slipped in, I see right through you." As the Dyer's Wife sings, a viola fiddles along a chromatic scale in rapid semiquavers, simulating the slippery deceit of the Nurse.[45] The latter, however, is undeterred in her flattery, expressing mock amazement to learn that Barak is the husband, not the servant, of the house.

The Nurse now sings lyrically of her astonishment to the Empress in an ascending D-major phrase, with flourishes from the violins and flutes—"O meine Tochter!"—Oh my daughter!—as if the child she once nursed were actually her real daughter. The Empress, however, has only one single line to sing, only one personal phrase of passionate intensity, accompanied by the harps: "I want to kiss the shadow that she casts."[46] For the Empress, the

Dyer's Wife really is a princess, really is a peerless beauty, because she possesses that most desirable of all attributes, a human shadow.

The Nurse descends to the bottom of her range to hint to the Dyer's Wife at a hidden mystery—*das Geheimnis*—and the triangle, tambourine, and snare drum enter to build the magical suspense. The mystery lies in "your shadow"—*deinen Schatten*—the Nurse reveals, her words ornamented with a rising and falling coloratura figure. By selling her shadow the Dyer's Wife may acquire power without limits over men, sings the Nurse, now soaring over the orchestra on the word "limits" (*Schranken*), which takes her to the sustained G-sharp at the upper limit of her vocal register.[47] Hofmannsthal conceived the Nurse as demonic and grotesque, but Strauss endowed her in this scene with treacherously beautiful music, the better to deceive and seduce the Dyer's Wife and conclude the fateful bargain.

The woodwinds offer magical accompaniment as the Nurse promises silks and brocades, slaves and lovers, gardens and fountains—with harps to evoke the spray of the fountains.[48] Out of thin air the Nurse produces a hairband ornamented with pearls and jewels, and the celesta enters the score to surround the Dyer's Wife with a cascade of notes to suggest her new illusionary beauty. And now the Nurse demonstrates the full extent of her sorcery as she, together with the Straussian orchestra, transforms Barak's humble dwelling into the richly decorated pavilion of a princess. The lilting 6/8 time slows to a hypnotic 3/4 waltz time, and the celesta, the flutes, and trilling violins bring about the scenic transformation, with triangle, tambourine, glockenspiel, harps, and timpani joining to convey the magical atmosphere. There is some echo of the conjuring of the magical garden in the second act of *Parsifal*, the Nurse singing with the voice of Kundry (whose vocal range, like that of Brangäne, seems to fit the Nurse). To confirm the resemblance, a chorus of female slaves appears and begins to sing gently, sounding very much like the Flower Maidens from *Parsifal*.[49]

As the chorus reaches its climax and the Dyer's Wife gazes upon her newly contrived beauty in a mirror, the voice of the Empress is heard singing one single waltzing line, accompanied by the harp and the English horn: "For the image in the mirror, wouldn't you give up your insubstantial shadow?" The score, peculiarly, specifies that this is the "Voice of the Empress" rather than simply the Empress, as if her voice is being conjured by the sorcery of the Nurse as a means of seducing the Dyer's Wife. That is certainly true for the "Voice of the Youth," a tenor fantasy lover, who seems to echo the Empress's voice when he now sings: "I would give up even my soul for the image in the mirror."[50]

The Nurse was not just a diabolical force within the opera and not just a fifth wheel in the balanced symmetrical drama of two couples. As the first act moved toward its conclusion, the Nurse appeared to be almost the dominant figure in the opera, seducing the Dyer's Wife with flatteries and conjurings while reducing the Empress to the role of a maidservant. The Nurse was both the Freudian genius who could discover the inner fantasies and longings of unhappy humans and also the theatrical impresario who could bring about magical transformations of scene—precisely the transformations that Hofmannsthal and Strauss would require from the production when the opera finally came to the stage. In spite of her lifelong devotion to the Empress, whom she had nursed as an infant, her allegiances were uncertain and ambivalent, while her treacherousness, malevolence, and deceit were all too readily apparent. Indeed, the malevolence of the Nurse seemed almost intended by Hofmannsthal as the literary means for emphasizing the innocence of the Empress, as if to absolve her in advance for the intended theft of the shadow, to assign the blame to an underling. When Hofmannsthal presented the Nurse to Strauss in the New Year's letter for 1914—"between the demonic and the grotesque"—he could not know that the New Year would also witness the advent of the demonic war that would, eventually, bring about the dissolution of the Habsburg Empire.

6

Hexentanz

**THE RENUNCIATION OF MOTHERHOOD
AND THE ASSASSINATION AT SARAJEVO**

"The Destiny of the Empress"

"The more you can cut the better, in this scene and in every other, without essentially damaging the comprehensibility of the characters," wrote Hofmannsthal to Strauss on January 2, 1914, at the beginning of the new year. "I believe I will authorize every cut that seems possible to you."[1] After laboring for so long on the first scene of *Die Frau ohne Schatten*, Hofmannsthal now approved all possible trimming in advance; he worried that the fairy-tale scenario was already taking on unwieldy epic proportions.

Indeed, the epic poetry of Dante informed his sense of the opera's trajectory, as Hofmannsthal wrote to Strauss: "In the composition of these three acts your road will be exactly like Dante's: from hell, through purgatory, into the heaven of the third act."[2] The Nurse's Mephistophelean domination of act 1, scene 2, would give the first act its particularly hellish character, while the poverty and unhappiness of the Dyer's dwelling would also give the middle act some of its purgatorial atmosphere. It was, in fact, the Empress who would experience the human world as hell, would be morally tested by the trials of purgatory, and then reascend to the spiritual heights of imperial paradise in the third act. Hofmannsthal was about to travel to Berlin to bring Strauss the draft manuscript of the second scene of act 1 and was determined to read aloud to the composer the complete first act, as if only the poet's own voice could convey the spirit of the characters and the tone of the fairy tale.[3]

At the end of January Hofmannsthal reported from the Vienna Opera that conductor Franz Schalk—Anton Bruckner's pupil—was the only sincere advocate of the Strauss-Hofmannsthal collaborations and was conducting *Der Rosenkavalier*, making sure "from one performance to the next that this opera is kept intact." It was Schalk who disciplined the "laziness and reluctance" of Richard Mayr, the Austrian Baron Ochs who, in spite of his alleged laziness, would eventually create the role of the hardworking Barak in *Die Frau ohne Schatten*, with Schalk conducting. Schalk was also planning a new production of *Elektra*, with Maria Jeritza in the role of Elektra's sister Chrysothemis, who longs for motherhood and children. In February Hofmannsthal summoned a secretary to Rodaun to prepare the text of the full first act of *Die Frau ohne Schatten*.[4]

On April 4 Strauss wrote enthusiastically, "The first act is simply wonderful: so concentrated and unified that I cannot yet think of cutting or altering anything at all. For me it's just a matter of finding a new simple style which will make it possible to present your beautiful poetry to the listeners in its full purity and clarity."[5] Hofmannsthal wrote the libretto largely in verse, and Strauss intended to respect that versification in the music, using the restricted, transparent *Ariadne* orchestra for the upper sphere of the Emperor and the Empress, but also carefully arranging the forces of the larger orchestra deployed for the human world. Barak the Dyer, especially, sang almost with the clarity of folk style, accompanied by mellow horns, while the trio of night watchmen at the conclusion of the first act offered a hymn-like ensemble.

In April Strauss was working on the first scene of the act, navigating the end of the Emperor's aria and then the quick transition to the Empress's awakening. For the tenor piece he had already composed "a very dazzling conclusion," rising to high B-flat and leading immediately into a "very fiery" *fortissimo* orchestral statement of the Emperor's passion ("Denn meiner Seele"). Strauss then wanted to cut a whole page of the libretto and arrive at the awakening of the Empress: "sofort die Kaiserin" (immediately the Empress). He noted her opening line—"Ist mein Liebster dahin?" (Is my beloved gone?) The music would shift into the key of F-sharp, her music marked *grazioso*, and she would rise to high F-sharp on that first line, her exquisite entrance into the score. No sooner awake than the Empress thought

Figure 12. Roller's design for the Emperor in his hunting costume (*Jagdgewand*) was entirely in the spirit of the *Thousand and One Nights*, from his turban right down to his curled slippers. It was as a hunter that he first encountered the Empress, for she had taken the form of a gazelle. The Habsburgs were also avid hunters, especially Archduke Franz Ferdinand. (Lebrecht Music Arts/Bridgeman Images)

of returning to sleep, to perhaps dream her way back (*vielleicht träum' ich mich zurück*) into the form of a bird or a gazelle. Strauss referred to this text in his letter and would later elaborately compose the verb "to dream" running dreamily down and up the scale in shimmering thirty-second notes.[6]

Strauss expected to finish composing act 1 in the early summer and hoped to receive the libretto of act 2 by August 1914, without any idea, of course, of what that month would actually bring.[7] Hofmannsthal wrote back to agree, in principle, to the cuts and adjustments, and to observe that "in a collaboration like this I look upon you at the same time as my critic and my public."[8] He did, however, have one particular concern, and that related to the figure of the Empress, whose material Strauss was already revising. Hofmannsthal was almost chivalrous in his defense of his imperial heroine, as if she were at risk of lèse-majesté:

> There is only one thing you should never forget: the Empress, in a spiritual sense, is the main figure and her destiny the pivot of the whole opera. The Dyer's Wife and the Dyer are indeed the strongest figures, but the opera is not about them: their destiny is subordinate to the destiny of the Empress. This I must say, and you must always keep it in mind.[9]

Only by keeping this in mind throughout would it be possible to prepare for the Empress the climactic scenes in the third act—"the crown of the whole"—with poetry and music together leading, like Dante's epic poem, to "paradise."[10]

It was the Empress who would achieve this operatic coronation and apotheosis, learning humanity from her encounter with humans, and thus showing that she was worthy of being human herself and worthy to reign over humans. Historian Michael Steinberg has even suggested that "Hofmannsthal saw himself in the Empress."[11] She had been sheltered by her elevation from the human world, just as he had been sheltered by his early aestheticism. At the same time, however, her trials constituted an imperial legitimation, the implicit vindication of a dynasty.

"Will be happy to see you again!" wrote Strauss to Hofmannsthal. "I am already past the falcon's prophecy and am coming down to the human world [*herab zu den Menschen*]."[12] Thus Strauss, as he composed in April, associated himself with the descent of the Empress at the end of the first scene.

Figure 13. Roller's design for the Empress in her nightgown is a representation of fin de siècle sensuality. We first encounter the Empress as she is rising from her bed after a night of passion with the Emperor. While the image evokes some of the sexual presence of Beardsley's Salome (1893) or Klimt's Judith (1901), the pensive hand on the cheek suggests a spirit of sympathetic reflection. The very long dark hair would have immediately evoked memories of Habsburg Empress Elisabeth, assassinated in 1898. (Lebrecht Music Arts/Bridgeman Images)

Hofmannsthal in May was in touch with Roller about the set designs for the opera and particularly interested in how Roller would manage the scenic transformations during the orchestral interludes—as with the descent of the Empress.[13] Hofmannsthal and Strauss were preparing to meet in Paris in May for the premiere of the *Josephslegende* ballet, presented by Diaghilev with the Ballets Russes, choreographed by Michel Fokine, and starring as Joseph the eighteen-year-old Leonid Massine (instead of Nijinsky) defending his adolescent chastity. Contemplating Paris, Hofmannsthal asked a favor of Strauss—"since your name is bound to impress the manager of a Paris hotel, but mine not at all"—to book a room at the Hôtel de Crillon, "a not too expensive room, on one of the upper floors, not a servant's room, but rather a secretary's or librettist's room."[14] In 1919, the year of *Die Frau ohne Schatten* in Vienna, the Crillon would be an important site for the negotiations of the Paris Peace Conference.

Strauss and Hofmannsthal went to Paris in May, but Gavrilo Princip traveled from Sarajevo to Belgrade where he reported to the secret society of the Black Hand, directed by Colonel Dragutin Dimtrijević, known as Apis, an intelligence officer in the Serbian army. The visit of Franz Ferdinand to Sarajevo had been announced for June, and the Black Hand was planning his assassination, so Princip and two other young conspirators were given grenade bombs, Browning pistols, and suicide cyanide capsules in Belgrade, before being sent back to Sarajevo on May 28 to wait for the archduke.[15]

Hunters and Killers

Franz Ferdinand and his wife were spending the spring of 1914 becoming better friends with Karl and Zita. The two archdukes went hunting together that spring, like the Emperor whom Hofmannsthal had just created for his fairy-tale scenario—"he is the hunter and lover"—and for whom Strauss had just created an aria with a "very dazzling conclusion."[16] Franz Ferdinand was the supreme Habsburg hunter, tallying in his hunting journal 274,899 items of prey over the course of a shortened lifetime of fifty years, including a round-the-world tour in 1893 that involved hunting elephants in Ceylon, tigers in India, kangaroos in Australia, and grizzlies in Canada.[17] In the spring of 1914, the last hunting season of his life, he hunted less adventurously on

Austrian terrain, together with his nephew and designated imperial successor, Archduke Karl.

Because Karl and Zita were now in residence at Schloss Hetzendorf near Vienna, designed by Hildebrandt, they lived much closer to Franz Ferdinand and his family with their official residence at the Upper Belvedere Palace, originally built for Prince Eugene of Savoy by Hildebrandt. In the spring of 1914 the two archducal households in their two baroque palaces were in friendly family contact. "I was on very good terms with the Duchess of Hohenberg," recalled Zita later of Franz Ferdinand's wife. "She was not only a clever woman from much and bitter experience, but also a mature woman through motherhood and responsibility, and she stood by my side like an older friend."[18] In Zita's view, the two women were bonding over their common motherhood, Sophie with three children, ages ten to thirteen, and Zita with two under two; their shared sense of elite dynastic motherhood was reflected in a broader democratization of the cult of motherhood expressed at that very same time by Woodrow Wilson in Washington, DC, when he proclaimed Mother's Day to be an American national holiday in May 1914.

The spring of 1914, according to Zita's retrospective memory, was haunted by premonitions of assassination on the part of Franz Ferdinand himself.

> A terrifying, somber, fatally serious scene occurred one evening in the course of a visit to the Upper Belvedere. . . . When the Duchess of Hohenberg took the children off to put them to sleep, after a short silence Archduke Franz Ferdinand said, "I must let you know about one thing. . . . I will soon be murdered!" . . . We both gazed horrified, distraught, at Franz Ferdinand, and finally Archduke Karl said, as though he wanted to break the spell . . . "But Uncle, that is impossible! And besides: who would commit such a crime?"[19]

While Karl was innocent enough to doubt the older man's prophecy—"But Uncle, that is impossible!"—Zita was a connoisseur of dark premonitions. Already in 1911 the pope had predicted to her, before her marriage, that Karl would succeed Franz Joseph.

Now at the Belvedere, Franz Ferdinand informed Karl that there was a locked box of political papers set aside for him, to be opened after the foreseen assassination. "As you know," continued Franz Ferdinand, "in Artstetten everything is prepared, the crypt is waiting." Then he cut short the conversation, as his wife returned to the room: "And now we will speak no more about this. I don't want Sophie to become sad."[20] In Zita's remembering, all the ingredients of the fairy-tale form were present: the palace, the spell, the foreboding, the children, the locked box, the crypt. The members of the Habsburg dynasty, going back to the seventeenth century, were buried in the Kapuzinergruft, the Capuchin Crypt, in Vienna, though their hearts were buried separately in the Herzgruft in the Augustinerkirche at the Hofburg. Franz Ferdinand, however, would not be buried there, because his wife, ineligible to be empress, was also to be insultingly excluded from the imperial crypt. They were therefore to be buried together at Artstetten Castle, near Melk by the Danube.

Franz Ferdinand traveled to Bosnia in June 1914 for the same reason that Karl and Zita traveled to eastern Galicia in the summer of 1912, to provide a Habsburg presence at military maneuvers. Bosnia with its Serbian border, like Galicia with its Russian border, was a militarized frontier, and the troops here could be strategically deployed in the event of war—though some of their strategic planning had probably been already betrayed to Russia by Colonel Redl. Franz Ferdinand and Sophie traveled across Sarajevo in a motorcade on the morning of June 28—which also happened to be St. Vitus Day, an annual occasion of solemn Serbian remembrance of the battle of Kosovo, fought against the Ottomans in 1389. A half-dozen conspirators lined the route of the motorcade, and at 10:10 a.m. the nineteen-year-old Nedeljko Čabrinović threw a grenade that bounced off the archduke's car—a 32-horsepower Gräf & Stift Double Phaeton—and exploded without causing any deaths. With considerable relief it was now supposed that the assassination attempt had failed and that the danger was over, but when the motorcade set out again, after a short stop for a ceremonial reception at the Town Hall, the nineteen-year-old Princip opened fire with a Browning M1910 pistol around 11:00 a.m., and both the archduke and his wife were dead within the half hour.[21]

Karl and Zita received the news of the assassination by telegram in the gardens of Villa Wartholz, which had been built by Franz Ferdinand's father Karl Ludwig. Zita recalled the arrival of the telegram and declared this to be "one of the most moving moments of my life."[22] Stefan Zweig heard the news at the little spa town of Baden bei Wien just south of Vienna. He was reading in a public park while listening to a band concert in the distance—and "suddenly stopped reading when the music broke off abruptly."[23] An announcement of the assassination had been posted on a placard in the park. Zweig watched the people in the park react to the news:

> But to be honest, there was no particular shock or dismay to be seen on their faces, for the heir apparent was not at all well-liked. . . . Franz Ferdinand lacked everything that counts for real popularity in Austria: amiability, personal charm. . . . He had no sense for music, and no sense of humor, and his wife was equally unfriendly. They both were surrounded by an icy air; one knew that they had no friends, and also that the old Emperor hated him with all his heart, because he did not have sufficient tact to hide his impatience to succeed to the throne. . . . There were many on that day in Austria who secretly sighed with relief that this heir of the aged Emperor had been removed in favor of the much more beloved young Archduke Karl.[24]

Zweig strongly suggested that, if the war had not immediately intervened, the death of Franz Ferdinand might even have been regarded by some as a positive development for the Habsburg dynasty. The elevation of Karl and Zita to the status of immediate imperial heirs would also have signaled a generational shift of leadership for someone like Zweig, born in 1881, just six years older than Archduke Karl.

"To Renounce Motherhood Forever"

Zita's recollection of the burial rites at Artstetten on July 4, 1914, was focused with maternal sentimentality on the orphaned children: "And in all this black, among all these flowers and people, were the children of the deceased, and the pain of the orphans was heartrending."[25] On that same day, Hofmannsthal wrote to Strauss from Aussee with no mention of the assassination, the funeral, or the Habsburg dynasty, though perhaps pointedly emphasizing an Austrian identity: "Dear Dr. Strauss, Are you back? And peaceful? Have you already resumed work? At the end of act 1? If so, I have to keep my fingers crossed [*die Daumen halten*] for you—if you understand this Austrian expression. And how was London?"[26] Strauss had spent a large part of June in London, where he conducted the ballet *Josephslegende*, led additional concerts of his own music, received an honorary doctorate from Oxford marking his fiftieth birthday on June 11, and was generally celebrated as the greatest contemporary German composer—even as England and Germany were about to go to war.[27] Strauss had a large part of his savings in British banks—all about to be confiscated as the property of an enemy alien.

While Strauss at Garmisch was composing the first act of *Die Frau ohne Schatten*, Hofmannsthal in Aussee, with fingers crossed hopefully, had just finished a draft of the second act—concisely written in thirty pages—and given it over to his secretary. "You will never receive a more beautiful libretto," he wrote to Strauss, "neither from me nor from anyone else, it was a unique favor of destiny."[28] The day of Franz Ferdinand's funeral, with the war only a month away, Hofmannsthal was full of excitement at the prospect of *Die Frau ohne Schatten* and celebrated the favor of destiny.

Strauss replied the next day, Sunday, July 5, the day of the Potsdam meeting where German and Austrian officials discussed the possibility of a war against Serbia. The composer was worried, however, about the moral and musical implications of the dialogue between the Nurse and the Dyer's Wife at the conclusion of the first act. He wanted to cut six lines of verse in order to jump directly from the Dyer's Wife explaining that she has renounced sex with her husband—"So ist es gesprochen und geschworen in meinem Innern" (So it is spoken and sworn inside me)—to the Nurse's specification of the bargain for the shadow—"Abzutun Mutterschaft auf ewige Zeiten" (To renounce motherhood forever).[29] This was a matter of how Strauss envisioned the flow of the music, passing from the Dyer's Wife to the Nurse, and, though Hofmannsthal would ultimately allow the alteration, he was stubbornly resistant to having the Nurse begin her part with a grammatical infinitive: *abzutun*.

Strauss's other problem with the conclusion of the act involved the Nurse and the Dyer's Wife frying fish for Barak's dinner: the fish sing from the frying pan with the voices of children, crying out to the Dyer's Wife as their mother. Barak comments hungrily on the smell of the frying fish, and his wife says, "There is the food." Strauss worried over this and wrote to Hofmannsthal: "Won't this suggest that he is about to eat the fried little fish—which would be rather distasteful and disgusting [*ekelhaft*]?"[30] Taking the black magic of the Nurse very literally, Strauss feared that the audience would think that Barak was eating his own unborn children.

Hofmannsthal promptly replied from Aussee on July 8, as Franz Joseph's ministers in Vienna discussed the possibility of an ultimatum to Serbia that would likely lead to war. "The objection to the eating of the fish seems to me, speaking frankly, oversubtle," wrote Hofmannsthal. "The little fish are not, after all, children: they are only the vehicles of magic. I cannot think that anyone could take offense at this passage; it is always like that in fairy tales."[31] For Hofmannsthal, the magical elements of a fairy tale were not to be treated too seriously or literally. For Strauss, who was actually composing notes for live children to sing, as if coming from the frying pan, the vocal reality was harder to dismiss. Yet, for both Strauss and Hofmannsthal, this debate about the magical element of the singing children and the frying fish evaded the much more dangerous reality of the human world of July 1914—when parents were already aware that they might have to send their children to die in war.

Hofmannsthal divided the Nurse's text into four parts—A, B, C, D—and specified that the Nurse should turn in four different directions as she delivered the four parts, as if ritually casting a magic spell, for which Strauss would have to design appropriate dance music: "Here the Nurse dances a ritual witch dance [*Hexentanz*] until she cries out her triumph A, B, C, D, to all four points of the compass."[32] For Hofmannsthal this renunciation of motherhood—"Abzutun Mutterschaft"—was an evil moment of black sorcery, and he wanted Strauss to produce the appropriate musical accompaniment to complete the spell.

On July 10 the ministers in Vienna were already preparing an ultimatum to Serbia, anticipating a rejection that would lead to the evil moment of war, with the onus of responsibility on the Serbs for not accepting the terms. Strauss in Garmisch was still worried about Barak's problematic dinner: "You have not removed my concerns about Barak eating his own children. If one didn't hear the children singing you'd be right! But as it is, one must identify the unborn children with the little fish in the pan!" Barak's meal could be skipped altogether, suggested Strauss: "He goes to bed without supper." For Hofmannsthal, a fairy tale might allow for magical cannibal symbolism, as in the "Juniper Tree" from the Brothers Grimm, in which a father unwittingly eats the cooked body of his own child. For Strauss a fairy tale might offer a more prosaic reality, when poor families go to bed hungry, as in the tale "Hänsel and Gretel," also from the Brothers Grimm.[33]

"We're going next week for eight days in the Dolomites," wrote Strauss cheerfully on July 10. On July 12, as the draft of the ultimatum to Serbia was being completed in Vienna and presented for consideration in Berlin, Hofmannsthal was still worrying about the use of the infinitive in the passage "Abzutun Mutterschaft" and urging the composition of a witch dance for the Nurse. He did not want to leave this unresolved with Strauss about to depart for the Dolomites: "Please, a word about this point on a postcard: this is poetically, dramatically, gesturally, one of the most important points of the piece and I would like to be fully reassured [*beruhigt*] about it." Again, the irony was clear enough: the condition of Europe could not have been more unsettled at this moment when Hofmannsthal craved some becalming reassurance over the matter of the fairy tale. He hoped to be able to send off the second act in time for Strauss to take it with him to the Dolomites and promised also a note on the financial terms for *Die Frau ohne Schatten*.[34] Of course, their collaboration had a business aspect, and for both of them, in mid-July 1914, it was business as usual. On July 15 Hofmannsthal and his wife Gerty sent a vacation postcard to Arthur Schnitzler: "Under a cloudless sky we sit peacefully together and wish you the same."[35]

The Night Watchmen

In July Strauss was already composing the conclusion of the first act, when the Nurse's magically conjured world of fountains and gardens, lovers and slaves, triangle and tambourine suddenly collapses, and the Dyer's Wife finds herself back in her own miserable home, her world of striving without joy. In a nervously subjunctive question, her curiosity heightened by ascending triplets in the flutes, clarinets, harps, and cellos, she asks: "If I were willing—how would it even be possible to barter away a shadow?" The Nurse and the Dyer's Wife trade off vocal lines as the Nurse tries to make motherhood seem repulsive: "Should your body be used as an army road [*Heerstraße*] and your slenderness a heavily trodden path? Should your breasts wither and their glory be quickly gone?" These were the physiological consequences that

Figure 14. Strauss was determined to have the Nurse's words "Abzutun Mutterschaft" (to renounce motherhood) immediately following the Dyer's Wife's inner resolve ("geschworen in meinem Innern"), though Hofmannsthal worried about having the Nurse begin with a verb infinitive and stipulated that she would sing "as if completing the unspoken thoughts of the Dyer's Wife." When the Nurse declared that the renunciation must be forever (*ewige*), Strauss emphasized the solemnity of that dark Mephistophelean bargain with a *pianissimo* C-minor chord in the trumpets and trombones. (*Die Frau ohne Schatten*, 1919)

a wet nurse would have known well, and her winding phrases were darkly reflected in the cellos and basses, the basset horn and the bassoon. Finally, very quietly, with *pianissimo* accompaniment, the Dyer's Wife concedes, "My soul has become fed up [*satt geworden*] with motherhood." The tempo becomes even slower, the orchestration even more hushed, as she resolves to refuse to sleep with her husband; she descends to a low G and concludes "so ist es gesprochen und geschworen in meinem Innern."[36]

And then, without even pausing for a single measure of orchestral transition, the Nurse sings immediately, beginning with the infinitive: "Abzutun Mutterschaft." The notation in the score—"as if completing the unspoken thoughts of the Dyer's Wife"—was inserted to explain the grammatical as well as musical sense of Strauss's insistence on this particular splicing of lines. "The direct joining of the words 'Abzutun Mutterschaft' with the words of the Dyer's Wife suits me so well," wrote Strauss on July 16 "that I am convinced you'll agree when I have played it for you."[37]

The dancing rhythms of 6/8 and 3/4 ˆgive way to the steadiness of 4/4, and the solemn key is C minor, but the whole huge Straussian orchestra comes to a dead halt so that the Nurse may be understood with perfect clarity as she pronounces, *a cappella*, the precise condition of the Mephistophelean bargain of renouncing motherhood: "Abzutun" descends from C almost a full octave all the way down to D-flat, while "Mutterschaft"—with the first syllable spread out over six different notes—climbs all the way from low D to high G, imposing upon the word almost more extension than it can gracefully sustain. The Nurse's dark magic requires that the renunciation of motherhood, along with the release of the shadow, must be, definitively, forever: "auf ewige Zeiten." On the first syllable of *ewige*, the orchestra enters with pianissimo C-minor chords from the trumpets and trombones to signal the solemnity of the pact.[38] To impose the eternal renunciation of motherhood would have been the exemplary revenge of a wet nurse who had given over her own maternal love to someone else's child.

The Nurse seduces the Dyer's Wife with lyrical invocations: "O du Herrscherin!"—O you sovereign! she exclaims, with the harps and clarinets joining in as she sings in sensually extended notes, in the triple meter of 3/2 time. The rhythm is then enlivened by dotted phrases in the tubas and trombones and the entrance of the timpani, the bass drum, and three Chinese gongs, for the Nurse must invoke "powerful names" as she casts her spell. "I've adopted your idea of a kind of witch dance [*Hexentanz*]," wrote Strauss to Hofmannsthal on July 16.[39] That dance emerges from the orchestra, with dotted rhythms and trilling flutes and violas building to an incantatory climax as the Nurse stipulates the surrender of the shadow "from mouth to mouth, from hand to hand, with knowing hand, and willing mouth." The Nurse promises more fountains, gardens, slaves, and a treasury of gold—conjured to the accompaniment of the celesta, the triangle, and the tambourine—when suddenly her seductions are interrupted by Barak's return.[40]

There remains one more spell to cast before the end of the act: solemnly, with the accompaniment of the tam-tam, the wind machine, the timpani, and the tubas, the Nurse moves fish through the air into the frying pan, calls forth a fire at the hearth to cook them, and magically breaks apart the marital bed into two separate single berths. Flutes and clarinets create a magic fire music in restless and irregular rhythms, and the celesta signals the magical sounding of five children's voices, seeming to come from the frying pan. Strauss wrote five different harmonizing parts for the children's voices, beginning on an E-minor chord, as they cry, *pianissimo, Mutter, Mutter* . . . calling out from the frying pan with a plaintive octave descent. The Dyer's Wife is horrified by what she hears, just as Strauss himself feared that the audience might be horrified. Barak, however, relishes the smell of frying fish, while the flutes and violins keep returning to the octave descent associated with the children's voices, reminding the audience that his olfactory enthusiasm is more disturbing than he himself realizes.[41]

His wife tells him that he will be sleeping alone, and then the score specifies—as Strauss had insisted—that he takes a piece of bread from his pocket and sits down on the floor to eat it. He has no appetite for the fried fish that initially smelled so appetizing. As he sits down with his bread, however, a shimmering chord of horns, trombones, and tremolo strings announces a new musical presence: the offstage voices of three night watchmen. The key shifts to a very solemn A-flat major harmony, and the three watchmen, all of them bass-baritones like Barak himself, enter accompanied by exceptionally hushed (*ppp*) trumpets and trombones. The unison, the regular 4/4 time, the solemnity of the mood, and the very clear setting of each syllable with its own note are suggestive of a religious hymn. Yet, dramatically, these three are neither conventional watchmen, looking out for the security of the streets, nor any sort of traditional religious confraternity, for they are, above all, guardians of sex and reproduction, singing their tribute to the conjugal secrets of the night: "You spouses in the homes of this city, love one another more than your life, and know that the seed of life is entrusted (*anvertraut*) to you, not for the sake of your life but for the sake of your love!"[42]

Hofmannsthal and Strauss were surely thinking of the single watchman in the second act of Wagner's *Die Meistersinger*, preserving the peace of Nuremberg. Yet, the three watchmen in *Die Frau ohne Schatten* possess magical benedictions and charms which act as the counterforce to the dark sorcery of the Nurse, the scheming enemy of human marriage and reproduction. Barak asks his wife whether she hears the watchmen's call, their affirmation of marriage, sex, and childbirth. But his wife does not reply, and the watchmen resume "with the greatest solemnity"—even greater than before.[43]

Now the hushed trumpets and trombones play again, *pianississimo* (*ppp*), this time pushing the watchmen into the dominant key of E-flat, which was also the Masonic key of Mozart's *Die Zauberflöte*. Their message becomes both more erotic and more philosophical, as expressed in Hofmannsthal's beautifully wrought poetry:

> Ihr Gatten, die ihr liebend euch in Armen liegt,
> ihr seid die Brücke, überm Abgrund ausgespannt,
> auf der die Toten wiederum ins Leben gehn!

> You spouses who lie lovingly in each other's arms,
> you are the bridge that extends over the abyss,
> by which the dead return to life![44]

The lines were set by Strauss with hymnal simplicity, as Barak went to sleep alone, listening to the watchmen who articulated his own sense of conjugal piety. Neither Hofmannsthal nor Strauss could have known that between the time they wrote and composed this scene, and the time of its first performance five years later, some twenty million lives would have been lost in the war. Strauss conceived the final verse with greatest solemnity in 1914, but the watchmen singing of the bridge by which the dead return to life would have resonated with a different solemnity five years later, at the opera's premiere in 1919.

Figure 15. The watchmen sing in hymnal unison, in solemn A-flat major, as guardians of marriage and reproduction: "Ihr Gatten" (you spouses), they sing, "liebet einander mehr als euer Leben" (love one another more than your own life). They are gently accompanied by *pianissimo* (*ppp*) trumpets and trombones. (*Die Frau ohne Schatten*, 1919)

Strauss completed the rough score of act 1 on August 20, 1914, three weeks after the outbreak of war, when young men were being mobilized and when many Germans and Austrians still believed that the war would be short and triumphant. Dating the completion of act 1, Strauss wrote on the manuscript of the score: "The day of the victory at Saarburg. Hail to our brave troops. Hail to our great German fatherland."[45] Strauss and Hofmannsthal both, as they collaborated on their fairy-tale opera in the summer of 1914, were also susceptible to the bellicose spirit of the military moment.

Wartime

HABSBURG CATASTROPHE, OPERATIC TRANSFIGURATION

7

Menschenblut

THE SONS OF ADAM AND THE OUTBREAK OF WAR

"Pregnant with Disaster"

"The second act is wonderful," wrote Strauss on July 16, 1914. "The two scenes with the Emperor and the Empress are quite splendid, and the end of the act is extremely magnificent. It does set me a very difficult assignment, and, in particular, I don't know yet how I can manage both septets; also, strangely, for me the character of the Dyer's Wife has not yet quite translated itself into music, whereas Barak is excellent for me."[1] It was a complicated act with five scenes, the first, third, and fifth set in the lower world of Barak's dwelling, but the second and fourth in the upper sphere of the imperial hunting lodge, one scene for the Emperor and one for the Empress. The addition of Barak's three brothers allowed for the creation of septet ensembles in the lower sphere. The scene changes would be challenging, as also the alternation of musical combinations and textures, the two different orchestras of the upper and lower worlds.

"I will work hard, and I hope to manage it," wrote Strauss. "I hope my music will be worthy of your beautiful poetry." He had been eager—even importunate—to have the libretto from the moment he first heard the project described back in 1911. Now he was two-thirds of the way to having a complete libretto, as excited as he always imagined he would be, and, with the world falling apart around him, determined to coax, flatter, and extract the final act from Hofmannsthal: "I hope that after this highly dramatic second act, pregnant with disaster [*unheilschwangeren*], I will now receive a beautiful, lyrical, lively, concluding third."[2] In July 1914, as Strauss read through the second act, all of Europe was "pregnant with disaster."

Hofmannsthal responded nine days later on July 25 with gratitude for Strauss's enthusiasm over the second act and with no mention of all that had happened in the last forty-eight hours. On July 23 Austria had presented its ultimatum to Serbia, demanding the suppression of all "propaganda" against Austria-Hungary (including claims to Bosnia), the removal of Serbian officials considered hostile to Austria-Hungary, the arrest and prosecution of figures named as complicit in the assassination, and the active presence of police from Austria-Hungary in Serbia to enforce compliance.[3] It was intended as an ultimatum that Serbia would feel compelled to refuse and which would then lead to war. The deadline was set to expire on July 25, the same day that Hofmannsthal was writing to Strauss from Aussee, "Like you I believe that I have never achieved anything as dramatically successful as this work."[4] The completion and dispatch of the libretto for act 2 coincided precisely with the July Crisis of 1914, following the assassination on June 28 and preceding the declaration of war on July 28.[5] Contemporary events thus provided an emotional context to the sense of struggle, confusion, incomprehension, and imminent violence that so darkly colored the whole act.

"That you are frightened by the two septets in the fifth scene I very well understand," wrote Hofmannsthal. "Perhaps the earlier smaller one may have to be sacrificed to the mighty second septet."[6] As for the Dyer's Wife, Hofmannsthal had imagined her partly as a musical portrait of Strauss's wife Pauline:

> It surprises me that of all the characters it is the Dyer's Wife that gives you trouble, and I am actually disinclined to comment on a character whose sharp and definite contours speak for themselves. To represent in music precisely the moodiness, the jumpiness [*das Launische, Abspringende*] of such a fundamentally good female nature is a desire you have often mentioned. I would prefer not to say more about this.[7]

Indeed, there was little more to say without actually insisting that Strauss should regard the Dyer's Wife as a portrait of Pauline, whose moodiness, as the librettist hoped, could perhaps inspire the composer to create the changeable musical moods of this soprano role. The libretto, however, perhaps depicted a more discontented wife and a more troubled marriage than Strauss cared to recognize as his own

In the second act the Dyer's Wife would have to dominate the musical drama, for the whole act would be focused upon her and the question of whether she was going to renounce her shadow, her marriage, and her future children. Yet Hofmannsthal did not want the Dyer's Wife to distract Strauss from the crucial figure of the Empress. In the second act she would appear incognito, disguised as a servant in the Dyer's dwelling, with little to sing, largely an observer, but her significance remained fundamental.

> I would like to draw all your attention to the Empress. She has not much libretto text [in act 2] and yet is actually the most important figure in the opera as a whole. This is something you must never neglect. The opera is about how she becomes a human being: she—not the other one—is the woman without a shadow. The whole third act, in which she is central, will hang in the air, unless the composer does for her in the second act everything within the power of his wonderful, sensual-spiritual art. . . . There is always a spiritual light coming from her, and the stages on her road to humanity are marked as if by luminous flames.[8]

Hofmannsthal had written a libretto for the second act in which the character of the Empress seemed to be effaced, and yet now, when it was time for Strauss to compose the act, the poet rushed to the defense of the imperial heroine whom he himself had rendered not just shadowless but relatively voiceless.

Back in April 1914 Hofmannsthal had insisted that Strauss should "never forget" that the Empress was the central figure in the opera, and now in July her luminous centrality was reaffirmed.[9] Like the Marschallin, like Ariadne, the Empress was to become the third in a series of exquisite female figures for whom Hofmannsthal himself felt some combination of romantic infatuation and vassal devotion. The Marschallin was a deeply introspective Viennese aristocrat, the supreme mistress of elegance, manners, and tact, while Ariadne was a mythological princess, emotionally magnificent in her abandonment. The Empress, with a still more exalted title, had to command the drama, command the attention of the composer, eventually command the public; it was not just because the drama belonged to her—the drama of obtaining a shadow and acquiring humanity—but also because the mystique of an empress, even disguised as a servant, had to be commanding in itself.

Hofmannsthal reviewed for Strauss the Empress's presence, even when reticent, in each of the second act's five scenes. In the first scene the Empress watches the Nurse magically conjure a handsome young man out of a broom to satisfy the sexual fantasy of the Dyer's Wife. She is repelled by the sorcery and exclaims, "Alas! Must this happen before my eyes?"[10] She reacts as if she were a spectator at a drama being performed for her, as if she were a part of the public watching the opera, establishing the note of sympathy that would become the key to her own humanity. The second scene belongs to the Emperor in his hunting lodge—"she does not speak, but the whole scene is about her," noted Hofmannsthal—and the third scene returns to Barak's dwelling where the Empress is again a servant and a spectator.[11] She looks on without a single line to sing until the very end of the scene, when she is left alone with Barak and identifies herself to him as "your servant."[12] What began as a charade, the Empress costumed as a servant, now becomes emotionally real after what she has witnessed: she wants to serve and comfort him.

The fourth scene, set in the imperial hunting lodge, belongs to the Empress entirely—only ten minutes long—as she dreams, imagines, or hallucinates her husband turning to stone; and she acknowledges that in the upper sphere with the Emperor, as in the lower sphere with Barak, "here and there, everything is my fault." The acknowledgment of guilt and responsibility is part of her path toward becoming human.[13]

The fifth and final scene brings the Empress back to the human world, but with "higher powers in play"—and this scene, according to Hofmannsthal, had to emphasize the Empress's inner emotional experience. He reminded Strauss that "in the big septet it is entrusted to your mastery to give her voice the brilliance to soar and dominate over the whole." The Empress reflects on what she has learned from Barak about "the sons of Adam" and resolves to remain among humans, "to breathe their breath and bear their burdens."[14] Her descent has taken on a redemptive Christlike character, and she refuses to follow the Nurse's command to seize the shadow, seeing now that the coveted shadow is stained with blood. As Europe was about to go to war in July 1914, Hofmannsthal reminded Strauss not to forget the centrality and importance of the character of the Empress: he sent the composer the libretto for the second act, which concludes with her desperate attempt to keep her imperial hands unstained: "rein zu bleiben von Menschenblut!"—to remain clean of human blood.

"Outside at Schönbrunn"

Zita later recalled that during the July Crisis of 1914, when the decision to present the ultimatum and go to war was made in Vienna, Karl was excluded from the deliberations.

> During these fateful days, pregnant with destiny [*schicksalsschwangeren Tage*] we had nothing to do but wait at Wartholz. I know that there was much puzzling over this fact. Why did the old Emperor not draw the young heir into the deliberations? Did it not concern his future above all? I believe we should say today, with the passing of decades, that precisely this consideration was decisive for the determination of the Emperor. He wanted his heir and inheritor to be kept out of every entanglement. . . . [Later] Emperor Karl could truly and rightly say of himself that he had not the least to do with [causing] this war, bravely though he had fought on the front as the heir and successor.[15]

Karl and Zita played no role in the decision to go to war, and so, as Zita would insist years later, there was no blood on their hands. The climax of the July Crisis came to them simply as news:

> At last the report reached us at Wartholz from Vienna of the partial mobilization [July 27]. It is superfluous to say that we were convinced of the lawfulness of this step, convinced that we were fighting after being attacked, fighting for the survival and endurance of our homeland [*Heimat*]. Austria-Hungary, in the upcoming armed encounter, bore no guilt [*keine Schuld*].[16]

Zita's declaration of absolution from guilt echoed the preoccupation with guilt on the part of Hofmannsthal's fairy-tale Empress, her libretto lines scripted at this very moment of the July Crisis.

Finally, after the declaration of war on Serbia on July 28, Karl and Zita were summoned to Vienna, where Karl met with Franz Joseph on July 30, and Zita recalled that "people came again and again to our residence, little Schloss Hetzendorf, to cheer for us [*umjublen*] to give expression to their patriotic enthusiasm and confidence." On August 1 Germany declared war against Russia, anticipating Russian support of Serbia against Austria-Hungary. On August 2 Karl and Zita traveled by train to Budapest for a patriotic rally, now politically deployed with their first wartime assignment. On that day, as Germany occupied Luxembourg and delivered an ultimatum to Belgium, Karl and Zita were greeted at the station in Budapest with "roaring cheers." This was their first visit to Hungary as imperial heirs, and it was an important assignment, because Budapest had been more reluctant than Vienna to go to war. Hungary counted for half of the joint foreign policy of Austria-Hungary, and the Hungarian prime minister István Tisza (who was waiting at the train station for Karl and Zita) had initially resisted sending the provocative ultimatum to Serbia. Now he looked on as the Hungarians acclaimed Franz Joseph as King of Hungary, along with Karl and Zita: "Éljen a király! Éljen a trónörökös! Éljen Zita főhercegnő!" (Long live the King! Long live the Crown Prince! Long live Archduchess Zita!)[17] In Austria Karl and Zita would one day be emperor and empress, but in Hungary, under the dualist constitution, they would be crowned as king and queen.

Zita's conception of her own life was invested with a powerful sense of inexorable destiny, and, at least retrospectively, her experience was imbued with foreboding. "With Archduke Karl especially," she wrote, "I constantly had the feeling he was seeing the cheering people as they would soon become, as in consequence of the war it inevitably had to be: rundown, impoverished, wounded, dead."[18] His supposed prophetic vision, which she herself intuited alongside him, showed the cheering crowds spectrally transformed into lifeless corpses. That sense of foreboding extended to the political future as, according to Zita, "both the old Emperor and the young Archduke and heir stood under the impression, I would almost say under the great feeling, that such a violent war would mean the end of our great and beloved dual monarchy."[19] For Zita there was always a sense of higher forces in play and a sense of supernatural imminence in the course of current events.

Zita's feeling for the Habsburg "homeland," for the "beloved dual monarchy," was complicated by her family circle of Bourbon princes who, in many instances, considered themselves fundamentally French, though they had been residing in Austria, at Schwarzau and Frohsdorf, for decades. With the outbreak of war her brothers, Prince Xavier and Prince Sixtus, were planning to leave Austria for France, even as Xavier recorded in his diary, with some pride, that "Karl and Zita have gone to Budapest, and we hear of an unprecedented triumphal procession." On August 10 Xavier noted: "Sixtus visits Karl, who must depart for the army. Zita won't remain at Hetzendorf. The Emperor wants to have her with him at Schönbrunn."[20] Zita was pregnant again.

The French declaration of war against Austria-Hungary on August 12 shattered the royalist worldview of the Bourbon-Parma dynasty. Xavier observed on August 16:

> Karl will depart for Galicia today, a rather emotional departure. The whole thing is so terrible. But Zita is very very brave, she tried not to let it show. She has now finally relocated to Schönbrunn. Karl intends, as it is his duty, to depart for his army, so it is our duty to go to France. Where are they now, the days of Schwarzau and Frohsdorf![21]

Three years later in 1917 Sixtus and Xavier would serve as intermediaries when Karl and Zita, then the Emperor and Empress, attempted secretly to negotiate a peace agreement with France.

Now in 1914 Xavier looked back nostalgically to 1911, the year of Zita's marriage to Karl, as the last moment when their royalist world was ritually integrated in the pomp and circumstance of dynastic union.

> How we swore to one another to stand together even more closely; we wanted to build a ring around her, to protect her in these terrible times, because we guessed what would happen. And now it is here. They want to destroy us all: faith, church, state, Europe, humanity. But we won't give up, not ever.[22]

It was an unusual royalist's perspective on World War I, and one which Zita certainly shared in part: that the whole war was a revolutionary campaign against the *ancien régime* of Europe and, above all, against its most venerable dynasties. In fact, the war would ultimately displace them from the European political scene forever. For the moment it forced them into warring camps, and, while Zita remained at Schönbrunn, on August 28 Xavier and Sixtus arrived in France—where they made a distressing discovery: "All our friends seem to have become republicans!"[23]

Karl was sent to Galicia, where he had previously served with the army during 1912, when he had fallen from his horse with a concussion during the military maneuvers at Lviv. Those maneuvers were meant to prepare for precisely the war with Russia that was now beginning in 1914, and Karl found himself in August very close to Lviv at the fortress city of Przemyśl—which was soon besieged by the Russians in September. It would be the longest and most important siege of the war, falling to the Russians eventually in March 1915, with disastrous consequences for Austrian morale, but Karl was gone long before then. He was evacuated when the siege began and spent time in Vienna where Zita and the children were living with the Emperor in Schönbrunn. According to Zita, the imperial succession now became meaningful, as Karl reported to Franz Joseph about the troops, and Franz Joseph passed on the lessons of his political experience to his heir.[24]

Zita's family home at Schwarzau became a hospital during the war, and Zita herself visited hospitals in Vienna and sometimes further afield, closer to the military lines: "When I returned, I also had to make a precise report to the Emperor just as Archduke Karl did." She pondered the problem of how to report on the dire reality, when the hospitals themselves would make her visit into an occasion of semitheatrical dissimulation. "So one quickly became accustomed to distinguish the so-to-speak 'normal' in the hospital from what was arranged for the visit," she recalled.[25] Zita, who in the triumphal procession in Budapest was herself the theatrical event, could also—like the Empress in *Die Frau ohne Schatten*—find herself cast in the role of the theatrical spectator of human suffering.

Zita's recollections of the war were inevitably shaped by the retrospective knowledge that Austria-Hungary ultimately lost and the monarchy ceased to exist. When she congratulated Franz Joseph on a military victory in Galicia—perhaps the battle of Krasnik in late August 1914—he was not exultant:

> The old Emperor smiled kindly and said to me, "Yes, it begins like that. And then it gets worse and worse, and this time the war will end completely badly."
>
> "But Your Majesty! That is not possible," I answered. "We are standing up for such a just cause."
>
> But he only smiled and said in his characteristic kindly way, "You are still very young, so you believe in victory for the just cause, but this time it's the end. . . ."[26]

Zita's historical memory was made up of dark prophesies and ominous forebodings that she only gradually came to acknowledge and appreciate with age and experience, like the forgotten curse engraved on a lost talisman.

She brought the two-year-old Otto to see Franz Joseph and reported that it gave the Emperor pleasure, that they played with a music box together. A photograph of Franz Joseph with his great-grandnephew survives from this period, the frail emperor seated, the child—dressed in a rather feminine white frock, with curly blond hair—leaning into the imperial lap and gazing angelically at the camera. It was around this time, in September 1914, that the musical entertainment *Anno 14*, by the operetta composer Ralph Benatzky, introduced the popular song "Draußen in Schönbrunn" ("Outside at Schönbrunn") which paid melancholy tribute to the old Emperor:

> Draußen im Schönbrunner Park   Outside in the Schönbrunn Park
> sitzt ein alter Herr, sorgenschwer.   sits an old man, full of worries.[27]

Zita's account fit with this popular image of the Emperor burdened with worries, while Benatzky's song, with lyrics by Fritz Grünbaum, was also meant to rally the people of Vienna around the lonely figure of their emperor.

> Was wir können, woll'n wir tun, lass dir bisserl Zeit zum Ruh'n,
> lieber, guter, alter Herr von Schönbrunn.
>
> What we can, we will do, to leave you a little time to rest,
> dear, good old man of Schönbrunn.

The Hofburg palace was at the center of the city, but Schönbrunn, built as a summer palace in the eighteenth century, offered a sort of removal and

Figure 16. Ralph Benatzky's musical show *Anno 14* in September 1914 presented the song "Draußen in Schönbrunn" ("Outside at Schönbrunn"), which was intended to evoke sympathy for the old Emperor Franz Joseph, residing at the great Habsburg palace of Schönbrunn. He was supposedly "sorgenschwer," full of worries, as his empire went to war, though the photograph on the sheet music suggested good spirits. Franz Joseph had been reigning since 1848, a semi-mythological figure even in his own lifetime, and most of his subjects had never known any other emperor. (Property of the author)

elevation, a splendid separate sphere—a world of fountains and gardens, of mirrored rooms and Chinese porcelain—the upper imperial sphere that Hofmannsthal and Strauss sought to evoke in *Die Frau ohne Schatten*.

Soldier, Tailor, Embroiderer, Dyer

With Austrian mobilization, even Hofmannsthal, age forty, was summoned as a reserve officer to join his regiment in Istria on the Adriatic. Though entirely committed to the Austrian cause and what he sought to articulate as the "Austrian idea," he was not eager to go into combat, and, as a very well-known writer, was able to make use of his connections to obtain a transfer to the press office of the War Relief Authority (*Kriegsfürsorgeamt*). The fall of 1914, which had probably been intended for work on the third act of *Die Frau ohne Schatten*, was instead dedicated to writing propaganda essays for Austria at war. Already on September 8 his first article appeared on the front page of the *Neue Freie Presse* in Vienna, the great liberal newspaper of the Viennese elite: Hofmannsthal's "Appeal to the Upper Classes." He revisited the theatricality of the preceding month, as Zita herself might have experienced it: "It was beautiful, the cheering of maidens, children, the elderly with fruit and flowers in their hands, from the Salzach to the Dniester that is now drinking the blood of brave men; it was beautiful, the shy reverent gaze with which women and boys followed a wounded man, one of *ours*, as they saw him go by." And yet, after a month, "now it is time for life to continue, while the monstrousness takes place all around us."[28]

Hofmannsthal's injunction for the Viennese upper classes—partly in the spirit of "Manche freilich"—was to take note of the lower classes, in the streets of Vienna, and consider their economic circumstances:

> There is our tailor, there is the cleaner, there is the laundry, there is the feather worker [*Federschmückerin*]; they want to live. The trimmer-embroiderer and the leather worker want to live. The bookdealer and his assistants want to live. Five thousand people, or maybe seven thousand, who are ready, evening after evening, to play the fiddle and the flute for us and our wives, to act and to sing, people we could otherwise scarcely do without, they want to live. And it's up to us, to live and let them live.[29]

The responsibility of the upper classes was to generate income for the lower classes, to buy new suits and feather hats, to buy leather goods and books, to go to the theater and the opera, so that the economy of Vienna would not collapse. Barak the Dyer might have appeared on the list right in between the embroiderer and the leather worker. In fact, my maternal great-grandfather Leiser Erber was a leather worker with a leather shop in Vienna, and my paternal grandfather Joseph Wolff, born in Habsburg Galicia, was an embroiderer. Hofmannsthal's sense of upper-class responsibility extended to them: "to live and let them live."

Tailors and leather workers would, in fact, contribute to the war effort, making uniforms, boots, belts, and jackets. For Hofmannsthal, however, leather workers, like feather workers, were there to costume the upper classes, as if to set them on stage for the operatic performance of society itself: "Ostentation, otherwise so repulsive, now becomes a higher decorum. What was otherwise empty fuss, the duties of society, are now *something*. What was once presumption and appropriation now becomes duty."[30] Wearing a new suit or a feather hat was a patriotic duty, and patronizing the fiddler and the flautist, the actor and the singer, meant that going to the theater, the concert, the opera, was also a duty. The Vienna Opera began its season late, on October 18 with *Lohengrin*, and the Strauss-Hofmannsthal *Elektra* was performed on November 1.[31]

In October Hofmannsthal prepared a more political article, "The Affirmation of Austria," which appeared in the *Österreichische Rundschau* on November 1, 1914. Here he revisited the pessimistic political forebodings of his letter to Bodenhausen from the spring of 1912—"cloudy for our old Austria"—which had since been proved fully accurate: "this state, whose misfortune it was to have lost its political center of gravity and not to have found definitively a new one." Now, however, the center of gravity was clearly nothing other than the army, and Hofmannsthal reflected historically on the period of the Ottoman siege of Vienna in 1683: "The momentum of that great defensive action created for us a great artistic flowering . . . that persisted for more than a century, providing an incomparable inner strengthening and rebirth. 1683 is the beginning of that wave that first reached its full height under Maria Theresa." Reaching back to Habsburg baroque and rococo culture, to the epoch of the greatest empress and the scenario of *Der Rosenkavalier*,

Hofmannsthal tried to imagine a similar cultural resurgence arising from the spirit of the army fighting Austria's contemporary war. "A monstrous meteorological phenomenon has altered the atmosphere in which we breathe," he wrote, perhaps remembering the metaphor of cloudy weather from 1912.[32] Meteorology also defined the final scene of act 2 of *Die Frau ohne Schatten*, which began with darkening skies, howling dogs, flashes of lightning, and a sense of atmospheric pressure that led the Nurse to believe that "higher powers are in play."

Hofmannsthal's military reflections received further elaboration in his Christmas article of 1914 in the *Neue Freie Presse*, devoted to Prince Eugene of Savoy, the most celebrated commander in Habsburg history. In 1717 he conquered Belgrade, the city that was, of course, one of the first principal objects of the Habsburg armies in World War I. He built the baroque Belvedere Palace in which, most recently, Franz Ferdinand had his Vienna residence. Born in Paris, formed at the court of Louis XIV (the archenemy of the Habsburgs), Prince Eugene entered into the service of the Habsburg dynasty: "He came here and served the emperor and the empire. He came from a foreign land, he never learned to master the German language, and he became a German national hero."[33] Hofmannsthal, however, wanted to think of him as an Austrian hero, the bearer of an Austrian idea that transcended nationality and resided in the military spirit of the army, dedicated to the service of the dynasty, and linked to the cultural spirit of the Habsburg baroque age.

When Hofmannsthal was initially summoned to the army at the outbreak of the war, Strauss was unable to reach him, and—with Europe descending into the abyss—worried over the completion of the libretto for *Die Frau ohne Schatten*. Strauss wrote with wartime irony to Hofmannsthal's wife Gerty on August 22—a day of immense fatalities on the western front—"Hugo has the damned duty not to die for the fatherland before I have my third act which will bring him, I hope, more honor than a beautiful obituary in the *Neue Freie Presse*."[34] Though humorously phrased, Strauss clearly did take seriously the possibility that the war would provide yet another reason for delay in providing him with the libretto, all the more frustrating in that it was now two-thirds complete.

It was not until early October that Strauss wrote directly to Hofmannsthal to express his relief at learning—from Clemens von Franckenstein, director of the Munich opera—"that you are no longer in the field but in safety at a quiet post." The composer was therefore ready to impart the good news that he had completed the first four of the five scenes of the second act, most recently the fourth scene which belonged to the Empress. Hofmannsthal had versified her spiritual anxieties, and Strauss was taking up the challenge, giving the Empress "a great deal of inward-looking music"—her dreams and visions, her guilt and desperation. The composer was very happy with the second-act libretto: "The text is really brilliant, can be composed with marvelous ease," wrote Strauss. "You've really created your masterpiece here."[35]

With German troops advancing in the east on the Vistula and holding off the French in the west at the First Battle of Arras, Strauss in Germany, like Hofmannsthal in Austria-Hungary, believed that at this moment the army was the single fundamental institution:

> In the middle of all the unpleasant things which this war brings—excepting the brilliant deeds of our army—hard work is the only salvation. Otherwise one would die of rage at the inaction of our diplomacy, our press, the Kaiser's apologetic telegram to Wilson. . . . And how are the artists being treated? The Kaiser reduces salaries at the Hoftheater, the Duchess of Meiningen dismisses her orchestra, Reinhardt stages Shakespeare, the Frankfurt Theater performs *Carmen, Mignon, The Tales of Hoffmann*. . . . What's the mood in Vienna, by the way? One hears so much about despondency and treason. . . . You don't have to hurry with the third act: now that I know you are safe, I know I will somehow receive it. I won't need it before March 15.[36]

While Strauss was writing heroic music for the Emperor within the opera, he was jeering at the imperial government in Berlin, feeling that the kaiser had gone too far in excusing himself by telegram to Woodrow Wilson for the German destruction of Louvain in Belgium. Like Hofmannsthal, Strauss was concerned about salaries for actors and employment for musicians, and both believed that German and Austrian culture were a large part of what their respective countries were fighting to preserve and promote.

While Hofmannsthal publicly took a position against extreme wartime nationalism in Austria in the September 1914 article "Boycott Foreign

Languages?"—Strauss seemed more inclined to feel that Reinhardt should not be producing Shakespeare while Germany was at war with England, and that German opera houses should not be performing French operas.[37] Eventually, both sides would embrace the chauvinist rejection of the enemy's cultural traditions, and in England, where Strauss himself was so recently celebrated in June 1914, his music would largely disappear from the repertory during the war. In New York, after the United States entered the war in 1917, the Metropolitan Opera eliminated Wagner from the repertory and also canceled *Der Rosenkavalier* along with Beethoven's *Fidelio*.[38] Strauss himself was clearly attuned to such wartime nationalist preferences and, of course, stood to benefit from them within Germany. By March 1915 he could report to Hofmannsthal from Berlin on a veritable festival of Strauss-Hofmannsthal operas: *Elektra, Der Rosenkavalier*, and *Ariadne auf Naxos*.[39]

On October 14, 1914, Strauss informed Hofmannsthal that "the second act is almost finished: will be really splendid; really almost composes itself, the poetry is so good and so fit for music."[40] Hofmannsthal replied on October 19 to report that he was making progress on the third act, even in wartime, but the material was itself now entangled with his experience of the war: "It [the opera] ends in a powerful upsurge, in which many of the horrors [*Ungeheueren*] brought to us this year have been already mysteriously anticipated within my own being [*in mir selbst geheimnisvollerweise vorweggenommen ist*]."[41] Like Zita susceptible to the spirit of foreboding, Hofmannsthal in October 1914 now suspected that his conception for *Die Frau ohne Schatten*, dating back to 1911, somehow ("mysteriously") anticipated the outbreak of the war. The whole unconscious development of the material which made him so reticent, and made the project so difficult to develop, could be reinterpreted as an inner psychological premonition of the crisis that was about to erupt in world affairs.

On October 12, as Strauss finished composing the second act and Hofmannsthal worked on the libretto of the third act, the assassins and conspirators went on trial in Sarajevo. At the trial the nineteen-year-old Čabrinović appealed for forgiveness to Franz Ferdinand's three orphaned children. The oldest child, Sophie, only six years younger than Čabrinović himself, supposedly wrote a letter forgiving him.[42]

A total of twenty-five people were tried, and though the wartime climate was hardly in their favor, justice was sufficiently impartial for nine of them to be acquitted. Three were hung, and two had death sentences commuted by the clemency of Emperor Franz Joseph. Princip received a sentence of twenty years in prison, because he had been just under twenty at the time of the assassination and therefore could not be condemned to death. At the trial he was reported to have denounced the Habsburg monarchy for its record of oppression toward the South Slavs: "to trample on their nationality, culture, language, religion, and everything considered most sacred." He felt it was only possible to protest "by striking an individual who incarnated such a despotic, retrograde, and cruel organization," namely Franz Ferdinand, but Princip openly regretted that he had murdered the Duchess of Hohenberg, declaring her death to have been an accidental consequence.[43] Čabrinović, like Princip, received a sentence of twenty years' imprisonment on account of his youth, and both young men died of tuberculosis as prisoners at the fortress of Theresienstadt during the course of World War I.

As the French and British blocked the German advance at the first battle of Ypres in Flanders, Strauss wrote to Hofmannsthal from Garmisch on October 27, the day before the verdicts were issued in Sarajevo: "Second act finished according to schedule . . . When will I see you again? Could you come here for a visit for a few days? We are staying in Garmisch till Christmas. I very much want to play the two acts for you and discuss the third one."[44] The exigencies of wartime meant that Strauss would, once again, have to restrain his impatience, and Hofmannsthal—who pleaded his service obligations—would have to wait to hear the music of the first and second acts.[45]

"The Sons of Adam"

At the very end of act 2, scene 3, the Dyer's Wife expresses her contempt for her husband and then leaves him confused and distressed at home while she goes out with the Nurse, possibly in search of romantic adventures. The Empress, however, remains behind with Barak, and when he becomes aware of her and asks "Who's there?," she replies with her only line in the entire scene, "Ich, mein Gebieter, deine Dienerin!"—It is I, my master, your servant. She shapes her identification into an elegantly extended musical line, concluding with a lyrically dotted phrase on *Dienerin*. Her voice is supported by the woodwinds, the harp, and the solo violin, suggesting the comfort that an empress might bring to a wounded man of the people, but also perhaps the grace with which she embraced the role reversal, playing the part of a sympathetic servant.[46]

The Empress's compassionate vocal line leads into the restless orchestral interlude that accompanies the change of scene to her own bedroom in the imperial hunting lodge, as the fourth scene begins by entering directly into her dreams. The piccolo, the glockenspiel, and the celesta all convey the eerie magic of her dream, and the orchestra builds to a *fortissimo* climax as she recognizes the suffering face of Barak. The orchestra then stops dead, so that she may clearly acknowledge her guilt toward him—"Dir, Barak, bin ich mich schuldig"—ascending to a sustained high A-flat on "schuldig" (guilty) to express her distress.[47] She falls now into a deeper sleep and dreams that the Emperor is entering a mountain cave, carved with graves. The bassoons and contrabassoon, tubas and trombones, cellos and basses, all conjure the darkness of the cave, as if it were Fafner's lair in Wagner's *Siegfried*. The percussion rumbles, and the bass tuba is scored for a note so low that an annotation allows, "if not playable, then an octave higher."[48]

The Empress sees the Emperor passing through the funerary cave, a natural analogue to the Kapuzinergruft in Vienna. An unseen chorus of male voices, singing in the clarity of C major, leads him to the crossroads of "the water of life, the threshold of death," with the magical accompaniment of the tam-tam and the harps, while trombones, bassoons, horns, and tubas sound a dark and ominous rhythm: "dadada dum." As the men's chorus concludes, the soprano voice of the falcon sings on a monotone C-sharp, "The woman casts no shadow," and then, one half-tone higher, on a monotone D, "The emperor must turn to stone." In their highest registers the piccolos, flutes, oboes, and clarinets echo the falcon's quavering cry, each note rendered more plaintive by a preceding grace note.[49]

The Empress awakens and, now in woeful B minor, sings "Wehe mein Mann" (Alas my husband), "Welche Weg, wohin?" (Where is he going?) It might have been the lament of every wife in Europe at the moment that Strauss composed this music, every wife whose husband was being mobilized for war. The fairy-tale Empress, however, feels not only woe but guilt, and as she sings "meine Schuld," she descends stepwise in three notes to B, while the winds and horns accompany her descent and assuage her guilt with a beautiful B-minor chord.[50]

She either sees, imagines, or dreams that the Emperor is turning to stone, as predicted by the falcon, and she sings "Sein Leib erstarrt"—his body stiffens—with a dramatic descent on the last word, accompanied by the bass clarinet and *pianissimo* trombones.[51] This descent has been the motif of the Emperor's turning to stone ever since it was first announced by the messenger of Keikobad in the first scene of the opera, but it now becomes vivid for the Empress as she sees the Emperor's body stiffen, like the stiffness of the dead on the battlefield or the paralysis of the shell-shocked survivors in a wartime hospital ward.

The Empress thinks not only of her husband but also of Barak, whom she left down below, grieving and uncomforted in his home. Accompanied by chromatic descending scales in the solo violin, the Empress agonizes over her own guilt (*meine Schuld*), both above and below. Still accompanied by the solo violin, she laments, "Whatever I touch I kill," and declares that she would rather turn to stone herself. The tuba, trombones, bassoons, and bass clarinet immediately enter *fortissimo* to mark the end of her solo scene in the upper sphere, and the beginning of another orchestral interlude that will take her back, once more, to the human world.[52]

The upper world, however, exerts its influence down below, with a strange barometric pressure creating tension in the domestic atmosphere and a gathering storm that makes the scene darker and darker inside Barak's dwelling. The orchestral coloring is also dark—including timpani, bass drum, and the Chinese gongs—as the Nurse quietly comments to the Empress that higher forces are in play. The Empress, however, is now focused on the sufferings of the human world, and sings, in hypnotic 3/4 waltz time, "Womit ist die Welt der Söhne Adams erfüllt!" (With what is the world of the sons of Adam filled!) And thus the first septet is launched: Barak's three brothers joining Barak, the Dyer's Wife, the Nurse, and the Empress. It is the Empress who holds the highest part on the vocal staff, pronouncing in an arching musical phrase "Gepriesen sei der mich diesen Mann finden liess" (Praised be whoever has let me find this man), while Barak, the man himself, harmonizes with her on the bass clef. The Empress declares that for his sake she will

Figure 17. The Empress declares that she does not want the shadow, because there is blood on it. "Auf ihm ist Blut!" She is singing the top line of the great septet that concludes the second act, accompanied by Strauss's stormy orchestration. Hofmannsthal imagined her anguished conscience dominating the septet, and she rises dramatically to a high B-flat on *Schatten* (shadow) and a high A-flat on *Blut* (blood). (*Die Frau ohne Schatten*, 1919)

remain among humans and share their afflictions. At the word "afflictions"—*Beschwerden*—she ascends to a sustained high A, *fortissimo*, joined by the entire orchestra, triumphing musically over those afflictions and dominating the septet just as Hofmannsthal had insisted when writing to Strauss.[53]

With the conclusion of the first septet, the Dyer's Wife solemnly renounces her shadow and her fertility, and Barak wants to kill her on the spot. The second septet begins—"the great septet" as Hofmannsthal conceived it—and once again the Empress is dominant: "Ich will nicht den Schatten: auf ihm ist Blut" (I don't want the shadow, there is blood on it). She reaches up to a sustained high B-flat on *Schatten* and a sustained high A-flat on *Blut*. She is determined to keep her hands clean of human blood (*Menschenblut*) and, in spite of the urgent exhortation of the Nurse, refuses to seize the shadow.[54] The Empress again soars over the septet, and the words that rise above the ensemble at the top of her vocal range are *Schatten* and *Blut*. Strauss and Hofmannsthal, working on their opera as war enveloped Europe, gave dramatic expression to the inexorability of guilt and the horror of human blood.

8

"The Shadow Hovering in the Air"

WARTIME PROPAGANDA, MUSICAL PATRIOTISM, AND OPERATIC COLLABORATION

"After This War"

"You have not had a sign of life [*Lebenszeichen*] from me for a long time," wrote Hofmannsthal to Strauss on January 12, 1915, not having written since mid-October. "It was impossible for me to write, and even today I could not speak about why it was impossible to write—there were quite general, impersonal reasons."[1] This was very much the traumatic style and reasoning of the "Chandos Letter": an inability to write or speak, all inexplicable, even to oneself. Of course the last months of 1914 were traumatic for all of Europe, culminating in the unofficial Christmas truce in the trenches of the western front—with soldiers sometimes singing carols to their enemies—and the resumption of warfare after Christmas passed. For Austria-Hungary, on the eastern front, December was a month for trying to hold out against the ongoing Russian siege of Przemyśl in Galicia, while the Habsburg army also suffered a humiliating defeat by the Serbs and was forced to withdraw altogether from Serbia for a time. Hofmannsthal told Strauss it was impossible for him to write, but Strauss could perfectly well have been reading Hofmannsthal's assorted publications in the press, culminating in a tribute to Prince Eugene of Savoy on Christmas Day.

On New Year's Day Hofmannsthal published a piece in the *Neue Freie Presse*, "Build Up, Don't Tear Down," which affirmed the beauty of Vienna and Austria transfigured by the heroism of war. "Never was the beauty of

Austria more forcefully evident than in August 1914, and never was that beauty so purely and strongly registered in millions of hearts," declared Hofmannsthal. He evoked a hundred thousand "singing young men" traveling through Hungary to fight against Russia, revealing the unity of Austria-Hungary and sanctifying the territory of the empire by defending its borders.[2] Just as baroque Vienna was built in the aftermath of the Ottoman siege of 1683, so Hofmannsthal now anticipated a new and beautiful Vienna emerging after the war. Lovingly he described the inner city: "An old town is suited to the lively traffic that flows not in straight lines but presses through a thousand crooked veins" and "achieves heightened pulsing life, connecting so many people, and bringing a person a thousand wares, to profit a thousand sellers."[3] In *Die Frau ohne Schatten*, Hofmannsthal imagined the misery of urban life in the human world, but now he also envisioned the postwar Viennese cityscape transfigured by meaningful human connections.

Hofmannsthal regretted not having been able to accept Strauss's October invitation to come to Garmisch to listen to the newly composed music for *Die Frau ohne Schatten*, pleading military service and the impossibility, for the moment, of obtaining leave. At the same time, the ongoing war impeded the poet's progress on the libretto.

> I did the sketch for the third act in July [1914]. It was finished fourteen days before the Serbian ultimatum. Now, half a year later, I have finally been able to resolve to take it up again, and I am working on it: but everything essential was already there. This third act is by far the most beautiful and, in the music as in the poetry, must become the crown of the whole opera.[4]

In January 1915 Hofmannsthal was thinking back to July 1914 and retrospectively plotting his progress on the libretto against the timetable of the Serbian ultimatum—as if it had been also some sort of deadline for himself, as it was for Europe as a whole. As he worked he nostalgically looked back to peacetime, all the way back to the summer of 1913, to try to recover his own sense of the beauty of the opera. "Do you remember our conversations about it on our Italian journey?" he wrote to Strauss. "Now please come to Vienna in February for two days, and we will exchange our treasures [*unsere Schätze*]."[5] Even their collaboration could be envisioned as a sort of fairy tale.

On Saturday evening, January 16, there was a performance at the Vienna Konzerthaus to benefit the Red Cross and the Widows and Orphans Assistance Fund. The benefit was held under the patronage of no less than three Habsburg archduchesses—Blanca, the Spanish infanta who married Archduke Leopold Salvator; Marie Valerie, the daughter of Emperor Franz Joseph; and Zita, eight months pregnant. The *Neue Freie Presse* did not note Zita's actual presence in the concert hall. If she had been there, she would have heard the famous Moravian tenor Leo Slezak perform three songs by Richard Strauss, concluding with the rapturous "Cäcilie," ascending to a high B in the concluding phrase.[6] On February 27 the same three archduchesses sponsored another concert for the Red Cross—this time concluding with the "Blue Danube Waltz"—a few weeks after Zita had given birth to Archduke Robert.[7]

Hofmannsthal wrote to Strauss again on February 6, 1915, reiterating that "for my part a trip to Germany is impossible, because I am on active service, and an application for leave would have to be based on illness." Yet he was longing to hear the music for the first two acts: "I have in mind not my private curiosity or my private pleasure but the interest of the closest possible collaboration in this most important and most promising of all the works we have ever undertaken together." Hofmannsthal conceived of the collaboration almost as a matter of military strategic coordination, which would require the meeting of two generals to confer over the map of their joint campaign. He wanted to be sure that their operatic purposes and plans did not diverge (*auseinanderkommen*).[8] "Nobody could have expected," wrote Hofmannsthal, thinking strategically, "that during our most important common work, we would be cut off from one another for an unpredictable period. Please God that this monstrous affair, from which I suffer perhaps especially violently [*heftig*], may be nearing a decisive point."[9] Hofmannsthal pleaded his own sensitive nerves and, solipsistically, saw the war itself as an obstacle to the creation of *Die Frau ohne Schatten*.

The other urgent question of strategy that arose at this time was whether the ballet *Josephslegende* should be performed in Germany, or whether the prestige of the Strauss-Hofmannsthal collaboration would be better served by completing and presenting *Die Frau ohne Schatten*. Hofmannsthal worried that *Josephslegende* was both a lesser work and at the same time a work that might seem to have an unpatriotic history, given that it was commissioned by the Ballets Russes for Paris. This led him to the reflection that *Die Frau ohne Schatten*, originally conceived three years before the war, might now be the providentially ideal opera—in its fundamental "seriousness"—for the eventual postwar moment:

> After this war, first of all in Germany, there will be felt a quite definite atmosphere, with quite definite demands (and prejudices) regarding everything, and especially the arts. . . . *Die Frau ohne Schatten*, because of its theme and execution, may appear exceptionally good and honorable [*gut und ehrenvoll*] in this atmosphere.[10]

Hofmannsthal emphasized the atmosphere of Germany rather than Austria (though the opera would eventually have its premiere in Vienna), and he considered German seriousness (perhaps as opposed to the proverbial Austrian lightheartedness) as an important factor that made *Die Frau ohne Schatten* an opera destined to appear at the solemn conclusion of the war. In fact, the final chorus of unborn children could have been plausibly envisioned to give meaning to the rebirth and repopulation of Europe after a war that brought unprecedented loss of life.

Strauss had concerns of his own about the patriotic wartime atmosphere and what it meant for his musical work as a German composer. He replied to Hofmannsthal in February:

> Sad enough that we working artists who are true to mature, serious, and artistic ideals, must take such consideration of people for whom this great time [*die grosse Zeit*] is only a pretext for bringing their mediocre accomplishments into the open . . . [and] who forget that I wrote my "Heldenleben," the "Bardengesang," battle songs and military marches in peacetime but now, confronting these great events [*den grossen Ereignissen gegenüber*], preserve a respectful silence, whereas they, exploiting the present circumstances, and under the cloak of patriotism, are launching forth the most dilettantish stuff![11]

Strauss, with his established musical eminence, was well aware that a younger generation of musicians might attempt to exploit the wartime moment to amplify their own careers, and that patriotic culture might offer an opportune avenue for self-promotion. Ralph Benatzky, composing "Draußen in Schönbrunn" about Emperor Franz Joseph, would have been a good example in the Austrian context, while the young composer Fritz Lubrich wrote the anthem "Heil Kaiser dir!" for Kaiser Wilhelm in Germany.

"In this great time" (*in dieser grossen Zeit*) was a bombastic phrase taken up ironically in December 1914 by Karl Kraus in his journal *Die Fackel*, mocking the pompousness of wartime patriotism and the depravity of patriotic culture. To him this was not a great epoch at all, but rather an epoch of monstrously grandiose expression that seemed to trivialize the horrors of war:

> In these loud times which are booming with the nightmarish symphony of deeds causing reports and with the nightmarish symphony of reports responsible for deeds: in these times here, you should not expect any words of my own. None but these, which are intended to prevent my silence from being misinterpreted.[12]

Strauss in February employed the same phrases that Kraus had mocked in December—"this great time," "these great events"—though the composer was also aware that silence might be a more dignified response than patriotic noise.

Strauss felt personally threatened by patriotic demagoguery: "When one is conscious of how seriously one has always taken one's art (even if one actually once had a ballet premiere performed in Paris), then one is gripped by true disgust at all the hypocrisy and ignorance." Strauss, rather like Kraus, was horrified to hear people celebrate a "splendid" (*herrlich*) war, a war to bring about the "cleansing" and "purifying" of German culture—when young soldiers had to be first "cleansed of lice and bedbugs and cured of all infections and weaned from murder."[13] Hofmannsthal, as a propagandist, did sometimes write about the war as ennobling, but Strauss now saw it more brutally as a matter of lice, infection, and death. Yet he and Hofmannsthal together imagined that *Die Frau ohne Schatten* might, eventually, be a fittingly solemn response to the solemnity of the war.

Though Strauss appreciated some of the horrors of the war, he was not discouraged by the stalemate in the trenches of the western front, and he believed that the postwar moment might not be far off:

> Concerning the war itself, I believe we have every reason to look happily to the future. In our navy there prevails unbelievable confidence; the Russians will soon be finished; and in England itself the popular mood is already supposed to be extremely flat. What will February 18 bring?[14]

It had been announced on February 4 that, beginning on February 18, German U-boats would attack commercial shipping in British waters, and

Strauss wondered what that day would bring. In fact, unrestricted submarine warfare would lead to the German sinking of the *Lusitania* off the coast of Ireland on May 7, killing twelve hundred passengers and crew, including more than a hundred Americans—and initiating a major shift in American public opinion concerning the war.

In February 1915 Strauss in Berlin was eager to have the libretto for the third act of *Die Frau ohne Schatten*, whether or not it was possible to arrange a meeting with Hofmannsthal to discuss it.

> I believe it would be best if you sent me act 3 here as soon as possible: I will study it carefully, and whatever needs to be discussed we will work through verbally in the spring. . . . I know your wishes which are also my own—so you can calmly send me your third act even without commentary. I won't bungle anything [*nichts verpfuschen*].[15]

For Hofmannsthal this period of enforced wartime separation—"cut off from one another for an unpredictable period"—caused serious anxiety about misunderstandings in the collaboration. Strauss countered with the conviction that they were both so thoroughly attuned to one another ("I know your wishes which are also my own") that the physical separation was unimportant. He added a postscript to note that he had played the first act for some friends: "It's a pity though that I can't play both acts for you."[16] As of February 1915 it was already possible to offer an intimate partial performance of *Die Frau ohne Schatten*.

Friendly Interventions

On February 8 Zita had given birth in Vienna to her third child, Robert, attended again by Dr. Heinrich Peham. She was living with her children in Schönbrunn, and it was there in the palace that the baptism took place on February 10 in the Maria-Theresien-Zimmer, that is, the great ceremonial hall dominated by the Martin Meytens portrait from the 1740s, showing Empress Maria Theresa in a rose-pink gown frosted with white Belgian lace.[17] With her three crowns—Imperial, Bohemian, and Hungarian—on a crimson cushion before her, Maria Theresa looked down upon Zita who would, very soon, be assembling crowns of her own.

Hofmannsthal, who had conjured the age of Maria Theresa in *Der Rosenkavalier* and would look to her for inspiration in a wartime essay of 1917, was now, in 1915, looking for a way out of military service. On March 31 he wrote to Arthur Schnitzler, who had trained as a neurologist: "Tell me the name of someone you consider a good nerve doctor (psychiatrist) with whom I could speak confidentially about my really absurd nerves. It must also be someone who would count as an authority for the military, if possible someone in service, so that his evaluation eventually could lead to a long leave."[18] He had written to Strauss about his extreme sensitivity to the ongoing war—"from which I suffer perhaps especially violently"—but now writing to Schnitzler he sought the clinical diagnosis that would frame this sensitivity as a medical problem necessitating leave from the military.

In April Hofmannsthal noted that Reichsrat representative Joseph Redlich was intervening with Prime Minister Karl von Stürgkh to recommend a special dispensation for the poet.[19] By May 20 Redlich reported that Stürgkh would confirm Hofmannsthal's leave from military authority for an indefinite period and commented in a postscript: "you'll write a few friendly words to Count Stürgkh, won't you?" Hofmannsthal promised to do that and thanked Redlich for his "kind and friendly intervention" that relieved the poet of duties that "for my nature were doubly painful."[20] Still, he would continue to write on behalf of the Austrian military cause.

In early 1915 Hofmannsthal was particularly concerned with the Austrian-German alliance, insisting that Austria should not be considered a secondary partner. In fact, the German army had proved sturdier in combat, while the Austrians were driven back in Serbia in December 1914. In January Hofmannsthal published boldly in Berlin's *Vossische Zeitung* an affirmation of Austrian importance, regretting that in Germany Austria was sometimes "overlooked." Hofmannsthal reminded the German public of the historic importance of Prince Eugene and of Maria Theresa— though Maria Theresa had spent her reign at war against the Prussia of Frederick the Great.[21]

German submarine warfare offered another test of the Austrian-German alliance in 1915, challenging American neutrality, but Karl and Zita maintained a friendship with the American envoy in Vienna, Frederic Penfield. "He was one of our best personal friends," recalled Zita. "How often did we invite him to tea, him and his wife!" He and his wife were both American Roman Catholics, which must have made them seem particularly sympathetic to Zita. "He did everything for us," recalled Zita, "to the extent that was allowable for him, and maybe even a little more." The suggestion was that he informally compromised official American neutrality, because, according to Zita, "Penfield loved Austria, and we naturally undertook to do everything possible to strengthen this sympathy."[22] That sympathy would become more precarious after the German sinking of the *Lusitania* in May 1915, and Penfield would be recalled from Vienna when the United States entered World War I in April 1917.

"The Shadow Hovering in the Air"

"When shall I get act 3?" wrote Strauss in March from Berlin. "I arrive in Garmisch on March 24 and would be delighted to find it there!"[23] Hofmannsthal replied on March 26 with excuses and deferrals: he had hoped to finish by Easter, in spite of his father's recent illness, in spite of his own "depressed spirit," but now Easter was imminent. He proposed to dedicate himself religiously to the third act during Easter Week.[24] Strauss wrote from Garmisch on March 30, Holy Tuesday, to announce a thoroughly Habsburg conducting schedule that involved performing in Budapest, Vienna, and Prague during the last week in April.[25] At last they would see each other in Vienna, and Strauss would be able to play for Hofmannsthal the first two acts.

"Please send me immediately [*sofort*] what you have finished of act 3, so that I have time to get into the spirit [*mich hineinzuleben*]," Strauss requested. "I hope the third act will give me rich opportunities for lyrical outbursts as in the *Rosenkavalier* trio."[26] He was now openly impatient with Hofmannsthal's sensitive nerves:

> I am fresh, well-rested, and full of energy [*tatenfroh*]. Why are you letting your head hang low? You can rely on Germany. Naturally I understand that your father's illness has assailed you. . . . But as for politics: we should try to consider it a little from a distance and leave the worry to those it concerns. Only work can comfort us; only work can help us achieve victory. Please send me soon what is finished—if possible the first half.[27]

It was an oddly military message: with the command to deliver the libretto "immediately," the reproachful contrast between his own high energy—*tatenfroh*—and the poet's hanging head, the injunction to leave politics to the politicians, the implication that Austria should rely on the German alliance, and the concluding invocation of victory. Furthermore, Strauss purposefully confused the cultural work of the operatic collaboration (the work that brings comfort) with the national work that would lead to military victory, as if they were in fact mutually interdependent—all the more reason for the librettist to dispatch the third act. And yet, the spirit of the music that Strauss imagined was anything but military; he wanted to compose a *Rosenkavalier* trio for the last act of *Die Frau ohne Schatten*, something wistful, nostalgic, fervent, and sublime.

On Easter Sunday, April 4, Hofmannsthal published in the *Neue Freie Presse* an essay entitled "Deeds and Fame" (*Die Taten und der Ruhm*). He began from the premise that "after this war people will no longer speak of the heroes and deeds of the Greeks and Romans, but of ours; that the battles of Marathon and Plataea will be replaced by the battles on the San River and at Limanowa."[28] These Galician place names—sites of Austrian-Russian combat—would have once seemed particularly unheroic to Hofmannsthal, who had distasteful associations with his military service in that impoverished province. Yet now Galicia was imbued with the spirit of military heroism as the arena of Habsburg warfare. Hofmannsthal at Easter 1915, like Yeats in Ireland at Easter 1916, was writing about ordinary names transfigured by patriotic heroism—"to murmur name upon name"—such that even humble Galician place names "are changed, changed utterly: a terrible beauty is born."[29] Defining an Austrian identity and mission—especially within the Austrian-German alliance—remained fundamental for Hofmannsthal, and the wartime deeds of the Habsburg monarchy, he hoped, would be translated into a sense of postwar purpose.

The next day, Easter Monday, Strauss wrote from Garmisch with some concerns about the end of the second act and the still incomplete libretto for the third.

> What happens with the shadow that the Dyer's Wife has lost in act 2 and the Empress does not want to take? . . . The shadow therefore hovers

[*schwebt*] in the air. Moreover the Empress's words—"I don't want the shadow/there is blood on it"—are lost to the public, since they are sung in the ensemble. It would thus be very important to have the Empress in act 3 reiterate expressly this resolve to renounce the bloodstained shadow.[30]

It was perhaps a pedantic point to be worrying over in the fairy tale: if one woman has renounced her shadow, but the other woman has refused to accept it, what becomes of the shadow? What does it mean for the shadow to hang in the air, literally, and for the drama itself to hang in the air, figuratively, between the second and third acts? Strauss, composing the septet, would allow the Empress to take the words *Schatten* and *Blut* to the top of the staff, dominating the septet, though not necessarily yielding the necessary clarity of meaning.

Before leaving Berlin, Strauss had given the partial libretto to Nikolaus von Seebach, intendant of the Dresden opera, and to Georg von Hülsen-Haeseler, intendant of the Berlin opera, two likely stages for the completed work. The composer had been enthusiastic when he first received the libretto for the second act back in July 1914 but was now more skeptical after showing it to the intendants:

> Both stood in total incomprehension of the work, and Seebach understood it only after I had once more orally explained the subject to him and played the first act at the piano. I see from all this that the subject and its themes are difficult to understand and that everything must be done to make them quite clear. I ask you urgently therefore to recapitulate quite forcefully in act 3 (as Wagner often does) the decisive psychological processes, so that nothing remains in the dark, and especially the idea that the Empress, because she has learned to feel pity, has earned the shadow, that is, become a human being.[31]

Hofmannsthal had wanted to create a highly concise libretto, with some allusive mystery, but Strauss now wanted everything spelled out less subtly, with the plot points of the second act hammered home in the third act. Above all, he worried that the character of the Empress—whose centrality Hofmannsthal insisted upon back in July 1914—would be misunderstood. Implicitly the composer blamed his librettist: "It is so easy, while working, to identify with the subject, so that one believes that everything that is clear to oneself must also be comprehensible to the reader or listener."³²

Hofmannsthal was not pleased to learn that Strauss had been vetting the libretto with assorted opera intendants, but he was willing to confront the problem of clarification in *Die Frau ohne Schatten*:

> That is quite correctly understood: at the end of act 2 the shadow hovers in the air: the one woman has forfeited it, the other has not validly acquired it—this hovering transaction and its arbitration by the Solomonic judgment of higher powers, whose spokesmen are the unborn children, this is the central point of the third act, the great scene of the Empress in the Temple: this is the spiritual core of the whole piece.³³

The "Solomonic" reference further clarified that, in disputing possession of the shadow, the two women were each claiming the same child, the same fertility, the same line of progeny. This idea that the work should culminate in "Solomon's judgment" dated back to Hofmannsthal's earliest conception of the opera in 1911.³⁴

On April 15, Strauss finally received the text he had been pleading for, but not enough of it: "Your third act is magnificent: word, structure, and content equally wonderful. Only in the striving for brevity it has become too much a sketch." He wanted "absolutely more text" for what he saw as the big lyrical moments, notably the duet between Barak and his wife as well as the duet for the Emperor and the Empress.³⁵ At the same time Strauss felt he needed to understand better the elusive character of the Empress.

"What appears most questionable to me is the figure of the Empress, who does not step close enough to us humanly," wrote Strauss. She was entirely at home in her upper sphere, but if the human world really made her human, then Strauss needed to be able to convey that musically in the score. He wanted Hofmannsthal to help him focus on "her confessions of her own thoughtlessness [*Leichtsinn*], her guilt, and especially her vacillation between her pity for the dyer pair and her love of the Emperor." Strauss thus offered a variety of suggestions for text that might make the Empress seem more human in her great temple scene, but, as he went on to admit, the character actually left him cold, because he did not really believe in her love for the Emperor: "What I miss here is that the Empress says nothing about her relationship to the Emperor; here the whole psychological development of the Empress must be expressed in a monologue . . . how she had loved him beyond reason, without thinking, idolatrously, so that she lost the talisman."[36] This was a very detailed intervention in the text of the libretto, and Strauss pleaded his dissatisfaction with the Empress as something almost personal, as if he had been offended by the Empress for her failure to focus sufficiently on her husband.

"I can't help myself," he wrote, as if he knew he ought to like her better. "It strikes me as very unsympathetic that the Empress is so full of thoughts about her own humanity that she thinks only about the sufferings of the dyer pair and that she has completely forgotten the Emperor."[37] He simply expected an empress to be a devoted wife: if she renounced the shadow for fear of staining her hands, wasn't she condemning her husband to petrification, by the terms of the prophecy?

> The Empress sacrifices her beloved husband, because she doesn't want to obtain the shadow through deceit and the destruction of the happiness of the other couple. There is something unnatural and unsympathetic here. Therefore, the Empress's renunciation of love and of the Emperor's salvation, her resolve to do penance, ought to be more deeply motivated. Otherwise nobody will understand why Barak's happiness is more important to the Empress than her own happiness and the life of the Emperor."[38]

She was sensitive, she was righteous, but she was not sufficiently conjugal.

There were also other elaborations and clarifications that Strauss had in mind for the third-act libretto. He wanted a full farewell scene for the Nurse after the Empress finally recognized her treachery: to express "her love for the Empress whom she has now lost forever" and to pronounce "a more horrible and longer curse on humans." The Wagner libretto for *Lohengrin* was on Strauss's mind, and he referenced Ortrud's curse, imagining the Nurse as a witchlike creature. Strauss also puzzled over the choral voices of the unborn children in the third act, perhaps imagining the prospective confusion of the opera intendants. "How does the public know that it is the unborn children who are singing? The audience hears children's voices but doesn't understand the text."[39] He was looking forward to discussing all this with Hofmannsthal in person in Vienna and announced his arrival at the Hotel Imperial on

April 21, followed by a performance in Budapest on April 22 and a return to Vienna for a whole week from April 23 to 30, including a performance of *Elektra* at the Hofoper on April 28.[40]

On April 22, on the western front around Ypres, the Germans transformed the character of the war with the horrific first use of poison chlorine gas against the French lines. Hofmannsthal would have known nothing of that when he wrote to Strauss on April 23. They had already had one meeting, presumably on the twenty-first—"our recent conversation was very fruitful; act 3 will unfold very beautifully"—and were scheduling another, with a piano, for Sunday, April 25. The meeting was to take place at the home of the conductor Franz Schalk (eventually the conductor of the premiere) and was to include also Alfred Roller (eventually the stage designer)—so this was very much a preparation for performance, even though the premiere was still four years away. Hofmannsthal somewhat officiously reported that the meeting would have to be postponed till 12:30 p.m., since he had a military commitment, "an official appointment with Major Morath at eleven o'clock which cannot be postponed." The poet offered a suggestion for Strauss's morning walk: "Perhaps you could take your stroll in the Schönbrunn gardens beforehand."[41] From the gardens Strauss might have caught a glimpse of Archduchess Zita, the future empress, living in the Schönbrunn palace with her three children—just before he adjourned to the musical meeting to play through the piano score for the first two acts of *Die Frau ohne Schatten*.

The Composer at the Piano

Coming in from his walk in the Habsburg imperial gardens at Schönbrunn, Strauss would have arrived at the meeting with Hofmannsthal, Schalk, and Roller to sit down at the piano and begin to play: act 1, scene 1, set on the terrace over the fictive imperial gardens of the fairy-tale Emperor and Empress. The piano would have presented the syncopated leaping phrase that accompanied the rising curtain (later orchestrated for clarinets, basset horn, and bass clarinet). Strauss would have played piano octave tremolos (later composed for runs on the harp and celesta) to accompany the Nurse's opening words, "Licht über'm See" (light over the sea).[42] Strauss and Hofmannsthal could not have known that that very morning at dawn, on April 25,

Australian and New Zealander troops had made their amphibious landings on the Gallipoli Peninsula, launching an unsuccessful campaign against the Ottoman Empire that would result in massive casualties over the next six months.

Continuing with the first act, when the Emperor departed to hunt, Strauss would have played *fortissimo* octaves to simulate the full orchestra's E-flat presentation of the Emperor's passionate theme: "Denn meiner Seele." For the Empress's awakening, which immediately followed—"Ist mein Liebster dahin?"—the piano would have rendered what later became the line of the solo violin, while arpeggiated chords simulated the eventual accompaniment of the harp.[43] Possibly Strauss's just-finished stroll in the Schönbrunn gardens added coloring to the piano evocation of the operatic imperial gardens, and Roller might have been mentally contemplating the coloration for the eventual stage design.

Strauss had already let Hofmannsthal know of his affinity for the Dyer ("Barak is excellent for me") and now Strauss would have conveyed his sympathy at the piano: Barak listening to his wife's harsh words but invoking the "blessing of revocability." Barak's baritone role was perhaps the only one that Strauss could have comfortably sung from the piano for his small audience. Probably the composer could already imagine the characteristic Straussian horns, harmonizing in different parts, adding gorgeous coloring to Barak's phrasings.[44]

Barak returns to the same phrase—the "blessing of revocability"—in act 2, scene 1, when his wife despises the feast that he has triumphantly brought home. He is nevertheless celebrated as the working-class hero of the neighborhood by the full orchestra, the three brothers, and a chorus of beggar children, who anticipate the imminent feast: "O Tag des Glücks, O Abend der Gnade!" (O day of luck, O evening of grace!) Strauss at the piano would have had to present all the parts of the ensemble while hinting at a score that would need everything from trilling piccolos to clicking castanets, with enthusiastic horns and trumpets leading the celebration.[45] The prospect of the feast would have taken on some additional significance in the circumstances of wartime Vienna with its serious food shortages.

By the time Strauss got to the end of the second act, he would have been at the piano for well over two hours. It would have been challenging for him to perform the two septets, for how could he possibly render the seven voices? In the first septet he would have tried to suggest the power of the Empress's vocal line at the top of the staff, as she sang of Barak, 'Praised be whoever has let me find this man." He already knew that Barak himself would harmonize with her line—but did he envision the ascending horn phrase that would accompany them both?[46]

It was following this first septet that the Dyer's Wife renounced her shadow: the renunciation—"Abtu' ich von meinem Leibe die Kinder" (I put off children from my body)—could be sung on a monotone high F, easy enough for Strauss to suggest at the piano, while tremolo F octaves indicated the eventual *fortissimo* presence of the string section.[47] "Habe ich meinen Schatten verhandelt" (I have traded away my shadow) he could have recited in a sort of *Sprechstimme*, with no piano accompaniment at all. And, similarly, Barak's reply could have been merely spoken, "Das Weib ist irre" (the woman is mad). The three brothers could see that the Dyer's Wife spoke the truth, and they too spoke rather than sang: "She casts no shadow!" The Nurse then directs the Empress, "Take the shadow"—and Strauss may have suggested at the piano the eventual presence of flutes, oboes, and clarinets to emphasize the strange magic of this moment.[48]

It was the moment that Strauss and Hofmannsthal had discussed already in the correspondence: the moment when the shadow was hovering in the air. It was also the moment for the launching of the second septet in which the Empress sings, "I don't want the shadow, there is blood on it." For the brothers the shadow is an absence, something which cannot be seen, no longer attached to the Dyer's Wife—but for the Empress the shadow is visible, stained with blood. Strauss could have emphasized the word *Blut* as it rose above the septet, though he could hardly have sung the soprano's high A-flat; he might have hinted on the piano at the chromatic ascent in the horns and cellos that would lead up to that soaring note.[49] The black keys of the piano would have conveyed the majesty of D-flat major. At the same time, Strauss had to suggest all seven voices and a cacophonous orchestra while also insisting on the clarity of the scenario, conveying to his little audience the drama of the shadow hovering in the air, surrendered by the Dyer's Wife but refused by the Empress.

The septet must convey Barak's rage, for he is finally roused to such fury that he wants to kill his wife for having given up her shadow—while his brothers try to restrain him. He calls for a sack and some stones to drown her in the river, until finally, at the climax of the septet, with bass drum, crashing cymbals, and *fortissimo* trumpets, a flashing sword magically appears in his hand, and he is armed to execute her on the spot. She, however, suddenly has a change of heart, is moved by his rage, and no longer feels contempt. "Barak, ich hab' es nicht getan!" (I have not done it) she exclaims, emphasizing the note of denial—*nicht*—as a sustained high A-flat.[50] The Dyer's Wife has not yet given herself to another man, not yet forfeited her fertility, not yet renounced her shadow. Strauss might well have wondered about the problem of clarity: Had she or hadn't she? Was the shadow still hovering in the air? "Mighty Barak," she apostrophized him, with the first syllable of his name sung on a high B-flat; Strauss at the piano could have indicated the trumpet salute that would eventually accompany her high note.[51] If the dramatic situation was ambiguous, her musical phrasings were majestically clear, and she sang with a lucidity that recalled the phrases of Wagner's Brünnhilde in the Immolation Scene; she apostrophized her husband—"Mighty Barak"—as if he were her Siegfried, armed with his sword.

The tempo accelerates for the act's conclusion, and the full orchestra joins *fortissimo*: Barak stands ready to kill his wife, but the cymbals crash, the sword disappears, and the stage darkens. With a roaring noise the earth opens up—an earthquake in the spirit of baroque stagecraft—the river floods the dwelling, Barak and his wife sink and disappear into the darkness. Only the voice of the Nurse is heard over the orchestra exclaiming, "Übermächte sind im Spiel!" (Higher powers are in play!)—clarifying the circumstances for the audience and ending on a high F-sharp as the orchestra takes over entirely. Strauss might have indicated with octaves at the piano the offstage presence of six trumpets and six trombones sounding the call to judgment—Solomonic judgment—for, as the orchestra came crashing to a conclusion, the shadow still hovered in the air.[52]

9

"Spirit of the Carpathians"

MILITARY SERVICE, THE PREOCCUPATIONS OF WARTIME, AND THE TRIALS OF SEPARATION

"The Bust of the Emperor"

"My departure for Poland is somewhat postponed because of the great events," wrote Hofmannsthal to Strauss on May 14, 1915, "but I hope I can still send you the revised beginning of act 3." He wanted more time for the rest of the act, because he had been so moved in Vienna by Strauss's playing of the score that he now wanted to revise act 3 according to the "splendid after-feeling" left behind by the music.[1] His reference to the "great events"—the phrase that Karl Kraus regarded with such fierce satirical derision—indicated the Austrian-German offensive in the Polish lands. Following the fall of the Galician fortress of Przemyśl in March 1915—a blow to morale and a loss of prestige for Austria-Hungary—the Russians stood poised to cross the Carpathian Mountains and invade Hungary. At the beginning of May, therefore, the Germans and the Austrians launched an offensive in Galicia around the town of Tarnów. The campaign would have just begun as Hofmannsthal wrote his letter, and it was no time for a poet, even a poet writing wartime propaganda, to travel around the region. The German artillery dominated the Russians, who had to surrender Przemyśl at the beginning of June and Lviv by the end of the month. For the Austrians, perhaps the most important point was dislodging the Russians from the Carpathian mountain passes at the border between Galicia and Hungary.

Young men were fighting and dying in the Carpathians and in the trenches of Flanders, but Hofmannsthal, on May 14, was focused on the young man who, in act 2, scene 1, was magically conjured from a broom by the Nurse as a sexual temptation for the Dyer's Wife, to encourage her to reject her husband and renounce her shadow. In act 2, scene 3, the young man—"the apparition of a youth"—is conjured again, a sexual fantasy seemingly brought to life as a tenor. He sings a brief 3/4 time waltz trio with the Nurse and the Dyer's Wife, declaring his passionate love for the latter at the top of the staff in a series of ardent G-sharps and high As.[2] Hofmannsthal would have had some sense of this trio from the piano performance in April, and he was now, three weeks later, worrying over the musical characterization of the young man. "It was a serious mistake of mine, only explicable by the preoccupations of wartime," he wrote now to Strauss, "that I did not remind you sufficiently that the 'youth from afar' [*fremde Jüngling*] is a phantom to be played by a mime with utmost delicacy on stage—and sung from somewhere else (from the orchestra pit) with a ghostly [*geisterhaft*] voice."[3] The youth was *fremd* in the sense of strange, unknown, alien, foreign, from afar—in this case otherworldly, from the spirit world.

Hofmannsthal specified that the youth was related to such spirit creatures as the soprano falcon and the chorus of unborn children, and the poet was clearly displeased to think of the youth singing as a masculine tenor. "It is my heartfelt plea in this one scene where the phantom opens his mouth," wrote Hofmannsthal, "to recast the modulation of the voice, as singular, nonhuman, ghostly."[4] The ghostly voice would be disembodied, sung from the orchestra, while a mime performed on stage—and here Hofmannsthal was probably influenced by having seen the seventeen-year-old Leonid Massine perform the role of Joseph in Paris in May 1914, exactly one year earlier. Now, in May 1915, teenagers were fighting and dying in the trenches of the western front, and the phantom apparition of a strange youth from afar would have had powerful spectral associations with the war dead.

Much more satisfactory for Hofmannsthal was the Straussian musicalization of the Emperor: "The way you have created the Emperor in music gives me the most definite guidance for how to deal with this figure in the third act. After he is awakened from his petrifaction, he must have his aria, his (completely different) *Gralserzählung*."⁵ Not for the first time, *Lohengrin* was a point of reference for Hofmannsthal, for the *Gralserzählung* referenced Lohengrin's third-act aria, "*In fernem Land,*" identifying himself as a knight of the Holy Grail, from a distant land. Strauss had played for Hofmannsthal the Emperor's two scenes in the first and second acts, first as a passionate hunter and lover, then as a jealous and despairing husband, trusting himself only to his loyal falcon. In the third act he would be turned to stone in the temple of Keikobad and then brought back to life, resurrected, to herald the advent of the messianic empire of the future. He would appear seated, silent, and petrified upon his throne, till the moment when the Empress proved her humanity and cast her shadow, enabling him to arise and sing.

In 1915 Emperor Franz Joseph turned eighty-five, and while he was a powerful symbolic figure of unity within Austria-Hungary—in the sixty-seventh year of his reign—he was past the age of very active leadership. In Benatzky's song "Draußen in Schönbrunn" he was simply sitting in the park, *sorgenschwer*, full of worries, while the people of Vienna promised to do what they could to allow him "a little time to rest" (*bisserl Zeit zum Ruh'n*). Franz Joseph did not have very much time left, in any event, but would die in November 1916, the following year. In the song, for all intents and purposes, he might already have been a statue of himself, a monument to his own semi-mythological reign. He had been petrified on a grand scale in 1898 and in 1908, the years of his fiftieth and sixtieth jubilees, with the unveiling of stone busts in his honor all over his empire.⁶

The Galician writer Joseph Roth, in his story "The Bust of the Emperor," imagined Franz Joseph surviving the demise of his empire in the form of a stone bust in postwar Poland: "Every peasant who passed by doffed his cap to the sandstone bust of the old Emperor, and every Jew who passed by with his bundle murmured the prayer which a pious Jew will say on seeing an Emperor."⁷ The petrification of an emperor was the magical conceit of a fairy-tale opera, but it was also, in some sense, the historical experience of the Habsburg subjects of Franz Joseph, including Hofmannsthal himself, who had watched their emperor grow into extreme old age, seen him honored in stone monuments, and experienced his reign as an emperor of mythological status in his own lifetime.

Franz Joseph came to life and "spoke" to his peoples at crucial moments—most dramatically with the declaration of war on Serbia on July 28, 1914, issued as a poster declaration "To My Peoples" in all the languages of the empire. "It was my most ardent wish," he began, "to dedicate the years that by God's grace are still left to me to works of peace and to protect my peoples from the heavy sacrifices and burdens of war." He denounced the Serbs for their "hatred against me and against my house," and declared his confidence in "my peoples who in every storm have gathered around my throne in unity and loyalty."[8] It was the language of a statue brought to life for the moment of imperial crisis. In May 1915 the Emperor would address his peoples again, to denounce Italy's declaration of war. The Italians, previously allied with Germany and Austria-Hungary but remaining neutral at the outbreak of World War I, had now concluded a treaty with the Entente, agreed to reverse alliances, and declared war against Austria with the promise of receiving Habsburg lands. "The King of Italy has declared war against me," proclaimed Franz Joseph on May 23, the personal incarnation of the dynastic state.[9]

On that same day Hofmannsthal published in the *Neue Freie Presse* his essay, "Spirit of the Carpathians," about the recently concluded campaign against Russia. Beginning in January 1915, the Habsburg army undertook a disastrously costly winter campaign for control of the Carpathian mountain passes, fighting in deep snow and freezing temperatures, with huge casualties including death by frostbite and exposure. Now in May Hofmannsthal looked back upon a winter of Carpathian struggle, set with the "sublimity of nature around all these events: the starry winter nights, the hushed snowy birch woods, the silent mountaintops in the dawn light and the rising of the morning star in the icy clear air, great and magical here as never before and nowhere else." The Carpathians had become a "heroic landscape," theatrically "the stage [*Schauplatz*] where the war formed its heroes"—"the most experienced and invincible army since the days of Prince Eugene." The reports from the Carpathians were "engraved upon our souls," including the place names of the mountain region: "when we hear Dunajec or Biala, Ondawa and Orawa and Laborcza, Ung or Stryj, something trembles inside us deep down . . . we pronounce these names and we feel that they instill the sublime in us, not we in them."[10] The soldiers accomplished their heroic work in silence (*stumm haben sie es geleistet*), and now it was the poet's task to articulate their experience. As in Galicia, so too in the Carpathians Hofmannsthal anticipated the Yeatsian transfiguration of names—"to murmur name upon name / as a mother names her child"—with the birth of a terrible beauty in the toponyms of Habsburg geography.

Hofmannsthal also pronounced the roll call of ordinary men from everyday professions who made up the heroic army: coal miners, metalworkers, woodcutters, mountaineers, vineyard farmers, brewery men, gamekeepers, blacksmiths, locksmiths, butchers, wagoners, saddlers, gendarmes. One might have imagined Barak the Dyer among them, conscripted into the Habsburg army, fighting in the Carpathians but with a firearm, not a magical sword. Hofmannsthal listed the officers' professions as well, including the electrical technician, the judicial official, the station chief, the small-town salesman, the schoolteacher, and the musician—though not the poet—and he paid tribute to the priests and the doctors who attended the army. He described the "death prayer of the Bosnian Muslim, heard by no one except the imperial prince, who bent back the underbrush and found the lonely Muslim singing his death song."[11] Here was a fairy-tale scene indeed, from the *Thousand and One Nights*, transposed to the Habsburg Carpathians, with a Habsburg prince as Harun al-Rashid. The Habsburg prince could only have been Archduke Joseph August, the older cousin of Archduke Karl, commander of the Habsburg Seventh Corps in the Carpathians. It seemed to Hofmannsthal that the "spirit of the Carpathians"—linking the imperial dynasty to ordinary men in military service—might inspire a reburnished Habsburg patriotism.

Poets and Musicians at War

Hofmannsthal included musicians among the Habsburg military heroes, and, in fact, there was an exceptionally important Austrian musician who served on the eastern front in Galicia: the young concert pianist Paul Wittgenstein, older brother of Ludwig the future philosopher. Like Hofmannsthal, the Wittgenstein brothers came from a prosperous family of converts from Judaism, very involved in Viennese culture; their sister Margaret was painted by Klimt.[12] Paul Wittgenstein was tragically wounded in battle and had to have his right arm amputated, just before being taken prisoner by the

Russians and sent to Siberia. Surviving the war, Wittgenstein later undertook a series of commissions—most famously from Ravel, the left-handed piano concerto in D-major—but also from Richard Strauss, who created in the 1920s a piano concerto for the left hand based on his Sinfonia Domestica. Ravel himself served as a truck driver in the French army during the war.

Arnold Schoenberg, born in Vienna in 1874 just like Hofmannsthal, was conscripted into the Habsburg army in 1915 in spite of his asthma, and he spent some time in service though not in combat. "No foreign music ever meant anything to me," wrote Schoenberg to Alma Mahler on August 28, 1914, at the outbreak of the war. "It always seemed to me stale, empty, disgusting, cloying, dishonest, and amateurish." He named, for instance, Bizet, Stravinsky, and Delius, and exulted, "Now comes the reckoning! Now we throw these mediocre kitsch-mongers into slavery again, and they will need to revere the German spirit and learn to worship the German God."[13] His military service in 1915 was thus partly suffused with the spirit of cultural jingoism. He himself was already enough of a celebrity for his subversively atonal compositions to receive quizzical reactions within the military. An officer asked him whether he was the "notorious Schoenberg"—to which he supposedly replied, "Beg to report sir, yes. . . . Someone had to be, so I let it be me."[14] He was famous or notorious enough to get himself released from service and was eventually discharged.

His pupil Alban Berg, also asthmatic, likewise served during the war—with a desk job in the Vienna war ministry. There he became a pacifist and began to work on his atonal operatic masterpiece *Wozzeck*, about the brutality of military life, eventually to be performed in Berlin in 1925. As a wartime operatic project, *Wozzeck* was radically different from *Die Frau ohne Schatten*—with starkly atonal scoring, extreme textual conciseness, and a desperately tragic conclusion. These works offered completely different postwar visions of operatic modernism.[15]

Hofmannsthal did not mention poets among the professions that came together in the Habsburg army, for it would certainly have touched too closely on his own case at the very moment when he was securing his military release. Yet there was one very important Austrian writer who might have been cited here, the young expressionist poet Georg Trakl, who participated in the Galician campaign and died in Kraków in November 1914 of an overdose of cocaine, probably with suicidal intention.[16] Trakl had published a volume of expressionist verse just before the war in 1913—when he was twenty-six—and the style represented the aesthetic values of a new generation. He was exactly the same age (born 1887) as Paul Wittgenstein, and almost the same age as the expressionist painter Oskar Kokoschka (born 1886), who joined the Austrian cavalry and was wounded on the Russian front in 1915.

Trakl, born in Salzburg, was also trained as a pharmacist and served in that capacity in Galicia in 1914. His poem "Evening" conjured the ghosts of young men in the moonlight, like Hofmannsthal's operatic apparition of a beautiful youth:

> With the shapes of dead heroes,
> Moon, you fill
> The silent woods . . . .[17]

Among Trakl's final poems, published posthumously, "Grodek" was named for the town in eastern Galicia where an Austrian-Russian battle was fought.

> In the evening the autumnal woods resound
> With deadly weapons . . . .[18]

The final lines of "Grodek" seemed to echo the libretto of *Die Frau ohne Schatten*, which Trakl could not possibly have known.

> The hot flame of the spirit nourishes today tremendous grief,
> The unborn descendants [*die ungebornen Enkel*].[19]

Just as Hofmannsthal sought to convey pathos through the voices of the unborn children of the future, so Trakl indicated precisely what this would have meant in the context of the ongoing war: the unborn children were the descendants of the soldiers who died on the battlefield.

Galician Refugees

Hofmannsthal's friend Leopold von Andrian wrote to him on May 23 after reading "Spirit of the Carpathians" in the *Neue Freie Presse*: "Your feuilleton this morning gave me great joy, because it was at the same time so useful and so beautiful."[20] It was meant to be useful, of course, in articulating the achievements of the Austrian war effort, but the classification of the essay as a "feuilleton" rather than a piece of factual journalism or partisan propaganda placed the emphasis on Hofmannsthal's poetic impressions and subjective sensibility in reformulating the course of the war. Hofmannsthal and Andrian were linked artistically as fin de siècle writers of the 1890s and, remaining friends, they became politically compatible Habsburg patriots. Andrian served in the Habsburg diplomatic service and worked as far afield as Brazil and Argentina before being posted to Warsaw in Russian Poland in 1911. After 1914 Hofmannsthal and Andrian were both interested in trying to define an "Austrian idea" as the basis for wartime patriotism and postwar political life.[21]

In the spring of 1915 the German-Austrian offensive drove the Russians from Galicia, and, despite the unsteady performance of the Austrian army, Andrian and Hofmannsthal believed that Austria should not be shunted aside by its ally Germany in planning the future of the occupied Polish lands. Hofmannsthal's Polish visit in June 1915 was closely connected to this concern. He asked his publisher to have correspondence sent to him in care of Andrian at the Hotel Francuski in Kraków.[22]

On August 5 the German army took Warsaw from the Russians, and on August 8 Hofmannsthal published in the *Neue Freie Presse* an article entitled "Our Military Administration in Poland." Based on his June visit he believed that occupying the territories of Russian Poland, following the Russian retreat, would constitute an immense labor of reconstruction: "What was taken over was in a real sense not a land but a chaos." In fact, the notion of Poland as chaos was a long-standing German and Austrian stereotype, dating back to the partitions of Poland in the eighteenth century.[23] Yet Hofmannsthal believed that the Austrians, much more than the Germans, would have the capacity to create a successful military administration in Poland, based on the multinational, multilingual Habsburg army. A Habsburg military administration would speak to Poles in their own language.

> And there's something else, a certain generosity of heart and that which can scarcely be defined, that which weighs so heavily in the coexistence of nations: tact. It is given to us, more than to the Germans, to be able to

dwell with strangers: as neighbors, as masters, as temporary administrators, as friends.[24]

Here was a sense of mission for Austria-Hungary, to participate in the occupation of the Polish lands and show the Germans how to do it properly, with tact. Hofmannsthal himself had been exceptionally uncomfortable among the population of Galicia when he was doing his military service in the 1890s, describing a provincial world of beggars and Jews that appeared to him as "ugly, miserable and dirty." Now, however, twenty years later, Hofmannsthal declared that in the Polish lands, "among peasants, nobles, townsmen, industrialists, and Jews, the organs of our administration, our officers and soldiers, move with effortless tact."[25] In the spring of 1915 he was in Galicia being tactful himself.

Not only Hofmannsthal but likewise Stefan Zweig was sent on a service trip to Galicia in 1915, working for the War Archive to collect poster proclamations from the recently displaced Russian occupation. Zweig traveled in July, and, like Hofmannsthal, he afterward published an appropriately patriotic piece in the *Neue Freie Presse*—"Galiziens Genesung" ("The Healing of Galicia")—but, in retrospect, in his memoirs, Zweig described the impact of the trip as moving him toward his ultimate stance of principled pacifism. In Tarnów, Drohobych, and Lviv he was struck by "the terrible misery of the civilian population, upon whose eyes the horror of what they had experienced lay like a shadow." He sympathized with the misery of the Galician Jews, and even of the Russian prisoners of war, while he witnessed "the shelled cities and the plundered shops, whose contents lay about in the middle of the streets like broken limbs or torn-out entrails." He described soldiers who "while they were being led to the slaughter already looked like slaughtered cattle," and horrific hospital trains: "How little they resembled the well-lighted, white, carefully cleaned ambulance trains in which the archduchesses and the fashionable ladies of Viennese society had their pictures taken as nurses at the beginning of the war!"[26] Zweig might have been thinking of the publicized hospital visits of Archduchess Zita in Vienna.

Even as Hofmannsthal and Zweig were traveling to Galicia, Vienna was absorbing a massive rush of Galician refugees who had come during the first year of the war to escape from the advancing Russian army and ongoing military encounters. As many as 100,000 Galician Jews fled to the capital, often fearing pogroms under Russian occupation, but there were also Poles and Ukrainians displaced from Galicia, and the social and economic life of Vienna experienced new tensions from this influx.[27] On November 5, 1914, the orchestra, chorus, and soloists of the Vienna Opera held a benefit concert to raise money for the refugees from Galicia and the neighboring province of Bukovina—"without regard for nationality or confession," meaning Poles, Ukrainians, and Jews. One of the conductors was Franz Schalk, and three of the soloists were Maria Jeritza, Lucie Weidt, and Richard Mayr, who would eventually create the roles of the Empress, the Nurse, and Barak in *Die Frau ohne Schatten*. The concert naturally began with Haydn's imperial anthem "Gott erhalte"—but it concluded with two patriotic marches by Richard Strauss.[28]

On December 5, 1914, another concert was held to benefit the Galician refugees, this time combining vocal and chamber music, with the celebrated violinist Arnold Rosé. On December 10 the Galician-born pianist Ignaz Friedman gave a recital to benefit the refugees, with lots of Chopin on the program as a Polish reference but concluding with the piano transcription of a Johann Strauss waltz for Vienna.[29] A benefit event on December 17 took on a more pronounced Jewish character, billed as a Chanukah concert and starring Don Fuchs, the tenor and chief cantor of the Viennese community, singing some cantorial pieces, while the program also included an aria from Handel's *Judas Maccabeus* in honor of Chanukah. On March 24, 1915, the day after the fall of Przemyśl to the Russians, with all of Galicia at risk, Fuchs gave one more benefit concert, including Eleazar's aria from Halévy's *La Juive* and, perhaps more unexpectedly, the aria "In fernem Land" from Wagner's *Lohengrin*.[30] At the Vienna concert the "distant land" might have been Galicia itself, and Fuchs himself would later travel to an even more distant land, seeking to raise money for refugees from American Jews—and eventually emigrating to America after the war.

The very particular preoccupation of Fuchs with refugee cantors was amplified in an appeal that he published in the United States in January 1916 in *The Reform Advocate*, the leading American journal of Reform Judaism. Fuchs noted the wartime suffering of the Galicians in general, observing that "the most unfortunate among all these war victims are the cantors and the choir singers," since "beside the loss of their worldly possessions, of their incomes, and the destruction of their homes, they face the loss of their most precious gift, their only possession, the loss of their voice."[31] Fuchs counted six hundred Galician cantors who were refugees in Vienna and cited exile, illness, and even bad weather as likely dangers to their vocal cords, in addition to the "too well-founded fear that upon their return home they will find their congregations impoverished, their synagogues destroyed, their own dwellings looted and devastated."[32] In fact, by the time this appeal appeared, the Russians had been driven out of Galicia, and an Austrian administration would have been—according to Hofmannsthal's propaganda—restoring order in the aftermath of chaos.

On January 14, 1915, the *Neue Freie Presse* announced the opening of a refugee asylum (*Flüchtlingsheim*) by the Vienna Refugee Committee under the patronage of Zita herself.[33] She was also the patroness of a benefit for Galician refugees on January 27, 1915, an evening of poetry dedicated to "Young German and Austrian Heroes'"—starring the glamorously handsome Viennese actor (and later film director) Franz Höbling. He read poems on patriotic subjects, for instance "Dem alten Kaiser" (To the Old Emperor) by Marx Möller, "1914" by Heinrich Pekel, and "An Polen" (To Poland) by Richard Kralik.[34] Some of the poems were by actual combat soldiers, and none were by Hofmannsthal, whose patriotism at this moment was expressed in prose rather than verse. Kralik was a Catholic writer who would later belong to the cultural circle that advised Empress Zita in exile, while his son Heinrich Kralik would be one of the music critics who reviewed *Die Frau ohne Schatten* in 1919.

Difficult Marriages

On May 27 Strauss wrote to Hofmannsthal requesting more text for the first scene of the third act—a letter that the poet would not receive until he returned from his Polish tour. After the earth opened up and swallowed Barak and his wife at the end of the second act, they found themselves imprisoned in darkness at the opening of the third act and solitary in their separation from one another. The scene began with her monologue, and he then initiated a lyrical duet in which they would harmonize without actually being able to see or hear each other, without knowing that each was thinking longingly of the other. Strauss wanted more text for her monologue, and, though he was pleased with Barak's text for the duet—"Mir anvertraut" (Entrusted to me)—he wanted parallel text for her to sing.³⁵

The very next day, May 28, Strauss impatiently wrote again, now presuming to write some lines of verse for the Dyer's Wife to show Hofmannsthal what was needed: "Verstossen von ihm / in Nacht und Grauen / allein in Verzweiflung / allein in Reue" (Repudiated by him / by night and in terror / alone in despair / alone in regret). The librettist did not deign to use one single word of the composer's proposed text, but Strauss clearly had very strong ideas of what was needed, had already chosen the key of F minor, and could scarcely wait for Hofmannsthal to return from Poland. He suggested another pair of unsubtle lines that Hofmannsthal would never have accepted: "aller Menschenpflicht / hab' ich mich entäussert / nun bin ich ausgestossen / aus menschlicher Gemeinschaft" (all my human obligations / I have renounced, / now I have been ejected / from the human community). Strauss clearly knew that the lines were inadequate and urged Hofmannsthal to consider these words "only as a suggestion."³⁶

With Hofmannsthal in Poland, Strauss was so eager to compose the duet that he decided to let the Dyer's Wife simply adapt the lines already written for Barak (*mir anvertraut*). On June 8 he wrote to say that he had not waited for the poet's words:

> The first scene of act 3 is now musically finished. It turned out a very well-constructed and beautifully developing scene, for which I have laboriously rearranged the text. . . . Please decide whether you agree with all the carpentry, adjustments, and repetitions, or whether you want to create the desired verses for the designated places.³⁷

On the one hand, Strauss was courteous in deferring to Hofmannsthal's approval, but, on the other hand, the composer made very clear that he was capable of improvising text and proceeding on his own.

Strauss was even drawing on his own reading to rethink the libretto, mentioning *Mendel Gibbor*, a nineteenth-century novella of traditional Jewish life by Aaron Bernstein (uncle of the famous German socialist Eduard Bernstein), which referenced "the custom of Jewish coroners to ask the dead man's forgiveness for all misfortunes inflicted on him during his lifetime." He wondered whether this might be relevant to the Dyer's Wife, begging

Barak's forgiveness during the opening scene of the third act. Strauss wanted "an element of excited fanaticism [*etwas begeistert Fanatisches*]."[38]

Strauss's reference to *Mendel Gibbor* poses the important question of to what extent Barak, an urban craftsman from a city that might have been Vienna, could have been construed as a Jewish character. Barak (not so far from Baruch) and his brothers were throughout the opera associated with dance rhythms and woodwind timbres that seemed to hint at klezmer music. Mahler had already made use of klezmer material in his symphonies, and Strauss might also have been interested in those orchestral textures, though Hofmannsthal, with his carefully effaced Jewish ancestry, would probably have preferred to evade such associations.

On June 17 (with Hofmannsthal still in Poland), Strauss wrote to emphasize the Old Testament framing of *Die Frau ohne Schatten*: "The Judgment of Solomon keeps going around in my head."[39] In the third act the Empress would come for judgment to the temple of her father Keikobad, the spirit king, and there she would find her husband the Emperor turned to stone. For Strauss this had to be the climax of the opera: "There must be a powerful explosion here—such that in the end there is wrested from the breast of the Empress the first terrifying human cry [*Menschenschrei*], something like a woman in childbirth." This cry would be the crucial dramatic turning point of the act: "Please work on fulfilling my wishes immediately upon your return from Poland, so that I can quickly get to work."[40] It seems unlikely that Hofmannsthal imagined anything so graphic as the sonic simulation of labor pains in the Empress's climactic scene—though, in fact, the year 1915 had begun with a flesh-and-blood future empress in the throes of childbirth at Schönbrunn.

Hofmannsthal finally reported his return from Poland on June 22: "Returning from Poland yesterday, I found here your letters of May 26, May 27, June 8, and June 17." He was a little irritable about the importunateness of the onslaught ("you had told me you would not need the new material before the end of June") but promised to focus his attention on the libretto. He huffily refused to rework the lyrical duet between Barak and his wife, since Strauss had already done that himself: "If I must partly paint over some of the text that you have put together, this can happen later; probably I will be able to approve most of it."[41]

The third-act duet—"Mir anvertraut"—was the opera's most lyrical tribute to human love and marriage, as the dyer pair longed for each other in the darkness of isolation. In the first two acts Strauss had found his way to composing the harsh and difficult aspects of the Dyer's Wife—her dissatisfactions and resentments, her outbursts of contempt for her husband, her fantasized infidelity, and her ambivalence about motherhood—all the qualities that made her a difficult wife for Barak. In the third act, however, she realized that she loved him.

In Strauss's marriage to Pauline, the opera diva, she was the difficult one, making scenes, and he the one who calmed her nerves. Hofmannsthal's marriage to Gertrud (Gerty) Schlesinger was perhaps the reverse, for he was the difficult one. She was not an opera singer or any sort of an artist but the daughter of a Viennese Jewish financier and younger sister of an aesthete and painter, Hofmannsthal's friend Hans, who later converted to Catholicism and became a Dominican monk. "Your sister pleases me more than all other women," wrote Hofmannsthal to Hans in 1896 when she was only sixteen. "She is, externally and internally, in such an unbelievably happy balance and such naive security and confidence that she cheers one up." The next year, he saw her at a social gathering and wrote, "Your little sister went around among all those people like a child at the zoo." She converted to Christianity in 1900 to marry him in 1901, an ironic move in view of his own family history but characteristic of her conciliatory inclinations. In marriage she continued to conciliate, as he acknowledged in a letter to her of 1906: "I ponder over this incomprehensible strange bad nature in me that has so often tormented and offended you, whom I love most in the world."[42] Hofmannsthal and Strauss both were sensitive to the tensions that emerged in marriage when one spouse was more difficult and moodier, the other more composed and balanced.

Yet Hofmannsthal believed in the ultimate sturdiness of married life: "Marriage is a sublime institution and in our miserable existences it stands like a castle cut into a rock cliff," he wrote many years later.[43] Both Hofmannsthal and Strauss, with their very different wives and marriages, were true believers in the institution, and in the opening scene of the third act they created together an operatic tribute to sublime reconciliation, seized upon so urgently by Strauss that he could not even wait a few weeks for Hofmannsthal to supply him with the necessary text.

"Mir anvertraut"

The third act begins with the darkest timbres of the orchestra, introducing a scene in the vaults of some Piranesian prison. Subdued horns, trombones, and tubas suggest the subterranean spirit of the scene, accompanied by cellos and basses. There is a *pianissimo* drumroll, and a plaintive figure emerges from the bassoon, soon joined by the bass clarinet. Finally, in the sixteenth measure, the flutes and celesta offer a contrast to the darkness, in a reiterated dotted rhythm, and a notation in the score tells us that we are hearing the voices of the unborn children. This syncopated rhythm, growing louder and more forceful in the full orchestra, finally provokes a vocal cry in the darkness from the Dyer's Wife who recognizes those voices and needs to silence them: "Schweiget doch," she sings, be silent, as she mimics the syncopation of the voices themselves, setting off frenzied runs of triplets in the flutes, clarinets, and violins.[44]

Strauss then has the cellos introduce the lyrical melody of her romantic longing for her husband, as she begins to call to him, "Barak, mein Mann." With Hofmannsthal in Poland, Strauss had very little text to work with, so she sings over and over again about Barak's face—*dein Angesicht*—and the whole string section sings ecstatically along with her. The score is marked *molto appassionato*, and she chants his name accompanied by mysterious cadences in the woodwinds. She confesses that the youth from afar—recalled by the English horn—came to her while Barak was asleep but reassures her husband that she has remained faithful.[45] Certainly, the circumstances of wartime, with soldier husbands and their wives separated across the continent of Europe in 1915, would have added additional intensity to Strauss's composition of this duet of marital separation and mutual longing.

A lyrical figure in the French horns signals Barak's presence in the subterranean vault as he prepares to initiate their duet. It is the horns that bridge the two measures from the end of her monologue to his purring entrance on A-flat—"Mir anvertraut"—his melody accompanied by ascending phrases for harp, cello, and basset horn. His baritone voice reaches higher and higher, first up to C and D-sharp, then up to D and E-flat, finally up to E and F, expressing an ever more aching regret that he has failed in his solemn obligation to honor and protect his young wife. When he concludes his melody,

Figure 18. "Mir anvertraut" (entrusted to me), sang Barak, and Strauss was so impatient to compose this beautiful duet of marital reconciliation that he could not wait for Hofmannsthal to return from Poland to write the words for the Dyer's Wife. So Strauss had her almost echo the Dyer's words: "Mir anvertraut / Dir angetraut." Even as they both harmonized on the aching, ascending line, they were accompanied by the harp and joined by the expressive French horn. (*Die Frau ohne Schatten*, 1919)

thinking regretfully of how he should have acted "for the sake of her young heart" (*um ihres jungen Herzens willen*), it is the rueful oboe that descends stepwise along with him and then accompanies him gloriously across a whole octave on the word "heart." When he begins his melody again—"Mir anvertraut"—he is joined by the French horn, his alter ego, and then, in the second measure, by his wife, as if responding. She echoes his text—"Dir angetraut" (wedded to you) —in words that Strauss only slightly varied, because Hofmannsthal was in Poland and not replying to letters.[46]

The syncopation of their parts has her embroidering his melody, descending where he ascends, singing her note on the beat after his note, even as their texts also begin to diverge. When he again pays his gorgeous tribute to her young heart, she longs to see him, to breathe him in, and the verb "to breathe"—*atmen*—is lavishly extended from two syllables to a full eight-note octave descent, in itself an exercise in breathing for the soprano. As Barak again commences his series of aching ascents to the top of his baritone range, she harmonizes with him and articulates her suddenly discovered longing to give him children—with the verb "to give" (*geben*) extended across thirteen notes and five measures, as the flutes, oboes, and clarinets adorn her phrasing to make her regret all the more expressive.[47]

Her part concludes, and Barak is left to sing alone, wishing he could see her just one more time and say to her, "fürchte dich nicht," don't be afraid.

The orchestra goes silent as he speaks the words for the first time, softly, on a descending phrase. The strings and harps then join to cushion his phrasing as he reaches up to F-sharp, at the top of his baritone range, to tell her again, even more softly, not to be afraid. She cannot hear him across their separate imprisonments, but his voice has an incantatory power. Suddenly there is a gleam of light in the darkness, and Barak can see steps carved into the rock of his underground prison. The trumpets now herald the advent of a supernatural messenger whose angelic alto voice comes from somewhere above, commanding Barak to ascend the steps. A solemn chord from the horns confirms his resolve.[48]

But then, as he ascends, the full orchestra accelerates, explodes *fortissimo*, the rhythm shifts to passionate triple time, and the Dyer's Wife, from her isolation, almost as if she knows that he is on the move, sings with the "excited fanaticism" that Strauss imagined for this text: "Komm zu mir, Barak mein Mann," come to me, Barak my husband. It was the mood that Strauss associated with the repentant spirit of the Jewish novella *Mendel Gibbor*. The voice of the Dyer's Wife also proves to be incantatory, bringing her also a gleam of light, an alto voice from above, and a staircase cut into the rock so that she too may ascend.[49]

The difficult wife of Barak the Dyer has dissolved her own difficulty in a lyrical outpouring of marital love, has renounced her renunciation of the shadow, and declared her passionate longing to give her husband children. They will keep searching and calling to each other throughout the third act, and their actual meeting at the end of the act will consummate their reconciliation, but, by harmonizing them so movingly in the duet, Strauss has already anticipated the outcome, the renewal of their marriage. Even with Hofmannsthal away and unreachable in Poland in June 1915, Strauss found the musical means to reconcile husband and wife, at a time when husbands and wives were separated by the circumstances of war all over Europe.

10

The Empress at the Threshold

THE IMMINENCE OF CATASTROPHE
AND THE LAST ROMANTIC OPERA

"Contemporary Reflections on War and Death"

In July 1915 Hofmannsthal sent a simple postcard to Strauss to describe progress on the third act, noting the completion of the scene of the Nurse's dramatic departure, cursing humankind. "The whole scene now full of inner unrest, driving toward catastrophe," noted Hofmannsthal telegraphically.[1] A sense of unrest and catastrophe could easily have been conditioned by the ongoing wartime circumstances—the trenches of the western front, naval and submarine war in the Baltic and the North Sea, and armed aircraft encounters over eastern France, the earliest aerial warfare in military history. In 1915 Sigmund Freud in Vienna published his "Contemporary Reflections on War and Death," considering how the catastrophe of war produced disillusionment (*Enttäuschung*) with civilization itself. Freud, whose sons were conscripted into the Austrian army, was initially patriotic at the outbreak of the war in 1914, but by 1915 he was himself already disillusioned, writing that "no event had ever destroyed so much of the precious heritage of mankind, confused so many of the clearest intellects, or so thoroughly debased what is highest." While he would later reflect on the traumatic experiences of soldiers in combat, in 1915 he was more interested in providing some clarification for "the individual who is not himself a combatant, and therefore has not become a cog in the gigantic war machinery" but "feels confused in his bearings" by the horrors of the contemporary moment.[2]

During the summer of 1915 Strauss, still missing the full text for the third act, was busy orchestrating the first act from the piano-vocal score. When he wrote to Hofmannsthal on August 17, he was already at the end of the first act and wanted instructions for the trio of watchmen as he needed to know which of their verses would be sung offstage and which ones visibly onstage. He would orchestrate accordingly. With war being waged on the eastern front, the western front, in the Middle East, at Gallipoli, and in colonial Africa, Strauss initiated hostilities with the director of the Munich Opera, Clemens von Franckenstein. Strauss felt that his operas were being slighted by Franckenstein and that, after three years of misleading promises, there would have to be "firm written guarantees about the maintenance of my works in my native city—or else I will not enter the Munich Hoftheater so long as the present leadership holds office."[3] It was a sort of declaration of war.

Hofmannsthal replied four days later in barely restrained fury; he resented being caught between Strauss and Franckenstein, a personal friend. Hofmannsthal had been in touch with Franckenstein, who insisted he did not want to have a "conflict" with Strauss, but "if he were to be publicly attacked, he would defend himself." This was very much the language of war—conflict, attack, defense—with the respective parties on the brink of full hostilities. Hofmannsthal clearly sided with Franckenstein and believed that Strauss was being petty—nourishing wounds to his *amour propre* by pressing for more performances "in this abnormal year," that is, in wartime—but the poet was focused above all on the future of *Die Frau ohne Schatten*. He was furious at Strauss's readiness to break with Munich and thus "lose for the new work one of the few first-class German stages."[4]

Hofmannsthal in 1915 was collecting and conserving the literary culture of Austria-Hungary, and on August 15 he announced in the *Neue Freie Presse* the publication of the first six volumes of a projected series, the Austrian Library or Österreichische Bibliothek, including a Franz Grillparzer drama about Habsburg history and selections from the correspondence of Prince Eugene of Savoy. The purpose of the publication series was to demonstrate that Austria-Hungary did constitute a "fatherland" for its diverse peoples, that literature could consolidate a sense of patriotism: "Holy and fateful is the homeland. Now it has become even holier, for we have buried so many dead, who have shed their blood for Austria." The poet claimed that the peoples of Austria "have never felt so spiritually close to one another," that they were more than ever aware of their common historical past: "The countenance of Maria Theresa is directed at us, the falcon eye of Prince Eugene watches us, Papa Haydn is there and plays with semi-stiffened elderly fingers his *Gott erhalte.*" The great Austrians of the past, who formerly appeared as "legendary shadows," were now present and real for the Austrian peoples in time of war.[5] In honor of his own eighty-fifth birthday on August 18, Franz Joseph created a new nonmilitary wartime decoration, *Kriegskreuz für Zivilverdienste*, the War Cross for Civil Merits. The white-enameled cross bore the Latin inscription "Merito Civili tempore belli"—and there were four different classes of recognition. Hofmannsthal was to receive this decoration, second class, in May 1918 from Emperor Karl.[6]

But in September 1915 Strauss and Hofmannsthal were unsuccessfully trying to set up a meeting in Salzburg. Hofmannsthal on September 11 had the sense that he was being stood up: "Dear Dr. Strauss, you do not come, you do not telegraph, the whole thing is completely incomprehensible to me."[7] On September 17 Hofmannsthal was still trying to establish contact with Strauss, in order to send him the finally completed libretto of the third act. "If you will confirm receipt of this postcard by telegram," he wrote, fastidiously, "I shall accept that the irregularities of the postal service have ended and will entrust the only copy of the final scene (I have no copyist here) to the post."[8] The war was taking its further toll on the collaboration with the malfunctioning mail service, and Hofmannsthal, insisting on the security of the "only copy," found a new way to emphasize the precarious sensitivity of the whole project. When he received no reply from Strauss, Hofmannsthal decided to send the libretto by making use of the diplomatic offices of the Bavarian legation in Vienna.[9]

Having completed the text for the third act, Hofmannsthal, writing on September 19, had very specific suggestions for the musical composition, now principally focused on bringing out the supernatural aspects of the fairy-tale opera in its concluding scenes.

> I hope you will be satisfied with the Temple scene and that everything is realized as you wanted it. For the guardians of the threshold, who are deceitful sorcerers or demons, seducers, I imagine highly peculiar voices,

male-female, alluring and thereby repellent, as if a snake were singing. Perhaps one might employ a male voice in an especially high range (falsetto) or a female one of strange depth, or something far more beautiful than I can imagine. The place where the Emperor repeats the prophecy that the spirits "sang to him" during petrification must sound extremely ghostly [*geisterhaft*], a marvelous report from someone just returned to life.[10]

The temple scene of trial and temptation was always intended, from the first conception of the opera, to place the opera in relation to Mozart's *Die Zauberflöte*, with the Temple of Keikobad as the counterpart to the Temple of Sarastro. If the Temple of Sarastro, for Mozart and Schikaneder, clearly represented the Freemason temples of eighteenth-century Europe, the Temple of Keikobad more probably reflected for Hofmannsthal some aspects of the aesthetic religion of his own Viennese youth, as exemplified in the temple structure of the Sezession building of 1898, a temple of art. The Sezession presented in 1902 Gustav Klimt's Beethoven frieze that portrayed the alluring-repellent siren-gorgons and snakelike women who offered seductive and disturbing temptations. Hofmannsthal himself, as noted by historian Carl Schorske, had been one of the deities in the metaphorical temple of Viennese aestheticism in the 1890s.[11]

Hofmannsthal was looking for unsettling and supernatural effects in the music for these final scenes of the third act. The threshold of the temple, which was also the threshold between the natural and supernatural worlds, seemed to call for a music of stylized aestheticism, marvelous sounds for their own sake, like art for art's sake. The most ethereal effect, as Hofmannsthal imagined, was to come from the children's chorus:

> The first passages for the unborn children, "Hört, wir wollen sagen Vater" [Hear us, we want to say Father] I imagine as so tonally marvelous that it does not matter whether one understands them or not: as if birds were suddenly speaking from the sky, but the sound is more important than the sense. These passages could move quickly, as on the wings of the wind, then like silvery rejoicing. The main passage then—"Hört, wir gebieten euch" [Hear us, we command you]—is true singing, and will be repeated by the Emperor and the Empress. But in the first passage the

alienating-enchanting sound miracle [*das befremdlich-entzückende Klangwunder*] must predominate.[12]

The voices of the children were supposed to resemble birdsong, with a silvery coloring that was more important than the meaning, and Hofmannsthal's Viennese aestheticism invoked "the alienating-enchanting sound miracle." The Emperor, as he was coming back to life, would still sing with a supernatural ghostly sound, but once fully restored, together with the Empress, he would be able to articulate clearly the spirit messages that were being sung by the unborn children from beyond the threshold of human existence.

Birdsong belonged to the aesthetic sound world of *Die Frau ohne Schatten* from the opening scene, with the flutes and clarinets suggesting birds at the awakening of the Empress, who would herself be warbling coloratura phrases—recalling perhaps her previous history of metamorphosis as a bird. Maria Jeritza, the soprano who eventually created the role, wrote in her memoirs about an earlier moment of avian emissaries in Vienna in the Stadtpark in 1910: "a great number of people, myself among them, had come out to see thirty Chinese nightingales—'Sun Birds' they called them—turned loose in the park to make their home there, and teach the native birds some of the bird-songs of the Celestial Empire." Jeritza recalled their first singing in the park as if the birds were opera singers—"soft clear liquid notes, beginning softly and gradually swelling in tone"—and she wondered later whether they "subsisted through the trials and hardships of the war and the fall of empire, and still send up their hymn to the sun as their ancestors did in the Middle Kingdom."[13] Hofmannsthal was also interested in the "sound miracle" of a transcendent world that he attempted to imagine and describe even through the darkest years of the war.

"FroSch" the Problem Child

On December 8 Hofmannsthal's father, the bank director, died in Vienna, age seventy-three; his son, the poet, published a death notice announcing the funeral mass at the Church of Our Lady at the Schottentor and the burial at the family plot in the Zentralfriedhof.[14] By the beginning of the New

Year, Hofmannsthal was in Berlin to introduce an Austrian propaganda film about the Isonzo campaign against Italy and the defense of Tyrol. He wrote to Strauss, who was also in Berlin, to thank the composer for his letter of condolence, and noted that the deceased had truly appreciated the operatic collaboration as few others did: "If others who are my friends and wish me well sometimes feel there is something all too questionable about working for music or for a musician," wrote the poet, "my father felt only the beauty of it." Hofmannsthal seemed to want Strauss to know how insecure he himself felt about the value of their collaboration and perhaps to suggest that he felt even more uncertain about it now after his father's death. He asked Strauss to provide him with a ticket for the next evening's Beethoven concert in Berlin, with Strauss conducting. The tone was oddly self-effacing, and the letter concluded: "Please do not forget me."[15]

Later in January 1916 Hofmannsthal was again looking for tickets in Berlin, requesting them from Strauss for a performance of their own *Ariadne*: "full of hope that this problem child [*Schmerzenskind*] will be repaired."[16] In fact, much of the year 1916 would be dedicated to revising the work and achieving the final form in which the opera is still performed today, with the prologue replacing the Molière drama. *Ariadne*, however, was such a success that Strauss would later transfer the term *Schmerzenskind* to *Die Frau ohne Schatten*, following its mixed reception after the war: "the problem child [*Schmerzenskind*] was completed in grief and worries during the war."[17] The abbreviation *FroSch*, which Strauss sometimes used to signify *Fr(au) o(hne) Sch(atten)*, also meant "frog" (*Frosch*) in German.[18] Later, when the opera was produced, there would be some implication that the problem child was a poor frog whom the world failed to recognize as a fairy-tale prince.

In February 1916 Hofmannsthal, rather unusually, wrote a letter to Strauss's wife Pauline, an implicit acknowledgment that collaboration with the composer also inevitably involved her views and inclinations. Hofmannsthal was worrying about whether *Die Frau ohne Schatten* would be properly appreciated when it was finally produced. He was most sensitive to the question of whether it would be well received in Vienna, his native city, and was skeptical about whether Vienna should host the premiere: "Nowhere will the poetry find so little good will, so much preconceived miscomprehension, as in

Vienna. Now I have perhaps written more than the censorship allows."[19] In his wartime propaganda Hofmannsthal was the great proponent of Austria's cultural mission, but in his private correspondence he was prepared to argue the case against Vienna.

In April, with the premiere of the new version of *Ariadne* coming up in October, Strauss and Hofmannsthal disagreed sharply over the role of the young composer in the prologue. Strauss wanted it to be a trouser role for a female singer, like Octavian in *Der Rosenkavalier*, and Hofmannsthal, who perhaps identified too closely with the precocious young man, was outraged at the idea of making him into an "operetta-style travesty."[20] Strauss, however, was very sure that he was right, and asked Hofmannsthal to imagine the Composer "as a young Mozart," straight out of the *ancien régime*.[21]

In May—even as the French and Germans were fighting the long battle of Verdun, and the Austrians were opening an offensive against the Italians in South Tyrol—Strauss was already imagining that a peace conference might be the possible subject for a new opera with "lots of love." It would be set a hundred years ago at the time of the Congress of Vienna, following the Napoleonic wars:

> A diplomatic love intrigue in the milieu of the Vienna Congress with a genuine high aristocratic female spy as the main character—the beautiful wife of an ambassador as a traitor for the sake of love, exploited by a secret agent or something amusing like that, and then add to it the famous session of the Congress when Napoleon's return is announced—you are perhaps saying: Kitsch![22]

He then congratulated Hofmannsthal on Austria's military success against the Italians in South Tyrol—"we are delighted" (*wir freuen uns herzlich*)—as if the war were about to have a happy ending.[23] There was, in fact, already an operetta set at the Congress of Vienna, *Wiener Blut*, by Johann Strauss II, produced in 1899.

Hofmannsthal immediately replied on May 30, 1916, with derision for the proposed opera: "I had to laugh heartily over your letter. For my sensibility these are truly horrid things [*scheussliche Dinge*] that you are proposing to me, and could frighten me for life from becoming a librettist." He then offered his own understanding of the dynamics of collaboration:

> You must guide me, I must guide you, and maybe we will still come together in a quite new and bizarre domain. Just be glad that I bring to you (as now again with *Die Frau ohne Schatten*) the element that unsettles people, that calls forth a certain resistance [*Widerstand*], for you already have too many followers, you are already too much the master of the moment, too universally accepted.²⁴

Strauss had indeed been the cultural hero of his German generation, as summed up in his tone poem *Ein Heldenleben* of 1898. Hofmannsthal offered himself as the corrective antidote to Strauss's universal success, the collaborator who could help Strauss get beyond the obstacle of his own popularity, to explore the new, the bizarre, the unsettling, to move beyond his own easy mastery and let himself be guided through the deep and undiscovered facets of his own genius. It was a vision of artistic collaboration that owed something to psychoanalysis. Hofmannsthal believed in *Die Frau ohne Schatten* as the sort of innovative artistic achievement that might emerge from such challenging terms of collaboration—and he imagined that the opera might appear both bizarre and unsettling to a part of the musical public.

On May 31, 1916, Zita gave birth to a fourth child, Archduke Felix, at the Loew Sanatorium in Vienna, the same sanatorium where Mahler died in 1911. Zita stayed for three days, and the baptism then took place at Schönbrunn, with the king of Saxony (Karl's uncle) serving as baptismal godfather. Zita recalled the wartime moment of Felix's birth in 1916:

> The third year of the war made everything difficult. The supply situation became harder and harder for the population; for the wealthy it meant impoverishment, for the poor—infinitely harder—it meant destitution. The situation on the front required our complete commitment; every man even half fit for service was in the military.²⁵

Historian Maureen Healy has demonstrated the increasingly harsh impact of food shortages in wartime Vienna, especially as experienced by women and children on the home front; shortages of milk and potatoes were noted already in 1915, while in 1916 people were waiting in lines for coffee, sugar, eggs, and soap.²⁶

Zita did not wait in market lines, but she clearly identified with the soldier's wives who were separated from their husbands.

> When the arrival of my fourth child drew near, Archduke Karl found himself on the southern front, in the camp of Vielgereuth-Folgaria [in South Tyrol], and he saw his third [male] heir only when he came northeast to carry out a mission for the Emperor and could spend a few hours in Vienna on the way. . . . So as not to unsettle him with news of my giving birth, I left him somewhat unclear about the expected due date.[27]

Karl, now in a command position on the southern Isonzo Front, was notified after the birth by telephone, and the infant archduke supposedly cried into the mouthpiece so that his father could hear him from the field. The whole scenario had peculiar elements of the wartime operatic comedy that Strauss might have imagined and that Hofmannsthal would have considered kitsch: the comedy of purposeful confusion surrounding the baby's due date, the setting in the elite sanatorium, a crowned king as godfather, and even the theatrical prop of the telephone—which Strauss would in fact employ in *Intermezzo* in the 1920s.

On June 5, Strauss wrote to Hofmannsthal about wanting to compose comic operas, perhaps operettas, even political-satirical operettas—"after this war, tragedy in the theater would seem something rather stupid and childish." Therefore, Strauss aspired to become "the Offenbach of the twentieth century"—"and you will be and must be my poet." Strauss, however, had plenty of ideas of his own: "The glorious types that have revealed themselves in this war: the usurer as cultural patron, the spy, the diplomat, Prussian and Austrian against each other and yet with each other—they would make a splendid comedy and you've got the talent for it."[28] This comic *mélange* that Strauss envisioned bore some relation to the epic wartime satirical drama, *The Last Days of Mankind*, by Karl Kraus, another admirer of Offenbach. Knowing that Hofmannsthal was about to make one of his semiofficial wartime trips to the Polish lands, Strauss wrote: "Maybe bring me back a subject from your Warsaw trip. Study the Jewish-Galician interpreter and middleman on the spot: also a glorious figure." Hofmannsthal was unlikely to want to contemplate a Jewish-Galician subject for an operetta, and furthermore he was unlikely to view his rather serious travel to Warsaw as the occasion for collecting comic operetta material. "Long live the political-satirical-parodistic operetta!" concluded Strauss.[29] In fact, operettas were immensely successful as entertainment during the war, with big hits in Vienna for works like

Emmerich Kálmán's *Csárdásfürstin* in 1915, about cabaret culture in Budapest and Vienna, and Leo Fall's Turkish romance *Die Rose von Stambul* in 1916.[30]

Strauss suggested, half-jokingly, that Hofmannsthal wasn't writing enough and should therefore be eager to take on an operetta project. Hofmannsthal was deeply irritated and wrote a letter (that he never posted) listing the points where, five years earlier, he thought that Strauss had done a poor job with the music for *Der Rosenkavalier*. The chorus of Faninal servants in the second act, for instance, was a failure, as it should have been composed "in the transparent Offenbach style: what you did was to smother it with *heavy* music." Yet even in this letter, which he never sent, Hofmannsthal offered apologies for his severity and pleaded the tensions of wartime: "I am somewhat oppressed by the events on the eastern front."[31] The Russians had taken advantage of the Italian attack on Austria to launch a new offensive from the east, led by General Alexei Brusilov, eventually inflicting heavy casualties on the Austrian army—just as Hofmannsthal was about to return to the occupied Polish lands.

"The Last Romantic Opera"

Hofmannsthal went to Warsaw in July 1916 to give a lecture, hosted by his good friend Andrian, who continued to emphasize the Austrian role in the Austrian-German occupation of Poland. The Russians withdrew from Warsaw on August 5, 1915, and on August 18 Andrian was already organizing a Polish celebration for Franz Joseph's eighty-fifth birthday. In 1915 the German politician Friedrich Naumann had published his book *Mitteleuropa*, outlining a leading political and economic role for Germany in Central Europe. Andrian and Hofmannsthal were engaged in trying to formulate a rival Austrian role in the region, already suggested in the poet's 1915 article on Austria's military administration in Poland. Now he lectured in Warsaw at the neoclassical Teatr Wielki on July 7, 1916, offering "Austria in the Mirror of Its Literature," which proposed an Austrian cultural community as an implicit alternative to Naumann's German economic integration. Hofmannsthal spoke to an audience of Poles, Austrians, and Germans, civilian and military, and reported afterward, "I have got the impression that this difficult balancing act actually succeeded beyond all expectations."[32] Later in November 1916, Germany and Austria actually agreed to create a Kingdom of Poland with the possibility of assigning the crown to a Habsburg archduke. This, however, proved merely hypothetical, since after Germany and Austria lost the war in 1918, Poland became an independent republic.

In his 1916 Warsaw lecture Hofmannsthal used music to clarify what he meant by Austrian style: "Austria developed its spirit first in its music, and in this form it conquered the world: Haydn, Mozart, Schubert." Hofmannsthal summed up the spirit of Austrian music, which also, he believed, conditioned Austrian poetry: "The most charming happiness, bliss without ecstasy, joyfulness, almost merriment in Haydn's masses, a breath of the Slavic, a flash of the Italian, in this music created out of the deepest German spirit."[33] Austrian culture reflected the mingled currents of the German, Slavic, and Italian worlds, the particular aspects of the diverse landscapes of the Habsburg monarchy, from Bohemia to Tyrol, from the imperial metropolis of Vienna to the remote hinterlands of Transylvania. Hofmannsthal proposed an all-embracing Austrian idea of cultural unity in diversity: "The formulation of an Austrian idea is the geometric locus for all possible Austrianisms."[34] The lecture would be published in the *Neue Freie Presse* in November.

On the day of the lecture, July 7, Hofmannsthal wrote to Strauss from Warsaw to let him know that plans for *Ariadne* and *Der Rosenkavalier* were in progress in Poland, and that he might be able to pass through Garmisch on his way back from Warsaw and Berlin.[35] On the visit to Garmisch Strauss played for him the music for the prologue of *Ariadne* alongside music for the third act of *Die Frau ohne Schatten*, and, once home in Vienna, Hofmannsthal was disturbed by the juxtaposition of the two operas:

> The memory of the music for the Singspiel [*Ariadne*] is as charming as can be imagined: like fireworks in a beautiful park, on a charming, all too fleeting summer evening. The memory of the scenes of the third act [of *Die Frau ohne Schatten*] (with the exception of the first scene) sticks in my head—I can't help it, dear Dr. Strauss—as something heavy and gloomy [*etwas Beschwerendes und Trübes*].[36]

The heaviness of *Die Frau ohne Schatten*, contrasting with the lightness of *Ariadne*, left Hofmannsthal feeling troubled.

Strauss, replying on July 28, conceded that he also loved the prologue to *Ariadne* as marking their "peculiar new path"—the path of Offenbach and comic operetta. It was, however, too late to rethink the fairy-tale opera:

> But to change the style in *Die Frau ohne Schatten* . . . really will not work. It isn't a matter of more or less music or text; it's about the subject itself with its Romanticism and its symbols, characters like the Emperor and the Empress, and also the Nurse, can't be filled with red corpuscles, like a Marschallin, an Octavian, or an Ochs. I can exert my brain as much as I want, and I'm struggling with it, sifting and sifting, but my heart is only half in it.[37]

For Strauss the problem was inherent in the fairy-tale scenario and characters, with their unnamed allegorical profiles: the problem of how to make an empress into an operatic figure of flesh and blood, if her whole dramatic premise was that she was not human, that she had to learn how to be a warm-blooded childbearing human being. In fact, when the opera was first conceived in 1911, Europe was full of red-blooded royalty leading lives that were not at all allegorical. The possibility for transfusing these fairy-tale figures had clearly been easier for both Strauss and Hofmannsthal to imagine when they first embarked on the project, and it seemed that the war itself, now entering into its third year, was taking its toll on their capacity for realizing the imperial framework of the opera.

While Hofmannsthal may have wanted the opera to be more charming, like *Ariadne*, Strauss wanted it to be more sentimentally moving, like *Der Rosenkavalier*.

> I now have the whole conclusion of the opera (the quartet and the choruses). It has vigor [*Schwung*] and great upward sweep [*Steigerung*]—but my wife finds it cold and misses the heart-stirring melody of the *Rosenkavalier* trio. I believe her, and I search and seek—but believe me:
>
> >   Schatten zu werfen   To cast shadows
> >   beide erwählt . . .   both chosen . . .
>
> does not go to music like:
>
> >   Hab mir's gelobt   I have promised myself
> >   ihn lieb zu haben.   to love him.

I will make every effort to shape act 3 according to your view, but let us make the resolve that *Die Frau ohne Schatten* is to be the last Romantic opera.[38]

Strauss's own self-confessed disillusionment with the opera was striking as he contrasted the verses of the final quartet of *Die Frau ohne Schatten* and the concluding trio of *Der Rosenkavalier*. The declaration that *Die Frau ohne Schatten* would be the last Romantic opera suggested that European culture itself had irrevocably changed, that, after the collapse of Europe in 1914, it would no longer be possible to retrace one's creative path.

Hofmannsthal, replying on August 1, tried to reassure the composer, praising the first two acts as "beautiful beyond all expectation." He attributed Strauss's doubts about the opera to a "small depression, which even the mature artist may not be spared, a mood of fearfulness and sadness that touches me closely."[39] In fact, these doubts occurred in the broader context of a continent in the deepest quagmire of collective despair.

Hofmannsthal had heard Strauss play for him the music of the first two acts in Vienna, more than a year earlier, and remembered "the wonderfully beautiful music with which you outfitted even a character who, as you say, felt remote (I mean the Emperor)."[40] The problem of the third act was not to sentimentalize the characters in the manner of *Der Rosenkavalier*, Hofmannsthal felt, and he urged Strauss to consider instead the magical dimensions of *Die Zauberflöte*.

> In the third act it is the spiritual element which offers the solution, the soaring into the light harmonic region, the changing of fairy-tale scenes, the intervention of the children's voices finally, all these form a combination of elements that the public will not be able to resist, even if the music were to fall off (as I am sure it will not). Do not on any account let yourself be daunted, either by your own hesitations . . . or even by the perhaps all too rash and all too spontaneous (though always important to me) judgment of your wife.[41]

Strauss had mentioned in his letter that Pauline found the music "cold," and now Hofmannsthal worried that she was exercising an undue influence on her husband's mood. With some condescension he invited Strauss to take the opening of the final quartet—"Schatten zu werfen / beide erwählt"—and, for the sake of inspiration, while cunningly keeping the same rhythm, pretend that the words were "more trivial" in the spirit of the *Rosenkavalier* trio—"Selig zu werden / beide vermählt" (To become blissful / both married). "Perhaps that would stir you more!" he suggested, as if Strauss might be a better composer with a "more trivial" text.[42]

Already in 1915 Strauss had worried that the Empress seemed to care more about Barak than her own husband, and now, in 1916, he attempted to remedy this as he composed her declaration of marital devotion to the Emperor in the third act: "Was er leidet, will ich leiden / Ich bin in ihm, er ist in mir!" (What he suffers, I want to suffer/ I am in him, he is in me). The Empress, Strauss explained to Hofmannsthal, would sing in the melodic spirit of "heroic, excited resolve (E-flat major)"—the key generally associated with the Emperor.[43] Hofmannsthal responded skeptically on July 24, not eager to extend the Empress's lines or to have her sing with heroic fervor: "Now a new extension of the earlier passage? More and always more! Must it be? Dear Dr. Strauss! Even if the idea of E-flat major is certainly powerful and beautiful—think twice! Think about our many conversations."[44] Hofmannsthal was concerned about excess and imbalance, about Strauss's music overwhelming rather than enhancing the drama of the final act.

As August progressed Hofmannsthal was at Aussee worrying over the staging of the new version of *Ariadne*, upcoming in Vienna in October. Meanwhile he had reread his own libretto for the third act of *Die Frau ohne Schatten* and was personally "quite satisfied."[45] As summer ended Strauss wrote that he had finished composing the third act: "but after our very beneficial conversation, I have become so uncertain that I no longer rightly know what's successful and what's bad." He was more excited about *Ariadne* with the new prologue and, encouraged by Hofmannsthal, looked forward to composing in the future only "un-Wagnerian" operas of human emotions: "I promise you that I have now definitively stripped off the Wagnerian musical armor [*Musizierpanzer*]." Strauss's whole career as a composer had been inspired and dominated by the revolutionary masterpieces of Wagner, but now his doubts about *Die Frau ohne Schatten*, experienced in the context of European Armageddon, made him determined to put Wagnerian operatic Romanticism behind him.[46]

Hofmannsthal replied on September 16 from Aussee, expressing satisfaction at Strauss's letter, having just "reread it once again with joy."[47] The stripping off of Wagnerian armor was certainly something that the poet welcomed, for that armor was both "heavy" and extremely German, in contrast to the spirit of lightness that he himself understood as fundamentally Austrian. Possibly the reference to armor also had some military significance for them both at that wartime moment. In late August the Habsburg monarchy betrayed new vulnerability when Romania declared war and invaded Habsburg Transylvania. Meanwhile, on the western front, at the Somme in mid-September, the British introduced armored tanks into military combat.

On October 4 the revised version of *Ariadne auf Naxos* had its premiere in Vienna and was reviewed the next day in the *Neue Freie Presse* by Julius Korngold. Above the fold on page one, the newspaper patriotically reported victory over the Romanians along the lower Danube, while grimly observing that "the battlefield was covered with enemy corpses." Below the fold Korngold began his review by observing that "Richard Strauss did not want his Ariadne, abandoned by Theseus, to be abandoned by the public." Therefore the original version with the Molière scenario—"a strange theatrical mishmash"—had been revised for Vienna. Korngold admired the orchestral score for its "enchanting delicacy and grace," and he had only praise for the conductor Franz Schalk, for Maria Jeritza as Ariadne, for Selma Kurz as Zerbinetta, and for the young Lotte Lehmann (originally the understudy) in the trouser role of the Composer. Jeritza and Lehmann, three years later, would create the roles of the Empress and the Dyer's Wife in *Die Frau ohne Schatten*. Now Korngold concluded his review by declaring *Ariadne auf Naxos* a triumph, noting that the public "stormily celebrated the creators."[48] At a moment of grimly ongoing war on multiple fronts, the creators, Strauss and Hofmannsthal, had presented an operatic comedy of sweetness, delicacy, and grace, and they were enthusiastically cheered at the triumphant conclusion.

October 4, 1916, the date of the premiere, was also the feast day of St. Francis of Assisi and therefore the name day of Emperor Franz Joseph. While the public at the opera celebrated Strauss and Hofmannsthal, the military sponsored celebrations of the Emperor in Vienna, including of course the playing and singing of the Haydn imperial hymn. It was to be Franz Joseph's last name day, for he died at Schönbrunn on November 21, at the age of eighty-six, after a reign of sixty-eight years. Karl and Zita became the Emperor and Empress of Austria, immediately and automatically. Zita later recalled:

176 Chapter 10

On the morning of November 21, 1916, Kaiser Franz Joseph received Archduke Karl and myself one last time. He sat at his desk in uniform working on a recruitment decree. He was burning with fever, and still he did not stop working. He told us how happy he was that great progress was being made in Romania, that the offensive was going well. Furthermore, he was happy about the blessing that the Holy Father had sent him and told us that he had received holy communion that same morning. Then he dismissed us with much warmth, and that was the last time that we saw him alive and conscious. That same evening the life of Emperor Franz Joseph slowly expired. Archduke Karl and I were present, and it was moving to see with what peace and calm he passed over. At that same moment the whole burden that had been borne till then by Emperor Franz Joseph was transferred to the shoulders of Emperor Karl.[49]

There was not a moment's interregnum between the reign of Franz Joseph and that of Karl as Emperor of Austria, but Zita's assumption of her role now gave the Habsburg monarchy an empress for the first time since the assassination of Empress Elisabeth in Geneva in 1898.

The Empress at the Threshold

Following the love duet of Barak and his wife in their separate imprisonments, the scene changes: there is a river, and a boat appears bearing the Nurse and the Empress, the latter asleep. The boat is guided by higher powers and brings them to the foot of a flight of steps carved into the cliffs, steps leading up to a bronze door, marking the entrance to Keikobad's temple. The Nurse recognizes immediately where they are and, fearful of judgment, cries out in hurried 3/4 time, "Fort von hier"—let's get away from here.[50]

The Empress, however, awakens to a sense of destiny, compels a slowing of the tempo and a change of rhythm to a steady 4/4 common time, observing "der Kahn will bleiben," the boat wants to remain. Six offstage trombones issue a summons, the key shifts solemnly to A-flat, and Strauss marks the score *maestoso*, as the Empress discovers in herself her own imperial majesty. "Don't you hear the tone?" she asks. "It is a call to judgment [*Gericht*]," and she ascends to a majestic A-flat on the final syllable of *Gericht*, demonstrating that, unlike the Nurse, she is not afraid. She recognizes the presence of her father, Keikobad, whose trisyllabic name is signaled by a dotted three-note descent, *pianissimo*, in the timpani, the cellos, and the basses. The score is marked *feierlich* (solemn), as the Empress envisions her father sitting on his throne in judgment like Solomon—though he will never actually appear in the opera.[51]

The Empress, acknowledging the higher authority of her father the spirit king, but also arraying herself in her own sense of personal majesty, prepares to meet him face to face. "Ich bin sein Kind," I am his child, she sings, as the violins leap up in tribute to her spirit. "Ich fürchte mich nicht," I am not afraid, she sings, now ascending all the way up to A-natural, in the innocence and confidence of A major. As she reaches her high note, the offstage trombones summon her once more to the presence of her father.[52]

Now the key signature shifts to E-flat, the heroic key of the Emperor himself, as ardent hunter and lover, and the Empress launches herself into a long melodic line, the very passage for which Strauss required more text from Hofmannsthal in July. In an extended romantic melodic phrase, she sings the text that Hofmannsthal had adjusted for Strauss:

Was ihn bindet, bindet mich.	What binds him, binds me.
Was er leidet, will ich leiden.	What he suffers, I want to suffer.
Ich bin in ihm, er ist in mir!	I am in him, he is in me!
Wir sind eins. Ich will zu ihm.	We are one. I want to go to him.[53]

The whole orchestra accompanies her, with racing triplets in the strings to suggest her excitement, as she builds to a Wagnerian climax with another high B-flat on "eins," returning to E-flat for "ihm."[54]

The Nurse, along with a nervously trilling piccolo, in restless 6/8 time, tries to distract the Empress from her newfound sense of focused purpose, to urge her away from the threshold of her father's temple.[55] "So you recognize this threshold?" asks the Empress, suddenly realizing that the Nurse knows more than she admits, that she has perhaps been playing a treacherous game all along, scheming for the petrification of the Emperor. The threshold leads to "the water of life," the Nurse concedes, and the harps depict that magical fountain with a *glissando* run up and down the scale. Is it the fountain of life or the threshold of death, wonders the Empress, fearing for the death of the Emperor. She escapes from confusion into D major and clarifies her sense of purpose in magnificent phrasing: "Hell, hell ist vor mir" (Bright, bright the way before me).⁵⁶ As in Mozart's *Die Zauberflöte*, the way to enlightenment is a path from darkness and confusion to clarity and light.

The Nurse makes one last desperate effort, assisted by tremolo strings and rumbling percussion, to warn the Empress away from the temple of judgment, attempting to frighten her with the terrible powers of her father and the punishments she would suffer for having mingled with accursed human beings. The Empress, however, is unintimidated; she is "transformed, resolved" (*verklärt, entschlossen*), according to the score.⁵⁷ "Nurse, I am separating myself from you forever," she announces, ascending the steps of the temple, affirming her own emancipation. For the Nurse knows nothing about the needs of humans (*Menschen*) and the mysteries of the human heart. On the word *Menschen* the Empress executes a lovely and affectionate ornamental turn, echoed by her alter ego, the solo violin, returning now to accompany her to the next stage of her personal transformation. She knows that human beings, though tormented by guilt, are able to renew themselves spiritually

Figure 19. "Amme, auf immer scheid' ich mich von dir." "Nurse, I am separating myself from you forever," sings the Empress, her declaration introduced by the harps. "What humans need, you know too little." On the word "humans"—*Menschen*—she executes an ornamental turn, accompanied by the solo violin, as if to express her sympathy for humans and to demonstrate her own humanity. (*Die Frau ohne Schatten*, 1919)

like the phoenix. The soprano sings a joyously expansive articulation of the verb of renewal—*erneuen*—and then the cellos and horns play ascending scales to accompany the resurrection of the phoenix from the ashes of death, while ascending arpeggios on the harps offer the promise of new life.[58]

The Empress stands ready not just to defend herself and her husband before her father, Keikobad, but to defend all of humankind. "Ich gehöre zu ihnen," I belong to them, she sings, the orchestra pausing for her to articulate her sense of identity with maximum clarity. Now, at the top of the temple steps, she crosses the threshold and passes through the bronze door which closes behind her.[59] She will make her case for herself as a human empress, ready to reign alongside her husband, the human emperor, over their human subjects.

II

Empress Zita

IMPERIAL MOTHERHOOD AND THE PURSUIT OF PEACE

Succession and Coronation

With the succession of Karl and Zita in November 1916, the nineteen-year-old Erich Korngold composed the "Kaiserin Zita Hymne"—the "Empress Zita Hymn"—in honor of the new empress. Korngold prepared the piece very grandly for orchestra, organ, children's chorus, and tenor soloist—though the full score has been lost, leaving only a piano reduction. The introduction evoked the spirit of Haydn's hymn for the Emperor, "Gott erhalte," and the first verse, beginning "Noch stehen wir in Gewittern" (We're still in the storm), was a martial tribute to the Austrian army. The second verse evoked a "young Austria," the younger generation represented by Korngold himself, gathered together to sing chorally in honor of the young Empress. The third verse saluted the Empress as the maternal protectress of Austria's children—children who were supposedly ready to give their lives "for their good Empress."[1] Zita's maternity—she was already the mother of four—was undeniable, and motherhood would also be fundamental for Strauss and Hofmannsthal's operatic Empress, the key to her pursuit of true humanity.

Korngold's "Empress Zita Hymn," patriotic and sentimental, had some of the flavor of an operetta creation, as if the composer suspected that the operetta stage was where imperial royalty would be most comfortably at home. Twenty years later he would refashion the same music for the Hollywood

Figure 20. The "Empress Zita Hymn" was composed by Erich Korngold in November 1916 to honor Zita at the moment of her accession as Empress of Austria. Prepared for orchestra, organ, children's chorus, and tenor, the hymn represented the enthusiasm of "young Austria" for their young empress; it was also intended as an anthem of patriotism in wartime. Zita's picture appeared on the sheet music, an icon of youthful and sympathetic elegance. Korngold later reused some of the score as movie music for the Hollywood film *The Private Lives of Elizabeth and Essex* in 1939. (Reproduced with the kind permission of the Österreichische Nationalbibliothek)

film *The Private Lives of Elizabeth and Essex,* starring Bette Davis and Errol Flynn. Composer Hermann Dostal had already created the operetta-style "Zita Waltz" for her wedding in 1911, and now she became even more of a musical icon.

Zita herself recalled leaving Franz Joseph's deathbed at Schönbrunn with Karl on November 21, 1916, and immediately hearing the title "Your Majesty" on the lips of the court.

> Our life changed now completely. A monstrous burden was transferred to the Emperor. My life also changed a lot. As the successor of Empress Elisabeth, who was so revered by the people, especially the Hungarian people, the situation for me was not so easy. Certainly I had great love for the people engraved upon my heart, and for all those who suffered; and, all the more so now that I had become the mother of the country [*Landesmutter*], the difficulties and hardships of the people weighed upon us.[2]

The title "Emperor of Austria" was only a hundred years old, dating from 1804, when Napoléon crowned himself as the Emperor of the French, and Habsburg Emperor Franz made himself Emperor of Austria. Franz had originally been crowned as Holy Roman Emperor, but he proceeded to abolish that title in 1806, partly for fear that Napoléon would claim it for himself. Thus the Habsburgs effectively replaced the traditional title of Holy Roman Emperor, dating back to Charlemagne, with the new title of Emperor of Austria. Zita as Empress of Austria—the very last one—also incorporated into her role the modern gendered identity of *Landesmutter*.

There was no formal imperial coronation in Vienna when Karl became Emperor of Austria in 1916—the succession was automatic—but in Budapest a royal coronation was required. Hungary was ruled not by the Emperor of Austria but rather by the King of Hungary, even though those two titles happened to converge upon the same Habsburg successor. Now Karl and Zita, who had visited Budapest together immediately after the outbreak of the war in August 1914, returned two years later for their coronation, arriving by train from Vienna just after Christmas. Zita was welcomed as a "guardian angel," and she replied in Hungarian using the same gracious words of acknowledgment that Empress Elisabeth had spoken fifty years before, at the 1867 coronation that consummated Austro-Hungarian dualism. The coronation itself took place in the Gothic Matthias Church with a musical program that featured the mass composed by Franz Liszt for the coronation of 1867. Film and photography documented the traditional splendor of the occasion, which was intended as a ratification of dualism and included the presence of four-year-old Otto, the prospective heir in the next generation. One photograph showed Karl wearing the Hungarian crown with its tilted cross, Otto in a plumed Hungarian headpiece, and Zita in a voluminous trailing gown and magnificent high crown that somehow disappeared during the twentieth century.[3] After the coronation Karl and Zita returned immediately to Vienna rather than staying for further celebration, for, as Karl declared, "At a moment when so many of our people are dying on the front, it is not the time to rejoice with wine and music."[4]

From Vienna Zita and Karl traveled to visit and encourage the soldiers at the front. "I went, whenever possible, out there to the front, and I saw the infinite suffering in Siebenbürgen [Transylvania], in Tyrol, in the Karst [Slovenia]," she recalled. "We had to deal with it all, we had to intervene to help. Above all, however, we had to make peace as quickly as possible."[5] Like the operatic fairy-tale Empress who was humanized through her own appreciation of the suffering of humankind, so Zita claimed to undergo a transformation through her exposure to the sufferings at the front.

Zita vividly recollected her encounters with the army: "I remember a visit to the front in the Karst, right after a battle, corpses and rats, rats and corpses, everywhere—and a horrible indescribable stink. Wherever I looked, the silent corpses of fallen soldiers, among rats, rats, rats." For Zita the war was a "nightmare" as she confronted its "indescribably terrible inhuman face." The story of Karl and Zita, as she recalled it, was the fairy tale of a young emperor and empress—at their accession they were twenty-nine and twenty-four—who encountered the bestial nightmare of human suffering and became committed to trying to end the war: "We simply had to make peace."[6] In 2004 when Karl was beatified, Pope John Paul II declared, from St. Peter's Square in Rome, that Karl "strove to promote the peace initiative of my predecessor, Benedict XV." In his Lenten letter of March 1916, Pope

Figure 21. In December 1916, one month after becoming Emperor and Empress of Austria, Karl and Zita traveled to Budapest to be crowned as King and Queen of Hungary, affirming the solidarity of the dual monarchy Austria-Hungary in wartime. In this photograph they appear together with their son Otto, age four, in Hungarian ceremonial costume and regalia. The coronation was a spectacular piece of fairy-tale pageantry that must have already seemed incongruous and almost anachronistic, as the Battle of Verdun concluded that same month with 300,000 deaths. (Sueddeutsche Zeitung Photo/Alamy Stock Photo)

Figure 22. Empress Zita and Emperor Karl were photographed here visiting the Habsburg troops during the war. Zita stands out as a sober and striking figure in her austerely tailored dark suit, white blouse with expansively ruffled neckline, and broad-brimmed hat. Like the Empress in *Die Frau ohne Schatten*, Zita had to confront the difficult ordeal of her subjects in wartime and try to convey sympathy as a humane empress. Zita recalled, "I went, whenever possible, out there to the front." At the same time she worked together with Karl in a vain attempt to negotiate peace. (Reproduced with the kind permission of the Österreichische Nationalbibliothek)

Benedict had declared the war to be the "suicide of civilized Europe"—and, from the moment of their accession in November, Karl and Zita would begin to lend their support to a negotiated peace.[7]

Zita as empress stood at the center of Karl's peace plans, because her Bourbon-Parma family bridged the two warring camps; at the very beginning of the war, her brothers Prince Sixtus and Prince Xavier had left Austria to fight for the Entente, while other members of her family fought along with the Austrian army. Now Sixtus and Xavier became intermediaries between the court of Karl and Zita in Vienna and the French government in Paris. While Karl's newly appointed foreign minister, Bohemian Count Ottokar Czernin, urged peace considerations on Austria's ally in Berlin, the

Viennese court worked together with Zita's family to pursue a secret channel for peace discussions with France.

In February 1917, with Germany resuming unrestricted submarine warfare, Zita was confronted by German Admiral Henning von Holtzendorff, who declared, "I know already you are an opponent of submarine war. You are generally against the war." She then allegedly replied, "I am against the war like every other woman who prefers to see human beings happy rather than in such misfortune as this war, in which so many are suffering."[8] In March 1917 Karl and Zita met with Princes Sixtus and Xavier at the imperial summer palace of Laxenburg, just south of Vienna, and Karl wrote a letter addressed to Sixtus about peace terms, to show secretly to French leaders. The Emperor agreed in principle to the return of Alsace-Lorraine from Germany to France, and when the "Sixtus letter" was later made public the German government was outraged.[9]

Zita acknowledged the open antagonism between herself and the German general staff, led by Generals Paul von Hindenburg and Erich Ludendorff. She also faced resentment from the Austrian military leadership. When General Conrad von Hötzendorf, who played such a large role in pushing Austria into war against Serbia in July 1914, was dismissed by Karl as chief of staff, the general blamed Zita and her family: "Especially dangerous were the machinations pursued by Empress Zita, hand in hand with her brother Sixtus, and the weak Emperor allowed himself to be drawn in, which also put him in a crooked position with Germany: a textbook example of what happens when women, even with the best intentions, meddle in serious political and military affairs."[10] The German general staff and the Austrian war party would ultimately endorse the view that Zita, as a princess of Bourbon-Parma, was fundamentally disloyal to Austria on account of her French and Italian family affiliations, and that the imperial peace initiatives were implicitly treasonous.

In December 1916 the almost yearlong German campaign to take Verdun on the western front had definitively failed, and the resumption of submarine warfare in February 1917 was intended to try to achieve a breakthrough at sea after the failure on land. On February 7, Richard Strauss used strangely military language to announce to Hofmannsthal that "I have just finished a splendid victory progress (*Siegeszug*) with your works." He brought *Der*

Rosenkavalier to the Hague and to Amsterdam, then *Der Rosenkavalier* and *Ariadne* to Mannheim, and then *Ariadne* and *Elektra* to Switzerland: "with downright triumphal success."[11] Neutral Switzerland was also a meeting place for people from both of the warring sides. It was in Switzerland, in Neuchâtel, that Zita's mother, Maria Antónia, met with her sons, Prince Sixtus and Prince Xavier, on January 29—one day after the January 28 performance of *Ariadne* in Zurich—and delivered to them the initial message from Emperor Karl indicating his willingness to initiate secret peace negotiations.[12]

"At the Swiss performances there were lots of French and Russians!" wrote Strauss. "God grant that the whole world may become reasonable again." Stefan Zweig's pacifist play *Jeremiah* was produced in Zurich in February, and in March Hofmannsthal was in Zurich to deliver his already well-practiced lecture on "Austria in the Mirror of Its Literature." Strauss believed that the Strauss-Hofmannsthal operas could provide a point of common cultural appreciation for audiences in Switzerland that included the French and the Russians, already anticipating a postwar moment when the world would be reasonable again, the moment for which *Die Frau ohne Schatten* was being prepared.[13]

The Birthday of the Empress

On May 9, 1917, Empress Zita turned twenty-five, and—in advance of Karl turning thirty in August—her birthday became the first occasion since the coronation for fostering patriotism by celebrating the young imperial pair. The army chief of staff General Arthur Arz von Straussenburg, who had been named to replace Conrad von Hötzendorf in March, presented Zita with flowers on behalf of the troops. A *Te Deum* was performed in her honor at the Theresianum, the elite school created by Empress Maria Theresa. The *Neue Freie Presse* noted not only church services but also synagogue appreciations of the Empress, with Rabbi Israel Taglicht delivering a sermon entitled "Kaiserin Zita als wahre Landesmutter"—as the true mother of her country.[14]

Her birthday was celebrated as the Kaiserin Zita Kindertag: Empress Zita Children's Day. The holiday was consistent with the international children's movement established by Swedish reformer Ellen Key in 1900, declaring the

Figure 23. Zita's twenty-fifth birthday on May 9, 1917, was celebrated as *Kaiserin Zita Kindertag*, Empress Zita Children's Day, emphasizing her particular role as *Landesmutter*, the mother of her country. The occasion was used for fundraising for children's charities in wartime, especially for children of fallen or fighting soldiers. One prominent fundraising activity involved selling lottery tickets with the picture of young Crown Prince Otto framed by the Habsburg double eagle. For the occasion of the birthday a children's chorus participated in the performance of Korngold's "Empress Zita Hymn." The cherishing of children was central to the opera *Die Frau ohne Schatten*, which would also require a children's chorus. (Property of the author)

twentieth century to be the "Century of the Child." Zita was quoted in the *Neue Freue Presse* as affirming that "the care and nurture of infants assures us of a healthy future generation." The events of the day involved fundraisers for children's charities under the general umbrella of the Kriegspatenschaft, founded soon after the outbreak of the war as a sort of godmothership (*Paten* meaning "godparents") for children in need. The principal fundraising formula was the sale of inexpensive badges and lottery tickets with an image of the four-year-old crown prince Otto, and, according to the *Neue Freie Presse*, "on Zita Day no one will want to be seen on the streets without wearing the charming little image." The funding supported impoverished children whose fathers were fighting at the front or had died in the war. One of the concerns of the charity was infant mortality, and it was noted that 20 percent of infants in Austria-Hungary died before the age of one, with the claim that charitable care could bring the statistic down to 3 percent.[15] Zita thus took the occasion of her birthday to emphasize her imperial relation to Austrian children as *Landesmutter* by presiding over a charity of general godmothership.

On the morning of May 8, the day before her birthday, Zita received more than a hundred members of the Kriegspatenschaft in the Grosse Galerie of Schönbrunn, the Hall of Mirrors modeled on that of Versailles. Viennese schoolgirls were assembled to welcome the Empress, and six-year-old girls dressed in white with baskets of flowers sat before her throne. A children's chorus give the first performance of Korngold's "Empress Zita Hymn"—with lyrics by Baroness Hedda von Škoda, who was herself an officer of the Kriegspatenschaft (and the wife of Karl von Škoda, the Bohemian munitions manufacturer). After the singing of the hymn, there was a children's dance, and the Empress gave a short speech of gratitude.[16] Zita spoke beneath the ceiling fresco of Empress Maria Theresa and Emperor Franz Stefan, surrounded by the personifications of their virtues.

The next day, May 9, was the actual birthday, Empress Zita Children's Day, and the date coincided with a fundraising concert given by tenor Leo Slezak together with soprano Lotte Lehmann, just recently featured in the role of the Composer in *Ariadne*. They performed the wedding duet from *Lohengrin* together, and Slezak sang two Richard Strauss songs, "Morgen" and "Cäcilie." Slezak was, in fact, one of the tenors whom Strauss considered for the role of the Emperor in *Die Frau ohne Schatten*—though the role ultimately went to Karl Oestvig in 1919.[17] In 1917 the *Neue Freie Presse* took special note of the fact that the concert on Zita's birthday featured Slezak in the first major public performance of Korngold's "Empress Zita Hymn," following the more private performance at Schönbrunn the day before. Among the audience at the concert, there were noted at least three archduchesses and five government ministers, including Foreign Minister Count Czernin.[18]

Though she was present at Schönbrunn on the morning of May 8 to welcome the Kriegspatenschaft and to hear the "Empress Zita Hymn," the Empress was at Laxenburg on her birthday May 9, and there her special guest was her brother Prince Sixtus. He was taking advantage of the occasion of his sister's birthday to come to Austria to discuss peace initiatives, as Zita later recalled:

> During the whole day Kaiser Karl and my brother Sixtus carried on their conversation outside at Laxenburg. . . . I believe that the good weather also helped to put us in an optimistic mood, to believe in successfully achieving peace. My brother Sixtus noted down: "After our conversation, my sister joined us. Both the Emperor and the Empress expressed their certainty that peace would soon be concluded. . . . Understandably, the Emperor insisted on absolute discretion."[19]

The gardens were in the style of English landscape gardening, with artificial ponds and islands to underscore the charm of nature, with solitary paths ideal for private walks and confidential conversations. In this case discretion was essential, since Karl and Zita were maneuvering for peace behind the backs of their German ally.

Four days after Zita's twenty-fifth birthday came the two hundredth birthday of Empress Maria Theresa on May 13. It was celebrated with an essay in the *Neue Freie Presse* by Hofmannsthal, who emphasized that the chief characteristics of Maria Theresa's reign were ongoing warfare, constantly recurring motherhood (she gave birth sixteen times), and deep Catholic piety. Hofmannsthal also emphasized Maria Theresa's "conscience" (*Gewissen*) and sense of justice (*Gerechtigkeit*)—which brought her closer to his own vision of the Empress in *Die Frau ohne Schatten*, who achieves her humanity by discovering her conscience. Hofmannsthal concluded by suggesting that the Austrian spirit of Maria Theresa's reign—a spirit that was natural and proud, but not stiff or hard—was expressed in the music of Haydn, Gluck, and Mozart.[20]

On May 11 Strauss wrote to Hofmannsthal in mock military style, "Beg to report (*Melde Ihnen gehorsamst*) that the score of the third act is approaching completion."[21] On June 28, the third anniversary of the assassination of Franz Ferdinand at Sarajevo, Strauss reported that the orchestration of the score was complete.[22] Since both composer and librettist had agreed that this was an opera to inaugurate the postwar era, they now had to wait for the war to end to put their imperial fairy tale on the stage, even as Karl and Zita, the real-life Emperor and Empress, were trying to hasten that end.

Hofmannsthal's "Austrian Idea"

In the spring of 1917, the Russian February Revolution led to the imperial abdication of Nicholas and Alexandra on March 15 and the establishment of a provisional government—which might have been read as an ominous sign for emperors and empresses elsewhere in Europe. For the moment, however, Germany and Austria could take some encouragement from the destabilization of an enemy power. At the same time, however, on April 6, Woodrow Wilson in Washington declared war against Germany, shifting the balance of the alliances in play. During the summer and fall the British failed to break through the German lines in Belgium, in the long third battle of Ypres, but in October Austria-Hungary achieved a major victory against the Italians on the Isonzo Front at Caporetto. Lenin's Bolshevik Revolution in early November (the "October Revolution" by the Russian Julian calendar) also suggested the imminent possibility of Russia's removal from the war on the eastern front.

On September 4 Hofmannsthal was thinking about the eventual premiere of *Die Frau ohne Schatten*.

> It becomes ever more clear to me that Munich is the place where one could at least hope to find the diverse elements of the public for a work like *Die Frau ohne Schatten*, with its spiritual values that are unreachable for the average Viennese-Jewish horizon [*dem wienerisch-jüdischen Durchschnittshorizont unerreichbare Werte*]—not the disgusting [*ekelhaft*] "wanting to understand" in the sense of 2 x 2 = 4, but entering into a higher sense where the mystery lies in the "fractions"—but Vienna by no means, I would defend myself against that with my hands and feet and even my teeth.[23]

Hofmannsthal's mathematical conception of the mysteries of *Die Frau ohne Schatten* was meant to suggest that the meaning of the opera could not be understood as simple, straightforward, or self-evident. With a frankly anti-Semitic slur he declared that the Viennese Jewish public would be particularly incapable of appreciating the spiritual dimensions or complex mathematics of the opera.

Vienna had been a city of potent anti-Semitism, at least as far back as the 1890s, when Karl Lueger's Christian Socialist party took power in the municipal government. The wartime Galician Jewish refugees in Vienna often met with anti-Semitism in the capital.[24] Yet Hofmannsthal's anti-Semitism was not aimed at the poor Galician immigrants but rather at the established Viennese Jewish middle class who might be likely to go to the opera.

On September 2, 1917, two days before writing to Strauss, Hofmannsthal wrote to the philosopher Rudolf Pannwitz, who was just publishing his book, *The Crisis of European Culture*. He warned Pannwitz against the prospective enthusiasm of the Viennese Jews—"a certain intellectual Viennese Jewish milieu, that for me is the worst of the worst." Hofmannsthal frankly admitted his own hereditary kinship: "I myself have blood as mixed as possible, also Jewish, as well as Italian, Lower Austrian peasant blood, and the blood of urban Germans, so I am not speaking of something about which I know nothing, but something I know with true hatred and disgust." With increasing savagery Hofmannsthal wrote, "The Augean Stables would not be more dirtying than these people and their salons and country houses," with their "simian groping curiosity, accursed money-changing restlessness"—"no substance, no reverence, no piety." They would be "groping everything, licking everything, turning everything into chatter, this horrible clique of Jewish doctors and stockbrokers, females, school reformers, music scholars, psychoanalysts, feuilletonists, usurers, neo-idealists . . . which, in part at least, is my world and the Austrian world."[25] After trotting all over Europe, from Warsaw to Zurich, to lecture on the grace, the elegance, the clarity of Austrian culture, Hofmannsthal now seemed to see the Viennese Jewish middle class as the philistine enemy, indeed the despoilers, of his own Austrian world. With his anti-Semitic vitriol he actually seemed to put himself at odds with himself and his own Austrian family history—at a moment when Habsburg Jews were notably loyal Austrians, organizing synagogue celebrations of the Empress's birthday.[26] The Jews of Austria-Hungary would be devoted to the dynasty to the very end of the empire, rightly seeing Habsburg rule as impartially protective and rightly fearing their fate in the national successor states.

On December 2, Hofmannsthal published not in the *Neue Freie Presse* (the newspaper most enthusiastically patronized by the Viennese Jewish middle class) but in the *Neue Zürcher Zeitung* (for the neutral foreign public) his brief essay "The Austrian Idea." He affirmed that Austria had proved its strength and importance in the war, that its contribution to Europe was in the sphere of the spiritual (*das Geistige*), and that that was all the more important "now at the end of the war." It was Austria's mission to establish a balance between the Latin-German peoples of Western Europe and the Slavic peoples of Eastern Europe. Hofmannsthal was looking toward the end of the war, and he declared that "this Europe, that wants to form itself anew, needs an Austria"—that Europe needed Austria "to grasp the polymorphous East" and establish the dominion of European "spiritual values."[27] His own public commitment to imperial rule was framed by his sense of the polymorphous mix of peoples who constituted the monarchy, even as his private anxieties were colored by anti-Semitism.

While Hofmannsthal was writing as if he believed the war was about to end, the final phase of the war was only just beginning. On December 7, 1917, the United States declared war against Austria-Hungary, the logical but delayed corollary of fighting against Germany. On December 22 the Bolsheviks opened peace negotiations with Germany at Brest-Litovsk, preparing to withdraw from the Entente, even as America became more engaged. On that same day in Vienna there was a ceremonial distribution of Christmas presents to war orphans that took place in the Konzerthaus, with Empress Zita listed on the program for the viewing of the gifts. She was the star of the performance, playing the role of the Empress, and the musical program began with Haydn's imperial hymn and a Christmas song, followed by Korngold's "Empress Zita Hymn." After the performance of her hymn, the Empress ritually inspected the gifts for the orphans.[28]

On Christmas Day Hofmannsthal published a schematic comparison between "The Prussian and the Austrian" in Berlin's *Vossische Zeitung*, summing up the two different cultural perspectives. Austrians had a sense of history that Prussians lacked, no talent for abstraction, a greater sense of balance, and a sense of self-irony. Overall, the Prussians had more virtue and efficiency, the Austrians more piety and humanity (*Menschlichkeit*).[29] Hofmannsthal was at this time writing his play *Der Schwierige* (*The Difficult One*) in which the reticent aristocrat, Count Hans Karl, appeared as the incarnation of Hofmannsthal's spirit of Austria—in clear contrast to his negative counterpart, the north German Baron Theophil Neuhoff.

As the war entered what was to be its final year, Hofmannsthal was making the case for Austria's essential role in defining the values of the postwar era, values of humanity. Strauss reported in December on a sold-out hundredth Dresden performance of *Der Rosenkavalier*—in the house where the opera had its first performance in 1911, seemingly ages ago, in the remote and irretrievable prewar world. The composer was also thinking about the end of the war, observing in a postscript, "I have already begun probing slowly and carefully in Dresden concerning *Die Frau ohne Schatten*."[30]

Woodrow Wilson and the Habsburg Monarchy

On January 8, 1918, Woodrow Wilson presented the Fourteen Points that summed up his American vision for postwar peace in Europe. In Point Ten he declared that "the peoples of Austria-Hungary, whose place among the nations we wish to see safeguarded and assured, should be accorded the freest opportunity to autonomous development." On the one hand, such a proposition involved a remarkably meddling presumption of intervention in the internal politics of a sovereign state, even an enemy sovereign state, and, on the other hand, it gave no suggestion that the United States was committed to the dissolution of Austria-Hungary, the abolition of the Habsburg monarchy, or the displacement of the dynasty. Czernin as foreign minister responded with some sympathy to Wilson's Fourteen Points, noting that "to some of them Austria-Hungary could joyfully give her approval"; he demurred with regard to Point Ten, observing that "we courteously but resolutely reject the advice as to how we are to govern ourselves," and that "we have in Austria a parliament elected by universal, equal, direct and secret franchise"—"with the right to decide upon the internal affairs of Austria."[31]

Yet, later in January the Austrian legal scholar Heinrich Lammasch arrived in Switzerland and arranged for a meeting with the American theologian and former Protestant minister George Herron, in order to try to send a message from Emperor Karl to Woodrow Wilson—altogether circumventing the Austrian parliament, and even Czernin, but especially Berlin. Lammasch and Herron met on Sunday, February 3, at a chateau near Bern, and the American reported to Washington that "the Emperor, urged on by the Empress, was getting more and more anxious for a change, and they wanted to find some way of getting a confidential message through to President Wilson that would not be known by Germany." Zita was described as "extraordinarily clever and forcible." Furthermore, Lammasch reported to Herron that Karl fully endorsed Wilson's Point Ten concerning national autonomy in Austria-Hungary.[32]

Herron, however, was skeptical about Karl's sincerity and suspicious of his Roman Catholicism, wondering if the Emperor was "playing the Pope's game" in cooperation with the peace initiative of Benedict XV. Herron was also wary of any American engagement with the Habsburg regime and warned Wilson that "across the golden bridge between Vienna and Washington it seemed to me that Austria wouldn't be walking into the future, but America would be walking into the past."[33] Later in February Karl would send a secret letter to Wilson, seeking a "direct exchange of views" toward the establishment of peace negotiations. But when Lammasch tried to make the case for negotiations in the Herrenhaus, the Austrian House of Lords, he was shouted down—"We want war and victory!"—by the militarist members who would have been all the more enraged if they knew that Karl was secretly corresponding with the American president.[34]

On February 10 the Vienna Konzerthaus optimistically presented a benefit for "refugees returning home," as if the war were about to end, as if Galician refugees were about to depart. This particular charity was under the patronage of Princess Hanna von Liechtenstein, but the conductor of the concert was Erich Korngold, and he put his own patriotic "Empress Zita Hymn" on the program, which also included two Richard Strauss songs and concluded with Johann Strauss's "Blue Danube Waltz."[35] On February 16 the Hofoper presented the Viennese premiere of Leoš Janáček's Czech opera *Jenufa* in a German translation by Franz Kafka's friend Max Brod. The plot concerned illegitimate birth and infanticide in a Moravian village, and the Moravian-born Maria Jeritza sang the title role, while Lucie Weidt (later the Nurse in *Die Frau ohne Schatten*) sang the role of the stern stepmother. The staging of the opera in Vienna was intended as a gesture toward Czech culture and Czech autonomy, and, according to Jeritza, *Jenufa* "would not have been performed had not the Emperor Karl interested himself in it."[36]

On March 1 and 2, Maria Jeritza appeared at the Konzerthaus in Richard von Goldberger's one-act operetta, *Die Modebaronin* (*The Fashion Baroness*); she sang the role of the director of a fashion atelier that catered to the aristocracy. The staging was designed by the Wiener Werkstätte, the studio for the applied arts that had emerged alongside Gustav Klimt's Sezession movement. The operetta was followed by a fashion show, and the proceeds benefited widows and orphans of the Viennese Deutschmeister battalion—with the band of the battalion participating in the performance.[37] At a moment when Strauss was contemplating operetta, Jeritza applied her glamorous presence and gorgeous voice to a new operetta in wartime.

Jeritza, who had been noticed by Emperor Franz Joseph while singing in *Die Fledermaus*, made her impression on Karl before he succeeded to the throne, later observing that "Emperor Karl, though by no means appreciative of other music, was especially fond of those tuneful operettas" and "always showed me the greatest consideration and courtesy." She further recalled meeting him and Zita at the Alpine winter resort of Semmering, when he gallantly worried about the diva being exposed to the cold: "It would never do for you to catch a chill in your voice!" She claims he was shocked to learn that she was not a Kammersängerin, one of the specially designated star performers of the court opera, and when she explained that she was still too young for that honor, he promised to remedy that "if ever I have the opportunity." He then made her an imperial Kammersängerin when he became Emperor, perhaps the very last one to be imperially designated, since he was the last Habsburg Emperor.[38]

In Bertita Harding's romanticized chronicle of Karl and Zita from the 1930s, written after Karl's death, the Emperor was actually presented as imperially lusting after Jeritza on the stage in *Tosca*: "At the sight of that magnificent body, swelling voluptuously under folds of revealing satin, male senses could not but reel. Karl, too, had felt himself stricken with that sensuous ache recognized so easily by all wives. Zita had recognized it. That night, on leaving the imperial box, she had worn the parched and slightly bilious face of jealousy."[39] The story is unlikely, since Jeritza did not seriously take up the role of *Tosca* in Vienna until 1920—after Karl and Zita had gone into exile—but it was clearly considered plausible to depict the diva as worthy of imperial attentions, as Zita's operatic rival.

On March 10, 1918, Zita had another baby, Archduke Karl Ludwig, and his birth was announced to the city of Vienna with cannon salutes. He was born at Baden bei Wien, the spa town near Vienna which had become the army headquarters, and where the Emperor and the Empress were in residence. Zita recalled, "The first thing I heard, as everything became a little more normal in my room, was from the town square where, right after hearing the report of my successful childbirth, a pious Muslim spread out his prayer rug and publicly performed his prayer of thanks." This was a fairy-tale moment in Zita's family life, but it was also a parable of imperial solidarity, juxtaposed with the report of a *Te Deum* in the Baden church and a religious service in her honor at the local synagogue. The birth of the little archduke was further celebrated the next day with an amnesty for prisoners.[40] Karl had issued an earlier amnesty in July 1917, which freed political prisoners, and notably Czech nationalists, who had been charged with treasonous hostility to the monarchy—part of the Emperor's program of reconciliation within the empire.

If Karl and Zita allowed themselves to imagine that the birth of the baby in March was attended by good omens, in April they were confronted with political disaster. On April 12, 1918, the French prime minister Georges Clemenceau published Karl's letter of the previous year to Prince Sixtus, in which the Emperor had indicated peace terms without consulting his German ally. German fury at this revelation severely constricted Karl's room for maneuver in peace negotiations, while the reminder of Sixtus's role further compromised the reputation of the Empress, his sister.

Joseph Maria Baernreither, recently part of the Vienna government, wrote in his diary on April 13, 1918, the day after the publication of Karl's compromising letter:

> Much is being said about the Parmas being caught up in old émigré illusions, thinking it possible that in France the monarchy might be reestablished and that a Bourbon-Parma could be called to the throne, if he could bring Alsace-Lorraine as a dowry. "As likely as me becoming Emperor of China," said Prince Liechtenstein to me recently, when we were discussing these rumored combinations.[41]

The Bourbon-Parma fantasies, however fantastic, inevitably led to the aggravation of Austrian and German suspicions about Karl and especially about Zita. Baernreither noted in his diary on April 19: "Lèse majesté in abundance, and a flood of rumors. But certain Parma plans become ever clearer. This family works with all its means for itself." Because of Zita, the Bourbon-Parma family influence was presumed to be very great in Vienna. Baernreither would even compare Austrian hostility to Zita to the French vilification of Marie Antoinette in the eighteenth century, another instance of a Habsburg-Bourbon marital connection gone awry.[42] A British Foreign Office report observed that Zita "could not be expected to realize that the days are long gone by, when women and priests could sway the destinies of nations."[43]

According to Baernreither, writing on April 27, "What's bad is due to the Parma influence. The Parmas are always looking for a throne, formerly the Portuguese, now the French. But the Emperor of Austria can't pursue a Bourbon policy."[44] The problem of treasonous influence upon the Emperor inevitably focused on the Empress. On May 7 the German embassy in Vienna sent Kaiser Wilhelm in Berlin a memorandum on "Kaiser Karl and the Bourbons," which noted that "Kaiser Karl is married to a Bourbon princess, who is under the influence of her numerous family." Wilhelm was urged to undertake a "serious but at the same time benevolently paternal" conversation with Karl on this subject.[45]

On May 8, the day before Zita's twenty-sixth birthday, Baernreither reflected that the Bourbon-Parma aspirations belonged to a wider network of papal and Roman Catholic calculations for the future of Europe. He thought that "the masterminds know for sure that Sixtus will never come to the French throne, but such illusions chain the Parmas to their plans, and flatter the Empress. In these castles in the air, however, dwells the betrayal of our whole policy till now."[46] Zita's birthday on May 9 thus took place at a moment when she was regarded increasingly as a figure of particular suspicion, even with insinuations of treason and betrayal. There was a celebratory *Jause*—a late afternoon tea—at home in Baden bei Wien for members of the Habsburg family to pay their respects, and there was an evening concert at the Carmelite church in Döbling with tenor Leo Slezak as well as a chorus and organ—probably including the "Empress Zita Hymn" on the program. In Vienna proper there were church services, military bands playing patriotic marches, and the founding of a Soldatenheim, a soldier's home for invalids. It was in May 1918 that Hofmannsthal received his imperial war cross for civil merit.[47]

On May 10, unknown to Karl and Zita, Robert Lansing, the American secretary of state, began to press Wilson to consider openly endorsing the abolition of the Habsburg monarchy as part of the peace program. "My dear Mr. President," wrote Lansing. "I feel that the time has arrived when it is wise to assume a definite policy in relation to the various nations which make up the Austro-Hungarian Empire." Karl's amnesties had failed to conciliate national leaders who dreamed of independence, and if the Czechs, Poles, and South Slavs were to form independent states after the war—Czechoslovakia, Poland, and Yugoslavia—the Habsburg monarchy would effectively cease to exist. Now Lansing asked Wilson, "Should we or should we not favor the disintegration of the Austro-Hungarian Empire into its component parts?"[48] While it would take Wilson still some time to come to a conclusion, the posing of the question was itself an important turning point for the future of the monarchy.

Voyage to Constantinople

Later that month, from May 19 to 21, Karl and Zita undertook their first and last important foreign travel as Emperor and Empress. At a moment when they were radically unpopular in Berlin for their alleged efforts to undermine the common war effort, they traveled to visit Austria's other ally, the Ottoman Empire. Zita understood this to be part of their peace initiative:

> To bring peace, at least to help to prepare for peace, to spread the mood of readiness for negotiation and reconciliation—that was the main reason for our trip to Constantinople. . . . In the middle of these sad times our stay in Constantinople became a triumphal acknowledgment of peace and confirmation of our alliance, which, after centuries of bitter enmity, was transformed over decades of connection, of communal destiny, into a heartfelt friendship.[49]

Zita came prepared with a diamond diadem and magnificent pearl necklace for the thousand-person reception at the Dolmabahçe Palace on the Bosphorus, while Karl was ready to step off the train at the Istanbul station in his Hungarian fur-trimmed gala uniform and tall Kalpak cap with a diamond clasp.

Zita recalled the striking impression that Karl made: "His appearance called forth from the Orientals—so susceptible to theatrical effects and splendid entrances—stormy admiration that turned into enthusiastic fervor." Karl greeted them in Turkish, and there were "joyful cries" in response. "The whole town was covered with roses for us," according to Zita. "We saw many things, heard the music of the picturesquely costumed Janissaries, admired the tact of the Turks who with this theatrical performance appeared to confirm, centuries later, that we once defeated them outside Vienna."[50] The Janissaries had played fierce military music outside the walls of Vienna in 1683 but now performed as picturesque entertainment for Karl and Zita. The players were only costumed as Janissaries, since the actual Janissaries, along with their musical bands, had been abolished in the 1820s—though they lived on in Viennese music thanks to Mozart, who made use of their rhythms in *The Abduction from the Seraglio*.[51]

The details of the imperial visit in May 1918—splendid jewels and picturesque costumes, along with music and roses and snatches of Turkish dialogue—strongly suggested the world of Viennese operetta. Maria Jeritza would have been well prepared to play the part of Empress Zita in Constantinople, including the Empress's inevitable visit to the Ottoman harem, chatting with the harem women about raising children and women's concerns.[52] In December 1916, immediately following Zita's accession, the operetta *Die Rose von Stambul (The Rose of Istanbul)* by Leo Fall had been presented in Vienna, set partly in Constantinople—though not with Jeritza. On May 19, 1918, the day that Zita arrived in Constantinople, Jeritza was singing as Ariadne in Vienna.[53]

In May Strauss was relieved to learn that his son Franz (known as "Bubi"), now twenty-one, had been declared medically exempt from military service. In June Strauss was playing the score of *Die Frau ohne Schatten* at the piano and thinking that it was "above the level of the present cultural world, or at least those who feel obliged to fill the theaters." He was now working on a comic opera about his own wife, *Intermezzo*, and writing the libretto himself—"until I receive a new Hofmannsthal."[54] The composer was also working on a group of songs to texts by the Romantic poet Clemens Brentano, including "Lied der Frauen (wenn die Männer im Krieg sind)"— "Song of the Women (when the Men Are at War)"—a frenzied composition with verses of despair, as the singer imagines her soldier husband dead on the battlefield.⁵⁵

On July 12 Strauss was still eager to have a new libretto from Hofmannsthal, so they could continue to produce their collaborative operas: "as it goes in *Die Zauberflöte*—another little Papageno, then another Papagena."⁵⁶ On July 16, Karl and Zita with their little family of archducal Papagenos and Papagenas made the short trip of fifty miles on the Danube River from Vienna to Bratislava for a charity event to benefit war invalids. The occasion took on the character of a popular festival in wartime. A military band prompted the crowd in singing the Haydn imperial hymn, and Zita later recalled the demonstrations of loyal enthusiasm as the Habsburg dynasty entered its final months of rule: "It is one of the most beautiful memories, one of the most moving moments in my recollection of the dying monarchy. The welcome exceeded all imagining." They returned to Vienna by boat also along the Danube, cherishing this sense of a popular loyalty, as village people gathered on the banks of the river to salute them as they passed—with children's choirs and wind bands—for the performance of devotion to a dynasty whose days were numbered.⁵⁷

On the night of July 16, in the early morning hours of July 17, after Zita and Karl and their five children returned from Bratislava to Vienna, more than two thousand miles to the east, in Ekaterinburg, in the region of the Ural Mountains at the boundary between Europe and Asia, the Bolshevik government of Russia executed Tsar Nicholas, Tsarina Alexandra, and their five children. In a basement room they were shot and bayoneted over the course of twenty minutes of butchery and then buried in an unmarked mass grave in the forest. The age of emperors and empresses was coming to a close.

The Empress in the Temple of Judgment

In the third act of *Die Frau ohne Schatten*, when the Empress passes through the bronze door, she leaves behind her Nurse, dismissed forever. Agitated triplets in the strings and flutes convey the spirit of rage and frustration as the Nurse calls out a curse upon humankind (*Fluch über sie!*) that dramatically descends from high A-flat down almost an octave to B-flat. Disconcertingly, however, she discovers that she is not alone: the voices of Barak and his wife are heard from offstage, still calling to one another in the aftermath of their duet. The Nurse curses human beings, but, ironically, she begins to find herself trapped in a trio with their invisible presences, with their heartfelt calls to one another. "Humans! Humans!" she exclaims, "How I hate them!"[58]

Barak appears in the fog to ask the Nurse if she has seen his wife, but the Nurse points him in the wrong direction and tells him his wife is cursing him. The Dyer's Wife then enters to ask the Nurse if she has seen Barak, and again the Nurse offers misdirection and tries to instill fear and mistrust. He wants to kill you, the Nurse lies, but the Dyer's Wife sings exultantly: "Swing your sword, kill me quickly [*töte mich schnell*]." The brilliant sustained high A on "töte"—across three measures—demonstrates that her passion will triumph over the Nurse's deceit with its irregular harmonies, dotted rhythms, and leaping octaves.[59]

Now Keikobad's Messenger—the same one who visited the Nurse at the very beginning of the opera to inform her of the Emperor's impending doom—appears at the bronze door, denounces the Nurse as a dog (*Hündin*), and banishes her from the spirit realm. Frenzied, she turns to the rhythm of 3/4 time and sings "Mir anvertraut" (entrusted to me), the crucial words of the duet for Barak and his wife, reminding the Messenger that the Empress had been entrusted to her care.[60] The key shifts to D-flat as rapid little runs on the woodwinds accompany the thickening of the fog and the coming of a storm—and the Nurse, excluded forever from the world of the spirits, suddenly finds herself again accompanied by the offstage human voices of Barak and his wife. The music re-creates the melody and spirit of their love duet—"Mir anvertraut"—shifting easily from D-flat into the original key of A-flat—with the Nurse again compelled to participate in a trio with the two humans she most despises.[61]

And then the Messenger, responding, joins the trio and makes it into a quartet: two baritones, a soprano, and a mezzo-soprano. With Barak and his wife longing for each other, the Nurse now longing for the Empress—"Weh, mein Kind!"—and the Messenger insisting that she will never see the Empress again, the quartet overflows with musical pathos. As it builds to a climax, the Dyer's Wife sings a sustained D-flat on the first syllable of "Kinder" (children), with the others harmonizing, and the swelling rhythm makes unmistakably clear that Strauss—who was always looking for a place to insert into the third act something like the *Rosenkavalier* trio in D-flat—found a glimmering of musical possibility here. Strauss stops the quartet abruptly at its climax, however, providing a pause in the orchestration for the Messenger to deliver, *a cappella*, the dramatically most important point of the scene: the punishment of the Nurse is that she must lead the rest of her life among human beings.[62]

Now the Messenger commands the boat to carry the wretched Nurse down to the human world, and, as the boat obeys his command, the orchestra explodes *fortissimo (fff)* in the storm that has been foggily threatening since the beginning of the scene; the trumpets ascend a chromatic scale, the piccolos execute short shrill runs, the percussion section drums fiercely, and the wind machine blows. With racing triplets in the woodwinds and the strings, the trumpets and trombones begin to signal the summons to justice, "dadada dum," three eighth notes, *marcato*, followed by a long sustained note. Barak and his wife can barely make themselves heard over the orchestra, as the storm envelops them.[63]

But then the storm passes, the orchestral fury subsides to *pianissimo* calm, and an expressively ascending phrase on the bass tuba, of all instruments, suggests that the Empress is about to appear on the scene—now the temple interior. It is Keikobad's temple, but the sounding of solemn chords in 3/2 time from the horns, the trombones, and the tubas darkly suggests some spiritual affinity with Sarastro's Masonic temple in *Die Zauberflöte*. Choral spirits offer Masonic messages—"Hab' Ehrfurcht! Mut!" (Have reverence! courage!)—like those that Mozart offered to Tamino. A soprano spirit sings a lovely ascending phrase: "Fulfill your destiny!"[64]

The Empress stands in the temple, unafraid, and asks of the invisible deity, "Father, is it you?" A gentle horn harmonizes along with her when she identifies herself: "Here, look at your child." Then it is again the solo violin that accompanies her as she sings, "I have learned to sacrifice myself (*mich hinzugeben*), but no shadow have I negotiated." She asks her father to show her her place among human beings who cast shadows, and as she sings she almost seems to cast her own shadow musically, jumping up to her favorite note, the gorgeous high F-sharp, on "werfen" (to cast)—while accompanied by the harmonizing horn, completing the F-sharp chord.[65]

A fountain of golden water appears before her, characterized by magical runs on the flutes, harps, and celestas. Now a solo violin, a solo viola, and a solo cello all accompany the Empress as she lyrically apostrophizes the fountain—"Golden drink, water of life"—but gently refrains from drinking. With spacious melody and elegant triplet ornamentation she sings, "I don't need you to strengthen me, love is in me, and that is more." The three solo string instruments create together with her soprano voice a sort of chamber quartet, while the harps and celestas continue their runs to suggest the rising and falling of the golden fountain waters.[66]

The Guardian of the Threshold—the score suggests a soprano, or even a male falsetto for magical effect—now urges her to drink so that the shadow of the other woman may become her own. A lovely octave leap to high A-flat on the clarinet brings the music back to the Empress, who is wondering what will become of that other woman. And then she hears the Dyer's Wife calling Barak's name from offstage, and Barak, now perhaps hearing for the first time, responds, "Where are you?" The Empress's sympathy goes out to him once again, and, gazing upon the fountain, she sees blood in the golden water and refuses to drink. Defiantly, she calls upon her father to show himself to her and—with a sustained high B-flat—she demands that he deliver judgment.[67]

Instead—with a frightening *crescendo* on an E-flat minor chord, accompanied by the Chinese gongs—Keikobad offers her a vision of her husband, the Emperor, enthroned and petrified, sitting as a statue in one of the niches of the temple. At the climax of the *crescendo* the trumpets and trombones sound, *fortississimo (fff)*, in the sinisterly prolonged four-note descent—from E-flat down to a low F-sharp—that originally accompanied the words "Er wird zum Stein" (He will turn to stone). The sight of her petrified husband has an equally paralyzing effect on the Empress who, suddenly, can no longer sing. Instead she speaks her lines while the orchestra continues to play as the accompaniment to her speech—a technique of melodrama (or *melologo*) that was often employed in the eighteenth century.[68]

Strauss, in a letter of July 1917, claimed that he had composed in this fashion according to Hofmannsthal's preference: "In the third act of *Die Frau ohne Schatten*, as soon as you twitched your eyelash, didn't I tear out large pieces of flesh and make the Empress's main scene into melodrama?"[69]

The calculation was that the climax of the Empress's inner struggle in the temple could be more forcefully represented—perhaps more humanly represented—by holding back from singing at the most dramatic moment. Arnold Schoenberg's experiments with *Sprechstimme*—introduced in *Pierrot Lunaire* in 1912—pointed the way toward a modern adaptation of the melodrama form. Strauss later suggested that the use of the melodrama was connected to the tensions of wartime, in his case his anxiety over whether his son would be conscripted or medically excused from service: "These war worries registered even on the score, especially in the middle of the third act where a certain nervous overexcitement was resolved in the form of melodrama."[70]

Having lost the power of song, the Empress can only speak her horror, her guilt, her helplessness, while the orchestra tries to support her with the musical emotions that she herself cannot express. "Lass mich sterben"—let me die—she declaims before Keikobad's seat of judgment, for she has passed harsh judgment upon herself.[71] Between the time that Strauss completed the opera in 1917, the year of the Russian Revolution, and its first performance in 1919, after the collapse of the Habsburg, Hohenzollern, Romanov, and Ottoman Empires, it had become very clear that emperors and empresses might sit before the judgment of history.

As the Empress stands before her stone husband, unable to sing, a chorus of male spirits, the spirits of judgment, chant the monotone prophecy of the

Figure 24. When the Empress refuses to drink from the golden fountain, it vanishes, leaving the stage in darkness and bringing about a long pause in the music. Then light returns from above, and the solo violin tenderly (*zart*) sounds the Empress's leaping theme, rising from F-sharp to B-natural, and then rising another full octave to high B. The glass harmonica creates the magical moment in which the prostrate Empress rises from the floor to see that now she casts a shadow. (*Die Frau ohne Schatten*, 1919)

Emperor's petrification—"The woman casts no shadow, the Emperor must turn to stone"—over a band of horns, trumpets, trombones, and the throbbing tam-tams. The Guardian of the Threshold urges the Empress again to drink the water of the fountain in order to obtain a shadow and bring her husband back to life. The Guardian's seductive ornamentations, assisted by harps, celestas, and glockenspiel, make the promised salvation of the fountain seem almost irresistible. The Empress, however, hears the voices of Barak and his wife, calling for help and for mercy, as if they know that their lives and futures are also at stake in the temple of judgment. The Empress joins in a strange trio with them, as they sing and she merely recites, all the time accompanied by the harps and celestas of the fountain.[72]

The orchestra builds to a great *fortississimo (fff)* climax, as the winds and brasses embrace a winding figure in broad 6/4 time, and the music then comes to a crashing halt so that the Empress, finally and definitively, can refuse to drink the golden water that would enable her to appropriate the shadow of another woman. The score goes silent, and the stage goes dark. When the orchestra resumes, with the Empress's leaping octave on the solo violin, and the mysterious entrance of the glass harmonica, the Emperor is already returning to life, and the crisis of the empire is past. As the light returns to the stage, it can be seen that the Empress now casts a human shadow of her own.[73] She has been judged, and she has been vindicated.

12

Departure from Schönbrunn

THE END OF THE HABSBURG MONARCHY
AND THE REBIRTH OF AUSTRIAN CULTURE

Postwar Succession at the Vienna Opera

"I remember an event at the Vienna Konzerthaus to benefit war victims, sometime in the summer of 1918," noted Zita much later. "Naturally I wanted to attend this occasion, but it was very secretly communicated to me that it would be better to stay away, that it would cause a scandal, that I would be booed and jeered . . . the mood was too agitated."[1] Zita, in retrospect, presented a narrative of the triumph of courage and principle over threats and malice. She claimed that she had in mind the case of her predecessor Empress Elisabeth, who had been driven by criticism to escape Vienna and avoid the public eye.

> Therefore it was my decision, without heeding the threats, to attend the event at the Konzerthaus. Kaiser Karl, who heard about these circumstances, announced that he would come too. It was certainly a tense evening for us, as we went there and entered the hall. How shall I describe it? Scarcely had we appeared under the portal than a huge cheer broke out. . . . At the end of the lectures and performances we entered into conversation with the soldiers who had come, especially those blinded in war. For several minutes they held our hands tight—I can still feel today the groping fingers on my face. . . . Yes, we could give these men, who had given what was most precious for their homeland, a little comfort . . . the feeling that their sacrifice was not in vain. And when we finally left this

event—it was already almost midnight—we had once more regained the conviction that the whole crazy wave of rumors with which the monarchy was flooded had entered the ears, but certainly not the hearts of our loyal people.²

In these waning months of the monarchy, clearly Zita herself had the sense that she was living through a fairy tale. At the same she saw herself as giving a performance—in this case at the concert hall—in which the boos or the cheers of the audience became a referendum on the political condition of the Habsburg Empire.

Zita specified the summer of 1918, but the summer months were slow at the Konzerthaus, and perhaps the most likely event would have been the Rosé Quartet (with violinist Arnold Rosé) performing Haydn, Brahms, and Schubert on August 16—in honor of Emperor Karl's thirty-first birthday on August 17. ³ The concert was to benefit impoverished musicians—not quite the same as war victims—and there is no evidence that the imperial pair attended that particular chamber music concert. In fact, the much more likely Konzerthaus event to fit the pattern of Zita's narrative took place in the spring of 1918, on May 6, a concert to honor Zita herself, for the occasion of her upcoming twenty-sixth birthday on May 9. This would have occurred a few weeks after Clemenceau's publication of the Sixtus letter, and Zita might well have been warned about the possibility of being booed in public. The concert featured a military band playing marches and waltzes, and also involved scenes of ballet-pantomime from Austrian musical history: like the young Mozart at the court of Empress Maria Theresa. Karl and Zita were both present, she in white lace with a diamond diadem, and both were cheered by the audience, according to the *Neue Freie Presse*, and by a crowd outside the theater afterward, "most warmly" (*auf das wärmste*). The Empress's spring birthday concert was, appropriately, a benefit for the Kriegspatenschaft.⁴ Later in the summer, on Karl's birthday in August, Zita was present for the opening of a war kitchen and received "enthusiastic ovations."⁵

In March 1918 the Germans had launched their spring offensive to try to break through the enemy lines on the western front, but by August the momentum was reversed and it was the Allies—French, British, Australians, Canadians, and now also Americans—who went on the offensive in the Battle of Amiens, inaugurating the final "Hundred Days" of World War I. Yet Viennese operatic life, after a summer pause, resumed in mid-August, presenting Wagner's *Tannhäuser* with Lotte Lehmann on August 16, then the *Marriage of Figaro* on August 17, the Emperor's birthday, with Figaro comically sending Cherubino off to fight in an imaginary war: "Non più andrai, farfallone amoroso" (You won't be going about anymore, you amorous butterfly).[6] Jeritza sang in *The Flying Dutchman* on August 22 and *Lohengrin* on August 27, and while Czech nationalists agitated for independence from the Habsburg monarchy, the Vienna Opera presented Smetana's *Dalibor* in September.[7] Richard Strauss was surely pleased to note that *Salome*, *Elektra*, and *Der Rosenkavalier* were being performed in October. *Salome*, considered too scandalous for Vienna when it was composed in 1905, was now finally presented on October 14, 1918, starring Jeritza and conducted by Schalk. The Viennese premiere thus had to wait for the imminent collapse of the empire to be deemed acceptable at the imperial opera.[8]

The violence and psychopathology of *Salome*—concluding with the bloody decapitated head of John the Baptist on a silver platter—now dominated the final weeks of the war at the Vienna Opera, with performances on November 3, 6, 9, and 12.[9] The performance on November 12 marked the beginning of the postwar operatic era, coming the day after the armistice, the day after Emperor Karl withdrew from political life. The Hofoper—the opera of the imperial court—ceased to exist in November 1918 along with the court, and today it is the Wiener Staatsoper.

On August 1, 1918, with the war still ongoing, Hofmannsthal raised the question of the future of the Vienna Hofoper in his correspondence with Strauss. It was a letter that began darkly with a confession of the poet's own depressions (*Verdüsterungen*): "all contact with the outside world, sociability, business, visiting, the newspapers, everyday life just makes it worse; only rest, solitude and the right books can heal this." Of course he could not produce a new libretto for Strauss in such a frame of mind, and his mood of epistolary depression shifted into a tone of frank hostility. Hofmannsthal had heard that Strauss was being considered for the musical directorship of the Hofoper—perhaps jointly with Schalk—and the poet declared his own disapproval.[10]

"I believe that about fifteen years ago you would have been the ideal person for the urgently needed rebirth of the Vienna institution," wrote

Hofmannsthal, "but I cannot believe that you still are today." Hofmannsthal insultingly suggested that "today you would put your own personal comfort and above all the egoism of the creative musician above the difficult fight for the higher benefit of the institution." Rather than the composer dedicating himself to reviving the works of Mozart and Wagner, Hofmannsthal wondered whether Strauss would use such a position in Vienna only to the advantage of his own operas.[11] It was an extremely strange declaration of opposition, in part because it was directed against someone who had to be considered a friend and close collaborator, and in part because the operas that Strauss might favor, if he favored his own works, would include important works by Hofmannsthal himself: *Elektra, Der Rosenkavalier, Ariadne auf Naxos*, and, eventually, *Die Frau ohne Schatten*.

Hofmannsthal's friend Andrian had been named in July by Emperor Karl as intendant of the Imperial Court Theater, and Hofmannsthal certainly imagined himself playing a role in shaping Austrian theater, together with Andrian, according to their own ideas about a distinctly Austrian cultural identity. Strauss, born in Munich, conducting for many years in Berlin, would have represented, even to his close collaborator, a German force within Austrian cultural politics. Hofmannsthal's hostility to Strauss's prospective role at the Vienna Opera was shaped by some sense of an imminent postwar struggle for power, which would take place in the cultural realm as well as in the political sphere.[12]

"I mean well by you, as few people in your life have meant well," concluded Hofmannsthal, striking a conciliatory note in conclusion. "You have sought few friends and have had few. I wish you could convince me that I am wrong in what I have written above."[13] Strauss replied on August 5 with almost ironic courtesy: "Many thanks for your kind letter. Though it rather anticipates matters which have not yet in any way taken concrete shape." Writing deferentially, as if he were applying to Hofmannsthal for the position, he began by agreeing that "I no longer could, nor would want to, fill this post today in the way that Mahler did"—that is, dedicating the larger part of his life to it. He planned to spend his summers composing but would work for five winter months as a conductor, dividing his commitments between Vienna and Berlin; he left unstated the need to compensate financially for the funds that he had lost in England at the outbreak of the war. In Vienna Strauss would undertake "the reorganization and rejuvenation of the magnificent orchestra," with regularly scheduled new productions. "Since people generally consider me to be a very good Mozart and Wagner conductor," he wrote, modestly enough, "the works of these masters (alongside Gluck and Weber) would be the first to be attacked for revival."[14] Hofmannsthal was apparently won over, for in the next letter, written from Aussee in early September, he was full of the sense of himself as the power broker who was arranging matters between his friend Andrian, the imperial intendant, and his collaborator Strauss, the famous composer. Ultimately, during the Strauss-Schalk years in Vienna from 1919 to 1924, Wagner would be the most performed composer, with Strauss coming second and Puccini close behind.[15]

When Andrian was offered the theater intendancy in July 1918, he reported to Hofmannsthal that Hermann Bahr was going to write a testimonial to the cardinal-archbishop of Vienna, Friedrich Gustav Piffl, stating that "though I [Andrian] would not create Catholic theater, it would be theater in which the Catholic religion and Catholic literature would receive more consideration than hitherto."[16] Andrian's maternal grandfather was the composer Giacomo Meyerbeer, so like Hofmannsthal, he was partly Jewish by descent. The two friends expected to collaborate on reorienting Austrian culture in a conservative and Catholic spirit, though Hofmannsthal, who lacked Andrian's long experience of government service, worried about the burdens of the intendancy: "the weight of responsibility, so many tormenting things, the impossibility of improving anything quickly, the tormenting dissonances."[17] Yet Hofmannsthal was also excited at the opportunity to play a role in cultural politics and eagerly offered to assist his friend.

When Strauss wrote his letter of August 5, justifying himself as a plausible candidate for the Hofoper, Hofmannsthal immediately showed the letter to Andrian, commenting that "Strauss has very great flaws and weaknesses, but he is a person of stature and does not lie. I infer from the letter that he would gladly come."[18] Hofmannsthal thus almost implied to Andrian that his whole strategy of declaring himself to be an opponent was to determine whether Strauss was sincerely interested.

On August 27 Hofmannsthal was at Aussee, fifty miles from Salzburg, writing to Andrian excitedly about the idea for a Salzburg Festival that they might create together with Max Reinhardt, an Austrian festival summing up the Austrian idea and realizing "all my hopes for a rebirth of the Austrian theater."[19] Hofmannsthal was already counting on a Strauss-Schalk partnership at the Vienna Opera, and he was convinced that they would have a role to play at the Salzburg Festival. The poet was writing to Andrian almost every day at this time, excited to be conspiring about the future of theater and opera in Vienna. "Do you see, Poldy, for me this is not just any old theater matter," wrote Hofmannsthal, as they discussed Reinhardt's role, "but the thing on which everything depends for me, both for my moral balance and for my nerves."[20] By September, Hofmannsthal was interested in playing a role in mediating discussions with Strauss about the Hofoper, acting almost as an agent: "Strauss's demand was for 60,000 kronen for five months." When Hofmannsthal wrote to Andrian about the concerns of the Vienna Opera, it was suggested that the poet knew best how to handle the problematic composer: "Strauss is often frivolous and heedless, but if you ask him with proper seriousness, he will answer properly."[21]

Hofmannsthal was also urging Strauss to cooperate with Andrian: "I say to you both: don't be narrow-minded, but do seek, both of you, to realize the high and the beautiful."[22] The poet presented himself as the supreme mediator, but, in fact, he seemed rather to be attempting to advance the directorship on his own artistic terms. Furthermore, *Die Frau ohne Schatten* was very much on his mind: "He [Andrian] regards as his obvious responsibility the care for your own works, but says you must relieve him of the fear that when, for example, *Die Frau ohne Schatten* is in the repertory, you would be conducting mostly just your own works and not the classics."[23] Hofmannsthal's scheming for and against Strauss's appointment in Vienna thus revealed some anxiety, just below the surface, about the presentation of *Die Frau ohne Schatten*, which, the librettist believed, should occur in the context of the classics.

The Liquidation of Austria-Hungary

On September 26, 1918, Karl and Zita appeared at the Prater steamship station on the Danube to welcome back to Vienna 450 Viennese children who had been evacuated from the city and had been living in the countryside in Hungary. A Viennese crowd gathered for this imperial public appearance, as Karl and Zita boarded the steamship upon its arrival and greeted the children. The children had learned enough Hungarian for a singing of the Haydn hymn in Hungarian—invoking God's protection for Karl as King, not as Emperor—and he expressed the hope that their evacuation would constitute a new bond between the peoples of Austria and Hungary within Austria-Hungary.[24]

On October 16, Karl issued a manifesto transforming the Austrian or "Cisleithanian" lands of Austria-Hungary into a federal state with full autonomy conceded to its national components. The posted proclamation was addressed "To my loyal Austrian peoples" and promised the "reconstruction of the fatherland" in the form of a "federal state in which each national group [*Volksstamm*] upon its own territory forms its own political community." This was Karl's formula for envisioning the ongoing constitutional existence of the multinational empire. With a musical metaphor, he promised that "the wishes of the Austrian peoples are carefully to be given satisfaction and brought into harmony [*Einklang*] with one another."[25] Hungary was excluded, as the idea of such a federal structure would have been unacceptable to the Hungarians in relation to their own national minorities, and on October 17, the next day, the Hungarian Parliament declared its independence from Austria-Hungary (though Karl and Zita remained the King and Queen of Hungary). On October 18 Czech political leader Tomáš Masaryk, lobbying in the United States, issued a Declaration of Independence, signifying the secession of the Czech lands from Austria and the Slovak lands from Hungary. "The Hapsburg dynasty, weighted down by a huge inheritance of error and crime, is a perpetual menace to the peace of the world," declared the Czechoslovaks, "and we deem it our duty toward humanity and civilization to aid in bringing about its downfall and destruction."[26]

On October 24, the Italians launched the Battle of Vittorio Veneto in northeastern Italy, north of Venice and Treviso, and over the course of the following week the Austrian army was crushed. On November 3, the collapsing Habsburg army suffered the loss of 30,000 dead and 300,000 prisoners and agreed to a humiliating armistice that gave over vast territories to Italian occupation; this also meant that the government in Vienna was in no condition to resist the claims to independence coming from the Slavic provinces of the monarchy. On October 27 Emperor Karl named the last

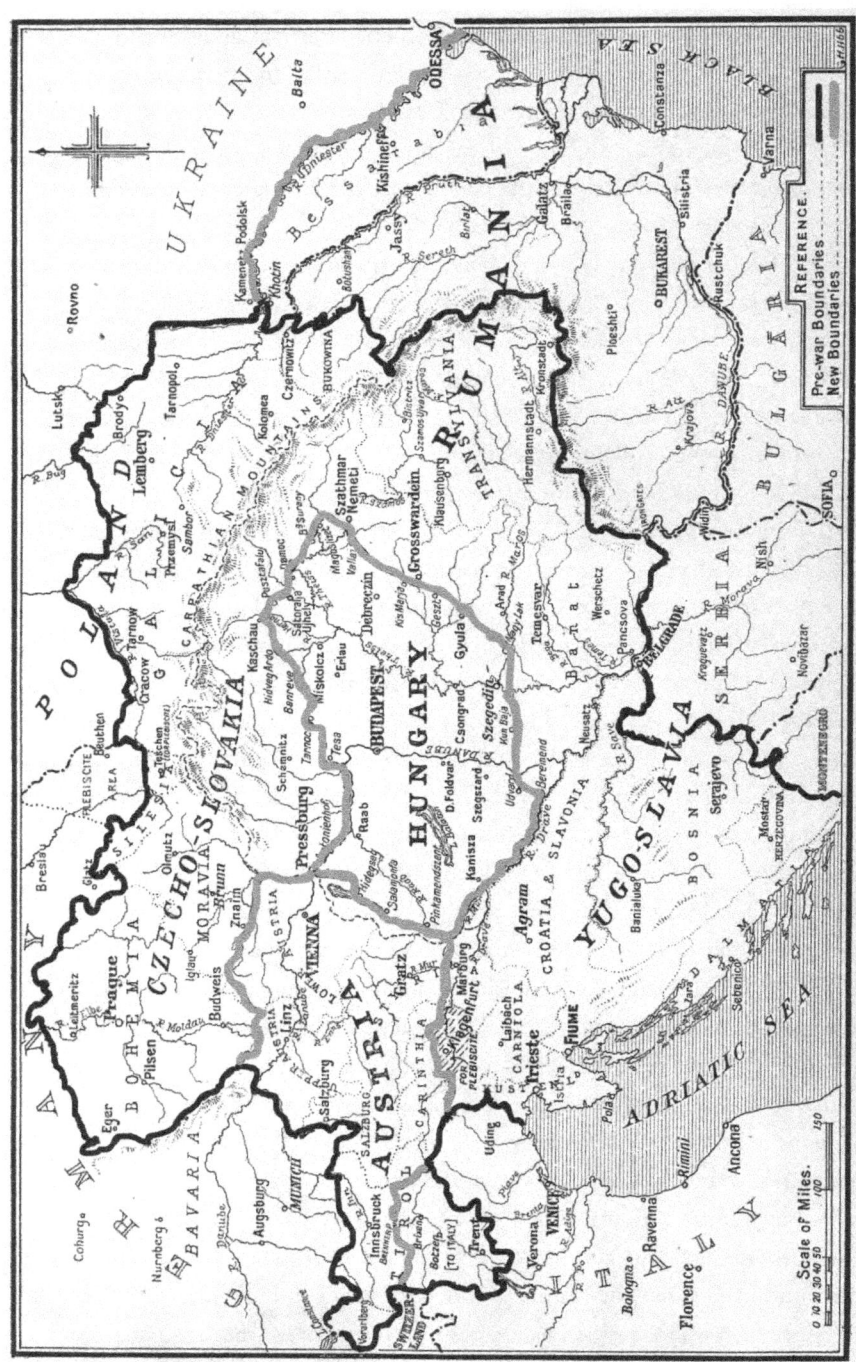

THE PARTITION OF AUSTRIA-HUNGARY: SHOWING THE BOUNDARIES AS DEFINED IN THE TREATIES.

Figure 25. The extent of the Habsburg monarchy of Karl and Zita, as it existed before and during World War I, is shown here by the dark border superimposed upon the map of the new national states that emerged following the imperial collapse in 1918. On their honeymoon in 1911, Karl and Zita traveled along the Adriatic Dalmatian coast and then went inland to Sarajevo in Bosnia at the monarchy's southern frontier with Serbia. Afterward Karl rejoined his regiment in Bohemia in the northwest of the monarchy, and in 1912 he and Zita traveled to Galicia in the northeast of the monarchy, arriving at the provincial capital of Lemberg (today Lviv in Ukraine) for the army summer maneuvers. After November 1918 these territories were divided among the successor states of Yugoslavia, Czechoslovakia, and Poland, while Austria and Hungary also became independent countries. (Wikimedia Commons)

minister president (or prime minister) of the Habsburg monarchy: the law professor Heinrich Lammasch, who had been working covertly for a separate Austrian peace since 1917. Karl and Zita returned from their Hungarian palace at Gödöllő to Vienna in order to receive Lammasch at Schönbrunn. Now Lammasch would certainly achieve an armistice, though it would be an armistice of unconditional defeat and surrender, but, even as he was named minister president, he was being called in the *Neue Freie Presse* the "Liquidator" of Austria and his government a "Liquidationsministerium."[27] His job would be not just to arrive at an armistice but to wind up the affairs of the Habsburg monarchy before it passed into history.

Hungary was already an independent Habsburg kingdom as of October 17, but on October 31 Karl and Zita were deposed as the King and Queen of Hungary, and a republic was established under Prime Minister Mihály Károlyi. On November 1 Baernreither in Berlin noted in his diary, "Talk about the Empress. The Empress, the destiny of Marie Antoinette, though not to the end, one hopes. But her carelessness gives the grounds for her unpopularity."[28] He hoped Zita would not go to the guillotine, but she had been careless about visiting the wounded from the disastrous Italian front:

> She began with the division where the Italians lay, and spoke for a long time with the wounded Italians, and then there was no more time to speak with the others in the other divisions. Conclusion: The Empress speaks only with wounded Italians. The whole thing of course terribly awkwardly and thoughtlessly arranged.[29]

It was the moment of the horrific conclusion of the Battle of Vittorio Veneto, the decisive Habsburg defeat by the Italians, but the wounded Habsburg soldiers would have included many Habsburg Italians—a national group that, like the Czechs, was now seen increasingly as a treasonous Fifth Column within the monarchy. Zita, even attending to the wounded soldiers of the Habsburg army, presumably speaking Italian, called forth criticism for disloyalty. As the dynasty was about to be deposed, her reputation remained at best ambivalent.

A popular revolution in Berlin led to the abdication of Kaiser Wilhelm on November 9. Karl and Zita were at Schönbrunn, where the imperial guards were abandoning their posts even as Karl refused to abdicate. Zita recalled the departure of "the imperial bodyguard with its men so splendid to look at in their uniforms covered with gold," and she noted, "I remember going through a hall and seeing a halberd leaning alone in a corner, because the man who had carried it had simply gone away." Outside of Schönbrunn she heard there was "disorder and chaos," caused partly by marauding soldiers as they retreated from the front. "For us it was a matter of persisting as well and as long as possible," she observed. "For as long as the Emperor was in Schönbrunn, he gave by his presence a sign of order and orientation, and so we persisted, ever more alone, ever more abandoned."[30]

Hofmannsthal's daughter Christiane, sixteen years old in 1918, recorded in her diary for November 5 that all the family valuables in the house at Rodaun were packed up and sent to Vienna for fear of marauding soldiers: "Papa carried his manuscripts in his hands, and all in all looked rather comical."[31] Hofmannsthal himself, in a letter to Ottonie Degenfeld on November 26, attempted to put his own anxieties in perspective, looking back over the month:

> Twenty-eight hundred people were dying of the flu each week in Vienna; four of the seven of us here were bed-ridden. In addition there were constant plunder alarms and shootings in the area . . . thousands of wandering hungry prisoners of war all around, escaped criminals by the hundreds in the little villages . . . all this, hungering, freezing, threatening and yet, *au fond*, of an astonishing good nature, otherwise much worse would have happened. . . . The future is extremely uncertain. . . . Throughout this entire time Goethe has been incredibly valuable to me . . .[32]

The Spanish flu may have killed as many as 50 million people worldwide in 1918 and 1919, intersecting in Europe with the terrible social circumstances of the last year of the war and the postwar economic collapse. Among the victims of the Spanish flu in Vienna was Egon Schiele, the brilliant expressionist artist, who died on October 31 at the age of twenty-eight. Gustav Klimt had already died in February, possibly also from the Spanish flu.

While Zita saw the chaos as proceeding from the withdrawal of Habsburg authority, Hofmannsthal saw it as a verdict on Habsburg rule: "The whole thing has for me something redeeming, in that I have learned to truly hate and despise that which is now collapsing in these days."[33] On November 11, the day of the armistice, Emperor Karl, still refusing to abdicate, instead renounced his role in political life, while preserving—for himself at least—the idea that he remained Emperor of Austria. According to the document of renunciation, he declared, "I renounce all participation in the affairs of state [*Ich verzichte auf jeden Anteil an den Staatsgeschäften*]. At the same time I release my Austrian Government from its office."[34] The last imperial ministry—under Lammasch—thus concluded its existence after a mere two weeks. Karl and Zita departed from Schönbrunn to resettle in the baroque imperial hunting lodge at Eckartsau, once the dwelling of Archduke Franz Ferdinand, thirty miles east of Vienna along the Danube, close to the border that now emerged between German Austria and the new state of Czechoslovakia. The day after Karl's renunciation and departure, November 12, German Austria was declared a republic, Austria without the Habsburgs. On November 13 Karl issued a parallel renunciation of political participation in his role as King of Hungary, again without formal abdication. There was some public confusion about whether or not he had abdicated, and Hofmannsthal's daughter Christiane noted sentimentally in her diary: "Emperor Karl has abdicated, and he is the only one whom I regret, because he always only wanted the good, though he lacked genius and advisers.... He did not even quite reign for two years, but sacrificed his youth and freshness."[35]

Karl's formula of renunciation without abdication was intended to leave open the possibility of returning to political life at some future date. In fact, Karl and Zita would make two unsuccessful attempts to return to power as King and Queen of Hungary in 1921. After Karl's death in 1922, Zita would spend the next generation focused on trying to reclaim a throne in Austria or Hungary for her oldest son Otto. Zita, after all, a Bourbon by descent and the daughter of the deposed duke of Parma, had a whole family tree of royal pretenders. When *Die Frau ohne Schatten* was first performed in Vienna in 1919, in the brand-new Austrian republic, it was not altogether unthinkable to imagine the political restoration of the recently deposed Karl and Zita. The Emperor's awakening from petrifaction to animation on the stage was a fairy-tale happening, but it took place in a political context in which the resurrection of emperors had a contemporary significance.

The Chorus of the Unborn Children

The glass harmonica sounds the magical notes that convey the casting of the Empress's shadow. At the same time, the Emperor gradually returns to life: ascending chords in the winds and horns lead to his opening his mouth and singing, the operatic proof that he is alive again. As he begins to sing the glass harmonica offers an A-major chord and then an F-sharp minor chord to endow him with magical harmony. The glass harmonica, with its spinning glass bowls, was a rarity in opera (Donizetti intended to use it for Lucia's mad scene, but had to settle for a flute), and it required significant additional expense to add to the orchestra for *Die Frau ohne Schatten*. For Strauss it offered part of the magical musical intonation of the Emperor's resurrection; he opens his mouth and produces cryptic words of oracular significance:

Wenn das Herz aus Kristall	When the heart of crystal
zerbricht in einem Schrei,	is shattered with a cry,
die Ungebornen eilen	the unborn children hurry
wie Sternenglanz herbei.	over like starlight.
Die Gattin blickt zum Gatten,	The wife looks to her husband,
ihr fällt ein irdischer Schatten	she casts an earthly shadow
von Hüfte, Haupt und Haar.	from hips, head, and hair.
Der Tote darf sich heben	The dead man shall rise
aus eignen Leibes Gruft.	Out of the tomb of his own body.[36]

The Emperor explains that these were the last words he heard as he lay dying, the prophecy of his resurrection, and these religiously suggestive phrases are set in a manner reminiscent of Lohengrin's magical tenor solemnity. The staged resurrection must in itself have been very powerful as performed on a continent that had just witnessed a war with twenty million deaths.

"Now I may live again," sings the Emperor in a sweeping phrase that lavishes three measures on the verb "to live" (*leben*), ascending first to a sustained F-natural, and then all the way up to high B-flat, accompanied by the flutes, clarinets, oboes, and the first violin, shifting to 9/4 triple time to make the third measure even more expansive.[37] Yet his own return to life, crucial though it may be for the fairy-tale ending, is not the point of this scene on the stage. His song of resurrection, the quotation of the oracular words that he heard at the moment of petrification, is actually an annunciation to herald the musical arrival of the unborn children. "Here comes the heavenly host, singing and fluttering [*mit Singen und mit Schweben*]," sings the Emperor. Triplets in the strings and flutes suggest the fluttering, and the triangle chimes in, while the word *Schweben* makes a beautiful two-syllable octave descent from high A, landing on the A-major chord that concludes the song of the Emperor's resurrection and brings on the unborn children.[38] For Hofmannsthal, the entrance of the children's chorus here was conceived as the most magical moment in the opera, as he noted back in September 1915 when he was working on the libretto: "as if birds were suddenly speaking from the sky . . . the alienating-enchanting sound miracle."[39]

Since both Strauss and Hofmannsthal were very consciously thinking about the relation of *Die Frau ohne Schatten*, as a fairy-tale opera, to *Die Zauberflöte*, they cannot have failed to consider Mozart's very original use of children's roles and voices. The three boys in *Die Zauberflöte* inaugurate the second act finale by heralding the messianic dawn of a world transformation in the spirit of the late Enlightenment:

Bald prangt, den Morgen zu verkünden,	Soon to proclaim the morning,
die Sonn' auf goldner Bahn . . .	The sun on its golden course . . .
Dann ist die Erd' ein Himmelreich,	Then earth will become heaven
und Sterbliche den Göttern gleich.	And mortals like gods.[40]

Mozart's three boys, who first appear holding silver palm branches, were closely associated with the artistic tradition of the putti, the figures of winged children (often with palms of victory) who colonized the canvases of Renaissance art, from the upper margin of the *Primavera* of Botticelli to the lower margin of Raphael's *Sistine Madonna*.[41] The putti have both a pagan significance in relation to Eros and a religious meaning as cherubim, and their marginal placement often denotes their unusual status on the threshold between the worldly and the otherworldly. Their most spectacular appearance in Renaissance art came with Correggio's heavenly host of putti, seen from below, in the sixteenth-century frescoes of the cathedral dome in Parma—where Zita's ancestors had prayed in ducal devotion.

The putti were still very much present in eighteenth-century rococo art, and Mozart in *Die Zauberflöte*, in 1791, could cast a trio of boys as musical putti in his fairy-tale opera, giving voice—the voice of actual singing children—to figures who were otherwise silent in painting and sculpture. One century later in 1893, Richard Strauss conducted in Weimar the premiere of the most famous fairy-tale opera of the nineteenth century, Engelbert Humperdinck's *Hänsel und Gretel*. The principal characters, Hänsel and Gretel, are children, but they are sung by adults, and Humperdinck held back the children's chorus until the very final scene, when the witch had been killed and the *Kuchenkinder*—the children she had baked into sweets—came back to life. "Erlöst, befreit, für alle Zeit" (saved, freed, for all time), they sing, with "erlöst" suggesting not just rescue but religious salvation. The children's chorus thus enters—like the three boys in *Die Zauberflöte*—to announce a salvific and messianic moment with the defeat and destruction of the evil witch. Indeed, their coming to vocal life constitutes a resurrection, even as it gives to the opera the crucial musical element that was lacking till this moment: the voices of children. The children sing "sehr leise, wie im Traume" (very softly, as if in a dream), and though they begin in D major, the harmony shifts to E major, and the rhythm is enlivened, as the children beg Hänsel and Gretel to touch them and bring them back to life.[42] Thus the *Kuchenkinder* awaken from the liminal sphere in which they seemed to be suspended: between death and life, as if asleep, as if in a dream.

Strauss, who conducted the premiere of *Hänsel und Gretel*, must surely have had that opera in mind, along with *Die Zauberflöte*, when he composed the chorus of unborn children, brought to life, brought to voice, in the final scene of *Die Frau ohne Schatten*. In the libretto's implicit cosmology the unborn children, passing from nonexistence into existence, replenish mankind. In the opera the unborn children of the Dyer's Wife are first condemned to death, are heard crying out from the frying pan in the first act, because their putative mother has heartlessly renounced her shadow. Now, however, with the Dyer's Wife reconciled to motherhood, and the Empress acquiring a shadow of her own, a whole troop of unborn children are ready to be born, are fluttering and hovering, and finally able to break into choral voice:

Hört, wir wollen sagen: Vater!	Listen, we want to say, Father!
Hört, wir wollen Mutter rufen!	Listen, we want to call Mother!
Steiget auf!	Climb up!
Nein, kommt herunter!	No, come down!
Zu uns führen alle Stufen!	All stairs lead to us![43]

Figure 26. In 1915, in the murderous depths of World War I, Hofmannsthal imagined the voices of the unborn children: "as if birds were suddenly speaking from the sky . . . as on the wings of the wind, then like silvery rejoicing . . . the alienating-enchanting sound miracle." When the chorus of children sang in the final scene—"hört wir wollen sagen Vater, hört wir wollen Mutter rufen" (hear us we want to say Father, hear us we want to call Mother)—Strauss created an orchestral sound miracle of trilling flutes, of triangle and celesta, suggesting the supernatural sphere of spirits waiting to be born into the world. (*Die Frau ohne Schatten*, 1919)

The triangle and the celesta emphasize the magic of the children's vocal presence, while the flutes perform triplets and trills. As with the putti of previous centuries, the unborn children belonged to the supernatural frontier, between existence and nonexistence, the liminal space between this world and another dimension.

The score specifies the lighting direction that "the light coming down from the dome [*Kuppel*] has become stronger and stronger"—thus revealing that the temple is domed, and the dome is filled with fluttering, hovering putti.[44] The score further directs that the voices of the unborn children should come "from above out of the dome" [*von oben aus dem Kuppel*]. It was as if the putti that Correggio painted in the dome of the cathedral in Parma now found voice in Strauss's chorus of unborn children and marked the happy ending of the fairy-tale opera.

> KAISERIN *deutet nach oben*
> Sind das die Cherubim,
> die ihre Stimmen heben?
>
> KAISER *von der untersten Stufe*
> Das sind die Nichtgeborenen,
> nun stürzen sie ins Leben
> mit morgenroten Flügeln
> zu uns, den fast Verlorenen.

> EMPRESS *indicates above*
> Are those the cherubim
> Who are lifting their voices?
>
> EMPEROR *from the lowest step*
> Those are the not-born,
> now they fall to life
> with dawn-red wings
> to us, who are almost lost.[45]

The harps return to accompany the Empress as she looks up and wonders if she is seeing the heavenly cherubim, her voice leaping to her favorite note, high F-sharp, for the final syllable of "cherubim." The Emperor's petrification has taught him secrets of the universe that she does not know, and he can recognize the unborn children—including his own unborn children—and, as he responds to the Empress, the orchestra, including the harp, unites them in the first musical exchange, almost a duet, that they have been permitted so far in the entire opera.[46]

Zita, the Habsburg empress from 1916 to 1918, while *Die Frau ohne Schatten* awaited its premiere, believed that her own relation to the children of Austria was crucial to the prestige of the dynasty. She made her birthday in 1917 into a Children's Day, *Kindertag*, and dynastically loyal committees of civic-minded women arranged for children's tributes, including those of children's choruses, paeans to Zita as *Landesmutter*, the mother of her country. Korngold's "Empress Zita Hymn," performed for her birthday, also deployed a children's chorus to celebrate the Empress, who was herself constantly pregnant. A fifth child was born in 1918 while she still reigned, and a sixth in 1919 after Karl and Zita had given up their thrones, with two more still to follow before Karl's death in 1922. Childbirth for Zita was the literal future of the dynasty, but children were also the symbolic emblems of the very uncertain post-Habsburg future in the lands of Austria-Hungary. Like Mozart's three boys, who "proclaim the morning," so the children's chorus in *Die Frau ohne Schatten* hopefully heralded a new day for postwar Europe in the aftermath of World War I.

Postwar

THE AFTERLIVES OF EMPRESSES

13

The Emperor and the Empress

IN EXILE IN SWITZERLAND AND ON STAGE IN VIENNA

Departure by Train

Stefan Zweig, who left wartime Austria for neutral Switzerland in 1917 as a committed pacifist, returned home to the brand-new German Austrian republic in March 1919. Having crossed the border, he got out of the train at the Austrian frontier station of Feldkirch in far western Austria on March 24:

> I became aware of an odd restlessness among the customs officers and police. They paid small attention to us and made their inspection in a most negligent manner; plainly something important was to happen. At last came the bell that announced the approach of a train from the Austrian side. The police lined up, the officials piled out of their office; their womenfolk, evidently in the know, crowded together on the platform. . . . Slowly, almost majestically, it seemed, the train rolled near. . . . Then I recognized behind the plate glass window of the car Emperor Karl, the last Emperor of Austria, standing with his black-clad wife, Empress Zita. I was startled; the last Emperor of Austria, heir of the Habsburg dynasty which had ruled for seven hundred years, was forsaking his realm![1]

Zweig described one elderly woman sobbing on the platform, but otherwise a mood of curiosity rather than legitimist devotion seemed to govern the small crowd. Behind glass Karl and Zita appeared almost as their own paired portraits on the wall, already royalty from a receding epoch, traveling in

Einsteinian space-time—in a moving train, the emblematic vehicle of special relativity—out of Austria and into history. Zita, inevitably, was pregnant, but the future of the imperial family would have seemed already irrelevant to those who experienced the moment of their imperial passing from the station's platform.

Zweig was only briefly the subject of Karl and Zita but had lived most of his Viennese life in the reign of Emperor Franz Joseph.

> Innumerable times had I seen the old emperor in the long since legendary splendor of elaborate celebrations; I had seen him on the great staircase of Schönbrunn, surrounded by his family and brilliantly uniformed generals, receiving the homage of the eight thousand Viennese school children, massed on the broad green plain, singing, their thin voices united in touching chorus, Haydn's "Gott erhalte." . . . And now I saw his heir, the last Emperor, banished from his country.[2]

Zweig was thinking back on the children's choruses that once celebrated the Emperor, even as Hofmannsthal was about to present a children's chorus on the operatic stage to sing to the Emperor, "Hört, wir wollen sagen: Vater!" For Hofmannsthal and Zweig both, with their privileged Viennese childhoods, the Habsburg Emperor, as they remembered him, was a figure both politically real and magically legendary at the same time. Zweig relished the coincidence that his homecoming intersected so precisely with Karl and Zita's exile, but Hofmannsthal would be involved in another coincidence of timing: the Emperor and Empress departed from Austria in the flesh in the very same year that they stepped onto the stage in Vienna, as figures from a fairy tale, in *Die Frau ohne Schatten*.

Karl's renunciation of political life and retreat to Eckartsau in November 1918—refusing to abdicate—predictably did not give satisfaction to the coalition government of the new republic under the socialist leadership of Karl Renner. When Renner traveled to Eckartsau to speak with Karl and Zita in January 1919, they actually refused to meet with him, because he had not requested a formal audience; that is, he had treated them as private persons rather than as Emperor and Empress.[3] On March 15 Renner secured his government by forming a coalition between his own Social Democrats and the Christian Socialists, and he now felt himself secure enough to propose to

Eckartsau an ultimatum: either Karl could abdicate and remain in Austria, or he could go into exile. If he remained without abdicating there was the implicit possibility of arrest, and, following on the murder of the Romanovs, there were even insinuations that it might be difficult to guarantee the safety of the Habsburg imperial family. This was sufficiently concerning for Zita's brothers to ask King George V to assign a British officer to travel with Karl and Zita and their children to Switzerland. The officer, Lieutenant Colonel Edward Lisle Strutt, also a noted Alpine mountaineer, was on the train at Feldkirch.[4]

From the station on the border Emperor Karl wrote out a secret "Feldkirch Manifesto," dated March 24, which he entrusted only to Pope Benedict XV and King Alfonso XIII of Spain. He offered a "solemn protest" against his own dethronement, declaring illegitimate the republican government that was established after his withdrawal from politics. He regarded the acts of that government as "null and void for me and for my dynasty," and offered an affirmation of "confidence in the people with whom my family and I have borne the suffering and sacrifice of this unhappy war." The pope replied from the Vatican on March 26, praising Karl, "after such serious political upheavals," for preserving his ongoing good will toward "the peoples entrusted to you by Divine Providence." Cardinal Gaetano Bisleti—who had performed the marriage of Karl and Zita in 1911—sent a separate letter to Zita from the Vatican, offering appreciation for "the sublime beauty of most spirited faith and heroic Christian strength."[5] While these letters were piously sympathetic, they did not explicitly recognize the imperial rights of Karl and Zita.

"We could not console ourselves," recalled Zita, "for having had to take leave of our homeland . . . but we hoped it would not last too long, that we would soon be able to return to our dear homeland." Karl, on the train, changed out of his Austrian uniform adorned with his Habsburg Order of the Golden Fleece and put on civilian clothes in preparation for his Swiss exile.[6] The homeland for which they could not be consoled was Austria-Hungary, which, in fact, no longer existed, but Zita's family was, of course, at home all over Europe. In Switzerland Zita's mother occupied a Bourbon-Parma castle, Schloss Wartegg, on Lake Constance, though Zita and Karl ultimately resided in a villa of their own, further from the Austrian border, Villa Prangins on Lake Geneva. When Zita imagined them returning soon to "our dear homeland," she implicitly meant that they would return as the Emperor and Empress.

Though Austrians were unaware of the Feldkirch Manifesto, the government of the republic certainly knew that Karl had not abdicated when he withdrew from politics back in November and that he had again refused to abdicate before leaving the country. By the "Habsburg Law" of April 3, 1919, ten days after the family departed from Austria, the dynasty was formally deposed, Karl was exiled forever, no member of the family was permitted to return without renouncing all dynastic claims, and the family's dynastic property was confiscated by the government.[7] The Habsburg Law constituted a sharp legal break with the past, rendered more plausible by the departure of Karl and Zita from Austria, but the republic still had to reckon with the persistence of institutional and sentimental continuities, even as Austria developed its postimperial form and identity over the course of 1919.

"This New Era"

Hofmannsthal wrote to Strauss on December 5, 1918, and noted the volatile Austrian political situation, the revolutionary transition from empire to republic, as if it were merely the background to the more important question of transition at the Vienna Opera:

> I consider it certain that—whatever regime here may rule—they will not back off from summoning you, and I firmly believe . . . that you and Schalk, truly working together, can bring about a beautiful era for this precious institution, so extremely dear to me.[8]

Before receiving this, on December 6 Strauss sent a telegram from Berlin asking whether Hofmannsthal agreed that the premiere of *Die Frau ohne Schatten* could take place in Vienna in October 1919.[9] Hofmannsthal noted his agreement on December 7, as if it were a self-evident corollary of Strauss's appointment at the Vienna Opera:

> I have worked all these weeks like a horse for this thing: to save the Strauss-Roller-Schalk team! In fact, I am full of hopes for this regime, I *want* to have you here—so what is all this nonsense? I am thoroughly in agreement about a Vienna premiere . . .[10]

As recently as August 1917 Hofmannsthal had doubts about Vienna, fearing that the opera's spiritual values would not be appreciated in the imperial capital, but now, with the advent of the postwar republic, Vienna appeared as the focus for a new postwar Austrian culture. Hofmannsthal's anticipation of a new regime at the opera house allowed him to contemplate bringing *Die Frau ohne Schatten* home to Vienna.

On December 22, as Christmas approached, the Vienna Symphony Orchestra performed at the Konzerthaus, offering Mozart's Symphony no. 39 in E-flat, Beethoven's Second Piano Concerto, Wagner's overture to *Rienzi*, and Richard Strauss's tone poem *Death and Transfiguration*. Such a concert already represented a sort of apotheosis of Strauss, elevated in his own lifetime to the pantheon of greatest German composers. On that same day *Der Rosenkavalier* was presented at the opera with Schalk conducting and Richard Mayr giving his already acclaimed interpretation of Baron Ochs.[11]

On Christmas Day Hofmannsthal sent a letter of reconciliation, thanking Strauss for "the measure of kindness and patience with which you reacted to my (supposed) opposition to your coming [to Vienna]," further declaring (not quite correctly) that "my position the whole time was the opposite." Hofmannsthal now claimed to believe that Strauss's directorship in Vienna was a crucial element in establishing the postwar culture of the new Austrian republic: "It may be that from here [Vienna], far more than from Berlin, the whole nature of theater could receive a new look for a new generation—and precisely from a combination like Strauss-Schalk-Roller, which has something symbolic in its mingling of tradition and progress." The poet also expected to increase his own influence through Strauss's presence in Vienna: "It will strengthen my power in cultural-political questions."[12] Having attempted to articulate an Austrian identity during the war, under the auspices of the Habsburg monarchy, Hofmannsthal considered himself in a position to hold some sort of unofficial portfolio for cultural affairs in the postwar republic.

Hofmannsthal was also keen to conciliate Hermann Bahr, the literary leader who had been his own patron, indeed discoverer, back in the 1890s, and who continued to be culturally influential in postwar Austria. Bahr was married to the Wagnerian soprano Anna Mildenburg, once Mahler's lover— and also Mahler's Isolde in 1903 in the celebrated production designed by

Roller for the Vienna Opera. Now that Mildenburg was married to Bahr, and now that her Isolde days were behind her, Hofmannsthal observed, "it often occupies my thoughts whether... Mildenburg could sing the Nurse—but probably it is impossible!" It was somewhat outside his sphere as librettist to be casting the roles for *Die Frau ohne Schatten*, but Hofmannsthal was thinking very politically about culture at this moment and was eager to conciliate someone as influential as Bahr. For it was now definitively settled that *Die Frau ohne Schatten* would be performed first in Vienna: "I have telegrammed my agreement to the Vienna world premiere," wrote Hofmannsthal. He was discussing set designs with Roller: "He [Roller] will accomplish what is possible in the shortest possible time, also taking into account the altered material circumstances."[13]

The reference to material circumstances alluded to the economic catastrophe of postwar Austria and Germany, and Christmas 1918 was certainly a Christmas of general hardship. Zita claimed that even at Eckartsau her little family of archdukes and archduchesses experienced the economic misery: "We actually suffered from the acute lack of foodstuffs. . . . It was bitter when the children began to suffer from undernourishment, but these hardships had to be borne by the whole population, and the Emperor would have been the last to complain about these things, especially since his concern was not just for us, but for all of his peoples."[14] With the premiere of *Die Frau ohne Schatten* in postwar Austria, Barak's determination to provide food for his impoverished family would now be performed in the context of postwar food shortages:

Gib du mir Kinder, dass sie mir hocken	Give me children, to come sit with me
um die Schüsseln zu Abend,	around their bowls in the evening,
es soll mir keines hungrig aufstehn.	not one of mine will stand up hungry.[15]

In 1919 even Karl and Zita were worrying about feeding their children.

Stefan Zweig, who remarked upon the obvious economic misery from the moment he crossed the border from Switzerland into Austria, also left an account of operatic performance under the Austrian material circumstances:

> I shall never forget what an opera performance meant in those days of direst need. . . . The theater was not heated, thus the audience kept their

overcoats on and huddled together. . . . The Philharmonic players were like gray shadows in their shabby dress suits, undernourished and exhausted by many privations, and the audience, too, seemed to be ghosts in a theater which had become ghostly. Then, however, the conductor lifted his baton, the curtain parted, and it was as glorious as ever.[16]

Roller's task, as Hofmannsthal suggested, would be not just to stage the very recognizable poverty of Barak's family, but also, with limited budget and supplies, to suggest the splendor of the vanished imperial sphere by conjuring with illusionary stagecraft. Roller himself noted that "all the designs originated in the prewar period"—along with the conception of the opera itself—and these would be difficult to realize in the postwar economic situation.[17]

In January 1919, as the leading statesmen of the victorious Allies gathered in Paris for the coming peace conference, Hofmannsthal wrote to Strauss full of preoccupations with music politics in Vienna surrounding the opera directorship. On January 4 he was advising Strauss about the importance of some friendly overture to the *Wunderkind* composer Erich Korngold, age twenty-one, who might feel flattered by Strauss's attention; such friendliness could be the perfect ploy for winning over Julius Korngold, the composer's father, at the *Neue Freie Presse*. Hofmannsthal wanted Strauss present in Vienna for discussions about the directorship, noting that "then I will gladly participate in everything, and I hope that this new era will also be a good and productive era for us."[18] The new era in Austrian political life was thus associated with the imminent new era at the Vienna Opera, which was also purposefully connected to the future of the Strauss-Hofmannsthal collaboration.

Writing about the "new era" immediately made Hofmannsthal think of *Die Frau ohne Schatten*, and, though he was hopeful about the intended Roller production in Vienna, he was already cringing at the thought of how the opera might be presented in Berlin. He was worried about ugliness—"as with the production of all our works in Berlin"—worried that "the child of my imagination [*Phantasie*] may be exposed to common, ugly, vulgar business."[19] Here, insisting on his own acknowledged position as one of the most sensitive artists of Viennese aestheticism in the 1890s, he exercised his animus against Berlin—pent up over the wartime years of writing Austrian propaganda in the shadow of German military dominance.

Hofmannsthal was suspicious of the Berlin stage design team, including Hans Kautsky, the brother of the leading German Marxist theoretician Karl Kautsky ("The Pope of Marxism"), both of them originally from the Habsburg lands.[20] Their father Johann made stage designs for the Vienna Opera in the nineteenth century. Now, however, Hofmannsthal was consumed with rage at the thought of Kautsky and his team in Berlin adapting, and ruining, Roller's stage designs for *Die Frau ohne Schatten* in Vienna. Hofmannsthal was particularly protective of this opera, "the child of my imagination," which would be challenging for the public, would likely be misunderstood, and would only slowly gain appreciation. It would be better, he suggested scathingly, to let "the voiceless Mildenburg" sing the role of the Nurse than to turn over the whole production to the "barbarism" of Kautsky in Berlin: "A whole regime does not collapse so that only this swinishness may remain."[21] The political collapse of the old imperial regime, from Hofmannsthal's aesthetic perspective, had to be considered in relation to the menace of "barbarism" and "swinishness" in opera production.

The Ethnographic Museum

Hofmannsthal was deeply invested in *Die Frau ohne Schatten* at this moment, dedicating his writing hours to finishing the fairy tale which, at over a hundred pages, would be the length of a novella and excite much less interest than the opera. Because of the length it was possible to add details and whole scenes that were not included in the opera at all. For instance, as he concluded the fairy tale Hofmannsthal graphically described the Emperor's experience of paralysis: "Since he could not feel the fingers of his right hand, he wanted to bring those of the left to assist, but neither hand any longer obeyed him, his petrifying arms lay already stiff at his petrified sides and no sound came from his petrified lips."[22] This narration of the experience of paralysis was also perhaps a reflection on the millions of war-wounded.

In the fairy tale, even more than in the opera libretto, Hofmannsthal strongly suggested that the Emperor had been transformed into a stone statue of himself. His petrified body appeared in the middle of the fountain of golden water:

It appeared weighty like a funerary monument [*Grabmal*] built of stone in the middle of a pond. The statue was set upon a rectangular dark stone. It was stripped of all weapons, wearing only light hunting armor, as if for decoration. But even the silver-scaled leg pieces, that might protect from the tusks of a boar or the teeth of a lynx, were gone, and the legs were naked and fully of marble; so also the shoulders and the neck, from which the cape had fallen away. The Empress cried out, and threw herself into the gentle golden waves of the pool; like a swan with lifted wings she rushed upon her beloved. She bent over him, but did not dare to kiss him. . . . She leaned over him, didn't know for how long, didn't move at all. She herself was like a statue, part of a funerary monument.[23]

In the published fairy tale of 1919, after the withdrawal of Karl and Zita from politics, Hofmannsthal's "funerary monument" seemed to evoke an imperial past that was very recent but also increasingly alien and remote, perhaps a funerary monument from the Habsburg Kapuzinergruft. The intricately overlong tale of *Die Frau ohne Schatten* emerged at the moment when emperors and empresses were receding into the domain of historical legends and commemorative statues.

It was also the moment of postwar hardship, and Hofmannsthal conjured for Strauss a picture of himself laboring in January over his fairy tale "in rooms almost unheatable, with no gas and almost no electric light."[24] As he worked in the cold and the dark, as he awaited the premiere of the opera, Hofmannsthal was nominated for the Nobel Prize in 1919, his first nomination, submitted by German writer Gerhart Hauptmann.[25] The nomination was snubbed by the Swedish judges who awarded no prize at all in 1919.

In his letter of January 4, 1919, Hofmannsthal was already, nine months in advance, awkwardly distancing himself from the October premiere of *Die Frau ohne Schatten*, explaining to Strauss that he could not possibly return from Aussee in time for the early rehearsals: September had to be dedicated to writing. The poet would work with Roller to prepare a director's book (*Regiebuch*) with full instructions for the rehearsals.[26] Hofmannsthal would be in the mountains at Aussee, but he would be micromanaging the rehearsals through Roller and the book of instructions. Intent upon preparing for all complications in advance, Hofmannsthal suggested that it would be well to identify a backup for Jeritza as the Empress—"the unpredictable Jeritza"—so unpredictable that she might "run away" a month after the premiere.²⁷ In fact, she was reliably singing in *Ariadne, Salome, Lohengrin,* and *La Juive* at the Vienna Opera in January 1919.²⁸

On January 6, at Epiphany, Karl Kraus gave an afternoon public reading in the Schubert Hall of the Konzerthaus to benefit the Children's Friends (*Kinderfreunde*), a workers' charity—with children's causes now cut loose from their former imperial patronage. That evening Leo Slezak, tenor star of the Vienna Opera, gave a recital at the Konzerthaus, concluding with a series of Richard Strauss *Lieder*, including "Morgen" and "Cäcilie."²⁹ Korngold's "Empress Zita Hymn" had now disappeared from Slezak's repertory.

On January 7 Strauss wrote to Hofmannsthal, promising to try to make Berlin respect Roller's vision for *Die Frau ohne Schatten*, but also noting the need for political expedience—"because Kautsky is above all the brother of the minister and has political influence over the whole character of the opera house."³⁰ Hans Kautsky, the stage designer, could not be offended at a moment when his brother Karl Kautsky held a post in the socialist postwar German government. As Strauss was writing on January 7, the Spartacus Uprising was launched in Berlin, an unsuccessful attempt to replace the socialist government with a more thoroughly revolutionary regime, guided by Rosa Luxemburg and Karl Liebknecht—who would both be arrested and murdered one week later.

Strauss, however, was focused on *Die Frau ohne Schatten*, taking up the question of a second cast and a possible replacement for Jeritza. As he wrote to Hofmannsthal, he took into consideration the demands of the score: "Would you trust the second Empress to Kiurina and the Dyer's Wife to Schoder? Or the other way round? The Empress needs a lot of dramatic power in the third act and the Dyer's Wife much vocal brilliance in the top range. Accursed dilemma!"³¹ The exclamation "Accursed dilemma!" (*Verfluchte Klemme!*) was Mime's phrase from Wagner's *Siegfried* as the dwarf attempted to figure out how best to induce Siegfried to slay the dragon and obtain the treasure. There was some suggestion that choosing second casts was a scheming dwarf's dilemma. In the end, Marie Gutheil-Schoder—also a celebrated Octavian and Elektra—would sing the Dyer's Wife after Lotte Lehmann, while Berta Kiurina, with a lighter voice—often cast as Eva in *Die Meistersinger*—would back up Jeritza as the Empress.

In February 1919 Strauss reported to Hofmannsthal the unwelcome news that Kautsky in Berlin was eager to consider an ethnographic staging of *Die Frau ohne Schatten*. "I once hinted to him about Chinese fairy-tale themes," wrote Strauss, exasperated—and now Kautsky "wants to drag me to the Ethnographic Museum." The composer urgently needed advice from Hofmannsthal on how to rebut this conception "graciously but crushingly" (*schonend aber niederschmetternd*).[32] The Berlin Royal Museum of Ethnography (*Völkerkunde*) was one of the great collections in Europe, dating back to the 1880s. After the war the museum would move to its twentieth-century home in Dahlem, with exhibits dedicated to the arts and crafts of the Americas, Africa, Asia, and Oceania—the latter potentially relevant to the "Emperor of the Southeastern Islands" in *Die Frau ohne Schatten*. Yet, both Strauss and Hofmannsthal agreed that ethnography would offend their traditional sense of a fairy-tale scenario, and Strauss, additionally, was clearly determined to avoid having to spend a day in the museum.

Hofmannsthal replied on February 12, which happened to be the twentieth birthday of Hencze "Lucy" Erber, born a subject of Franz Joseph in 1899 in Galicia and after the war a citizen of the Austrian republic in Vienna. She was even a voting citizen, since with the declaration of the republic on November 12, 1918, women were given the right to vote, starting at the age of twenty. Lucy would have been eligible to vote in the elections for the constituent assembly—to create a new constitution for Austria—on February 16, four days after her birthday. The Social Democrats would win a plurality of seats, with the Christian Socialists coming second: I do not know whether my grandmother voted but, if she did, she certainly would not have voted for the openly anti-Semitic Christian Socialists. Hofmannsthal's sixteen-year-old daughter Christiane, too young to vote, went to a Social Democratic election campaign meeting in late January and heard people cheering at denunciations of Zita.[33]

Hofmannsthal's letter of February 12 had nothing to say about the imminent elections, for he was too distressed by Kautsky's interest in the ethnographic museum. The poet was appalled by the pedantry of the museum proposal and urged Strauss to explain that the opera "did not present a historical anecdote but an eternal, that is, timeless, symbolic subject," requiring "idealized costume and an idealized setting." Hofmannsthal believed that it

Figure 27. The imperious Lucy in furs, my grandmother, was born Hencze Erber in eastern Galicia in 1899, a subject of Franz Joseph. As a teenager she lived through the brief reign of Karl and Zita from 1916 to 1918. She migrated with her parents to the Viennese metropolis, where her father had a prosperous leather goods shop on the Rauscherstraße after the war. Photographs show Lucy smoking, skiing, traveling around Europe, and enjoying the Adriatic beaches of the former Habsburg monarchy. She married my grandfather Martin (Moses) Stier in 1933, and they left Austria forever after the Anschluss in 1938. (Property of the author)

would be appropriate to seek some sort of theatrical style combining classical antiquity and the Orient, and it was therefore necessary to avoid absolutely "the historically and ethnographically precise," but rather to suggest "the remote, the mysterious, the immense, the religious."[34]

By June Strauss had the idea of engaging a truly modern Austrian artist, Oskar Kokoschka, to stage *Die Frau ohne Schatten*. Strauss conceded that "Kautsky is reluctantly executing Roller's designs"—but even Roller belonged to the older Austrian generation of the Klimtian Sezession, while Kokoschka, the pioneer of Viennese expressionism, was twenty years younger, age thirty-three in 1919.[35] Hofmannsthal immediately agreed in principle to the "Kokoschka experiment," expecting that he would bring "the fantastic, the baroque, the timeless" (*das Phantastische, Barocke, Zeitlose*) into the staging of the opera.[36]

Hofmannsthal did however have practical concerns, as with the "unpredictable" Jeritza: "Kokoschka is, as I hear everywhere, a genius but not a reliable person, does not feel bound by contracts, stays away from his job for days, treats everything as an improvisation."[37] In fact, Kokoschka, after being wounded in the war in Austrian uniform in 1915 and experiencing shell shock, was in fragile psychological condition, and by 1918 he had created for himself a life-sized doll of his former lover Alma Mahler, which served as a model, a companion, and possibly a sexual surrogate.[38] Hofmannsthal was rightly skeptical about whether Kokoschka could be counted on to collaborate in designing *Die Frau ohne Schatten*.

Hofmannsthal himself had a modest collection of paintings, including what turned out to be a forged Van Gogh, but in 1916, in a letter to his wife, the poet made clear his contempt for contemporary Austrian art: "the dreadful perfumed Klimt, the half-swindler Kokoschka, the common swindler Schiele."[39] Three years later in 1919 Klimt and Schiele were both dead, and Kokoschka—only a half-swindler—seemed to be the survivor of Austrian modernist painting. "I have from Kokoschka still no answer," wrote Strauss to Hofmannsthal, discouraged, on June 27; they were worrying about stage designs in Berlin the day before the Treaty of Versailles was to be signed in France, confirming Germany's humiliation and setting the stage for a generation of political rage and resentment.[40]

Kunstpolitik

In June, with the cast for the Vienna October premiere already selected, Hofmannsthal was thinking ahead to rehearsals. He asked Strauss to begin offering private rehearsals to some of the performers: "above all Weidt (whose role depends entirely on clarity of enunciation), and if possible also Lehmann, to come and study the roles under your oversight, so that they, the least talented actors, will be almost ready when they come to rehearsals." Hofmannsthal worried that Lucie Weidt as the Nurse and Lotte Lehmann as the Dyer's Wife would fail to give satisfaction in their dramatically complex roles. He thought special rehearsals were less essential for the other principals, as "Jeritza, Mayr, and Aagard should not create any difficulties."[41] The veteran Austrian bass-baritone Richard Mayr in the role of Barak did not worry him, and likewise the young Norwegian tenor Karl Aagard Oestvig in the role of the Emperor—possibly because those two male roles seemed less dramatically challenging even to their creator.

Mayr had a career at the Vienna Opera dating back to Mahler's directorship and was still singing his signature Mozart roles of Figaro, Leporello, and Sarastro, but he had also made a great success of Baron Ochs in Vienna. Oestvig had joined the company only in 1917 and had performed as Lohengrin and Don José, though he had also sung heroically in *Ariadne* as Bacchus. Lehmann, beginning in Vienna in 1916, had been a Wagnerian Rhinemaiden and Flowermaiden, but had also that year jumped in as the understudy (for Marie Gutheil-Schoder) as the Composer in *Ariadne*. Only thirty-one when she took on the daunting role of the Dyer's Wife, her great career lay still before her in the 1920s and 1930s. Lehmann was intimidated by the role of the Dyer's Wife, and she even tried to back out of the premiere, but Strauss both persuaded her to accept and coached her through the part in Garmisch during August 1919.[42]

Lucie Weidt had been a major Wagnerian soprano during the Mahler decade in Vienna, in fact, the slightly younger rival of Anna Mildenburg. Weidt's suitability for the role of the Nurse meant that Hofmannsthal was still worrying over what to do about Mildenburg and her influential husband Hermann Bahr. The poet proposed that Strauss pay Mildenburg a twenty-minute visit in the interest of "art politics" (*Kunstpolitik*) and offer her some "crumbs" (*Brosamen*), namely the possibility of a role in some future season.[43] Hofmannsthal had become a practitioner of *Kunstpolitik* in the postwar operatic circumstances, attending to the egos of aging divas.

It was notable that Hofmannsthal had no concerns about coaching the opera's supreme diva, "the unpredictable Jeritza," in the role of the Empress. Jeritza, who had captured the attention of Emperor Franz Joseph and been honored as a court Kammersängerin by Emperor Karl, was so much a product of the imperial *ancien régime* that the role of the Empress may now have seemed almost natural for her. She regarded Strauss as a personal friend and recalled that "he and Schalk often came to my house in Vienna to run over my roles with me at the piano."[44]

Strauss was certainly prepared to begin rehearsing singers for *Die Frau ohne Schatten* during the summer of 1919, and his letter to Hofmannsthal of June 27 offered a schedule.

> Concerning *Die Frau ohne Schatten*, I am hoping to receive Fräulein Lehmann here for private study at the beginning of August and Frau Weidt at the end of August. Schalk is here with me, and we have extensively discussed all the important questions. I am thinking I'll be in Vienna on August 28 for the first blocking rehearsal. But before then I must have your and Roller's director's book [*Regiebuch*] in hand . . .[45]

There was perhaps a sense of picking teams here, with Strauss and Schalk together, composer and conductor, personally settling "all the important questions"—while Hofmannsthal and Roller were asked to mail in their comments on the production. Hofmannsthal explained that the director's book would take the form of an annotated piano score, to map the correspondences of gesture and music.[46]

When Strauss was writing to Hofmannsthal at the end of June 1919, an Austrian delegation at Saint-Germain-en-Laye was awaiting the harsh outcome of the peace treaty process, a German national assembly at Weimar was preparing to adopt a republican constitution, and in Budapest a Hungarian Bolshevik government had seized power under Béla Kun.[47] Strauss was not altogether oblivious to the contemporary political situation, commenting: "I should so much like to have a political satire in late-Grecian costume, with Jeritza as a hetaera from Lucian—today's operetta governments cry out for musical setting and ridicule [*Vertonung und Verhöhnung*]."[48] In the aftermath of empires, with the rise and sometimes rapid fall of new republican governments—even Bolshevik governments—politics appeared to Strauss as a subject for satirical operetta.

On September 5 Zita gave birth to her sixth child, Archduke Rudolf, at Villa Prangins on Lake Geneva. The oldest, Archduke Otto, was not yet seven years old. Rudolf was the first child born outside the Habsburg monarchy and the first one born without the obstetrical assistance of Heinrich Peham. In 1918 Peham had been ennobled by Emperor Karl in reward for his services, and he would succeed in 1920 to a professorship of obstetrics at the university in Vienna, where he would serve with the reputation of a post-Habsburg monarchist.[49] On September 10, five days after Rudolf's birth, the Treaty of Saint-Germain-en-Laye was signed in France, bringing about peace between the Allies and the "former Imperial and Royal Austro-Hungarian Government," confirming that the empire "has now ceased to exist, and has been replaced in Austria by a republican government."[50] Karl and Zita in Switzerland, removed from political life, were curiously sheltered from responsibility for the terms of the treaty. Their empire had ceased to exist, but the Emperor and the Empress seemed to float freely in the European imagination, in a dissociated dimension of postimperial space-time.

On September 18, with rehearsals already under way in Vienna, Hofmannsthal excused himself to Strauss, insisting that he was recovering from illness and depression but also immersed in writing: "So you must fully understand if I exclude myself from the joy of listening to the rehearsals until the last three or four, and renounce the joy, the magic, of seeing my words and characters blossom out in your music." In a phrase of hyperbolic pleading he insisted that to return to Vienna—"rehearsals, people, reality, would be like falling from heaven into hell." He was nervous about how the opera would be received in Vienna, whether it would be appreciated and understood. He was braced for the "stupid frustration" of people trying to "interpret and puzzle over" what was supposed to be a simple fairy tale.[51] At the same time, he wrote to Arthur Schnitzler on September 19 not only that he needed to preserve his time for writing in Aussee but also that he would feel like a "fifth wheel" at the rehearsals.[52]

Even at a distance Hofmannsthal in Aussee was agitated by reports from the rehearsals in Vienna and wrote to Strauss: "People tell me that you want, at the end of the first scene on the terrace, to have the Empress and the Nurse sink down [*versinken*] instead of going off into the bedchamber." Hofmannsthal insisted to Strauss that this would be a major mistake in staging and laid out the reasons against it. Wrestling with the stagecraft of astronomical and aviational displacement, the poet observed that "the orchestra takes up their 'earth flight,' meaning a flight through the air, gradually nearing the human sphere—not slipping through the dark interior of the earth." The flight would require time—the time of the duet between the Empress and the Nurse, plus the duration of the orchestral interlude—and they could not simply "sink down" from the upper sphere to lower, suddenly rematerializing from above to below.[53] Hofmannsthal, like Karl and Zita, was attuned to aerodynamics in an age of aviation, and he wanted Strauss to be sure that the fairy-tale scenario respected the dynamics of magical flight.

Hofmannsthal promised to write for Strauss new libretti for lighter works, "not giant burdens [*Riesenlasten*] on your shoulders, as *Die Frau ohne Schatten* must have been, though you carried it up the steepest mountain as if it were play." In fact, *Die Frau ohne Schatten* seemed to have been a greater strain, an uphill Sisyphean burden, for Hofmannsthal himself, who struggled to produce the libretto over the course of years. Now he wrote to Strauss, "I hope you will have more joy [*Freude*] from this piece than torment [*Qual*] from the inevitable frictions [*Reibungen*]."[54] Again, it was more likely to be Hofmannsthal himself—like the Composer from the prologue of *Ariadne*—who painfully experienced the torments and frictions of real performances before real publics.

On Tuesday, September 30, ten days before the premiere, Hofmannsthal was still at Aussee, but now his return to Vienna was imminent: "PS Sunday morning I will be in Vienna Stallburggasse 2." He had acquired an apartment there during the war, in a building where Maria Jeritza, rehearsing as the Empress, also kept an apartment.[55] It was in the inner city, roughly between St. Stephen's and the opera house, and around the corner from the Kapuzinergruft, the imperial crypt of the Habsburg emperors.

Finale in C Major

Strauss had composed the opera's finale back in July 1916: "I now have the whole conclusion of the opera (the quartet and the choruses); it has thrust and great upward sweep; but my wife finds it cold." Working in the middle of the war, four months before Franz Joseph was put to rest in the Kapuzinergruft, Strauss was ready to resolve that *Die Frau ohne Schatten* was to be the "last Romantic opera."[56] By the time of the premiere in 1919, the celebratory final quartet could have been a *Te Deum* to inaugurate a counterfactual postwar era, the historical outcome that never actually occurred: the Emperor and the Empress enthroned in triumphant glory, joined in sentimental solidarity with their happy subjects.

The enthronement of the finale is almost an apotheosis, with the Emperor and Empress appearing at the summit of a steep landscape, just above a golden waterfall as the flutes, oboes, and clarinets sound a spacious B-major phrase of half-notes.[57] Barak and his wife meet each other down below, crossing a magically conjured golden bridge that spans the abyss that separated them. The key shifts to C major and the trumpets and trombones issue a heralding summons *fortissimo*, while the triangle, glockenspiel, celestas, and harps sustain the magic of the moment. The orchestra reaches a climax and then stops dead so that the time can shift to the compound meter of 6/4 and Barak can initiate the final quartet with an energetic melody of celebration—"nun will ich jubeln" (now I want to rejoice)—receiving its pulse from the trumpets and trombones hitting all six of the quarter notes in each bar. The passage was marked fiery (*feurig*), perhaps because Strauss, back in 1916, feared that the conclusion would seem cold—especially in comparison to the *Rosenkavalier* trio.[58]

Strauss fully realized the inevitable difference: the *Rosenkavalier* trio is dominated by the glamorously nostalgic renunciation of the Marschallin, while the quartet of *Die Frau ohne Schatten* looks forward joyously to a future of marriage and procreation, happy subjects and enlightened rulers. The Marschallin's ethereally extended opening lines of the trio could not have been further in spirit from Barak's earthily happy tune, pulsing with sexual energy as he concludes, "Ich zerschwelle mit heiliger Kraft" (I am bursting with holy strength). He is ready to jump into bed and make babies. The

Emperor, however, takes up the second part in the quartet in a very different spirit, for though he too is now eligible for fatherhood, he is also interested in his paternal relation to his subjects. He tenderly looks down upon Barak and his wife, then "further down upon the human world," and is moved by the music of humanity. In the spirit of Beethoven's "Ode to Joy" he greets his human subjects as "brothers, companions!" (*Brüder, Vertraute!*) The solo violin accompanies him with delicate triplets: he offers a set of gently swelling phrases that take him up to high G and then back down to rest on C as the Empress and the Dyer's Wife enter the quartet together on G.[59]

Their first words, "Schatten zu werfen"—to cast shadows—show that they are in perfect accord, beginning in unison, then harmonizing (with the Empress a third above) and singing a spacious melody of half and whole notes. There is even a spirit of bel canto as they celebrate together having passed through their trials—"both steeled by trial of fire"—expressed in an elegant run of notes, sung together along with the oboes and ornamented by harps.[60] The serenity of the women, now ready for motherhood, easily harmonizes with the tender beneficence of the tenor Emperor, and it is left to Barak, in his masculine baritone, to recall the quartet to its energetic opening: "Nun will ich jubeln," accompanied by pulsing horns and trumpets.[61] Now, as all four parts harmonize, the quartet recalls again the celebratory quality of the quartet in the "Ode to Joy." Here, however, it is not an affirmation of revolutionary solidarity in which all men are brothers but rather a

Figure 28. The four principal characters harmonize in the final quartet, Barak returning to his opening sally, "Nun will ich jubeln" (now I want to rejoice), while the two women also rejoice that they have both been chosen to cast shadows (*Schatten zu werfen, beide erwählt*), the Empress singing at the top of the staff. The concluding C-major quartet also recalls the quartet of Beethoven's "Ode to Joy" in the finale of the Ninth Symphony. (*Die Frau ohne Schatten*, 1919)

celebration of the political and social order with the Emperor and Empress on high in harmony with their subjects down below.

As the quartet builds to a climax, the Dyer's Wife sings the word "Mütter" (mothers) across ten bars, rising from D-flat to high A-flat and descending again. The four soloists are joined by the chorus of unborn children, who now echo the Emperor, singing "Brüder, Vertraute!" The two sopranos conclude the quartet on unison high Cs, joined by the Emperor, with Barak taking a lower C and the unborn children striking a C-major chord *fortississimo* (*fff*).[62]

The horns and cellos almost waltz in 6/4 time as the orchestra swells "mit grossem Schwung" (with great vigor). The woodwinds and strings sound the octave leap that signals the Empress's sublime presence. The trumpets and violas offer an ornamented ascent, heralding the return of the choral voices of the unborn children, accompanied by organ, glass harmonica, harps, and celestas. The orchestra has calmed itself now—"allmählich ruhiger" (gradually more peaceful)—with the harps, the celestas, and the glass harmonica all participating in the final *pianissimo* C-major chord as the curtain falls.[63]

The conclusion is fully affirmative, for Strauss and Hofmannsthal, working on the third act during the war, imagined that they would be presenting their opera in the context of victory, peace, and a renewed popular appreciation of emperors and empresses. This was a fairy-tale world in which imperial rulers looked down upon their human empires from perches high above golden waterfalls, not the real postwar world in which emperors and empresses took trains into exile in Switzerland. The premiere in Vienna took place on October 10, 1919. One year earlier, Karl and Zita were reigning over the Habsburg monarchy, as Karl's ancestors had done for centuries. By the time the opera was actually performed the imperial past was already being reconceived in the fairy-tale spirit of long ago and far away.

14

Premiere 1919

DIE FRAU OHNE SCHATTEN, THE MÄRCHENKAISER, AND THE VIENNESE CRITICS

Die Neue Freie Presse: *"Overburdened with Meaning"*

The premiere of *Die Frau ohne Schatten* took place on Friday, October 10, 1919, and the next day the *Neue Freie Presse* published a long review essay by Julius Korngold, beginning below the fold on the front page, and continuing below the fold for the first four pages of the edition. Critical of Hofmannsthal's libretto, Korngold felt that *Die Frau ohne Schatten* was a fairy tale "overburdened with meaning"—with "not always comprehensible meaning." Hofmannsthal had been nervous in advance that the public would not know how to understand a simple fairy tale, and Korngold now immediately indicted the libretto for its incomprehensibility. It was, Korngold suggested, a matter of Hofmannsthal's poetic preciousness: "the sensitive and sympathetic poet's soul vibrates like Venetian glass at every poetic tone of world literature."[1] Hofmannsthal, who had spent twenty years seeking to transcend the reputation for aesthetic oversensitivity that attended his precocious youth in the 1890s, could still be caricatured even in the grim aftermath of World War I.

At the top of the front page, juxtaposed with the beginning of the review, were the comments of Chancellor Karl Renner: "I believe that this winter we will reach the lowest point of our poverty, the lowest point of our helplessness. There are still terrible things that lie before us." The front page also noted that in Paris the leaders at the peace conference were calling for a blockade of Soviet Russia, inasmuch as its "widespread program for international revolution creates a serious danger for every country's national security." The newspaper reported further on Woodrow Wilson, once the great hope of postwar Europe, who had just suffered an incapacitating stroke on October 2 in the course of his passionate but hopeless American campaign on behalf of the Treaty of Versailles and the League of Nations.[2] It was in this disturbing context—on the very same front page—that Korngold reviewed *Die Frau ohne Schatten* as a fairy-tale opera.

Korngold recognized the relation of the new opera to *Die Zauberflöte*, comparing the "spirit power" of Keikobad to that of Sarastro and the Queen of the Night.[3] In fact, by coincidence, *Die Zauberflöte* was actually being performed at the Vienna Volksoper on the evening of October 10, at the same time as the premiere of *Die Frau ohne Schatten*. Strauss's opera began at 5 p.m. and Mozart's at 6 p.m., so the rejoicing finales might have roughly coincided.[4] "And why shouldn't Richard Strauss have wanted to write his own *Die Zauberflöte*?" asked Korngold rhetorically, ironically.[5]

Korngold had already had his reservations about *Der Rosenkavalier* in 1911, had been opposed to Strauss's directorship of the Vienna Opera in 1919, and probably saw *Die Frau ohne Schatten* as a competitive work with his own son Erich's imminent new opera *Die tote Stadt*.[6] The critic gently mocked *Die Frau ohne Schatten* as a consumer product—"outfitted with every musical dramatic comfort of the modern age." Yet, at the same time, Korngold really doubted that the opera was particularly modern, noting "an expedient [*zweckdienlich*] unmodern inclination toward diatonic, symmetrical, almost popular folk rhythms, even downright amiable song melodies, and tonal and vocal harmony."[7] Arthur Schnitzler, who attended the dress rehearsal, noted in his diary that the music was "brilliant, melodious, with a tendency to banality."[8]

Korngold conceded that Strauss had wrested (*abgerungen*) much beauty from the flawed book—"never before has Strauss brought such energy, such intensity to his artistic work"—but the opera was simply too long:

> For example: one counts eight orchestral interludes that became necessary for the excess [*Übermass*] of scene changes. They have a retarding effect; the opera is stretched out [*dehnt sich*]. This overabundance [*Überfülle*]

discourages also any attempt to seek out and go into the striking details of the score.⁹

Korngold further pointed out that just as the characters had to undergo their trials, in the spirit of *Die Zauberflöte*, so the score offered a series of trials for the leading singers, not least the challenge of rising above the Straussian orchestra.¹⁰

Korngold admired the Empress's opening scene of awakening, which was accompanied by the lighter orchestration of the upper sphere: "The first aria of the Empress shimmers in delightful beauty, pervaded by a tenderly intimate fairy-tale tone [*zart-heimlichen Märchenton*], then completely colored in the most individual way by the clipped sobbing C-sharp cry of the falcon." The Empress was for Korngold the figure for whom the fairy-tale opera seemed most suitable, and he also admired Jeritza's imperial qualities, the "nobility" of her performance, the "splendor" of her voice.¹¹ The falcon, who brought word in the opening scene of the Emperor's imminent petrification, must also have been sung with admirable nobility: the Hungarian soprano Felicie Hüni-Mihacsek, creating this small role at an early stage of her career, was later celebrated as the Queen of the Night, the Countess Almaviva, and the Marschallin.

Jeritza, in her memoirs, particularly appreciated her own aria in the first scene: "a good deal of coloratura work . . . an exquisite melodic bit." She also remembered her costume: "I wore a beautiful gold-studded Persian robe, with my hair trailing to the ground."¹² That trailing hair was a famous attribute of Empress Elisabeth, known for her extremely long and beautiful dark hair. It was natural for Jeritza to feel—as Hofmannsthal did—that the Empress was the central character in the opera. She claimed that Strauss had originally written the role of the Dyer's Wife for her and then shifted her to the role of the Empress, because nobody else was imaginable. "You simply will have to sing the Empress," he told her. "You must do it to please me." She claimed she would have sung both roles—"if a singer could possibly have sung two roles at once."¹³

For Hofmannsthal himself Jeritza made a striking impression at the premiere, as he wrote in a letter to Princess Marie von Thurn und Taxis. Hofmannsthal praised the "tender silver gleam of the orchestra," the beauty of

Figure 29. Maria Jeritza, costumed as the Empress, wore her hair all the way down her back, according to Roller's design, in the style of Empress Elisabeth. Here Jeritza appears in the nightgown (with a plunging neckline) that Roller conceived for her awakening in the first scene. Jeritza was one of the most glamorous as well as vocally brilliant performers of the age, and the Czech soprano was closely associated with the operas of Strauss and Hofmannsthal, creating the roles of Ariadne and the Empress. Supposedly discovered by Emperor Franz Joseph while singing in *Die Fledermaus* at the spa town of Bad Ischl, she had a great career in Vienna but also at the Metropolitan Opera in New York. (Reproduced with the kind permission of the KHM-Museumsverband, Theatermuseum Vienna)

the staging ("you absolutely must see this production"), and the magical appearance of the phantom youth from afar. The poet's deepest appreciation, however, was reserved for "the wonderful gestures of Jeritza on the steps of the temple or her standing alone with the murmuring, almost speaking, golden water inside the temple."[14] Her gestures and her presence, as much as her voice, portrayed the Empress for Hofmannsthal as he had always lovingly imagined her.

For Korngold, however, the heart of the opera lay in the figure of Barak, for it was only with Barak that "the heart opens up, a good sentimental German heart." With Barak the music became "vigorous to the point of overflowing [*Überschwung*]"—again the note of excess—Strauss composing in the early nineteenth-century Romantic style of Mendelssohn. The music of the three night watchmen was also in this spirit, very moving for Korngold with its soft trombones and A-flat harmony, creating the musical mood for the conclusion of the first act. Korngold found the role of Barak well suited to Richard Mayr's "gentle bass, his simplicity, and his warmth of heart," and suggested that Mayr "brought out the Austrian, the Viennese, from the Oriental character."[15] In an age of social class polarization, the age of the Bolshevik Revolution, Barak was perhaps the sort of poor but good-hearted Viennese proletarian who could still be cherished by bourgeois Viennese operagoers—and critics.

Lehmann, in Korngold's view, domesticated the role of the Dyer's Wife by making her into a little madcap creature (*Tollköpfchen*): "Her unlovableness [*Unliebenswürdigkeit*] received a housewifely pouting tone, that made her almost lovable." Korngold claimed to discern in the Dyer's Wife symptoms of "hysteria"—a diagnosis which had become increasingly complex in Vienna during the previous two decades as Freud placed cases of hysteria at the center of his discovery and formulation of psychoanalysis. Leaving glamour to Jeritza as the Empress, Lehmann, along with Mayr, managed to make their troubled working-class marriage into something that could win the sympathy of elite Viennese operagoers. Oestvig as the Emperor obtained less sympathy, with Korngold noting "something of the petrified about him from the beginning."[16]

Korngold had no doubt that there was supposed to be a portentous message written into the scenario of the fairy-tale opera, and he observed that the unborn children were given the last word in the opera.

Figure 30. Creating the role of the Dyer's Wife as costumed by Roller, Lotte Lehmann wore a sort of sarong, with its colored pattern perhaps showing off the Dyer's craft while suggesting the "Empire of the Southeastern Islands." Lehmann made a great success of the difficult role of the Dyer's Wife, moody and dissatisfied, deeply ambivalent about childbirth and motherhood until she was reconciled with her husband in the third act. It was her shadow that the Empress coveted and the Nurse attempted to obtain. Lehmann, who created the role of the Composer in *Ariadne auf Naxos* for Strauss and Hofmannsthal in 1916, would also become a famous Marschallin in *Der Rosenkavalier*, in both Vienna and New York. She died in California in 1976. (Tully Potter/Bridgeman Images)

Salvation through pity, salvation for true marriage, salvation for humanity by means of the child—one can make one's choice. There is advocacy for motherhood and reproduction, the guardianship for unborn children, a gynecological argument, so to speak, that no longer makes sense at a time when a mother's love for her born children is seen as a moral issue, but not the desire for motherhood in itself. Thus, in *Die Frau ohne Schatten* the naive self-evident comprehensibility of a fairy tale is lost.[17]

Korngold recognized that Hofmannsthal's fairy tale was partly intended as a contemporary social and political statement about motherhood, in fact a conservative statement. Women were fully emancipated as citizens in the new postwar Austrian republic, voting for the first time in 1919. For Hofmannsthal, however, in *Die Frau ohne Schatten*, women were very much, as Korngold suggested, gynecologically defined, and the desire for motherhood was indeed a moral issue: the Empress was humanized by her desire for motherhood, while the Dyer's Wife was unhappily alienated from herself by her readiness to surrender her fertility.

For Korngold, *Die Frau ohne Schatten* was driven by its stage effects, and, as he quoted the Nurse—"Higher powers are in play!"—he wrote sarcastically, "The higher powers above all: the scene painter, the stage technician, the lighting director." Yet the staging was also reviewed as a point of Viennese pride: "No other opera stage in the world could accomplish something like this." Roller's sets were praised for the simplicity of their stylization but some were "so ascetically stylized that one seemed to recognize more the hardship of the times."[18] It was one of the few points in the review that intersected with Renner's reported speech on the anticipated hardship of the imminent winter. In another review, written by musicologist Egon Wellesz for *Der Neue Tag*, the set for Barak's dwelling was described as "built into a dilapidated palace." The conception of poor people living in the ruins of a former palace was particularly striking for Vienna in the postimperial moment of 1919.[19] Hofmannsthal's daughter Christiane was at the premiere and thought the opera was "fabulously beautiful, the stage designs wonderful, especially the Dyer's house." She had been unsure whether "the dumb people would applaud" (an anxiety perhaps transmitted by her father) and was pleased by the enthusiastic reception. Still, she regretted that people were not able to enjoy things simply because they were beautiful: "they want symbols and interpretations."[20] Korngold, however, blamed Hofmannsthal himself for having created a libretto "overburdened with meaning."

Korngold's predecessor as music reviewer at the *Neue Freie Presse* was Eduard Hanslick, who had been famously critical of Wagner. Strauss now declared that "if he [Korngold] really wants to play Hanslick, it can only be the greatest honor for me to be scolded [*hinaufgeschimpft*] as the Richard Wagner of 1919."[21] Yet Korngold faithfully reported that there were repeated ovations for Strauss at the conclusion of the *Die Frau ohne Schatten*. In a final conceit Korngold suggested that the Straussian melodies were like the children in the opera, only waiting to be born, that melody itself had a therapeutic role to play in the contemporary world. The opera, thus, had a "healing" (*heilsam*) effect, bringing melody into the postwar world, and the fertile Strauss, according to Korngold, was determined not to become "a composer without a shadow."[22]

Arbeiter-Zeitung: "Morality in the Highest Sense"

The social democratic newspaper, the *Arbeiter-Zeitung*, gave the opera just a brief notice on page 7 in the edition of October 11. The author was identified as D. B., signifying David Josef Bach, the principal music reviewer of the newspaper since 1904, a close friend of Arnold Schoenberg, and a dedicated socialist who now emerged as a powerful cultural figure in Red Vienna with its social democratic municipal government.[23] Bach, in his notice, claimed to find that *Die Frau ohne Schatten* was musically similar to *Der Rosenkavalier*—but offering "thanks to the poetry, a more strongly emphasized ethos, that is, morality [*Sittlichkeit*] in the highest sense."[24] The moral values of humanity that the Empress learned in the lower world of urban proletarians was meaningful for the *Arbeiter-Zeitung*.

Bach felt that the response of the public was mixed, and he observed some tension between the enthusiastic younger members of the audience and the more conventionally elite operagoers in the boxes, "the people who absolutely must be present at a premiere." Noting that prices were raised for the premiere, Bach declared, on behalf of the working-class newspaper, that "we have no objection to making such people pay higher prices, though the price increase was not evenly applied."[25] For the *Arbeiter-Zeitung*, the prices of the tickets offered a lesson in socioeconomic class relations, while the contested appreciation of the opera suggested a tension between the *ancien régime* of operagoers at the former Hofoper and a new generation that represented the public of the future, applauding a new opera in the context of a new social and political order.

Bach's notice appeared in the left column of page 7 of the *Arbeiter-Zeitung*. Facing it at the top of the right column was an advertisement for a Viennese dyer: "Färberei Schnek"—which was probably a typo for "Färberei Schenk."[26] The business of the dyer was still part of the economic life of postwar Vienna, and the Schnek-Schenk operation was busy enough to have two branches, one centrally located on Kleebattgasse, in the First District, close to the Graben and St. Stephen's, and another on Raffaelgasse in the Twentieth District, on the other side of the Danube Canal, where one might have found Jewish craft businesses like Leiser Erber's leather shop on the Rauscherstraße, also in the Twentieth District. Leather could, of course, be dyed, so it was not impossible that my great-grandfather had some connection with the Schnek-Schenk business.

Though the Färberei topped the page, the advertisements below were all focused on a very different sort of business: jewelry. At this moment of postwar hardship, with winter approaching, these firms were not selling jewelry—but buying it, from people who could no longer sustain themselves economically. "Persons who are now selling their jewels and pearls will be astonished by the high prices they receive at the Politzer business, Augustinerstraße 12." The "Better" Jeweler and Watchmaker at Mariahilferstraße 98 sought diamonds, pearls, gold, silver, platinum, watches, corals, garnets, coins, and even teeth, while the Guttmann jewelry business on the Graben in the Trattnerhof (where Mozart once lived) promised the highest price for diamonds, large and small.[27] The Viennese elite in their boxes at the opera premiere were possibly appearing without some of the prized jewelry they would have worn before the war.

Bach's single-paragraph notice concluded by observing that the opera required "more detailed examination," and, in fact, by the next day, October 12, he had prepared a full review for the *Arbeiter-Zeitung*. While Korngold in the *Neue Freie Presse*—the great organ of the Viennese bourgeoisie—was full of reservations about the opera, Bach in the *Arbeiter-Zeitung* one day later offered a generally favorable review, embracing both Strauss and Hofmannsthal. Born into a Galician Jewish family in Lviv in 1874, exactly the same age as Hofmannsthal, Bach came to Vienna to study at the university. Committed as he was throughout his career (which concluded in England after 1939) to classical music for the working classes, he can hardly have thought that the masses were going to show up at the opera for *Die Frau ohne Schatten*, but he was mindful of the importance of the fairy-tale element as having a possibly popular appeal. The socialist *Arbeiter-Zeitung* was not sympathetic to the Habsburgs, but Bach was careful to emphasize that the opera was about a fairy-tale empire: "the fairy daughter who as empress lives alongside the fairy-tale emperor [*Märchenkaiser*]."[28] The word "Märchenkaiser" was particularly meaningful at a moment when emperors and empresses were largely relieved of their political places.

Barak was the central figure for a workers' newspaper, and Bach reported on Mayr's performance as something "real" rather than something out of a fairy tale: "he is really, really, and truly (*wirklich, wirklich und wahrhaftig*) the bearer of the destiny that threatens to crush the simple and lowly man, but elevates him on account of his good heart." This observation appeared below the fold, while, above, the newspaper elaborated upon the shortages of meat, sugar, and flour facing the people of Vienna. For Bach, as for Korngold, the production of the opera in its every aspect was a point of Viennese pride: "that it might be possible to put on a better production in any other opera house in the world," declared Bach, "is unthinkable."[29] Having grown up in Lviv, in eastern Galicia, he embraced Viennese metropolitan pride with adoptive enthusiasm, perhaps all the more so when the imperial capital had been shorn of its former provinces, including Galicia.

For Bach the importance of the Viennese working man went beyond the performance of Mayr as Barak on stage. Viennese pride extended to all the Viennese working men who labored behind the scenes. "But this time we must not forget the humble people, on whose work so much depends," wrote Bach, at the conclusion of his review.

> I mean the stage workers. From this production, people will be able to measure the worth of these men by their accomplishment not according

to their part in the division of labor [*Arbeitseinteilung*]. They helped to realize the sets that Alfred Roller devised.³⁰

Thus even a recognizable element of Marxist terminology—"division of labor"—entered into the opera review in the *Arbeiter-Zeitung*, just as the reality of working-class lives—on stage and behind the scenes—entered into the fairy-tale scenario devised and designed, versified and composed by Roller, Hofmannsthal, and Strauss.

Wiener Abendpost: *"Uncanny"*

October at the opera, for the triad of Roller, Hofmannsthal, and Strauss, began with a performance of *Elektra* on October 2, starring Marie Gutheil-Schoder, who would, later in the month, alternate with Lehmann in the role of the Dyer's Wife. Orestes was sung by bass-baritone Josef von Manowarda, who created the small role of Keikobad's Messenger in the very first scene of *Die Frau ohne Schatten* but would eventually move into the role of Barak in later seasons.³¹ Between performances of the Emperor, Karl Oestvig gave an October recital at the Konzertsaal of songs by Hugo Wolf, Edvard Grieg, and, of course, Richard Strauss. Also at the Konzertsaal in October, in the smaller Mozart-Saal, Karl Kraus was reading from his fierce satirical drama about the war, *The Last Days of Mankind*, and architect Adolf Loos gave a series of lectures on modern design.³² On October 9, the night before *Die Frau ohne Schatten* premiered, the first Viennese performance of Stefan Zweig's pacifist drama *Jeremiah* (originally performed in Zurich in 1917) took place at the Volkstheater.³³

The *Wiener Abendpost* was the evening edition of the *Wiener Zeitung*, which had been founded as the *Wienerisches Diarium* in 1703, and was closely associated with the Viennese court, functioning as a semiofficial government newspaper up until the end of the monarchy.³⁴ The review of *Die Frau ohne Schatten* appeared in the October 11 evening edition, that is the *Wiener Abendpost*, and the reviewer was the thirty-two-year-old Heinrich Kralik, a member of the Habsburg nobility born Heinrich Ritter Kralik von Meyrswalden; he would become one of the most important music critics in interwar Austria.[35] At the time of the Habsburg Law of April 3, 1919, titles of nobility were abolished in the new Austrian republic, so Kralik wrote his review simply as Heinrich Kralik, just as Hugo von Hofmannsthal appeared on the program for *Die Frau ohne Schatten* as simply Hugo Hofmannsthal. Kralik's father Richard, a religiously inspired Roman Catholic writer, founder of the journal *Der Gral* (*The Grail*), worked with Hofmannsthal on the Austrian Library publishing project during the war.

Heinrich Kralik, reviewing the opera, focused on the moral judgment of the Emperor and the Empress—"too proud and too far from earth"—and therefore incurring a guilt that they must expiate "through soul purification in the school of hard trials stipulated by the spirit world."[36] Kralik's reading of the story, as recounted in what had once been the official journal of the Habsburg court, could have been interpreted as a veiled commentary on the fate of emperors and empresses in the contemporary world, six months after Karl and Zita went into exile.

Kralik was full of praise for the dramatic and musical success of Jeritza and Lehmann as the Empress and the Dyer's Wife, but he could barely conceal his evidently greater fascination with the character of the Nurse, "a witch of Mephistophelean character." He was struck by the fact that while she desired only evil—to steal the shadow by cunning deceit—the Nurse ultimately brought about everyone's salvation, by bringing the Empress down to the human world where it was possible for her to discover her own humanity. Kralik was overwhelmed by Lucie Weidt's performance—"the artist, equipped with spirit, ideas, and playful terseness, developing the demonic with splendor and without exaggeration, grew almost into the main character, became in any event the strongest role in the piece." For him Barak's "golden heart" seemed less believable than the maleficence of the Nurse which paradoxically produced the happy ending.

Kralik also celebrated the conductor Schalk as "magnificent, unsurpassable" and was fascinated by the orchestral scoring of the opera: "The Straussian orchestra gets it right every time and always with the first blow. No prelude, no introduction. Just an A-flat minor chord, to which the bass instruments chant their muffled *Keikobad!*—and the move into the dark, uncanny, threatening spirit and magic world has been executed."[37] The musical atmosphere of *Die Frau ohne Schatten*, introduced by the bass instruments, and dominated by the demonic nurse, was clearly one that Kralik recognized as both familiar and disturbing, the realm of the spirit king Keikobad, whose presence was darkly declared by the syncopated three-note descent. The "uncanny" (*unheimlich*) effect of the opening bars on the reviewer might be read in the light of Freud's famous essay "The Uncanny," published that same year in 1919, on the particular forms of horror and dread that play upon the human imagination. Freud referenced E. T. A. Hoffmann, the Romantic writer of disturbing fairy tales, mentioned the uncanny doubling effect of the human shadow, and cited the disturbing implications of animism, magic, and witchcraft. All these aspects of the uncanny were psychoanalytically correlated with the anxieties that emerged from the human unconscious.[38] *Die Frau ohne Schatten*, which presented the unsettling proximity of supernatural and ordinary worlds, was calculated to elicit precisely the uncanny effects that Freud was writing about at the very same time.

Neues Wiener Tagblatt: *"Strauss Needs Hofmannsthal"*

"Unheimlich" was also a word that occurred in the long review by the important music critic Ludwig Karpath in the *Neues Wiener Tagblatt*, a journal which had been founded half a century earlier as an organ of Habsburg liberalism at the constitutional moment of the Austro-Hungarian compromise in 1867. Karpath, born in Budapest in 1866, had a career as an opera singer already behind him when he emerged as a major critic. Strauss valued Karpath as a friend and in 1924 dedicated the ballet *Schlagobers* (*Whipped Cream*) to him.[39]

Karpath characterized the score of *Die Frau ohne Schatten* as combining the symphonic dissonance of *Elektra* and the lyrical quality of *Ariadne*, but new for Strauss in its "tremendous and unprecedented polyphony." It was the presence of melodic themes in the inner voices of the polyphonic orchestra, where one might have expected simpler harmonizing, that had an "uncanny" effect for Karpath: "Uncanny [*unheimlich*] is the relocation of the themes to the inner voices."[40] For Karpath, as for Kralik, *Die Frau ohne Schatten* was an opera which made an uncanny and unsettling impression.

Karpath was very explicitly psychoanalytic in his understanding of the collaborative creation of the opera. For the Hungarian-born critic it was a point of Viennese pride that the opera had its premiere in Vienna and also that the librettist was a Viennese poet.

> The fact that Strauss believes in the poetic greatness of Hofmannsthal, follows his suggestions and takes fire from his inspirations, gives one something to think about. And I have thought about it a lot and often. And I have become convinced that the story of Strauss's nature is completed by Hofmannsthal. Strauss needs Hofmannsthal. The latter prepares the colors, as the former desires them for his palette. For that reason we always have to consider the connection here. A psychoanalysis of Strauss's deepest essence, not in the clinical sense, but seen through his expressive temperament . . . would lead to the conclusion that the poetic subjects that Hofmannsthal hands over to Strauss, as composer, engage with the true nature of Strauss, who thus becomes intuitive, thus finds the tonal expression for sleeping [*schlummernde*] feelings and ideas.[41]

This psychoanalytic reading of the relation between composer and librettist suggested that Hofmannsthal understood how to appeal to the "sleeping" unconscious materials that Strauss had to discover in himself as he exercised his creative genius.

Karpath recognized that Hofmannsthal's writing was "controversial" for some, considered sometimes "confusing" and "knotted," but these were the same qualities that supposedly inspired Strauss to explore his own psychoanalytic depths.

> He is provoked by the manifold entanglements, the apparent mental leaps, the always somewhat symbolically inspired solutions in Hofmannsthal's poetic works, that would be designated in musical terminology as dissonance-rich creations. Between Strauss and Hofmannsthal there exists an elective affinity [*Wahlverwandtschaft*] that flows not from arbitrariness but from an identity of nature. They both attract each other magnetically. The poet creates consciously that which struggles for release in the unconscious of the composer.[42]

From the uncanny to the unconscious, Karpath proposed a conception of the Strauss-Hofmannsthal collaboration that was fully consistent with the dynamics of psychoanalysis as formulated in Freud's Vienna.

Karpath noted that the production of the opera was a long-awaited event, because "for more than two years it was lying completed in the writing desk of the master," waiting for the end of the war. Writing in the aftermath of the recent treaty of Saint-Germain, Karpath observed that "peace has been proclaimed," but the new peace "weighs upon us": it was as if the opera were being presented "to test the peace after the immeasurably enormous world events."[43] The slaughter of the war had given way to the misery of the postwar period, and the disturbing and uncanny aspects of the opera mirrored the anxious aspects of a peace that had been proclaimed but not achieved.

Karpath praised "the heavenly [*sphärenhaften*] final quartet," which "created for the public a rare feast for the ears [*Ohrenschmaus*]."[44] The metaphorical feast at a moment of hunger and privation in Vienna emphasized the alternative reality of the opera production. Strauss and Hofmannsthal had intended the premiere to take place in a happier peacetime, in an alternative historical reality that did not include the ignominious and humiliating defeat of Germany and Austria.

Above the fold from Karpath's review, the *Neues Wiener Tagblatt* published an open letter to French Prime Minister Clemenceau from the Austrian Society for the League of Nations.

> In the note by which you transmitted the final peace terms to the Austrian delegation at Saint-Germain, the allied and associated governments work from the assumption that the Austrian people are also responsible for the war that was waged by their government. We regret deeply together with the representatives of all other civilized peoples that through the confluence of unfortunate circumstances and forces not susceptible to our influence it became possible to unleash the war that we saw with horror raging for four years in almost all countries and parts of the world. All the more do we lodge a solemn protest against the quite undemonstrated assertion that the Austrian people participated in the war with enthusiasm from beginning to end.[45]

The open letter strongly opposed holding "the people" (*das Volk*) responsible for the war, and observed that "the sufferings that innocent people have now borne for five years should not be thereby magnified."[46] The Viennese newspaper spoke particularly for the people of Vienna.

Strauss, according to Karpath, had bestowed his new opera on Vienna as an "act of love for this hard hit, severely pressed city"—a bridegroom's gift (*Morgengabe*), an offering from the "future artistic generalissimo of the opera theater." Strauss's leadership at the Vienna Opera was conceived in military and marital terms; he was both generalissimo and bridegroom.

> For there can be no doubt about it: the location where a new creation by Richard Strauss is heard for the first time attracts the interest of the whole world. If we lived in a true peace instead of a merely apparent peace, we would now be able to welcome music scholars, theater directors, and friends of art from all over the world, as formerly in Dresden where most of Strauss's works were baptized. But even if this is not possible, the musical circles in Germany, in Paris, London, Rome, and New York will listen up today, waiting impatiently for the report that, even indirectly, will now fly out over the whole world about the first performance of the new opera.[47]

Vienna had been the capital of a vast multinational empire up until 1918, one of Europe's great powers, and arguably the musical capital of Europe with a tradition that looked back to the presence of Haydn, Mozart, and Beethoven. Austria-Hungary had a population of fifty million in 1914, while the new republic of Austria had a population of six and a half million people in 1918. The city's major musical critics—including Julius Korngold born in Brno, Moravia, David Bach born in Lviv, Galicia, Ludwig Karpath born in Budapest, Hungary—demonstrated the extent to which the city's musical life was created by men from places that were now politically separated from the new Austrian republic.

Yet the premiere of *Die Frau ohne Schatten* offered some compensation for the collapse of empire by nostalgically refurbishing the former prestige of the imperial capital. Karpath noted that the production, designed by Mahler's former collaborator Roller, "reminds one of the glorious days of Gustav Mahler," the age of the imperial court opera. Karpath also mentioned by name the concertmaster violinist Arnold Rosé, who played the solo violin line that magically accompanied the Empress's vocal part; he had played with the orchestra since he was eighteen in 1881, under Emperor Franz Joseph and Empress Elisabeth.[48] Rosé was married to Mahler's sister Justine.

Karpath singled out Jeritza and Oestvig as especially credible in their fairy-tale roles: "Frau Jeritza the Empress and Herr Oestvig the Emperor, already believable by their external appearances, both overflowing with graceful youth and vocally excellent, constitute an ornament of the conception."[49] They were precisely believable as a young emperor and empress, as if, in 1919, those offices had already become a matter of theatrical representation. Jeritza was just five years older than Zita, and Oestvig two years younger than Karl, as the singers now represented to Vienna the ornamental conception of imperial sovereigns.

Karpath described the ovations that greeted Strauss himself following the opera, though there was no mention of Hofmannsthal taking a bow. Taking a cue from Barak's opening line in the final quartet—"nun will ich jubeln" (now I want to rejoice)—Karpath remarked that "this public now gave the opera a rejoicing [*jubelnde*] reception."[50] The Viennese public also implicitly celebrated Vienna itself as it regained some of its cultural prestige with *Die Frau ohne Schatten*.

Prague-born critic Richard Batka, writing in the *Wiener Allgemeine Zeitung*, emphasized Viennese pride at a time of postwar hardship: "There must be an invincible strength in the Austrian, in the Viennese character [*im Wienertum*]. Devastated in the most terrible of wars, mutilated, robbed of its former riches, hungering, freezing, going blind, this city can still make music [*musizieren*] like no other city."[51] *Die Frau ohne Schatten* represented a triumph of the Viennese spirit in defiance of military defeat and economic disaster.

Karl and Zita on the Ringstraße

The Roller premiere production received thirty-nine performances over the course of the next decade—until a new production by Lothar Wallerstein was introduced in 1931. Strauss was disappointed in the 1919 production, feeling that Roller was too restrained in presenting the spectacular and magical aspects of the production. "The music alone cannot do everything," commented Strauss later. "Unless one just writes an oratorio and renounces completely the stage setting!"[52] Hofmannsthal—who had been Roller's great advocate beforehand—later agreed that the designer had failed at producing the magical effects, had little feeling for the fantastic.[53] Strauss was even more unhappy with the Dresden premiere which quickly followed on October 22, noting that "it was a serious blunder to entrust this opera, difficult as it was to cast and produce, to medium and even small theaters immediately after the war."[54]

Roller himself distinguished *Die Frau ohne Schatten* from *Der Rosenkavalier* as a "Machine Comedy" rather than a "Room Comedy," but worried that Vienna had inadequate command of stage machinery to produce the supernatural effects required by the libretto. While Kautsky in Berlin proposed to make the Empress and the Nurse appear to be in flight, as they descended to the city in the first act, Roller avoided such stage tricks partly out of economic necessity and preferred to make use of lighting effects "which I can control myself." He recognized, however, that such effects might have a lesser impact on the audience.[55]

With the year coming to an end in December 1919, Hofmannsthal, in a letter to his friend Rudolf Pannwitz, declared himself satisfied with his collaboration with Strauss:

> I am very clear about the fact that I have staked a lot on this collaboration—above all, my prestige . . . but it is also clear to me what I might win. These things conceived for the theater now stand really there, much of the poetry is here and there clouded over, he has not always understood me, here and there he has coarsened the delicacy, ignored the spiritual, diminished the wit—but he has also given much: so many places are so beautiful and right and forever there . . . and above all the characters are there: the Marschallin and Octavian, Ariadne and Zerbinetta, and the five characters of *Die Frau ohne Schatten*—these all have an actual life, at least for one or two generations, maybe three, that is a great gain for me.[56]

The characters might be remembered for one, two, or three generations, but even for Hofmannsthal the five principal characters of *Die Frau ohne Schatten* had no names. The Emperor and the Empress would allegorically represent all emperors and empresses to future generations.

The Ringstraße, the great avenue that encircles the old city of Vienna, had been developed in the late nineteenth century in the space where the city walls once stood, and there were different names for the different segments.

The stretch of the Ringstraße that runs from the opera house to the Schwarzenbergplatz was given the name of the Kärntner-Ring in the nineteenth century, intersecting the Kärntnerstraße. On the other side of the opera house, the stretch of the Ringstraße that extended to the Volksgarten was called simply the Opern-Ring. They are still called the Kärntner-Ring and the Opern-Ring today. Yet in 1917, they were, for a brief period, renamed as the Kaiserin-Zita-Ring and the Kaiser-Karl-Ring respectively, and then on November 6, 1919, roughly a month after the premiere of *Die Frau ohne Schatten*, Zita's and Karl's names were removed from the Ringstraße, and those stretches became the Kärntner-Ring and the Opern-Ring once again and ever after.[57] The renaming was cited as "the obliteration of Byzantinism" in the *Arbeiter-Zeitung*, firmly committed to the new republic.[58] The names of the Emperor and the Empress were erased from the map of the city in which they had briefly reigned.

Five days later, on November 11, the Austrian republic reached the anniversary of the armistice that ended the war—also the anniversary of the day on which Emperor Karl withdrew from politics without actually abdicating. The name changes on the Ringstraße were likely timed to this anniversary. On the evening of November 11, *Die Frau ohne Schatten*, featuring an unnamed emperor and empress, was performed at the opera house—no longer situated between the Kaiser-Karl-Ring and the Kaiserin-Zita-Ring.

15

Imperial Afterlife

THE POLITICS OF HUNGARIAN HABSBURG RESTORATION AND AUSTRIAN OPERATIC REPERTORY

Varieties of Afterlives

In 1874, the year of Hofmannsthal's birth, during the reign of Franz Joseph and Elisabeth, a competition was held in Vienna for an imposing bronze monument to commemorate Empress Maria Theresa, almost a hundred years after her death. The completed work, showing the crowned and enthroned Empress, attended by a crowd of female allegorical virtues and male historical ministers, unveiled in 1888, still stands in front of the Kunsthistorisches Museum.[1] It served as a site of patriotic commemoration for Austria-Hungary while solidifying (in bronze) the historic afterlife of the most important Habsburg empress. Hofmannsthal himself would attend to her legend, notably in his patriotic wartime essay for the bicentennial of her birth in 1917. At that moment Zita was the living Empress, attempting to play her own role in the fostering of wartime Austrian patriotism.

Empress Elisabeth, in the aftermath of her 1898 assassination, became a figure of legendary martyrdom, with diverse associations that touched upon her glamorous beauty, her artistic temperament, and her wandering inclinations. She was the dead wife of the reigning Emperor Franz Joseph. Her ghost haunted the final period of Franz Joseph's reign, and her image remains omnipresent in Vienna even today. While she still lived and reigned in the 1860s, Franz Joseph's brother Maximilian had participated in an ill-fated transatlantic adventure, becoming briefly the Emperor of Mexico, until he was executed in 1867 by a firing squad of Mexican soldiers fighting under republican leader Benito Juárez. Maximilian was married to the daughter of the king of Belgium, Princess Charlotte, who reigned briefly alongside Maximilian as Empress Carlota of Mexico but then returned to Europe, had a mental breakdown, and lived for sixty years after her husband's death, dying after a very long imperial afterlife in Belgium in 1927.

The Mexican adventure of Maximilian and Carlota was keenly supported by French Emperor Napoléon III and his Spanish wife, Empress Eugénie, both dethroned when the Franco-Prussian war brought about the advent of the French Third Republic in 1870. Napoléon III died three years later, but Eugénie survived her husband by almost fifty years, mostly in England, living long enough to lend her support to British and French military hospitals during World War I. Following her death in 1920, the afterlife of this Empress continued in fashion, with the tilted and feathered "Eugénie hat," and in outer space with the "45 Eugenia" asteroid that was named for her during her reign. The afterlife of an empress could take the form of legend, as in the case of Elisabeth, or of actual widowed survival, as in the cases of Carlota and Eugénie. Zita would outlive Karl by sixty-seven years and die in Switzerland in 1989. Twenty years after her death, the Roman Catholic Church began to consider the possibility of her beatification and canonization as a saint.

Sainthood creates a uniquely religious form of afterlife, involving altars, images, miracles, and prayers for intercession, and there have not been many worldly empresses who have attained that status. Fundamental for the Roman Catholic Church is Empress Helena, the mother of Emperor Constantine, the Roman Emperor who converted to Christianity in 312 AD. Helena traveled to Jerusalem in 326 to search for the wooden cross on which Christ was crucified three centuries earlier. She was still formally an empress as she carried out this religious mission, for it was her son Constantine who had made her "Augusta," rather than her husband Emperor Constantius, who actually divorced her before he began to reign.

Her success in discovering the true cross—along with the nails from the crucifixion—led to her sainthood after her death in 330. Her feast day, August 18, became accidentally a special holiday in the late Habsburg monarchy, because it was also the birthday of Emperor Franz Joseph. Furthermore, one of the nails that St. Helena supposedly brought back from Jerusalem ended up in Vienna in the Middle Ages and was kept in a bejeweled reliquary in the Habsburg imperial treasury, today in the Kunsthistorisches Museum. Helena is considered the patron saint of troubled marriages.

Some Byzantine empresses are recognized as Orthodox saints, and Empress Theodora, beginning her life as a sixth-century actress and prostitute according to Procopius, married Emperor Justinian, presided with him over the creation of the great cathedral of Hagia Sophia in Constantinople, and became a saint after her death. Some fifteen centuries later, in the year 2000, Tsarina Alexandra of Russia was canonized in the Russian Orthodox Church, along with her husband Tsar Nicholas and their children, eight decades after they were murdered by the Bolsheviks at Ekaterinburg in July 1918, while Zita was reigning as empress in Vienna.

The age of Napoléon as Emperor of the French gave France empresses instead of queens: first, Josephine de Beauharnais, crowned in Notre Dame along with Napoléon who then divorced her, and, second, the Habsburg Archduchess Marie Louise who gave Napoléon his desired son and heir. Napoléon, in the spirit of imperial improvisation, decided that Josephine, even after their divorce in 1809, would still preserve the title of empress, and she remained a divorced empress in retirement for the remaining five years of her life, at the chateau of Malmaison, near Paris.

Marie Louise became Napoléon's second empress, because her father, Habsburg Emperor Franz, had to reconcile himself with France following the French defeat of the Austrian army at the battle of Wagram in 1809. The marriage of Marie Louise to Napoléon in 1810 was distasteful to the Habsburgs because they regarded him as an utterly illegitimate Corsican adventurer whose titles were of no meaningful value. From a Habsburg perspective, Marie Louise as "Empress of the French" was really no empress at all, but simply a pawn in international diplomacy. Napoléon thought that the marriage would protect him from future hostilities on the part of the Habsburgs, but Emperor Franz nevertheless joined the coalition that defeated Napoléon at Leipzig in 1813. Napoléon was then deposed and exiled to Elba. After returning to France for the Hundred Days, and then losing the battle of Waterloo, he would abdicate definitively in 1815 and be exiled to St. Helena in the remote southern Atlantic Ocean, between Africa and

Brazil. The island had been named by Portuguese explorers after the mother of Emperor Constantine, the empress-saint who discovered the true cross.

The divorced Empress Josephine died at Malmaison in May 1814, allegedly from grief at the downfall of Napoléon. Marie Louise, however, only nineteen when she married Napoléon, would live for another three decades. Rather than continuing to bear the title of Empress of the French, she was assigned a sovereign role of her own as the Duchess of Parma, a position that she held until her death in 1847. Following Napoléon's death on St. Helena in 1821, she was free to marry again, but as the daughter of the Habsburg emperor and sovereign Duchess of Parma—somewhat soiled by her marriage to Napoléon—the question of eligible future partners was complicated, and she made an unacceptable morganatic marriage to a one-eyed Austrian general. In Parma she presided over the building of the city's great neoclassical opera house which opened in 1829 with the premiere of Bellini's *Zaira*.[2] In the eighteenth century Parma had been governed by a branch of the Bourbon dynasty, and it was given over to Marie Louise for the first half of the nineteenth century. Upon her death in 1847 Parma reverted to the Bourbons—in fact, to the grandfather of Zita—before being incorporated into the unified kingdom of Italy.

On June 4, 1920, the Treaty of Trianon was signed at Versailles, ratifying the dismemberment of Habsburg Hungary, stripping away two-thirds of the territory of the historical kingdom—assigning, for instance, Slovakia to Czechoslovakia, Croatia to Yugoslavia, and Transylvania to Romania. It was a huge blow to Hungarian national sentiment and is still remembered painfully a hundred years later, with the word "Trianon" signifying national humiliation. For Karl and Zita, ritually crowned as King and Queen of Hungary, the territorial diminution of the lands of the Crown of St. Stephen was something they could not help taking seriously and personally—though somewhat abstractly, since they themselves were living in exile in Switzerland. Zita recalled that the treaties of Saint-Germain and Trianon "naturally caused concern in the same way."[3]

Hungary had become a republic in November 1918, like Austria, and then a communist republic for four months under Béla Kun in 1919—but when Kun was toppled by the rightist authoritarian government of Admiral Miklós Horthy, the country became formally a kingdom again in March

1920, a kingdom without a king. The crowned king and queen were in exile in Switzerland, and Horthy governed Hungary as "regent" in the name of the crown. As Zita recalled, "The preparations for the attempt to restore the King to his full governing power began already in the summer of the year 1920, as an immediate consequence of the insane dictated peace treaty of Trianon, recognized immediately by reasonable politicians as scarcely second to the Treaty of Saint-Germain in its senselessness."[4] The severity of the treaties that ratified the dismemberment of the Habsburg lands—Trianon for Hungary, Saint-Germain for Austria—was experienced as a personal affront by Karl and Zita. The radical unsettling of national political sentiment by the Treaty of Trianon in 1920 encouraged Karl and Zita to contemplate a return to Hungary as King and Queen in 1921.

Hofmannsthal at the Salzburg Festival

Die Frau ohne Schatten presented the legendary afterlives of emperors and empresses on the operatic stage, following their general departure from European political life. After its premiere in the fall of 1919, the opera was part of the repertory in 1920, beginning already on January 6, though on that date Maria Jeritza did not sing the role of the Empress. Instead she was preparing for a new production of *Tosca*, opening on January 10, and she then performed as Ariadne on January 15, with Oestvig as Bacchus, Lehmann as the Composer, and Strauss conducting.[5]

On February 6, 1920, Jeritza sang the role of the Empress in *Die Frau ohne Schatten*, with most of the performers from the premiere: Richard Mayr and Lotte Lehmann as Barak and his wife, Lucie Weidt as the Nurse. With a very demanding schedule, Jeritza sang in *Lohengrin* on February 8 (with Weidt as Ortrud), in *Ariadne* on February 10 (with Lehmann as the Composer), and in *Salome* on February 12 (with Weidt as Herodias). She was the Empress again in Vienna on March 24 (and Tosca three days later), though Strauss himself was by then in Berlin preparing for *Die Frau ohne Schatten* to open there in April.[6] He urged Hofmannsthal to join him for the production that was being prepared—not by Kautsky, not by Kokoschka—by the young Greek designer Panos Aravantinos, who came from the island of Corfu, the beloved retreat of Habsburg Empress Elisabeth, site of her fantasy palace, the Achilleion. Strauss believed that Aravantinos could deliver in Berlin the magical effects that Roller had underplayed in Vienna: "All the magic will be there."[7] Hofmannsthal did not come, complaining of exhaustion, nervous depression, and "a lingering influenza and rheumatism with some constant fever for five weeks."[8]

In spring 1920 Vienna presented *Die Frau ohne Schatten* on May 4 (starring Jeritza and Lehmann), followed on May 5 by the opera that Strauss and Hofmannsthal regarded as their fairy-tale inspiration, Mozart's *Die Zauberflöte*, with Strauss conducting.[9] The juxtaposition of the two operas, with their magical scenarios, must have been Strauss's conception, and both productions were designed by Roller. For Jeritza the performance on May 4 turned out to be her last in the role of the Empress in Vienna.

That summer, in August 1920, the Salzburg Festival was inaugurated; it was Hofmannsthal's most cherished cultural project. The featured dramatic work was the poet's very own Christian mystery play *Jedermann* (*Everyman*), directed by Reinhardt, designed by Roller, and performed, as it is still performed today, in front of the Salzburg Cathedral. Hofmannsthal's conception of the Salzburg Festival grew out of his wartime writings about the special role that Austria could play in European culture: deploying the legacy of baroque Catholicism, fully evident in the monuments of Salzburg, and the transcendent spirit of European classicism as represented by the figure of Mozart, born and raised in Salzburg. The festival also reflected Hofmannsthal's own operatic collaboration with Strauss, as the poet suggested in his promotional brochure: "If a festival, why then in Salzburg? The Bavarian-Austrian tribe [*Stamm*] was always the bearer of the theatrical wealth of all the German peoples."[10] His collaboration with Strauss was a Bavarian-Austrian collaboration, and Salzburg was located right on the border between Bavaria and Austria, conveniently close to where Hofmannsthal and Strauss spent their working summers in the mountains.

The brochure also preserved a lingering outline of the poet's former Austrian idea, the idea of bringing together diverse cultures:

> Salzburg is the heart of Europe's heart. It lies halfway between Switzerland and the Slavic lands, halfway between northern Germany and Lombard Italy; it lies in the middle between North and South, between

mountains and plains, between the heroic and the idyllic; it stands as a construction between the urban and the rural, the ancient and the modern, the princely baroque and the lovely peasant folk: Mozart is the expression of all that. The middle of Europe has no more beautiful region, and Mozart had to be born here.[11]

Thus Hofmannsthal refurbished his wartime Austrian idea of cultural transcendence for postwar Europe following the abolition of the Habsburg monarchy.

Historian Michael Steinberg, writing about the origins of the Salzburg Festival, has noted the cultural tensions in the 1920s between Red Vienna and the more conservative, more Catholic spirit of the western and mountainous areas of Austria.[12] The performance of *Jedermann* in front of the Salzburg Cathedral attracted the ire of local observers because the director was Reinhardt, born a Viennese Jew, and the star was one of Reinhardt's favorite actors, Alexander Moissi from Trieste whose Mosaic name suggested the possibility of some Jewish ancestry. He had played the role of Shylock for Reinhardt in Berlin in November 1918, as the war was ending, and the actor joined the revolutionary Spartacus movement there. *Jedermann* became an annual event at Salzburg, and local commentators protested against "the return of the Jews Max Reinhardt and Moissi" and even against "the poetry of the Jew Hofmannsthal"—or, similarly, against "smoking Jewesses inside our Christian houses of God, collected by the Semites Max Reinhardt, Moissi, and Hofmannsthal."[13] Hofmannsthal, in spite of his dedication to the Catholic culture of Austria, in spite of his own family's Catholicism for the last three generations, in spite of his own occasional anti-Semitic comments, was still marked by the Judaism of his great-grandfather, the eighteenth-century silk merchant. Removed after 1918 from the Habsburg context of his own family fairy tale, by 1920 the simple fact that Hofmannsthal was a Viennese intellectual made it seem plausible in Salzburg that he might be Jewish.

Strauss on Tour in Rio de Janeiro

Strauss, as one of the directors of the Vienna Opera, was also one of the founders of the Salzburg Festival, but he was absent from that first summer festival of 1920—which had no musical program—and, from August to

December, was occupied with a South American tour, conducting in Rio de Janeiro and Buenos Aires. He wrote to Hofmannsthal from Rio on October 5 to report on a production of *Der Rosenkavalier* there, with Tullio Serafin conducting and Claudia Muzio "as an extremely elegant and charming Marschallin"—singing in Italian. Hofmannsthal, with his fevers and depressions, could not even be tempted from Vienna to Berlin, so it was unlikely that he would contemplate a trip to Brazil, but Strauss enthusiastically dangled the possibility of a "free passage on a Brazilian steamer from Trieste to Rio"—as if Trieste were still Vienna's Habsburg port, though it had been seized by Italy after the war.[14]

Strauss promised Hofmannsthal that he was publicizing the Salzburg Festival in Brazil:

> For Salzburg we are working industriously, distributing our propaganda writings to the ladies of the Salvation Army [*Heilsarmee*]—so far without visible success. What's Salzburg to a Brazilian or, even worse, to a German living in Brazil?! A trip like this has one good feature: one recovers one's full pride as a European, and one longs even for hunger, coal shortages, and Bolshevism.[15]

Strauss, leading his Vienna orchestra into the New World, clearly had the sense that he was engaged in a sort of campaign for European culture, even using with some sense of irony the word "propaganda," so familiar from the recent years of the war, and especially to Hofmannsthal. Now they were both engaged in propaganda for Salzburg, a revindication of German and Austrian culture after wartime defeat and postwar poverty. What did Salzburg mean to a Brazilian? Stefan Zweig might have pondered that question twenty years later, when he left his home in Salzburg in the 1930s, fleeing from Nazi Europe, and settled in Brazil where he committed suicide in 1942 in Petrópolis, just north of Rio de Janeiro.

Die Frau ohne Schatten was on Strauss's mind in Rio in 1920. According to Hofmannsthal's conception, the Emperor and Empress reigned over a mythological "Empire of the Southeastern Islands," and Strauss was thinking of that empire in Rio:

> For its fairy tale splendor I can only compare Rio to the "Empire of the Eastern Islands," where I believe myself to be transplanted every day, when I look out over the bay from our roof terrace. . . . I have often

thought of you and wished you were here, so that you could see your beautiful poetic dream become reality.[16]

In a postcard from Rio to Roller, Strauss made the same reference to finding himself "in the Empire of the Emperor of the Eastern Islands."[17] Brazil was no longer an empire, for the last Brazilian emperor, Pedro II, was deposed in 1889. Pedro belonged to the Brazilian branch of the Portuguese Braganza dynasty and was therefore related to Zita on the side of her mother, the Portuguese infanta. For Strauss, however, the New World was where mythological empires became real in an exotic landscape. He looked out upon the fairytale imperial landscape from his roof terrace in Rio, certainly well aware that the very first scene of *Die Frau ohne Schatten* was set on the roof terrace of the imperial palace.

The performance of *Der Rosenkavalier* in Rio in October 1920 was a reminder of the importance of opera in the Americas, but *Der Rosenkavalier* had not been performed at the Metropolitan Opera in New York since the United States entered the war against Germany in 1917. Opening its season in November 1920, the Met affirmed its power and importance in the opera world with casts of glittering celebrities: Enrico Caruso and Rosa Ponselle together in *La Juive* for opening night November 15, and then together again in *La Forza del Destino* later in the month.[18] Cultured New Yorkers might also have been aware of a much smaller theatrical event taking place downtown in November in Greenwich Village, the opening of Eugene O'Neill's play *The Emperor Jones*, about an African American train porter and murderer who escapes from prison to a Caribbean island where he declares himself "emperor": the Emperor Jones. The play was being staged in the aftermath of European empires, and the protagonist was emotionally driven and psychologically haunted by his own imperial fears, ambitions, fantasies, and delusions. "Ain't I de Emperor?" he asks proudly, in dialect, as if parodying the claims of all the European pretenders nourishing their ambitions in exile.[19] In 1922 Luigi Pirandello would offer an even more unsettling perspective on the fate of emperors in his play *Enrico IV*, about a contemporary Italian who seems to believe that he is the medieval Holy Roman Emperor Henry IV—while his family and servants accommodatingly act the medieval roles that permit him to preserve his delusion. The afterlives of Habsburg empresses were refracted in a new medium in 1921 with the German silent film *Kaiserin Elisabeth von Österreich*, which included a dramatic treatment of Empress Elisabeth's assassination.

Nostalgia: The First Attempted Restoration

With Strauss returning to Vienna in December 1920, the very last opera performance of the year was supposed to be *Die Frau ohne Schatten*, canceled at the last minute because there was no one who could sing the role of the Empress. Kiurina was indisposed, and Jeritza was apparently unavailable though she had sung Rosalinde in *Die Fledermaus* on December 26, the day after Christmas, with Strauss conducting. On December 30 *Lohengrin* was substituted for *Die Frau ohne Schatten*, with Oestvig shifting from the Emperor to the role of Lohengrin.[20]

Jeritza would never sing the role of the Empress in Vienna again after a total of just nine performances. On January 10, 1921, she presented a brand-new role in the Vienna premiere of Erich Korngold's new opera *Die tote Stadt* (already performed in Hamburg and Cologne in December)—the tale of a troubled tenor who becomes infatuated with a mysteriously seductive woman, Marietta, who resembles his dead wife. Jeritza performed both roles, the dead wife and the dangerous siren, singing Marietta's lute song in a spirit of passionate nostalgia, a song she remembers from "younger and happier days." The team that produced *Die Frau ohne Schatten* was reassembled here, with Oestvig as the troubled tenor Paul, Mayr as the performing Pierrot Fritz, Schalk conducting, and Roller and Kautsky both involved in designing the sets.[21]

Jeritza as Marietta, with her nostalgic lute song, embodied the temptations of personal nostalgia in the postwar decade of the 1920s. In 1921 Karl and Zita believed that they could still regain their lost crowns in Hungary and Austria, that their nostalgic former subjects, traumatized by postwar hardship, would restore them to their sovereign roles. On March 1 Zita gave birth to Archduchess Charlotte in Switzerland, with Dr. Peham traveling from Vienna to attend the birth as he had done for Zita so many times before in Austria.[22] By the end of the month, when Jeritza sang Marietta on March 29 in Vienna, Karl was in Hungary trying to regain his throne.

"The Hungarian people cried out for their king," recalled Zita. "People begged him to consider that as king he had promised to protect his people and preserve a just order in the land."[23] On March 26, Holy Saturday, traveling incognito, Karl made his way from Switzerland (through Austria) to western Hungary and established himself at Szombathely where, the next day, Easter Sunday, he confronted Admiral Horthy in Budapest and demanded to be recognized and reestablished as the rightful king of Hungary. Horthy, the "regent," supposedly bargained for posts and honors for himself, including the Order of the Golden Fleece. In the end, however, the regent refused to turn over power to Karl, the latter did not receive diplomatic support from the French government as he had hoped, and Hungary's neighbors, Czechoslovakia and Yugoslavia, threatened to invade if the Habsburg dynasty were restored in Budapest. In fact, "Habsburg Hungary" included large territories that had been incorporated into those neighboring countries by the Treaty of Trianon. There was a standoff between Karl back in Szombathely and Horthy in Budapest, and then Karl came down with pneumonia.[24] By early April it was clear that Karl had failed, and he left Hungary to return to his family in Switzerland.

In Vienna Strauss conducted *Die Frau ohne Schatten* on April 29, with the Emperor and Empress concluding in triumphant possession of their empire. Now, as the opera came around again on May 13, Kiurina was the Empress of choice, Jeritza's successor, though perhaps lacking Jeritza's glamorous star quality.[25] Three days later Hofmannsthal wrote to Strauss defensively about *Die Frau ohne Schatten*, which had been condemned in a recent publication by German music critic Paul Bekker for "inner unclarity, artistic complexity, the contradictory ambiguity and speculative excess of its symbolism."[26] Bekker thus echoed some of Julius Korngold's criticism of the libretto at the premiere.

Hofmannsthal found such criticism distressing and worried that *Die Frau ohne Schatten* was undermined by its complicated second act:

> The second act is overburdened with poetry, heavy, tiring. But the first act is so fortunate, the third so beautiful, the whole thing so beautifully conceived, leading to moral good . . . the characters so well rounded: the Dyer, the Empress, the Children, the Falcon. Is that a *failed* libretto?

Does a failed libretto look like that? And doesn't it always please wherever it is performed?[27]

Hofmannsthal acknowledged the daunting construction of the second act, with its five separate scenes and complex ensembles, but he placed his faith in the audiences that applauded the work in the opera house. The public, however, was not always easy to read, as Karl and Zita also discovered. Zita had been convinced that the Hungarian people were crying out for their king.

The physical production of *Die Frau ohne Schatten*, with all of its scene changes, was daunting, and between the Vienna premiere in October 1919 and the Berlin premiere in April 1920, productions in Dresden, Munich, and Cologne revealed the costs and challenges of staging the work.[28] The intendant of the Weimar theater wrote to Strauss directly in 1919 to regret that *Die Frau ohne Schatten* could not be included in a planned cycle of Strauss operas: "In a time of extreme material poverty it is completely out of the question to fulfill even partly the necessary stage sets and transformations. Indeed, I fear that even without poverty only very few theaters will be able to satisfy the technical requirements." Darmstadt staged a production in 1920, and the local press declared it to be an enterprise of "bold daring."[29]

Die Frau ohne Schatten had sixteen performances in Vienna during its premiere season of 1919–20, but in 1921 the fickle public was excited about *Die tote Stadt*, which received eighteen performances across that year (and *Die Frau ohne Schatten* only four). With the arrival of the fall season Jeritza sang Marietta in *Die tote Stadt* on September 22, Aida on October 14, and then left the Vienna Opera for the rest of the year to proceed to New York where she would make her triumphant Metropolitan debut as Marietta in November. On October 27 *Die Frau ohne Schatten* was performed in Vienna with Oestvig as the Emperor singing opposite the Swedish soprano Lilly Hafgren as the Empress.[30] On that date Jeritza was already on board ship crossing the Atlantic: "I did not know a single, solitary soul in the United States, and felt anything but brave when I landed in Hoboken after a ten days' trip on the *Rotterdam* on November 4." She began rehearsing at the Met the very next day and had a successful debut on November 19 as Marietta.[31] In 1922 when *Der Rosenkavalier* finally returned to the Met repertory for the first time since the war, Jeritza sang Octavian.[32] Korngold too would have a great career in America, after fleeing from Nazi Europe: he would become one of the brilliant pioneers of Hollywood movie music, winning the Oscar for *The Adventures of Robin Hood* in 1939.

Aviation: The Second Attempted Restoration

While Jeritza made the voyage to New York by ship in October 1921—still six years before Lindbergh first crossed the Atlantic by plane—Karl and Zita, early fans of aviation, actually obtained an aircraft to make their second and final attempt to regain the Hungarian throne. Before traveling, Karl made his will, establishing Zita as regent in the event of his death, on behalf of Archduke Otto. Of course Zita was pregnant again in the fall of 1921, but on October 20 she accompanied Karl in a plane from an airfield near Zurich to a wheatfield in western Hungary, near Sopron. In a later interview she described their near motor failure over Bavaria at 11,000 feet, and then, over Vienna, the moving sight of Schönbrunn down below.[33] Karl regarded the restoration attempts as "the path of duty," but Zita, generally considered the more determined of the pair, was supposed to have taken as her motto the hunter's adage (today a sports adage): *Wer nicht schiesst, kann nicht treffen* (If you don't shoot, you can't score).[34]

On the next day, October 21, Zita was welcomed with flowers by Hungarian girls in folk costume. It happened to be Karl and Zita's tenth wedding anniversary. Karl formed a "government" of loyalists, and the royal couple set out by train for Budapest to challenge Admiral Horthy and Prime Minister István Bethlen. Army units joined Karl and Zita along the way and declared their loyalty to the King and Queen. "What did I feel as I climbed onto the locomotive?" Zita later reflected. "What should I say about that? People were up on it, and it drove off. The whole thing was simply self-evident [*selbstverständlich*], there's really nothing to say about it."[35] From Zita's perspective she and Karl were the crowned King and Queen of Hungary; it was self-evident that they would seek to reclaim their throne. One of the leading royalist Hungarian officers was Anton Lehár, brother of the famous operetta composer Franz Lehár, and, indeed, there were some romantic elements of operetta scenario in Karl and Zita's enterprise.

From a practical point of view, however, there were not enough trains available to transport all their supporters promptly to Budapest—probably due to the October harvest, with trains full of agricultural products. Later in January the *New York Times* published an account of an interview with Zita on the front page under the whimsical headline, "ZITA SAYS TURNIPS KEPT CHARLES [KARL] FROM REGAINING THE THRONE."[36] Because of the delay, Horthy's troops were prepared to confront the royalists outside Budapest, and, instead of resuming their reign, Karl and Zita became prisoners in their own kingdom and were held at a monastery on Lake Balaton.[37]

In *Die Frau ohne Schatten* the Empress makes her entrance, in the second scene of the third act, by coming on stage in a boat that seems to move by itself. The next act in Zita's life involved an extraordinary odyssey by boat, its itinerary beyond her control. She and Karl were taken from the monastery on Lake Balaton and put on a Danube ship, flying the British flag, traveling to the east, toward the mouth of the river on the Black Sea. As they proceeded along the Danube through Hungary, then Yugoslavia, then Romania, they looked out upon lands of their own former empire, as Zita recalled.

> It was a great solace that the Danube that bore us greeted our old homeland on the left and on the right. We passed through all the many places in which barely three years earlier we had been so warmly greeted. So we saw for instance Újvidék [Novi Sad] again, the city that had once prepared for us such a magnificent welcome. Then, to our surprise, a chaplain came to us and said that the Danube River pilots had refused to take our ship through the rapids; both the Hungarian and the Croatian pilots said that they did not want to steer a ship that was taking their king by force out of his country. . . . The loyalty of these men moved us deeply.[38]

For Zita even deportation took on the air of a triumphal tour, nostalgically imbued with the memories of her actual reign. The persistent loyalty of the multinational Habsburg peoples was a matter of conviction for her, and, to be sure, she would have interpreted the slightest signs of interest as the deepest manifestations of loyalism. "When the ship once again could travel no further, because of low water levels in the Danube," she recalled, "the people said: 'It's clear that the Danube does not want to carry the king out of his land.'"³⁹ This was already the language of fairy-tale royalty, with magical interventions and landscapes that exercised incantatory powers.

At Galatz Karl and Zita were placed on a Romanian ship that turned out to be "an old Austrian ship that the Romanians took over and rechristened."⁴⁰ They recognized it as formerly their own, and Zita believed that in some sense the ship recognized them:

> We were especially touched when suddenly on this ship we received our midday meal that consisted of nothing but Viennese cooking. When we inquired how that was possible, it came out that the ship's cook was Viennese and had once worked for the court. So that we would "feel at home" this cook had prepared for us a "court dinner" in the Viennese style.⁴¹

Again, the fairy-tale quality of her story was evident in the retelling: the King and Queen could still be recognized and honored in spite of all efforts to hurry them quickly out of their former kingdom, and the rechristened ship could be reconstituted as the old imperial court with real Viennese cooking.

Eventually the ship arrived at the mouth of the Danube opening onto the Black Sea. There at Sulina Karl and Zita boarded the *Cardiff*, an English warship which was to bring them to Constantinople. They had been there in May 1918, during the war, as Emperor and Empress, in the simultaneous spirit of wartime alliance and oriental fairy tale. Zita now recalled that earlier visit:

> Constantinople presented indeed a very different aspect from three years before. . . . The sultan disempowered, the buildings neglected, and the beautiful roses of May were faded. What days those were, when we were here, on the Golden Horn, still hoping for peace and compromise, when we were still speaking of the position of Austria in the future new Europe. . . . Now we saw foreign warships, French, English, Italian. . . . The White Palace, where we were served precious and fragrant tea, we could recognize over on the Asiatic side . . .⁴²

The Ottoman Empire had been humiliated in 1920 by the Treaty of Sèvres, which divided the empire into foreign mandates and spheres of influence. The Constantinople that Zita gazed upon from the deck of the *Cardiff* in 1921 was still under Allied occupation, as she could see from the foreign warships. Sultan Mehmed VI would reign for one more year before Atatürk fully overturned the Treaty of Sèvres, abolished the sultanate, and established modern Turkey in 1922. Like Karl and Zita, the last sultan would be deported from his former empire on a British warship. For Zita in 1921, the view of Constantinople, with its memories of roses in May and fragrant palace tea, was a fairy-tale city, even an operetta city experienced in the spirit of bittersweet nostalgia.

The *Cardiff* continued through the Dardanelles, passing from the Black Sea to the Mediterranean. Karl and Zita crossed the entire Mediterranean, past Malta, past Italy, and finally touched land when they reached British soil at Gibraltar, supposedly uninformed of their ultimate destination. It lay beyond the Straits of Gibraltar: the Portuguese island of Madeira, four hundred miles off the Atlantic coast of Morocco. After using Switzerland as a base for two attempts to recover the Hungarian throne, creating awkward international incidents each time, they were now to be banished from Europe altogether.

Madeira: "Europe Disappearing"

"From the bridge the Emperor and I saw Europe disappearing slowly in the distance," recalled Zita of their departure from Gibraltar. "I said to the Emperor, it was a very sad thing for us that now we had to leave not just our homeland but also Europe. And the Emperor answered very calmly: 'If God wants to bring us back, he certainly will do it. And if not, then I give myself over to his will.'" As they approached Madeira from the ocean, they saw the high-lying church of Nossa Senhora do Monte at Funchal, and Karl supposedly exclaimed with nostalgia, "What melancholy remembrances does this church waken in me! It reminds me so much of the churches of my own land." There is actual film footage of Karl and Zita landing on Madeira, with Zita, now in the third month of her pregnancy, wearing a broad-rimmed black hat to shelter her from the semitropical Atlantic sun.[43] They arrived at their place of exile on Madeira on November 19, thinking nostalgically of Austria-Hungary, and by chance on the very same date that Maria Jeritza made her Metropolitan Opera debut in New York singing her celebrated Viennese aria of nostalgia in Korngold's *Die tote Stadt*.

Napoléon was exiled to Elba in 1814, but then, after the Hundred Days and after Waterloo, he was sent to the much more remote island of St. Helena. The exile of Karl and Zita followed the Napoleonic pattern of a century earlier, first exiled to nearby Switzerland, but then more definitively and remotely banished to Madeira. (Supposedly, St. Helena was actually considered for Karl and Zita.[44]) Napoléon went into exile alone, without either of his empresses. Karl and Zita were shipped to Madeira together in November 1921, though they arrived without their children, who had been left in Switzerland when their parents took the plane to Hungary in October.

Zita returned to Switzerland in January 1922 because six-year-old Robert had to have an appendectomy in Zurich. Her travel required the special permission of the Swiss government, which ruled that "the entry of Frau Zita at the present moment has no danger for the country"—while reserving the right to monitor her movements.[45] The *New York Times* described her arrival, "traveling incognito with a maid and handbag." According to the *Times*, the Swiss were watching Zita closely, as she was "considered an intriguer, and the real head of the Habsburg restoration movement."[46] Furthermore, the Paris Conference of Ambassadors, associated with the implementation of the Versailles Treaty, was reportedly worried that "Zita's trip was merely a blind, her real intention being to seize the opportunity to formulate a fresh plot for a royalist rising in Hungary, and that she traveled from Funchal with the intention of placing herself at the head of an expedition to recapture the throne." Zita, however, disappointed any expectations of political drama.[47] After Robert's surgery Zita returned to Madeira, and the children were also sent to Madeira from Switzerland, thus reuniting the imperial family.

The children, however, were susceptible to infections on Madeira, and were soon laid low by an outbreak of flu in early 1922. Karl also fell sick. He was already in poor health, aggravated by the Madeira subtropical climate, and suffered psychologically from homesickness and severe "nervous depression"—the latter a consequence of his failed adventure in Hungary and his accumulating debts.[48] He was thirty-four years old, and he died of pneumonia on April 1, 1922.

Zita, in the last trimester of her last pregnancy, was accompanied by a loyal nurse who attended to the children and could also play the role of midwife: Franziska Kral. According to Kral, on April 1, "the poor Empress" held the body of the Emperor in her arms, all morning long, from sunrise until his death a little after noon: "She called out, 'Karl, what will I do alone?' and she whispered in his ear for hours." His heart was removed for separate burial (and eventually joined together with Zita's heart in Switzerland after her death); his corpse was dressed in Habsburg uniform, and he was laid out in his coffin wearing the Order of the Golden Fleece. "How young and beautiful he looks," lamented Zita, "and I must give him up."[49] He was buried in the church of Nossa Senhora do Monte, the same church he had seen from the ocean as he arrived, reminding him nostalgically of the churches of Austria-Hungary.

The *Neue Freie Presse* in Vienna published an obituary story on the front page the day after Karl's death, on Sunday, April 2, titling him "Exkaiser Karl." The obituary began theatrically: "Far from the homeland a lonely man has died, a man who was chosen by fate to rule over a great empire." Though Karl had been dethroned and banished, the *Neue Freie Presse* was now prepared to appreciate him sympathetically ("a deep tragedy lies in this life"), but that spirit of sympathy was accompanied by skepticism concerning his political qualities. "It is probable that even a spirit of talent, a titan of strength, would not have been able to give events a different course, to prevent the collapse of the monarchy, to forestall the dissolution of Austria-Hungary," observed the newspaper, implicitly doubting that Karl possessed either talent or strength. The recent ill-considered attempts to regain the Hungarian throne were held up as evidence of his political ineptitude. The end of Austria-Hungary thus hovered over the sad conclusion of Karl's own life: "So his death far away on a forgotten island provokes the melancholy that every person must feel who remembers what we have lost, lost because of inexorable destiny, but also in part because of him, the man who today lies alone on the funeral bier." The obituary was a sympathetic but critical indictment of Karl and an aria of nostalgia for Habsburg Austria-Hungary. There were requiem masses for Karl in both Vienna and Budapest.[50]

The *Neue Freie Presse* reported that circles close to the Habsburg family wanted to bring Karl's body to Vienna to be buried in the Kapuzinergruft with his Habsburg ancestors: "It is still uncertain how the state authorities in Austria will respond to this question." Karl's resting place, however, still remains, one hundred years later, the church of Nossa Senhora do Monte on

Madeira. Also uncertain in 1922 was the question of whether Karl's banishment from Austria—for refusing to abdicate—still applied after his death to his widow and children. This was summed up in the newspaper as the question of "The Future Residence of Exkaiserin Zita and Her Children." Whether Zita could return to Austria might turn on the issue of whether she was willing to renounce all claims as Empress of Austria and take an oath of loyalty to the republic, and in this regard the *Neue Freie Presse* was rightly skeptical: "It is very much in question whether the former Empress will be inclined to fulfill this condition."[51] Indeed Zita would maintain the claims of her son Otto for decades to come.

"Are You the Goddess of This Island?"

In late March 1922, as Karl lay dying on Madeira, Strauss and Hofmannsthal were enjoying the Vienna Opera premiere of their biblical ballet *Josephslegende*, first produced in Paris in 1914, just before the outbreak of the war. Strauss conducted the ballet in Vienna on a double bill with his own early opera *Feuersnot*, from 1901, and Hofmannsthal wrote to him afterward about the ballet, "Yesterday evening I had great great joy! It's a wonderfully beautiful thing!" Hofmannsthal in 1922 was ready for a new collaboration with Strauss, which was to be *Die ägyptische Helena* (*The Egyptian Helena*), a mythological comedy of Helen's reconciliation with Menelaus after the Trojan War. "Now there is added for me a third work certain to have a long future," wrote the poet, "along with *Rosenkavalier* and *Ariadne*."[52] The absence of *Die Frau ohne Schatten* from the list cannot have been accidental but reflected his ongoing concerns about whether the opera would be a continuing success.

Hofmannsthal's anxieties about the opera emerged explicitly in a letter to Strauss of April 15, actually dated "Holy Saturday," that is, the day before Easter. "For me the finished works are not dead but living cares and joys [*Sorgen und Freuden*], like children," wrote Hofmannsthal, and *Die Frau ohne Schatten* was more care than joy. "What is burdensome [*das Beschwerende*] is the second act, above all the rhythmic return to the Dyer's home. Here I was wrong." He was oddly unsure that the opera could succeed in Germany and Austria but claimed to believe in its future in France and Italy—"this is a work that in the Latin lands would be able to have great effect and great value."⁵³

For a work so notably Wagnerian in its proportions, orchestrations, dynamics, and mythological content, it was an unusual notion to insist that it belonged more properly to the spheres of Latinate culture and Mediterranean entertainment. The opera had certainly been composed to present to the victorious German and Austrian publics at the end of the war, and that Hofmannsthal now preferred to appeal to the cultural taste of the French and Italian publics was perhaps driven by a sense that *Die Frau ohne Schatten* had missed its cultural and geopolitical moment. Hofmannsthal's letter made no reference to the recent death of Emperor Karl in a Latin land, the Portuguese island of Madeira.

Easter week, as Hofmannsthal was writing to Strauss, was a moment in the Viennese calendar closely associated with the Habsburg family, as the emperors had traditionally made public appearances on Holy Thursday to wash the feet of the poor, following Christ's example.⁵⁴ Franz Joseph was meticulous in carrying out this exercise into his old age, and Karl assumed this imperial role together with Zita at Easter 1917 and Easter 1918. This aspect of their brief reign has been purposefully recalled in relation to Karl's beatification in 2004 and the ongoing cause of Zita's beatification. The Kaiser-Karl-Gebetsliga (Emperor Karl League of Prayer) narrated this imperial Easter activity on Facebook at Easter 2014:

> After attending Mass, Emperor Karl and Empress Zita would enter the Ceremonial Hall at 8:00 a.m. In the presence of ambassadors, the aristocracy, court officials, and many ceremonial military guards, the Emperor and Empress served the twenty-four poor people a ritual four-course meal, taking the time to talk to each guest, who was frequently overwhelmed with the honor and attention. Karl served the men, and Zita served the women. After the meal, the tables were removed and the Emperor and Empress would get on their knees to wash the feet of their guests.⁵⁵

Franz Joseph had paid particular attention to this tradition as a means of enhancing the mystique of imperial rule in the modern world of the nineteenth century, and Karl and Zita, according to the Gebetsliga, took this even further in the context of a modern commitment to social welfare and war relief;

> For Karl and Zita, these were no hollow rituals ... performed once a year and then not thought of again until the calendar rolled around. They actively cared for their people and the poorest among them. They founded and worked in soup kitchens and homeless shelters, they actively sought the improvement of the living conditions for all of their people, founding churches, hospitals, and government ministries to distribute aid among wounded veterans, widows, orphans, and the sick. Their Holy Thursday ritual was part of their everyday life. Even on his death bed, his thoughts and prayers were on his people, whom he loved as a father.[56]

Karl's death, in early April 1922, came close to the Easter holiday, which later would become a particular moment for remembering the Emperor.

The washing of feet on Easter weekend 1922 took place on the stage of the Vienna Opera, in Wagner's *Parsifal*, when Kundry washed Parsifal's feet in the third act, set on Good Friday and including Wagner's famous music for *Karfreitagszauber*, Good Friday Magic. In 1922 the Vienna Opera gave performances of *Parsifal* on Holy Saturday, Easter Sunday, and Easter Monday. On Saturday Franz Schalk conducted *Parsifal* with Richard Mayr (the original Barak) as Gurnemanz and Lucie Weidt (the original Nurse) as Kundry, washing Parsifal's feet. The production was designed by Roller. By Easter Monday, April 17, Karl Oestvig had joined the cast as Parsifal.[57]

On Thursday April 20 Jeritza returned to the Vienna Opera, after her season in New York at the Metropolitan. She had had great success there with some of her trademark roles: Marietta in *Die tote Stadt*, Sieglinde in *Die Walküre*, Elsa in *Lohengrin*, Santuzza in *Cavalleria Rusticana*, and Tosca of course. She returned to the Vienna Opera as Elisabeth in *Tannhäuser*, receiving a huge ovation as she stepped on stage at the opening of the second act, before she began to sing, "Dich teure Halle, grüß' ich wieder," (Precious hall, I greet you again). The Viennese press spoke of the audience responding with "a demonstration that has scarcely ever been experienced," an expression of *Wiedersehensfreude* (the joy of reunion): the sort of return to Vienna that Zita might have imagined in her political fantasies of restoration. Jeritza sang Ariadne on April 27, Salome on May 5, Rachel in *La Juive* on May 10,

Marietta on May 17, and Tosca on May 26. On May 12, 1922, however, it was Kiurina who sang the role of the Empress, opposite Oestvig, in *Die Frau ohne Schatten*.[58]

In the second act the Empress, sleeping in the hunting lodge, has her vision of what it would mean to outlive the Emperor, to lose him, the joyous hunter, in the athletic prime of his youthful masculinity, to a sinister paralysis that would kill him by turning him to stone. With triplets in the bass clarinet and a dark winding figure for the bassoons and contrabassoon, she dreams that the Emperor is approaching a cave with a bronze door, which is identified by an offstage chorus as the "threshold of death."[59]

The sleeping Empress cries out in D major, "Wehe, mein Mann!" (Alas, my husband). She sings the dark musical line associated from the beginning of the opera with the words "Er wird zum Stein" (he will turn to stone), a stepwise descent that suddenly drops precipitously on the last syllable, the word "Stein." Here, however, she sings "als wär's ein Grab" (as if it were a grave), dropping down on "Grab"—accompanied by dark trombones, with the final note reinforced by the bass tuba. Now she can actually envision as a nightmare his paralysis and describe it almost clinically. She employs the descending phrase again, twice in succession: "Ihm stockt der Fuss/ Sein Leib erstarrt" (His foot falters / His body stiffens). The final drop on the word "erstarrt" takes her down to middle C in her chest voice. But then she is suddenly roused to the Emperor's need for her help. She leaps up to a sustained high B on the first syllable of "Hülfe"—the cry for help that he cannot vocalize—but her high notes have no power to save him from the creeping death of paralytic petrification.[60] In the third act she herself will arrive by boat at the bronze door, the threshold of death, and will bring her paralyzed husband back to life.

Though Jeritza, returning from New York, did not sing the role of the Empress opposite Oestvig on May 12, she had already been reunited with him in *Ariadne auf Naxos* on April 27.[61] He sang the role of Bacchus with Jeritza as Ariadne, delivering the same Straussian chemistry that they had once brought to the roles of the Emperor and the Empress. In *Ariadne auf Naxos* Jeritza would have presided over a barely populated island—Naxos, in fact—alone and abandoned after the departure of Theseus. At this moment in 1922 the public might have noted the uncanny dramatic correspondence to the situation of Zita who suddenly found herself alone and abandoned on her own island, Madeira, after the death of Karl.

While Zita had her seven children to keep her company, and one more on the way, Ariadne has three singing nymphs and a *commedia dell'arte* troupe of entertainers captained by Zerbinetta and Harlequin. For Ariadne, a Cretan princess, the island of Naxos becomes the empire of her loneliness, but she dreams of a different empire—"Es gibt ein Reich"—the empire of death and oblivion. When the god Bacchus appears on her island, she mistakes him for the god of death and gives herself over to him, and they join in a rapturous duet of mutual metamorphosis. Hofmannsthal had explained the character of Ariadne to Strauss back in 1911, contrasting her to the "frivolous Zerbinetta" with her cheerful spirit of romantic promiscuity: "Ariadne could only be the wife or lover of *one* man, just as she can be left behind, abandoned only by *one* man. One thing, however, remains for her: the miracle, the god."[62] Hofmannsthal had no doubt about Ariadne's supreme fidelity, and, later, when he wrote the libretto for the operatic prologue, he had the character of the Composer sing about Ariadne in terms that echoed the earlier letter to Strauss—"she is one among a million, the woman who does not forget"— and Strauss set the words to a swelling musical line of fervent sincerity.

"Are you the goddess of this island?" Bacchus asks Ariadne, and Jeritza surely presided magnificently over the island stage setting at the Vienna Opera on April 27.[63] Zita was not interested in presiding over island society on Madeira. She had an invitation from the King of Spain, but her banishment from Europe had not been formally revoked, and in the British Foreign Office there were some who felt that she should be kept on Madeira unless she pledged to "behave herself"—that is, refrain from royalist machinations. There were also, however, those who felt that the banishment to Madeira without stipulated means of support had helped to bring about Karl's death. Ultimately, the governments of England and France conceded Zita's right to leave the island.[64]

On May 19 she arrived in Spain, and there she gave birth to her eighth and last child, Archduchess Elisabeth, on May 31 in Madrid. Zita would now reside in Spain, still a Bourbon monarchy in the 1920s. Like Ariadne, Zita was an empress who believed in fidelity to one man only, and she now embarked upon the next stage of her imperial afterlife, her widowhood. Named regent by Karl's testament for the nine-year-old Crown Prince Otto, she became the empress-regent-pretender-in-exile for the crown-prince-pretender-in-exile. She had been born into a family of exiled royalty, the Bourbon-Parma dynasty, and now, just turning thirty, became the presiding matriarch of her own banished Habsburg family. As Karl's widow she wore black for the rest of her long life.

16

"The Thread of Past Time"

POSTIMPERIAL PERSPECTIVES IN THE 1920S

"For the Ears of Normal Humans"

In the 1920s Zita raised her family of eight children in a palace on the Bay of Biscay in the little Basque town of Lekeitio in Spain. King Alfonso XIII of Spain was Zita's distant cousin. The last reigning Bourbon in Europe, from 1923 the king presided over the military dictatorship of General Miguel Primo de Rivera but would himself have to go into royal exile in 1931 when Spain was declared a republic. By then Zita would have moved on, but until 1929 she lived in Lekeitio by the sea in the Uribarren Palace, built by a French architect in the 1890s in Second Empire style.[1] Lekeitio is ten miles from the inland town of Guernica, and the Uribarren Palace would be destroyed during the Spanish Civil War.

Zita raised her children as Habsburg archdukes and archduchesses with the eldest, Archduke Otto, brought up to understand that he was the heir to all the Habsburg crowns and titles. His mother dedicated herself to the cause of his restoration during the following decades, and though her efforts were ultimately unavailing, it should be noted that in the 1970s, when Otto became a member of the European Parliament, Juan Carlos, the Bourbon grandson of Alfonso XIII, was brought back to the throne of Spain following Franco's death. Twentieth-century restorations were always unlikely but not absolutely unimaginable.

In 1925 a "Gebetsliga," or prayer league, was officially established in Austria, for the post-Habsburg purpose of promoting Karl as a possible Roman Catholic saint.² The Habsburg dynasty had been closely associated with the Catholic Church since the age of the Counter-Reformation, and Karl himself was certainly pious, but now it was also suggested that his unsuccessful efforts on behalf of a negotiated peace to end World War I might provide some grounds to consider him as saintly. Zita was no less pious, and in 1926, even while raising her family at Lekeitio, she became an oblate, or lay affiliate, of the Benedictine convent of St. Cecilia at Solesmes in France. Three of Zita's sisters were nuns there, and though Zita was content to remain an oblate, she would visit Solesmes for periods of prayer throughout her life. The balance of maternal commitment, restoration politics, permanent mourning, and convent piety would constitute the fundamental themes of her imperial afterlife.³

Die Frau ohne Schatten was presented in Vienna on November 9, 1922, with Schalk and Oestvig from the original cast. On that same day Schalk wrote to Strauss, affirming the importance of the opera, in spite of "the countless difficulties of this greatest and most powerful work of the post-Wagnerian operatic repertory." The role of the Empress on November 9 was sung by soprano Fanny Cleve, the daughter of an Austrian rabbi, probably the first Jewish Empress; she had trained with the great Wagnerian soprano Lilli Lehmann and would go on to star in the sensational jazz opera of the 1920s, Ernst Krenek's *Jonny spielt auf* (*Jonny Strikes Up*). Cleve would have to leave Nazi Austria after 1938, and she then emigrated to the United States.⁴ The role of the Dyer's Wife—with Cleve as the Empress in 1922—was taken by Nelly Pirchoff-Manowarda, the wife of bass-baritone Josef von Manowarda, who had sung the role of Keikobad's Messenger at the premiere; both husband and wife would become dedicated Nazis. Josef von Manowarda was supposed to have been particularly admired by Hitler.⁵

On November 26 Lucie Weidt sang the Marschallin in *Der Rosenkavalier*, opposite Lotte Lehmann as Octavian—with Manowarda as Baron Ochs.⁶ Strauss, still the director of the Vienna Opera, kept his own works in the repertory, and *Die Frau ohne Schatten* had its turn roughly once a month. In 1922 it came back after Christmas, on December 28, with Strauss conducting, Oestvig as the Emperor, and Weidt returning to the role of the Nurse.⁷

In 1922 Strauss set about building for himself a villa in Vienna, actually in the former garden of Archduke Franz Ferdinand at the Belvedere. He ended up donating the autograph score of *Der Rosenkavalier* to the Austrian State Library as part of the financial terms of the arrangement, confirming his place as a leading cultural figure in Vienna.[8] Yet Hofmannsthal felt that they were both embattled in Vienna, and he wrote to Strauss on September 4 to denounce the *Spiessbürger*, the bourgeois philistines, who could not appreciate the "spiritual" significance of the Vienna Opera. Hofmannsthal might once have meant the Viennese Jewish public who could only imagine that $2 \times 2 = 4$, as he wrote in September 1917, but in Salzburg he now saw the *Spiessbürger* philistines as the German nationalists and anti-Semites who hated Reinhardt because he was Jewish.[9] For Hofmannsthal, the cosmopolitan Austrian culture represented by Salzburg was antithetical to any sort of strident nationalism, and he now recognized the vulnerability of high culture to extreme political movements. In October 1922 Mussolini would stage his March on Rome, and the age of European fascism would begin.

Hofmannsthal rejected the philistines, but he was not at all aligned with the 1920s avant-garde. In fact, he was moving toward a position of pronounced cultural conservatism, fully articulated in 1927 in his address "The Written Word as the Spiritual Space of the Nation."[10] For him and for Strauss the notion of a postwar philistine public would become entangled with some elements of public failure to appreciate their operas, and notably *Die Frau ohne Schatten*, which seemed to be struggling to maintain its place in the repertory.

In July 1923 Strauss was in South America again, traveling by ship along the coast from Buenos Aires to Rio de Janeiro, writing to Hofmannsthal about the triumph of *Salome* and *Elektra* in Buenos Aires.[11] Two months later, on September 8, Strauss's ship stopped in Dakar on the way home, and he seized the opportunity to write to Hofmannsthal full of eagerness for the new libretto for *Die ägyptische Helena*.[12] The opera was to focus on Helen of Troy after the Trojan War, and, anticipating Strauss's return, Hofmannsthal wrote to Garmisch on September 14 to insist that "the style must be light." He was emphatic on this point: "The more lightly, the more lightheartedly you take the work, the better it will be." At the same time Hofmannsthal was imagining Jeritza and Oestvig—the stars of *Die Frau ohne Schatten*—as Helena and Menelaus.[13]

On September 22, 1923, Hofmannsthal urged Strauss to compose *Helena* "as if it were only supposed to be an operetta," and he was explicit about the example to be avoided: "Over *Die Frau ohne Schatten* we both became too heavy." Future collaborations should be prepared "for the ears of normal humans and for the throats, not of the most artistic singers, but of many singers."[14] By implication *Die Frau ohne Schatten* was fit neither for a normal public nor for normal singers. It continued to be produced—Darmstadt in 1920, Hamburg in 1921, Stuttgart in 1923, Nuremberg in 1924—but the music eluded consensus, with "many ear-whipping dissonances" heard in Darmstadt, but with "tonal beauty and magic" in Nuremberg.[15]

In 1923 there were three performances of *Die Frau ohne Schatten* in Vienna, the first with Strauss conducting the Hungarian Jewish soprano Rose Pauly as the Empress.[16] Pauly, however, possessed the dramatic qualities that made her even more successful as the Dyer's Wife, and in the heavier roles of Salome and Elektra—the latter a role that she brought to New York to public acclaim in 1938 and 1939.[17] After Pauly's single performance as the Empress in January 1923, German soprano Gertrud Geyersbach assumed the role and appeared as the Empress five times between 1923 and 1925.[18] She had something of Jeritza's personal glamour and also regularly performed the role of Korngold's Marietta in Vienna.

Hofmannsthal at Fifty, Strauss at Sixty

Hofmannsthal turned fifty on February 1, 1924, and Strauss wrote to congratulate him on behalf of their joint operatic creations: "Chrysothemis, the Marschallin, Ariadne, Zerbinetta, the Empress, and not least the so much admired and chided H [Helena] may join with me and thank you for all that you have dedicated to me from your life's work."[19] For Strauss, the Empress remained one of their great collaborative creations, and he conjured her to life in his letter to join him in wishing Hofmannsthal a happy birthday.

In 1924 Zita's cultural advisers (at the urging of Leopold von Andrian) considered the possibility of having her send congratulations from her

Spanish exile to Hofmannsthal on the occasion of his birthday. An opinion was solicited, on behalf of Zita in Lekeitio, from the Catholic writer Richard von Kralik, who had worked with Hofmannsthal on the Austrian Library project during the war (and whose son Heinrich had reviewed *Die Frau ohne Schatten* for the *Wiener Abendpost*). The elder Kralik now advised against congratulations to Hofmannsthal, noting that "his reputation is even in his own (Jewish liberal) circles not uncontested." Touchily, Kralik further observed that "although he is known to be of Jewish descent, he behaved with me as if he came from an old landed family."[20] Baron Erwein Gudenus, Zita's adviser, noted accordingly that there would be no birthday wishes from the former Empress. Instead, it was the fairy-tale Empress from *Die Frau ohne Schatten* whom Strauss invoked as joining him—and his other operatic heroines—in congratulating the poet.

Hofmannsthal had been nominated for the Nobel Prize in 1919, the year of *Die Frau ohne Schatten*, and was nominated again in 1924 by German literature professor Walther Brecht, but the prize went to Polish novelist Władysław Reymont, author of the four-volume novel *Peasants*. Hofmannsthal would be considered again in 1926 and 1927 but his name would not prevail in Stockholm. It has been suggested that he did not receive the Nobel Prize in the 1920s in part because one of the Swedish judges took note of Hofmannsthal's remote Jewish ancestry.[21]

Strauss turned sixty on June 11, 1924, and a performance of *Die Frau ohne Schatten* on May 13 (with Mayr as Barak, Weidt as the Nurse, and Strauss conducting) was part of the season of celebration.[22] Yet, for Strauss it was also a year of mixed appreciation, with his lighthearted new ballet *Schlagobers* (*Whipped Cream*) receiving negative reviews from, among others, Karl Kraus: "There has not been a nastier desolation of the spirit of the ballet or a more thoroughgoing degradation of theater to a level of pre-school than this *Schlagobers*."[23] As musicologist Michael Kennedy has observed, Strauss at sixty—"he who had been in tune with the times in the first decade of the century"—was now at risk of seeming old-fashioned and irrelevant. In 1924 he was even edged out of the directorship of the Vienna Opera by the maneuvering of his Viennese codirector Franz Schalk. Though Schalk was a great advocate of Strauss's work and the first conductor of *Die Frau ohne*

Schatten, their codirectorship had inevitably involved personal and professional frictions.[24]

For Hofmannsthal's fiftieth birthday, Fischer Verlag in Berlin published his collected works (*Gesammelte Werke*) in six volumes. Strauss and Hofmannsthal, after two decades of collaboration, now discussed the publication of a selection of their letters, going up until 1918, to the end of the war, the collapse of the Habsburg monarchy, and the completion of *Die Frau ohne Schatten*. By September 1925 Hofmannsthal was preparing the text and feeling "wistful" (*wehmütig*) about the past years of their collaboration.[25] Correcting the proofs in November, he reflected on "how this is all lined up on the thread of passing time [*am Faden der vergehenden Zeit*]: the first meeting, *Elektra*, *Rosenkavalier*, then *Ariadne*, *Die Frau ohne Schatten*, *Joseph*, the second *Ariadne*."[26] Thus Hofmannsthal became himself like the Marschallin, meditating on the fleeting nature of time, with each opera revisited in the logical and historical order of its creative emergence in a past world that itself had been completely transformed. "Sometimes I get up in the middle of the night and stop all the clocks," sang the Marschallin.[27]

Hofmannsthal worried about frank passages in the correspondence where Strauss had momentarily criticized the libretti for *Ariadne* and for *Die Frau ohne Schatten*; the poet was nervous that if those letters were published it would provide "a fearful weapon in the hands of philistine criticism [*philisterhafte Kritik*]"—to be used against those operas.[28] He remained insecure about the reception of *Die Frau ohne Schatten*, even though Strauss reassured him in January 1925 that the opera "still has a future" (*hat noch ihre Zukunft*), that it was successful again in Hamburg and had good prospects in Munich.[29] The operatic event of 1925 was Berg's *Wozzeck*, with its very dark drama of military life and its austerely atonal score, radically different from *Die Frau ohne Schatten*, which had been conceived before the war in the spirit of post-Wagnerian late Romanticism.

In January 1926 Hofmannsthal was revising the conclusion of *Helena*, and he proposed several cuts from his own libretto, including the lines of "Menelaus's anxiety that, if Helena is a phantom, then all the Greeks have died for the sake of a ghost (indeed an important, profound theme)." These lines were, in fact, cut from the second-act libretto—"Um ein Gespenst, starben sie hin?"³⁰—and certainly when Hofmannsthal and Strauss contemplated a reckoning with the Trojan War, they were also thinking of the terrible war that they themselves had witnessed, reflecting on the illusions for which so many men had given their lives.

"In Berlin I conducted a magnificent *Rosenkavalier*," Strauss boasted on March 19, 1926, "and a completely sold-out *Die Frau ohne Schatten*."³¹ In the fall of 1927, Strauss notified Hofmannsthal that *Die Frau ohne Schatten* was a "great success" during a "Strauss week" in Frankfurt in August and alerted him to upcoming performances of the opera in Stuttgart and Dresden.³² On October 25, after conducting the Stuttgart performance, he reported that it was "as musically brilliant as it was visually bleak," noting parenthetically that "the cursed war" was still to blame for the scenographic disappointment of what was supposed to be a spectacular opera: "we can only hope for a better future."³³

Spectacular staging marked the operatic sensation of 1926, Puccini's posthumous last opera *Turandot*, the cruel Chinese princess making her first appearance at La Scala under Toscanini in a fairy-tale scenario set in the imperial palace of the Forbidden City in Beijing. At the La Scala premiere in April 1926 the title role was sung by Polish Jewish soprano Rosa Raisa, born Raitsa Burchstein in Bialystok, but Jeritza always claimed that Puccini wrote the role for her, and it was she who sang the New York premiere in November at the Met. Jeritza had given up the role of the Empress in *Die Frau ohne Schatten* to apply her imperial glamour to the role of Puccini's Chinese princess—who must also discover her humanity through love. Olin Downes in the *New York Times* declared *Turandot* to be a "brilliant spectacle" and was full of admiration for Jeritza's "resplendent" gowns and charismatic stage presence—"she was shimmering magnificence, imperiousness, allurement personified when she appeared a brief instant on the balcony in the first act"—though he had reservations about her vocal performance.³⁴

A year later, in October 1927, Hofmannsthal was still eager to recruit Jeritza for the role of Helena, but Strauss responded with some skepticism, offering the counterproposal of the younger German soprano Elisabeth Rethberg who was more likely to be available for the Dresden premiere in 1928. Rethberg, Strauss noted, had recently been "splendid" as the Empress in *Die Frau ohne Schatten* in Dresden.³⁵ Hofmannsthal, however, seemed to feel

Figure 31. Jeritza's personal glamour enhanced her stage charisma and vocal artistry. This postcard dates from the late 1920s when she had given up the role of Strauss's Empress but taken on the spectacular imperial role of Puccini's Chinese princess Turandot. Strauss and Hofmannsthal both believed in her as a compelling interpreter of their work. After World War II in 1948, one year before his death, Strauss dedicated one of his *Four Last Songs*—"September"—to her in the personae of the roles she had sung for him: "To the most beautiful woman in the world [Helena], the sublime Empress [in *Die Frau ohne Schatten*], the most powerful Princess [Ariadne]. . . ." She herself, by then, was married to an American umbrella manufacturer and living in New Jersey, where she died in 1982. (Property of the author)

that only Jeritza could offer the ideal incarnation of Ariadne, the Empress, and now Helena, heroines whom he sometimes feared that Strauss did not properly appreciate.[36]

With regard to *Helena*, Hofmannsthal was determined to impress upon Strauss the fateful importance of the premiere: "The main point is the complete resounding success of the premiere, and the music unfortunately is not enough to achieve that (otherwise *Die Frau ohne Schatten*, whose score is supposed to be a true miracle, would be your most successful opera)."[37] The parenthetical aside indicated that anxiety about *Die Frau ohne Schatten* remained always in the back of Hofmannsthal's mind. In spite of Jeritza, in spite of Strauss's miraculous music, the premiere of *Die Frau ohne Schatten* had not quite established the lasting success of the opera which remained, for both collaborators, a "problem child."

In a letter of October 31, Strauss expressed confidence that *Die Frau ohne Schatten* would still find "appreciation" (*Würdigung*) in the context of their collaborative oeuvre: "That our operas (even if you are no Schiller and I no Richard Wagner) have now stayed in the repertory for over twenty years is at least a sign that there is nothing better."[38] Strauss showed himself perhaps purposely oblivious to what was taking place in the opera world even as he wrote in 1927. After the artistic triumph of *Wozzeck* in 1925, and the huge public success of Puccini's posthumous *Turandot* in 1926, there followed in 1927 the premieres of Krenek's *Jonny spielt auf*, Kurt Weill's *Mahagonny-Songspiel*, Darius Milhaud's *Le pauvre matelot*, Arthur Honegger's *Antigone*, Stravinsky's *Oedipus Rex*, and Erich Korngold's *The Miracle of Heliane*. Indeed Strauss's brand of late-Romantic operatic modernism—which brought him sensational success before the war—was being overtaken by a younger generation of classical composers.

While Hofmannsthal affirmed that *Die Frau ohne Schatten* might be a "true miracle" on the strength of its music, Strauss replied on November 2 with an affirmation of confidence in the libretto.

> In spite of all the stupid reviews, I still today believe that *Die Frau ohne Schatten* is not only beautiful poetry but also a theatrically effective opera libretto. . . . We can't do anything about the fact that today the times are generally bad for art, and that the public—the people who can today afford a seat at the opera—are stupid and uneducated![39]

Strauss made the case for *Die Frau ohne Schatten* with confident snobbism, but he also seemed to raise the disturbing possibility that he and Hofmannsthal together might constitute a pair of prewar geniuses awkwardly out of step with the new decade of the 1920s.

The Habsburg Past on the Operatic Stage

In 1927 there was violent social conflict in Vienna: encounters between paramilitary forces of the Left and Right, a general strike, demonstrations at the Reichsrat, the burning of the Palace of Justice, and fatal police firing on protestors. On December 22, as 1927 drew to a close, Hofmannsthal was thinking back to older and more peaceful times, Habsburg times, as he contemplated the libretto for *Arabella*—to be set in the Vienna of the 1860s. For the romantic baritone role of Mandryka, a Croatian nobleman, Hofmannsthal had in mind some text from Slavic folk songs.[40] This was the sort of material that once belonged to Hofmannsthal's Austrian Library project during the war, reconciling the diverse Habsburg nations within one literary publishing project, defining a unified Austrian culture, an "Austrian idea"—that would serve as a bulwark of patriotic unity during the war and after. Now that the multinational Habsburg monarchy no longer existed, Hofmannsthal could only nostalgically revisit the empire by writing a libretto that took him back into the reign of Franz Joseph.

There were four performances of *Die Frau ohne Schatten* in Vienna in 1927 and two more in the first half of 1928. The role of the Empress was sung all six times by the Berlin-born soprano Wanda Achsel, who now became the preferred performer for the role in Vienna. Lucie Weidt, who had created the role of the Nurse, was now in her early fifties and sang her last performance in that role in 1927. Barak at this time was usually sung by Alfred Jerger, who would later create the role of Count Mandryka in *Arabella*.[41]

As 1927 came to an end, Hofmannsthal urged Strauss not to rush him over the libretto for *Arabella*: "Have some confidence after so many on the whole (despite several mistakes in *Die Frau ohne Schatten*) fairly successful works."[42] With 1928 about to begin, with *Helena* scheduled to have its premiere in Dresden in June, and with *Arabella* evolving in his creative imagination, Hofmannsthal believed that it was important to acknowledge and try to understand the mistakes of *Die Frau ohne Schatten*. The premiere of *Helena* in Dresden would take place on June 6, 1928, with Rethberg, followed immediately by Vienna on June 11 with Jeritza, who would also introduce the role in New York on November 6.

On April 25, 1928, anticipating the Dresden premiere, Strauss wanted Hofmannsthal to write about *Helena* in advance and explain the libretto, so that it would not be misunderstood by the public. Strauss noted that opera houses were now publishing with the playbill a synopsis of the plot (the modern practice that still prevails), and he wanted Hofmannsthal himself to write the synopsis for *Helena*: "Please allow me to convince you that everything must be done now to confront in advance all malicious or clueless misinterpretations of your poetry . . . as with *Die Frau ohne Schatten*."[43] Strauss was ever more contemptuous of the stupidity of the philistine critics and publics, and he was firmly convinced that their inevitable misunderstandings had undermined the success of *Die Frau ohne Schatten* in 1919.

Julius Korngold, reviewing the Dresden premiere of *Die ägyptische Helena* for the *Neue Freie Presse* in Vienna, thought that Hofmannsthal's libretto was too full of "dark symbolism and artful psychology," further noting, with disapproval, that the opera displayed "the mingling of symbolism and magical creatures from *Die Frau ohne Schatten*."[44] Korngold was one of the critics who had failed to appreciate properly *Die Frau ohne Schatten* in 1919, and he continued to regard it as a negative reference for comparison. Though *Die Frau ohne Schatten* had still never been produced in New York, *Helena* was performed there promptly, offered as a vehicle for Jeritza after her triumph in *Turandot*. Olin Downes, reviewing the American premiere in November for the *New York Times*, noted the "spectacular production" but found the libretto "somewhat rambling and dramatically futile," with Strauss "not wholly to be blamed if he found himself helpless before the redundancies and futilities of the text of Hofmannsthal." Even Jeritza, though she "assumed many a picturesque pose," was judged to be "unsteady in tone and frequently off pitch."[45]

By June 1928 the collaborators were back at work on *Arabella* with a libretto that offered minimal symbolism and no magical creatures. It was to be a romantic comedy, culminating in marriage, and on June 24 Strauss worried that the first-act libretto was "not brilliant enough"—but sent congratulations to Hofmannsthal on his own daughter's marriage.[46] Christiane

Hofmannsthal married Heinrich Zimmer, a Heidelberg University professor of South Asian philology and culture, a scholar of Oriental mythology and symbolism. Within a decade the young couple would end up in the United States, refugees from Nazi Germany. Strauss's own son Franz (Bubi) had gotten married already in 1924—to Alice Grab von Hermannswörth from a Prague family of Jewish manufacturers ennobled by Franz Joseph.

Hofmannsthal tried to impress upon Strauss the reason why the libretto for *Arabella* did not seem more elevated in tone: this was a different Vienna from the Vienna of *Der Rosenkavalier*. "Vienna under Maria Theresa—and the Vienna of 1866!" wrote Hofmannsthal on July 13. "The atmosphere of *Arabella*, already very close to our own time as it is, is more normal, more earnest, more ordinary."[47] The Vienna of *Arabella*, set in the 1860s in the reign of Franz Joseph, belonged to the vanished imperial age which was becoming increasingly remote—and by 1933, when *Arabella* had its premiere in Dresden, Hitler had already come to power in Germany.

"As If I Were Stepping on Someone's Grave"

In the later 1920s the collaborators more regularly began to address one another as "my dear friend" (instead of Dear Dr. Strauss and Dear Herr von Hofmannsthal), but they never arrived at the informal and intimate German pronoun *Du* in their letters. When Hofmannsthal showed himself willing to revise the libretto for *Arabella*, Strauss wrote to him on July 3, 1928, almost romantically, "I find we understand each other better from year to year. What a pity such good continuous work toward perfection must come to an end some day, and that others must start again from the beginning."[48] It was perhaps in part a reflection on mortality, the conviction that one of them would die and the other would need to learn to work with new collaborators—as eventually occurred, and sooner than anticipated. Perhaps there was also some implicit sense that the opera world itself—corrupted by the supposed philistinism of the 1920s—was no longer as conducive to their collaborative efforts as before, however perfect their reciprocal understanding. In August Kurt Weill and Bertolt Brecht would present in Berlin the sensational premiere of their *Threepenny Opera*—utterly remote from the cultural premises of the Strauss-Hofmannsthal collaborations.

In the fall of 1928 Strauss noted a production of *Helena* in Hamburg and reported to Hofmannsthal about an exchange with one philistine critic:

> A Hamburg critic commiserated with me, that my "splendid music" was burdened by your "incomprehensible text." I answered that *Helena* was easier to understand than *Die Frau ohne Schatten*. He replied: "Oh but I now understand *Die Frau ohne Schatten* quite well!" Well, I hope he doesn't need another ten years for *Helena*![49]

It was perhaps unnecessarily provocative of Strauss to suggest to the critic the difficulty of understanding *Die Frau ohne Schatten*, and Hofmannsthal may not have been altogether pleased to hear that his collaborator was bantering about the alleged incomprehensibility of the libretto.

On November 7 Strauss complained that he was not sufficiently engaged by the title character Arabella, blaming Hofmannsthal's libretto: "Everything is weaker and more conventional than in *Der Rosenkavalier*—unless you can still succeed in making Arabella a truly interesting figure like our good Marschallin."[50] Hofmannsthal was deeply offended, and wrote in reply on November 19, offering Strauss something like epistolary psychoanalysis:

> The thought comes to me, whether perhaps entirely without your will, even without your consciousness, something may have occurred which sometimes also occurs in marriages after about fifteen years, and against which both partners are entirely helpless: an inner fatigue, a chilling—so that suddenly my whole palette, the way that I draw characters and the kind of characters I draw . . . may have suddenly become unpalatable and unexciting to you.[51]

Hofmannsthal thus regarded their collaboration as a sort of creative marriage between two men, mediated by their invented heroines. If Strauss was unable to respond to Arabella but was still pining for the Marschallin, Hofmannsthal almost doubted whether they could continue to collaborate.

In 1929, as the decade approached its conclusion, Hofmannsthal's daughter Christiane was settling in Heidelberg, and the poet was thinking about his sons, Franz and Raimund, who both spent some time in the United States in the 1920s. Raimund was at ease in Hollywood society and later made a sensational American marriage to Ava Alice Astor, the daughter of multimillionaire Titanic victim John Jacob Astor IV. Franz, Hofmannsthal's older son, born in 1903, found his life more stressful and returned to Europe feeling sick and depressed in 1927; he was living at home in Rodaun with his parents in 1929. On July 13, after lunch, Franz went to his room and shot himself. In a letter to his friend Carl Burckhardt on July 14, Hofmannsthal wrote, "There was something infinitely sad and infinitely noble in the way that the poor child took leave of life. He could never communicate. Even his departure was silent [*schweigend*]."[52] On July 15 Hugo von Hofmannsthal had a stroke, at home, and died at the age of fifty-five.

"The main thing is the act endings," the widow Cosima Wagner had once said to Richard Strauss, emphasizing the importance of operatic conclusions, the coordination of the music and the drama to the moment at the end of each act when the curtain would fall. Strauss passed on this piece of Wagnerian wisdom to Hofmannsthal in 1928 when they were discussing the libretto of *Arabella*, and on July 6, 1929, one week before the poet's death, the composer had been writing to stress the importance of the curtain scene to the first act. "Arabella must absolutely close the first act with a longer aria, monologue, contemplation," wrote Strauss. "In a three-act opera the first-act closing must be very effective. So I ask you urgently [*dringend*] to shape the whole act so that it culminates with compelling necessity in the lyrical solo scene for Arabella."[53] Strauss might have been thinking of the Marschallin left alone on stage at the first-act curtain of *Der Rosenkavalier*, suddenly distressed that she had neglected to kiss Octavian as he departed. Possibly he thought of *Die Frau ohne Schatten* and the moving trio of night watchmen outside Barak's dwelling at the first-act curtain: "You spouses who lie lovingly in each other's arms, you are the bridge that extends over the abyss, by which the dead return to life!"

Hofmannsthal had been fully in agreement about the end of the first act of *Arabella*: "I was aiming to create just such a quiet, peaceful conclusion, but I was not certain that it would please you. Your letter was therefore a stone lifted from my heart."[54] The poet, just before his death, had prepared the text for the soliloquy—"Mein Elemer"—dismissing one suitor and then fantasizing in the key of D-flat (the key of the *Rosenkavalier* trio) about "der fremde Mann" (the unknown man), the Croatian nobleman Arabella has not yet met.[55] The monologue, which concludes by anticipating the waltzing Viennese carnival ball of the second act, remains beloved by all

Strauss sopranos—but Hofmannsthal never had the chance to hear Strauss's setting.

Before the shift in the music to the concluding carnival waltz, there occurs a beautiful and eerie phrase that Hofmannsthal submitted with the revision just before his death: "Was rührt mich denn so an, als trät' ich einem übers Grab?" (What is it that touches me so, as if I were stepping on someone's grave?) Strauss has Arabella sing all the way down to low B-flat and then ascend the scale to reach the word "Grab"—her voice accompanied by the solo viola, a faithful companion through the whole soliloquy.[56] On July 14 Strauss sent an enthusiastic telegram to Hofmannsthal: "First act excellent. Warm thanks and congratulations."[57] But the poet died on July 15, before he could receive and open the telegram.

Strauss wrote to Gerty von Hofmannsthal the next day, July 16, to offer his condolences to the widow on the deaths of both her son and her husband—"this brilliant man, this great poet, this sensitive collaborator, this kind friend, this unique talent"—and he promised to make a final glorious monument out of the "splendid poetry that he sent me just before his death," that is, the libretto of *Arabella*.[58] In September 1929 Strauss wrote to her again to affirm his support: "It is for me an obligation of honor to preserve true friendship for the wife of the precious Hugo."[59] He had never called Hofmannsthal "Hugo" in their correspondence but now used his Christian name posthumously in correspondence with the poet's widow.

On the other side of Europe, in September 1929, another widow, the former Empress, packed up her family in Spain and moved to Belgium. Spain was about to depose its Bourbon king in 1931 and become a republic, and Zita's sense of the instability of the monarchy was one of the considerations behind her relocation. It was also true that her children were growing up, and Otto, born in 1912, was ready to begin studying at the Catholic University of Louvain.[60] He would soon attain the age of majority at eighteen and would be able to claim the Habsburg crown in his own right. The little court of retainers in exile moved from Spain to Belgium, along with Otto's seven siblings and, of course, his mother.

17

Nazi Germany and Austrian Anschluss

POLITICAL AND OPERATIC PROSPECTS IN THE 1930S

New Production

The 1930s was a decade of overwhelming economic depression and deep political polarization; it witnessed the rise of Nazism in Austria and Germany and, finally in 1938, the annexation of Austria by Nazi Germany. The decade began, however, with a new production of *Die Frau ohne Schatten* in 1931 at the Vienna Opera, an affirmation of the importance of the work whose viability and survival had been a cause of some concern to its creators in the 1920s.[1] The new musical director of the Vienna Opera, replacing Schalk in 1930, was Clemens Krauss, who had first worked there as an assistant conductor during the Strauss regime of the early 1920s. Krauss would be the preeminent Strauss conductor of the 1930s, not least because of his convenient ability to get along with the Nazi regime, taking over jobs from less deferential conductors who refused to collaborate: he left Vienna for the Berlin Opera in 1934, replacing Erich Kleiber, and then took over Munich in 1937 from Hans Knappertsbusch. Krauss's wife, the Romanian soprano Viorica Ursuleac, became the leading Strauss soprano of the decade, performing under her husband's baton in close consultation with the composer.

Krauss was the conductor and Ursuleac the Empress for the new production of *Die Frau ohne Schatten* in Vienna in 1931. Two years later he would be the conductor and she the eponymous heroine for the premiere of *Arabella* in Dresden in 1933. Both artists were born as Habsburg subjects in the 1890s, and Krauss, born in Vienna, had a tangential connection to the Habsburg dynasty as the illegitimate cousin of Baroness Mary Vetsera, the seventeen-year-old girl at Mayerling with Crown Prince Rudolf.[2] Ursuleac was born in a city that had been virtually created by the Habsburgs: Czernowitz, capital of the province of Bukovina, with its important university—the Franz Joseph University—and mixed population of Germans, Jews, Ukrainians, and Romanians. It was the quintessentially multinational dynastic metropolis which only made sense in the context of the Habsburg monarchy. As Cernăuți the city belonged to Romania in the 1920s and 1930s, and it became part of Ukraine, as Chernivtsi, after World War II. Ursuleac could bring to the role of the Empress a powerful sense of the imperial legacy, and her long lifespan (1894–1985) roughly corresponded to that of Zita (1892–1989). The role of the Empress, as conceived by Strauss and Hofmannsthal, belonged to Ursuleac in the 1930s and usually under the baton of Krauss.

The new production, conceived by the Prague-born stage director Lothar Wallerstein, opened in Vienna at the end of February in 1931 and ran in repertory until June, thus overlapping with the bankruptcy of the Austrian Credit-Anstalt bank on May 11.[3] Founded by the Rothschilds in the early nineteenth century, the bank had always had close connections to the Habsburg government and after 1918 remained central to the Austrian economy. Its collapse in 1931 was the signal for the onset of the Great Depression in Austria and in Europe as a whole, and the world of Barak the Dyer, representing the precariously employed poor craftsmen of Vienna, was suddenly undermined even as the opera was being staged.

The role of the Dyer's Wife was taken by Lotte Lehmann, who had created the part in 1919 and now returned to the role in Vienna for the first time in a decade. The role of the Dyer, however, passed from Richard Mayr to Josef von Manowarda, who had originally sung the role of Keikobad's Messenger at the 1919 premiere.[4] Manowarda would be an enthusiastic advocate of Nazism as the decade continued, while Lehmann would leave Europe altogether in the 1930s and move to the United States, even becoming an American citizen. Returning to the Dyer's Wife in 1931, Lehmann, born in 1888, was already turning forty-three, and Jeritza, who was still singing Salome in Vienna in 1931, was one year older. What was beginning to appear as a probability in both of their life trajectories was that Jeritza and Lehmann, who had competed for the symbolic shadow of fertility and motherhood at the premiere of *Die Frau ohne Schatten* in 1919, were, like many operatic divas of their generation, never going to have biological children of their own.

A review of *Die Frau ohne Schatten* appeared in the *Neue Freie Presse* on February 27, 1931, and Julius Korngold, now in his early seventies, reviewed the opera again, as he had at its premiere in 1919, again just below the fold on the front page. Whereas in 1919 Korngold had been skeptical about the work, especially Hofmannsthal's libretto, in 1931 he claimed to be won over by Wallerstein's new production—which finally endowed the opera with the "magic" that had been missing at the premiere. Korngold praised the intensity of Krauss's conducting, the charm, the nobility, the passion of Ursuleac as the Empress, and especially the maturity of Lehmann's performance as the Dyer's Wife, no longer manifesting the "hysteria" that he had noted at the premiere in 1919.[5]

Strauss, whom Korngold had criticized as insufficiently modernist in 1919, was now praised for having heralded a new age of Romantic opera with *Die Frau ohne Schatten*. In fact, Korngold's son Erich was himself a neo-Romantic modernist composer. Following *Die tote Stadt*, the Vienna Opera presented *The Miracle of Heliane* between 1927 and 1930 in a production by Wallerstein with the role of Heliane interpreted by Lehmann. Julius Korngold was thus also promoting the operatic success of his son when he produced his reversal of opinion on *Die Frau ohne Schatten*. The critic recalled Barak's beautiful musical phrase in the first act, after his wife's harsh words: "They are blessed with the blessing of revocability [*Widerruflichkeit*]." Korngold now borrowed the phrase for his own recantation: "Happily, even a critic may enjoy the blessing of revocability."[6]

The Wallerstein production of *Die Frau ohne Schatten* was presented fifteen times between 1931 and 1934, always with Krauss conducting and Ursuleac in the role of the Empress, an extraordinary conjugal dedication to the work which was itself an operatic study in conjugality. Lehmann did not sing all of the performances of the Dyer's Wife, alternating in 1931 with Nelly Pirchoff-Manowarda, who thus sang opposite her husband Josef von Manowarda as Barak.[7] In 1934, however, Manowarda, with his political commitment to Nazism, would be singing Barak opposite the Hungarian Jewish soprano Rose Pauly in the role of the Dyer's Wife. The tensions within the operatic marriage would have played out differently with different casts in the volatile and evolving political climate of the 1930s.

In the summer of 1932 the new production was brought to the Salzburg Festival with Krauss conducting, and with Ursuleac, Lehmann, and Manowarda in the cast; for Hofmannsthal, had he been still alive, it would have represented an important vindication of *Die Frau ohne Schatten* at the festival that he had done so much to create.[8] The opening performance on August 19 fell one day after the birthday of Franz Joseph and two days after the birthday of Karl, imperial dates that Austrians would have likely recalled. The production returned to Salzburg in August 1933, with Krauss, Ursuleac, Manowarda, and Pauly.[9] It was scheduled to come back again in August 1934 but was canceled "for technical reasons" and replaced with *Don Giovanni*. Yet 1934 was the year of Strauss's seventieth birthday, and Salzburg featured works of the Strauss-Hofmannsthal collaboration: *Der Rosenkavalier* (with Lehmann), *Die ägyptische Helena* (with Ursuleac), and *Elektra* (with Pauly).[10]

In February 1934 there was also the Austrian Civil War, several days of fighting between socialists and right-wing paramilitary groups assisted by the police and the army—especially in Red Vienna—bringing about the consolidation of power by the Fatherland Front of Chancellor Engelbert Dollfuß. His authoritarian leadership was sometimes characterized as Austrofascism. Such was the political context for the performance of *Die Frau ohne Schatten* on June 11, 1934. The turmoil continued, however, for on July 25 Dollfuß was assassinated by Austrian Nazis, who hoped (but failed) to seize power and join Austria to Nazi Germany.[11]

Because of Dollfuß's funeral, the opening of the Salzburg Festival—with Krauss conducting Lehmann in *Fidelio*—was postponed one day until July 29.[12] Bruno Walter then conducted *Tristan* on July 30. On July 31, 1934, a child was born at the Viennese maternity hospital called the Rudolfinerhaus after Archduke Rudolf, who had died at Mayerling in 1889. That child, Renee Stier, was my mother, born into a Viennese Jewish family at the moment of extreme political unrest immediately following the assassination of Dollfuß.

My mother's mother Lucy was the daughter of Leiser Erber, who had come from Galicia to open his leather shop in Vienna. My mother's father, Martin or Moses Stier, a doctor, was trained at the University of Vienna, after graduating from high school (*Gymnasium*) in Czernowitz, the Habsburg

Figure 32. Franzensbad (named for Habsburg Emperor Franz) was the spa town in Bohemia where Karl and Zita began their romance in the early twentieth century, after she left her convent school and when he was serving as an officer in the Habsburg army. After World War I the town became Františkovy Lázně in Czechoslovakia, and in this photo the strolling romantic pair are Leiser Erber, on vacation from his leather shop in Vienna, and his wife Malka, Lucy's parents and my great-grandparents. They were deported from Vienna to Theresienstadt during World War II and murdered by the Nazis in the Holocaust. (Property of the author)

city of Viorica Ursuleac. Both Martin and Lucy, my grandparents, were born as subjects of Franz Joseph in the Habsburg monarchy in the 1890s. My mother was born into a post-Habsburg family in the post-Habsburg capital of Austria, a country that was then, in 1934, only barely clinging to its deeply polarized and precarious political existence.

Richard Strauss in Hitler's Germany

In the autumn of 1934, the Vienna Opera went on tour to Italy and presented *Die Frau ohne Schatten* in Venice at La Fenice, with Krauss and Ursuleac, Manowarda and Pauly.[13] Hofmannsthal and Strauss, who laid the artistic foundations of the opera during their trip to Italy in 1913, had later been interested in the idea that their fairy-tale opera might have some Mediterranean success. In 1934 the idea of an Austrian-Italian political alliance was particularly prominent, with Italy supporting Austria as it sought to maintain its independence from Nazi Germany. There is even one source that reports Mussolini's possible presence at *Die Frau ohne Schatten* in Venice, speaking to the Viennese guests the next day about his support for independent Austria following the Dollfuß assassination.[14]

Strauss himself, generally acknowledged as the greatest living German composer, held an official position in the cultural life of Nazi Germany, serving from 1933 to 1935 as the president of the Reichsmusikkammer (Reich Music Chamber). That institution was created by Joseph Goebbels to glorify German music and suppress "degenerate" modern music, including of course all music by Jewish composers, dead or alive, from Mendelssohn and Mahler to Korngold and Schoenberg. The Berlin Philharmonic celebrated Strauss's seventieth birthday in June 1934, and Strauss was quoted in the *Völkischer Beobachter*: "Ten years ago was a tough time of inner disintegration and collapse, but now that Adolf Hitler has achieved the unification of the whole German Volk, we are again striving upward; he has established the conditions for a new zenith of German art."[15] When Roller designed a new production of *Parsifal* for Bayreuth in 1934, and Toscanini withdrew in protest against the Nazi regime, Strauss stepped in to conduct. In 1935, however, he was removed as the president of the Reichsmusikkammer for private criticism of the regime: he had written in a letter to Stefan Zweig—which was read by the Gestapo—"Do you suppose Mozart was consciously 'Aryan' when he composed?"[16]

Hofmannsthal—though anti-Semites sometimes denounced him as a Jewish poet—was just barely racially acceptable by the standard of the Nuremberg Laws; he had one grandfather who was born Jewish but converted to Christianity. His operatic collaborations with Strauss could therefore still be performed in the Third Reich, and, at the Vienna Opera, between the Anschluss in 1938 and the bombing of the opera house in 1945, there were seventy-three performances of *Der Rosenkavalier*, thirty-seven performances of *Ariadne*, thirteen performances of *Elektra*, seven performances of *Arabella*, and eight performances of *Die Frau ohne Schatten*, including a new wartime Vienna production in November 1943.[17] If Hofmannsthal was acceptable as a librettist in Nazi Germany and Austria, Strauss's collaboration with Stefan Zweig—following Hofmannsthal's death—on *Die schweigsame Frau* was completely unacceptable. Thereafter Strauss worked principally with Joseph Gregor, the director of the Austrian National Library.[18] While Strauss, who outlived Hofmannsthal by twenty years, would never find another equally inspiring collaborator, it was also true that the oppressive cultural climate of the Third Reich drastically reduced the literary possibilities.

After leaving the Reichsmusikkammer in 1935, Strauss turned to mythological characters like Daphne and Danae and entered into the rococo spirit of *Capriccio*, remote from the ideological concerns of the Nazi regime. Ursuleac, who already sang the roles of the Marschallin, the Empress, Chrysothemis, Helena, and Arabella, would also create the new Strauss soprano roles of the Nazi period: Maria in *Friedenstag* (*Peace Day*) in Munich in July 1938, just before the Munich conference that brought about the destruction of Czechoslovakia; the Countess in *Capriccio* in Munich in October 1942, while Europe's Jews were being murdered in the gas chambers of Auschwitz; and the eponymous heroine of *Die Liebe der Danae* (*The Love of Danae*) which received just one dress rehearsal in Strauss's presence in Salzburg in August 1944 as the Third Reich confronted its own imminent catastrophic defeat.[19]

Strauss's private preoccupation was the protection of his Jewish daughter-in-law Alice and his half-Jewish grandchildren. In 1942 he established himself in Vienna in the hope of being better able to protect his family there, and he actually traveled to Theresienstadt to try—in vain—to save Alice's grandmother who was interned there.[20] Hofmannsthal's widow, Gerty, who converted from Judaism when she married him, had to flee from Austria after the Anschluss; she lived in England during the war, as did Hofmannsthal's surviving younger son Raimund. Hofmannsthal's daughter Christiane, with her husband the Indologist Heinrich Zimmer (who lost his academic job in Heidelberg under the Nazis), emigrated to the United States.

Lotte Lehmann renounced her German citizenship when Hitler came to power and then left Austria at the time of the Anschluss, also resettling in the United States. Her husband Otto Krause was a retired Austrian cavalry officer, and his four children, who became Lehmann's stepchildren, were half-Jewish through their mother.[21] Lehmann made a sensational Metropolitan Opera debut in 1934, singing Sieglinde opposite the Siegmund of

Lauritz Melchior, and in 1935 she appeared on the cover of *Time Magazine* costumed as the Marschallin, which she sang at the Met that year.[22] Her last performance in Vienna, conducted by Hans Knappertsbusch, was also in the supremely Viennese role of the Marschallin in September 1937.[23]

Lehmann was a regular summer performer at Salzburg and she often appeared there in the Strauss-Hofmannsthal operas. With Krauss conducting and with Richard Mayr as Baron Ochs, she sang five performances of the Marschallin in August 1929, just one month after Hofmannsthal's death in July.[24] In 1930 and 1931 she shared the role of the Marschallin with Ursuleac. In 1932 they sang together in *Die Frau ohne Schatten*.[25] In 1933 Lehmann sang the Marschallin again at Salzburg, and she gave a *Lieder* recital with Bruno Walter at the piano.[26] In 1936 she sang in *Die Meistersinger* and *Fidelio* with Toscanini conducting, and she gave a recital with Walter that included songs by Mendelssohn, who was now banned in Germany. This was her penultimate summer in Salzburg and was also the summer that she discovered the Trapp Family Singers and urged them to enter the Salzburg Festival choral competition.[27]

Georg von Trapp was born in 1880, a contemporary of Otto Krause and Emperor Karl, all born in the 1880s, all Habsburg officers, all serving in World War I as the empire went down to defeat. Georg was the widower father of seven children in the 1920s when he fell in love with Maria, the novice nun who was tutoring his children. She became their stepmother (as Lotte Lehmann did for Krause's four children) and then had three more children of her own to add to the Trapp family singing ensemble. Following their success at the Salzburg Festival in 1936, the Trapp family went on tour, singing especially Austrian folk songs and religious hymns.[28] They emigrated to the United States after the Austrian Anschluss with Nazi Germany, and their fame as a singing group was later amplified by the Rodgers and Hammerstein Broadway musical and the Oscar-winning Hollywood film *The Sound of Music*. Maria von Trapp died in Vermont in 1987, the same year that her Austrian contemporary, Hofmannsthal's daughter Christiane, died in New York.

Steenokkerzeel

Photographs of the widowed Empress Zita with her eight children in the 1920s and 1930s—the boys in sailor suits, the girls in frilly white frocks—bear

Figure 33. The widow Zita and her eight children were photographed together in 1929, the year that they left Lekeitio in Spain for Steenokkerzeel in Belgium. Zita, who wore black for the rest of her life following Karl's death in 1922, appeared utterly sober of purpose; she still thought of herself as the Empress of Austria and Queen of Hungary though she had given up her thrones, if not her claims, a decade earlier. Her family of young archdukes and archduchesses, in their sailor suits and white frocks, evoked some of the spirit of the tragic family of Nicholas and Alexandra, murdered by the Bolsheviks in 1918, but there is also an undeniable costumed resemblance to the exactly contemporary Austrian family of children who would eventually become famous as the Trapp Family Singers. Zita and her family, like the Trapp family, would find refuge in America during the war and, like them, would symbolically represent anti-Nazi Austrian traditions and values during the war years when Austria was a part of Hitler's Third Reich. (Sueddeutsche Zeitung Photo/Alamy Stock Photo)

some resemblance to the Trapp Family Singers assembled in their folk costumes. Both families were international emblems of Austrian values—the values of nobility and piety that harkened back to the Habsburg era—and both offered some foundations for opposition to Nazi Austria after 1938. Maria von Trapp left behind her Salzburg convent novitiate at Nonnberg Abbey, the Benedictine convent near Salzburg, when she married Georg in 1927, while Zita affirmed her religious vocation in 1926 when she took her vow as an oblate at the Benedictine convent of Solesmes. The spirit of the convent hovered over them both as they raised their very large families with traditional Roman Catholic values.

Zita had been established in Belgium since 1929 in the little Flemish town of Steenokkerzeel, where she rented Ham Castle (Kasteel ter Ham) with its towers, parapets, and moat. The decade of the 1930s, with the Depression and the rise of Hitler, offered some opportunities to the imperial pretenders, just because the peacemakers of 1919 were no longer secure in their postwar settlement; the possibility of imperial restoration no longer seemed like the worst of all possible political eventualities. At the beginning of the decade Zita was still living in relative political obscurity and some degree of genteel poverty, but the shifting political circumstances gave a dramatic trajectory to her imperial afterlife.

Empresses exercised a particularly romantic appeal on the postimperial cultural public in the 1930s. The German film star, Lil Dagover, who had already appeared in the 1929 silent film *The Favorite of Schönbrunn* as Empress Maria Theresa, now starred in the role of Empress Elisabeth in the 1931 talkie *Elisabeth of Austria*. The leading writer of romantic imperial biographies was Bertita Harding, daughter of a German engineer and a Hungarian countess, married to an American and writing from Indianapolis. Her 1934 book *Phantom Crown* told the nineteenth-century story of Habsburg Emperor Maximilian and Empress Carlota of Mexico. The book then became the basis of the 1939 film *Juarez*, with Bette Davis playing Empress Carlota and movie music by Erich Korngold. In 1937 Harding wrote *Golden Fleece*, about Franz Joseph and Elisabeth, and in 1939 she published *Imperial Twilight*, an account of Karl and Zita.

Making use of the contemporary press and contemporary gossip, Harding conveyed Zita's passionate obsession with recovering the Habsburg crowns for future generations of the dynasty. At the very end of the book Harding even slipped into Zita's dreams: "Thus dreamed the Empress in a twilight that precedes both darkness and a dawn."[29] Though Harding wrote in English, the German word *Dämmerung* signifies both twilight and dawn—and the lingering Habsburg twilight of the 1930s seemed to offer, at moments, the promise of a new dawn. Zita's dreams, as imagined by Harding, might have been accompanied by Korngold's Hollywood music—or the glorious exclamation of the Empress in the first scene of *Die Frau ohne Schatten*: "Ein Tag bricht an."

As the 1930s began, Zita and her family were living hand to mouth at Steenokkerzeel, scraping together the funding—"contributions from innumerable monarchist die-hards"—to pay for Otto's tuition at Louvain. For Harding there was an element of incongruous comedy to the former Empress raising her family in humble poverty: "Desserts were banished from the imperial menu with a stern phrase: 'We must not eat up Otto's Ph.D.'" The ironic benefit of such abstemiousness was the "lean and aristocratic look" of the whole imperial family: "Other royal dowagers saw their ankles thicken and their figures wane, while Zita remained slender as a reed beside her wiry sons and gazelle-limbed daughters."[30] Zita modestly assumed the incognito title of the "Duchess of Bar"—with reference to "Bar-le-Duc," once a duchy of the Holy Roman Empire associated with the Habsburgs.

On Monday, August 18, 1930, the hundredth birthday of Emperor Franz Joseph was quietly observed in the *Neue Freie Presse*, a date that had once been celebrated across the entire Habsburg monarchy. Some six hundred people gathered the Sunday before for a commemorative mass in the Votivkirche in Vienna, and the Kaisertreue Volkspartei (Emperor-Loyal People's Party), led by Colonel Gustav Wolff in his Habsburg uniform, placed a marble plaque in the church to mark the centennial: the Emperor remembered in stone. As they left the church they saluted one another—"Hoch Habsburg!" and "Hoch Kaiser Otto!" There was another outdoor mass to commemorate Franz Joseph at the Schwarzenberg Palace Garden attended by some twelve hundred people, including fascist paramilitary fighters (*Frontkämpfer*) and Austrian boy scouts (*Pfadfinder*). There was also a procession across the city, past the Vienna Opera on the Ringstraße—everyone singing the Haydn imperial hymn—to the Kapuzinergruft where the Habsburgs lay buried.[31] The *Neue Freie Presse* further reported on church services to honor Franz Joseph in Budapest.[32]

At just this moment, in mid-August 1930, there were rumors of a coming Habsburg restoration attempt in Hungary, which surfaced even in the *New York Times* under the headline, "HUNGARY ALARMED BY TALK OF A COUP," with the subheads, "Otto's Return Feared: Country Stirred as Automobiles Are Searched for Archduke and the Ex-Empress Zita."[33] Some supposed that Otto and Zita would arrive by airplane or, alternatively, were already hiding in a former Habsburg palace in Budapest. The Budapest police were on full alert, watching all roads into the city for Zita and Otto, and actually arrested a woman dressed in black together with an eighteen-year-old boy—who turned out to be innocent Budapest residents.[34] At the moment of Franz Joseph's centennial both Zita and Otto exercised some power over the fears, fantasies, and political imaginations of former Habsburg subjects.

On November 20, 1930, Otto turned eighteen and became an adult pretender in his own right, no longer under Zita's pretended regency. He was congratulated by the persistent party of Hungarian royalists who sent him a uniform with gold braid and sable fur. The next day the *Neue Freie Presse* in Vienna offered the front-page headline "THE COMING OF AGE OF OTTO VON HABSBURG." The newspaper began by recalling the funeral of Franz Joseph on November 30, 1916:

> Behind the coffin of the Emperor Franz Joseph walked the young Emperor and the young Empress and, led by them both, a child with bright blond hair.... The joy of hope [*Hoffnungsfreude*] seemed to radiate from these young figures.... In good faith the whole monarchy awaited peace and salvation from the new government.[35]

The *Neue Freie Presse* was sufficiently nostalgic to wish that Karl and Zita might have succeeded in saving the monarchy. The newspaper blamed Karl—once again, as in the obituary of 1922—for his political clumsiness, and it faulted him anew for having prematurely attempted a restoration in Hungary in 1921: "he wanted to pluck the fruits before they ripened, he did not recognize the fully unfavorable nature of the historical conjuncture." The newspaper seemed to be warning young Otto that the imperial fantasies of the past had now become fairy tales: "The vision is extinguished, the fairy tale is over [*das Märchen ist zu Ende*]."[36] In February 1931, the Vienna Opera would present its new production of *Die Frau ohne Schatten*, featuring the Emperor and the Empress as fairy-tale figures.

The *New York Times* covered Otto's coming of age from across the Atlantic with interest but without urgency: "Habsburg Prince Called Ruler of Austria and Hungary at Ceremony in Exile: Budapest Is Apathetic: Legitimists Celebrate, but Public Shows Little Concern." The *Times* reported from Steenokkerzeel, describing Zita as she appeared in black together with Otto to receive the assembled family and monarchist guests. The account further dramatized the relation of mother and son: "In a few quietly spoken words the Empress handed over to her son all the rights which she has enjoyed as regent. Turning toward his mother, the Prince thanked her for having 'with great devotion and sacrifice taken the place of his father for eight years.'"[37] The *Times* not only seemed to have an informant in the room, straining to hear when Zita spoke quietly, but also clearly felt that its American readers would be interested in Zita.

A year later, on November 25, 1931, the *Times* reported the rumor of an imminent Habsburg "royalist coup," mentioning a meeting of Austrian and Hungarian legitimists with Zita at Steenokkerzeel: "These leaders told the former Empress that the economic situation of Austria and Hungary was so bad that a popular rising was more probable than ever before. They said everyone was longing for the return of Otto."[38] In July 1932 the *Times* featured a report from the Viennese press that Zita in Belgium was speaking with Bavarian, Hungarian, and Austrian representatives about the possibilities of restoration, noting that "Zita plays a very active part in supervising and coordinating these legitimist activities." Otto was reported to be "planting a black and yellow flag in the name of each village on his map which confers honorary citizenship on him," thus making a sort of board game out of restoration politics. Zita announced herself as "strongly opposed to the whole Hitler movement, to which she attributes a Bolshevist character."[39] In the German presidential elections that spring General von Hindenburg (whom Zita would also have hated from the time of the war) defeated Hitler, temporarily keeping him out of power. The German Communist party candidate for president, Ernst Thälmann, would certainly have been surprised to hear Hitler described as a Bolshevist.

Hitler's rise to power in Germany as chancellor in January 1933 was a turning point for Habsburg prospects in Austria, as Habsburg restoration offered a possible bulwark against Nazism. Hitler had hated the Habsburgs ever since his early formative years as an aspiring artist in early twentieth-century Vienna and a subject of Franz Joseph. "Who could retain his loyalty to a dynasty which in past and present betrayed the needs of the German people?" Hitler asked rhetorically in *Mein Kampf.* He believed that the Habsburg state had favored the Slavs over the Germans, and he always maintained his youthful antipathy to the dynasty: "The House of Habsburg was destined to be the misfortune of the German nation."[40] After the war Hitler celebrated the demise of the Habsburg monarchy and keenly sought the union of Germany and Austria as one single German national community.

On September 24, 1933, journalist Emil Lengyel, born in Habsburg Budapest in 1895, published a long article in the Sunday *New York Times Magazine* under the headline "ZITA LOOKS TOWARD AUSTRIA—AND HOPES" with the subhead, "Will the Fight against Hitlerism, Europe Asks, Enable the Former Empress to Put Young Otto on the Throne?" A large picture showed Zita together with Otto. Lengyel began descriptively:

> On a private beach near the Belgian city of Ostend a mother and her eight children have been spending morning hours of the summer days. The mother has just turned forty-one, but her youthful features belie her age. The bold cut of her chin bespeaks fortitude of character; gray streaks in her hair tell of past tragedies.[41]

For the American public Zita was a figure of romance, and Lengyel seemed to expect the public to be sympathetic even to her imperial ambitions. Though Otto had come of age as an imperial pretender, the drama was still about Zita:

> Despite years of disappointment, Zita has never given up hope for a restoration. With her ears close to the ground, she awaits the call for Otto to assume the throne. There were times when Empress Zita was extolled as the hope of Europe, the angel of peace. But in more recent times she was denounced as an arch-conspirator, the mind behind the schemes of the Habsburgs to regain their lost power.[42]

It was even reported that Hitler had tried to establish contact with Zita, but that she had refused to receive his envoy at Steenokkerzeel. One informant told Lengyel that Zita, though preoccupied with restoration, was not scheming to seize power: "It is unfair to describe her as trying to upset the European applecart. She is relying on Divine Providence to enable her family to bring peace to the valley of the Danube."[43]

After reviewing her life, marriage, reign, and exile, Lengyel concluded: "Will the threat of Hitlerism force Austria into the arms of the Hapsburgs? Are the great powers playing the game of Zita? The near future may give the answers to these questions; meanwhile the world pauses for a moment and thinks of Zita, one of the most picturesque women in contemporary history."[44] The modern afterlife of an empress was partly a matter of picturesqueness—but the element of the providential was also relevant to a figure like Zita, who stood outside the structural dynamics of modern politics, a surviving fairy-tale figure from another era. *Die Frau ohne Schatten* was performed just one week earlier in Vienna, on September 17, 1933, with Ursuleac as the Empress—an Empress discovering that she could not fully control her own imperial destiny, recognizing, along with the Nurse, that higher powers were in play: "Übermächte sind im Spiel."

The Throne Room

Dating back to 1918, Karl and Zita had been always opposed to Austrian political union with Germany, seeing Anschluss as the political undoing of the dynastic patrimony. The Habsburg record of opposition to Anschluss meant that, following the assassination of Dollfuß in 1934, his successor Kurt Schuschnigg considered more seriously the possibility of imperial restoration with Otto.[45] In Bertita Harding's account, the shift in Austrian policy toward the Habsburgs in 1934 appeared to Zita as her supreme opportunity: "Like a tense gambler scanning the green tables, Zita sat waiting; her heart was set on playing *va banque*."[46] Harding, writing from America, also recorded the American perspective on Zita at this moment:

> The feeling of expectancy communicated itself to the outside world and gave rise to a maze of rumors. Even America shared the general hubbub; newspaper correspondents from Boston, New York and San Francisco hovered about Steenokkerzeel, armed with pencils and candid cameras. They clamored for interviews. With regal condescension Zita granted an occasional audience to the gentlemen whose readers (mostly feminine) longed to know if Otto's coronation would revive the Vienna of Strauss waltzes, Lehár operettas, dashing guardsmen and romance.[47]

While recognizing that Zita's restoration politics were under new consideration in the 1930s, Harding clearly suggested that the afterlife of an empress belonged to the public sphere as a subject of romance with a particularly gendered appeal.

Harding also perceived an association between restoration politics and musical nostalgia. The operettas that were themselves vehicles of nostalgia were here associated with the programmatic aim of restoration, emblems of the world to be restored. Franz Lehár's *Merry Widow*, perennially performed ever since 1905, would hardly have suited Zita's sense of pious widowhood—even though the composer's brother Anton had been such a stalwart supporter of Karl's claims in Hungary—and she probably would not have approved of the new operettas of the 1930s that boldly (and frivolously) took on the lives of actual empresses. Fritz Kreisler's *Sissy* opened in Vienna in 1932, presenting Franz Joseph and Elisabeth as operetta figures, while Emmerich Kálmán's *Kaiserin Josephine*, about Napoléon's first empress, had its premiere in Zurich in 1936.[48]

Though Harding certainly had in mind the waltzes of Johann Strauss II, the *Rosenkavalier* waltzes of Richard Strauss were no less relevant for nostalgic fantasies of the Viennese past. *Arabella* in 1933 was a vehicle of operatic nostalgia, and *Die Frau ohne Schatten*, presented that year in both Vienna and Salzburg, also offered nostalgic imperial evocations. In January 1935 Lotte Lehmann gave her first performances as the Marschallin in New York, to a public that also read about Zita, Otto, and Habsburg restoration politics in the *New York Times*.

In 1934 Italian dramatist Luigi Pirandello won the Nobel Prize for Literature and donated the gold medal to the Italian fascist government to be melted down—in support of the Italian war of imperial conquest in Ethiopia. Back in 1922, the year of Mussolini's March on Rome, Pirandello had presented in Milan his drama of delusion *Enrico IV*. The curtain rose on the imperial throne room: that is, the room that the madman's family had designed for him, in order to preserve his conviction that he was the medieval emperor. Eugene O'Neill's *The Emperor Jones*, opening in Greenwich Village in 1920, raised the curtain on the emperor's audience chamber on the Caribbean island, with no furniture but a big wooden chair: "This is very apparently the Emperor's throne. It is painted a dazzling, eye-smiting scarlet."[49] In 1933 *The Emperor Jones* was made into a movie starring Paul Robeson, and the film sets included the throne room, with the throne itself in baroque style. In 1933 American composer Louis Gruenberg created a short opera out of *The Emperor Jones*, performed with American baritone Lawrence Tibbett in blackface, singing from his throne room on the stage of the Metropolitan Opera House.⁵⁰

In the 1930s, with a renewed European interest in Habsburg restoration politics, Zita arranged for herself a throne room at Ham Castle in Steenokkerzeel. Bertita Harding, who suggested that Zita had become "unhinged" by the new influx of funding and support, described her as if she were an imaginary or deluded sovereign of the stage, in the spirit of Pirandello or O'Neill:

> Zita assumed a long-forgotten air of majesty and played the empress. She employed all the trappings of the old school, transforming the cramped parlor of her rented castle into a "throne room." When visitors arrived they were bidden to wait in the hall, while she swept dramatically down the stairway in front of them without casting a glance to left or right. Striding into the "throne room," she seated herself upon a creaking armchair and waved through the open door to her chamberlain, Count von Degenfeld, who, in turn, announced the callers. The fact that the entire pantomime took place within sight and earshot of the visitors themselves did not shatter Her Majesty's poise. With grotesque seriousness Zita registered bland surprise at their presence and inquired into their reasons for seeking an audience. More than once Otto smiled at his mother's performance, though she failed to see the slightest cause for merriment.⁵¹

For Harding, Zita's throne room was a stage set and her role as imperial pretender a theatrical role: she "played the empress," she "swept dramatically down the stairway," she performed an "entire pantomime," while Otto watched his mother's "performance." Among the sources that Harding lists for her book is "Count von Degenfeld: personal correspondence with the author"—so it is possible that her account came directly from the person who assumed the Pirandellian role of the chamberlain at Steenokkerzeel. The age of empresses was sufficiently remote by the 1930s so that Zita's sense of herself as an empress could only register on Harding and her readers as a matter of performance.

Heinrich von Degenfeld-Schonburg had been Otto's tutor going back to the time in Lekeitio and was now promoted to the role of Zita's chamberlain. His cousin Christian Martin von Degenfeld-Schonburg had died in 1908, leaving behind a young widow, Countess Ottonie Degenfeld, who had become both operatic muse and extramarital infatuation for Hofmannsthal.

She was the poetic model for the spiritually exquisite and nobly faithful Ariadne.[52] In the 1920s and 1930s it was her husband's cousin Heinrich who faithfully attended to Zita and Otto.

In March 1934 Zita was in France at the deathbed of her older brother Prince Sixtus, who had played such a significant intermediary role in the peace efforts of Karl and Zita during the war. He died at the age of forty-seven from a bacterial infection, following a voyage of exploration in Africa.[53] In August Zita was in Italy, pursuing the possibility of a royal Italian marriage for Otto—to Princess Maria Francesca of Savoy, the daughter of King Vittorio Emanuele III of Italy—in the hope that Mussolini would look favorably upon a Habsburg restoration in Austria.

That summer Otto, Zita, and Austrian Chancellor Schuschnigg were all in Italy, seeking to conciliate Mussolini's favor. Otto was, according to the *New York Times*, "Reported Seeking to Consult Mussolini on Restoration or Woo Princess Maria." Zita was reported at Viareggio—probably at Villa Pianore, the Bourbon palace where she was born—coordinating her summer travel with Otto's aspirations.[54] In August Schuschnigg met with Mussolini in Florence, and then, as reported in the *New York Times*, drove right past Viareggio on his way north without stopping to meet with Zita. The *Times* headline—"SCHUSCHNIGG SHY ON MONARCHY TALK"—was followed by subheads, "Avoided Meeting Zita: Drove at Night through Town Where Ex-Empress Lives."[55] The political conjuncture for the Habsburg marriage was also not quite right, and in the end the Italian princess would marry Zita's younger brother Prince Louis of Bourbon-Parma.

On July 13, 1935, the Austrian government, contemplating the possible utility of the Habsburgs in fending off German annexation, rescinded the Habsburg Law of 1919, which had banned the family from returning to Austria and had confiscated their property.[56] The repeal went almost unmentioned in the Austrian press, which was dominated by the tragic automobile accident that also took place on July 13: the chancellor's Gräf & Stift automobile went off the road and crashed into a pear tree. Schuschnigg and his wife Herma were thrown from the car; he was injured and she was killed. The front pages of the newspaper the next day, on July 14, were dedicated to the tragedy of Herma, from the liberal *Neue Freie Presse* to the Catholic monarchist *Reichspost*.[57] The latter also reported some news from Nazi

Germany: that Richard Strauss was resigning his office as president of the Reichsmusikkammer and that Goebbels accepted his resignation out of consideration for his age. The newspaper reflected that Strauss might now "come to the realization that in the Third Reich there were powers at work with whom even a man of his musical stature cannot easily bind himself in a lasting alliance."[58] Yet Strauss would compose an Olympic hymn for the Berlin Olympics the following year.

Along with the Social Democratic Party, the socialist *Arbeiter-Zeitung* had been suppressed in 1934 by the Dollfuß regime following the Austrian Civil War in February. The *Arbeiter-Zeitung* then published a weekly edition in Czechoslovakia, and it was smuggled illegally across the border into Austria.[59] On July 14, Bastille Day, it was the illegal *Arbeiter-Zeitung* alone that spotlighted and denounced the revocation of the Habsburg Law. The front-page headline was "RETURN OF THE HABSBURGS" (*Habsburgs Wiederkehr*) and the newspaper offered a Marxist interpretation:

> Thus the meaning of Austrian fascism is complete: it restores the domination of the old precapitalist ruling classes, the nobility and the clergy. But so far there was still the lack of the Emperor himself: now it brings the Emperor back and gives him back his castles. . . . Nothing is more urgent than that the do-nothing Habsburg family should get back its treasures![60]

Dripping with sarcasm, the *Arbeiter-Zeitung* was particularly outraged about the restoration of Habsburg property, noting that one of the family castles, Schloss Hetzendorf (where Karl and Zita were living before the war), had been put to use as a home for war invalids in the postwar republic. "Nothing is more just than that the state, which lets the unemployed starve, should make giant presents to the Habsburgs!" exclaimed the *Arbeiter-Zeitung*.[61]

The fairy-tale imperial family, according to the *Arbeiter-Zeitung*, were now the dramatis personae of a political nightmare:

> Otto and Zita are not yet in Austria. They will first send ahead a pair of their numerous cousins. Each of these archdukes will get his castle, his court, his princely appanage. Each will become an agitator for the restoration of the "Emperor." . . . Then, one fine day, Otto Habsburg will move his residence to Austria. And on another day the world will learn as a *fait*

accompli that the Habsburgs are again residing at Schönbrunn. The war dead will have fallen in vain. The world wants to persuade the Austrian fascist government that Habsburg is always better than Hitler, and that the restoration of the monarchy is the only means to prevent the conquest of Austria by the Nazis.[62]

The *Arbeiter-Zeitung* was, notably, even willing to suggest that the Habsburgs might not be preferable to Hitler.

Tracking the movements of Zita and Otto became a matter of particular interest now that their return to Austria was no longer out of the question. It was reported in January 1936 in the *New York Times* that the Austrian vice chancellor, Prince Ernst Rüdiger Starhemberg, one of the leaders of the Fatherland Front, might be holding secret meetings at undisclosed locations: "It is believed he left London after the funeral of King George [V] to meet former Empress Zita and Archduke Otto, but the meeting place has not been revealed. Zita is in Italy but is leaving immediately for Paris."[63] In August the *Times* reported from Castel Gandolfo that Zita, dressed as usual in black, was meeting with Pope Pius XI for a private audience of forty-five minutes. It was further noted that "Vatican prelates always have supported the restoration of the Catholic dynasty in Austria."[64]

While Zita and Otto remained based in Belgium, the two members of the family who went back to Austria to test the waters, after the repeal of the Habsburg Law in 1935, were Archduchess Adelheid and Archduke Felix. While Felix attended the Austrian military academy at Wiener-Neustadt, Adelheid made a tour of Austria representing the family in the general spirit anticipated by the *Arbeiter-Zeitung*: "each will become an agitator." Both Adelheid and Felix, however, fled from Austria—into neighboring Hungary—following the Anschluss in March 1938.[65] Their cousins, the two sons of Franz Ferdinand, Ernst and Maximilian, were also known opponents of the Anschluss and supporters of Habsburg restoration; they were arrested and sent to Dachau.[66]

Opera after the Anschluss

Zita's and Otto's hopes for a restoration, pursued between 1934 and 1938, were definitively derailed by the Anschluss. On February 12 Schuschnigg met with Hitler at Berchtesgaden and was compelled to agree to a powerful Nazi presence within the Austrofascist government, and on February 17 Otto wrote a letter to Schuschnigg, which was enough of a public document for Harding to be able to quote it in the final pages of her 1939 book. "From my standpoint as Austria's rightful emperor, I regard our foreign policy as of the utmost importance," wrote Otto to Schuschnigg, as pretender to chancellor:

> Should you be unable to withstand further pressure . . . I ask you then . . . to hand over to me the office of chancellor. I am not demanding a restoration of the monarchy, which would require a long drawn-out process of recognition by the Powers. I call on you only to give me the chancellorship, so that we could gain the same advantages achievable through a formal restoration of the monarchy but without any change in the constitution.[67]

In fact, within the authoritarian state of the Austrofascist Fatherland Front, the power of the chancellor in 1938 was probably greater than the power of the emperor in the old Habsburg monarchy.

Schuschnigg did not accept Otto's proposal and instead, on March 9, called for an Austrian referendum on political independence. Hitler responded by invading Austria, declaring the Anschluss on March 12. Otto later claimed that he and his mother disagreed sharply over what was to be done: Zita audaciously argued that Otto should take a private plane to Vienna and rally the Austrians to resist the Nazis, but Otto reminded her of the utter failure of her own plane flight into Hungary with Karl in 1921.[68]

On March 15 Hitler spoke from the balcony of the Habsburg palace, the Hofburg, to a crowd of cheering Austrians in the Heldenplatz, while Viennese Jews were assaulted and humiliated in the streets of the city. Rabbi Israel Taglicht, who in May 1917 had delivered the synagogue sermon for Zita's birthday—on Zita as the true mother of her country—was now in March 1938 made to scrub the sidewalks of Vienna on his knees.[69] Zita herself in Steenokkerzeel was praying "for a miracle to save Austria for the Habsburgs," while the Nazis in Austria placed Otto on a wanted list for arrest.[70]

The Vienna Opera suspended performances for a week as the Anschluss occurred, but resumed on March 19 with *Der Rosenkavalier*, and *Arabella* soon followed on March 30. Knappertsbusch was conducting *Der Rosenkavalier*, and the Marschallin was Viennese soprano Anny Konetzni who, together with her sister, soprano Hilde Konetzni, would dominate German dramatic repertory in Vienna during the Nazi period. On March 19 the role of Octavian was sung by twenty-four-year-old American mezzo-soprano Risë Stevens, born in New York and Jewish by descent through her mother. She had just made her Vienna debut in the role on March 8, presenting the silver rose that Hofmannsthal had invented as an Austrian aristocratic custom, and now she sang her second and very last performance with the Vienna Opera—though she would go on to a great career with the Met and would die in New York in 2013 at the age of ninety-nine.

The great emigration was about to begin, as Adelheid and Felix crossed the border into Hungary and the Nazis undertook a major round of arrests. Lotte Lehmann had already sung her last performance in Vienna, and before the end of 1938 she would be singing the Marschallin opposite the Octavian of Risë Stevens in New York. Sigmund Freud emigrated to England, as did Gerty von Hofmannsthal. Rose Pauly was singing Elektra in New York on March 3, 1938, as the Anschluss was about to occur.[71] Arnold Schoenberg and Erich Korngold were already in California. The entire singing Trapp family emigrated to the United States, where they would soon settle in Vermont.

Following the terrible pogrom of Kristallnacht in November 1938, my grandparents, together with their four-year-old daughter, prepared to leave Austria, now part of Nazi Germany. They traveled to Hamburg, and on November 28 they sailed on the ship *Orinoco* of the Hamburg-America Line, all the way to Havana where they lived for some years before eventually coming to New York. They are named in the passenger list of the *Orinoco* as Herr Dr. Moses Stier, Frau Moses Stier, and Renee Stier.[72] The ship's farewell dinner on December 13, before arrival in Havana, included caviar, turtle soup, fillet of sole in Rheinwein, and lobster Newburg.[73] My grandfather bought first-class tickets, because Nazi Germany would not allow him to take his savings out of the country, while my grandmother, whose family had a leather shop, smuggled out her diamond jewelry in the heels of her shoes.

In April 1938, one month after the Anschluss, *Die Frau ohne Schatten* had its first performance in Rome, performed in Italian as *La donna senz'ombra*. It must have been planned as a project of Austrian-Italian cultural cooperation, coming to fruition now only after Austria had ceased to exist. The

Figure 34. Lucy, Martin, and Renee, age four, left Austria after the Anschluss, and are photographed here in Hamburg in November 1938, as they are about to sail to Havana, escaping from Nazi Germany to save their lives. Lucy, the daughter of a leather craftsman, has her diamonds concealed in the heels of her shoes. Lucy and Renee (my mother) spent two years in Havana, arriving in New York in 1940, the same year that Zita arrived in New York from Lisbon. (Property of the author)

conductor was Italian Gino Marinuzzi, with Spanish-Italian tenor Giovanni Voyer as the Emperor and Italian baritone Benvenuto Franci as Barak—but, from the Vienna casts, Rose Pauly as the Dyer's Wife and Viorica Ursuleac as the Empress. The three night watchmen at the conclusion of the first act included the young Tito Gobbi, just twenty-four, and the young Giuseppe Taddei, almost twenty-two. In fact, the Emperor and Empress were labeled in the program as the King (*il Re*) and the Queen (*la Regina*), as if imperial titles might have been misunderstood in the Kingdom of Italy. The costume design for Ursuleac was bejeweled and embroidered, heavy with silver ornamentation, and topped by a winged crown of orientalist inspiration that gave Strauss's Empress a notable resemblance to Puccini's Turandot.[74]

Richard Strauss presented his new opera *Friedenstag* in Munich in July 1938. The subject was the end of the Thirty Years' War in 1648 and the coming of peace to the Holy Roman Empire of Germany, ruled by the Habsburg Emperor (who was only an offstage presence). Strauss's celebration of peace meant that the opera would have to be shelved as soon as World War II began in September 1939, but there was occasion for a single performance in Vienna in June 1939, in honor of Strauss's seventy-fifth birthday, with Hitler attending as well as the composer.[75] *Der Rosenkavalier* was also presented in Vienna in June for Strauss's birthday, the dedicated Nazi Manowarda in the role of Baron Ochs. Krauss offered new productions of *Arabella* and *Die Frau ohne Schatten* in Munich in July and August of 1939, in honor of Strauss's birthday, roughly coinciding in July with the opening of the Nazi "Great German Art Exhibit" in Munich—following the "Degenerate Art" exhibit of 1937. The Great German Art Exhibit opened on July 14; the Munich Opera presented *Tannhäuser* on July 15 (with Hitler in attendance) and *Arabella* on July 16 (with Strauss in attendance). *Die Frau ohne Schatten* was performed on July 29 and repeated on August 15 and August 26, as World War II was about to begin.[76]

Die Frau ohne Schatten would also return to Vienna in Strauss's seventy-fifth year, but not until October 1939, after the outbreak of the war. There was a new staging by Viktor Pruscha, and the opera was conducted by Rudolf Moralt, who was about to become the musical director of the Vienna Opera.[77] Pruscha's restaging, not actually a new production, was presumably intended to erase the name of Lothar Wallerstein, the Jewish son of a Prague cantor. Wallerstein spent the war years directing at the Met in New York, mostly Wagner operas but also *Der Rosenkavalier,* and usually working with Jewish refugee conductors like George Szell and Erich Leinsdorf, both born as subjects of Franz Joseph.[78] The Empress at the Vienna Opera in 1939, seeking a shadow in the darkness of the Third Reich, was the twenty-five-year-old Serbian soprano Daniza Ilitsch, who would later participate in Austrian underground activity against the Nazi regime.[79]

Hitler invaded Poland on September 1, 1939, marking the beginning of World War II, and France and England declared war against Germany on September 3. There then followed eight months of "Phoney War," however, without active fighting on Germany's western front until Hitler attacked Holland and Belgium in May 1940, on his way to conquer France in June. In March, still during the Phoney War, Otto flew to the United States, and the *New York Times* headline heralded his arrival for a three-week study trip: "OTTO, PRETENDER, IS HERE BY PLANE: HABSBURG ARCHDUKE TO STUDY OUR DEMOCRACY AS MODEL FOR A FEDERATED EUROPE." Gently mocking him as "pretender to the nonexistent throne of Austria," the *Times* cited Otto as proposing a European federation of Danubian lands to include "parts of Bohemia, Moravia, Slovakia, Yugoslavia, and Austria," that is, something like a reconstituted Habsburg monarchy.[80] The war had barely begun, and the Habsburgs were already looking to the postwar political settlement as a possible framework for reconstituting the empire and engineering a dynastic restoration.

It was in the period of the Phoney War, with its uncanny sense of suspended history, of menaced sovereignties, of political somnambulism, that La Scala presented its first production of *Die Frau ohne Schatten*—in Italian—at Epiphany in January 1940. Richard Strauss was present himself in Milan for the rehearsals; the conductor was Gino Marinuzzi, and the Empress was Stella Roman, a Romanian soprano born in 1904 in the city of Cluj or Kolozsvár in Habsburg Transylvania. The Milanese reviewer in the *Corriere della Sera* skeptically observed that "the opera did not succeed in being comprehensible to any listener."[81] A scratchy recording still exists from 1940 of Benvenuto Franci and Iva Pacetti, as the Dyer and his wife, singing their moving third-act duet in Italian.

Zita's castle at Steenokkerzeel was confiscated by the Nazis when they conquered Belgium in May 1940—as the locality was important to military planning for the development of nearby Zaventem airport—but Zita was already gone. She and her children left Belgium as soon as the Nazis invaded, crossing the border into France, which was soon also under attack. On June 22, the French government agreed to an armistice that involved surrendering all of northern and western France, including Paris, to German occupation, while allowing the government of Marshal Philippe Pétain to preserve a nominally independent rump state at Vichy. Three days earlier, on June 19, Zita and her family had crossed the international bridge at Irun over the Bidasoa River, from France into Spain.[82] The imperial family had been issued visas for Portugal by Aristides de Sousa Mendes, the Portuguese consul at Bordeaux, who ignored the directives of António Salazar's government in Lisbon by giving out some 30,000 visas at this crucial juncture, ultimately saving the lives of many European Jews. Zita's party was issued a total of eleven visas: Zita traveling incognito as the "Duchess of Bar," with seven of her children, Count Heinrich von Degenfeld, the chamberlain, Countess Therese von Kerssenbrock, the governess, and, finally, Zita's mother Maria Antónia, a displaced Portuguese princess returning to Portugal, though not for long.[83] Zita and her family were on their way to America.

18

The Empress in America

ESCAPE FROM NAZI EUROPE

World's Fair

On July 20, 1940, Zita arrived in New York, and the *New York Times* heralded her arrival under the headline "EX-EMPRESS ZITA HERE AS REFUGEE: WAR-BUFFETED ROYAL AUSTRIAN ARRIVES WITH DAUGHTER ON THE *DIXIE CLIPPER*."[1] The *Clipper* was a boat-plane, a vehicle that floated as well as flew, produced by Boeing in the late 1930s and operated mostly by Pan Am during the 1940s. It was the New York–Lisbon route that inaugurated the era of transatlantic commercial air travel, with just twenty-two passengers on the first flight of June 1939. There were dining tables with white table cloths and convertible bed-seats—and the whole flight took about twenty-four hours. For Zita there was nothing incongruous about an empress on an airplane in 1940; she and Karl had been interested in early Austrian aviation at Wiener Neustadt dating back to the time of their marriage in 1911. The moment of Zita's *Dixie Clipper* flight in 1940 was certainly a time for appreciating the modern importance of aviation, as the *Times* front-page headline made very clear: "BRITISH BEAT OFF MASS RAIDS BY SWARMS OF NAZI PLANES; R.A.F. BOMBS GERMAN BASES: SKY BATTLES FIERCE."[2]

The *Times* took a long historical view of Zita's arrival in New York in 1940, describing her as "a refugee at last from a world that began to crumble under her throne a quarter-century ago."[3] The substance of the article—though it appeared in the Sunday news section—lay somewhere between

Figure 35. In July 1940 Zita arrived at La Guardia Airport in New York from Lisbon, a widow in black, traveling on the *Dixie Clipper* to escape from Hitler's Europe. She was welcomed by her sons Otto (right) and Felix (left), who were already in America. The *New York Times* described Zita as "a refugee at last from a world that began to crumble under her throne a quarter-century ago." Zita herself was forty-eight years old and would live to be ninety-six. (Sueddeutsche Zeitung Photo/Alamy Stock Photo)

the news of the war and the society pages. There was a large picture of Zita arriving at La Guardia Airport in a turban cap and a dark belted coat, carrying a business-like leather briefcase in one hand. Archduchess Elisabeth alongside her looked like a schoolgirl in her white broad-brimmed hat, gazing downward as she walked, while Zita had a professionally imperial smile for whoever was greeting her. In fact, she was being met at the airport by her sons Otto and Felix, who had traveled to the United States earlier and now welcomed their mother by kissing her hand, as empress, before kissing her cheek, as mother.

Another Austrian mother and daughter arrived in New York by boat earlier that year: Lucy Stier and her five-year-old daughter Renee, my grandmother and my mother. They had left Austria in 1938, had crossed the Atlantic to Cuba, and had been living in Havana for the past two years. They now traveled on the SS *Mexico* from Havana to New York, listed on the Manifest of Alien Passengers as German by nationality, since Austria no longer existed.[4] My grandfather, born in Habsburg Bukovina, fell under a different immigration quota and had to remain alone in Havana for several more years.

There was a five-year-old child selected to greet Zita at La Guardia in July as she deplaned, Vera Nickich, who, according to the 1940 US census, was the daughter of New Yorkers John and Rose Nickich, born as Habsburg subjects in the lands that then became Yugoslavia and Czechoslovakia respectively.[5] The same generation as my grandparents, John and Rose (possibly Ivan and Ružena) were born in the 1890s. Their daughter Vera now presented carnation leis to Zita and Elisabeth for them to wear around their necks in an improvised Habsburg "aloha" welcome to the United States. Little Vera also "put into their hands two slightly moist tickets"—for an upcoming event to benefit the Milk Fund at the New York World's Fair, which was then taking place at Flushing Meadows in Queens.[6]

Four more of Zita's children were announced as due to arrive on July 29, though a mechanical problem held them up at the Azores and also served as a reminder that the boat-plane (this time the *Yankee Clipper*, not the *Dixie Clipper*) was still a technological novelty.[7] The *New York Times* on July 29 also offered news from the World's Fair in Queens, where political speeches denouncing Nazi Germany were delivered by Czech statesmen in exile (including Jan Masaryk, the son of Tomáš Masaryk), speaking in the name of Czechoslovakia—"first of the original participants in the Fair to become a ghost nation."⁸ The pavilions of the World's Fair, intended as showcases for national pride, were one by one—Czechoslovakia, Poland, France—becoming spectral representations of countries conquered by Hitler. In a continent of ghost nations, the phantom former dynasty of the Habsburgs could begin to imagine a role for itself in the purely hypothetical postwar world.

Zita, after arriving in New York, immediately proceeded to Massachusetts, where she was to be a guest at the New England country estate of Calvin Bullock, a seventy-three-year-old Wall Street investor who managed mutual funds and collected Napoleonic memorabilia.⁹ On September 15, 1940, Zita reappeared in the *New York Times* in the Sunday real estate section as the unlikely doyenne of the Bullock home in the appropriately named small town of Royalston, Massachusetts. The headline was "ZITA FINDS REFUGE IN BAY STATE HOME: EX-EMPRESS OF AUSTRIA STILL DREAMS OF RESTORATION OF HABSBURG THRONE." The article reported on the Massachusetts state troopers assigned to guard Zita's residence and described the "changing of the guard" at Royalston:

> A sturdy Massachusetts State Trooper drives up, says "How's it [going], Frank?" to another trooper, who asks how the Red Sox came out, and drives away. It has been so since mid-July when Zita, one-time mistress of 50,000,000 subjects, came to this peaceful New England village as a refugee.¹⁰

The *Times* meant to highlight the incongruity between Zita's pretensions to grandeur ("two courtiers of the old days are with her, a countess and a count") and the popular classes who were rooting for the Red Sox.

"It is peaceful here," commented Zita about Royalston. "These hills and mountains remind me of the Austrian landscape." The Trapp family would settle down in New England, in Stowe, Vermont, just two years later. Zita, the *Times* reported, had seven of her eight children with her (Robert was in England), though Otto and Felix came up to Royalston from New York only on weekends, playing golf on the course that adjoined the Bullock estate. From the dining room the imperial family could look out the window at the New England common with its little white church, but of course Zita traveled on Sunday to a Roman Catholic church, located in the nearby town of Athol—"where she and her family occupy a front pew, and at communion time file to the altar rail."[11] Even in Massachusetts Zita practiced the demonstrative piety of a former empress, establishing her ceremonial precedence in the front pew. The house in Royalston is today nicknamed the "Bastille," as if it continues to represent the *ancien régime*.[12]

The 1940 article about Zita in Royalston emphasized that her afterlife as an empress had not been an easy one, that "Zita had to do her own cooking, scrub floors, pinch pennies for food"—though the implication was that such hard times were over, that imperial family life in Royalston was a version of the American good life, including golf.[13] Oddly, Zita's story was refashioned in the image of the conventional American immigrant narrative: hardship and poverty in Europe led to immigration to America with the chance for a better life, as represented by the gracious homes of the real estate section. My grandmother and my mother, who also arrived in New York in 1940, lived rather differently. They moved into a shared apartment in Washington Heights, first on 157th Street, then on 161st Street, and my mother started first grade while my grandmother went to work at a sewing machine in a leather goods factory, which was soon busy preparing military equipment for American soldiers. My great-grandfather had owned a leather goods store in Vienna, so my grandmother knew the business, but now in New York she was one of the workers and joined the union.

My mother Renee, starting first grade in September 1940, knew German, her family language from Austria, and Spanish after two years in Havana, but not English. The *Times* in September 1940 noted that Zita's children, now young adults, could speak "German, French, Spanish, Italian, Hungarian, Czech, and Croatian—schooled at Zita's orders in the many tongues of the old empire." They were refugees from an Austro-Hungarian homeland that no longer existed, a geopolitical phantom, without even a ghost pavilion at the World's Fair. The other reason that Zita could not go home, for now at least, was because, as the article noted, "Hitler, who now rules Austria, charged Zita with treason for having opposed Anschluss with the Reich."[14] In a very different mode from my Austrian Jewish grandmother, one of her former fifty million subjects, Zita was also an Austrian refugee fleeing from Hitler.

Prospective Beatification

Zita's immigration to the United States in 1940 was also, retrospectively, the moment at which she entered into my life and became the object of my particular interest. In 2009, almost seventy years later, I received an unexpected email message from a French priest:

> Dear Professor Wolff, You will probably be surprised to receive this e-mail. I am actually looking for an American historian who could collaborate for searching in North America on the Servant of God, H. M. Empress and Queen Zita (1892–1989). You probably know that the Church has beatified the Blessed Emperor Charles in 2004. Now we are beginning the process for her, so that the holiness of this venerable couple may be acknowledged and given to the faithful as an example. I am the legitimately constituted postulator of this cause of beatification and canonization, which will run in France, in Le Man's diocese, since the Servant of God was an oblate of Solesmes abbey, located in that very diocese.[15]

I was indeed surprised, and also intrigued, to learn that the Roman Catholic Church required a team of research historians to study the documents of the life of a prospective saint. Since Zita had come to America in 1940, it was necessary to have an American historian of the Habsburg Empire on the committee.

> We are constituting the committee of experts in history whose very important job (especially for a semi-historical cause like this) is to search sources in all possible archives so that we may collect as many documents of interest related to her life as possible. . . . I know that you are a specialist of the Habsburg Empire, but also of Church History and you live pretty close to the cities where the Servant of God used to live. That is the reason why I thought you could be the appropriate person for my American expert. Has this request any chance to make sense in your eyes?[16]

In 2009 I was actually living in New York City, where Zita had arrived in 1940 at La Guardia airport. I was teaching the history of the Habsburg monarchy and Eastern Europe at New York University, having moved there in 2006 from Boston, where I had been teaching at a Catholic and Jesuit university, Boston College—and where I was, of course, a Red Sox fan who experienced the semi-miraculous championship season of 2004, the first World Series victory since 1918.

Zita's marriage had lasted for only eleven years, followed by sixty-seven years of pious widowhood, as the course of Karl's beatification moved slowly across the twentieth century. He was finally beatified in 2004, fifteen years after Zita's death, during the reign of Pope John Paul II, who had been born in post-Habsburg Galicia in 1920. As Karol Wojtyła he was thought to have been named for Emperor Karl following the Emperor's dethronement.

The decisive miracle in Karl's case occurred in 1960 when a disabled Polish nun in Brazil, Sister Maria Zita Gradowska, recovered the power to walk after praying for the intercession of the former emperor.[17] When Karl was beatified in 2004 the date chosen for his feast day was not his birthday, his name day, or the date of his death but, unusually, the date of his marriage to Zita, October 21. The cause for her own beatification was then opened in 2009 when she became a "Servant of God," and it was possible to imagine that, someday, they might both be canonized as saints, a model of pious marriage for Roman Catholics. The Empress recast in the role of a "servant" was also one of the plot points of *Die Frau ohne Schatten*.

As a member of the historical commission for Zita's beatification, one of the first scholarly services that I was able to perform was to obtain Zita's file at the United States Department of Immigration and relevant alien registration papers from the Department of Homeland Security. The Alien Registration Act, or Smith Act, was signed by Franklin Roosevelt and became law on June 28, 1940, just before Zita arrived in the United States. It was aimed at the surveillance of foreigners who might attempt to overthrow the American government, including fascists and communists. Zita—whose own imperial government had been overthrown in 1918, and who had herself twice tried to overthrow the government of Hungary in 1921—now had to fill out an Alien Registration Form that was certified in Athol, Massachusetts, on September 25, 1940, two months after her arrival on the *Dixie Clipper*.

It was noted that she had entered the United States incognito under the name of the "Duchess of Bar." Asked whether she was known by any other names, she mentioned being known as "Queen of Hungary" and as "Princess of Bourbon-Parma." She gave her citizenship as "Austria and Hungary" without specifying whether she conceived that as one country or two. Her height was given as 5 feet, 5½ inches, weight 135 pounds, brown hair and

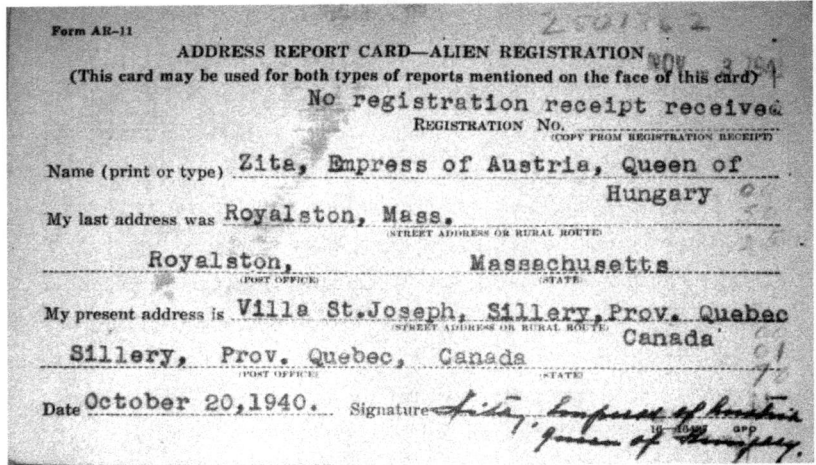

Figure 36. Under the Alien Registration Act of June 1940, Zita, who arrived in July, was required to register her address upon arrival in the United States. She listed Royalston, Massachusetts, though she had already moved on to Quebec by the time she filled out the form in October. Her typed name and signature imperiously specified her titles. In her own eyes she was always "Empress of Austria, Queen of Hungary." (Immigration and Naturalization Service, National Archives, Washington DC)

brown eyes (though another government form gave her hair as fair and her eyes as blue). She listed her occupation as "none," affirmed that she had not been arrested, indicted, or convicted of any offense, and further that she had not been affiliated with any organization furthering the political activity of a foreign government (which would have been true only if restricted to currently existing foreign governments). She signed her name as "Zita, Empress of Austria, Queen of Hungary" and gave her right index fingerprint for identity. She was then issued an Alien Registration Receipt Card with name and address: Zita, Empress of Austria, Royalston, Mass.[18]

My work for the historical commission was never about looking for the kinds of miracles that qualify a person for sainthood; that was apparently the concern of some other constituted body of researchers. In fact, an internet posting of 2009 issued a call for miracles:

> Any graces received through the intercession of the Servant of God, Empress Zita—especially those which are possibly miraculous—should contact:

Association for the Beatification of Empress Zita
Abbaye Saint-Pierre
1, place Dom Guéranger
72300 Solesmes, France.[19]

I had the impression (though this was never stated explicitly) that part of the purpose of the strictly historical commission was to make sure that there was nothing awkward on the record that would make the candidate appear unsaintly at some later stage of the process. In Zita's case there was always perhaps the small chance that research would turn up a postmarital American romantic life, but, in fact, if there was anything unsaintly about Zita's imperial afterlife, in America or elsewhere, it was the sheer worldly intensity of her political focus on Otto's prospective restoration. On September 8, 1940, some weeks before submitting her Alien Registration Form, she traveled from gracious Royalston, Massachusetts, to even more gracious Hyde Park, New York, to have lunch with President Roosevelt, along with Otto, Adelheid, Felix, and Rudolf.[20]

By December 1940, when *Life Magazine* published a Christmas photo of Zita surrounded by five of her children, she had already left Royalston and was settled in Quebec, where she would remain until 1948. The story was more generally about refugees and showed the family gazing out of a window into a happier future, with a caption noting that "Empress Zita (center) in mourning black, has never let Europe or her children forget their Hapsburg claim to the throne."[21] *Life* also humorously issued some "rules for refugees, royal or otherwise," which outlined the American perspective. For instance: "Refugees should remember that they are nothing special. Broadly speaking, all U.S. citizens except Indians, who do not count, are either refugees or descendants of refugees." Or: "Celebrated refugees must learn U.S. manners and customs. They should not suggest to natives that civilized people take three hours for lunch, that what the U.S. needs is art and culture such as only Europeans can contribute, and that Americans do not really know how to live." Or even: "Refugees should remember that Americans' nerves are on edge. They must not band together in little swarms, chattering and squealing in their foreign bird-talk." There was one rule with specific reference to Austrians, though perhaps more for the Trapps than the Habsburgs: "At all costs, let those refugees and imitation refugees who insist on sliding in the snow in Tyrolean costume stop yodeling."[22] *Life* was partly satirizing American attitudes toward refugees and partly satirizing the refugees themselves, but the rules suggested that the phenomenon of Habsburg refugees might be discomfiting for some part of the American public.

For Zita, Quebec was more familiarly Francophone and more generally Roman Catholic than Massachusetts—though Otto remained in America, and his mother continued to take an interest in American policy. In Quebec the family lived piously in the Villa Saint-Joseph which belonged to the Sisters of St. Joan of Arc.[23] Yet Zita traveled to the White House in September 1943 and discussed the future of Central Europe with Roosevelt, and she had tea with him in Quebec in September 1944 when he came to meet with Churchill to discuss postwar plans.[24] Her daughter Archduchess Elisabeth later claimed that Zita's chief objects were to interest the president in the reestablishment of Austria as an independent state after the war, to recognize that Austria had been violently occupied by Nazi Germany and therefore had to be liberated, and then to support the reconstruction of postwar Austria. Elisabeth recalled her mother being welcomed to the White House by Eleanor Roosevelt, noting that "even for the First Lady it meant something quite extraordinary to receive Empress and Queen Zita." Eleanor Roosevelt was known to have a weakness "for everything that was Russian or communist," according to Elisabeth, but she had sympathy for oppressed and exploited peoples, and Zita was able to bring about "the small miracle [*das kleine Wunder*] of persuading even Frau Roosevelt of the necessity of a free and independent Austria."[25] This was, of course, not quite the kind of miracle to be considered later for beatification.

In fact, by 1943 Zita already had an American political enemy denouncing her for her political maneuvering. Emanuel Celler, the longtime Democratic congressman from New York City, took the trouble to attack the Habsburg restoration politics of Zita and Otto on the floor of Congress. Celler had been receiving letters from constituents complaining about American recruitment for an "Austrian Battalion" that was being formed to participate in the military effort in Europe:

> Unfortunately that battalion has been tied up with the pretensions of Archduke Otto von Hapsburg . . . and this pretender, now in this country, is making of our country a political arena to further his ambitions to

ascend the old throne of the Austro-Hungarian Empire. His pretensions, and the machinations of the flunkies surrounding him, and the monarchists surrounding him, are driving deeply a wedge between our own country and our allies, the governments in exile of the Czechs, Yugoslavs, and the Poles.... Some of the things that are happening in New York are outrageous where this man holds forth.[26]

Otto's plan for the battalion failed to attract soldiers, though his brothers Archduke Felix and Archduke Karl Ludwig enthusiastically enlisted.[27]

Celler was critical of American quota restrictions that restricted Jewish immigrants from Nazi Europe, and perhaps for that reason all the more indignant at the pretensions of royalist refugees. Outraged at Otto, Celler also linked him inevitably to Zita: "I have information which I have submitted to the FBI. There are, I am informed, five or six ruling families in Germany today who have been contributing large sums to the attempts of the Empress Zita, the mother of Otto, and her son Otto to restore the Austro-Hungarian Empire."[28] J. Edgar Hoover did open a file on Zita, for this latter charge was a very serious one: if Zita and Otto were being funded by families within "Germany today," then they were perhaps entangled with forces inside Nazi Germany, America's wartime enemy. In any event, Celler was probably right in affirming that Zita during the war, like Otto, was very much concerned with the prospect of imperial restoration.

Following tea with Roosevelt in Quebec in 1944, Zita conscientiously wrote to the president:

> I want to tell you how much I enjoyed talking to you and how grateful I am for the words of encouragement, for your promise to act to safeguard the lives of the Hungarians and Austrians from the Communist danger. Your words have taken a heavy burden off my heart.
>
> May God help and protect you, dear Mr. President, in this noble task, which will secure you the undying friendship and gratitude of my countries.
>
> With kindest regards to Mrs. Roosevelt...[29]

In the final years of the war against Nazism Zita was well aware that Soviet communism would play a powerful role in postwar Central Europe. The only allusion to her own dynastic claims was the reference to "the undying friendship and gratitude of my countries"—without specifying whether she was simply a citizen of those plural countries or their empress and queen.

According to Archduchess Elisabeth, Roosevelt, in his conversations with Zita, "gradually came over to the significance of crowned rulers, and thus gradually came to speak of the significance of dynasties and their function in exile, and decidedly represented the view that the dispossessed might be just as concerned for their former lands as those currently governing." When they spoke of the successor states to the Austro-Hungarian monarchy, "it was clear to see how much he wanted to justify himself to the Empress and Queen"—as if her dethronement was partly America's fault—but the precise nature of American responsibility went unmentioned: "about President Wilson they did not speak."[30]

"I am Richard Strauss"

While Zita was meeting with Roosevelt in the White House in September 1943, the Vienna Opera was preparing a new production of *Die Frau ohne Schatten* that would have its premiere on November 18, at a time when the Allies were already fighting their way up the Italian peninsula and the balance of the war was clearly shifting against the Nazis. There were six performances over the course of the 1943–44 season, with the sixth taking place on June 13, during the week of Richard Strauss's eightieth birthday, one week after the Allies made their D-Day landing on the beaches of Normandy, three days before the Allied bombing of Vienna began. The conductor was the Austrian Karl Böhm, born in Graz in 1894 as a Habsburg subject; he had made all the mandated ideological statements necessary for career advancement in Nazi Germany and was music director in Dresden from 1934 to 1942, becoming very close to Strauss and conducting in Dresden the premieres of *Die schweigsame Frau* and *Daphne*. In Vienna in 1943 the Empress was Hilde Konetzni alongside the Swedish tenor Torsten Ralf as the Emperor. Böhm—following his prescribed period of denazification—would be the crucial figure for postwar revivals of *Die Frau ohne Schatten*.[31] He lived long enough for me to have heard him conducting Mozart's *Marriage of Figaro* in New York in the 1970s, an opera he had conducted in Nazi Salzburg and Nazi Vienna during the war.

"Unfortunately we still need him," wrote Goebbels in his diary about Strauss in February 1944, "but one day we shall have our own music and then we shall have no further need of this decadent neurotic."[32] What did it mean for Nazi Vienna to produce *Die Frau ohne Schatten* at the height of World War II, during the 1943–44 opera season, as the tide of the war was turning against Germany? The fairy-tale scenario of emperors and empresses would have reminded the Viennese public of the now remote imperial world in which the opera had been first conceived. *Der Rosenkavalier* likewise received a new staging in May 1944, with Anny Konetzni and Hilde Konetzni alternating in the role of the Marschallin (and with one closed performance reserved for soldiers of the Nazi Wehrmacht).[33] At the end of May 1944 Maria Josepha of Saxony, Archduchess of Austria and the mother of Emperor Karl, died in Bavaria and was quietly buried in the Kapuzinergruft in Vienna, alongside her husband Archduke Otto, who had died in 1906. Habsburg dynastic rituals, like imperially nostalgic operas, could still be performed even during the last apocalyptic year of the war.

Strauss's operas were performed in Nazi Germany for the glory of German music, while he had settled largely in Vienna in 1942, composing a brass fanfare for the Vienna Trumpet Corps with a dedication to the Vienna City Council: *Festmusik der Stadt Wien*.[34] Hofmannsthal's libretti for Strauss belonged to Austrian literature and reflected a sense of Austria's specific identity—as distinct from Germany's. The performances of *Die Frau ohne Schatten* and *Der Rosenkavalier* in 1943 and 1944 in Vienna would thus have served as a reminder of a set of distinctive Austrian historical and cultural concerns—even as Zita, simultaneously, was trying to convey her sense of that distinctiveness to Roosevelt in Washington and Quebec. Like Zita herself, the public in Vienna would have been already wondering what was to become of Austria following the increasingly likely defeat of Nazi Germany.

In the 1920s Hofmannsthal had worried that *Die Frau ohne Schatten* was doomed to be misunderstood by the "philistine" public—but the public of 1943 and 1944 in Nazi Vienna represented a kind of philistinism that he could scarcely have imagined. It was a public that had conformed ideologically to the slogans and rituals of Nazism, and it was, of course, a public that had been entirely purged of Jews—for some 120,000 Viennese Jews had emigrated and

60,000 were deported and murdered by the Nazis. There would have been Viennese Jews in New York to hear Lotte Lehmann sing her farewell performance at the Met on February 23, 1945—as the Marschallin. The costumes were by Roller, the sets by Kautsky, the direction by Wallerstein.[35]

On March 12, 1945, American bombers over Vienna destroyed the opera house. On March 29 the Soviet army, which had already occupied Hungary, entered Austrian territory and took Vienna in April—with Soviet soldiers engaging in mass looting and rape. American and British troops reached Austria later that month, and the country was divided into four occupation zones: Soviet, American, British, and French. Vienna was to be "international" with rotating forces of occupation troops. The socialist Karl Renner, who presided over the post-Habsburg government in 1918, now formed a government again in 1945, with Stalin's approval and with some key communist ministers.[36] The tense balance of power among the occupying forces meant that the occupation would last for a full decade until 1955, with Austria remaining an unresolved political problem in the age of the early Cold War. From Zita's perspective in Quebec, between 1945 and 1948, she would have seen almost every other piece of her former empire fall under communist government—Galicia and Bukovina, Bohemia and Slovakia, Transylvania and Hungary, Croatia and Slovenia—all beyond any imaginable cultivation of Habsburg presence or influence.

Zita during these postwar years was engaged in helping to raise money for humanitarian aid to occupied Austria. In 1948 she moved from Canada back to the United States, settling in Tuxedo Park, New York, thirty-five miles northwest of New York City, a wealthy little town that gave its name to the "tuxedo" jacket in America. Her house, built in 1904 with wrap-around porches amid woods and lakes, belonged to the Bullock family, who first invited Zita, as in Royalston, and then sold the property to the Habsburg family. It can be rented today as "The Empress's Palace."[37]

In 1948 Zita went to Washington to speak at a luncheon for the wives of American congressmen, and she later claimed some political credit for Austria's inclusion in the Marshall Plan. Her daughter Elisabeth was there: "I remember how warmly the women greeted my mother at her entrance. After all, it meant something to them, just the fact that there was a genuine empress sitting across from them and one who spoke such charming English."

For them, she could have been an empress from a fairy tale, describing the beauties of Austria and then the hardships of the postwar period. According to Elisabeth, her mother at a certain point just departed from her script and spoke freely, conveying her enthusiasm about Austria:

> I saw at the beginning the burning curiosity with which they marveled at the "Empress & Queen"; the miraculous being [*Wunderwesen*] . . . from another world, and how they gradually forgot the "Empress" and saw more and more only the mother, who was fighting for her children, for millions of disenfranchised, hungry, battered human children.[38]

Zita was replaying her role from Children's Day in 1917, but now as a fairy-tale empress—in fact, as the fairy-tale empress in *Die Frau ohne Schatten* who comes to appreciate that motherhood and children are what make an empress into a human being.

In 1946, immediately after the war, Strauss nostalgically took up the score of *Die Frau ohne Schatten* and produced a gorgeous twenty-minute "symphonic fantasy" of its major themes. The duet for Barak and his wife—"Mir anvertraut"—lies at the romantic heart of the musical arrangement, which elides the agonies and conflicts of the opera. Strauss composed the symphonic fantasy in Switzerland, where Karl and Zita had spent an important part of their exile, and the piece was performed in Vienna at the Konzerthaus in 1947.[39]

Richard Strauss died in Garmisch in September 1949 at the age of eighty-five. When American soldiers had first arrived to confront him in Garmisch in April 1945, he had simply announced, "I am Richard Strauss, the composer of *Der Rosenkavalier* and *Salome*"—but it was not until 1948 that a denazification tribunal in Munich ruled him innocent of collaboration with the Nazis. According to Strauss himself: "I only managed with great difficulty to rescue my family from being exterminated by the Nazis." During the difficult postwar years he received some financial support from Maria Jeritza, who was married to a wealthy American umbrella manufacturer in New Jersey.[40]

It was impossible for the postwar world to take stock of Strauss's career without addressing the fact that he had spent twelve years living and composing within the Third Reich. The *New York Times* obituary in September 1949 dedicated more than a third of its content to those twelve years, concluding with the account of the Munich denazification verdict, as if that were the best way to sum up his life: "It found that Strauss had taken no part in the Nazi movement and had received no benefits from it. Evidence was introduced to show that he had devoted himself solely to music during the years of Nazi power."[41] The *Times* critic Olin Downes wrote an essay of querulous appreciation the following week in which he insisted that "it has long been acknowledged that Richard Strauss had outlived his creative period at least a quarter of a century before he died last week." Downes considered *Salome* and *Elektra* to be the only operas of major significance, with *Der Rosenkavalier* and *Ariadne* both lesser works, and *Die Frau ohne Schatten* not even worth mentioning.[42] Nevertheless, in November 1949 the Metropolitan Opera presented *Der Rosenkavalier* for the opening night of the season as tribute.[43]

In 1949, the Viennese Jewish impresario Rudolf Bing, who spent the war years in England, came to the United States to prepare to take over as general manager of the Met. In December 1950, his first season, Bing paid tribute to Vienna with a new production of Johann Strauss's operetta *Die Fledermaus*. Later that season, on February 22, 1951, Bing presented Maria Jeritza in that same production of *Die Fledermaus*, her farewell performance at the Met. It was the same opera in which she had made such a favorable impression on Emperor Franz Joseph in 1910.[44] Born in Habsburg Vienna in 1902 as a subject of Franz Joseph, Bing lived through the reign of Zita and Karl as a teenager. It would be Bing who would introduce the missing works of the Strauss-Hofmannsthal collaboration for the very first time at the Met: *Arabella* in 1955, *Ariadne* in 1962, and finally, after initial hesitations, *Die Frau ohne Schatten* in 1966.[45]

19

The Empress Returns

ZITA AND *DIE FRAU OHNE SCHATTEN* AFTER WORLD WAR II

Zita in Zizers

In 1949, the year that Strauss died in Garmisch, *Die Frau ohne Schatten* came to the Americas with a performance in Buenos Aires under the baton of Viennese conductor Erich Kleiber.[1] The NATO treaty was signed in 1949, the Cold War was well under way, and there was no chance of a Habsburg restoration in the former lands of the monarchy. Zita, however, still living in Tuxedo Park, was focused on a different milestone. The campaign of the Gebetsliga, established back in 1925 to promote Karl as a possible saint, was now advancing. In 1949 the Vatican, under Pope Pius XII, formally established a "cause" to consider the beatification and eventual canonization of Karl, and designated him as a "Servant of God."[2] Zita's long widowhood acquired a new spiritual intensity with the hypothetical possibility that she had been married to a saint.

With the end of the 1940s Zita was preparing to return to Europe, to leave behind gracious American living at Tuxedo Park, abandoning the challenges of American political lobbying, and beginning the more saintly next stage of her long life, dedicated to family and piety. Zita was in Europe in 1951 when Otto married Princess Regina of Saxe-Meiningen in Nancy, the bride wearing Zita's magnificent diamond tiara.[3] Zita had worn the tiara, a gift from Franz Joseph, at her own wedding in 1911, and, like my Viennese grandmother, she had managed to preserve some of her diamond jewelry through all the years of emigration and postimperial poverty. My grandmother went to work when she got to New York in 1940 but never sold her diamonds because, she claimed, she never knew whether she might have to emigrate again. The diamonds, which could be carried in the heels of her shoes, were her insurance.

In 1952, the year after Otto's wedding, Zita established herself in Luxembourg to care for her own mother Maria Antónia, Infanta of Portugal, Duchess of Parma, who died in 1959 at the age of ninety-six. Back in Europe, Zita spent as much as two months every year living among the nuns of Solesmes, where she had now for decades been affiliated as a lay oblate.[4] In 1962 Zita turned seventy and took up residence at the St. Johannes-Stift in Zizers, Switzerland, a religious foundation that also served as an old-age home. The baroque castle with its octogonal tower would be her home for the rest of her life, placing Zita in Zizers only some thirty miles from Feldkirch, where she and Karl had crossed over from Austria into Switzerland by train in the spring of 1919, at the very beginning of her long exile.

Zita's return to Europe in 1952 preceded the death of Stalin in Moscow in 1953, which then facilitated the negotiation of an end to the long postwar occupation of Austria. By the Austrian State Treaty of 1955 Austria was restored as an independent country, and the occupying armies departed, including the Soviet Army, on the understanding that Austria would remain diplomatically neutral in the Cold War world. Zita, however, could not return to Austria, since, although the Habsburg Law of 1919 had been rescinded by Schuschnigg in 1935, it had been restored by Hitler after 1938 and was specifically included in the 1955 State Treaty, remaining the law of the land.[5] The Habsburgs could not return to Austria without renouncing their claims. When Zita traveled she sometimes carried a passport honorarily conferred by the royal family of Monaco, at other times a passport issued by the Knights of Malta. When she reentered the United States in 1951, following Otto's wedding, the immigration papers listed her nationality as Maltese.[6]

The Reopening of the Vienna Opera

The State Treaty establishing Austria's independent sovereignty was signed on May 15, 1955, and on November 5 the Vienna Opera reopened, another occasion of major symbolic significance for the country's postwar identity. The opera house had been bombed in 1945 but was now restored to its nineteenth-century neo-Renaissance glory on the Ringstraße. The opera company had been performing for the last decade in the halls of the Volksoper and the Theater an der Wien, with Jeritza returning to sing as Tosca and Salome in 1951: "It seemed as if all Vienna was demonstrating its undying affection for Jeritza," recalled dramaturge Marcel Prawy. "There were crowds round her hotel all day long."[7] Finally, in 1955 the Vienna Opera was reinstated in its own historic home, under the musical direction of Karl Böhm—who was chosen over Clemens Krauss, both of them Austrians with compromising career histories as important conductors during the Nazi period.

The opening-night opera in 1955, inaugurating the restored opera house, was Beethoven's *Fidelio*, conducted by Böhm and staged by Heinz Tietjen, the artistic director of Bayreuth during the whole Nazi period. It was the opening of a new era, but with some disturbing continuities, and the new republic itself rested on the precarious fiction of Austria as Hitler's innocent victim rather than enthusiastic collaborator. Lotte Lehmann, who sang thirty-five performances of *Fidelio* in that opera house between 1927 and 1936, returned to Vienna to witness the reopening of the theater in 1955.[8]

After *Fidelio* on November 5, Böhm conducted Mozart's *Don Giovanni* on November 6, came back to *Fidelio* on November 8, and then on November 9 led *Die Frau ohne Schatten* in a new production designed by Emil Preetorius, who had also worked at Bayreuth during the Nazi period.[9] In the role of the Empress Böhm presented the twenty-nine-year-old Viennese soprano Leonie Rysanek; born in 1926, she was actually too young to remember the world of Habsburg emperors and empresses. She would be closely associated with the role of the Empress in *Die Frau ohne Schatten* for the next quarter of a century, singing the part with fierce dramatic intensity and thrilling top notes, making the Empress the undeniable star at the center of the opera—as Hofmannsthal had intended all along. In 1955 Decca Records made the first studio recording of the opera with Böhm and Rysanek in state-of-the-art stereophonic sound, and *Die Frau ohne Schatten* for the first time became available to the wider public outside the opera house.

Böhm himself was driven by a sense of mission in seeking to make *Die Frau ohne Schatten* a defining masterpiece of the postwar era—not for the aftermath of World War I as Strauss and Hofmannsthal had originally imagined, but following World War II. By the 1950s emperors and empresses had been gone from the political stage for a whole generation. Böhm had presented *Die Frau ohne Schatten* in Nazi Vienna in 1943 and 1944 in the midst of the European apocalypse, but now, in 1955, he made the work into a postwar affirmation of social and political renewal for governments and societies in search of a new humanity, leaving behind the violence and brutality of the recent past. The Nuremberg Trials of 1945–46 had highlighted the importance of holding political leaders responsible for "crimes against humanity." Even musical leaders, like Karl Böhm himself, faced denazification tribunals—and Böhm was actually banned from performance for a two-year period of postwar purgation.

The Böhm and Preetorius production of *Die Frau ohne Schatten* was presented fourteen times between 1955 and 1959, with its last performance on September 8, 1959, the tenth anniversary of Richard Strauss's death. A new production was then created for the Richard Strauss centennial in 1964, led by Austrian conductor Herbert von Karajan, who had also faced a denazification tribunal after the war. Karajan now undertook large cuts and significant rearrangements in the operatic score. Present in Vienna in 1964 to appreciate the new production was Heinrich Kralik, who had reviewed the original 1919 premiere for the *Wiener Abendpost*. Writing as the elder statesman of Viennese music criticism, Kralik fiercely regretted Karajan's cuts in the score: "Anyone who is somewhat familiar with the work will feel wounded in the heart over the missing parts." Kralik felt that Karajan had particularly compromised the final scene of the second act, "when the Empress is left alone with Barak, and feels pity for the suffering man, and becomes aware of this human emotion."[10] For Kralik it was crucial to be able to believe in the humanizing transformation of the Empress.

Karl Böhm had ceded his position as musical director of the Vienna Opera to Karajan in 1956, and in 1957 Rudolf Bing brought Böhm, his fellow Austrian, to New York and entrusted him with crucial parts of the Met's German and Austrian repertory. Böhm made his Met debut with *Don Giovanni* in October 1957, quickly followed by *Der Rosenkavalier* in November. In March 1959 he conducted the Met premiere of the Austrian modernist masterpiece, Berg's *Wozzeck*, and in December of that year he conducted

Tristan for the debut of Swedish soprano Birgit Nilsson, who was to become the Met's reigning Wagnerian diva. In December 1962 Bing and Böhm presented the Met premiere of *Ariadne auf Naxos*, half a century after Strauss and Hofmannsthal collaborated in its creation.[11]

In 1962 Maria Jeritza was living in New Jersey and Lotte Lehmann in California, and the Met brought them together in New York for a radio broadcast interview during the intermission of *Ariadne*, rival divas for decades, now reminiscing as Mizzi and Lottchen in their seventies.[12] Like Böhm himself, they had known Strauss well. They had created the roles of Ariadne and the Composer before creating the roles of the Empress and the Dyer's Wife in *Die Frau ohne Schatten*. Singing the role of Ariadne for Bing and Böhm in 1962 was Leonie Rysanek.

Böhm thus had enormous artistic credit with Bing as the Met approached the great turning point in its company history, the move to a new opera house at Lincoln Center, leaving behind the old building on Broadway at Thirty-Ninth Street, which had opened in 1883 and witnessed the great performances from the Golden Age of opera, from Caruso and Ponselle to Jeritza and Lehmann. The New Met was designed with an enormous backstage area and a sophisticated rotating stage for set changes, and Böhm persuaded a hesitant Bing that the opening season of the new house would be the ideal occasion to present the Met premiere of *Die Frau ohne Schatten*. According to Bing, it became "the triumph of our first season," in fact, "for the first time anywhere an authentic popular hit."[13] The stage machinery and technology of the later twentieth century finally seemed to realize the spectacular theatrical conception of Strauss and Hofmannsthal.

When Bing declared the opera "an authentic popular hit," he had in mind the American box office metrics of success, and, in fact, the opera achieved its success partly in spite of the critics. The *New York Times* published its review on October 3 under the headline "MARVEL AT THE MET," and Harold Schonberg, the *New York Times* critic, declared the work to be "the most elaborate production ever put on by the company" and an "unqualified success."[14] He did, however, have serious reservations about the opera itself:

> *Die Frau ohne Schatten* has always been a problem opera. There are those who cannot stand it, and there are those who consider it the finest of all

the Strauss-Hofmannsthal collaborations. Admittedly, the allegory of the libretto is hard to take; and the last act, with its backstage choral apotheosis, is admittedly weak. Not only weak: actually vulgar, and no better than a great MGM finale of the nineteen-thirties. But elsewhere in the opera Strauss has written some of his finest, most beautiful music.[15]

The allegory of a fairy-tale empress in search a shadow as the emblem of her humanity, as conceived by Hofmannsthal in Habsburg Vienna before World War I, was simply not compelling for a New York critic after World War II. Schonberg, born in Washington Heights in 1915, educated at Brooklyn College, was New York's arbiter of musical taste, and he clearly disliked the final quartet with the chorus of unborn children.

Schonberg claimed to be thinking of a Hollywood film finale from the 1930s. The Hollywood supersuccess of 1965, however, winning the Oscar and becoming in 1966 the biggest box office film in cinema history, was that epic celebration of Austrian singing, *The Sound of Music*, filmed on location in Salzburg. The Hollywood ending showed the Trapp family climbing the Alps to escape from the Nazis while an invisible chorus sang the inspirational hymn "Climb Every Mountain"—the sort of "backstage choral apotheosis" that was perhaps on Schonberg's mind while reviewing *Die Frau ohne Schatten*. The actual Trapp family did not climb over the Alps to freedom but, less dramatically, took a train to Italy.

My Vienna-born mother went with my father to see *Die Frau ohne Schatten* at Lincoln Center in 1966, and it was then that the opera first entered my nine-year-old consciousness: I remember hearing the fairy tale from my parents, and some of the music in our living room in New Jersey when it was broadcast on the radio from the Met. I was taken to see *The Sound of Music* by my Viennese grandmother, who told me that she remembered those Salzburg settings, which made the movie seem less like a fairy tale to me. My grandmother, who left Austria in 1938, never returned. Her parents, my great-grandparents, who probably rubbed shoulders with dyers and their wives in the world of Viennese craftspeople, were murdered in Hitler's concentration camps.

The Emperor and the Empress in San Francisco and Tokyo

In 1966, the year of *Die Frau ohne Schatten* in New York, Otto von Habsburg returned to Austria for the first time since going into exile with his parents in 1919 when he was a child. In 1961 Otto had issued a tactical renunciation of the Austrian throne, seeking an Austrian passport and preparing for a political career in Europe that did not necessarily involve becoming emperor. Austria, however, had been governed, ever since the years of occupation, by a coalition government of Left and Right, the Socialist Party of Austria and the Austrian People's Party, and the socialists were determined not to let Otto return. In March 1966, however, the People's Party—fundamentally a Christian Democratic party which attracted the political allegiance of religious Roman Catholics—won the legislative elections with enough seats to form a government without the socialists.[16] The month of October 1966 began on October 2 with the Emperor and the Empress appearing in the fairy-tale opera on stage in New York and concluded on October 31 with Otto returning to Austria as an ordinary citizen, no longer a fairy-tale figure seeking to reclaim his lost empire. November 1966 would bring more performances of *Die Frau ohne Schatten* in New York, while on November 21, 1966, members of the Habsburg family noted the fiftieth anniversary of the death of Franz Joseph and accession of Karl and Zita as the Emperor and Empress of Austria, events that now receded into the increasingly remote and semilegendary past.

Following the Lincoln Center triumph, Karl Böhm continued on his artistic crusade to establish *Die Frau ohne Schatten* in the global operatic repertory. In 1972 Böhm brought the opera to Paris for the first time, to the Palais Garnier.[17] He conducted the opera in Salzburg at the summer festival of 1974, Hofmannsthal's centennial year, and then again for the festival of 1975.[18] In the spring of 1975 I was a freshman at Harvard and was introduced to the Strauss-Hofmannsthal correspondence in a seminar about their artistic collaboration.

In October 1976 Böhm and Rysanek traveled to California for *Die Frau ohne Schatten*. The general director of the San Francisco Opera was Kurt Herbert Adler, born a Viennese Jew and subject of Franz Joseph in 1905. He was the son of Freud's patient Ida Bauer, known as "Dora" in the famous

Freudian case study of hysteria.[19] Both Adler and his mother left Austria after the Anschluss in 1938; she died in New York in 1945, while he ended up in San Francisco, where he presented *Die Frau ohne Schatten* with Böhm and Rysanek three decades later.

Lotte Lehmann died in August 1976, just down the California coast at Santa Barbara, and my Viennese grandmother, Lucy, died in September in New York. Böhm, who belonged to their generation, led a new production of *Die Frau ohne Schatten* in Vienna in 1977, bringing Rysanek back to her hometown, where the work was first conceived by Hofmannsthal. In the role of the Dyer's Wife Böhm now cast the world's most celebrated Wagnerian soprano, Birgit Nilsson, his Met Isolde, and, in an intricate piece of Viennese casting, the voice of the falcon was sung by Rysanek's older sister Lotte, also a soprano, so that the Empress's opening scene involved a short and haunting duet between the two sisters.[20]

In 1955 when Lotte Lehmann returned to Vienna for the reopening of the opera house, the company presented her with a commemorative ring to mark her return and honor her extraordinary contributions to opera in Vienna before the war; when Lehmann died in 1976, the ring was passed on to Rysanek, a kind of Viennese operatic investiture, just as she was about to return to Vienna as the Empress in 1977.[21] Now the opera was a hit in Vienna too, and though Böhm conducted it for the last time in the Austrian capital in 1978, Rysanek would continue to sing the role of the Empress there until 1984—the year that she traveled to Tokyo with *Die Frau ohne Schatten*.[22] For the first time it was being performed in a country with a real emperor and empress, not fairy-tale figures: Emperor Hirohito and Empress Kojun, reigning since 1926. On September 8, 1979, Rysanek sang the Empress in Vienna in a performance marking the thirtieth anniversary of Richard Strauss's death. In September 1980 Rysanek returned to California to sing the Empress once again in San Francisco. I was a graduate student in European history at Stanford in 1980, living in San Francisco, and that was when I went to see *Die Frau ohne Schatten* for the first time in my life.[23] I was deeply moved by the beauty of the music and by a sense that the fairy tale of an imperiled emperor, a compassionate empress, and their struggling subjects belonged to the world of my grandparents.

Like Otto, numerous members of the very reproductive Habsburg family had waived their dynastic rights, as specified by the Habsburg Law, so that they could return to Austria. Zita, of course, refused to make any such renunciation, and therefore remained at Zizers just beyond the Austrian border, while diverse members of her family settled themselves on the other side. She particularly regretted not being able to attend the funeral or visit the grave of her daughter Adelheid, who died in 1971 in Bavaria but was buried in Austria.[24] In 1972 Zita, turning eighty, appeared in Austria—but only on television—in a filmed interview conducted by Viennese journalist Erich Feigl, who came to the project with a monarchist perspective. His extensive interviewing allowed Zita to shape retrospectively the narrative of her own imperial and postimperial life.[25] The year 1972 marked the fiftieth anniversary of Karl's death, and on Madeira his coffin was opened and his body examined as part of the ongoing cause for his beatification. Otto was present, along with the Austrian bishop of Feldkirch, the Portuguese bishop of Funchal, and two medical doctors: the body, embalmed in 1922, was found to be still well preserved (which would be consistent with hypothetical sanctity), and was placed in a new uniform before the sarcophagus was closed again.[26]

Kurt Waldheim's Austria

Zita, in Switzerland, turned ninety on May 9, 1982—and, presumably by chance, *Die Frau ohne Schatten* was being performed at the Vienna Opera on her birthday. The Bourbon king of Spain Juan Carlos, her distant cousin, now appealed to the Austrian government to permit Zita to return without signing the dynastic waiver. It was argued that since she herself was a Bourbon by birth, and a Habsburg only by marriage, she technically had no dynastic rights in Austria to renounce.[27] By this reasoning she could have returned to Austria any time in the previous seven decades. Suddenly, the ban was dropped, and on May 16, 1982, a week after her ninetieth birthday, with failing eyesight, she entered Austria to visit Adelheid's grave, sixty-three years after leaving Austria to go into exile in 1919. In November she appeared in Vienna and attended mass in St. Stephen's Cathedral with Cardinal Archbishop of Vienna Franz König (born a Habsburg subject in 1905). Zita's presence attracted a crowd of thousands of onlookers, and there was even a singing of the Haydn Habsburg hymn, "Gott erhalte," expressing some complex mélange of loyalism and nostalgia. An Austrian journalist asked her during this year of her return to Austria whether she still felt she was the Empress of Austria, to which she replied, "Man ist, was man ist." One is what one is.[28]

In July 1982 Maria Jeritza, the woman for whom Strauss and Hofmannsthal created the role of the Empress in 1919, died in New Jersey at the age of ninety-four. Strauss had dedicated one of his *Four Last Songs*—"September"—to Jeritza, back in 1948, and after her death a letter of dedication from Strauss was found in her estate: "Der schönsten Frau der Welt, / der erhabenen Kaiserin, / grossmächtigsten Prinzessin . . ." (To the most beautiful woman in the world, the sublime Empress, the most powerful Princess . . .). For Strauss, in the last year of his life, Jeritza was still vividly present in the roles that Hofmannsthal had conceived: the beautiful Helena, Ariadne the Princess of Crete, and, sublimely, the Empress in *Die Frau ohne Schatten*.[29]

In 1983 Zita continued to make visits to Austria, including a visit to the Kapuzinergruft.[30] She would have seen the great baroque conjugal tomb of Empress Maria Theresa and Emperor Franz Stefan. Nearby lay the only non-Habsburg tomb in the crypt: that of Maria Theresa's governess, Countess Fuchs, whose little palace in Rodaun had later become the residence of Hugo von Hofmannsthal. Zita would have seen the many tiny tombs of Habsburg children who died in infancy or childhood, not the unborn children but the just barely born children of the past centuries of infant mortality—whereas Zita's eight children had all lived to grow up. She would have seen the dignified sarcophagus of Emperor Franz Joseph, whom she lived with at Schönbrunn during the war, of Empress Elisabeth, who was assassinated during Zita's childhood, and of Archduke Rudolf who committed suicide at Mayerling before Zita was born. Now, in 1983, the ninety-one-year-old Zita managed to create a small sensation when she indiscreetly told a journalist that she possessed secret information that the death of Rudolf at Mayerling had been an act of political assassination.[31]

In 1984, the year that Leonie Rysanek sang her last performances of the Empress in Vienna, the ninety-two-year-old Zita went to Rome for an audience with Pope John Paul II, who would not allow her to kneel down before him, supposedly saying, "Empress of my parents, it is I who should kneel before you."[32] Very much on her mind was the "cause" for Karl's beatification, and John Paul II was the pope who set records in this regard, with 482 canonizations and 1338 beatifications during his twenty-seven-year papacy. John Paul may perhaps also have been thinking about his Galician parents as Habsburg subjects when he beatified Emperor Karl in 2004.[33]

In 1986, as Zita turned ninety-four, seventy years after her accession as Empress of Austria, there emerged a sudden and profound crisis in Austrian politics. The most celebrated Austrian stateman in the world, Kurt Waldheim, who had formerly served as Secretary General of the United Nations in the 1970s, ran for president of the republic in the elections of 1986, and the presidential campaign led to the revelation that for decades he had suppressed the circumstances of his military service in the Wehrmacht during World War II. It now turned out that he had served as an intelligence officer in the Nazi occupation of Yugoslavia, in a military landscape that involved the massacre of civilians and the perpetration of war crimes. The postwar Austrian republic had rested on the fiction that Austria had been Hitler's first victim, conquered and coerced by Nazi Germany, and that fiction involved suppressing any suggestion that Austrians participated as enthusiastically as Germans in the Third Reich, forgetting the fact that Hitler had been welcomed by cheering crowds in Vienna at the moment of the Anschluss.[34] Now the suppressed secret history of the world's leading Austrian statesman became a metaphor for the suppressed secret history of the whole country.

Waldheim won the presidential election in 1986 as the candidate of the Austrian People's Party, in spite of the revelations about his past—or even because of those revelations. The Austrian public did not reject him, perhaps even identified with him, though he was ostracized by world leaders after becoming president. Furthermore, in a strange reversal of the situation of the Habsburgs who, for decades, were prevented from entering Austria, Waldheim, as president from 1986 to 1992, found that he could not easily leave Austria, since he was unwelcome elsewhere; the United States officially declared him persona non grata in 1987. Maria von Trapp, the paragon of Austrian innocence, died in Vermont in 1987 at the age of eighty-two.

The embarrassment of having a president in such deep international disgrace compelled Austrians to look seriously for the first time at their own history within the Third Reich. Waldheim himself took the lead on March 10, 1988, issuing a public apology for "Nazi crimes committed by Austrians"—though he made no mention of his own Nazi service. He acknowledged that there were hundreds of thousands of Austrians "who welcomed the Anschluss."[35] Two days later, on March 12, Austrians marked the fiftieth anniversary of the Anschluss with an exhibit at the Vienna Town Hall that showed the actual filmed and photographed evidence of the Viennese crowds cheering for Hitler, while Jews were forced to their knees to scrub the sidewalks of the city.[36] It was the most serious reckoning that Austria had ever undertaken with its Nazi past, and a need for acknowledgment and reconciliation would continue to accompany Austria's path toward European Union membership, eventually achieved in 1995.

While Austria confronted its demons during the Waldheim presidency from 1986 to 1992, the Cold War came to an end with the collapse of communism in Eastern Europe in 1989. Perhaps Austria's most notable moment came with the "Pan-European Picnic" of August, when the Iron Curtain at the Austrian-Hungarian border was unexpectedly opened for free transit out of the Eastern Bloc. Otto, an elected member of the European Parliament (representing Bavaria) since 1979, was the presiding figure of the Pan-European Movement which sponsored the picnic in 1989.[37] In the 1980s Czech writer Milan Kundera, in his essay "The Tragedy of Central Europe," had promoted the idea that Czechoslovakia and Hungary, former Habsburg lands, had no historical connection to Russia but were closely connected to Austria within a Habsburg cultural tradition. Now in 1989 the sense of former Habsburg lands toppling their communist governments and rejoining Europe became ever more powerful.[38] Zita had once ruled over these lands as empress and queen, and now in March 1989, still at the beginning of the annus mirabilis that would transform her former realm, she died at Zizers in Switzerland, ninety-six years old.

There were notable deaths in 1989 of more obviously epochal significance. When Emperor Hirohito died in Tokyo in January, his reign was part of the history of the twentieth century, for he had participated in the terrifying rise, the apocalpytic fall, and the complete metamorphosis of the Japanese imperial presence in Asia. He had reigned since 1926, though Zita, in her mind at least, had reigned since 1916. Among legendary Austrians, Herbert von Karajan died at Anif near Salzburg in July 1989: one of the denazified wonders of the postwar musical world, directing the Berlin Philharmonic, the Vienna Opera, the Vienna Philharmonic, the Salzburg Festival, and recording prolifically with Deutsche Grammophon. Zita, when she died in 1989, had long outlived her political moment, surviving in exile and oblature over many decades, weaving an imperial cloak of invisibility, so that the news of her death in Switzerland was like a report from another galaxy: Hadn't it already happened long ago?

Kapuzinergruft

Zita died on March 14, during Lent, twelve days before Easter Sunday, while March 1989, in popular culture, was blasphemously dominated by the release of Madonna's music video "Like a Prayer." The former Empress was promptly embalmed, and her heart was removed from her body so that it could be buried later, together with Karl's heart, in the Swiss Benedictine monastery of Muri, near Basel. Since the seventeenth century, Habsburg hearts had been traditionally entombed separately from bodies, and there is a special "Heart Crypt" or Herzgruft at the Augustinian Church in the Vienna Hofburg. Zita's heartless body traveled from Switzerland to Vienna, to be buried on April 1, after Easter, in the Kapuzinergruft with the whole Habsburg family. Karl's grave in Madeira was already a shrine, as part of the ongoing cause for his beatification, and there were no plans to exhume and rebury him in Vienna.

It turned out that a committee had already been formed to prepare for Zita's death, under the chairmanship of Georg von Hohenberg, the grandson of Archduke Franz Ferdinand. Hohenberg was serving in 1989, at Waldheim's appointment, as Austrian ambassador to the Vatican of John Paul II.[39] Now the committee swung into action, meeting with the Viennese municipal government to plan a funeral that turned out to be a much larger event than anyone anticipated.

The funeral train coming from Switzerland, bearing Zita's embalmed corpse, stopped first at the Augustinian monastery at Klosterneuburg, closely associated with the Habsburg dynasty. The abbot preached over Zita's body a eulogy of Austrian patriotism: "We turn our thoughts to Empress Zita's faith in Austria. For her, Austria was a great mission—in the last days of the First World War, when she together with Emperor Karl bore responsibility for the empire of peoples. She always believed in Austria, even during the days and years when she had to abandon Austria. Do we not have to thank her for such a strong faith in Austria?"[40] Zita's Habsburg sense of Austria was transmuted into a more contemporary sense of Austria at a moment when the whole country was feeling diplomatically abandoned and ostracized by the wider world. Zita thus became an emblem of national affirmation in 1989.

A government official of Lower Austria, Siegfried Ludwig of the Austrian People's Party (who like Waldheim had fought in the Nazi Wehrmacht), also spoke at Klosterneuburg about Zita's service to Austria:

> Her greatest concern in the First World War was alleviating and abbreviating the immeasurable suffering that came to innumerable people and especially the poorest of the poor. Tirelessly she supported the last Emperor of Austria, her husband Karl, in his honorable and upright struggle for peace and reconciliation. The deceased struggled just as tirelessly in her exile for the preservation of Austrian independence and, during the Nazi occupation and the war years, for the restoration of a free and independent Austria. Nevertheless it apparently remained her fate to be misunderstood in the crucial periods and only much later to be rightly judged in her actions.[41]

Ludwig unashamedly referenced the Austrian victim myth—characterizing the wartime period as one of Nazi "occupation" of Austria—but further implied that just as Zita was misjudged and misunderstood, so also was Austria itself misjudged and misunderstood.

Following the stop at Klosterneuburg, the funeral train continued to Vienna and arrived in the evening for a torchlight procession to St. Stephen's Cathedral. There Zita was to lie in state, visited by tens of thousands of people, culminating in a funeral mass on April 1, which was also the precise anniversary of the death of Karl in 1922. This was not an official state funeral, but Kurt Waldheim was present in the cathedral, as were the leaders of Austria's regional governments and a large part of the diplomatic corps.[42] The Cardinal Archbishop of Vienna Hans Hermann Groër presided over the funeral mass, while the papal nuncio delivered the pope's apostolic blessing.

Groër eulogized Zita as a "marvelous example of faith," as "the immortalized [*verewigte*] Empress Zita"—as a figure who belonged already to the realm of religious and historical mythology. He declared the occasion to be not an official funeral but a "people's funeral" (*Volksbegräbnis*).⁴³ It was estimated that 40,000 people were present in the church and the square, while Austrian television brought the funeral to the rest of the population.

The *New York Times*, providing international coverage, characterized the popular aspect as almost folkloric, almost an operetta, in its harkening back to the colorful world of the Habsburg monarchy: "princes and dukes in formal mourning attire, farmers in feathered caps and multicolored national costumes, members of Catholic student clubs in embroidered caps, old soldiers in antique uniforms, members of ancient orders in flowing capes." Furthermore, the *Volk* who gathered for the *Volksbegräbnis* were not nationally Austrian in any narrow sense of the word: "The many tongues of the old empire that had covered most of central Europe mingled in the great church and the streets outside—mostly German and Hungarian, but also Croat, Czech, Polish, Italian, Slovenian. Thousands of Hungarians were there, evidence of a new fascination with the monarchy that has come with the loosening of the Soviet bonds."⁴⁴ Habsburg nostalgia became intertwined with the contemporary political struggle against communism.

The funeral mass at St. Stephen's concluded with the singing of the Haydn imperial hymn, and Cardinal Groër assured the assembled mourners that singing the hymn was not an act of disloyalty to the Austrian republic, though there were a few protesters outside carrying signs that said "The Empire is dead, the Republic lives."⁴⁵ It was probably just a coincidence that, in the spirit of Habsburg nostalgia, *Der Rosenkavalier* was playing at the Vienna Opera the day of Zita's funeral.⁴⁶

Cardinal Groër was born in Vienna on October 13, 1919, three days after the premiere of *Die Frau ohne Schatten* with its celebration of motherhood and childbirth, six months after Karl and Zita went into exile. Ordained in 1942, he served as a young priest in the final years of the Third Reich and made his ecclesiastical career in the postwar republic, teaching at a seminary—and was finally named archbishop of Vienna in 1986, the same year that Waldheim became president of Austria. Like Waldheim, Groër had his secrets, and, as with Waldheim, those secrets were revealed. In the 1990s there were numerous charges that Groër had sexually abused young boys in the seminary, and Groër had to step down as archbishop in 1998.⁴⁷

Hubertus Czernin—the journalist who helped to expose Waldheim's secret past as well as Groër's pedophile record—was the grandnephew of Count Ottokar Czernin who, as Habsburg foreign minister in 1917 and 1918, worked with Emperor Karl and Empress Zita in pursuit of a negotiated peace.⁴⁸ Later, in the 1990s, Hubertus Czernin would begin to study the history of the Klimt paintings during the Nazi period and would help Maria Altman, the niece of Adele Bloch-Bauer, achieve the restitution of the famous portrait that once hung at the Belvedere in Vienna and now hangs at the Neue Galerie in New York.⁴⁹

Following Zita's funeral mass at St. Stephen's, there was a procession to the Kapuzinergruft for Zita's final entombment in the crypt of the Habsburg family. The procession involved borrowing the black imperial catafalque carriage from the Schönbrunn Carriage Museum—which opened in 1922, the year that Karl died on Madeira, when it seemed that there would be no more imperial funerals in Vienna and the carriage hearse could be consigned to the museum.⁵⁰ Just as there was a Guardian of the Threshold at Keikobad's temple in *Die Frau ohne Schatten*, so there was a Guardian at the entrance to the Kapuzinergruft in Vienna. The crucial piece of ritual for entering the crypt involved the Guardian ritually asking: Who seeks entry?

There was a ceremonial reply, by convention, with the full list of Zita's titles: Zita, Empress of Austria, Apostolic Queen of Hungary, Queen of Bohemia, Dalmatia, Croatia, Slavonia, Galicia and Lodomeria, Illyria, and Jerusalem; Archduchess of Austria; Grand Duchess of Tuscany and Kraków; Duchess of Lorraine and Bar, of Salzburg, Styria, Carinthia, Carniola, and Bukovina; Grand Princess of Transylvania; Margravess of Moravia; Duchess of Upper and Lower Silesia, of Modena, Piacenza, and Guastalla; of Auschwitz and Zator, of Teschen, of Friuli, of Dubrovnik, and of Zadar; Princely Countess of Habsburg, of Tyrol, of Kyburg, of Gorizia and Gradisca; Princess of Trent and of Brixen; Margravess of Upper and Lower Lusatia and of Istria; Countess of Hohenems, of Feldkirch, of Bregenz, and of Sonnenberg; Lady of Trieste, of Kotor and of the Windic March; Grand Voivodess of Serbia; Infanta of Spain; Princess of Portugal; Princess of Parma. There were a lot of titles to recite, and it would have served as a reminder of how far-flung and complex the Habsburg world had once been.

Zita had crossed many borders in her long lifetime, geographical, political, historical, and epochal—but when all her titles were recited at the door to the Kapuzinergruft, the Guardian did not grant her admission: "I do not recognize her." There was a second ceremonial knocking on the door, and a second long recitation of the titles, and once again she was not recognized, once again refused admission: "I do not recognize her." After the third knocking, and third questioning—Who seeks entry?—the ceremonial reply was very simple: "Zita, a mortal and sinful human being [*ein sterblicher, sündiger Mensch*]."[51] And finally she was permitted to enter the crypt. It was traditional religious and dynastic ritual that played out as fairy tale in the news reports of 1989. The Vienna Boys Choir, celebrated all over the world as the musical emblem of innocent Austrian childhood, then sang "Salve Regina" at the Kapuzinergruft.[52]

Coming home from exile to be buried in Vienna was a fairy-tale ending in itself. Lotte Lehmann, who died in Santa Barbara in 1976, was brought back to Vienna to be buried in the Zentralfriedhof, the central cemetery, where Beethoven, Schubert, and Brahms are buried, where Mozart's remains lie somewhere in an unmarked grave. Lehmann's tombstone is engraved with Strauss's eulogy: "Her singing touched the stars." Maria Jeritza—Strauss's "sublime Empress"—lies buried in Holy Cross Cemetery in North Arlington, New Jersey.

The return of Zita's body to Vienna was always focused on the particular funerary charisma of the Kapuzinergruft. She was not the first Habsburg who died abroad and was brought home to be buried there: Marie Louise, Napoléon's second empress, died as the Duchess of Parma in 1847 and was carried back to the Kapuzinergruft to be buried along with her father, Haydn's Emperor Franz. Habsburg Emperor Maximilian of Mexico, executed by the army of Benito Juárez in 1867, was sent back across the Atlantic Ocean to be buried in the Kapuzinergruft.

By the time Zita died in 1989, there were few people alive who could still clearly remember the Habsburg world in which she had reigned as empress. One person who probably remembered was Vaso Čubrilović, one of the conspirators in the assassination of Franz Ferdinand in 1914. Born in Habsburg-occupied Bosnia in 1897, he was seventeen at the time of the assassination; he came out of his Habsburg prison as a citizen of Yugoslavia after World War I. He became a history professor at Belgrade University, and, after spending most of World War II as a prisoner of the Nazis, became the minister of agriculture in Tito's postwar communist government. When asked what he thought in retrospect about the assassination of Franz Ferdinand, which brought on World War I and destroyed the Habsburg monarchy, Čubrilović supposedly commented, "We destroyed a beautiful world that was lost forever."[53] He outlived Zita by one year and died in Belgrade in 1990 at the age of ninety-three.

"As If Birds Were Suddenly Speaking from the Sky"

Zita, a reigning empress for only two years, had multiple imperial afterlives: the afterlife of her exile with Karl in 1919, trying to regain their thrones; the afterlife of her widowhood and motherhood after 1922, nourishing Otto's claims as the Habsburg pretender; the afterlife of her American and Canadian exile during World War II as a refugee from Hitler; the afterlife of her postwar return to Europe and pious retreat to Switzerland; and finally the posthumous afterlife that began with her entrance into the Kapuzinergruft as an imperial legend and culminated in the cause for her beatification, still ongoing.

Zita could only enter the Kapuzinergruft ceremonially shorn of her titles, as "Zita, a mortal and sinful human being." Hofmannsthal certainly knew this traditional formula, as he would have remembered Empress Elisabeth's entrance into the Kapuzinergruft in 1898 and would have been reminded of it again in 1916, while still working on *Die Frau ohne Schatten*, when Franz Joseph was entombed. The formula must surely have been somewhere in the back of his mind when he imagined a fairy tale about an empress in search of her humanity, a spirit trying to understand mortal humans, an empress costuming herself as a servant, a woman with a sense of her own guilt and responsibility, ultimately refusing to steal the shadow of another woman. The year of Zita's death in 1989 was the sixtieth anniversary of Hofmannsthal's death in 1929 and the fortieth anniversary of Strauss's death in

1949. Hofmannsthal was buried at the Viennese Kalksburg Cemetery near Rodaun—wearing the robe of a Franciscan monk, as he himself had specified. At Strauss's funeral in Munich in 1949 the young Georg Solti—born a Hungarian Jewish subject of Franz Joseph in Budapest in 1912—conducted the final trio from *Der Rosenkavalier*, imparting a spirit of Habsburg nostalgia to the occasion. Strauss was cremated and his ashes interred in Garmisch, where he composed his operas in correspondence with Hofmannsthal.

Forty years later, in 1989, Solti undertook a new digital recording of *Die Frau ohne Schatten* with the Vienna Philharmonic; it would require three years to complete. The recording sessions took place in the great hall of the Vienna Musikverein—and the chorus of unborn children was entrusted to the Vienna Boys Choir, who had performed at the Kapuzinergruft when Zita entered as a mortal and sinful human being. In 1989 the funeral of the former Empress had some of the character of a fairy tale, while the same children's chorus moved easily from the actual funeral to the fairy-tale opera recording. Zita, at the time of her death, left a lineage of some sixty great-grandchildren, a whole Habsburg children's chorus.[54] Hofmannsthal wrote to Strauss in 1915, from the depths of the world war, imagining that the chorus of the unborn children would sound "so tonally marvelous that it does not matter whether one understands them or not: as if birds were suddenly speaking from the sky."[55] Together as composer and librettist Strauss and Hofmannsthal created a fairy-tale opera in which emperors and empresses, discovering their own humanity, would be able to hear the marvelous voices of the unborn children of the twentieth century.

Notes

Introduction
Translations from the German, unless otherwise noted, are by the author.

1. Hugo von Hofmannsthal, "Aufzeichnungen aus dem Nachlass 1911," February 25, 1911, in Hugo von Hofmannsthal, *Gesammelte Werke: Reden und Aufsätze III (1925–29), Buch der Freunde, Aufzeichnungen (1889–1929)* (Frankfurt: Fischer Taschenbuch Verlag, 1980), 506; Hugo von Hofmannsthal, "Zur Entstehungsgeschichte der *Frau ohne Schatten*," in Hofmannsthal, *Gesammelte Werke: Dramen V: Operndichtungen* (Frankfurt: Fischer Taschenbuch Verlag, 1979), 388.

2. Hofmannsthal, "Aufzeichnungen aus dem Nachlass 1911," February 25, 1911, 388.

3. Hermann Dostal, *Zita-Walzer: Ihrer kaiserlichen und königlichen Hoheit der durchlauchtigsten Frau Erzherzogin Zita ehrfurchstvoll gewidmet* (Vienna: Musikhaus Ludwig Doblinger, 1911). Copy held by the Bibliothèque Nationale de France.

4. Krishan Kumar, *Empires: A Historical and Political Sociology* (Cambridge: Polity Press, 2021).

5. Strauss to Hofmannsthal, March 17, 1911, in Richard Strauss and Hugo von Hofmannsthal, *Briefwechsel: Gesamtausgabe*, ed. Franz Strauss, Alice Strauss, Willi Schuh (Zurich: Atlantis Verlag, 1964), 112; Richard Strauss and Hugo von Hofmannsthal, *A Working Friendship: The Correspondence*, trans. Hanns Hammelmann and Ewald Osers (New York: Random House, 1961), 75.

6. Hofmannsthal to Strauss, March 20, 1911, Strauss and Hofmannsthal, *Briefwechsel*, 112; Strauss and Hofmannsthal, *A Working Friendship*, 76.

7. Walter Werbeck, ed., *Richard Strauss Handbuch* (Stuttgart: Verlag J. B. Metzler, 2014).

8. Hofmannsthal to Strauss, 20 March 1911, Strauss and Hofmannsthal, *Briefwechsel*, 113; Strauss and Hofmannsthal, *Working Friendship*, 76.

9. Richard Strauss, "Erinnerungen an die ersten Aufführungen meiner Opern" (1942), in Richard Strauss, *Betrachtungen und Erinnerungen*, ed. Willi Schuh (Mainz: Schott, 2014), 244.

10. Modris Eksteins, *Rites of Spring: The Great War and the Birth of the Modern Age* (Boston: Houghton Mifflin, 1989); on the war and Austria, see also Edward Timms, *Karl*

Kraus, Apocalyptic Satirist: Culture and Catastrophe in Habsburg Vienna (New Haven, CT: Yale University Press, 1986); Maureen Healy, *Vienna and the Fall of the Habsburg Empire: Total War and Everyday Life in World War I* (Cambridge: Cambridge University Press, 2004); Steven Beller, "The Tragic Carnival: Austrian Culture in the First World War," in *European Culture in the Great War: The Arts, Entertainment, and Propaganda, 1914–1918*, ed. Aviel Roshwald and Richard Stites (Cambridge: Cambridge University Press, 1999); see also Pieter Judson, "Austria-Hungary," *International Encyclopedia of the First World War*, 1914–1918—Online: https://encyclopedia.1914-1918-online.net/article/austria-hungary?version=1.0.

11. On Habsburg political culture, see Daniel Unowsky, *Pomp and Politics of Patriotism: Imperial Celebrations in Habsburg Austria* (West Lafayette, IN: Purdue University Press, 2005); Adam Kożuchowski, *The Afterlife of Austria-Hungary: The Image of the Habsburg Monarchy in Interwar Europe* (Pittsburgh: University of Pittsburgh Press, 2013).

12. Erich Feigl, ed., *Zita: Kaiserin und Königin* (Vienna: Amalthea Verlag, 1991); Cyrille Debris, *Zita: Portrait intime d'une impératrice* (Paris: Les Éditions du Cerf, 2013). It is notable that Zita's photograph (with Karl) was featured on the cover of Pieter Judson's important scholarly reframing of Austro-Hungarian history, *The Habsburg Empire: A New History* (Cambridge, MA: Harvard University Press, 2016).

13. Carl Schorske, "Politics and the Psyche in Fin-de-siècle Vienna: Schnitzler and Hofmannsthal," *American Historical Review* 66, no. 4 (July 1961): 930–46; Michael Steinberg, *Austria as Theater and Ideology: The Meaning of the Salzburg Festival* (1990; Ithaca NY: Cornell University Press, 2000); Hermann Broch, *Hugo von Hofmannsthal and His Time: The European Imagination, 1860–1920*, trans. Michael Steinberg (Chicago: University of Chicago Press, 1984).

14. Ulrich Weinzierl, *Hofmannsthal: Skizzen zu seinem Bild* (2005; Frankfurt: Fischer Taschenbuch Verlag, 2007).

15. Strauss to Hofmannsthal, July 28, 1916, Strauss and Hofmannsthal, *Briefwechsel*, 353–54; Strauss and Hofmannsthal, *Working Friendship*, 258–59. Recent studies of Strauss include Bryan Gilliam, *Rounding Wagner's Mountain: Richard Strauss and Modern German Opera* (Cambridge: Cambridge University Press, 2014), and Laurenz Lütteken, *Strauss* (Oxford: Oxford University Press, 2019). For Strauss's life and work, see Michael Kennedy, *Richard Strauss: Man, Musician, Enigma* (Cambridge: Cambridge University Press, 1999). For the specific study of *Die Frau ohne Schatten*, see Jakob Knaus, *Hofmannsthals Weg zur Oper "Die Frau ohne Schatten": Rücksichten und Einflüsse auf die Musik* (Berlin: Walter de Gruyter, 1971); Sherrill Pantle, *"Die Frau ohne Schatten" by Hugo von Hofmannsthal and Richard Strauss: An Analysis of Text, Music and Their Relationship* (Bern: Peter Lang, 1978); Claudia Konrad, *"Die Frau ohne Schatten" von Hugo von Hofmannsthal und Richard Strauss: Studien zur Genese, zum Textbuch und zur Rezeptionsgeschichte* (Hamburg: Verlag der Musikalienhandlung Karl Dieter Wagner, 1988); Wolfgang Perschmann, *Hugo von Hofmannsthal und Richard Strauss: "Die Frau ohne Schatten": Sinndeutung aus Text und Musik* (Graz: Österreichische Richard Wagner Gesellschaft, 1992); Olaf Enderlein, *Die Entstehung der Oper "Die Frau ohne Schatten" von Richard Strauss* (Frankfurt: Peter Lang, 2017). Methodologically crucial for the historian studying opera are the classic works of Paul Robinson, *Opera and Ideas: From Mozart to Strauss* (New York: Harper and Row, 1985) and James Johnson, *Listening in Paris: A Cultural History* (Berkeley, CA: University of California Press, 1996).

16. Maria Jeritza, *Sunlight and Song: A Singer's Life* (New York: D. Appleton, 1924); Robert Werba, *Maria Jeritza: Primadonna des Verismo* (Vienna: Österreichischer Bundesverlag, 1981); Michael Kater, *Never Sang for Hitler: The Life and Times of Lotte Lehmann* (Cambridge: Cambridge University Press, 2008).

Chapter 1: Hofmannsthal's Viennese Celebrity and Princess Zita's Habsburg Marriage

1. Mark Twain to Joseph Twichell, September 13, 1898, in *Mark Twain's Letters*, vol. 2, ed. Albert Bigelow Paine (New York: Harper & Brothers, 1917), 667.

2. Mark Twain, "The Memorable Assassination" (1898) in Twain, *What Is Man? And Other Essays* (New York: Harper & Brothers, 1917), 172; Edmund Burke, *Reflections on the Revolution in France* (Oxford: Oxford University Press, 1999), 75.

3. Alma Mahler-Werfel, *Diaries 1898–1902*, trans. Antony Beaumont (Ithaca, NY: Cornell University Press, 1999), 57.

4. Hugo von Hofmannsthal, translation of Gabriele D'Annunzio, "Kaiserin Elisabeth," in Hugo von Hofmannsthal, *Gesammelte Werke: Reden und Aufsätze I: 1891–1913* (Frankfurt: Fischer Taschenbuch Verlag, 1979), 602–6; see also Andrea Carrozzini, "Carducci, Pascoli, D'Annunzio e il mito tragico di Elisabetta d'Austria," *Misure critiche*, nuova serie, anno 10, no. 1–2 (2011), 123–36.

5. Redlich to Hofmannsthal, March 18, 1911, in Hugo von Hofmannsthal and Josef Redlich, *Briefwechsel*, ed. Helga Ebner-Fussgänger (Frankfurt: Fischer, 1971), 11–12.

6. Redlich to Hofmannsthal, March 18, 1911, 11–12.

7. Dorrit Cohn, "Als Traum Erzählt: The Case for a Freudian Reading of Hofmannsthal's 'Märchen der 672. Nacht,'" *Deutsche Vierteljahrsschrift für Literaturwissenschaft und Geistesgeschichte* 54 (1980): 284–305; Walter Naumann, "Die Quelle von Hofmannsthals *Frau ohne Schatten*," *Modern Language Notes* 59, no. 6 (June 1944), 385–86.

8. Hofmannsthal to Harry Kessler, June 10, 1911, cited in Claudia Konrad, *"Die Frau ohne Schatten" von Hugo von Hofmannsthal und Richard Strauss: Studien zur Genese, zum Textbuch und zur Rezeptionsgeschichte* (Hamburg: Verlag der Musikalienhandlung Karl Dieter Wagner, 1988), 110.

9. "Aufzeichnungen aus dem Nachlass 1911," February 25, 1911, in Hofmannsthal, *Gesammelte Werke: Reden und Aufsätze III (1925–29), Buch der Freunde, Aufzeichnungen (1889–1929)* (Frankfurt: Fischer Taschenbuch Verlag, 1980), 506; "Zur Entstehungsgeschichte der *Frau ohne Schatten*," in Hofmannsthal, *Gesammelte Werke: Dramen V: Operndichtungen* (Frankfurt: Fischer Taschenbuch Verlag, 1979), 388.

10. Adolf Hitler, *Mein Kampf*, trans. Ralph Manheim (1943; Boston: Houghton Mifflin, 1971), 19.

11. Frederic Grunfeld, *Prophets without Honor: Freud, Kafka, Einstein, and Their World* (New York: Holt, Rinehart, and Winston, 1979), 2.

12. Hermann Broch, *Hugo von Hofmannsthal and His Time: The European Imagination, 1860–1920*, trans. Michael Steinberg (Chicago: University of Chicago Press, 1984), 92.

13. Stefan Zweig, *The World of Yesterday* (1943; Lincoln: University of Nebraska Press, 1964), 46–47.

14. Zweig, *World of Yesterday*, 48.

15. Carl Schorske, "Politics and the Psyche in Fin-de-siècle Vienna: Schnitzler and Hofmannsthal," *American Historical Review* 66, no. 4 (July 1961): 941, reprinted in Schorske, *Fin-de-siècle Vienna: Politics and Culture* (New York: Alfred A. Knopf, 1980), 3–23.

16. Zweig, *World of Yesterday*, 52–53.

17. Hofmannsthal, "Prolog zu dem Buch Anatol" (1892), in Hugo von Hofmannsthal, *Gedichte und kleine Dramen* (Frankfurt: Suhrkamp Verlag, 1966), 44–46.

18. Erich Feigl, ed., *Zita: Kaiserin und Königin* (Vienna: Amalthea Verlag, 1991), 18.

19. Feigl, *Zita: Kaiserin und Königin*, 19, 62–63.

20. James Bogle and Joanna Bogle, *A Heart for Europe: The Lives of Emperor Charles and Empress Zita of Austria-Hungary* (1990; Herefordshire: Gracewing, 2004), 19–20; Feigl, *Zita: Kaiserin und Königin*, 64–65.

21. Feigl, *Zita: Kaiserin und Königin*, 69.

22. Feigl, *Zita: Kaiserin und Königin*, 23–27.

23. Michaela Vocelka and Karl Vocelka, *Sisi: Leben und Legende einer Kaiserin* (Munich: C. H. Beck, 2014), 87; see also Georg Hamann, *Grosser Herren Häuser: Hinter den Fassaden prunkvoller Palais* (Vienna: Amalthea Verlag, 2017); and Martin Sommer, "Pilger auf dem Weg zu Romy: Audienz bei Kaiserin Elisabeth," *Zeit* online, April 24, 1992, https://www.zeit.de/1992/18/pilger-auf-dem-weg-zu-romy.

24. *Die Frau ohne Schatten*, orchestral score (Berlin: Adolph Fürstner, 1919; repr. Mainz: Fürstnermusikverlag, 1987), act 1, scene 1, 8–9; see also Wolfgang Perschmann, *Hugo von Hofmannsthal und Richard Strauss: "Die Frau ohne Schatten": Sinndeutung aus Text und Musik* (Graz: Österreichische Richard Wagner Gesellschaft, 1992), 17–32; Sherrill Pantle, *"Die Frau ohne Schatten" by Hugo von Hofmannsthal and Richard Strauss: An Analysis of Text, Music and Their Relationship* (Bern: Peter Lang, 1978), 104–14; Olaf Enderlein, *Die Entstehung der Oper "Die Frau ohne Schatten" von Richard Strauss* (Frankfurt: Peter Lang, 2017), 322–24.

25. *Die Frau ohne Schatten*, orchestral score, act 1, scene 1, 11–12.

26. *Die Frau ohne Schatten*, orchestral score, act 1, scene 1, 17, 19, 28–30.

27. *Die Frau ohne Schatten*, orchestral score, act 1, scene 1, 35–36.

28. *Die Frau ohne Schatten*, orchestral score, act 1, scene 1, 52–53, 60–62.

Chapter 2: Emblems of Imperial Marriage

1. Hofmannsthal to Strauss, March 20, 1911, in Richard Strauss and Hugo von Hofmannsthal, *Briefwechsel: Gesamtausgabe*, ed. Franz Strauss, Alice Strauss, Willi Schuh (Zurich: Atlantis Verlag, 1964), 113; Richard Strauss and Hugo von Hofmannsthal, *A Working Friendship: The Correspondence*, trans. Hanns Hammelmann and Ewald Osers (New York: Random House, 1961), 76.

2. Carl Schmidt, "Antonio Cesti's *Il pomo d'oro*: A Reexamination of a Famous Hapsburg Court Spectacle," *Journal of the American Musicological Society* 29, no. 3 (Autumn 1976): 383.

3. Schmidt, "Antonio Cesti's *Il pomo d'oro*," 383.

4. R. J. W. Evans, *The Making of the Habsburg Monarchy, 1550–1700: An Interpretation* (Oxford: Oxford University Press, 1979), 152–54.

5. Egon Wellesz in *Musikblätter des Anbruch* (1919), cited in Claudia Konrad, *"Die Frau ohne Schatten" von Hugo von Hofmannsthal und Richard Strauss: Studien zur Genese, zum Textbuch und zur Rezeptionsgeschichte* (Hamburg: Verlag der Musikalienhandlung Karl Dieter Wagner, 1988), 198.

6. Erich Feigl, ed., *Zita: Kaiserin und Königin* (Vienna: Amalthea Verlag, 1991), 87–88; *Gazzetta Ufficiale del Regno d'Italia*, October 24, 1911, telegrams from Vienna and Schwarzau, 6958.

7. James Bogle and Joanna Bogle, *A Heart for Europe: The Lives of Emperor Charles and Empress Zita of Austria-Hungary* (1990; Herefordshire: Gracewing, 2004), 36.

8. Feigl, *Zita: Kaiserin und Königin*, 87, 99.

9. Gordon Brook-Shepherd, *The Life and Times of Otto von Habsburg* (London: Hambledon and London, 2003), 23.

10. Feigl, *Zita: Kaiserin und Königin*, 80.

11. Bryan Gilliam, *Rounding Wagner's Mountain: Richard Strauss and Modern German Opera* (Cambridge: Cambridge University Press, 2014), 85–126; see also Richard Strauss, "Erinnerungen an die ersten Aufführungen meiner Opern" (1942), in Richard Strauss, *Betrachtungen und Erinnerungen*, ed. Willi Schuh (Mainz: Schott, 2014), 235–36; Andreas Halsch, "Die Uraufführung des 'Rosenkavalier': Eine Chronologie in Dokumenten," University of Frankfurt, http://manskopf.uni-frankfurt.de/rosenkavalier.html; and Archivio Storico del Teatro dell'Opera di Roma, *"Il cavaliere della rosa (Der Rosenkavalier)*, 1911," Teatro dell'Opera di Roma, https://archiviostorico.operaroma.it/edizione_opera/il-cavaliere-della-rosa-der-rosenkavalier-1911/.

12. *The New International Year Book: A Compendium of the World's Progress for the Year 1911*, ed. Frank Moore Colby (New York: Dodd, Mead and Company, 1912), 479.

13. Julius Korngold, "Feuilleton: Hofoperntheater: *Der Rosenkavalier*," *Neue Freie Presse*, April 9, 1911, 1–4.

14. Julius Korngold, review of *Der Rosenkavalier*, *Neue Freie Presse*, April 9, 1911, included in Bryan Gilliam, ed., *Richard Strauss and His World* (Princeton, NJ: Princeton University Press, 1992), 354–56.

15. Korngold, *Neue Freie Presse*, April 9, 1911, in Gilliam, *Richard Strauss and His World*, 356.

16. Hofmannsthal to Strauss, March 20, 1911, Strauss and Hofmannsthal, *Briefwechsel*, 112–14; Strauss and Hofmannsthal, *A Working Friendship*, 75–77; Jack Stein, "Adaptations of Molière-Lully's *Le Bourgeois gentilhomme* by Hofmannsthal and Strauss," *Comparative Literature Studies* 12, no. 2 (June 1975), 101–21.

17. Hugo von Hofmannsthal, "Zur Entstehungsgeschichte der *Frau ohne Schatten*," in Hugo von Hofmannsthal, *Gesammelte Werke: Dramen V: Operndichtungen* (Frankfurt: Fischer Verlag, 1979), 388–89.

18. Hofmannsthal, "Zur Entstehungsgeschichte," 388–89; Jakob Knaus, *Hofmannsthals Weg zur Oper "Die Frau ohne Schatten": Rücksichten und Einflüsse auf die Musik* (Berlin: Walter de Gruyter, 1971), 73.

19. Hofmannsthal to Strauss, March 20, 1911, Strauss and Hofmannsthal, *Briefwechsel*, 112–13; Strauss and Hofmannsthal, *Working Friendship*, 76.

20. Knaus, *Hofmannsthals Weg zur Oper*, 75.

21. Strauss to Hofmannsthal, May 15, 1911, Strauss and Hofmannsthal, *Briefwechsel*, 114; Strauss and Hofmannsthal, *Working Friendship*, 77.

22. Hofmannsthal to Strauss, May 15, 1911, Strauss and Hofmannsthal, *Briefwechsel*, 115–16; Strauss and Hofmannsthal, *Working Friendship*, 78.

23. Hugo von Hofmannsthal, "Letter from Lord Chandos" (1902), in *Selected Tales*, trans. J. M. Q. Davies (London: Angel Books, 2007), 89; Allan Janik and Stephen Toulmin, *Wittgenstein's Vienna* (New York: Simon and Schuster, 1973).

24. Strauss to Hofmannsthal, May 20, 1911, Strauss and Hofmannsthal, *Briefwechsel*, 119; Strauss and Hofmannsthal, *Working Friendship*, 81; see also Charles Youmans, *Mahler and Strauss: In Dialogue* (Bloomington: Indiana University Press, 2016).

25. Strauss to Hofmannsthal, March 17, 1911, Strauss and Hofmannsthal, *Briefwechsel*, 112; Strauss and Hofmannsthal, *Working Friendship*, 75.

26. Feigl, *Zita: Kaiserin und Königin*, 80.

27. Feigl, *Zita: Kaiserin und Königin*, 81.

28. *Die Frau ohne Schatten*, orchestral score (Berlin: Adolph Fürstner, 1919; repr. Mainz: Fürstnermusikverlag, 1987), act 1, scene 1, 38–39.

29. *Die Frau ohne Schatten*, orchestral score, act 1, scene 1, 41–44; see also Wolfgang Perschmann, *Hugo von Hofmannsthal und Richard Strauss: "Die Frau ohne Schatten": Sinndeutung aus Text und Musik* (Graz: Österreichische Richard Wagner Gesellschaft, 1992), 26–28; Sherrill Pantle, *"Die Frau ohne Schatten" by Hugo von Hofmannsthal and Richard Strauss: An Analysis of Text, Music and Their Relationship* (Bern: Peter Lang, 1978), 110–11; Olaf Enderlein, *Die Entstehung der Oper "Die Frau ohne Schatten" von Richard Strauss* (Frankfurt: Peter Lang, 2017), 325; Hugo Shirley, "Melancholy and Allegory in *Die Frau ohne Schatten*," *Cambridge Opera Journal* 24, no. 1 (2012): 67–97.

30. *Die Frau ohne Schatten*, orchestral score, act 1, scene 1, 45.

Chapter 3: Descent from the Imperial Heights

1. Erich Feigl, ed., *Zita: Kaiserin und Königin* (Vienna: Amalthea Verlag, 1991), 100.

2. Feigl, *Zita: Kaiserin und Königin*, 101.

3. Feigl, *Zita: Kaiserin und Königin*, 101.

4. *Die österreichisch-ungarische Monarchie in Wort und Bild: Bosnien und Hercegovina* (Vienna: Verlag der kaiserlich-königlichen Hof- und Staatsdruckerei, 1901).

5. Feigl, *Zita: Kaiserin und Königin*, 75–76.

6. Edin Hajdarpasic, *Whose Bosnia? Nationalism and Political Imagination in the Balkans 1840–1914* (Ithaca, NY: Cornell University Press, 2015); see also Mark Cornwall, ed., *Sarajevo 1914: Sparking the First World War* (London: Bloomsbury, 2020).

7. Strauss to Hofmannsthal, May 22, 1911, and Hofmannsthal to Strauss, June 15, 1911, in Richard Strauss and Hugo von Hofmannsthal, *Briefwechsel: Gesamtausgabe*, ed. Franz Strauss, Alice Strauss, Willi Schuh (Zurich: Atlantis Verlag, 1964), 120, 130; Richard Strauss and Hugo von Hofmannsthal, *A Working Friendship: The Correspondence*, trans. Hanns Hammelmann and Ewald Osers (New York: Random House, 1961), 81, 90.

8. Hofmannsthal to Strauss, June 27, 1911, Strauss and Hofmannsthal, *Briefwechsel*, 130; Strauss and Hofmannsthal, *Working Friendship*, 91.

9. Strauss to Hofmannsthal, [July 2, 1911], Strauss and Hofmannsthal, *Briefwechsel*, 131; Strauss and Hofmannsthal, *Working Friendship*, 91.

10. Hofmannsthal to Strauss, July 5, 1911, Strauss and Hofmannsthal, *Briefwechsel*, 131; Strauss and Hofmannsthal, *Working Friendship*, 91–92.

11. Hofmannsthal to Strauss, [middle July 1911], Strauss and Hofmannsthal, *Briefwechsel*, 134; Strauss and Hofmannsthal, *Working Friendship*, 94.

12. Strauss to Hofmannsthal, July 19, 1911, Strauss and Hofmannsthal, *Briefwechsel*, 136; Strauss and Hofmannsthal, *Working Friendship*, 95–96.

13. Hofmannsthal to Strauss, July 23, 1911, Strauss and Hofmannsthal, *Briefwechsel*, 138; Strauss and Hofmannsthal, *Working Friendship*, 98.

14. Hofmannsthal to Strauss, July 23, 1911, Strauss and Hofmannsthal, *Briefwechsel*, 140; Strauss and Hofmannsthal, *Working Friendship*, 99.

15. Strauss to Hofmannsthal, July 24, 1911, Strauss and Hofmannsthal, *Briefwechsel*, 142; Strauss and Hofmannsthal, *Working Friendship*, 101.

16. Jack Stein, "Adaptations of Molière-Lully's *Le Bourgeois gentilhomme* by Hofmannsthal and Strauss," *Comparative Literature Studies* 12, no. 2 (June 1975): 109–10, 121n14.

17. "Ferstel, Heinrich von," in *Österreichisches Biographisches Lexikon 1815–1950*, Band 1 (Wien: Verlag der Österreichischen Akademie der Wissenschaften, 1957), 303–4.

18. Feigl, *Zita: Kaiserin und Königin*, 435.

19. "Audienz bei Karl I auf Schloss Brandys nad Labem," Radio Prague International, May 9, 2014, https://www.radio.cz/de/rubrik/tourist/audienz-bei-karl-i-auf-schloss-brandys-nad-labem.

20. Hofmannsthal to Strauss, November 4, 1911, Strauss and Hofmannsthal, *Briefwechsel*, 147; Strauss and Hofmannsthal, *Working Friendship*, 105.

21. Hofmannsthal to Ottonie Degenfeld, November 1, 1911, in *The Poet and the Countess: Hofmannsthal's Correspondence with Countess Ottonie Degenfeld*, ed. Marie-Therese Miller-Degenfeld, trans. W. Eric Barcel (Rochester, NY: Camden House, 2000), 145; Claudia Konrad, *"Die Frau ohne Schatten" von Hugo von Hofmannsthal und Richard Strauss: Studien zur Genese, zum Textbuch und zur Rezeptionsgeschichte* (Hamburg: Verlag der Musikalienhandlung Karl Dieter Wagner, 1988), 19; Hofmannsthal to Strauss, November 4, 1911, Strauss and Hofmannsthal, *Briefwechsel*, 148; Strauss and Hofmannsthal, *Working Friendship*, 106.

22. Hofmannsthal to Strauss, December 18, 1911, Strauss and Hofmannsthal, *Briefwechsel*, 149–51; Strauss and Hofmannsthal, *Working Friendship*, 106–8.

23. Strauss to Hofmannsthal, January 2, 1912, Strauss and Hofmannsthal, *Briefwechsel*, 159; Strauss and Hofmannsthal, *Working Friendship*, 113.

24. Hofmannsthal to Strauss, February 7, 1912, and February 10, 1912, Strauss and Hofmannsthal, *Briefwechsel*, 168–69; Strauss and Hofmannsthal, *Working Friendship*, 118–20.

25. Feigl, *Zita: Kaiserin und Königin*, 104.

26. Larry Wolff, *The Idea of Galicia: History and Fantasy in Habsburg Political Culture* (Stanford, CA: Stanford University Press, 2010), 308–50.

27. Wolff, *Idea of Galicia*, 231–79.

28. Hofmannsthal to Andrian, May 4, 1896, in Hugo von Hofmannsthal and Leopold von Andrian, *Briefwechsel* (Frankfurt: S. Fischer Verlag, 1968), 63; see also Stefan Simonek, "Hugo von Hofmannsthals Galizische Implikationen," Kakanien Revisited online, March 2004, http://www.kakanien.ac.at.

29. Werner Volke, *Hugo von Hofmannsthal in Selbstzeugnissen und Bilddokumenten* (Reinbek bei Hamburg: Rowohlt, 1967), 54.

30. Volke, *Hugo von Hofmannsthal*, 55.

31. Feigl, *Zita: Kaiserin und Königin*, 105.

32. Alison Fleig Frank, *Oil Empire: Visions of Prosperity in Austrian Galicia* (Cambridge, MA: Harvard University Press, 2005).

33. Feigl, *Zita: Kaiserin und Königin*, 105.

34. Feigl, *Zita: Kaiserin und Königin*, 106–7.

35. *Die Frau ohne Schatten*, orchestral score (Berlin: Adolph Fürstner, 1919; repr. Mainz: Fürstnermusikverlag, 1987), act 1, scene 1, 52–53; see also Wolfgang Perschmann, *Hugo von Hofmannsthal und Richard Strauss: "Die Frau ohne Schatten": Sinndeutung aus Text und Musik* (Graz: Österreichische Richard Wagner Gesellschaft, 1992), 30–32; Sherrill Pantle, *"Die Frau ohne Schatten" by Hugo von Hofmannsthal and Richard Strauss: An Analysis of Text, Music and Their Relationship* (Bern: Peter Lang, 1978), 113–16; Olaf Enderlein, *Die*

Entstehung der Oper "Die Frau ohne Schatten" von Richard Strauss (Frankfurt: Peter Lang, 2017), 326–29.

36. *Die Frau ohne Schatten*, orchestral score, act 1, scene 1, 56–60.
37. *Die Frau ohne Schatten*, orchestral score, act 1, scene 1, 60–66.
38. *Die Frau ohne Schatten*, orchestral score, act 1, scene 1, 78.
39. *Die Frau ohne Schatten*, orchestral score, act 1, scene 1, 94; see also Wolff, *Idea of Galicia*, 241–46.
40. *Die Frau ohne Schatten*, orchestral score, act 1, scene 1, 86–90.
41. *Die Frau ohne Schatten*, orchestral score, act 1, scene 2, 93–95.

Chapter 4: Marriage and Childbirth in the Imperial Dynasty and the Fairy-Tale Opera

1. Hofmannsthal to Strauss, April 22, 1912, in Richard Strauss and Hugo von Hofmannsthal, *Briefwechsel: Gesamtausgabe*, ed. Franz Strauss, Alice Strauss, Willi Schuh (Zurich: Atlantis Verlag, 1964), 178–79; Richard Strauss and Hugo von Hofmannsthal, *A Working Friendship: The Correspondence*, trans. Hanns Hammelmann and Ewald Osers (New York: Random House, 1961), 127.

2. Ulrich Weinzierl, *Hofmannsthal: Skizzen zu seinem Bild* (2005; Frankfurt: Fischer Taschenbuch Verlag, 2007), 174–75.

3. Hofmannsthal to Strauss, May 18, 1912, Strauss and Hofmannsthal, *Briefwechsel*, 182; Strauss and Hofmannsthal, *Working Friendship*, 130.

4. Michael Hamburger, *Hofmannsthal: Three Essays* (Princeton, NJ: Princeton University Press, 1971), 79–80.

5. Laird Easton, *The Red Count: The Life and Times of Harry Kessler* (Berkeley: University of California Press, 2002), 203–4.

6. Hofmannsthal to Strauss, July 9, 1912, Strauss and Hofmannsthal, *Briefwechsel*, 193; Strauss and Hofmannsthal, *Working Friendship*, 138–39.

7. Hofmannsthal to Strauss, September 8, 1912, Strauss and Hofmannsthal, *Briefwechsel*, 197; Strauss and Hofmannsthal, *Working Friendship*, 141.

8. Strauss to Hofmannsthal, September 11, 1912, Strauss and Hofmannsthal, *Briefwechsel*, 198; Strauss and Hofmannsthal, *Working Friendship*, 142.

9. Strauss to Hofmannsthal, September 11, 1912, Strauss and Hofmannsthal, *Briefwechsel*, 198; Strauss and Hofmannsthal, *Working Friendship*, 142.

10. Hofmannsthal to Strauss, September 13, 1912, Strauss and Hofmannsthal, *Briefwechsel*, 199; Strauss and Hofmannsthal, *Working Friendship*, 143.

11. Hofmannsthal to Strauss, October 9, 1912, Strauss and Hofmannsthal, *Briefwechsel*, 200; Strauss and Hofmannsthal, *Working Friendship*, 144.

12. Hofmannsthal to Strauss, October 9, 1912, Strauss and Hofmannsthal, *Briefwechsel*, 201; Strauss and Hofmannsthal, *Working Friendship*, 145.

13. Richard Hall, *The Balkan Wars 1912–1913: Prelude to the First World War* (London: Routledge, 2000).

14. Richard Strauss, "Erinnerungen an die ersten Aufführungen meiner Opern" (1942), in Richard Strauss, *Betrachtungen und Erinnerungen*, ed. Willi Schuh (Mainz: Schott, 2014), 241.

15. Nigel Douglas, *More Legendary Voices* (London: Andre Deutsch, 1995), 111; Robert Werba, *Maria Jeritza: Primadonna des Verismo* (Vienna: Österreichischer Bundesverlag,

1981), 47–48; John Rockwell, "Obituary: Maria Jeritza, Star of Opera's 'Golden Age,' Dies at 94," *New York Times*, July 11, 1982, 24.

16. Larry Wolff, *Woodrow Wilson and the Reimagining of Eastern Europe* (Stanford, CA: Stanford University Press, 2020), 56–114.

17. Emmerich Deimer, *Chronik der Allgemeinen Poliklinik in Wien im Spiegel der Medizin- und Sozialgeschichte* (Vienna: Verlag Dieter Göschl, 1989); Marlene Jantsch, "Heinrich Peham," in *Österreichisches Biographisches Lexikon 1815–1950*, Band 7 (Vienna: Verlag der Österreichischen Akademie der Wissenschaften, 1978), 390–91; see also Marlene Jantsch, "Peham, Heinrich von," *Österreichisches Biographisches Lexikon* online: https://www.biographien.ac.at/oebl/oebl_P/Peham_Heinrich_1871_1930.xml;internal&action=hilite.action&Parameter=peham*.

18. Erich Feigl, ed., *Zita: Kaiserin und Königin* (Vienna: Amalthea Verlag, 1991), 107–8.

19. E. C. Helmreich, "An Unpublished Report on Austro-German Military Conversations of November, 1912," *Journal of Modern History* 5, no. 2 (June 1933): 199–200.

20. Feigl, *Zita: Kaiserin und Königin*, 110.

21. George Perle, "Alban Berg," in *The New Grove Second Viennese School* (New York: Norton, 1983), 144.

22. Modris Eksteins, *Rites of Spring: The Great War and the Birth of the Modern Age* (Boston: Houghton Mifflin, 1989).

23. Arnold Schoenberg to Alma Mahler, February 24, 1914, in *Schoenberg's Correspondence with Alma Mahler*, trans. and ed. Elizabeth Keathley and Marilyn McCoy (New York: Oxford University Press, 2019), 106.

24. Hofmannsthal to Strauss, January 20, 1913, Strauss and Hofmannsthal, *Briefwechsel*, 212; Strauss and Hofmannsthal, *Working Friendship*, 153–54.

25. Hofmannsthal to Strauss, January 20, 1913, Strauss and Hofmannsthal, *Briefwechsel*, 212–13; Strauss and Hofmannsthal, *Working Friendship*, 154.

26. Michael Gordin, *Einstein in Bohemia* (Princeton, NJ: Princeton University Press, 2020).

27. Hugo von Hofmannsthal, "Manche freilich" (1895), in Hugo von Hofmannsthal, *Gedichte und kleine Dramen* (Frankfurt: Suhrkamp Verlag, 1966), 22.

28. Carl Schorske, "Politics in a New Key: An Austrian Triptych," *Journal of Modern History* 39, no. 4 (December 1967): 355–65.

29. Strauss to Hofmannsthal, [March 1, 1913], Strauss and Hofmannsthal, *Briefwechsel*, 217; Strauss and Hofmannsthal, *Working Friendship*, 158.

30. Hofmannsthal to Strauss, March 5, 1913, Strauss and Hofmannsthal, *Briefwechsel*, 220–21; Strauss and Hofmannsthal, *Working Friendship*, 161.

31. Hofmannsthal to Strauss, March 5, 1913, Strauss and Hofmannsthal, *Briefwechsel*, 221; Strauss and Hofmannsthal, *Working Friendship*, 161.

32. Danny Bird, "The October Revolution," *Time Magazine*, November 6, 2017.

33. Jakob Knaus, *Hofmannsthals Weg zur Oper "Die Frau ohne Schatten"* (Berlin: De Gruyter, 1971), 82; Michael Kennedy, *Richard Strauss: Man, Musician, Enigma* (1999; Cambridge: Cambridge University Press, 2006), 99.

34. Knaus, *Hofmannsthals Weg*, 82.

35. Kennedy, *Richard Strauss*, 86.

36. Ernst Krause, *Richard Strauss: Gestalt und Werk* (Leipzig: Breitkopf und Härtl, 1963), 202; Kennedy, *Richard Strauss*, 92.

37. Kennedy, *Richard Strauss*, 99–100.
38. Kennedy, *Richard Strauss*, 92.
39. Willi Schuh, *Richard Strauss: A Chronicle of the Early Years 1864–1898* (Cambridge: Cambridge University Press, 1982), 429.
40. *Die Frau ohne Schatten*, orchestral score (Berlin: Adolph Fürstner, 1919; repr. Mainz: Fürstnermusikverlag, 1987), act 1, scene 2, 102–4; see also Wolfgang Perschmann, *Hugo von Hofmannsthal und Richard Strauss: "Die Frau ohne Schatten": Sinndeutung aus Text und Musik* (Graz: Österreichische Richard Wagner Gesellschaft, 1992), 38–40; Sherrill Pantle, *"Die Frau ohne Schatten" by Hugo von Hofmannsthal and Richard Strauss: An Analysis of Text, Music and Their Relationship* (Bern: Peter Lang, 1978), 118–20.
41. *Die Frau ohne Schatten*, orchestral score, act 1, scene 2, 109–11.
42. *Die Frau ohne Schatten*, orchestral score, act 1, scene 2, 111–12.
43. *Die Frau ohne Schatten*, orchestral score, act 1, scene 2, 112–13.
44. *Die Frau ohne Schatten*, orchestral score, act 1, scene 2, 113.

Chapter 5: "A Traitor Wind"
1. Strauss to Hofmannsthal, June 1, 1913, in Richard Strauss and Hugo von Hofmannsthal, *Briefwechsel: Gesamtausgabe*, ed. Franz Strauss, Alice Strauss, Willi Schuh (Zurich: Atlantis Verlag, 1964), 231; Richard Strauss and Hugo von Hofmannsthal, *A Working Friendship: The Correspondence*, trans. Hanns Hammelmann and Ewald Osers (New York: Random House, 1961), 166.
2. Hofmannsthal to Strauss, June 3, 1913, Strauss and Hofmannsthal, *Briefwechsel*, 231; Strauss and Hofmannsthal, *Working Friendship*, 166.
3. Georg Markus, *Der Fall Redl* (Vienna: Amalthea, 1984); Hannes Leidinger, "The Case of Alfred Redl and the Situation of Austro-Hungarian Military Intelligence on the Eve of World War I," in *1914: Austria-Hungary, the Origins, and the First Year of World War I*, ed. Günter Bischof and Ferdinand Karlhofer (New Orleans: University of New Orleans Press, 2014), 35–54.
4. Hofmannsthal to Strauss, June 3, 1913, Strauss and Hofmannsthal, *Briefwechsel*, 231–32; Strauss and Hofmannsthal, *Working Friendship*, 166.
5. Hofmannsthal to Strauss, June 3, 1913, Strauss and Hofmannsthal, *Briefwechsel*, 232; Strauss and Hofmannsthal, *Working Friendship*, 167.
6. Hofmannsthal to Strauss, June 3, 1913, Strauss and Hofmannsthal, *Briefwechsel*, 232; Strauss and Hofmannsthal, *Working Friendship*, 167.
7. *Die Frau ohne Schatten*, orchestral score (Berlin: Adolph Fürstner, 1919; repr. Mainz: Fürstnermusikverlag, 1987), act 1, scene 1, 35, 61.
8. Hofmannsthal to Strauss, June 3, 1913, Strauss and Hofmannsthal, *Briefwechsel*, 232; Strauss and Hofmannsthal, *Working Friendship*, 167.
9. Jakob Knaus, *Hofmannsthals Weg zur Oper "Die Frau ohne Schatten": Rücksichten und Einflüsse auf die Musik* (Berlin: Walter de Gruyter, 1971), 90, 107, 125.
10. Hofmannsthal to Strauss, June 3, 1913, Strauss and Hofmannsthal, *Briefwechsel*, 233; Strauss and Hofmannsthal, *Working Friendship*, 167–68.
11. Hofmannsthal to Strauss, June 3, 1913, Strauss and Hofmannsthal, *Briefwechsel*, 232–33; Strauss and Hofmannsthal, *Working Friendship*, 168.
12. Hofmannsthal to Strauss, June 3, 1913, Strauss and Hofmannsthal, *Briefwechsel*, 233; Strauss and Hofmannsthal, *Working Friendship*, 168.

13. Hofmannsthal to Strauss, June 3, 1913, Strauss and Hofmannsthal, *Briefwechsel*, 233; Strauss and Hofmannsthal, *Working Friendship*, 168.
14. Hofmannsthal to Strauss, June 12, 1913, Strauss and Hofmannsthal, *Briefwechsel*, 235–36; Strauss and Hofmannsthal, *Working Friendship*, 170–71.
15. Strauss to Hofmannsthal, June 15, 1913, Strauss and Hofmannsthal, *Briefwechsel*, 238; Strauss and Hofmannsthal, *Working Friendship*, 171–72.
16. Strauss to Hofmannsthal, July 10, 1913, Strauss and Hofmannsthal, *Briefwechsel*, 239; Strauss and Hofmannsthal, *Working Friendship*, 173.
17. Hofmannsthal to Strauss, September 24, 1913, Strauss and Hofmannsthal, *Briefwechsel*, 239–40; Strauss and Hofmannsthal, *Working Friendship*, 173–74.
18. Hofmannsthal to Strauss, September 24, 1913, Strauss and Hofmannsthal, *Briefwechsel*, 241; Strauss and Hofmannsthal, *Working Friendship*, 174.
19. Hofmannsthal to Strauss, September 24, 1913, and September 30, 1913, Strauss and Hofmannsthal, *Briefwechsel*, 239, 243; Strauss and Hofmannsthal, *Working Friendship*, 173, 176.
20. Marc Sageman, *Turning to Political Violence: The Emergence of Terrorism* (Philadelphia: University of Pennsylvania Press, 2017), 340.
21. Hofmannsthal to Leopold von Andrian, August 24, 1913, in *Leopold von Andrian: Korrespondenzen, Notizen, Essays, Berichte*, ed. Ursula Prutsch and Klaus Zeyringer (Vienna: Böhlau Verlag, 2003), 214–15; Hugo von Hofmannsthal and Leopold von Andrian, *Briefwechsel* (Frankfurt: Fischer Verlag, 1968), 198–200.
22. Carl Schorske, "Politics in a New Key: An Austrian Triptych," *Journal of Modern History* 39, no. 4 (December 1967): 355–65.
23. Hofmannsthal to Andrian, 24 August 1913, Andrian, *Briefwechsel*, 198–200.
24. Hofmannsthal to Andrian, 24 August 1913, Andrian, *Briefwechsel*, 198–200.
25. Hofmannsthal to Andrian, 24 August 1913, Andrian, *Briefwechsel*, 198–200.
26. Hugo von Hofmannsthal, *Der Tod des Tizian* (1892); see also Carl Schorske, "Politics and the Psyche in Fin-de-siècle Vienna: Schnitzler and Hofmannsthal," *American Historical Review* 66, no. 4 (July 1961): 941–42.
27. Hofmannsthal to Strauss, September 30, 1913, and October 25, 1913, Strauss and Hofmannsthal, *Briefwechsel*, 242–44; Strauss and Hofmannsthal, *Working Friendship*, 176–77.
28. Hofmannsthal to Strauss, December 8, 1913, Strauss and Hofmannsthal, *Briefwechsel*, 247; Strauss and Hofmannsthal, *Working Friendship*, 178–79.
29. Hofmannsthal to Strauss, December 26, 1913, and December 28, 1913, Strauss and Hofmannsthal, *Briefwechsel*, 254–55; Strauss and Hofmannsthal, *Working Friendship*, 183–84.
30. Hofmannsthal to Strauss, December 28, 1913, Strauss and Hofmannsthal, *Briefwechsel*, 255; Strauss and Hofmannsthal, *Working Friendship*, 184.
31. Hofmannsthal to Strauss, December 28, 1913, Strauss and Hofmannsthal, *Briefwechsel*, 255; Strauss and Hofmannsthal, *Working Friendship*, 184.
32. Hofmannsthal to Strauss, December 28, 1913, Strauss and Hofmannsthal, *Briefwechsel*, 255; Strauss and Hofmannsthal, *Working Friendship*, 184–85.
33. *Die Frau ohne Schatten*, libretto, act 1, scene 1 (Berlin: Adolph Fürstner, 1919), 18–20.
34. Sigmund Freud, *Totem and Taboo*, trans. Abraham Brill (1913; London: George Routledge, 1919), 1, 174.
35. Edmund de Waal, *The Hare with Amber Eyes: A Hidden Inheritance* (New York: Farrar, Straus and Giroux, 2010).

378   Notes to Chapter 6

36. Erich Feigl, ed., *Zita: Kaiserin und Königin* (Vienna: Amalthea Verlag, 1991), 115.

37. Wilhelm Franz Exner, *Erlebnisse* (Berlin: Springer Verlag, 1929), 142.

38. Feigl, *Zita: Kaiserin und Königin*, 116.

39. Brigitte Hamann, *The Reluctant Empress: A Biography of Empress Elisabeth of Austria* (New York: Alfred A. Knopf, 1986), 82; see also: https://royalcentral.co.uk/features/royal-wet-nurses-2-128756/.

40. Ulrich Weinzierl, *Hofmannsthal: Skizzen zu seinem Bild* (2005; Frankfurt: Fischer Taschenbuch Verlag, 2007), 220.

41. Hofmannsthal to Strauss, December 28, 1913, Strauss and Hofmannsthal, *Briefwechsel*, 255; Strauss and Hofmannsthal, *Working Friendship*, 184–85.

42. Alfred Roller, "Die Amme" (1919): https://commons.wikimedia.org/wiki/Category:Die_Frau_ohne_Schatten#/media/File:Amme_van_Alfred_Rollerkopie.jpg. See also Valerie Fildes, *Breasts, Bottles, and Babies: A History of Infant Feeding* (Edinburgh: Edinburgh University Press, 1987); Prophecy Coles, *The Shadow of the Second Mother: Nurses and Nannies in Theories of Infant Development* (New York: Routledge, 2015).

43. Sigmund Freud to Wilhelm Fliess, letters of October 3, 1897, October 4, 1897, October 15, 1897, in *The Complete Letters of Sigmund Freud to Wilhelm Fliess 1887–1904*, trans. Jeffrey Moussaieff Masson (Cambridge, MA: Harvard University Press, 1985), 267–73; Sigmund Freud, *Aus den Anfängen der Psychoanalyse: Briefe an Wilhelm Fliess und Notizen aus den Jahren 1887–1902* (Frankfurt: Fischer Verlag, 1950), 189–94.

44. *Die Frau ohne Schatten*, orchestral score, act 1, scene 2, 120.

45. *Die Frau ohne Schatten*, orchestral score, act 1, scene 2, 122–25; see also Wolfgang Perschmann, *Hugo von Hofmannsthal und Richard Strauss: "Die Frau ohne Schatten": Sinndeutung aus Text und Musik* (Graz: Österreichische Richard Wagner Gesellschaft, 1992), 42–48; Sherrill Pantle, *"Die Frau ohne Schatten" by Hugo von Hofmannsthal and Richard Strauss: An Analysis of Text, Music and Their Relationship* (Bern: Peter Lang, 1978), 135–39.

46. *Die Frau ohne Schatten*, orchestral score, act 1, scene 2, 126–28.

47. *Die Frau ohne Schatten*, orchestral score, act 1, scene 2, 131–34.

48. *Die Frau ohne Schatten*, orchestral score, act 1, scene 2, 139.

49. *Die Frau ohne Schatten*, orchestral score, act 1, scene 2, 143–48.

50. *Die Frau ohne Schatten*, orchestral score, act 1, scene 2, 156–60.

Chapter 6: Hexentanz

1. Hofmannsthal to Strauss, January 2, 1914, in Richard Strauss and Hugo von Hofmannsthal, *Briefwechsel: Gesamtausgabe*, ed. Franz Strauss, Alice Strauss, Willi Schuh (Zurich: Atlantis Verlag, 1964), 256; Richard Strauss and Hugo von Hofmannsthal, *A Working Friendship: The Correspondence*, trans. Hanns Hammelmann and Ewald Osers (New York: Random House, 1961), 186.

2. Hofmannsthal to Strauss, January 2, 1914, Strauss and Hofmannsthal, *Briefwechsel*, 256; Strauss and Hofmannsthal, *Working Friendship*, 186.

3. Hofmannsthal to Strauss, January 2, 1914, Strauss and Hofmannsthal, *Briefwechsel*, 257; Strauss and Hofmannsthal, *Working Friendship*, 186.

4. Hofmannsthal to Strauss, January 24, 1914, and February 18, 1914, Strauss and Hofmannsthal, *Briefwechsel*, 259, 263; Strauss and Hofmannsthal, *Working Friendship*, 188–91.

5. Strauss to Hofmannsthal, April 4, 1914, Strauss and Hofmannsthal, *Briefwechsel*, 263–64; Strauss and Hofmannsthal, *Working Friendship*, 191.

6. Strauss to Hofmannsthal, April 20, 1914, Strauss and Hofmannsthal, *Briefwechsel*, 264; Strauss and Hofmannsthal, *Working Friendship*, 191–92; *Die Frau ohne Schatten*, orchestral score (Berlin: Adolph Fürstner, 1919; repr. Mainz: Fürstnermusikverlag, 1987), act 1, scene 1, 28–36; Olaf Enderlein, *Die Entstehung der Oper "Die Frau ohne Schatten" von Richard Strauss* (Frankfurt: Peter Lang, 2017), 172–73.

7. Strauss to Hofmannsthal, April 20, 1914, Strauss and Hofmannsthal, *Briefwechsel*, 264–65; Strauss and Hofmannsthal, *Working Friendship*, 192.

8. Hofmannsthal to Strauss, April 22, 1914, Strauss and Hofmannsthal, *Briefwechsel*, 265; Strauss and Hofmannsthal, *Working Friendship*, 192–93.

9. Hofmannsthal to Strauss, April 22, 1914, Strauss and Hofmannsthal, *Briefwechsel*, 265; Strauss and Hofmannsthal, *Working Friendship*, 192–93.

10. Hofmannsthal to Strauss, April 22, 1914, Strauss and Hofmannsthal, *Briefwechsel*, 265; Strauss and Hofmannsthal, *Working Friendship*, 192–93.

11. Michael Steinberg, *Austria as Theater and Ideology: The Meaning of the Salzburg Festival* (1990; Ithaca, NY: Cornell University Press, 2000), 178.

12. Strauss to Hofmannsthal, April 25, 1914, Strauss and Hofmannsthal, *Briefwechsel*, 267; Strauss and Hofmannsthal, *Working Friendship*, 194.

13. Hugo von Hofmannsthal, Alfred Roller, and Richard Strauss, *"Mit dir keine Oper zu lang": Briefwechsel*, ed. Christiane Mühlegger-Henhapel and Ursula Renner (Salzburg: Benevento Verlag, 2021), 152–53.

14. Hofmannsthal to Strauss, April 22, 1914, Strauss and Hofmannsthal, *Briefwechsel*, 266–67; Strauss and Hofmannsthal, *Working Friendship*, 193–94.

15. Marc Sageman, *Turning to Political Violence: The Emergence of Terrorism* (Philadelphia: University of Pennsylvania Press, 2017), 344.

16. Erich Feigl, ed., *Zita: Kaiserin und Königin* (Vienna: Amalthea Verlag, 1991), 121.

17. Catherine Curzon, "Franz Ferdinand Killed Almost Everything . . ." History Answers online, https://www.historyanswers.co.uk/kings-queens/franz-ferdinand-killed-almost-everything-on-his-1893-world-tour/.

18. Feigl, *Zita: Kaiserin und Königin*, 122.

19. Feigl, *Zita: Kaiserin und Königin*, 123.

20. Feigl, *Zita: Kaiserin und Königin*, 123.

21. Tim Butcher, *The Trigger: Hunting the Assassin Who Brought the World to War* (New York: Grove Press, 2014), 271–77.

22. Feigl, *Zita: Kaiserin und Königin*, 124.

23. Stefan Zweig, *The World of Yesterday* (1943; Lincoln: University of Nebraska Press, 1964), 215.

24. Zweig, *World of Yesterday*, 215–17.

25. Feigl, *Zita: Kaiserin und Königin*, 125–26.

26. Hofmannsthal to Strauss, July 4, 1914, Strauss and Hofmannsthal, *Briefwechsel*, 274; Strauss and Hofmannsthal, *Working Friendship*, 199–200.

27. David Gordon and Peter Gordon, *Musical Visitors to Britain* (London: Routledge, 2005), 194–95.

28. Hofmannsthal to Strauss, July 4, 1914, Strauss and Hofmannsthal, *Briefwechsel*, 274; Strauss and Hofmannsthal, *Working Friendship*, 200.

29. Strauss to Hofmannsthal, July 5, 1914, Strauss and Hofmannsthal, *Briefwechsel*, 275; Strauss and Hofmannsthal, *Working Friendship*, 201.

30. Strauss to Hofmannsthal, July 5, 1914, Strauss and Hofmannsthal, *Briefwechsel*, 275; Strauss and Hofmannsthal, *Working Friendship*, 201; Enderlein, *Die Entstehung der Oper "Die Frau ohne Schatten,"* 198–200.

31. Hofmannsthal to Strauss, July 8, 1914, Strauss and Hofmannsthal, *Briefwechsel*, 276; Strauss and Hofmannsthal, *Working Friendship*, 202.

32. Hofmannsthal to Strauss, July 8, 1914, Strauss and Hofmannsthal, *Briefwechsel*, 277–78; Strauss and Hofmannsthal, *Working Friendship*, 203.

33. Strauss to Hofmannsthal, July 10, 1914, Strauss and Hofmannsthal, *Briefwechsel*, 279–80; Strauss and Hofmannsthal, *Working Friendship*, 204–5; see also Maria Tatar, *The Hard Facts of the Grimms' Fairy Tales* (Princeton, NJ: Princeton University Press, 1987).

34. Hofmannsthal to Strauss, [July 12, 1914], Strauss and Hofmannsthal, *Briefwechsel*, 281; Strauss and Hofmannsthal, *Working Friendship*, 205–7.

35. Hugo von Hofmannsthal to Arthur Schnitzler, July 15, 1914, Hugo von Hofmannsthal and Arthur Schnitzler, *Briefwechsel* (Frankfurt: Fischer Taschenbuch, 1983), 276; see also Christopher Clark, *The Sleepwalkers: How Europe Went to War in 1914* (London: Allen Lane, 2012).

36. *Die Frau ohne Schatten*, orchestral score, act 1, scene 2, 164–70; see also Wolfgang Perschmann, *Hugo von Hofmannsthal und Richard Strauss: "Die Frau ohne Schatten": Sinndeutung aus Text und Musik* (Graz: Österreichische Richard Wagner Gesellschaft, 1992), 49–56.

37. *Die Frau ohne Schatten*, orchestral score, act 1, scene 2, 170; Strauss to Hofmannsthal, July 16, 1914, Strauss and Hofmannsthal, *Briefwechsel*, 278–79; Strauss and Hofmannsthal, *Working Friendship*, 207.

38. *Die Frau ohne Schatten*, orchestral score, act 1, scene 2, 170.

39. *Die Frau ohne Schatten*, orchestral score, act 1, scene 2, 172–73; Strauss to Hofmannsthal, July 16, 1914, Strauss and Hofmannsthal, *Briefwechsel*, 279; Strauss and Hofmannsthal, *Working Friendship*, 207.

40. *Die Frau ohne Schatten*, orchestral score, act 1, scene 2, 174–76.

41. *Die Frau ohne Schatten*, orchestral score, act 1, scene 2, 179–92.

42. *Die Frau ohne Schatten*, orchestral score, act 1, scene 2, 194–96.

43. *Die Frau ohne Schatten*, orchestral score, act 1, scene 2, 196.

44. *Die Frau ohne Schatten*, orchestral score, act 1, scene 2, 196–97.

45. Michael Kennedy, *Richard Strauss: Man, Musician, Enigma* (1999; Cambridge: Cambridge University Press, 2006) 188.

Chapter 7: Menschenblut

1. Strauss to Hofmannsthal, July 16, 1914, in Richard Strauss and Hugo von Hofmannsthal, *Briefwechsel: Gesamtausgabe*, ed. Franz Strauss, Alice Strauss, Willi Schuh (Zurich: Atlantis Verlag, 1964), 285; Richard Strauss and Hugo von Hofmannsthal, *A Working Friendship: The Correspondence*, trans. Hanns Hammelmann and Ewald Osers (New York: Random House, 1961), 207–8.

2. Strauss to Hofmannsthal, July 16, 1914, Strauss and Hofmannsthal, *Briefwechsel*, 283–84; Strauss and Hofmannsthal, *Working Friendship*, 208.

3. "The Austro-Hungarian Ultimatum to Serbia," July 23, 1914, https://wwi.lib.byu.edu/index.php/The_Austro-Hungarian_Ultimatum_to_Serbia_(English_translation).

4. Hofmannsthal to Strauss, July 25, 1914, Strauss and Hofmannsthal, *Briefwechsel*, 284; Strauss and Hofmannsthal, *Working Friendship*, 208.

5. Christopher Clark, *The Sleepwalkers: How Europe Went to War in 1914* (London: Allen Lane, 2012).

6. Hofmannsthal to Strauss, July 25, 1914, Strauss and Hofmannsthal, *Briefwechsel*, 284–86; Strauss and Hofmannsthal, *Working Friendship*, 209–10.

7. Hofmannsthal to Strauss, July 25, 1914, Strauss and Hofmannsthal, *Briefwechsel*, 284–86; Strauss and Hofmannsthal, *Working Friendship*, 209–10.

8. Hofmannsthal to Strauss, July 25, 1914, Strauss and Hofmannsthal, *Briefwechsel*, 284–85; Strauss and Hofmannsthal, *Working Friendship*, 209.

9. Hofmannsthal to Strauss, April 22, 1914, Strauss and Hofmannsthal, *Briefwechsel*, 265; Strauss and Hofmannsthal, *Working Friendship*, 192–93.

10. *Die Frau ohne Schatten*, libretto, act 2, scene 1 (Berlin: Adolph Fürstner, 1919), 46.

11. Hofmannsthal to Strauss, July 25, 1914, Strauss and Hofmannsthal, *Briefwechsel*, 285; Strauss and Hofmannsthal, *Working Friendship*, 209.

12. *Die Frau ohne Schatten*, libretto, act 2, scene 3, 60.

13. *Die Frau ohne Schatten*, libretto, act 2, scene 4, 62.

14. *Die Frau ohne Schatten*, libretto, act 2, scene 5, 63; Hofmannsthal to Strauss, July 25, 1914, Strauss and Hofmannsthal, *Briefwechsel*, 285; Strauss and Hofmannsthal, *Working Friendship*, 209.

15. Erich Feigl, ed., *Zita: Kaiserin und Königin* (Vienna: Amalthea Verlag, 1991), 134–35.

16. Feigl, *Zita: Kaiserin und Königin*, 135.

17. Feigl, *Zita: Kaiserin und Königin*, 136–37.

18. Feigl, *Zita: Kaiserin und Königin*, 137.

19. Feigl, *Zita: Kaiserin und Königin*, 138.

20. Prince Xavier of Bourbon-Parma, diary, August 6 and 10, 1914, cited in Feigl, *Zita: Kaiserin und Königin*, 130.

21. Prince Xavier of Bourbon-Parma, diary, August 16, 1914, cited in Feigl, *Zita: Kaiserin und Königin*, 131.

22. Prince Xavier of Bourbon-Parma, diary, August 20, 1914, cited in Feigl, *Zita: Kaiserin und Königin*, 132.

23. Prince Xavier of Bourbon-Parma, diary, August 29, 1914, cited in Feigl, *Zita: Kaiserin und Königin*, 133.

24. Feigl, *Zita: Kaiserin und Königin*, 138–39.

25. Feigl, *Zita: Kaiserin und Königin*, 140; James Bogle and Joanna Bogle, *A Heart for Europe: The Lives of Emperor Charles and Empress Zita of Austria-Hungary* (1990; Herefordshire: Gracewing, 2004), 57.

26. Feigl, *Zita: Kaiserin und Königin*, 141.

27. Fritz Hennenberg, *Ralph Benatzky: Operette auf dem Weg zum Musical* (Vienna: Edition Steinbauer, 2009); Egon Gartenberg, *Johann Strauss: The End of an Era* (University Park: Penn State University Press, 1974), 226.

28. Hugo von Hofmannsthal, "Appell an die oberen Stände," *Neue Freie Presse*, September 8, 1914, in Hugo von Hofmannsthal, *Reden und Aufsätze II, 1914–1924* (Frankfurt: Fischer Taschenbuch Verlag, 1979), 348.

29. Hofmannsthal, "Appell an die oberen Stände," 349.

30. Hofmannsthal, "Appell an die oberen Stände," 349.

31. Wiener Staatsoper, October 18, 1914, November 1, 1914, Spielplanarchiv, https://archiv.wiener-staatsoper.at/search?since=01.10.1914.

32. Hugo von Hofmannsthal, "Die Bejahung Österreichs," *Österreichische Rundschau*, November 1, 1914, in Hofmannsthal, *Reden und Aufsätze II, 1914–1924*, 357–58.

33. Hugo von Hofmannsthal, "Worten zum Gedächtnis des Prinzen Eugen," *Neue Freie Presse*, December 25, 1914, in *Reden und Aufsätze II, 1914–1924*, 377.

34. Jakob Knaus, *Hofmannsthals Weg zur Oper "Die Frau ohne Schatten"* (Berlin: De Gruyter, 2015), 96.

35. Strauss to Hofmannsthal, October 8, 1914, Strauss and Hofmannsthal, *Briefwechsel*, 289; Strauss and Hofmannsthal, *Working Friendship*, 211.

36. Strauss to Hofmannsthal, October 8, 1914, Strauss and Hofmannsthal, *Briefwechsel*, 289–90; Strauss and Hofmannsthal, *Working Friendship*, 211.

37. Hugo von Hofmannsthal, "Boykott fremder Sprachen?," *Neue Freie Presse*, September 27, 1914, in *Reden und Aufsätze II, 1914–1924*, 351–55; Steven Beller, "The Tragic Carnival: Austrian Culture in the First World War," in *European Culture in the Great War: The Arts, Entertainment, and Propaganda, 1914–1918*, ed. Aviel Roshwald and Richard Stites (Cambridge: Cambridge University Press, 1999), 136–37.

38. J. E. Vacha, "When Wagner Was Verboten: The Campaign against German Music in World War I," *New York History* (April 1983), 174–75; John Dizikes, *Opera in America: A Cultural History* (New Haven, CT: Yale University Press, 1993), 406–8; Metropolitan Opera Archives, online, *Der Rosenkavalier* (January 8, 1917–November 17, 1922): http://archives.metoperafamily.org/archives/scripts/cgiip.exe/WService=BibSpeed/gisrch2f.r.

39. Strauss to Hofmannsthal, March 12, 1915, Strauss and Hofmannsthal, *Briefwechsel*, 299; Strauss and Hofmannsthal, *Working Friendship*, 217.

40. Strauss to Hofmannsthal, October 14, 1914, Strauss and Hofmannsthal, *Briefwechsel*, 290; Strauss and Hofmannsthal, *Working Friendship*, 212.

41. Hofmannsthal to Strauss, October 19, 1914, Strauss and Hofmannsthal, *Briefwechsel*, 290; Strauss and Hofmannsthal, *Working Friendship*, 212.

42. James Longo, *Hitler and the Habsburgs: The Führer's Vendetta against the Austrian Royals* (New York: Diversion Books, 2018), 94–95; Greg King and Sue Woolmans, *The Assassination of the Archduke* (New York: St. Martin's Press, 2013), 245–46.

43. "Man Accused of Murdering Archduke Ferdinand Goes on Trial," *The Guardian*, October 17, 1914: https://www.theguardian.com/world/2017/oct/17/archduke-ferdinand-trial-princip-archive-1914.

44. Strauss to Hofmannsthal, October 27, 1914, Strauss and Hofmannsthal, *Briefwechsel*, 291; Strauss and Hofmannsthal, *Working Friendship*, 212.

45. Hofmannsthal to Strauss, January 12, 1915, Strauss and Hofmannsthal, *Briefwechsel*, 291; Strauss and Hofmannsthal, *Working Friendship*, 213.

46. *Die Frau ohne Schatten*, orchestral score (Berlin: Adolph Fürstner, 1919; repr. Mainz: Fürstnermusikverlag, 1987), act 2, scene 3, 328–29; see also Wolfgang Perschmann, *Hugo von Hofmannsthal und Richard Strauss: "Die Frau ohne Schatten": Sinndeutung aus Text und Musik* (Graz: Österreichische Richard Wagner Gesellschaft, 1992), 85–100; Sherrill Pantle, *"Die Frau ohne Schatten" by Hugo von Hofmannsthal and Richard Strauss: An Analysis of Text, Music and Their Relationship* (Bern: Peter Lang, 1978), 160–66.

47. *Die Frau ohne Schatten*, orchestral score, act 2, scene 4, 340–46.
48. *Die Frau ohne Schatten*, orchestral score, act 2, scene 4, 351–54.
49. *Die Frau ohne Schatten*, orchestral score, act 2, scene 4, 356–62.
50. *Die Frau ohne Schatten*, orchestral score, act 2, scene 4, 364–65.
51. *Die Frau ohne Schatten*, orchestral score, act 2, scene 4, 367.
52. *Die Frau ohne Schatten*, orchestral score, act 2, scene 4, 373–77.
53. *Die Frau ohne Schatten*, orchestral score, act 2, scene 5, 381–89.
54. *Die Frau ohne Schatten*, orchestral score, act 2, scene 3, 410–14.

Chapter 8: "The Shadow Hovering in the Air"

1. Hofmannsthal to Strauss, January 12, 1915, in Richard Strauss and Hugo von Hofmannsthal, *Briefwechsel: Gesamtausgabe*, ed. Franz Strauss, Alice Strauss, Willi Schuh (Zurich: Atlantis Verlag, 1964), 291; Strauss and Hofmannsthal, *A Working Friendship: The Correspondence*, trans. Hanns Hammelmann and Ewald Osers (New York: Random House, 1961), 213.

2. Hofmannsthal, "Aufbauen, nicht einreissen," *Neue Freie Presse*, January 1, 1915, in Hugo von Hofmannsthal, *Reden und Aufsätze II, 1914–1924* (Frankfurt: Fischer Taschenbuch Verlag, 1979), 384.

3. Hofmannsthal, "Aufbauen, nicht einreissen," 388.

4. Hofmannsthal to Strauss, January 12, 1915, Strauss and Hofmannsthal, *Briefwechsel*, 291; Strauss and Hofmannsthal, *Working Friendship*, 213.

5. Hofmannsthal to Strauss, January 12, 1915, Strauss and Hofmannsthal, *Briefwechsel*, 291–92; Strauss and Hofmannsthal, *Working Friendship*, 213.

6. "Das erstes Bundeskonzert im grossen Konzerthaussaale," *Neue Freie Presse*, January 17, 1915, 20; Wiener Konzerthaus, Archivdatenbank, January 16, 1915: https://konzerthaus.at/datenbanksuche.

7. Wiener Konzerthaus, Archivdatenbank, February 27, 1915: https://konzerthaus.at/datenbanksuche.

8. Hofmannsthal to Strauss, February 6, 1915, Strauss and Hofmannsthal, *Briefwechsel*, 295; Strauss and Hofmannsthal, *Working Friendship*, 214.

9. Hofmannsthal to Strauss, February 6, 1915, Strauss and Hofmannsthal, *Briefwechsel*, 297; Strauss and Hofmannsthal, *Working Friendship*, 215.

10. Hofmannsthal to Strauss, February 6, 1915, Strauss and Hofmannsthal, *Briefwechsel*, 295–96; Strauss and Hofmannsthal, *Working Friendship*, 214–15.

11. Strauss to Hofmannsthal, [February 1915], Strauss and Hofmannsthal, *Briefwechsel*, 297–98; Strauss and Hofmannsthal, *Working Friendship*, 216.

12. Karl Kraus, "In dieser grossen Zeit," in *Die Fackel*, December 5, 1914; Steven Beller, "The Tragic Carnival: Austrian Culture in the First World War," in *European Culture in the Great War: The Arts, Entertainment, and Propaganda, 1914–1918*, ed. Aviel Roshwald and Richard Stites (Cambridge: Cambridge University Press, 1999), 150–54.

13. Strauss to Hofmannsthal, [February 1915], Strauss and Hofmannsthal, *Briefwechsel*, 298; Strauss and Hofmannsthal, *Working Friendship*, 216.

14. Strauss to Hofmannsthal, [February 1915], Strauss and Hofmannsthal, *Briefwechsel*, 298; Strauss and Hofmannsthal, *Working Friendship*, 216.

15. Strauss to Hofmannsthal, [February 1915], Strauss and Hofmannsthal, *Briefwechsel*, 298–99; Strauss and Hofmannsthal, *Working Friendship*, 216.

16. Strauss to Hofmannsthal, [February 1915], Strauss and Hofmannsthal, *Briefwechsel*, 298–99; Strauss and Hofmannsthal, *Working Friendship*, 216.

17. Michael Yonan, *Empress Maria Theresa and the Politics of Habsburg Imperial Art* (University Park: Penn State University Press, 2011), 33–43.

18. Hofmannsthal to Schnitzler, March 31, 1915, Hugo von Hofmannsthal and Arthur Schnitzler, *Briefwechsel* (Frankfurt: Fischer Taschenbuch, 1983), 277: "(psychiatrist)" is Hofmannsthal's parenthetical; Fredrik Lindström, *Empire and Identity: Biographies of the Austrian State Problem in the Late Habsburg Empire* (West Lafayette, IN: Purdue University Press, 2008), 134–38.

19. Hofmannsthal to Andrian, April 21, 1915, Hugo von Hofmannsthal and Leopold von Andrian, *Briefwechsel* (Frankfurt: Fischer Verlag, 1968), 211–12.

20. Redlich to Hofmannsthal, May 20, 1915, Hugo von Hofmannsthal and Josef Redlich, *Briefwechsel*, ed. Helga Ebner-Fussgänger (Frankfurt: Fischer, 1971), 15–16.

21. Hugo von Hofmannsthal, "Wir Österreicher und Deutschland," *Vossische Zeitung*, January 10, 1915; in Hofmannsthal, *Reden und Aufsätze II, 1914–1924*, 391–93.

22. Erich Feigl, ed., *Zita: Kaiserin und Königin* (Vienna: Amalthea Verlag, 1991), 143.

23. Strauss to Hofmannsthal, March 12, 1915, Strauss and Hofmannsthal, *Briefwechsel*, 299; Strauss and Hofmannsthal, *Working Friendship*, 217.

24. Hofmannsthal to Strauss, March 26, 1915, Strauss and Hofmannsthal, *Briefwechsel*, 299; Strauss and Hofmannsthal, *Working Friendship*, 217.

25. Strauss to Hofmannsthal, March 30, 1915, Strauss and Hofmannsthal, *Briefwechsel*, 301; Strauss and Hofmannsthal, *Working Friendship*, 218.

26. Strauss to Hofmannsthal, March 30, 1915, Strauss and Hofmannsthal, *Briefwechsel*, 300–301; Strauss and Hofmannsthal, *Working Friendship*, 218.

27. Strauss to Hofmannsthal, March 30, 1915, Strauss and Hofmannsthal, *Briefwechsel*, 301; Strauss and Hofmannsthal, *Working Friendship*, 218.

28. Hofmannsthal, "Die Taten und der Ruhm," *Neue Freie Presse*, April 4, 1915, in Hofmannsthal, *Reden und Aufsätze II, 1914–1924*, 397.

29. William Butler Yeats, "Easter 1916."

30. Strauss to Hofmannsthal, April 5, 1915, Strauss and Hofmannsthal, *Briefwechsel*, 301; Strauss and Hofmannsthal, *Working Friendship*, 218–19.

31. Strauss to Hofmannsthal, April 5, 1915, Strauss and Hofmannsthal, *Briefwechsel*, 301–2; Strauss and Hofmannsthal, *Working Friendship*, 219.

32. Strauss to Hofmannsthal, April 5, 1915, Strauss and Hofmannsthal, *Briefwechsel*, 302; Strauss and Hofmannsthal, *Working Friendship*, 219.

33. Hofmannsthal to Strauss, [beginning April 1915], Strauss and Hofmannsthal, *Briefwechsel*, 302; Strauss and Hofmannsthal, *Working Friendship*, 220.

34. Hofmannsthal, "Zur Entstehungsgeschichte der *Frau ohne Schatten*," in Hugo von Hofmannsthal, *Gesammelte Werke: Dramen V: Operndichtungen* (Frankfurt: Fischer Verlag, 1979), 388–89; Jakob Knaus, *Hofmannsthals Weg zur Oper "Die Frau ohne Schatten": Rücksichten und Einflüsse auf die Musik* (Berlin: Walter de Gruyter, 1971), 73.

35. Strauss to Hofmannsthal, April 15, 1915, Strauss and Hofmannsthal, *Briefwechsel*, 304–7; Strauss and Hofmannsthal, *Working Friendship*, 221–24.

36. Strauss to Hofmannsthal, April 15, 1915, Strauss and Hofmannsthal, *Briefwechsel*, 304–7; Strauss and Hofmannsthal, *Working Friendship*, 221–24.

37. Strauss to Hofmannsthal, April 15, 1915, Strauss and Hofmannsthal, *Briefwechsel*, 306; Strauss and Hofmannsthal, *Working Friendship*, 223–24.
38. Strauss to Hofmannsthal, April 15, 1915, Strauss and Hofmannsthal, *Briefwechsel*, 307; Strauss and Hofmannsthal, *Working Friendship*, 223–24.
39. Strauss to Hofmannsthal, April 15, 1915, Strauss and Hofmannsthal, *Briefwechsel*, 306–7; Strauss and Hofmannsthal, *Working Friendship*, 222–23.
40. Strauss to Hofmannsthal, April 15, 1915, Strauss and Hofmannsthal, *Briefwechsel*, 304; Strauss and Hofmannsthal, *Working Friendship*, 221.
41. Hofmannsthal to Strauss [April 23, 1915], Strauss and Hofmannsthal, *Briefwechsel*, 307; Strauss and Hofmannsthal, *Working Friendship*, 224.
42. *Die Frau ohne Schatten*, orchestral score (Berlin: Adolph Fürstner, 1919; repr. Mainz: Fürstnermusikverlag, 1987), act 1, scene 1, 2.
43. *Die Frau ohne Schatten*, orchestral score, act 1, scene 1, 35.
44. *Die Frau ohne Schatten*, orchestral score, act 1, scene 2, 113.
45. *Die Frau ohne Schatten*, orchestral score, act 2, scene 1, 241–44.
46. *Die Frau ohne Schatten*, orchestral score, act 2, scene 5, 386.
47. *Die Frau ohne Schatten*, orchestral score, act 2, scene 5, 402–3.
48. *Die Frau ohne Schatten*, orchestral score, act 2, scene 5, 405–8.
49. *Die Frau ohne Schatten*, orchestral score, act 2, scene 5, 410–11.
50. *Die Frau ohne Schatten*, orchestral score, act 2, scene 5, 417–18; see also Wolfgang Perschmann, *Hugo von Hofmannsthal und Richard Strauss: "Die Frau ohne Schatten": Sinndeutung aus Text und Musik* (Graz: Österreichische Richard Wagner Gesellschaft, 1992), 104–6; Sherrill Pantle, *"Die Frau ohne Schatten" by Hugo von Hofmannsthal and Richard Strauss: An Analysis of Text, Music and Their Relationship* (Bern: Peter Lang, 1978), 170–72.
51. *Die Frau ohne Schatten*, orchestral score, act 2, scene 5, 423–24.
52. *Die Frau ohne Schatten*, orchestral score, act 2, scene 5, 431–32.

Chapter 9: "Spirit of the Carpathians"

1. Hofmannsthal to Strauss, May 14, 1915, in Richard Strauss and Hugo von Hofmannsthal, *Briefwechsel: Gesamtausgabe*, ed. Franz Strauss, Alice Strauss, Willi Schuh (Zurich: Atlantis Verlag, 1964), 308; Richard Strauss and Hugo von Hofmannsthal, *A Working Friendship: The Correspondence*, trans. Hanns Hammelmann and Ewald Osers (New York: Random House, 1961), 224.
2. *Die Frau ohne Schatten*, orchestral score (Berlin: Adolph Fürstner, 1919; repr. Mainz: Fürstnermusikverlag, 1987), act 2, scene 3, 300–302.
3. Hofmannsthal to Strauss, May 14, 1915, Strauss and Hofmannsthal, *Briefwechsel*, 309; Strauss and Hofmannsthal, *Working Friendship*, 225.
4. Hofmannsthal to Strauss, May 14, 1915, Strauss and Hofmannsthal, *Briefwechsel*, 309; Strauss and Hofmannsthal, *Working Friendship*, 225–26.
5. Hofmannsthal to Strauss, May 14, 1915, Strauss and Hofmannsthal, *Briefwechsel*, 308; Strauss and Hofmannsthal, *Working Friendship*, 224–25.
6. Daniel Unowsky, *The Pomp and Politics of Patriotism: Imperial Celebrations in Habsburg Austria 1848–1916* (West Lafayette, IN: Purdue University Press, 2005), 118–19.
7. Joseph Roth, "The Bust of the Emperor," trans. John Hoare, in *Three Novellas* (New York: Overlook Press, 2003), 63–64.

8. Franz Joseph, "An meine Völker!" July 28, 1914, https://de.wikisource.org/wiki/An_Meine_V%C3%B6lker!.

9. Franz Joseph, "An meine Völker! Der König von Italien hat Mir den Krieg erklärt," May 23, 1915, https://digitalcollections.hoover.org/objects/10088.

10. Hugo von Hofmannsthal, "Geist der Karpathen," *Neue Freie Presse*, May 23, 1915, in Hugo von Hofmannsthal, *Reden und Aufsätze II, 1914–1924* (Frankfurt: Fischer Taschenbuch Verlag, 1979), 412–13.

11. Hofmannsthal, "Geist der Karpathen," 414–15.

12. Allan Janik and Stephen Toulmin, *Wittgenstein's Vienna* (New York: Simon and Schuster, 1973), 169–74.

13. Arnold Schoenberg to Alma Mahler, August 28, 1914, in *Schoenberg's Correspondence with Alma Mahler*, trans. and ed. Elizabeth Keathley and Marilyn McCoy (New York: Oxford University Press, 2019), 127–28.

14. "Arnold Schoenberg (1874–1951)," Mahler Foundation, https://mahlerfoundation.org/mahler/contemporaries/arnold-schoenberg/.

15. Carl Schorske, "Operatic Modernism," *Journal of Interdisciplinary History* 36, no. 4 (Spring 2006): 675–81.

16. Steven Beller, "The Tragic Carnival: Austrian Culture in the First World War," in *European Culture in the Great War: The Arts, Entertainment, and Propaganda, 1914–1918*, ed. Aviel Roshwald and Richard Stites (Cambridge: Cambridge University Press, 1999), 146–47.

17. Georg Trakl, "Der Abend," https://www.textlog.de/17590.html.

18. Trakl, "Grodek," https://www.textlog.de/17596.html.

19. Trakl, "Grodek," https://www.textlog.de/17596.html.

20. Andrian to Hofmannsthal, May 23, 1915, Hugo von Hofmannsthal and Leopold von Andrian, *Briefwechsel* (Frankfurt: S. Fischer Verlag, 1968), 216.

21. Fredrik Lindström, *Empire and Identity: Biographies of the Austrian State Problem in the Late Habsburg Empire* (West Lafayette, IN: Purdue University Press, 2008), 120–53.

22. Hofmannsthal an den Insel Verlag, [May 28? 1915], *Hofmannsthal/Insel-Verlag Briefwechsel* in *Archiv für Geschichte des Buchwesens*, Band 25, ed. Monika Estermann, Reinhard Wittmann, and Marietta Kleiss (Frankfurt: Buchhändler-Vereinigung, 1984), item 502, 553–54, https://books.google.it/books?id=T39dDwAAQBAJ&pg=PA497&dpg=PA497&dq=hofmannsthal+andrian+krakau+1915&source=bl&ots=jfcTwdxM6d&sig=ACfU3U1SzSqxktORGfBln-mt3Faw79Ut5g&hl=en&sa=X&redir_esc=y#v=onepage&q=hofmannsthal%20andrian%20krakau%201915&f=false.

23. Hugo von Hofmannsthal, "Unsere Militärverwaltung in Polen," *Neue Freie Presse*, August 8, 1915, in Hofmannsthal, *Reden und Aufsätze II, 1914–1924*, 422–23; Larry Wolff, *Inventing Eastern Europe: The Map of Civilization on the Mind of the Enlightenment* (Stanford, CA: Stanford University Press, 1994); Vejas Liulevicius, *The German Myth of the East* (Oxford: Oxford University Press, 2009).

24. Hofmannsthal, "Unsere Militärverwaltung in Polen," 427.

25. Hofmannsthal to Andrian, May 4, 1896, Hofmannsthal and Andrian, *Briefwechsel* 63; Hofmannsthal, "Unsere Militärverwaltung in Polen," 428.

26. Stefan Zweig, *The World of Yesterday* (1943; Lincoln: University of Nebraska Press, 1964), 247–49; Leon Botstein, "Stefan Zweig and the Illusion of the Jewish European," *Jewish Social Studies* 44, no. 1 (Winter 1982): 72–73; Eva Plank, *"Ich will euch eine Zukunft*

und eine Hoffnung geben" (Jer 29:11): Die biblische Prophetengestalt und ihre Rezeption in der dramatischen Dichtung "Jeremias" von Stefan Zweig (Göttingen: Vandenhoeck and Ruprecht, 2018), 41–42.

27. David Rechter, "Galicia in Vienna: Jewish Refugees in the First World War," *Austrian History Yearbook* 52 (2021): 113–30; Pieter Judson, "Austria-Hungary," *International Encyclopedia of the First World War*, 1914–1918—Online: https://encyclopedia.1914-1918-online.net/article/austria-hungary?version=1.0.

28. Wiener Konzerthaus Archiv, November 5, 1914: https://konzerthaus.at/datenbanksuche.

29. Wiener Konzerthaus Archiv, December 5, 1914, and December 10, 1914: https://konzerthaus.at/datenbanksuche.

30. Wiener Konzerthaus Archiv, December 17, 1914, and March 24, 1915: https://konzerthaus.at/datenbanksuche.

31. *Reform Advocate* 50, January 8, 1916, 682–83:
https://books.google.com/books?id=s1ccAQAAMAAJ&pg=PA682&lpg=PA682&dq=fuchs+cantors+galicia+1915&source=bl&ots=B8LQho8ztZ&sig=ACfU3U11MOFiUymBx8PcKaMAsAXO1XZL-Q&hl=en&sa=X&ved=2ahUKEwi6-rzv-ITqAhXRSTABHcNGApoQ6AEwDnoECA8QAQ#v=onepage&q=fuchs%20cantors%20galicia%201915&f=false.

32. *Reform Advocate* 50, January 8, 1916, 682–83.

33. "Das Flüchtlingsheim in der Wallnerstraße," *Neue Freie Presse*, January 14, 1915, 9.

34. Wiener Konzerthaus Archiv, January 27, 1915: https://konzerthaus.at/datenbanksuche.

35. Strauss to Hofmannsthal, May 27, 1915, Strauss and Hofmannsthal, *Briefwechsel*, 303–04; Strauss and Hofmannsthal, *Working Friendship*, 226; Olaf Enderlein, *Die Entstehung der Oper "Die Frau ohne Schatten" von Richard Strauss* (Frankfurt: Peter Lang, 2017), 257–63.

36. Strauss to Hofmannsthal, May 28, 1915, Strauss and Hofmannsthal, *Briefwechsel*, 311–12; Strauss and Hofmannsthal, *Working Friendship*, 227–28.

37. Strauss to Hofmannsthal, June 8, 1915, Strauss and Hofmannsthal, *Briefwechsel*, 312; Strauss and Hofmannsthal, *Working Friendship*, 228–29.

38. Strauss to Hofmannsthal, June 8, 1915, Strauss and Hofmannsthal, *Briefwechsel*, 313; Strauss and Hofmannsthal, *Working Friendship*, 228–29; Aaron Bernstein, *Mendel Gibbor* (Berlin: Louis Gerschel, 1865).

39. Strauss to Hofmannsthal, June 17, 1915, Strauss and Hofmannsthal, *Briefwechsel*, 313; Strauss and Hofmannsthal, *Working Friendship*, 230.

40. Strauss to Hofmannsthal, June 17, 1915, Strauss and Hofmannsthal, *Briefwechsel*, 314; Strauss and Hofmannsthal, *Working Friendship*, 230.

41. Hofmannsthal to Strauss, June 22, 1915, Strauss and Hofmannsthal, *Briefwechsel*, 315; Strauss and Hofmannsthal, *Working Friendship*, 231.

42. Ulrich Weinzierl, *Hofmannsthal: Skizzen zu seinem Bild* (2005; Frankfurt: Fischer Taschenbuch Verlag, 2007), 211–13.

43. Weinzierl, *Hofmannsthal*, 213.

44. *Die Frau ohne Schatten*, orchestral score, act 3, scene 1, 433–36; see also Wolfgang Perschmann, *Hugo von Hofmannsthal und Richard Strauss: "Die Frau ohne Schatten": Sinndeutung aus Text und Musik* (Graz: Österreichische Richard Wagner Gesellschaft, 1992),

108–15; Sherrill Pantle, *"Die Frau ohne Schatten" by Hugo von Hofmannsthal and Richard Strauss: An Analysis of Text, Music and Their Relationship* (Bern: Peter Lang, 1978), 173–78.

45. *Die Frau ohne Schatten*, orchestral score, act 3, scene 1, 437–44.
46. *Die Frau ohne Schatten*, orchestral score, act 3, scene 1, 444–45.
47. *Die Frau ohne Schatten*, orchestral score, act 3, scene 1, 445–48.
48. *Die Frau ohne Schatten*, orchestral score, act 3, scene 1, 450–51.
49. *Die Frau ohne Schatten*, orchestral score, act 3, scene 1, 451–55.

Chapter 10: The Empress at the Threshold

1. Hofmannsthal to Strauss, July 7, 1915, in Richard Strauss and Hugo von Hofmannsthal, *Briefwechsel: Gesamtausgabe*, ed. Franz Strauss, Alice Strauss, Willi Schuh (Zurich: Atlantis Verlag, 1964), 316; Richard Strauss and Hugo von Hofmannsthal, *A Working Friendship: The Correspondence*, trans. Hanns Hammelmann and Ewald Osers (New York: Random House, 1961), 231–32.

2. Sigmund Freud, *Zeitgemässes über Krieg und Tod* (Leipzig: Internationaler Psychoanalytischer Verlag, 1924); Sigmund Freud, *Thoughts for the Times on War and Death*, http://www.panarchy.org/freud/war.1915.html; Sigmund Freud, *Reflections on War and Death*, trans. A. A. Brill and Alfred Kuttner (New York: Moffat, Yard, 1918), 1–2.

3. Strauss to Hofmannsthal, August 17, 1915, Strauss and Hofmannsthal, *Briefwechsel*, 319; Strauss and Hofmannsthal, *Working Friendship*, 232.

4. Hofmannsthal to Strauss, August 21, 1915, Strauss and Hofmannsthal, *Briefwechsel*, 320–21; Strauss and Hofmannsthal, *Working Friendship*, 233–34.

5. Hugo von Hofmannsthal, "Österreichische Bibliothek: Eine Ankündigung," *Neue Freie Presse*, August 15, 1915, in Hugo von Hofmannsthal, *Reden und Aufsätze II, 1914–1924* (Frankfurt: Fischer Taschenbuch, 1979), 433–38.

6. "Hofmannsthal: Chronik zu Leben und Werk," http://www.navigare.de/hofmannsthal/chro.htm.

7. Hofmannsthal to Strauss, [September 11, 1915], Strauss and Hofmannsthal, *Briefwechsel*, 324; Strauss and Hofmannsthal, *Working Friendship*, 234.

8. Hofmannsthal to Strauss, September 17, 1915, Strauss and Hofmannsthal, *Briefwechsel*, 325; Strauss and Hofmannsthal, *Working Friendship*, 235.

9. Hofmannsthal to Strauss, September 19, 1915, Strauss and Hofmannsthal, *Briefwechsel*, 325–26; Strauss and Hofmannsthal, *Working Friendship*, 236.

10. Hofmannsthal to Strauss, September 19, 1915, Strauss and Hofmannsthal, *Briefwechsel*, 326; Strauss and Hofmannsthal, *Working Friendship*, 236.

11. Carl Schorske, "Politics and the Psyche in Fin-de-siècle Vienna: Schnitzler and Hofmannsthal," *American Historical Review* 66, no. 4 (July 1961): 930–46.

12. Hofmannsthal to Strauss, September 19, 1915, Strauss and Hofmannsthal, *Briefwechsel*, 326; Strauss and Hofmannsthal, *Working Friendship*, 236.

13. Maria Jeritza, *Sunlight and Song: A Singer's Life* (New York: D. Appleton, 1924), 21–22.

14. "Hugo August Peter Hofmann Edler von Hofmannsthal" (1841–1915), website Geni: https://www.geni.com/people/Hugo-Hofmann-Edler-von-Hofmannsthal/6000000009616855433.

15. Hofmannsthal to Strauss, January 5, 1916, Strauss and Hofmannsthal, *Briefwechsel*, 327–28; Strauss and Hofmannsthal, *Working Friendship*, 237.

16. Hofmannsthal to Strauss, January 18, 1916, Strauss and Hofmannsthal, *Briefwechsel*, 329; Strauss and Hofmannsthal, *Working Friendship*, 238.

17. Richard Strauss, "Erinnerungen an die ersten Aufführungen meiner Opern" (1942), in Richard Strauss, *Betrachtungen und Erinnerungen* (Mainz: Schott, 2014), 244; see also Hartmut Haenchen, "Opera and Operette: *Die Frau ohne Schatten*" (2004): https://www.opusklassiek.nl/opera_operette/haenchen_strauss_frauohneschatten.htm.

18. Strauss to Hofmannsthal, June 5, 1916, Strauss and Hofmannsthal, *Briefwechsel*, 344–45; Strauss and Hofmannsthal, *Working Friendship*, 251.

19. Hofmannsthal to Pauline Strauss, February 18, 1916, Strauss and Hofmannsthal, *Briefwechsel*, 332; Strauss and Hofmannsthal, *Working Friendship*, 239–40.

20. Hofmannsthal to Strauss, April 13, 1916, Strauss and Hofmannsthal, *Briefwechsel*, 334; Strauss and Hofmannsthal, *Working Friendship*, 242.

21. Strauss to Hofmannsthal, April 16, 1916, Strauss and Hofmannsthal, *Briefwechsel*, 335; Strauss and Hofmannsthal, *Working Friendship*, 243.

22. Strauss to Hofmannsthal, May 25, 1916, Strauss and Hofmannsthal, *Briefwechsel*, 342; Strauss and Hofmannsthal, *Working Friendship*, 248–49.

23. Strauss to Hofmannsthal, May 25, 1916, Strauss and Hofmannsthal, *Briefwechsel*, 342; Strauss and Hofmannsthal, *Working Friendship*, 249.

24. Hofmannsthal to Strauss, May 30, 1916, Strauss and Hofmannsthal, *Briefwechsel*, 342–43; Strauss and Hofmannsthal, *Working Friendship*, 249.

25. Erich Feigl, ed., *Zita: Kaiserin und Königin* (Vienna: Amalthea Verlag, 1991), 155–56.

26. Maureen Healy, *Vienna and the Fall of the Habsburg Empire: Total War and Everyday Life in World War I* (Cambridge: Cambridge University Press, 2004), 31–86; Pieter Judson, "Austria-Hungary," *International Encyclopedia of the First World War, 1914–1918*—Online: https://encyclopedia.1914-1918-online.net/article/austria-hungary?version=1.0.

27. Feigl, *Zita: Kaiserin und Königin*, 155–56; Pieter Judson, *The Habsburg Empire: A New History* (Cambridge, MA: Harvard University Press, 2016), 399–402.

28. Strauss to Hofmannsthal, June 5, 1916, Strauss and Hofmannsthal, *Briefwechsel*, 344; Strauss and Hofmannsthal, *Working Friendship*, 250–51.

29. Strauss to Hofmannsthal, June 5, 1916, Strauss and Hofmannsthal, *Briefwechsel*, 344–45; Strauss and Hofmannsthal, *Working Friendship*, 250–51; Harry Zohn, *Karl Kraus* (New York: Frederick Ungar, 1971), 68–85; Edward Timms, *Karl Kraus: Apocalyptic Satirist: Culture and Catastrophe in Habsburg Vienna* (New Haven, CT: Yale University Press, 1986); Micaela Baranello, *The Operetta Empire: Music Theater in Early Twentieth-Century Vienna* (Berkeley: University of California Press, 2021).

30. Steven Beller, "The Tragic Carnival: Austrian Culture in the First World War," in *European Culture in the Great War: The Arts, Entertainment, and Propaganda, 1914–1918*, ed. Aviel Roshwald and Richard Stites (Cambridge: Cambridge University Press, 1999), 154–59; Baranello, *Operetta Empire*, 93–121.

31. Hofmannsthal to Strauss, June 11, 1916 (not sent), Strauss and Hofmannsthal, *Briefwechsel*, 345–46; Strauss and Hofmannsthal, *Working Friendship*, 251–53.

32. Fredrik Lindström, *Empire and Identity: Biographies of the Austrian State Problem in the Late Habsburg Empire* (West Lafayette, IN: Purdue University Press, 2008), 146–49; "Hofmannsthal: Chronik zu Leben und Werk," http://www.navigare.de/hofmannsthal/chro.htm.

33. Hugo von Hofmannsthal, "Österreich im Spiegel seiner Dichtung," Warsaw lecture, July 7, 1916, published in *Neue Freie Presse*, November 15/16, 1916, in Hofmannsthal, *Reden und Aufsätze II, 1914–1924*, 13.

34. Hofmannsthal, "Österreich im Spiegel seiner Dichtung," 25.

35. Hofmannsthal to Strauss, July 7, 1916, Strauss and Hofmannsthal, *Briefwechsel*, 347; Strauss and Hofmannsthal, *Working Friendship*, 253.

36. Hofmannsthal to Strauss, July 24, 1916, Strauss and Hofmannsthal, *Briefwechsel*, 351; Strauss and Hofmannsthal, *Working Friendship*, 256.

37. Strauss to Hofmannsthal, July 28, 1916, Strauss and Hofmannsthal, *Briefwechsel*, 353; Strauss and Hofmannsthal, *Working Friendship*, 258.

38. Strauss to Hofmannsthal, July 28, 1916, Strauss and Hofmannsthal, *Briefwechsel*, 354; Strauss and Hofmannsthal, *Working Friendship*, 258–59.

39. Hofmannsthal to Strauss, August 1, 1916, Strauss and Hofmannsthal, *Briefwechsel*, 355; Strauss and Hofmannsthal, *Working Friendship*, 259–60.

40. Hofmannsthal to Strauss, August 1, 1916, Strauss and Hofmannsthal, *Briefwechsel*, 355; Strauss and Hofmannsthal, *Working Friendship*, 260.

41. Hofmannsthal to Strauss, August 1, 1916, Strauss and Hofmannsthal, *Briefwechsel*, 355–56; Strauss and Hofmannsthal, *Working Friendship*, 260.

42. Hofmannsthal to Strauss, August 1, 1916, Strauss and Hofmannsthal, *Briefwechsel*, 356; Strauss and Hofmannsthal, *Working Friendship*, 260.

43. Strauss to Hofmannsthal, July 18, 1916, Strauss and Hofmannsthal, *Briefwechsel*, 348–49; Strauss and Hofmannsthal, *Working Friendship*, 254.

44. Hofmannsthal to Strauss, July 24, 1916, Strauss and Hofmannsthal, *Briefwechsel*, 351; Strauss and Hofmannsthal, *Working Friendship*, 257.

45. Hofmannsthal to Strauss, August 13, 1916, Strauss and Hofmannsthal, *Briefwechsel*, 357; Strauss and Hofmannsthal, *Working Friendship*, 261.

46. Strauss to Hofmannsthal, [middle August 1916], Strauss and Hofmannsthal, *Briefwechsel*, 358–59; Strauss and Hofmannsthal, *Working Friendship*, 262; Bryan Gilliam, *Rounding Wagner's Mountain: Richard Strauss and Modern German Opera* (Cambridge: Cambridge University Press, 2014).

47. Hofmannsthal to Strauss, September 16, 1916, Strauss and Hofmannsthal, *Briefwechsel*, 359; Strauss and Hofmannsthal, *Working Friendship*, 262.

48. Julius Korngold, "Feuilleton: Hofoperntheater: *Ariadne auf Naxos*," *Neue Freie Presse*, October 5, 1916, 1–5.

49. Feigl, *Zita: Kaiserin und Königin*, 169–70; Judson, *Habsburg Empire*, 417–19.

50. *Die Frau ohne Schatten*, orchestral score (Berlin: Adolph Fürstner, 1919; repr. Mainz: Fürstnermusikverlag, 1987), act 3, scene 2, 469; see also Wolfgang Perschmann, *Hugo von Hofmannsthal und Richard Strauss: "Die Frau ohne Schatten": Sinndeutung aus Text und Musik* (Graz: Österreichische Richard Wagner Gesellschaft, 1992), 117–24; Sherrill Pantle, *"Die Frau ohne Schatten" by Hugo von Hofmannsthal and Richard Strauss: An Analysis of Text, Music and Their Relationship* (Bern: Peter Lang, 1978), 180–88.

51. *Die Frau ohne Schatten*, orchestral score, act 3, scene 2, 469–73.

52. *Die Frau ohne Schatten*, orchestral score, act 3, scene 2, 474–75.

53. *Die Frau ohne Schatten*, orchestral score, act 3, scene 2, 475–79.

54. *Die Frau ohne Schatten*, orchestral score, act 3, scene 2, 478–79.

55. *Die Frau ohne Schatten*, orchestral score, act 3, scene 2, 479–81.

56. *Die Frau ohne Schatten*, orchestral score, act 3, scene 2, 484–88.
57. *Die Frau ohne Schatten*, orchestral score, act 3, scene 2, 499–505.
58. *Die Frau ohne Schatten*, orchestral score, act 3, scene 2, 506–9.
59. *Die Frau ohne Schatten*, orchestral score, act 3, scene 2, 510–13.

Chapter 11: Empress Zita

1. Brendan Carroll, *The Last Prodigy: A Biography of Erich Wolfgang Korngold* (Portland, OR: Amadeus Press, 1997), 116; "Kaiserin Zita Hymne," in Erich Korngold, *Lieder aus dem Nachlass 2* (Mainz: Schottverlag, 2011), 33–37.
2. Erich Feigl, ed., *Zita: Kaiserin und Königin* (Vienna: Amalthea Verlag, 1991), 170.
3. "Emperor Karl, Empress Zita, and Archduke Otto in the Hungarian Coronation Regalia," photograph of 1916, https://www.habsburger.net/en/media/emperor-karl-empress-zita-and-archduke-otto-hungarian-coronation-regalia-photograph-1916.
4. Feigl, *Zita: Kaiserin und Königin*, 175–78.
5. Feigl, *Zita: Kaiserin und Königin*, 170.
6. Feigl, *Zita: Kaiserin und Königin*, 188.
7. "12 marzo 1916: La guerra è 'il suicidio dell'Europa,'" *La Difesa del popolo*, Settimanale della Diocesi di Padova, October 10, 2021, https://www.difesapopolo.it/Rubriche/Grande-guerra/12-marzo-1916-la-guerra-e-il-suicidio-dell-Europa; "Blessed Emperor Karl I and Empress Zita," catholicism.org, October 25, 2004, https://catholicism.org/karl-hapsburg.html.
8. Feigl, *Zita: Kaiserin und Königin*, 195.
9. Tibor Frank, "C'est la paix! The Sixtus Letters and the Peace Initiative of Emperor Karl I," *Hungarian Review* 6, no. 5 (September 11, 2015), http://hungarianreview.com/article/20150911_c_est_la_paix_the_sixtus_letters_and_the_peace_initiative_of_emperor_karl_i.
10. Feigl, *Zita: Kaiserin und Königin*, 185.
11. Strauss to Hofmannsthal, February 7, 1917, in Richard Strauss and Hugo von Hofmannsthal, *Briefwechsel: Gesamtausgabe*, ed. Franz Strauss, Alice Strauss, Willi Schuh (Zurich: Atlantis Verlag, 1964), 363; Strauss and Hofmannsthal, *A Working Friendship: The Correspondence*, trans. Hanns Hammelmann and Ewald Osers (New York: Random House, 1961), 265.
12. "*Ariadne auf Naxos*: Ytelseshistorikk for den andre versjonen," Wikipedia, https://no.qwe.wiki/wiki/Ariadne_auf_Naxos; Robert Rill, "Sixtus Afair," *International Encyclopedia of the First World War*, 1914–1918—Online: https://encyclopedia.1914-1918-online.net/article/sixtus_affair
13. Strauss to Hofmannsthal, February 7, 1916, Strauss and Hofmannsthal, *Briefwechsel*, 363–64; Strauss and Hofmannsthal, *Working Friendship*, 265–66; Steven Beller, "The Tragic Carnival: Austrian Culture in the First World War," in *European Culture in the Great War: The Arts, Entertainment, and Propaganda, 1914–1918*, ed. Aviel Roshwald and Richard Stites (Cambridge: Cambridge University Press, 1999), 149–50; "Hofmannsthal: Chronik zu Leben und Werk," http://www.navigare.de/hofmannsthal/chro.htm.
14. Angela von Glaser-Lindner, "Der Zita-Tag," *Neue Freie Presse*, May 9, 1917, 7–8; "Das Geburtsfest der Kaiserin," *Neue Freie Presse*, May 10, 1917, 7; Feigl, *Zita: Kaiserin und Königin*, 219–20.
15. Glaser-Lindner, "Der Zita Tag," *Neue Freie Presse*, May 9, 1917, 7–8; "Das Geburtsfest der Kaiserin," *Neue Freie Press*, May 10, 1917, 7; Ellen Key, *Das Jahrhundert des Kindes*,

trans. Francis Maro (Berlin: Fischer Verlag, 1902); Maureen Healy, *Vienna and the Fall of the Habsburg Empire: Total War and Everyday Life in World War I* (Cambridge: Cambridge University Press, 2004), 211–57; see also Perri Klass, *A Good Time to Be Born: How Science and Public Health Gave Children a Future* (New York: W. W. Norton, 2020).

16. Glaser-Lindner, "Der Zita Tag," *Neue Freie Presse*, May 9, 1917, 7–8; "Das Geburtsfest der Kaiserin," *Neue Freie Presse*, May 10, 1917, 7; see also Maureen Healy, "Becoming Austrian: Women, the State, and Citizenship in World War I," *Central European History* 35, no. 1 (2002): 1–35.

17. Claudia Konrad, *"Die Frau ohne Schatten" von Hugo von Hofmannsthal und Richard Strauss: Studien zur Genese, zum Textbuch und zur Rezeptionsgeschichte* (Hamburg: Verlag der Musikalienhandlung Karl Dieter Wagner, 1988), 158.

18. "Konzert Lehmann-Slezak," *Neue Freie Presse*, May 10, 1917, 9; Claudia Maria Korsmeier, "Zu Korngolds frühem Liedschaffen," in *Erich Wolfgang Korngold, "Der kleine Mozart": das Frühwerk eines Genies zwischen Tradition und Fortschritt*, ed. Ute Jung-Kaiser and Annette Simonis (Hildesheim: Georg Olms Verlag, 2017), 142; Brendan Carroll, foreword to Korngold, *Lieder aus dem Nachlass 2*.

19. Feigl, *Zita: Kaiserin und Königin*, 221.

20. Hugo von Hofmannsthal, "Maria Theresia," *Neue Freie Presse*, May 13, 1917, in Hugo von Hofmannsthal, *Reden und Aufsätze II, 1914–1924* (Frankfurt: Fischer Taschenbuch, 1979), 445–53.

21. Strauss to Hofmannsthal, May 11, 1917, Strauss and Hofmannsthal, *Briefwechsel*, 364; Strauss and Hofmannsthal, *Working Friendship*, 266.

22. Strauss to Hofmannsthal, June 28, 1917, Strauss and Hofmannsthal, *Briefwechsel*, 367; Strauss and Hofmannsthal, *Working Friendship*, 269.

23. Hofmannsthal to Strauss, September 4, 1917, Strauss and Hofmannsthal, *Briefwechsel*, 392; Strauss and Hofmannsthal, *Working Friendship*, 288.

24. David Rechter, "Galicia in Vienna: Jewish Refugees in the First World War," *Austrian History Yearbook* 28 (1997): 113–30; Marsha Rozenblit, *Reconstructing a National Identity: The Jews of Habsburg Austria during World War I* (Oxford: Oxford University Press, 2001).

25. Ulrich Weinzierl, *Hofmannsthal: Skizzen zu seinem Bild* (2005; Frankfurt: Fischer Taschenbuch Verlag, 2007), 37–38.

26. Weinzierl, *Hofmannsthal*, 30–48; Martin Stern, "Verschwiegener Antisemitismus," *Hofmannsthal Jahrbuch* 12 (2004): 243–53; John Milfull, "Juden, Österreicher und andere Deutsche: Anmerkungen zum Identitätsproblem am Beispiel der Prosa Hofmannsthals 1912–1916," *Geschichte und Gesellschaft* 7, no. 3/4 (1981): 582–89; David Österle, "The Stranger in the Self: Hofmannsthal's Relationship to Jewishness," *European Journal of Life Writing* 5 (2016): 1–12.

27. Hugo von Hofmannsthal, "Die österreichische Idee," *Neue Zürcher Zeitung*, December 2, 1917, in Hofmannsthal, *Reden und Aufsätze II: 1914–1924*, 454–58.

28. Wiener Konzerthaus, Archivdatenbank, December 22, 1917, https://konzerthaus.at/datenbanksuche.

29. Hugo von Hofmannsthal, "Preusse und Österreicher," December 25, 1917, *Vossische Zeitung*, in Hofmannsthal, *Reden und Aufsätze II: 1914–1924*, 459–61.

30. Strauss to Hofmannsthal, December 19, 1917, Strauss and Hofmannsthal, *Briefwechsel*, 401; Strauss and Hofmannsthal, *Working Friendship*, 295–96.

31. Larry Wolff, *Woodrow Wilson and the Reimagining of Eastern Europe* (Stanford, CA: Stanford University Press, 2020), 68–70.

32. Wolff, *Woodrow Wilson and the Reimagining of Eastern Europe*, 74–76.

33. Wolff, *Woodrow Wilson and the Reimagining of Eastern Europe*, 76–77.

34. Wolff, *Woodrow Wilson and the Reimagining of Eastern Europe*, 84–85; Dieter Köberl, "Zur Erinnerung an Heinrich Lammasch," February 13, 2019, https://www.uibk.ac.at/newsroom/zur-erinnerung-an-heinrich-lammasch.html.de.

35. Wiener Konzerthaus, Archivdatenbank, February 10, 1918, https://konzerthaus.at/datenbanksuche.

36. Maria Jeritza, *Sunlight and Song: A Singer's Life* (New York: D. Appleton, 1924), 90; Wiener Staatsoper, Spielplanarchiv, February 16, 1918, https://archiv.wiener-staatsoper.at/performances/29095.

37. Wiener Konzerthaus, Archivdatenbank, March 1, 1918, March 2, 1918, https://konzerthaus.at/datenbanksuche; "*Die Modebaronin*: Aufführung der Operette von Richard von Goldberger im Konzerthaus; Anschließend Modeschau," https://www.europeana.eu/de/item/9200290/BibliographicResource_3000095282820; Micaela Baranello, *The Operetta Empire: Music Theater in Early Twentieth-Century Vienna* (Berkeley: University of California Press, 2021), 93–121.

38. Jeritza, *Sunlight and Song*, 96–100; Robert Werba, *Maria Jeritza: Primadonna des Verismo* (Vienna; Österreichischer Bundesverlag, 1981), 103.

39. Bertita Harding, *Imperial Twilight: The Story of Karl and Zita of Hungary* (1939; New York: Blue Ribbon Books, 1941), 156.

40. Feigl, *Zita: Kaiserin und Königin*, 234–35.

41. Joseph Maria Baernreither, *Tagebuch*, April 13, 1918, in Feigl, *Zita: Kaiserin und Königin*, 247.

42. Baernreither, *Tagebuch*, April 19, 1918, and November 1, 1918, in Feigl, *Zita: Kaiserin und Königin*, 248–50.

43. Horace Rumbold to A. J. Balfour, May 9, 1918, cited in James Bogle and Joanna Bogle, *A Heart for Europe: The Lives of Emperor Charles and Empress Zita of Austria-Hungary* (1990; Herefordshire: Gracewing, 2004), 98.

44. Baernreither, *Tagebuch*, April 27, 1918, in Feigl, *Zita: Kaiserin und Königin*, 249.

45. "Kaiser Karl und die Bourbonen," May 7, 1918, in Feigl, *Zita: Kaiserin und Königin*, 267–68.

46. Baernreither, *Tagebuch*, May 8, 1918, in Feigl, *Zita: Kaiserin und Königin*, 249.

47. Feigl, *Zita: Kaiserin und Königin*, 240–41; "Hofmannsthal: Chronik zu Leben und Werk," http://www.navigare.de/hofmannsthal/chro.htm.

48. Wolff, *Woodrow Wilson and the Reimagining of Eastern Europe*, 87–88.

49. Feigl, *Zita: Kaiserin und Königin*, 250.

50. Feigl, *Zita: Kaiserin und Königin*, 253.

51. Larry Wolff, *The Singing Turk: Ottoman Power and Operatic Emotions on the European Stage from the Siege of Vienna to the Age of Napoleon* (Stanford, CA: Stanford University Press, 2016).

52. Feigl, *Zita: Kaiserin und Königin*, 255.

53. Baranello, *Operetta Empire*, 126–34; Wiener Staatsoper, Spielplanarchiv, May 19, 1918, https://archiv.wiener-staatsoper.at/performances/23736.

54. Strauss to Hofmannsthal, May 23, 1918, and June 6, 1918, Strauss and Hofmannsthal, *Briefwechsel*, 406–10; Strauss and Hofmannsthal, *Working Friendship*, 300–302.

55. Michael Kennedy, *Richard Strauss: Man, Musician, Enigma* (1999; Cambridge: Cambridge University Press, 2006), 199.

56. Strauss to Hofmannsthal, July 12, 1918, Strauss and Hofmannsthal, *Briefwechsel*, 415–16; Strauss and Hofmannsthal, *Working Friendship*, 306.

57. Feigl, *Zita: Kaiserin und Königin*, 256–57; "Reise des österreichischen Kaiserpaares Karl und Zita nach Pressburg," website *Kulturpool: Österreichs Portal zu Kunst, Kultur, und Bildung*, http://www.kulturpool.at/plugins/kulturpool/showitem.action?itemId=124554455016&kupoContext=default.

58. *Die Frau ohne Schatten*, orchestral score (Berlin: Adolph Fürstner, 1919; repr. Mainz: Fürstnermusikverlag, 1987), act 3, scene 2, 514–18; see also Wolfgang Perschmann, *Hugo von Hofmannsthal und Richard Strauss: "Die Frau ohne Schatten": Sinndeutung aus Text und Musik* (Graz: Österreichische Richard Wagner Gesellschaft, 1992), 126–34; Sherrill Pantle, *"Die Frau ohne Schatten" by Hugo von Hofmannsthal and Richard Strauss: An Analysis of Text, Music and Their Relationship* (Bern: Peter Lang, 1978), 188–93.

59. *Die Frau ohne Schatten*, orchestral score, act 3, scene 2, 519–23.

60. *Die Frau ohne Schatten*, orchestral score, act 3, scene 2, 527.

61. *Die Frau ohne Schatten*, orchestral score, act 3, scene 2, 529–32.

62. *Die Frau ohne Schatten*, orchestral score, act 3, scene 2, 532–38.

63. *Die Frau ohne Schatten*, orchestral score, act 3, scene 2, 541–46.

64. *Die Frau ohne Schatten*, orchestral score, act 3, scene 3, 549–52.

65. *Die Frau ohne Schatten*, orchestral score, act 3, scene 3, 553–54; see also Perschmann, *Hugo von Hofmannsthal und Richard Strauss*, 136–42; Pantle, *"Die Frau ohne Schatten" by Hugo von Hofmannsthal and Richard Strauss*, 194–99.

66. *Die Frau ohne Schatten*, orchestral score, act 3, scene 3, 555–60.

67. *Die Frau ohne Schatten*, orchestral score, act 3, scene 3, 562–70.

68. *Die Frau ohne Schatten*, orchestral score, act 3, scene 3, 571; Gastone Rossi-Doria, "Melologo," *Enciclopedia Italiana*, Treccani, 1934, https://www.treccani.it/enciclopedia/melologo_%28Enciclopedia-Italiana%29/.

69. Strauss to Hofmannsthal, July 10, 1917, Strauss and Hofmannsthal, *Briefwechsel*, 373; Strauss and Hofmannsthal, *Working Friendship*, 273; Olaf Enderlein, *Die Entstehung der Oper "Die Frau ohne Schatten" von Richard Strauss* (Frankfurt: Peter Lang, 2017), 667–778.

70. Richard Strauss, "Erinnerungen an die ersten Aufführungen meiner Opern" (1942), in *Betrachtungen und Erinnerungen*, ed. Willi Schuh (Mainz: Schott, 2014), 244–45.

71. *Die Frau ohne Schatten*, orchestral score, act 3, scene 3, 574–75.

72. *Die Frau ohne Schatten*, orchestral score, act 3, scene 3, 577–83.

73. *Die Frau ohne Schatten*, orchestral score, act 3, scene 3, 588–90.

Chapter 12: Departure from Schönbrunn

1. Erich Feigl, ed., *Zita: Kaiserin und Königin* (Vienna: Amalthea Verlag, 1991), 291.

2. Feigl, *Zita: Kaiserin und Königin*, 291.

3. Wiener Konzerthaus, Archivdatenbank, August 16, 1918, https://konzerthaus.at/datenbanksuche; "Theater und Kunstnachrichten," *Neue Freie Presse*, August 16, 1918, 7; "Der Geburtstag des Kaisers," *Neue Freie Presse*, August 17, 1918, 1.

4. Wiener Konzerthaus, Archivdatenbank, May 6, 1918, https://konzerthaus.at/daten banksuche; "Kaiserinhuldigungsabend der Kriegspatenschaft: In Anwesenheit des Kaiserpaares," *Neue Freie Presse*, May 7, 1918, 7.

5. "Die Einweihung der Kaiserin Zita Kriegsküche," *Neue Freie Presse*, August 17, 1918, 7.

6. Wiener Staatsoper, Spielplanarchiv, August 16, 1918, and August 17, 1918, https://archiv.wiener-staatsoper.at/performances/37914.

7. Wiener Staatsoper, Spielplanarchiv, August and September 1918, https://archiv.wiener-staatsoper.at/search/page/1?since=01.08.1918.

8. Wiener Staatsoper, Spielplanarchiv, October 1918, https://archiv.wiener-staatsoper.at/search?since=01.10.1918.

9. Wiener Staatsoper, Spielplanarchiv, November 1918, https://archiv.wiener-staatsoper.at/search?since=01.10.1918.

10. Hofmannsthal to Strauss, August 1, 1918, in Richard Strauss and Hugo von Hofmannsthal, *Briefwechsel: Gesamtausgabe*, ed. Franz Strauss, Alice Strauss, Willi Schuh (Zurich: Atlantis Verlag, 1964), 416–18; Richard Strauss and Hugo von Hofmannsthal, *A Working Friendship: The Correspondence*, trans. Hanns Hammelmann and Ewald Osers (New York: Random House, 1961), 307–9; Claudia Konrad, *"Die Frau ohne Schatten" von Hugo von Hofmannsthal und Richard Strauss: Studien zur Genese, zum Textbuch und zur Rezeptionsgeschichte* (Hamburg: Verlag der Musikalienhandlung Karl Dieter Wagner, 1988), 152–53.

11. Hofmannsthal to Strauss, August 1, 1918, Strauss and Hofmannsthal, *Briefwechsel*, 417; Strauss and Hofmannsthal, *Working Friendship*, 308.

12. Michael Kennedy, *Richard Strauss: Man, Musician, Enigma* (1999; Cambridge: Cambridge University Press, 2006), 205–12.

13. Hofmannsthal to Strauss, August 1, 1918, Strauss and Hofmannsthal, *Briefwechsel*, 418; Strauss and Hofmannsthal, *Working Friendship*, 309.

14. Strauss to Hofmannsthal, August 5, 1918, Strauss and Hofmannsthal, *Briefwechsel*, 418–19; Strauss and Hofmannsthal, *Working Friendship*, 309–11.

15. Konrad, *"Die Frau ohne Schatten" von Hugo von Hofmannsthal und Richard Strauss*, 154.

16. Andrian to Hofmannsthal, July 9, 1918, in Hugo von Hofmannsthal and Leopold von Andrian, *Briefwechsel* (Frankfurt: Fischer Verlag, 1968), 263; Fredrik Lindström, *Empire and Identity: Biographies of the Austrian State Problem in the Late Habsburg Empire* (West Lafayette, IN: Purdue University Press, 2008), 156–59.

17. Hofmannsthal to Andrian, July 15, 1918, in Hofmannsthal and Andrian, *Briefwechsel*, 263–64.

18. Hofmannsthal to Andrian [August 8, 1918], in Hofmannsthal and Andrian, *Briefwechsel*, 265–66.

19. Hofmannsthal to Andrian, August 27, 1918, in Hofmannsthal and Andrian, *Briefwechsel*, 267–68.

20. Hofmannsthal to Andrian, August 28, 1918, in Hofmannsthal and Andrian, *Briefwechsel*, 271.

21. Hofmannsthal to Andrian, September 19, 1918, and September 24, 1918, in Hofmannsthal and Andrian, *Briefwechsel*, 285–86.

22. Hofmannsthal to Strauss [September 1918], Strauss and Hofmannsthal, *Briefwechsel*, 421; *Working Friendship*, 311–12.

23. Hofmannsthal to Strauss [September 1918], Strauss and Hofmannsthal, *Briefwechsel*, 421; *Working Friendship*, 312.

24. Feigl, *Zita: Kaiserin und Königin*, 294.

25. Emperor Karl, "An meine getreuen österreichischen Völker!" October 16, 1918, https://europecentenary.eu/to-my-faithful-austrian-peoples-emperor-karls-manifesto/.

26. "Declaration of Independence of the Czechoslovak Nation by Its Provisional Government," October 18, 1918, (New York: Czechoslovak Arts Club, Marchbanks Press, 1918), 5, https://archive.org/details/declarationofindooczec/page/4/mode/2up.

27. "Ein Ministerium Lammasch," *Neue Freie Presse*, October 26, 1918, 1; "Die Verhandlungen über ein Liquidierungsministerium Lammasch," *Neue Freie Presse*, October 26, 1918, 2.

28. Josef Maria Baernreither, *Tagebuch*, November 1, 1918, in Feigl, *Zita: Kaiserin und Königin*, 250.

29. Baernreither, *Tagebuch*, November 1, 1918, in Feigl, *Zita: Kaiserin und Königin*, 250.

30. Feigl, *Zita: Kaiserin und Königin*, 296–98.

31. Ulrich Weinzierl, *Hofmannsthal: Skizzen zu seinem Bild* (2005; Frankfurt: Fischer Taschenbuch Verlag, 2007), 76; Christiane von Hofmannsthal, *Tagebücher 1918–1923 und Briefe des Vaters an die Tochter 1903–1929* (Frankfurt: S. Fischer Verlag, 1991), November 5, 1918, 22–23.

32. Weinzierl, *Hofmannsthal*, 76–77; Hofmannsthal to Degenfeld, November 26, 1918, in *The Poet and the Countess: Hugo von Hofmannsthal's Correspondence with Countess Ottonie Degenfeld*, ed. Marie-Therese Miller-Degenfeld, trans. W. Eric Barcel (Rochester, NY: Camden House, 2000), 325.

33. Weinzierl, *Hofmannsthal*, 77; Hofmannsthal to Degenfeld, November 26, 1918, *The Poet and the Countess*, 326.

34. Emperor Karl, Renunciation of Political Affairs, November 11, 1918, https://www.bl.uk/collection-items/emperor-karl-abdication-proclamation#.

35. Christiane von Hofmannsthal, *Tagebücher*, November 12, 1918, 25.

36. *Die Frau ohne Schatten*, orchestral score (Berlin: Adolph Fürstner, 1919; repr. Mainz: Fürstnermusikverlag, 1987), act 3, scene 3, 589–95; Konrad, *"Die Frau ohne Schatten" von Hugo von Hofmannsthal und Richard Strauss*, 159.

37. *Die Frau ohne Schatten*, orchestral score, act 3, scene 3, 597–98.

38. *Die Frau ohne Schatten*, orchestral score, act 3, scene 3, 598–99.

39. Hofmannsthal to Strauss, September 19, 1915, *Briefwechsel*, 326; *Working Friendship*, 236.

40. Wolfgang Amadeus Mozart and Johann Emanuel Schikaneder, *Die Zauberflöte* (Berlin: Holzinger, 2014), 50 (act 2, finale).

41. Mozart and Schikaneder, *Die Zauberflöte*, 20 (act 1, finale), "Drey Knaben führen den Tamino herein, jeder hat einen silbernen Palmzweig in der Hand."

42. Engelbert Humperdinck and Adelheid Wette, *Hänsel und Gretel*, orchestral score (Leipzig: Ernst Eulenburg, 1928?), act 3, scene 4, 505–6.

43. *Die Frau ohne Schatten*, orchestral score, act 3, scene 3, 601–2; see also Wolfgang Perschmann, *Hugo von Hofmannsthal und Richard Strauss: "Die Frau ohne Schatten": Sinndeutung aus Text und Musik* (Graz: Österreichische Richard Wagner Gesellschaft,

1992), 146–47; Sherrill Pantle, *"Die Frau ohne Schatten" by Hugo von Hofmannsthal and Richard Strauss: An Analysis of Text, Music and Their Relationship* (Bern: Peter Lang, 1978), 200–201.

44. *Die Frau ohne Schatten*, orchestral score, act 3, scene 3, 601–2.
45. *Die Frau ohne Schatten*, orchestral score, act 3, scene 3, 602–5.
46. *Die Frau ohne Schatten*, orchestral score, act 3, scene 3, 602–5.

Chapter 13: The Emperor and the Empress

1. Stefan Zweig, *The World of Yesterday* (1943; Lincoln: University of Nebraska Press, 1964), 283–84.
2. Zweig, *World of Yesterday*, 284.
3. Gordon Brook-Shepherd, *Uncrowned Emperor: The Life and Times of Otto von Habsburg* (London: Hambledon and London, 2003), 45–46.
4. Brook-Shepherd, *Uncrowned Emperor*, 45–47; Erich Feigl, ed., *Zita: Kaiserin und Königin* (Vienna: Amalthea Verlag, 1991), 304.
5. "Feldkircher Manifest Kaiser und König Karls," March 24, 1919; Benedict XV to Karl, March 26, 1919; Cardinal Gaetano Bisleti to Zita, March 27, 1919, https://de.readkong.com/page/feldkircher-manifest-kaiser-und-konig-karls-9260338; "Vermählung Erzherzogs Karl Franz Josef mit Zita" (Fotografie) October 21, 1911, Österreichische Nationalbibliothek, https://onb.digital/result/BAG_14627689; "Cardinale Gaetano Bisleti," website Ordine di Malta: Italia, https://www.ordinedimaltaitalia.org/gran-priorato-di-roma/veroli/article/cardinale-gaetano-bisleti.
6. Feigl, *Zita: Kaiserin und Königin*, 307–8.
7. Michael Kadgien, *Das Habsburgergesetz* (Bern: Peter Lang, 2005).
8. Hofmannsthal to Strauss, December 5, 1918, in Richard Strauss and Hugo von Hofmannsthal, *Briefwechsel: Gesamtausgabe*, ed. Franz Strauss, Alice Strauss, Willi Schuh (Zurich: Atlantis Verlag, 1964), 424; Richard Strauss and Hugo von Hofmannsthal, *A Working Friendship: The Correspondence*, trans. Hanns Hammelmann and Ewald Osers (New York: Random House, 1961), 312.
9. Strauss to Hofmannsthal, December 6, 1918, in Richard Strauss and Hugo von Hofmannsthal, *Briefwechsel: Neuausgabe*, ed. Willi Schuh (München: Piper, 1990; Mainz: Schott, 1990), 717; all following notes to Strauss and Hofmannsthal, *Briefwechsel*, are to the 1964 edition.
10. Hofmannsthal to Strauss, December 7, 1918, Strauss and Hofmannsthal, *Briefwechsel*, 425–26; Strauss and Hofmannsthal, *Working Friendship*, 314; Michael Kennedy, *Richard Strauss: Man, Musician, Enigma* (1999; Cambridge: Cambridge University Press, 2006), 206–8.
11. Wiener Konzerthaus, Archivdatenbank, December 22, 1918, https://konzerthaus.at/datenbanksuche; Wiener Staatsoper, Spielplanarchiv, December 22, 1918, https://archiv.wiener-staatsoper.at/performances/22059.
12. Hofmannsthal to Strauss, December 25, 1918, Strauss and Hofmannsthal, *Briefwechsel*, 426–28; Strauss and Hofmannsthal, *Working Friendship*, 315–16; Wiener Staatsoper, Spielplanarchiv, December 25, 1918, https://archiv.wiener-staatsoper.at/performances/50956.
13. Hofmannsthal to Strauss, December 25, 1918, Strauss and Hofmannsthal, *Briefwechsel*, 428; Strauss and Hofmannsthal, *Working Friendship*, 316; "Anna Bahr-Mildenburg

(1872–1947)," Mahler Foundation, online, https://mahlerfoundation.org/mahler/contemporaries/anna-bahr-von-mildenburg/.

14. Feigl, *Zita: Kaiserin und Königin*, 308–9.

15. *Die Frau ohne Schatten*, orchestral score (Berlin: Adolph Fürstner, 1919; repr. Mainz: Fürstnermusikverlag, 1987), act 1, scene 2, 102–3.

16. Zweig, *World of Yesterday*, 296.

17. Hugo von Hofmannsthal, Alfred Roller, and Richard Strauss, *"Mit dir keine Oper zu lang": Briefwechsel*, ed. Christiane Mühlegger-Henhapel and Ursula Renner (Salzburg: Benevento Verlag, 2021), 196–97.

18. Hofmannsthal to Strauss, January 4, 1919, Strauss and Hofmannsthal, *Briefwechsel*, 435; Strauss and Hofmannsthal, *Working Friendship*, 317–18.

19. Hofmannsthal to Strauss, January 4, 1919, Strauss and Hofmannsthal, *Briefwechsel*, 435; Strauss and Hofmannsthal, *Working Friendship*, 318.

20. "Kautsky, Hans (1864–1937), Theatermaler," *Österreichisches Biographisches Lexikon 1815–1950*, Band 3 (Vienna: Österreichische Akademie der Wissenschaften, 1963), 274.

21. Hofmannsthal to Strauss, January 4, 1919, Strauss and Hofmannsthal, *Briefwechsel*, 437; Strauss and Hofmannsthal, *Working Friendship*, 320; Hofmannsthal, Roller, Strauss, *"Mit dir keine Oper zu lang,"* 210–13.

22. Hugo von Hofmannsthal, *Die Frau ohne Schatten (Märchen)*, in *Die Frau ohne Schatten und andere Erzählungen* (Berlin: Holzinger Verlag, 2016), 93.

23. Hofmannsthal, *Die Frau ohne Schatten (Märchen)*, 122–23.

24. Hofmannsthal to Strauss, January 4, 1919, Strauss and Hofmannsthal, *Briefwechsel*, 437; Strauss and Hofmannsthal, *Working Friendship*, 319–20.

25. Ulrich Weinzierl, *Hofmannsthal: Skizzen zu seinem Bild* (2005; Frankfurt: Fischer Taschenbuch Verlag, 2007), 41; "The Nobel Prize: Nomination Archive," Literature, 1919, https://www.nobelprize.org/nomination/archive/list.php?prize=4&year=1919.

26. Hofmannsthal to Strauss, January 4, 1919, Strauss and Hofmannsthal, *Briefwechsel*, 438; Strauss and Hofmannsthal, *Working Friendship*, 320; Hofmannsthal, Roller, Strauss, *"Mit dir keine Oper zu lang,"* 215–17.

27. Hofmannsthal to Strauss, January 4, 1919, Strauss and Hofmannsthal, *Briefwechsel*, 438; Strauss and Hofmannsthal, *Working Friendship*, 320.

28. Wiener Staatsoper, Spielplanarchiv, January 1919, https://archiv.wiener-staatsoper.at/search/person/1324?since=01.01.1919&until=31.01.1919.

29. Wiener Konzerthaus, Archivdatenbank, January 6, 1919, https://konzerthaus.at/datenbanksuche.

30. Strauss to Hofmannsthal, January 7, 1919, Strauss and Hofmannsthal, *Briefwechsel*, 439; Strauss and Hofmannsthal, *Working Friendship*, 321.

31. Strauss to Hofmannsthal, January 7, 1919, Strauss and Hofmannsthal, *Briefwechsel*, 440; Strauss and Hofmannsthal, *Working Friendship*, 322.

32. Strauss to Hofmannsthal, February 5, 1919, Strauss and Hofmannsthal, *Briefwechsel*, 440–41; Strauss and Hofmannsthal, *Working Friendship*, 322–23.

33. Christiane von Hofmannsthal, *Tagebücher 1918–1923 und Briefe des Vaters an die Tochter 1903–1929* (Frankfurt: S. Fischer Verlag, 1991), January 21, 1919, 41.

34. Hofmannsthal to Strauss, February 12, 1919, Strauss and Hofmannsthal, *Briefwechsel*, 441–42; Strauss and Hofmannsthal, *Working Friendship*, 323–24.

35. Strauss to Hofmannsthal, June 17, 1919, Strauss and Hofmannsthal, *Briefwechsel*, 444; Strauss and Hofmannsthal, *Working Friendship*, 325; Carl Schorske, "Explosion in the Garden: Kokoschka and Schoenberg," *Fin-de-siècle Vienna: Politics and Culture* (1980; New York: Vintage Books, 1981), 322–66.

36. Hofmannsthal to Strauss, June 21, 1919, Strauss and Hofmannsthal, *Briefwechsel*, 444; Strauss and Hofmannsthal, *Working Friendship*, 326.

37. Hofmannsthal to Strauss, June 21, 1919, Strauss and Hofmannsthal, *Briefwechsel*, 444–45; Strauss and Hofmannsthal, *Working Friendship*, 326; Hofmannsthal, Roller, Strauss, *"Mit dir keine Oper zu lang,"* 218.

38. "Alma Mahler Doll Made for Oskar Kokoschka by Hermine Moos (1919)," Metropolitan Museum of Art, https://www.metmuseum.org/art/collection/search/811532.

39. Weinzierl, *Hofmannsthal*, 78–79.

40. Strauss to Hofmannsthal, June 27, 1919, Strauss and Hofmannsthal, *Briefwechsel*, 446; Strauss and Hofmannsthal, *Working Friendship*, 327.

41. Hofmannsthal to Strauss, June 21, 1919, Strauss and Hofmannsthal, *Briefwechsel*, 445; Strauss and Hofmannsthal, *Working Friendship*, 326–27.

42. Michael Kater, *Never Sang for Hitler: The Life and Times of Lotte Lehmann* (Cambridge: Cambridge University Press, 2008), 55–56; Claudia Konrad, *"Die Frau ohne Schatten" von Hugo von Hofmannsthal und Richard Strauss: Studien zur Genese, zum Textbuch und zur Rezeptionsgeschichte* (Hamburg: Verlag der Musikalienhandlung Karl Dieter Wagner, 1988), 159.

43. Hofmannsthal to Strauss, [late March 1919], Strauss and Hofmannsthal, *Briefwechsel*, 443; Strauss and Hofmannsthal, *Working Friendship*, 325.

44. Maria Jeritza, *Sunlight and Song: A Singer's Life* (New York: D. Appleton, 1924), 81–82; Robert Werba, *Maria Jeritza: Primadonna des Verismo* (Vienna; Österreichischer Bundesverlag, 1981), 112; "Jeritza, Maria," in *Biografia: Lexikon Österreichischer Frauen*, vol. 2, ed. Ilse Korotin (Vienna: Böhlau Verlag, 2016), 1492.

45. Strauss to Hofmannsthal, June 27, 1919, Strauss and Hofmannsthal, *Briefwechsel*, 446–47; Strauss and Hofmannsthal, *Working Friendship*, 328.

46. Hofmannsthal to Strauss, July 1, 1919, Strauss and Hofmannsthal, *Briefwechsel*, 448; Strauss and Hofmannsthal, *Working Friendship*, 329.

47. Jamie Bulloch, *Karl Renner: Austria* (London: Haus Histories, 2009), 73–91.

48. Strauss to Hofmannsthal, June 27, 1919, Strauss and Hofmannsthal, *Briefwechsel*, 447; Strauss and Hofmannsthal, *Working Friendship*, 328.

49. Feigl, *Zita: Kaiserin und Königin*, 330–31; Katharina Kniefacz, "Heinrich Peham, Ritter von Bojernberg, Prof. Dr.," website "History of the University of Vienna," https://geschichte.univie.ac.at/en/persons/heinrich-peham-ritter-von-bojernberg-prof-dr.

50. Treaty of Saint-Germain-en-Laye, preamble, https://en.wikisource.org/wiki/Treaty_of_Saint-Germain-en-Laye/Preamble.

51. Hofmannsthal to Strauss, September 18, 1919, Strauss and Hofmannsthal, *Briefwechsel*, 449–52; Strauss and Hofmannsthal, *Working Friendship*, 330–32.

52. Hofmannsthal to Schnitzler, September 19, 1919, in Hugo von Hofmannsthal and Arthur Schnitzler, *Briefwechsel*, ed. Therese Nickl and Heinrich Schnitzler (Frankfurt: Fischer Taschenbuch Verlag, 1983), 284–85.

53. Hofmannsthal to Strauss, September 18, 1919, Strauss and Hofmannsthal, *Briefwechsel*, 451; Strauss and Hofmannsthal, *Working Friendship*, 331–32.

54. Hofmannsthal to Strauss, September 18, 1919, Strauss and Hofmannsthal, *Briefwechsel*, 450–52; Strauss and Hofmannsthal, *Working Friendship*, 331–32.

55. Hofmannsthal to Strauss, September 30, 1919, Strauss and Hofmannsthal, *Briefwechsel*, 452; Strauss and Hofmannsthal, *Working Friendship*, 332–33; "Verworrene Stimmungen: Eine Ausstellung in Goethemuseum Frankfurt beleuchtet Hugo von Hofmannsthal im Ersten Weltkrieg," *Frankfurter Rundschau*, April 8, 2014, https://www.fr.de/kultur/verworrene-stimmungen-11212108.html; "Bräunerhof, Stallburggasse 2," Wien Geschichte, https://www.geschichtewiki.wien.gv.at/Br%C3%A4unerhof.

56. Strauss to Hofmannsthal, July 28, 1916, Strauss and Hofmannsthal, *Briefwechsel*, 354; Strauss and Hofmannsthal, *Working Friendship*, 258–59.

57. *Die Frau ohne Schatten*, orchestral score, act 3, scene 4, 629.

58. *Die Frau ohne Schatten*, orchestral score, act 3, scene 4, 639–42; see also Wolfgang Perschmann, *Hugo von Hofmannsthal und Richard Strauss: "Die Frau ohne Schatten": Sinndeutung aus Text und Musik* (Graz: Österreichische Richard Wagner Gesellschaft, 1992), 151–55; Sherrill Pantle, *"Die Frau ohne Schatten" by Hugo von Hofmannsthal and Richard Strauss: An Analysis of Text, Music and Their Relationship* (Bern: Peter Lang, 1978), 203–4.

59. *Die Frau ohne Schatten*, orchestral score, act 3, scene 4, 644–46.

60. *Die Frau ohne Schatten*, orchestral score, act 3, scene 4, 646–48.

61. *Die Frau ohne Schatten*, orchestral score, act 3, scene 4, 651.

62. *Die Frau ohne Schatten*, orchestral score, act 3, scene 4, 658–60.

63. *Die Frau ohne Schatten*, orchestral score, act 3, scene 4, 661–68.

Chapter 14: Premiere 1919

1. Julius Korngold, "Feuilleton: Operntheater: *Die Frau ohne Schatten*," *Neue Freie Presse*, October 11, 1919, 1–4.

2. "Der Winter als Tiefpunkt der Not," "Blockade von Russland," "Anhaltende Besserung im Befinden Wilsons," *Neue Freie Presse*, October 11, 1919, 1; Jamie Bulloch, *Karl Renner: Austria* (London: Haus Histories, 2009), 96–97.

3. Korngold, *Neue Freie Presse*, October 11, 1919, 1–4.

4. "Theater," *Wiener Zeitung*, October 9, 1919, 4.

5. Korngold, *Neue Freie Presse*, October 11, 1919, 1–4.

6. Jessica Duchen, *Erich Wolfgang Korngold* (London: Phaidon, 1996), 12–94.

7. Korngold, *Neue Freie Presse*, October 11, 1919, 1–4.

8. Schnitzler to Hofmannsthal, October 1, 1919, in Hugo von Hofmannsthal and Arthur Schnitzler, *Briefwechsel* (Frankfurt: Fischer Taschenbuch, 1983), 286; Arthur Schnitzler, *Tagebuch*, October 8, 1919, online edition, https://schnitzler-tagebuch.acdh.oeaw.ac.at/entry__1919-10-08.html.

9. Korngold, *Neue Freie Presse*, October 11, 1919, 1–4.

10. Korngold, *Neue Freie Presse*, October 11, 1919, 1–4.

11. Korngold, *Neue Freie Presse*, October 11, 1919, 1–4.

12. Maria Jeritza, *Sunlight and Song: A Singer's Life* (New York: D. Appleton, 1924), 82.

13. Jeritza, *Sunlight and Song*, 81–82.

14. Hofmannsthal to Princess Marie von Thurn und Taxis, October 27, 1919, in Hugo von Hofmannsthal, "Briefe an Freunde," *Merkur*, Jahrgang 9, Heft 92 (1955): 968–69; also cited in Claudia Konrad, *"Die Frau ohne Schatten" von Hugo von Hofmannsthal und Richard Strauss: Studien zur Genese, zum Textbuch und zur Rezeptionsgeschichte* (Hamburg: Verlag der Musikalienhandlung Karl Dieter Wagner, 1988), 224.

15. Korngold, *Neue Freie Presse*, October 11, 1919, 1–4.
16. Korngold, *Neue Freie Presse*, October 11, 1919, 1–4.
17. Korngold, *Neue Freie Presse*, October 11, 1919, 1–4.
18. Korngold, *Neue Freie Presse*, October 11, 1919, 1–4.
19. Egon Wellesz, "Hofmannsthal-Strauss, *Die Frau ohne Schatten*: Uraufführung im Operntheater," *Der Neue Tag*, October 11, 1919 (Morgen-Ausgabe), 7–8.
20. Christiane von Hofmannsthal, *Tagebücher 1918–1923 und Briefe des Vaters an die Tochter 1903–1929* (Frankfurt: S. Fischer Verlag, 1991), October 11, 1919, 59.
21. Konrad, *"Die Frau ohne Schatten" von Hugo von Hofmannsthal und Richard Strauss*, 167.
22. Korngold, *Neue Freie Presse*, October 11, 1919, 1–4.
23. Christian Glanz, "David Josef Bach and Viennese Debates on Modern Music," *Modern Humanities Research Association* 14 (2006), 185–95.
24. David Josef Bach, "Kunst und Wissen: Opentheater: *Die Frau ohne Schatten*," *Arbeiter-Zeitung*, October 11, 1919, 7.
25. Bach, *Arbeiter-Zeitung*, October 11, 1919.
26. "Färberei Schnek" (advertisement), *Arbeiter-Zeitung*, October 11, 1919, 7.
27. "Juwelen," "Brillanten," "Perlen" (advertisements), *Arbeiter-Zeitung*, October 11, 1919, 7.
28. Bach, "Feuilleton: *Die Frau ohne Schatten*: Zur ersten Aufführung im Operntheater," *Arbeiter-Zeitung*, October 12, 1919, 3–4.
29. Bach, *Arbeiter-Zeitung*, October 12, 1919, 3–4.
30. Bach, *Arbeiter-Zeitung*, October 12, 1919, 3–4.
31. Wiener Staatsoper, Spielplanarchiv, October 1919, https://archiv.wiener-staatsoper.at/search?since=01.10.1919&until=31.10.1919.
32. Wiener Konzerthaus, Archivdatenbank, October 1919, https://konzerthaus.at/datenbanksuche.
33. Theatermuseum, Vienna, Onlinesammlung, Deutsches Volkstheater, October 9, 1919, Stefan Zweig, *Jeremias*, https://www.theatermuseum.at/onlinesammlung/detail/971966/.
34. *AEIOU: Österreich Lexikon*, online, "Wiener Zeitung," http://www.aeiou.at/aeiou.encyclop.w/w648255.htm.
35. Austria-Forum, online, "Kralik, Heinrich," https://austria-forum.org/af/AEIOU/Kralik%2C_Heinrich.
36. Heinrich Kralik, "Feuilleton: Operntheater: *Die Frau ohne Schatten*," *Wiener Abendpost* (*Wiener Zeitung*), October 11, 1919, 1–3.
37. Kralik, *Wiener Abendpost*, October 11, 1919, 1–3.
38. Sigmund Freud, *The Uncanny*, trans. David McLintock (New York: Penguin Classics, 2003).
39. "Ludwig Karpath," *Österreichisches Biographisches Lexikon 1815–1950*, vol. 3 (Vienna: Austrian Academy of Sciences, 1965), 247.
40. Ludwig Karpath, "Feuilleton: *Die Frau ohne Schatten*: Uraufführung im Operntheater," *Neues Wiener Tagblatt*, October 11, 1919, 2–6.
41. Karpath, *Neues Wiener Tagblatt*, October 11, 1919, 2–6.
42. Karpath, *Neues Wiener Tagblatt*, October 11, 1919, 2–6.
43. Karpath, *Neues Wiener Tagblatt*, October 11, 1919, 2–6.
44. Karpath, *Neues Wiener Tagblatt*, October 11, 1919, 2–6.

45. "Ein offener Brief an Clemenceau," *Neues Wiener Tagblatt*, October 11, 1919, 2–3.

46. "Ein offener Brief an Clemenceau," *Neues Wiener Tagblatt*, October 11, 1919, 2–3; Larry Wolff, *Woodrow Wilson and the Reimagining of Eastern Europe* (Stanford, CA: Stanford University Press, 2020), 100–110.

47. Karpath, *Neues Wiener Tagblatt*, October 11, 1919, 2–6.

48. Karpath, *Neues Wiener Tagblatt*, October 11, 1919, 2–6; "Arnold Josef Rosé," *Österreichisches Biographisches Lexikon 1815–1950*, vol. 9 (Vienna: Austrian Academy of Sciences, 1988), 243–44.

49. Karpath, *Neues Wiener Tagblatt*, October 11, 1919, 2–6.

50. Karpath, *Neues Wiener Tagblatt*, October 11, 1919, 2–6.

51. Richard Batka, *Wiener Allgemeine Zeitung*, October 11, 1919, cited in Konrad, *"Die Frau ohne Schatten" von Hugo von Hofmannsthal und Richard Strauss*, 217–18.

52. Strauss to Hofmannsthal, March 8, 1920, in Richard Strauss and Hugo von Hofmannsthal, *Briefwechsel: Gesamtausgabe*, ed. Franz Strauss, Alice Strauss, Willi Schuh (Zurich: Atlantis Verlag, 1964), 456; Richard Strauss and Hugo von Hofmannsthal, *A Working Friendship: The Correspondence*, trans. Hanns Hammelmann and Ewald Osers (New York: Random House, 1961), 335.

53. Hofmannsthal to Strauss, March 10, 1920, Strauss and Hofmannsthal, *Briefwechsel*, 456; Strauss and Hofmannsthal, *Working Friendship*, 336.

54. Michael Kennedy, *Richard Strauss: Man, Musician, Enigma* (1999; Cambridge: Cambridge University Press, 2006), 213; playbill, *Die Frau ohne Schatten*, Dresden, October 22, 1919, https://www.alamy.com/stock-image-richard-strauss-s-opera-die-frau-ohne-schatten-the-woman-without-a-163557940.html.

55. Hugo von Hofmannsthal, Alfred Roller, and Richard Strauss, *"Mit dir keine Oper zu lang": Briefwechsel*, ed. Christiane Mühlegger-Henhapel and Ursula Renner (Salzburg: Benevento Verlag, 2021), 210–13.

56. Hofmannsthal to Rudolf Pannwitz, cited in Jakob Knaus, *Hofmannsthals Weg zur Oper "Die Frau ohne Schatten"* (Berlin: Walter de Gruyter, 1971), 140.

57. "Kärntner Ring," Wien Geschichte Wiki, https://www.geschichtewiki.wien.gv.at/K%C3%A4rntner_Ring.

58. "Tagesneuigkeiten: Ausmerzung des Byzantinismus," *Arbeiter-Zeitung*, November 8, 1919, 3.

Chapter 15: Imperial Afterlife

1. Michael Yonan, *Empress Maria Theresa and the Politics of Habsburg Imperial Art* (University Park: Penn State University Press, 2011), 189–90.

2. Larry Wolff, *The Singing Turk: Ottoman Power and Operatic Emotions on the European Stage from the Siege of Vienna to the Age of Napoleon* (Stanford, CA: Stanford University Press, 2016), 368–71.

3. Erich Feigl, ed., *Zita: Kaiserin und Königin* (Vienna: Amalthea Verlag, 1991), 323.

4. Feigl, *Zita: Kaiserin und Königin*, 346.

5. Wiener Staatsoper, Spielplanarchiv, January 2020, https://archiv.wiener-staatsoper.at/search?since=01.01.1920&until=31.01.1920.

6. Wiener Staatsoper, Spielplanarchiv, February and March 2020, https://archiv.wiener-staatsoper.at/search?since=01.02.1920&until=31.03.1920; *Richard Strauss Handbuch*, ed. Walter Werbeck (Stuttgart: Verlag J. B. Metzler, 2014), xxv; specifies April 18 as Berlin premiere of *Die Frau ohne Schatten*.

7. Strauss to Hofmannsthal, March 8, 1920, in Richard Strauss and Hugo von Hofmannsthal, *Briefwechsel: Gesamtausgabe*, ed. Franz Strauss, Alice Strauss, Willi Schuh (Zurich: Atlantis Verlag, 1964), 456; Richard Strauss and Hugo von Hofmannsthal, *A Working Friendship: The Correspondence*, trans. Hanns Hammelmann and Ewald Osers (New York: Random House, 1961), 335.

8. Hofmannsthal to Strauss, March 10, 1920, Strauss and Hofmannsthal, *Briefwechsel*, 457; Strauss and Hofmannsthal, *Working Friendship*, 336.

9. Wiener Staatsoper, Spielplanarchiv, May 1920, https://archiv.wiener-staatsoper.at/search?since=01.05.1920&until=31.05.1920.

10. Hugo von Hofmannsthal, "Die Salzburger Festspiele" (1919), in Hugo von Hofmannsthal, *Reden und Aufsätze II, 1914–1924* (Frankfurt: Fischer Taschenbuch Verlag, 1979), 260.

11. Hofmannsthal, "Die Salzburger Festspiele," 260–61.

12. Michael Steinberg, *Austria as Theater and Ideology: The Meaning of the Salzburg Festival* (1990; Ithaca, NY: Cornell University Press, 2000), 37–83.

13. Steinberg, *Austria as Theater and Ideology*, 166–67.

14. Strauss to Hofmannsthal, October 5, 1920, Strauss and Hofmannsthal, *Briefwechsel*, 460–62; Strauss and Hofmannsthal, *Working Friendship*, 339.

15. Strauss to Hofmannsthal, October 5, 1920, Strauss and Hofmannsthal, *Briefwechsel*, 460–62; Strauss and Hofmannsthal, *Working Friendship*, 340.

16. Strauss to Hofmannsthal, October 5, 1920, Strauss and Hofmannsthal, *Briefwechsel*, 460–62; Strauss and Hofmannsthal, *Working Friendship*, 339.

17. Strauss to Roller, September 20, 1920, in Hugo von Hofmannsthal, Alfred Roller, and Richard Strauss, *"Mit dir keine Oper zu lang": Briefwechsel*, ed. Christiane Mühlegger-Henhapel and Ursula Renner (Salzburg: Benevento Verlag, 2021), 235.

18. Metropolitan Opera Archives, online, November 1920, http://archives.metoperafamily.org/archives/scripts/cgiip.exe/WService=BibSpeed/gisrch2k.r.

19. Eugene O'Neill, *The Emperor Jones*, scene 1; Stephen Black, *Eugene O'Neill: Beyond Mourning and Tragedy* (New Haven, CT: Yale University Press, 1999), 264–66.

20. Wiener Staatsoper, Spielplanarchiv, December 30, 1920, https://archiv.wiener-staatsoper.at/performances/22870.

21. Wiener Staatsoper, Spielplanarchiv, January 10, 1921, https://archiv.wiener-staatsoper.at/performances/29928; Jessica Duchen, *Erich Wolfgang Korngold* (London: Phaidon, 1996), 76–79, 87–91.

22. Feigl, *Zita: Kaiserin und Königin*, 339–40.

23. Feigl, *Zita: Kaiserin und Königin*, 346.

24. Feigl, *Zita: Kaiserin und Königin*, 352; Eva Demmerle, *Kaiser Karl: Mythos und Wirklichkeit* (Vienna: Amalthea, 2016), 129–31; Miklós Zeidler, "Charles IV's Attempted Returns to the Hungarian Throne," in *Karl I (IV), der Erste Weltkrieg und das Ende der Donaumonarchie*, ed. Andreas Gottsmann (Vienna: Austrian Academy of Sciences, 2007), 269–84; Gordon Brook-Shepherd, *Uncrowned Emperor: The Life and Times of Otto von Habsburg* (London: Hambledon and London, 2003), 57–58.

25. Wiener Staatsoper, Spielplanarchiv, April and May 1921, https://archiv.wiener-staatsoper.at/search?since=15.04.1921&until=15.05.1921.

26. Hofmannsthal to Strauss, [May 16, 1921], Strauss and Hofmannsthal, *Briefwechsel*, 465–66; Strauss and Hofmannsthal, *Working Friendship*, 342–43; Paul Bekker, "Die Frau ohne Schatten," *Kritische Zeitbilder* (Berlin: Schuster and Loeffler, 1921), 120, 124–

25, https://archive.org/details/KritischeZeitbilderGesammelteSchriftenBand1/page/n121/mode/2up.

27. Hofmannsthal to Strauss, [May 16, 1921], Strauss and Hofmannsthal, *Briefwechsel*, 465–66; Strauss and Hofmannsthal, *Working Friendship*, 343.

28. Claudia Konrad, *"Die Frau ohne Schatten" von Hugo von Hofmannsthal und Richard Strauss: Studien zur Genese, zum Textbuch und zur Rezeptionsgeschichte* (Hamburg: Verlag der Musikalienhandlung Karl Dieter Wagner, 1988), 229, 391–93.

29. Konrad, *"Die Frau ohne Schatten" von Hugo von Hofmannsthal und Richard Strauss*, 224–25, 231–32.

30. Wiener Staatsoper, Spielplanarchiv, September and October 1921, https://archiv.wiener-staatsoper.at/search?since=15.09.1921&until=31.10.1921.

31. Maria Jeritza, *Sunlight and Song: A Singer's Life* (New York: D. Appleton, 1924), 138–40.

32. Metropolitan Opera Archives, online, November 17, 1922: http://69.18.170.204/archives/scripts/cgiip.exe/WService=BibSpeed/fullcit.w?xCID=82040&limit=2500&xBranch=ALL&xsdate=&xedate=&theterm=Der%20Rosenkavalier%3A&x=0&xhomepath=&xhome=.

33. "Zita Says Turnips Kept Charles from Regaining Throne," *New York Times*, January 24, 1922, 1; Feigl, *Zita: Kaiserin und Königin*, 361–65.

34. James Bogle and Joanna Bogle: *A Heart for Europe: The Lives of Emperor Charles and Empress Zita of Austria-Hungary* (1990; Herefordshire: Gracewing, 2004), 137; Brook-Shepherd, *Uncrowned Emperor*, 23.

35. Feigl, *Zita: Kaiserin und Königin*, 365.

36. "Zita Says Turnips Kept Charles from Regaining Throne," *New York Times*, January 24, 1922, 1.

37. Feigl, *Zita: Kaiserin und Königin*, 365.

38. Feigl, *Zita: Kaiserin und Königin*, 368.

39. Feigl, *Zita: Kaiserin und Königin*, 368.

40. Feigl, *Zita: Kaiserin und Königin*, 369.

41. Feigl, *Zita: Kaiserin und Königin*, 369.

42. Feigl, *Zita: Kaiserin und Königin*, 369.

43. Feigl, *Zita: Kaiserin und Königin*, 372; Paolo Mattei, "Carlo d'Asburgo, l'ultimo imperatore cattolico," *30Giorni*, no. 6 (2003), http://www.30giorni.it/articoli_id_997_l1.htm; Giuseppe Dalla Torre, *Carlo d'Austria: Una testimonianza cristiana* (Milan: Editrice Àncora, 1972); "Emperor of Austria and His Wife Zita in Exile in Funchal, Madeira Island," *YouTube*, https://www.youtube.com/watch?v=pvHoLhC2iMc.

44. Bertita Harding, *Imperial Twilight: The Story of Karl and Zita of Hungary* (1939; New York: Blue Ribbon Books, 1941), 251.

45. Feigl, *Zita: Kaiserin und Königin*, 143–50.

46. "Ex-Empress Zita at Zurich," *New York Times*, January 13, 1921, 10.

47. "Zita Says Turnips Kept Charles from Regaining Throne," *New York Times*, January 24, 1922, 1.

48. Feigl, *Zita: Kaiserin und Königin*, 396; "Exkaiser Karl," "Der Tod des Exkaisers," *Neue Freie Presse*, April 2, 1922, 1–2.

49. Feigl, *Zita: Kaiserin und Königin*, 398; Bogle and Bogle, *A Heart for Europe*, 146.

50. "Exkaiser Karl," "Der Tod des Exkaisers," *Neue Freie Presse*, April 2, 1922, 1–2; Bogle and Bogle, *A Heart for Europe*, 144–45.

51. "Exkaiser Karl," "Der Tod des Exkaisers," *Neue Freie Presse*, April 2, 1922, 1–2.

52. Hofmannsthal to Strauss, [March 21, 1922], Strauss and Hofmannsthal, *Briefwechsel*, 471–72; Strauss and Hofmannsthal, *Working Friendship*, 349–50.

53. Hofmannsthal to Strauss, [April 15, 1922], Strauss and Hofmannsthal, *Briefwechsel*, 476; Strauss and Hofmannsthal, *Working Friendship*, 350–52.

54. Daniel Unowsky, *The Pomp and Politics of Patriotism: Imperial Celebrations in Habsburg Austria 1848–1916* (West Lafayette, IN: Purdue University Press, 2005), 29–30.

55. Kaiser-Karl-Gebetsliga/Emperor Karl League of Prayers, *Facebook*, https://www.facebook.com/KaiserKarlGebetsliga/posts/happy-easterwe-have-just-completed-the-liturgical-celebration-of-the-easter-trid/875972205761760/.

56. Kaiser-Karl-Gebetsliga/Emperor Karl League of Prayers, *Facebook*.

57. Wiener Staatsoper, Spielplanarchiv, *Parsifal*, April 15, 1922, April 16, 1922, April 17, 1922, https://archiv.wiener-staatsoper.at/search/work/2/production/993?since=01.03.1922&until=01.05.1922.

58. Robert Werba, *Maria Jeritza: Primadonna des Verismo* (Vienna: Österreichischer Bundesverlag, 1981), 130; Wiener Staatsoper, Spielplanarchiv, April 1922, May 1922, https://archiv.wiener-staatsoper.at/search?since=19.04.1922&until=31.05.1922.

59. *Die Frau ohne Schatten*, orchestral score (Berlin: Adolph Fürstner, 1919; repr. Mainz: Fürstnermusikverlag, 1987), act 2, scene 4, 351–52, 356–57.

60. *Die Frau ohne Schatten*, orchestral score, act 2, scene 4, 364–69; see also Wolfgang Perschmann, *Hugo von Hofmannsthal und Richard Strauss: "Die Frau ohne Schatten": Sinndeutung aus Text und Musik* (Graz: Österreichische Richard Wagner Gesellschaft, 1992), 94–96; Sherrill Pantle, *"Die Frau ohne Schatten" by Hugo von Hofmannsthal and Richard Strauss: An Analysis of Text, Music and Their Relationship* (Bern: Peter Lang, 1978), 162–64.

61. Wiener Staatsoper, Spielplanarchiv, *Ariadne auf Naxos*, https://archiv.wiener-staatsoper.at/performances/23762.

62. Hofmannsthal to Strauss, [middle July 1911], Strauss and Hofmannsthal, *Briefwechsel*, 134; Strauss and Hofmannsthal, *Working Friendship*, 94.

63. "Bist du die Göttin dieser Insel?" *Ariadne auf Naxos*, in Hugo von Hofmannsthal, *Dramen V: Operndichtungen* (Frankfurt: Fischer Taschenbuch Verlag, 1979), 217.

64. Bogle and Bogle, *A Heart for Europe*, 149–50.

Chapter 16: "The Thread of Past Time"

1. Gordon Brook-Shepherd, *Uncrowned Emperor: The Life and Times of Otto von Habsburg* (London: Hambledon and London, 2003), 73–75.

2. "Steps toward Sainthood," Blessed Karl of Austria: Cause for Canonization, https://www.emperorcharles.org/steps-toward-sainthood.

3. Erich Feigl, ed., *Zita: Kaiserin und Königin* (Vienna: Amalthea Verlag, 1991), 64–66; "Benedictine Oblate," Association pour la Béatification de l'Impératrice Zita, http://www.beatification-imperatrice-zita.org/pages/english/spirituality/benedictine-oblate.html.

4. Claudia Konrad, *"Die Frau ohne Schatten" von Hugo von Hofmannsthal und Richard Strauss: Studien zur Genese, zum Textbuch und zur Rezeptionsgeschichte* (Hamburg: Verlag der Musikalienhandlung Karl Dieter Wagner, 1988), 226; Wiener Staatsoper, Spielplanarchiv, November 9, 1922, https://archiv.wiener-staatsoper.at/performances/45178; Josef Kern, "Ein Bildnis der Sopranistin Fanny Cleve," *David: Jüdische Kulturzeitschrift*, https://davidkultur.at/artikel/ein-bildnis-der-sopranistin-fanny-cleve.

5. "Manowarda (Edler von Jana), Josef," *Oesterreichisches Musiklexikon Online*, https://www.musiklexikon.ac.at/ml/musik_M/Manowarda_Josef.xml.

6. Wiener Staatsoper, Spielplanarchiv, November 1922, https://archiv.wiener-staatsoper.at/search?since=01.11.1922&until=01.12.1922.

7. Wiener Staatsoper, Spielplanarchiv, December 28, 1922, https://archiv.wiener-staatsoper.at/performances/45179#title.

8. Michael Kennedy, *Richard Strauss: Man, Musician, Enigma* (1999; Cambridge: Cambridge University Press, 2006) 221–22; Paul Thomason, "Richard Strauss and Vienna," San Francisco Opera website, https://www.sfopera.com/seasons/1819season/arabella/richard-strauss--vienna/.

9. Hofmannsthal to Strauss, September 4, 1922, in Richard Strauss and Hugo von Hofmannsthal, *Briefwechsel: Gesamtausgabe*, ed. Franz Strauss, Alice Strauss, Willi Schuh (Zurich: Atlantis Verlag, 1964), 481; Richard Strauss and Hugo von Hofmannsthal, *A Working Friendship: The Correspondence*, trans. Hanns Hammelmann and Ewald Osers (New York: Random House, 1961), 356.

10. Michael Steinberg, *Austria as Theater and Ideology: The Meaning of the Salzburg Festival* (1990; Ithaca NY: Cornell University Press, 2000), 79–80.

11. Strauss to Hofmannsthal, July 12, 1923, Strauss and Hofmannsthal, *Briefwechsel*, 491; Strauss and Hofmannsthal, *Working Friendship*, 363.

12. Strauss to Hofmannsthal, September 8, 1923, Strauss and Hofmannsthal, *Briefwechsel*, 492; Strauss and Hofmannsthal, *Working Friendship*, 364.

13. Hofmannsthal to Strauss, September 14, 1923, Strauss and Hofmannsthal, *Briefwechsel*, 494; Strauss and Hofmannsthal, *Working Friendship*, 365–66.

14. Hofmannsthal to Strauss, September 22, 1923, Strauss and Hofmannsthal, *Briefwechsel*, 495; Strauss and Hofmannsthal, *Working Friendship*, 366.

15. Konrad, *"Die Frau ohne Schatten" von Hugo von Hofmannsthal und Richard Strauss*, 248, 391–93.

16. Wiener Staatsoper, Spielplanarchiv, January 27, 1923, https://archiv.wiener-staatsoper.at/performances/45180#title.

17. Olin Downes, "'Elektra' Revived at Metropolitan," *New York Times*, January 8, 1938, 18.

18. "Geyersbach, Gertrude," *Grosses Sängerlexikon*, 4th edition, ed. K. J. Kutsch and Leo Riemens (Munich: K. G. Saur, 2003), 3: 1707–8.

19. Strauss to Hofmannsthal, January 29, 1924, Strauss and Hofmannsthal, *Briefwechsel*, 511; Strauss and Hofmannsthal, *Working Friendship*, 380.

20. Ulrich Weinzierl, *Hofmannsthal: Skizzen zu seinem Bild* (2005; Frankfurt: Fischer Taschenbuch Verlag, 2007), 41–43.

21. Weinzierl, *Hofmannsthal*, 41; "The Nobel Prize Nomination Archive," Literature, 1924, https://www.nobelprize.org/nomination/archive/list.php?prize=4&year=1924.

22. Wiener Staatsoper, Spielplanarchiv, May 13, 1924, https://archiv.wiener-staatsoper.at/performances/45185#title.

23. Kennedy, *Richard Strauss*, 226.

24. Kennedy, *Richard Strauss*, 224–28; Konrad, *"Die Frau ohne Schatten" von Hugo von Hofmannsthal und Richard Strauss*, 155.

25. Hofmannsthal to Strauss, September 15, 1925, Strauss and Hofmannsthal, *Briefwechsel*, 544; Strauss and Hofmannsthal, *Working Friendship*, 407.

26. Hofmannsthal to Strauss, November 17, 1925, Strauss and Hofmannsthal, *Briefwechsel*, 546; Strauss and Hofmannsthal, *Working Friendship*, 409.

27. Hugo von Hofmannsthal, *Der Rosenkavalier*, in Hugo von Hofmannsthal, *Gesammelte Werke: Dramen V: Operndichtungen* (Frankfurt: Fischer Taschenbuch Verlag, 1979), act 1, 42.

28. Hofmannsthal to Strauss, May 4, 1925, Strauss and Hofmannsthal, *Briefwechsel*, 538–39; Strauss and Hofmannsthal, *Working Friendship*, 402–3.

29. Strauss to Hofmannsthal, January 29, 1925, Strauss and Hofmannsthal, *Briefwechsel*, 534; Strauss and Hofmannsthal, *Working Friendship*, 399.

30. Hofmannsthal to Strauss, January 30, 1926, Strauss and Hofmannsthal, *Briefwechsel*, 552; Strauss and Hofmannsthal, *Working Friendship*, 413; Hugo von Hofmannsthal, *Die ägyptische Helena*, in *Dramen V: Operndichtungen*, act 2, 487.

31. Strauss to Hofmannsthal, March 19, 1926, Strauss and Hofmannsthal, *Briefwechsel*, 554; Strauss and Hofmannsthal, *Working Friendship*, 416.

32. Strauss to Hofmannsthal, September 20, 1927, and October 15, 1927, Strauss and Hofmannsthal, *Briefwechsel*, 584, 591; Strauss and Hofmannsthal, *Working Friendship*, 440, 446.

33. Strauss to Hofmannsthal, October 25, 1927, Strauss and Hofmannsthal, *Briefwechsel*, 591; Strauss and Hofmannsthal, *Working Friendship*, 446.

34. Olin Downes, "'Turandot' Opens; Scores a Triumph," *New York Times*, November 17, 1926, 21.

35. Strauss to Hofmannsthal, October 25, 1927, Strauss and Hofmannsthal, *Briefwechsel*, 591–92; Strauss and Hofmannsthal, *Working Friendship*, 446.

36. Hofmannsthal to Strauss, October 28, 1927, Strauss and Hofmannsthal, *Briefwechsel*, 595; Strauss and Hofmannsthal, *Working Friendship*, 449.

37. Hofmannsthal to Strauss, [October 29, 1927], Strauss and Hofmannsthal, *Briefwechsel*, 598; Strauss and Hofmannsthal, *Working Friendship*, 453.

38. Strauss to Hofmannsthal, October 31, 1927, Strauss and Hofmannsthal, *Briefwechsel*, 599; Strauss and Hofmannsthal, *Working Friendship*, 452.

39. Strauss to Hofmannsthal, November 2, 1927, Strauss and Hofmannsthal, *Briefwechsel*, 600; Strauss and Hofmannsthal, *Working Friendship*, 453–54.

40. Hofmannsthal to Strauss, December 22, 1927, Strauss and Hofmannsthal, *Briefwechsel*, 612–13; Strauss and Hofmannsthal, *Working Friendship*, 463–64.

41. Wiener Staatsoper, Spielplanarchiv, *Die Frau ohne Schatten*, https://archiv.wiener-staatsoper.at/search/work/65/production/1803?since=01.01.1927&until=01.12.1928; "Achsel, Wanda," *Grosses Sängerlexikon*, vol. 1, 8.

42. Hofmannsthal to Strauss, December 22, 1927, Strauss and Hofmannsthal, *Briefwechsel*, 609; Strauss and Hofmannsthal, *Working Friendship*, 461.

43. Strauss to Hofmannsthal, April 25, 1928, Strauss and Hofmannsthal, *Briefwechsel*, 621–22; Strauss and Hofmannsthal, *Working Friendship*, 472.

44. Julius Korngold, "Feuilleton: Die ägyptische Helena," *Neue Freie Presse*, June 7, 1928, 1–5.

45. Olin Downes, "American Premiere of 'Egyptian Helen': Mme. Jeritza Sings the Title Role," *New York Times*, November 7, 1928, 31.

46. Strauss to Hofmannsthal, June 24, 1928, Strauss and Hofmannsthal, *Briefwechsel*, 632–33; Strauss and Hofmannsthal, *Working Friendship*, 481.

47. Hofmannsthal to Strauss, July 13, 1928, Strauss and Hofmannsthal, *Briefwechsel*, 639; Strauss and Hofmannsthal, *Working Friendship*, 486.

48. Strauss to Hofmannsthal, July 3, 1928, Strauss and Hofmannsthal, *Briefwechsel*, 635; Strauss and Hofmannsthal, *Working Friendship*, 484.

49. Strauss to Hofmannsthal, November 1, 1928, and November 19, 1928, Strauss and Hofmannsthal, *Briefwechsel*, 670, 674; Strauss and Hofmannsthal, *Working Friendship*, 512–15.

50. Strauss to Hofmannsthal, November 7, 1928, Strauss and Hofmannsthal, *Briefwechsel*, 671; Strauss and Hofmannsthal, *Working Friendship*, 512–13.

51. Hofmannsthal to Strauss, November 19, 1928, Strauss and Hofmannsthal, *Briefwechsel*, 675; Strauss and Hofmannsthal, *Working Friendship*, 517.

52. Weinzierl, *Hofmannsthal*, 222–23.

53. Strauss to Hofmannsthal, May 3, 1928, and July 6, 1929, Strauss and Hofmannsthal, *Briefwechsel*, 625, 695; Strauss and Hofmannsthal, *Working Friendship*, 475, 534.

54. Hofmannsthal to Strauss, July 10, 1929, Strauss and Hofmannsthal, *Briefwechsel*, 696; Strauss and Hofmannsthal, *Working Friendship*, 534.

55. *Arabella*, orchestral score (Vienna; Verlag Dr. Richard Strauss, 1933), act 1, 172.

56. *Arabella*, orchestral score, act 1, 175.

57. Strauss to Hofmannsthal, [July 14, 1929], Strauss and Hofmannsthal, *Briefwechsel*, 696; Strauss and Hofmannsthal, *Working Friendship*, 536.

58. Strauss to Gerty von Hofmannsthal, July 16, 1929, in Strauss and Hofmannsthal, *Briefwechsel*, 698; Strauss and Hofmannsthal, *Working Friendship*, 537.

59. Strauss to Gerty von Hofmannsthal, September 13, 1929, in Strauss and Hofmannsthal, *Briefwechsel*, 700.

60. Brook-Shepherd, *Uncrowned Emperor*, 74–76.

Chapter 17: Nazi Germany and Austrian Anschluss

1. Wiener Staatsoper, Spielplanarchiv, February 25, 1931, https://archiv.wiener-staats oper.at/performances/45195.

2. "Clemens Krauss (Conductor)," Bach Cantatas website, http://www.bach-cantatas .com/Bio/Krauss-Clemens.htm.

3. Jamie Bulloch, *Karl Renner: Austria* (London: Haus Histories, 2009), 119.

4. "Manowarda (Edler von Jana), Josef," *Oesterreichisches Musiklexikon Online*, https:// www.musiklexikon.ac.at/ml/musik_M/Manowarda_Josef.xml.

5. Julius Korngold, "Feuilleton: Opernteater: Neuszenierung und Neustudierung der 'Frau ohne Schatten'" *Neue Freie Presse*, February 27, 1931, 1–3.

6. Korngold, *Neue Freie Presse*, February 27, 1931, 1–3.

7. Wiener Staatsoper, Spielplanarchiv, *Die Frau ohne Schatten*, 1931–1934, https://archiv .wiener-staatsoper.at/search/work/65/production/1805?since=01.06.1930&until=30.06 .1934.

8. Salzburg Festival Archive, 1932, https://archive.salzburgerfestspiele.at/en/archive/j/ 1932.

9. Salzburg Festival Archive, 1933, https://archive.salzburgerfestspiele.at/en/archive/ j/1933.

10. Salzburg Festival Archive, 1934, https://archive.salzburgerfestspiele.at/en/archive/ j/1934.

11. Wiener Staatsoper, Spielplanarchiv, June 11, 1934, https://archiv.wiener-staatsoper.at/performances/45207.
12. Salzburg Festival Archive, *Fidelio*, 1934, https://archive.salzburgerfestspiele.at/archive_detail/programid/5115/id/0/j/1934.
13. Wiener Staatsoper, Spielplanarchiv, September 16, 1934 (Teatro La Fenice), https://archiv.wiener-staatsoper.at/performances/49619.
14. Fritz Trümpi, *The Political Orchestra: The Vienna and Berlin Philharmonics during the Third Reich*, trans. Kenneth Kronenberg (Chicago: University of Chicago Press, 2016), 83–84.
15. Michael Kennedy, *Richard Strauss: Man, Musician, Enigma* (1999; Cambridge: Cambridge University Press, 2006), 280–91; David Dennis, *Inhumanities: Nazi Interpretations of Western Culture* (Cambridge: Cambridge University Press, 2012), 387.
16. Kennedy, *Richard Strauss*, 297.
17. Wiener Staatsoper, Spielplanarchiv, 1938–45, https://archiv.wiener-staatsoper.at/search/person/3452?since=10.03.1938&until=30.06.1945.
18. Kennedy, *Richard Strauss*, 305–33.
19. Kennedy, *Richard Strauss*, 305–56; Wiener Staatsoper, Spielplanarchiv, "Viorica Ursuleac," https://archiv.wiener-staatsoper.at/search/person/2968.
20. Kennedy, *Richard Strauss*, 339.
21. "O. Krause, Husband of Lotte Lehmann," obituary, *New York Times*, January 23, 1939, 13.
22. Michael Kater, *Never Sang for Hitler: The Life and Times of Lotte Lehmann 1888–1976* (Cambridge: Cambridge University Press, 2008), 150, 177.
23. Wiener Staatsoper, Spielplanarchiv, September 28, 1937, https://archiv.wiener-staatsoper.at/performances/22935.
24. Salzburg Festival Archive, 1929, https://archive.salzburgerfestspiele.at/en/archive/j/1929.
25. Salzburg Festival Archive, 1932, https://archive.salzburgerfestspiele.at/en/archive/j/1932.
26. Kater, *Never Sang for Hitler*, 118; Salzburg Festival Archive, 1933, https://archive.salzburgerfestspiele.at/en/archive/j/1933.
27. Maria Augusta Trapp, *The Story of the Trapp Family Singers* (1949; New York: Doubleday, 1990), 104–6.
28. Trapp, *Story of the Trapp Family Singers*, 110–11.
29. Bertita Harding, *Imperial Twilight: The Story of Karl and Zita of Hungary* (1939; New York: Blue Ribbon Books, 1941), 323.
30. Harding, *Imperial Twilight*, 305–6.
31. "Der hundertste Geburtstag Kaiser Franz Josephs," *Neue Freie Presse*, August 18, 1930, 2–3.
32. "Franz-Josef-Feier in Budapest," *Neue Freie Presse*, August 19, 1930, 4.
33. "Hungary Alarmed by Talk of a Coup," *New York Times*, August 23, 1930, 4.
34. "Hungary Alarmed by Talk of a Coup," *New York Times*, August 23, 1930, 4.
35. "Die Grossjährigkeit Ottos von Habsburg: Ein wichtiger Tag für den Legitimismus," *Neue Freie Presse*, November 21, 1930, 1–2; Harding, *Imperial Twilight*, 306.
36. "Die Grossjährigkeit Ottos von Habsburg," *Neue Freie Presse*, November 21, 1930, 1–2.

37. "Otto, 18, Is Hailed Emperor and King," *New York Times*, November 21, 1930, 10.

38. "Says Habsburgs Plan Royalist Coup Soon," *New York Times*, November 25, 1931, 9.

39. "Ex-Empress Rebuffs Hohenzollern Offers: Zita Keeps Close Watch on All Restoration Activity," *New York Times*, July 24, 1932, sect. 2 (foreign correspondence), E3.

40. Adolf Hitler, *Mein Kampf*, trans. Ralph Manheim (1943; Boston: Houghton Mifflin, 1971), 15–16; James Longo, *Hitler and the Habsburgs: The Führer's Vendetta against the Austrian Royals* (New York: Diversion Books, 2018), 11–53.

41. Emil Lengyel, "Zita Looks toward Austria—and Hopes," *New York Times Magazine* (sect. 6), September 24, 1933, 10, 22.

42. Lengyel, "Zita Looks toward Austria," 10, 22.

43. Lengyel, "Zita Looks toward Austria," 10, 22; Frank Gilbreth Jr. and Ernestine Gilbreth Carey, *Cheaper by the Dozen* (New York: Thomas Crowell, 1948).

44. Lengyel, "Zita Looks toward Austria," 10, 22.

45. Bulloch, *Karl Renner*, 133–36; Johannes Thaler, "Ally and Opposition: The Legitimist Movement under the Dollfuß-Schuschnigg Dictatorship," *Austrian History Yearbook* 52 (2014): 167–85; Janek Wasserman, "*Österreichische Aktion*: Monarchism, Authoritarianism, and the Unity of the Austrian Conservative Ideological Field during the First Republic," *Central European History* 47 (2014): 76–104.

46. Harding, *Imperial Twilight*, 314.

47. Harding, *Imperial Twilight*, 314.

48. Micaela Baranello, *Operetta Empire: Music Theater in Early Twentieth-Century Vienna* (Berkeley: University of California Press, 2021), 160.

49. Eugene O'Neill, *The Emperor Jones*, scene 1.

50. Metropolitan Opera Archives, online, *The Emperor Jones*, January 7, 1933, with photograph of Tibbett on throne: http://archives.metoperafamily.org/Imgs/TibbettEmperorJones.jpg.

51. Harding, *Imperial Twilight*, 314–15.

52. Ulrich Weinzierl, *Hofmannsthal: Skizzen zu seinem Bild* (2005; Frankfurt: Fischer Taschenbuch Verlag, 2007), 201–9; *The Poet and the Countess: Hugo von Hofmannsthal's Correspondence with Countess Ottonie Degenfeld*, ed. Marie-Therese Miller-Degenfeld, trans. W. Eric Barcel (Rochester, NY: Camden House, 2000).

53. "Prince Sixtus Dies in Paris Home, 47: Brother of Ex-Empress Zita of Austria Won Distinction as an Explorer," *New York Times*, March 15, 1934, 26.

54. Bertita Harding, *Imperial Twilight*, 312–13; "Archduke Otto on Trip to Italy," *New York Times*, August 8, 1934, 2.

55. "Schuschnigg Shy on Monarchy Talk," *New York Times*, August 23, 1934, 11; Gordon Brook-Shepherd, *Uncrowned Emperor: The Life and Times of Otto von Habsburg* (London: Hambledon and London, 2003), 88–90.

56. Dieter Kindermann, *Die Habsburger ohne Reich: Geschichte einer Familie seit 1918* (Vienna: Kremayr und Scheriau, 2010), 93.

57. "Frau Herma v. Schuschnigg tödlich verunglückt," *Neue Freie Presse*, July 14, 1935, 1; "Die Katastrophe von Ebelsberg," *Reichspost*, July 14, 1935, 1.

58. "Richard Strauss legt seine Aemter zurück," *Reichspost*, July 14, 1935, 5.

59. "Arbeiter-Zeitung," Weblexikon der Wiener Sozialdemokratie, http://www.dasrotewien.at/seite/arbeiter-zeitung-az.

60. "Habsburgs Wiederkehr," *Arbeiter-Zeitung*, July 14, 1935, 1–3.

61. "Habsburgs Wiederkehr," *Arbeiter-Zeitung*, July 14, 1935, 1–3.
62. "Habsburgs Wiederkehr," *Arbeiter-Zeitung*, July 14, 1935, 1–3.
63. "Starhemberg Moves Mystify Austrians; Vice Chancellor Reported to Be on Way to Meet Former Empress and Archduke Otto," *New York Times*, January 30, 1936, 10.
64. "Pope Pius Receives Zita," *New York Times*, August 25, 1936, 4.
65. Erich Feigl, ed., *Zita: Kaiserin und Königin* (Vienna: Amalthea Verlag, 1991), 116, 159.
66. Longo, *Hitler and the Habsburgs*, 164–67.
67. Brook-Shepherd, *Uncrowned Emperor*, 115–17; Harding, *Imperial Twilight*, 316–17.
68. Brook-Shepherd, *Uncrowned Emperor*, 129.
69. "Das Geburtsfest der Kaiserin," *Neue Freie Presse*, May 10, 1917, 7; "David Israel Taglicht," Jewish Virtual Library, https://www.jewishvirtuallibrary.org/taglicht-david-israel.
70. "Ex-Empress Zita Prays as Habsburg Hopes Fade," *New York Times*, March 14, 1938, 3.
71. Metropolitan Opera Archives, online, *Elektra*, March 3, 1938, http://archives.metoperafamily.org/archives/scripts/cgiip.exe/WService=BibSpeed/gisrch2k.r.
72. *Orinoco: Hamburg-Amerika Linie, Cuba-Mexico-Schnelldienst, Kapitän A. Jost, am 26 November 1938, Passagierliste, Liste der Reisenden*, Leo Baeck Institute Archives, Center for Jewish History Collections, New York City.
73. *Menu, An Bord M. S. Orinoco*, December 13, 1938.
74. Teatro dell'Opera di Roma, Archivio Storico, *La donna senz'ombra*, 1937–38, https://archiviostorico.operaroma.it/edizione_opera/la-donna-senzombra-die-frau-ohne-schatten-1937-38/.
75. Kennedy, *Richard Strauss*, 318–19; "Der Führer in der Wiener Staatsoper," *Neues Wiener Tagblatt*, June 11, 1939, 1.
76. Ferdinand Kösters, *Peter Anders: Biographie eines Tenors* (Stuttgart: Verlag J. B. Metzler, 1995), 87–89.
77. Wiener Staatsoper, Spielplanarchiv, October 30, 1939, https://archiv.wiener-staatsoper.at/performances/45209.
78. Metropolitan Opera Archives, online, "Lothar Wallerstein," http://archives.metoperafamily.org/archives/scripts/cgiip.exe/WService=BibSpeed/gisrch2f.r.
79. "Ilitsch, Daniza," *Grosses Sängerlexikon*, 4th edition, ed. K. J. Kutsch and Leo Riemens (Munich: K. G. Saur, 2003), 3:2188; "Ilitsch, Daniza," Androom Archive, https://androom.home.xs4all.nl/biography/p070796.htm.
80. "Otto, Pretender, Is Here by Plane," *New York Times*, March 5, 1940, 3.
81. Alberto Arbasino, "Hofmannsthal nello Specchio Magico," *La Repubblica*, archive, May 8, 1992, https://ricerca.repubblica.it/repubblica/archivio/repubblica/1992/05/08/hofmannsthal-nello-specchio-magico.html.
82. "Royalty Flees to Spain: Former Empress Zita among Those in Motor Caravan," *New York Times*, June 20, 1940, 5.
83. "Habsburg," Sousa Mendes Foundation, http://sousamendesfoundation.org/family/habsburg.

Chapter 18: The Empress in America

1. "Ex-Empress Zita Here as Refugee," *New York Times*, July 21, 1940, 25; "The Pan Am Clippers," https://www.clipperflyingboats.com/.

2. "British Beat Off Mass Raids by Swarms of Nazi Planes," *New York Times*, July 21, 1940, 1.

3. "Ex-Empress Zita Here as Refugee," *New York Times*, July 21, 1940, 25.

4. *S. S. Mexico, List or Manifest of Alien Passengers for the United States*, May 11, 1940.

5. Archives, Family History, 1940 US Census, Vera Nickich, http://www.archives.com/1940-census/vera-nickich-ny-59593359.

6. "Ex-Empress Zita Here as Refugee," *New York Times*, July 21, 1940, 25.

7. "Clipper Due Here Today: 4 Children of Ex-Empress Zita among 24 Passengers," *New York Times*, July 29, 1940, 15.

8. "Czech Will to Rise Reiterated at Fair," *New York Times*, July 29, 1940, 15.

9. John Brooks, "The Happy Venture" (profile of Hugh Bullock, son of Calvin Bullock), *The New Yorker*, March 8, 1958, 47–83.

10. "Zita Finds Refuge in Bay State Home: Ex-Empress of Austria Still Dreams of Restoration of Habsburg Throne," *New York Times*, September 15, 1940, sect. 11 (real estate), 16 RE.

11. "Zita Finds Refuge in Bay State Home," *New York Times*, September 15, 1940, sect. 11 (real estate), 16 RE.

12. Rob Brinkley, "All Is Calm," *New England Home*, April 30, 2012, https://www.nehomemag.com/all-is-calm/.

13. "Zita Finds Refuge in Bay State Home," *New York Times*, September 15, 1940, sect. 11 (real estate), 16 RE.

14. "Zita Finds Refuge in Bay State Home," *New York Times*, September 15, 1940, sect. 11 (real estate), 16 RE.

15. Email message to the author, May 14, 2009.

16. Email message to the author, May 14, 2009.

17. "Beatification Miracle for Blessed Karl: The Life and Healing of Sister Maria Zita Gradowska," website: Blessed Karl of Austria, Cause for Canonization USA/Canada, https://www.emperorcharles.org/beatification-miracle.

18. Alien Registration form, Zita, "Empress of Austria, Queen of Hungary, Duchess of Bar," certified in Athol, Massachusetts, September 25, 1940; from files of Department of Homeland Security, US Citizenship and Immigration Services, file number A-2501362; obtained under Freedom of Information Act, case number GEN-10108192.

19. "St. Zita? Church Opens Investigation into Sanctity of Zita of Bourbon-Parma, Wife of Blessed Charles and Last Empress of Austria-Hungary," December 13, 2009, Andrew Cusack website, https://www.andrewcusack.com/2009/zita-cause/.

20. Franklin D. Roosevelt Day by Day, FDR Presidential Library, September 8, 1940, http://www.fdrlibrary.marist.edu/daybyday/daylog/september-8th-1940/.

21. "Refugees," *Life Magazine*, December 16, 1940, 90–91, https://books.google.com/books?id=QEoEAAAAMBAJ&pg=PA88&source=gbs_toc_r&hl=en#v=onepage&q&f=false.

22. "Rules for Refugees, Royal or Otherwise, While in America," *Life Magazine*, December 16, 1940, 91, https://books.google.com/books?id=QEoEAAAAMBAJ&pg=PA88&source=gbs_toc_r&hl=en#v=onepage&q&f=false.

23. Yves Casgrain, "Zita, une impératrice au Québec," *LeVerbe*, September 15, 2017, https://le-verbe.com/reportage/zita-une-imperatrice-au-quebec/.

24. Steven Béla Várdy, "Hungarian Americans during World War II," in *Ideology, Politics, and Diplomacy in East Central Europe*, ed. Mieczysław Biskupski and Piotr Wandycz (Rochester, NY: University of Rochester Press, 2003), 138n47; US Department of State, Office of the Historian, Foreign Relations of the United States, conference at Quebec, 1944: https://history.state.gov/historicaldocuments/frus1944Quebec/d169.
25. Erich Feigl, ed., *Zita: Kaiserin und Königin* (Vienna: Amalthea Verlag, 1991), 406–8.
26. Congressional Record, House of Representatives, March 3, 1943, 1514.
27. Gordon Brook-Shepherd, *Uncrowned Emperor: The Life and Times of Otto von Habsburg* (London: Hambledon and London, 2003), 155–56.
28. Congressional Record, House of Representatives, March 3, 1943, 1515.
29. Feigl, *Zita: Kaiserin und Königin*, 407.
30. Feigl, *Zita: Kaiserin und Königin*, 408–9.
31. Wiener Staatsoper, Spielplanarchiv, *Die Frau ohne Schatten*, 1943–44, https://archiv.wiener-staatsoper.at/search/work/65/production/1806.
32. Michael Kennedy, "Richard Strauss: A Reluctant Nazi Collaborator," *New Statesman*, January 23, 2014, https://www.newstatesman.com/culture/2014/01/richard-strauss-reluctant-nazi-collaborator.
33. Wiener Staatsoper, Spielplanarchiv, *Der Rosenkavalier*, May 27, 1944, https://archiv.wiener-staatsoper.at/performances/21770.
34. Michael Kennedy, *Richard Strauss: Man, Musician, Enigma* (1999; Cambridge: Cambridge University Press, 2006), 342.
35. Metropolitan Opera Archives, online, *Der Rosenkavalier*, February 23, 1945, http://archives.metoperafamily.org/archives/scripts/cgiip.exe/WService=BibSpeed/fullcit.w?xCID=138960&limit=50&xBranch=ALL&xsdate=&xedate=&theterm=Altman,%20Thelma%20%5BMezzo%20Soprano%5D&x=0&xhomepath=&xhome=
36. Jamie Bulloch, *Karl Renner: Austria* (London: Haus Histories, 2009), 145–52; Harry Piotrowski, "The Soviet Union and the Renner Government of Austria: April–November 1945," *Central European History* 20, no. 3–4 (1987): 266–67.
37. "Tuxedo Park Estates," http://www.tuxedoparkestates.com/propertydetails.aspx?propertyid=77.
38. Feigl, *Zita: Kaiserin und Königin*, 410.
39. Kennedy, *Richard Strauss*, 372; Wiener Konzerthaus, Archivdatenbank, June 26, 1947, https://konzerthaus.at/datenbanksuche.
40. Kennedy, *Richard Strauss*, 363, 373, 383; John Rockwell, "Song by Richard Strauss Discovered," *New York Times*, September 15, 1984, 1, 11.
41. "Richard Strauss Dies at Age of 85," *New York Times*, September 9, 1949, 25.
42. Olin Downes, "Historic Figure: Richard Strauss' Place as One of the Great Composers Stands Secure," *New York Times*, September 18, 1949, sect. 2 (drama, music, etc.), X7.
43. Metropolitan Opera Archives, online, *Der Rosenkavalier*, November 21, 1949, http://archives.metoperafamily.org/archives/scripts/cgiip.exe/WService=BibSpeed/fullcit.w?xCID=152000&limit=5000&xBranch=ALL&xsdate=&xedate=&theterm=rosenkavalier%201949&x=0&xhomepath=https://us.search.yahoo.com/&xhome=https://us.search.yahoo.com/.
44. Metropolitan Opera Archives, online, *Die Fledermaus*, February 22, 1951, http://archives.metoperafamily.org/archives/scripts/cgiip.exe/WService=BibSpeed/fullcit.w

?xCID=156130&limit=5000&xBranch=ALL&xsdate=&xedate=&theterm=fledermaus%201951&x=0&xhomepath=https://us.search.yahoo.com/&xhome=https://us.search.yahoo.com/.

45. Thomas Voigt, "Die späte Karriere eines Schmerzenkindes: Zur Aufführungsgeschichte der *Frau ohne Schatten*," https://thomasvoigt.net/2019/04/die-spaete-karriere-eines-schmerzenskindes/.

Chapter 19: The Empress Returns

1. Claudia Konrad, *"Die Frau ohne Schatten" von Hugo von Hofmannsthal und Richard Strauss: Studien zur Genese, zum Textbuch und zur Rezeptionsgeschichte* (Hamburg: Verlag der Musikalienhandlung Karl Dieter Wagner, 1988), 335–36.

2. Eva Demmerle, *Kaiser Karl: Mythos und Wirklichkeit* (Vienna: Amalthea, 2016), 169–70.

3. Gordon Brook-Shepherd, *Uncrowned Emperor: The Life and Times of Otto von Habsburg* (London: Hambledon and London, 2003), 178–79.

4. Cyrille Debris, *Zita: Portrait intime d'une impératrice* (Paris: Les Éditions du Cerf, 2013), 133–52.

5. Austrian State Treaty (1955), article 10, paragraph 2; Brook-Shepherd, *Uncrowned Emperor*, 181; Dieter Kindermann, *Die Habsburger ohne Reich: Geschichte einer Familie seit 1918* (Vienna: Kremayr und Scheriau, 2010), 93; "Habsburger-Gesetz," AEIOU Encyclopedia, online: http://www.aeiou.at/aeiou.encyclop.h/h022680.htm;internal&action=_set-language.action?LANGUAGE=en.

6. Certificate of Alien Admission, US Department of Homeland Security, National Records Center, US Citizenship and Immigration Services, file no. 2501362, "Duchess Marie de Bar," arrival August 27, 1951, New York City; Brook-Shepherd, *Uncrowned Emperor*, 177.

7. Marcel Prawy, *The Vienna Opera* (Vienna: Verlag Fritz Molden, 1969), 174–75.

8. Michael Kater, *Never Sang for Hitler: The Life and Times of Lotte Lehmann 1888–1976* (Cambridge: Cambridge University Press, 2008), 276–77.

9. Prawy, *Vienna Opera*, 179–80.

10. Thomas Voigt, "Die späte Karriere eines Schmerzenkindes: Zur Aufführungsgeschichte der *Frau ohne Schatten*," https://thomasvoigt.net/2019/04/die-spaete-karriere-eines-schmerzenskindes/.

11. Paul Jackson, *Sign-Off for the Old Met: The Metropolitan Opera Broadcasts, 1950–1966* (Portland, OR: Amadeus Press, 1997), 318; Metropolitan Opera Archives, online, "Karl Böhm," http://archives.metoperafamily.org/archives/scripts/cgiip.exe/WService=BibSpeed/gisrch2k.r.

12. Jackson, *Sign-Off for the Old Met*, 322–23.

13. Rudolf Bing, *5000 Nights at the Opera* (New York: Doubleday, 1972), 308–9.

14. Harold Schonberg, "Marvel at the Met," *New York Times*, October 3, 1966, 61.

15. Schonberg, "Marvel at the Met," *New York Times*, October 3, 1966, 61.

16. Brook-Shepherd, *Uncrowned Emperor*, 181–83.

17. "*Die Frau ohne Schatten* (*La femme sans ombre*)," *Forum Opéra: Le magazine de l'opéra et du monde lyrique*, online, https://www.forumopera.com/v1/concerts/femme_ss_ombre_bastille.htm.

18. Salzburg Festival Archive, 1974 and 1975, https://archive.salzburgerfestspiele.at/en/archive/j/1974, https://archive.salzburgerfestspiele.at/en/archive/j/1975.

19. "Adler, Kurt Herbert," website: snac (social networks and archival context), https://snaccooperative.org/view/62101377.

20. Wiener Staatsoper, Spielplanarchiv, *Die Frau ohne Schatten*, January 16, 1977, https://archiv.wiener-staatsoper.at/performances/774.

21. "Notes on People: Tribute to Rysanek," *New York Times*, September 21, 1979, B4.

22. "Meine private Liste von R. Strauss-Aufführungen," http://www.ec.kagawa-u.ac.jp/~mogami/strauss-live.html.

23. Program, San Francisco Opera, Kurt Herbert Adler, general director, *Die Frau ohne Schatten*, September 10–September 30, 1980, War Memorial Opera House.

24. Erich Feigl, ed., *Zita: Kaiserin und Königin* (Vienna: Amalthea Verlag, 1991), 117.

25. Feigl, *Zita: Kaiserin und Königin*, 7–8.

26. "Steps toward Sainthood," website: Blessed Karl of Austria: Cause for Canonization USA/Canada, http://www.emperorcharles.org/steps-toward-sainthood.

27. Kindermann, *Die Habsburger ohne Reich*, 11–12.

28. Feigl, *Zita: Kaiserin und Königin*, 412–13; Kindermann, *Die Habsburger ohne Reich*, 13.

29. "Maria Jeritza: International gefeierte Sopranistin," website: *Richard Strauss: Erinnerungen*, http://www.richardstrauss.at/erinnerungen.html.

30. Feigl, *Zita: Kaiserin und Königin*, 413.

31. Feigl, *Zita: Kaiserin und Königin*, 416.

32. Facebook, Association for the Beatification of Empress Zita (Malta), Gabriele Testi, August 8, 2020, https://www.facebook.com/EmpressZitaMalta/.

33. Feigl, *Zita: Kaiserin und Königin*, 75.

34. Peter Pirker, "The Victim Myth Revisited: The Politics of History in Austria up until the Waldheim Affair," in *Myths in Austrian History: Construction and Deconstruction*, ed. Günter Bischof, Marc Landry, Christian Karner, *Contemporary Austrian Studies*, vol. 29 (New Orleans: University of New Orleans Press, 2020), 151–72.

35. Serge Schmemann, "Waldheim Apologizes for War Crimes by Austrians," *New York Times*, March 11, 1988, A3.

36. Serge Schmemann, "Austria Asks: Accomplice of Nazis, or Victim?," *New York Times*, March 10, 1988, A1, A6.

37. Brook-Shepherd, *Uncrowned Emperor*, 191–92.

38. Christian Hütterer, "Mitteleuropa—Nostalgia in New Disguises?," in *Myths in Austrian History: Construction and Deconstruction*, 243–60.

39. Feigl, *Zita: Kaiserin und Königin*, 418.

40. Feigl, *Zita: Kaiserin und Königin*, 420.

41. Feigl, *Zita: Kaiserin und Königin*, 421–22.

42. Feigl, *Zita: Kaiserin und Königin*, 423.

43. Feigl, *Zita: Kaiserin und Königin*, 424–25.

44. Serge Schmemann, "Habsburg Grandeur Is Dusted Off for Burial of 'Our Sister the Empress Zita,'" *New York Times*, April 2, 1989, 3.

45. Feigl, *Zita: Kaiserin und Königin*, 425–26; Schmemann, "Habsburg Grandeur Is Dusted Off," *New York Times*, April 2, 1989, 3.

46. Wiener Staatsoper, Spielplanarchiv, *Der Rosenkavalier*, April 1, 1989, https://archiv.wiener-staatsoper.at/performances/3249.

47. "Austrian Cardinal Quits in Sex Scandal," *New York Times*, April 15, 1998, A12; Hubertus Czernin, *Das Buch Groër: Eine Kirchenchronik* (Klagenfurt: Wieser Verlag, 1998); "Hubertus Czernin" (obituary), *Boston Globe*, June 16, 2006, http://archive.boston.com/news/globe/obituaries/articles/2006/06/16/hubertus_czernin_50_tracked_looted_art/.

48. "Hubertus Czernin," website: geni, https://www.geni.com/people/Hubertus-Czernin/6000000020363654726; son of Felix Theobald Czernin, who was the son of Paul Friedrich Czernin, who was the brother of Ottokar Czernin.

49. "Hubertus Czernin" (obituary), *Boston Globe*, June 16, 2006.

50. Schmemann, "Habsburg Grandeur Is Dusted Off," *New York Times*, April 2, 1989, 3.

51. Feigl, *Zita: Kaiserin und Königin*, 428–29; Martina Kirfel, "Ein sterblicher, sündiger Mensch: Das Begräbnis der letzten Kaiserin von Österreich," website: taz archiv (*Tageszeitung*), April 8, 1989, https://taz.de/Ein-sterblicher-suendiger-Mensch/!1816297/.

52. Feigl, *Zita: Kaiserin und Königin*, 432.

53. Travis Walton, "Professor, Minister, Assassin: The Fascinating Life of Dr. Vaso Čubrilović," website: Wessex Scene, November 11, 2018, https://www.wessexscene.co.uk/features/2018/11/11/professor-minister-assassin-the-fascinating-life-of-dr-vaso-cubrilovic; Larry Wolff, "If Gavrilo Princip Had Lived to Be a Hundred," *Aspen Review: Central Europe* (2018): https://www.aspen.review/article/2018/gavrilo-princip-lived-hundred; see also Peter Sugar, *East European Nationalism, Politics and Religion* (Aldershot: Ashgate Variorum, 1999) sect. XI, 348.

54. James Bogle and Joanna Bogle, *A Heart for Europe: The Lives of Emperor Charles and Empress Zita of Austria-Hungary* (1990; Herefordshire: Gracewing, 2004), 160.

55. Hofmannsthal to Strauss, September 19, 1915, in Richard Strauss and Hugo von Hofmannsthal, *Briefwechsel: Gesamtausgabe*, ed. Franz Strauss, Alice Strauss, Willi Schuh (Zurich: Atlantis Verlag, 1964), 326; Richard Strauss and Hugo von Hofmannsthal, *A Working Friendship: The Correspondence*, trans. Hanns Hammelmann and Ewald Osers (New York: Random House, 1961), 236.

Index

Note: Page numbers in italics indicate illustrative material.

Achilleion Palace, Corfu, Greece, 13, 21, 271
Achsel, Wanda, 299
Adelaide of Braganza, Princess, 20
Adelheid, Archduchess of Austria (daughter of Karl and Zita), 82, 324, 326, 339, 355
Adler, Kurt Herbert, 353–54
Adriatic coast, 40–41, 119, *215*, *238*
The Adventures of Robin Hood (film), 278
aestheticism: Hofmannsthal's, 79, 92, 233, 247; music of, 164, 165; Viennese cult of, 18, 49, 164–65
Die ägyptische Helena (Strauss and Hofmannsthal): as collaboration, 6; composition process, 284, 292–93, 295–96; performances, 296–98, 299–300, 302, 308
Alexandra, Tsarina of Russia, 7, 64, 191, 201, 268
Alfonso XIII, King of Spain, 229, 288, 290
Alien Registration Act, U.S. (1940), 337, *338*, 339
Allgemeine Poliklinik, 58
Altman, Maria, 362

Anatol, by Arthur Schnitzler, Hofmannsthal's prologue, 19
Andrian, Leopold von, 77, 78, 150–51, 170, 210, 211–12, 293
animals: falcon imagery, 37–39, *38*; gazelle 20, 22, 23, 37, 50, 81, 82, *91*, 92, 315; totem, 81–82. *See also* hunting
Anschluss, 308, 318, 319, 324–26, 358
anti-Semitism, 77, 191–92, 237, 272, 292, 294, 307–8, 325, 358
Arabella (Strauss and Hofmannsthal): composition process, 299, 300, 301, 302, 303–4; as nostalgic, 320; performances, 305, 310, 325, 328, 346
Aravantinos, Panos, 270–71
Arbeiter-Zeitung (newspaper), 254–57, 265, 323
Ariadne auf Naxos (Strauss and Hofmannsthal): Ariadne as character, 46, 288, 322; the Composer as character, 45, 46, 167, 175, 189, 240, 243, *252*, 270, 288, 351; composition process, 43–45, 75, 167; critical reception, 175, 346; *Die Frau ohne Schatten* comparison, 31, 73,

Ariadne auf Naxos (continued)
171, 259; performances, 57, 71, 171, 175, 187, 200, 236, 270, 286, 287, 310, 346, 351; prologue, 167, 171, 172, 174; Zerbinetta as character, 44, 45, 175, 264, 288

Arz von Straussenburg, Arthur, 187

Astor, Ava Alice, 302

Atatürk, Mustafa Kemal, 280–81

Auschwitz, 311

Australia, 141

Austria, Republic of: and Anschluss, 308, 318, 319, 324–26, 358; establishment of, 218, 237; and Habsburg Law, 230, 322, 323, 348, 355; Habsburg prospects in, 317–19, 322, 323–25, 340–41; Italian alliance interests, 310, 322, 326; Otto's return to, 353; postwar (after 1945) occupation of, 344, 348; rise of Nazism in, 305; and Treaty of Saint-Germain-en-Laye, 241, 242, 261, 270; victim myth, Austria as Hitler's victim, 349, 357–58, 360; Zita's return to, 355–56

Austria-Hungary. *See* Habsburg monarchy

Austrian Civil War (1934), 308

Austrian Glory (*La Gloria Austriaca*), in *Il pomo d'oro*, 26

Austrian State Treaty (1955), 344, 348

aviation: and attempted restoration in Hungary, 278, 282, 315, 325; Austrian, 29, 52, 331; and descent of the Empress in *Die Frau ohne Schatten*, 52, 243; falcon in *Die Frau ohne Schatten*, 37; Karl-Zita affinity for, *28*, 29, 36, 59 278, 331; operetta about, 59; transatlantic commercial air travel, 329, 331, 333

Bach, David Josef, 254–57, 262

Baernreither, Joseph Maria, 197–98, 216

Bahr, Hermann, 17, 211, 231–32, 240

Balkan Wars (1912, 1913), 57, 59, 76–77

ballet: *Josephslegende*, 55, 56, 76, 98, 130, 132, 284; *Nutcracker*, 15; *Schlagobers*, 259, 294; *The Snowman*, 30; for Zita's birthday, 208. *See also* Ballets Russes

Ballets Russes, 55, 60, 64, 94, 130

Barak, in *Die Frau ohne Schatten*, 66–70, *68*, *69*, 102–4, *104*, 141, 154–55, 156, 157, 158–60, *159*, 202, 204, 303; Mayr as, *67*, 153, 240, 251, 256, 270, 294, 306; sings of the "blessing of revocability," *69*, 69–70, 141, 307

baroque spectacles, 25–27, 56, 63. *See also* Cesti, Antonio, *Il pomo d'oro*

Batka, Richard, 263

Bauer, Ida ("Dora"), 353–54

Beardsley, Aubrey, "Salome" illustrations, *93*

beatification and canonization, 183, 267, 285, 291, 336–39, 347, 355, 357

Beethoven, Ludwig van: *Fidelio*, 35, 123, 308, 312, 349; grave, 363; Klimt's Beethoven frieze, 164; Ninth Symphony "Ode to Joy," 245; Second Piano Concerto, 231; in Vienna, 262

Bekker, Paul, 276

Belgium: in WWI, 122; in WWII, 329; Zita's exile at Steenokkerzeel, 304, *313*, 314, 315, 316, 317, 318, 319, 321, 325, 329

Belgrade, Serbia, 54, 94, 121

Bellini, Vincenzo, *Zaira*, 269

Belvedere Palace, Austria, 95, 121, 292

Benatzky, Ralph, "Draußen in Schönbrunn," 117, *118*, 131, 146

Benedict XV, Pope, 183–85, 195, 229

Berg, Alban, 60; *Wozzeck*, 149, 295, 298, 350

Berlin, Germany, 123, 233–34, 236, 237, 264, 270–71, 305

Berlin Olympics (1936), 322–23

Berlin Royal Museum of Ethnography, 237

Bernstein, Aaron, *Mendel Gibbor*, 155, 160

Bernstein, Leonard, 34

Bethlen, István, 278

Bing, Rudolf, 346, 350, 351

Bisleti, Gaetano, 229

Black Hand (Unification or Death), 43, 54, 94. *See also* Franz Ferdinand, Archduke of Austria: assassination of

Böhm, Karl, 342, 349–51, 353, 354

Bohemia, 16, 21, 34, 42, 45–46, 55, 133, 185, 189, *215*, *309*, 329, 344

Bolsheviks, 7, 191, 193, 201, 241, 242, 251, 268, 273, *313*, 317
Boryslav, Galicia, 49
Bosnia and Herzegovina, 41, 43, 77, 96, 110. See also Sarajevo
Botticelli, Sandro, *Primavera*, 220
Bourbon-Parma dynasty, 19–20, 115, 197–98, 218, 269. See also Robert of Bourbon-Parma, Duke; Sixtus, Prince of Bourbon-Parma; Xavier, Prince of Bourbon-Parma; Zita of Bourbon-Parma
Brandys, Bohemia, 45–46
Brecht, Bertolt, *Threepenny Opera* (with Weill), 301
Brecht, Walther, 294
Brentano, Clemens, "Lied der Frauen (wenn die Männer im Krieg sind)," 200–201
Britain. See England
Broch, Hermann, 7, 17, 18
Brod, Max, 195
Brothers Grimm, 15, 99–100
Brusilov, Alexei, 170
Bulgaria, 57, 77
Bullock, Calvin, 334, 344
Burckhardt, Carl, 303
Burke, Edmund, 14
Burnacini, Ludovico, 26, 29

Čabrinović, Nedeljko, 96, 123, 124
canonization and beatification, 183, 267, 285, 291, 336–39, 347, 355, 357
Carlota, Empress of Mexico, 267, 314
Carpathian Mountains, as military front, Hofmannsthal's essay, 144, 145, 147–48, 150
Caruso, Enrico, 83, 274, 351
Celler, Emanuel, 340–41
Cesti, Antonio, *Il pomo d'oro*, 25, 26, 27
charity and humanitarian aid, wartime, 130, 153, 187–89, 193, 195–96, 201, 207–8, 286, 344
Charlotte, Archduchess of Austria (daughter of Karl and Zita), 275

children: birth of Zita's, 50, 58, 82, 130, 133, 168–69, 196–97, 224, 242, 275, 288; chorus in *Die Frau ohne Schatten*, 98–99, 164–65, 220–23, *222*, 365; humanitarian aid for, 187–89, 193, 236. See also motherhood
China, Qing emperor and empire, 4, 165, 197
Chinese gongs, in orchestration of *Die Frau ohne Schatten*, 35, *52*, 53, 102, 126, 204
Chopin, Frédéric, 153
Churchill, Winston, 340
Clemenceau, Georges, 197, 208, 261
Cleve, Fanny, 291
Cold War, 344, 347, 348, 358
Cologne, Germany, 275, 277
commedia dell'arte, 31–32, 44, 288
communism, 269, 317, 337, 340, 341, 344, 358, 361, 364. See also Bolsheviks
Congress of Vienna (1814–1815), 167
Constantine the Great, Roman Emperor, 267
Correggio, Antonio da, 21, 220, 223
Čubrilović, Vaso, 363–64
Czechoslovakia: exiled statesmen from, 333–34; independence of, 199, 213; and Munich conference, 311; and Treaty of Trianon, 269, 276
Czernin, Hubertus, 362
Czernin, Ottokar, 185–86, 189, 194, 362
Czernowitz, Bukovina, 306, 308–9

Dagover, Lil, 314
D'Annunzio, Gabriele, 14
Dante Alighieri, *Divine Comedy*, 89
Darmstadt, Germany, 277, 293
Davis, Bette, 182, 314
Debussy, Claude, *Afternoon of a Faun*, 55
Degenfeld, Ottonie, 46, 217, 321–22
Degenfeld-Schonburg, Heinrich von, 321, 322, 330
Dehmel, Ida, 65–66
denazification, 342, 345, 346, 350, 359
Diaghilev, Sergei, 55, 56, 64, 76, 94

dirigible balloons, 29, 59
Dollfuß, Engelbert, 308, 310, 319, 323
Dostal, Hermann: *Der fliegende Rittmeister*, 59; "Zita Waltz," 2, *3*, 31, 59
Downes, Olin, 300, 346
Dresden, Germany, 194, 264, 277, 296, 300, 301, 305, 342
The Dyer's Wife, in *Die Frau ohne Schatten*, 66–70, *68*, *69*, 100-02, 102–4, *104*, 111, 141, 154–55, 157, 158–60, *159*, 202, 204, 303; Lehmann as, 175, 236, 240, 241, 25, *252*, 257, 258, 270, 306, 307, 312; as portrait of Pauline Strauss, 32, 64–65, 66, 110

Easter, 135, 136, 276, 285–86, 359
"Easter 1916" (Yeats), 136, 148
Einstein, Albert, 62, 228
Elektra (Strauss and Hofmannsthal): Downes on, 346; *Die Frau ohne Schatten* comparison, 259; performances, 90, 120, 123, 140, 187, 209, 257, 292, 308, 310
Elisabeth, Archduchess of Austria (daughter of Karl and Zita), 288, 340, 342, 344–45
Elisabeth, Empress of Austria and Queen of Hungary: and Achilleion Palace, 13, 21, 270–71; criticism of, 207; death of, 13–14, 356; and Empress character design in *Die Frau ohne Schatten*, *93*, 249, *250*; imperial afterlife of, 266–67, 275, 314, 320; and royal motherhood, 83
Elisabeth of Austria (film), 314
emigration. *See* refugees
The Emperor, in *Die Frau ohne Schatten*: as character, 80, *91*, 145–46; in key of E-flat major, 23, *23*, 174, *177*; petrification of, 126, 146, 204, 234–35, 287; relationship with Empress, 23, 138–39; resurrection of, 219–20
The Emperor Jones (film), 320
The Emperor Jones (Gruenberg, opera), 320–21
The Emperor Jones (O'Neill, play), 274, 320
The Empress, in *Die Frau ohne Schatten*: as character, 81, 92, *93*, 111–13, 138; guilt of, 124–27, *127*, 142, 205; relationship with Emperor, 23, 138–39; singing high F-sharp, 23, 24, 37, 90, 203, 223; and solo violin, 22, 23, 73, 125, 126, 141, 178, 203, 204, *205*, 206, 262; sympathy for humanity, *178*, 178–79, 204, 206, 364
England: declaration of war (WWII), 329; empire in India, 4; Jewish emigration to, 311, 326; Strauss celebrated in, 97–98; Strauss music during war, 123; western front developments (WWI), 124, 175, 191; and Zita's exile, 229, 280, 288
Erber, Leiser, 120, 255, 308, *309*, 335
Erber, Malka, *309*
Ermengarde, Holy Roman Empress, 26
Ernst, Prince of Hohenberg, 59, 324
eroticism, 55, 56, 60, *93*
Esperanto, 30
Ethiopia, 320
Eugene, Prince of Savoy, 95, 121, 128, 134, 147, 162
Eugénie de Montijo, Empress of the French, 267
Evans, R. J. W., 26
Exner, Wilhelm Franz, 82

fairy tale(s): emergence as genre, 15; Hofmannsthal's life as, 17–18; magic *vs.* reality, 99–100; qualities in *Die Frau ohne Schatten*, 6, 24, 31, 37, 39, 50, 52–53, 72, 75, 76, 80, 99, 137, 146, 163–64, 172–73; qualities in *Hänsel und Gretel*, 221; qualities in *Die Zauberflöte*, 2, 6, 16, 72, 173, 220, 248–49, 271
falcon, in *Die Frau ohne Schatten*: in the libretto, 24, *61*, 80, 82, 92, 146, 276; in the music, 37–39, *38*, 125–26, 145, 249, 354, 249
Fall, Leo: *The Dollar Princess*, 28; *Die Rose von Stambul*, 170, 200
The Favorite of Schönbrunn (film), 314
Feigl, Erich, 7, 36, 355
Feldkirch: Austrian frontier town, 227, 229, 348, 362; manifesto, 229, 230

Felix, Archduke of Austria (son of Karl and Zita), 168, 324, 326, 332, 334, 339, 341
Ferstel, Heinrich von, 45, 58
First Balkan War (1912), 57, 59, 77
Florence, Italy, 36, 63, 64, 322
Flynn, Errol, 182
Fokine, Michel, 94
Fourteen Points, 194–95
France: declaration of war (WWII), 329; as Napoleonic empire, 167, 182, 267, 268, 269, 320, 363; occupation of (WWII), 330; peace negotiations (WWI), 115, 185–86, 190, 197; performances of *Die Frau ohne Schatten* in, 284–85, 353; and Zita's exile, 288. *See also* Clemenceau, Georges
Franci, Benvenuto, 328, 329
Franckenstein, Clemens von, 121, 122, 162
Frankfurt, Germany, 122, 296
Franz II, Holy Roman Emperor (Franz I, Emperor of Austria), 182, 268, *309*, 363
Franz Ferdinand, Archduke of Austria: assassination of, 4, 41, 42, 43, 77, 95–97, 364; at the Belvedere, 95 121, 292; burial, 96; hunting interests, 42, 59, 94–95; at Karl-Zita wedding, 27; at Otto's christening, 58, 59
Franz Joseph, Emperor of Austria and King of Hungary: at Adelheid's christening, 82; annexation of Bosnia and Herzegovina, 41; celebrations of, 146, 175, 228, 315; death and burial, 146, 175–76, 316, 356; in "Draußen in Schönbrunn," 117, *118*; Easter Holy Thursday tradition, 285; imperial afterlife of, 314, 315, 316, 320; at Karl-Zita wedding, 2, 27, *28*; and Looshaus, 45; and Otto von Habsburg, 58, 59, 117; patronage of court opera, 8, 57–58, 83; titles, 13, 114; wartime concerns, 116–17, 147, 163
Franz Stefan (Franz I), Holy Roman Emperor, 189, 356
Franzos, Karl Emil, 53
Die Frau ohne Schatten (Strauss and Hofmannsthal)

– composition process: anticipated postwar significance and appreciation, 130–31, 187, 254, 261, 262, 298; artistic insecurities about, Hofmannsthal's, 33, 47, 54, 71–72, 75, 76, 171–72, 276–77, 298; artistic insecurities about, Strauss's, 172–74; Hofmannsthal's breakthroughs on, 46, 56, 60–62; influenced by baroque spectacles, 25, 26–27, 56–57; influenced by *Thousand and One Nights*, 16, 53; as "problem child," 6, 8, 166, 298; relation to *Lohengrin*, 139, 146, 219, 275; relation to *Tristan und Isolde*, 75, 85; relation to *Die Zauberflöte*, 2, 6, 16, 164, 173, 178, 203, 220–21, 248, 249, 271; Strauss's haste vs. Hofmannsthal's patience, 32–33, 55–56, 71, 72, 133, 135–36, 154–55; symphonic fantasy of major themes, 345; as a wartime work, 6–8, 113, 121, 123, 125, 126, 127, 129, 131, 133, 145, 158, 160, 161

– content analysis: Barak-Dyer's Wife relationship, 66–70, *68*, *69*, 102–4, *104*, 141, 154–55, 157, 158–60, *159*, 202, 204, 303; Barak the Dyer, as character, *67*, 156; children's chorus, 98–99, 164–65, 220–23, *222*, 365; commedia dell'arte in original conception, 31–32; Dyer's Wife, as character, 32, 65, 66, 110–11; Emperor, as character, 80, *91*, 145–46; Emperor, petrification of, 126, 146, 204, 234–35, 287; Emperor, resurrection of, 219–20; Emperor-Empress relationship, 23, 138–39; Empress, as character, 81, 92, *93*, 111–13, 138; Empress, guilt of, 124–27, *127*, 142, 205; Empress, sympathy for humanity, *178*, 178–79, 204, 206, 364; fairy-tale qualities, 6, 50, 75, 99, 172; falcon-Empress duet, 37–39, *38*; finale quartet, 244–46, *245*; human misery theme, 51–53, *52*, 89, 126–27; human shadow significance, 27, 87, 111, 112–13, 136–37, 142–43, 204, 205, 206, 259; hunting imagery, 20, 22–23, *91*; motherhood, renunciation of, 98, 99, 100–102, *101*, 142; Nurse, as

– *Die Frau ohne Schatten*—content analysis (*continued*)
character, *84*, 85, 89, 99, 139, 258; Nurse, punishment of, 201–3; Nurse-Dyer's Wife temptation scene, 86–88, 102; Nurse-Empress relationship, 85, 86, 88, 177–78; opening scene, 22–24, *23*, 80; relation of upper and lower worlds, 32, *61*, 62, 63, 72–74, 76, 126; Solomonic judgment, 138, 143, 156, 176–77, 204–6; temple scene, 163–64, 176–78, 203–6; treason theme, 74–75, 88; youth from afar, as character, 145, 158, 251

– critical reception: Bach's review, 254–57; Bekker's review, 276; Karpath's review, 259–63; Korngold's reviews, 247–54, 307; Kralik's review, 257–59, 350; Schonberg's review, 351–52; Strauss-Hofmannsthal disappointment in, 292, 295, 300, 302

– performances: costume designs, *84*, 85, *91*, *93*, *250*, *252*; in France, 284–85, 353; in Germany, 233–34, 236, 237, 264, 270–71, 277, 293, 295, 296, 328; in Italy, 284–85, 309–10, 326–28, 329; in Japan, 354; premiere casting decisions, *67*, 232, 236, 240–41, *250*, *252*; premiere rehearsals, 241, 242–43; premiere site selection, 166–67, 191, 194, 230–31, 232; in Salzburg, 308, 312, 320; stage designs, *61*, *94*, 140, 232, 233, 235, 239, 241, 253, 256–57, 262, 263–64, 271, 277, 328; studio recording, 349; in United States, 346, 351–52, 353; in Vienna Opera repertory, 1920s, 270, 271, 276, 277, 287, 291, 293, 294, 299; in Vienna Opera repertory, 1930s, 305–6, 307–8, 309–10, 316, 320, 328–29; in Vienna Opera repertory, during WWII, 310, 328–29, 342–43, 350; in Vienna Opera repertory, after WWII, 349–50, 354, 355

Die Frau ohne Schatten (Hofmannsthal, prose version), 79, 234–35
Frazer, James, *The Golden Bough*, 81
Freud, Sigmund, 85–86, 251, 326; "Contemporary Reflections on War and Death," 161; Dora case, 353–54; *Interpretation of Dreams*, 33; *Totem and Taboo*, 81–82; "The Uncanny," 259
Friedman, Ignaz, 153
Fuchs, Don, 153–54
Fuchs-Mollard, Marie Karoline von, 14, 356
Fuchs-Schlössl (Hofmannsthal residence, Rodaun), 14, 356
fundraising events and humanitarian aid, wartime, 130, 153, 187–89, 193, 195–96, 201, 207–8, 286, 344

Galicia: eastern front developments (WWI), 116, 128, 144, 151, 152; Hofmannsthal's military service in, 48–49, 51–52; military mobilization in eastern, 50, 72, 115, 116; as "oriental," 53; patriotic heroism in, 136; poverty and conflict in, 48–49, 152; refugees from, 152–54, 195; Zita's residence in, 48, 49–50
Galland, Antoine, *Thousand and One Nights*, 15
Gallipoli campaign, 141
George V, King of England, Emperor of India, 4, 229
German-Austria, Republic of. *See* Austria, Republic of
Germany: declaration of war against Russia (WWI), 114; declarations of war against (WWI), 191; eastern front developments (WWI), 144, 151–52; as empire, 2; occupation of Poland (WWI and WWII), 151–52, 170–71, 329; and peace negotiations (WWI), 186, 193, 197, 239; performances of Strauss-Hofmannsthal collaborations in, 123, 187, 233–34, 236, 237, 264, 270–71, 277, 293, 295, 296, 300, 301, 302, 328; and Prussian culture, 193; republican Weimar constitution, 241; Spartacus Uprising, 236; Strauss view of culture in wartime, 122–23; submarine warfare (WWI), 132–33, 134, 186; western front developments (WWI), 122, 124, 140, 186, 191, 208–9. *See also* Nazi Germany
Geyersbach, Gertrud, 293

glass harmonica, in orchestration of *Die Frau ohne Schatten*, 205, 206, 219, 246
Glinka, Mikhail, *A Life for the Tsar*, 64
Gobbi, Tito, 328
Goebbels, Joseph, 310, 323, 343
Goethe, Johann Wolfgang von, 60, 61–62, 63; *Faust*, 85
Goldberger, Richard von, *Die Modebaronin*, 195–96
Gozzi, Carlo, 16, 31
Der Gral (journal), 258
Great Britain. *See* England
Great Depression, 305, 306, 314
Greece: Achilleion Palace, 13, 21, 271; in Balkan League, 57; in Second Balkan War, 77
Gregor, Joseph, 311
Grieg, Edvard, 257
Grimm, Brothers. *See* Brothers Grimm
Grillparzer, Franz, 162
Groër, Hans Hermann, 360–62
Gruenberg, Louis, 320–21
Grünbaum, Fritz, 117
Gudenus, Erwein, 294
Gutheil-Schoder, Marie, 236, 240, 257,

Habsburg dynasty: burials in Kapuzinergruft, 96, 125, 243, 283, 315, 343, 356, 359, 362–63; dynastic rights waived by members of, 353, 355; Easter Holy Thursday tradition, 285–86; imperial title, 176, 182; restoration politics, 218, 315–18, 319, 320, 321, 322, 323–25, 329, 340–42; succession dynamics, 41–43, 59, 95–96, 97. *See also* Franz Ferdinand, Archduke of Austria; Franz Joseph, Emperor of Austria and King of Hungary; Karl I, Emperor of Austria and King of Hungary
Habsburg Law (1919), 230, 322, 323, 348, 355
Habsburg monarchy, Austria-Hungary: cultural identity and pride, 15, 120–21, 122, 162–63, 170–71, 192–93, 299; declaration of war against Serbia, 113–14; declarations of war against, 115, 147, 175, 193; dismantling (postwar), 199, 213–16, *214–15*, 217–18; eastern front developments, 116, 128, 144, 147, 151–52, 170; and Fourteen Points, 194–95; Italian Front developments, 167, 191, 213, 216; and Karl-Zita removal from throne, 216–18, 228–30, 284; occupation of Polish lands, 151–52, 170–71; peace negotiations, 183–86, 190, 194–95, 197; scholarship on cultural history of, 7–8; and Treaty of Saint-Germain, 241, 242, 261, 270; ultimatum to Serbia, 99, 100, 110, 113, 129. *See also* Galicia; Habsburg dynasty; Hungary; Vienna
Hafgren, Lilly, 277
Halévy, Fromental, *La Juive*, 153, 274, 286
Hamburg, Germany, 293, 295, 302
Ham Castle, Steenokkerzeel, Belgium, 314, 321, 329
Handel, George Frideric, *Judas Maccabeus*, 153
Hanna von Liechtenstein, Princess, 195
Hanslick, Eduard, 254
Harding, Bertita, 196; *Golden Fleece*, 314; *Imperial Twilight*, 314–15, 319–20, 321, 325; *Phantom Crown*, 314
harps, in orchestration of *Die Frau ohne Schatten*, 23, *23*, 38, 51, 55, 73, 86, 87, 100, 102, 125, 140, 141, 158, *159*, 160, 177, *178*, 179, 204, 206, 223, 244, 245, 246
Hauptmann, Gerhart, 235
Haydn, Joseph: "Gott erhalte," 49, 153, 163, 180, 315, 356, 361; as representative of Austrian style, 171, 190
Healy, Maureen, 168
Helena, Saint, 267–69. *See also* St. Helena (island)
Henry (Henri), Count de Chambord, 20
Herron, George, 194–95
Hildebrandt, Johann Lucas von, 82, 95
Hindenburg, Paul von, 186, 317
Hirohito, Emperor of Japan, 354, 358
Hitler, Adolf: and Anschluss, 318, 324–25; and art, 16, 310; hatred of Habsburgs, 317–18, 335; and opera, 291, 328; rise to power in Germany, 301, 317; and Strauss, 328; in Vienna, 16, 77
Höbling, Franz, 154

Hoffmann, E. T. A., 15, 259
Hofmann, Isaak Löw, 16
Hofmannsthal, Franz von, 83, 302–3
Hofmannsthal, Gertrud (Gerty) von, 83, 121, 157, 304, 311, 326
Hofmannsthal, Hugo von, *47*; aestheticism, 18, 48, 49, 63, 79, 92, 164, 165, 233, 234, 247; anti-Semitic views, 77, 191–92; on Austrian culture and spirit, 120–21, 122, 162–63, 170–71, 192–93, 210–12, 231, 271–72, 292, 299; birthday celebrations, 293–94, 295; civil merit award, 163, 198; collaboration dynamics with Strauss, 167–69, 259–60, 295; collaborations with Strauss, overview, 1–2, 6; crisis of language ("Chandos Letter"), 33–34, 35, 72, 78, 128; death and burial, 303, 364–65; death of father, 165–66; discovery as poetic genius, 17–19; and fairy tale literary tradition, 15–16; family background, 16–17, 63, 192, 272, 294, 310; on Habsburg monarchy, 217–18; on Jeritza, 235–36, 249–51; and *Kunstpolitik* ("art politics"), 240–41; on marriage, 157; military service, as propaganda writer, 119–21, 122–23, 128–29, 134, 136, 147–48, 150–52; military service, in Galicia, 48–49, 52; Nobel Prize nominations, 235, 294; political concerns, 55, 77–78; publication series on Austria-Hungary literature ("Austrian Library"), 162–63, 258, 294, 299; and Salzburg Festival, 7, 211–12, 271–72, 273; scholarship on, 7–8. *See also* Strauss-Hofmannsthal correspondence
– works: "Chandos Letter," 33–34, 35, 72, 78, 128; *The Death of Titian*, 79; *Die Frau ohne Schatten* (prose version), 79, 234–35; *Jedermann*, 271, 272; *Josephslegende* (with Strauss and Kessler), 55, 56, 76, 94, 130, 284; *Der Schwierige*, 193; "Tale of the 672nd Night," 15–16. See also *Die ägyptische Helena*; *Arabella*; *Ariadne auf Naxos*; *Elektra*; *Die Frau ohne Schatten*; *Der Rosenkavalier*
Hofmannsthal, Petronilla von (Rhò), 63

Hofmannsthal, Raimund von, 302, 311
Hohenberg, Georg von, 359
Holtzendorff, Henning von, 186
Holy Thursday, washing of feet, 285–86
Honegger, Arthur, *Antigone*, 298
Hoover, J. Edgar, 341
Horthy, Miklós, 269–70, 276, 278
Hötzendorf, Conrad von, 186, 187
Hülsen-Haeseler, Georg von, 137
humanitarian aid and fundraising events, wartime, 130, 153, 187–89, 193, 195–96, 201, 207–8, 286, 344
Humperdinck, Engelbert, *Hänsel und Gretel*, 221
Hungary: in dual monarchy Austria-Hungary, 13, 114, 182–83; independence from Austria-Hungary, 213, 216; Budapest visit of Karl and Zita, 114-15, 116; coronation of Karl and Zita, 182–83; restoration attempts of Karl and Zita, 275–76, 278–79; postwar government transformations, 241, 269–70; postwar status of Habsburgs in, 216, 270, 275–76, 278–79, 315–18; Soviet occupation of, 344; and Treaty of Trianon, 269, 270, 276. *See also* Habsburg monarchy
Hüni-Mihacsek, Felicie, 249
hunting: Habsburg interest in, 20, 42, 59, *91*, 94–95; imagery in *Die Frau ohne Schatten*, 20, 22–23, *91*

Ilitsch, Daniza, 329
Imperial Court Theater (Austria), 210, 211
imperial politics and culture: afterlives of emperors and empresses, 266–69, 274–75, 314, 319–21, 364; in landscape of prewar Europe, 2–4; postwar dismantling of, 7, 201, 216–18, 280; Zita's premonitions about, 35–37, 43, 95–96, 114. *See also* Habsburg monarchy
India, in British empire, 4
Industriellenball, 82
International Eucharistic Congress, Vienna (1912), 50
Italy: Austrian alliance interests, 310, 322, 326; and Ethiopia, 320; fascism in, 292,

320; performances of *Die Frau ohne Schatten* in, 284–85, 309–10, 326–28, 329; Strauss-Hofmannsthal trip to, 63–64; in WWI, 147, 167, 191, 213, 216. *See also* Milan; Mussolini

Janáček, Leoš, *Jenufa*, 195
Janik, Allan, 33
Janissaries, 200
Japan, 82, 354, 358
Jerger, Alfred, 299
Jeritza, Maria: in *Die ägyptische Helena*, 296–98, 300; in *Ariadne auf Naxos*, 57, 175, 200, 236, 270, 286, 287, 288; on bird song, 165; career in opera, overview, 8; in *Cavalleria Rusticana*, 286; death of, 356, 363; in *Die Frau ohne Schatten*, 5, 58, 235–36, 241, 249–51, 250, 258, 263, 270, 271; in *Elektra*, 90; financial support for Strauss, 356; in *Die Fledermaus*, 57, 250, 275, 346; in *The Flying Dutchman*, 209; fundraising concerts, 153, 195–96; in *Jenufa*, 195; in *La Juive*, 236, 286; as Kammersängerin, 196; in *Lohengrin*, 83, 209, 236, 270, 286; at the Met, 277, 281, 286, 346, 351; in *Die Modebaronin*, 195–96; personal life, *297*, 306–7, 345; in *Der Rosenkavalier*, 277; in *Salome*, 209, 236, 270, 286, 306, 349; in *Tannhäuser*, 286; in *Tosca*, 270, 286, 287, 349; in *Die tote Stadt*, 275, 277, 281, 286, 287; in *Turandot*, 296, *297*; in *Die Walküre*, 286
Jews: and Anschluss, 325, 358; anti-Semitism, 77, 191–92, 237, 272, 292, 294, 307–8; in Hofmannsthal's family background, 16–17, 63, 156, 192, 272, 294, 310; refugees (WWI), 153–54; refugees from Nazi Europe, 311, 326, 329, 335, 341, 343–44; in Strauss's family, 301, 311, 345
John Paul II, Pope, 183, 337, 356–57
Joseph August, Archduke of Austria, 148
Josephine de Beauharnais, Empress of the French, 268, 269, 320
Juan Carlos, King of Spain, 290, 355

Juarez (film), 314
Juárez, Benito, 267
July Crisis (1914), 99, 100, 110, 113–14, 129
Justinian I, Byzantine Emperor, 268

Kaiserin Elisabeth von Österreich (film), 275
Kaiser-Karl-Gebetsliga (Emperor Karl League of Prayer), 285–86, 291, 347
Kálmán, Emmerich: *Csárdásfürstin*, 170; *Kaiserin Josephine*, 320
Kapuzinergruft, Vienna, 96, 125, 243, 283, 315, 343, 356, 359, 362–63
Karajan, Herbert von, 350, 358–59
Karl I, Emperor of Austria and King of Hungary: accession and coronation as Emperor and King, 176, 180, 182–83, *184*; amnesty for prisoners, 197; beatification of, 183, 285, 291, 336, 337, 347, 355, 357; birthday celebrations, 208, 209; childhood and youth, 20, 21; in Constantinople, 199–200, 280–81; death and burial on Madeira, 4, 282–83, 355, 359; Easter Holy Thursday tradition, 285–86; in exile, 7, 227–30, 246, 279–82; honeymoon, 40–41; hunting interests, 20, 94, 95; and July Crisis, 113–14; in line of succession, 42–43, 95–96, 97; military service, 45–46, 48, 50, 115, 116, 168, *185*; patronage of court opera, 8, 196; peace negotiations, 183–86, 190, 194–95, 197; postwar withdrawal from political life, 216–18, 228–30, 284; postwar restoration attempts as King of Hungary, 270, 275–76, 278–79; titles, 182; wedding, 2, 27–29, *28*; and Zita's imperial premonitions, 35–37
Karl Ludwig, Archduke of Austria (father of Franz Ferdinand), 42, 58, 96
Karl Ludwig, Archduke of Austria (son of Karl and Zita), 196–97, 341
Károlyi, Mihály, 216
Karpath, Ludwig, 259–63
Kautsky, Hans, 234, 236, 237, 264, 344
Kautsky, Karl, 234, 236
Kennedy, Michael, 294
Kerssenbrock, Therese von, 330

Kessler, Harry, 16; *Josephslegende* (with Hofmannsthal and Strauss), 55, 56, 76, 94, 130, 284
Key, Ellen, "Century of the Child," 187–88
Kiurina, Berta, 236, 275, 276, 287
Kleiber, Erich, 305, 347
klezmer music, 156
Klimt, Gustav, 35, 148, 196, 217, 239, 362; *Beethoven Frieze*, 164; *Judith and the Head of Holofernes*, 93
Klosterneuburg Monastery, Austria, 359–60
Knappertsbusch, Hans, 305, 312, 325
Kojun, Empress of Japan, 354
Kokoschka, Oskar, 150, 239
Kolomiya, Galicia, 49, 50
Konetzni, Anny, 326, 343
Konetzni, Hilde, 326, 342, 343
König, Franz, 355
Korngold, Erich, 233, 277–78, 314, 326; *The Miracle of Heliane*, 298, 307; *The Snowman*, 30; *Die tote Stadt*, 248, 275, 277, 281, 286, 287; "Empress Zita Hymn," 2, 180–82, *181*, 189, 193, 195, 198, 236
Korngold, Julius, 30, 175, 233, 247–54, 262, 300
Kral, Franziska, 282–83
Kralik, Heinrich, 154, 257–59, 294, 350
Kralik, Richard, 258, 294; "An Polen," 154
Kraus, Karl, 236, 294; *Die Fackel*, 132, 144; *The Last Days of Mankind*, 169, 257
Krause, Otto, 311, 312
Krauss, Clemens, 305–6, 307, 308, 309, 312, 328, 349
Kreisler, Fritz, *Sissy*, 320
Krenek, Ernst, *Jonny spielt auf*, 291, 298
Kristallnacht (1938), 326
Kumar, Krishan, 4
Kun, Béla, 241, 269
Kunsthistorisches Museum, Vienna, 266
Kurz, Selma, 175

Lammasch, Heinrich, 194–95, 216, 218
Landesmutter role, for Zita, 182, 187, 189, 224
Lansing, Robert, 199

La Scala, 296, 329
leather shop, of Leiser Erber, 120, *238*, 255, 308, *309*, 326, *327*, 335
Lehár, Anton, 278, 320
Lehár, Franz, 28, 31, 54, 319; *Merry Widow*, 320
Lehmann, Lilli, 291
Lehmann, Lotte: in *Ariadne auf Naxos*, 175, 270; career in opera, overview, 8; death of, 354, 363; in *Die Frau ohne Schatten*, 5, 66, 236, 240, 241, 251, *252*, 258, 270, 271, 306, 307–8; in *Fidelio*, 312, 349; fundraising concerts, 189; in *Die Meistersinger*, 312; at the Met, 311–12, 326, 344, 351; personal life, 306–7, 311; in *Der Rosenkavalier*, 291, 312, 320, 326, 344; in *Tannhäuser*, 209
Leinsdorf, Erich, 329
Lekeitio, Spain, 290, 291, 294, *313*, 321
Lengyel, Emil, 318–19
Lenin, Vladimir, 191
Leopold I, Holy Roman Emperor, 25, 26, 27
Liebknecht, Karl, 236
Life Magazine, 339–40
Loos, Adolf, 45, 257
Looshaus, Michaelerplatz, Vienna, 45
Louis the Pious, Holy Roman Emperor, 26
Louis XIV, King of France, 2, 25, 31, 121
Louis, Prince of Bourbon-Parma, 322
Lubrich, Fritz, "Heil Kaiser dir," 131
Ludendorff, Erich, 186
Ludwig, Siegfried, 360
Lueger, Karl, 77, 191
Lusitania (ship), 133, 135
Luxembourg, 348
Luxemburg, Rosa, 236
Lviv, Galicia, 50, 116, 144, 152, *215*, 256

Madeira, 281–82, 283–84, 288, 355, 359
Mahler, Alma, 14, 60, 149, 239
Mahler, Gustav, 34–35, 168, 262; *Kindertotenlieder*, 60; "Symphony of a Thousand," 35
Malta, 348
Manowarda, Josef von, 257, 291, 306–7, 309, 328

Margarita Teresa of Spain, Holy Roman Empress, 25–26, 27
Maria Annunziata, Archduchess of Austria, 21
Maria Antónia, Infanta of Portugal (mother of Zita), 187, 330, 348
Maria Francesca, Princess of Savoy, 322
Maria Josepha of Saxony, Archduchess of Austria (mother of Karl I), 28, 343
Maria Theresa, Empress of Austria: historic importance of, 14, 15, 56, 134, 190, 301; Hofmannsthal on, 120, 134, 163, 190, 301; imperial afterlife of, 266, 314; in Kapuzinergruft, 356; portraits of, 133, 189; reign as period of *Der Rosenkavalier*, 6, 30, 134; Theresianum school established by, 187
Maria Zita Gradowska, Sister, 337
Marie Antoinette, Queen of France, 14, 198, 216
Marie Louise, Empress of the French, Duchess of Parma, 268, 269, 363
Marie Valerie, Archduchess of Austria, 130
Marie von Thurn und Taxis, Princess, 249–50
Marinuzzi, Gino, 328, 329
Marschallin (Marie Thérèse von Werdenberg), in *Der Rosenkavalier*: as character 14, 111, 172, 244, 264, 293, 295, 302, 303; Lehmann as, 252, 312, 320, 326, 344; as repertory soprano role, 249, 273, 291, 311, 326, 343
Marshall Plan, 344
Mary of Teck, Queen of England, Empress of India, 4
Masaryk, Jan, 333
Masaryk, Tomáš, 213, 333
Mascagni, Pietro, *Cavalleria Rusticana*, 286
Massine, Leonid, 94, 145
Maximilian, Duke of Hohenberg, 59, 324
Maximilian I, Emperor of Mexico, 266–67, 314, 363
Mayerling, 42, 306, 308, 356
Mayr, Richard: as Barak in *Die Frau ohne Schatten*, 67, 90, 240, 251, 256, 270, 294; as Baron Ochs in *Der Rosenkavalier*, 30, 67, 90, 231, 240, 312; fundraising concerts, 153; in *Parsifal*, 286; in *Die tote Stadt*, 275
Mehmed V, Ottoman Sultan, 2
Mehmed VI, Ottoman Sultan, 280–81
Melchior, Lauritz, 312
melodrama (*melologo*), 204–6
Metastasio, Pietro, 56
Metropolitan Opera, New York: Böhm at, 350–51; Caruso at, 274, 351; Jeritza at, 277, 281, 286, 346, 351; Lehmann at, 311–12, 326, 344, 351; performances of Strauss-Hofmannsthal collaborations, 274, 277, 344, 346, 350, 351–52, 353; performances of *Turandot*, 296; Stevens at, 326; Wallerstein at, 329
Meyerbeer, Giacomo, 77, 211
Meytens, Martin, 133
Milan, Italy, 30, 63, 64, 296, 320, 329
Mildenburg, Anna, 231–32, 240–41
modernism: architecture, 45, 257; ballet, 55, 60; music, 34, 35, 59–60, 149; and neo-Romanticism, 307; operatic modernism, 149, 298; Sezession movement, 35, 164, 196, 239
Moissi, Alexander, 272
Molière, *Le bourgeois gentilhomme*, as frame for *Ariadne auf Naxos*, 31, 57, 71, 75, 166, 175
Möller, Marx, "Dem alten Kaiser," 154
Montenegro, 57
Moralt, Rudolf, 328
motherhood: democratized cult of, 95; and *Landesmutter* role, for Zita, 182, 187, 189, 224; nursing, 83; renunciation of, in *Die Frau ohne Schatten*, 98, 99, 100–102, *101*, 142, 253; and Solomonic rivalry, 32, 138, 143, 156. *See also* children
Mother's Day, as American national holiday, 95
Mozart, Wolfgang Amadeus: *The Abduction from the Seraglio*, 200; *Don Giovanni*, 308, 349, 350; *Marriage of Figaro*, 6, 209, 342; as model for the Composer in *Ariadne* prologue, 167; as representative of Austrian style,

Mozart, Wolfgang Amadeus (*continued*) 171, 190; as represented in ballet-pantomime, 208; Strauss conducting, 210, 211; Symphony no. 39, 231; as *Wunderkind*, 18; *Die Zauberflöte*, 2, 6, 16, 103, 164, 173, 178, 203, 220–21, 224, 248, 249, 271

Munich, Germany, 277, 295, 305, 311, 328

Mussolini, Benito, 292, 310, 320, 322

Muzio, Claudia, 273

Nagl, Franz Xaver, 59

Napoléon, Emperor of the French, 182, 268, 282

Napoléon III, Emperor of the French, 267

nationalism: in Habsburg monarchy, 40, 48; Hofmannsthal's view of, 122, 292

NATO treaty (1949), 347

Naumann, Friedrich, *Mitteleuropa*, 170

Nazi Germany: and Anschluss, 308, 318, 319, 324–26, 358; and anti-Nazi sentiment at World's Fair, 333–34; Austria as supposed victim of Hitler, 349, 357–58, 360; cultural landscape in, 310, 323, 328, 343; declarations of war against, 329; denazification, 342, 345, 346, 350; emigration from, 311, 326, 329, 331, 335, 339–40, 341, 343–44; Holocaust, *309*, 311, 352; occupation of France, 330; occupation of Poland, 329; rise of, 305, 317; Strauss's career during, 310–11, 323, 342–43, 345–46

neo-Romanticism, late Romanticism, in music, 34, 35, 295, 298, 307

Netherlands, 187, 329

Neue Freie Presse (newspaper): on Franz Joseph's hundredth birthday, 315; on *Die Frau ohne Schatten*, 247–50, 251, 253–54, 255, 256, 276, 300, 307; on Habsburg restoration prospects, 284, 316; Hofmannsthal's Austrian Library publication announcement, 162; Hofmannsthal's Maria Theresa article, 190; Hofmannsthal's Warsaw lecture, 171; Hofmannsthal's wartime propaganda articles, 119–21, 128–29, 136, 147–48, 151–52; Jewish readership of, 192; on Karl's death, 283, 284; Korngold (Julius) opera reviews, 30, 175, 247–54, 300, 307; on Lammasch, 216; on Schuschnigg automobile accident, 322; on Zita's birthday celebrations, 187–89, 208

Neues Wiener Tagblatt (newspaper), 259–63

Der Neue Tag (newspaper), 253

Neue Zürcher Zeitung (newspaper), 192

New York City: Lucy and Renee Stier in, 333, 335; World's Fair (1940), 333–34; Zita's arrival in, 331–33, *332*. See also Metropolitan Opera, New York

New York Times (newspaper): Downes's opera reviews, 296, 300; Schonberg's opera reviews, 351–52; on Strauss, 345–46; on WWII, 331; on Zita-Otto Habsburg claims, 282, 315, 316–17, 322, 324, 329, 331, 334–35, 361

New York Times Magazine, 318

New Zealand, 141

Nicholas II, Tsar of Russia, 2, 7, 64, 141, 201, 268

Nickich family (John, Rose, Vera), 333

Nijinsky, Vaslav, 55, 56, 60, 64

Nilsson, Birgit, 351, 354

Nossa Senhora do Monte, Madeira, 281, 283–84

nostalgia: Habsburg, 275, 279, 281, 283, 299, 316, 320, 343, 356, 361, 365; musical, 136, 244, 262, 275, 281, 320, 343, 345; for world before war, 115, 129, 262, 275

Nuremberg, Germany, 103, 293

Nuremberg Laws, 310

Nuremberg Trials (1945–1946), 350

The Nurse, in *Die Frau ohne Schatten*: as character, *84*, 85, 89, 99, 139, 258; Mephistophelean, *84*, 85, 86, 89, *101*, 258; punishment of, 201–3; relationship with Empress, 85, 86, 88, 177–78; tempting of Dyer's Wife, 86–88, 100–102

Oestvig, Karl Aagard: in *Ariadne auf Naxos*, 240, 270, 287; in *Die Frau ohne Schatten*, 189, 240, 251, 257, 263, 277, 287,

Index   429

291; in *Lohengrin*, 275; in *Parsifal*, 286; in *Die tote Stadt*, 275
O'Neill, Eugene, *The Emperor Jones*, 274, 320
orientalism, 6, 41, 52–53, 55, 200, 237, 239, 251, 280, 301, 328
Orlando, Vittorio Emanuele. *See* Paris Peace Conference
Österreichische Rundschau (journal), 120
Otto, Archduke of Austria (father of Karl I), 42, 343
Otto von Habsburg (son of Karl and Zita): birth, 50, 58; education, 304, 315; and Franz Joseph, 58, 59, 117; Hungarian coronation, 183, *184*; imperial and monarchy claims, 218, 284, 290, 304, 315–18, 319, 321, 322, 323–25, 329, 340–41; political service in European Parliament, 358; return to Austria, 353; in United States, *332*, 334, 339, 340; wedding, 347–48; and Zita Children's Day, 188, *188*
Ottoman Empire, 2, 41, 57, 77, 96, 120, 129, 141, 199–200, 280–81

Pacetti, Iva, 329
Palisa, Johann, 29
Pan-European Movement, 358
Pannwitz, Rudolf, 264; *The Crisis of European Culture*, 192
Paris Peace Conference (1919), 58, 94, 233, 247
Parma, Duchy of, 2, 19, 269. *See also* Bourbon-Parma dynasty
Parma, Princess of (Proust), 21
patriotism, Austrian and Habsburg, 15, 46, 114, 121, 122–23, 131–32, 152, 153, 154, 161, 175, 187, 198, 266, 292, 359; Hofmannsthal's writings, 120, 136, 147–48, 151, 162–63, 299; Korngold's hymn, 2, 180, *181*, 195
Pauly, Rose, 293, 307–8, 309, 326, 328
Pedro II, Emperor of Brazil, 274
Peham, Heinrich, 58, 82, 133, 242, 275
Pekel, Heinrich, "1914," 154
Penfield, Frederic, 134–35

Perrault, Charles, 15
Pétain, Philippe, 330
Piffl, Friedrich Gustav, 211
Pirandello, Luigi, *Enrico IV*, 274, 320
Pirchoff-Manowarda, Nelly, 291, 307
Pius X, Pope, 42–43, 95
Pius XI, Pope, 324
Pius XII, Pope, 347
Poland: Hofmannsthal and, 144, 151, 155, 156, 158, 159, 160, 170, 171; independence of, 100; occupation of (WWI), 151–52, 170–71; occupation of (WWII), 329. *See also* Galicia
Ponselle, Rosa, 274, 351
Portugal, 198, 269, 274, 330, 331, *332*. *See also* Madeira
Potocki, Andrzej, 48
Prawy, Marcel, 349
Preetorius, Emil, 349
Przemyśl, siege of, 116, 128, 144, 153
Primo de Rivera, Miguel, 290
Princip, Gavrilo, 43, 54, 57, 77, 94, 96, 124
The Private Lives of Elizabeth and Essex (film), 182
propaganda articles, Hofmannsthal's, 119–21, 122–23, 128–29, 134, 136, 147–48, 151–52
Proust, Marcel, 21
Pruscha, Viktor, 328
Prussian culture (*vs*. Austrian), 169, 193
psychoanalysis, 33, 88, 168, 192, 251, 259–60, 302. *See also* Freud, Sigmund
Puccini, Giacomo, 75, 211; *La Bohème*, 83; *Madama Butterfly*, 45; *Tosca*, 45, 196, 270, 286, 287; *Turandot*, 16, 296, 298
putti, 220–223
Puyi, Qing Emperor, 4

Quebec, Canada, 340, 344

Raisa, Rosa, 296
Ralf, Torsten, 342
Raphael, *Sistine Madonna*, 220
Ravel, Maurice, 149
Red Cross, 130
Redl, Alfred, 72, 74, 75, 96

Redlich, Joseph, 15, 134
Reform Advocate (journal), 153
refugees: WWI, 152–54, 195; WWII, 311, 326, 329, 331, 335, 339–40, 341, 343–44
Regina von Habsburg, Archduchess of Austria, 347
Reichsmusikkammer (Reich Music Chamber), 310, 323
Reichspost (newspaper), 322–23
Reinhardt, Max, 30, 46, 48, 57, 122, 123, 212, 211, 271, 272, 292
Renner, Karl, 228–29, 247, 253, 344
Republic of Austria. *See* Austria, Republic of
Rethberg, Elisabeth, 296, 300
Reymont, Władysław, *Peasants*, 294
Ringstraße, Vienna, 264–65
Robert, Archduke of Austria (son of Karl and Zita), 130, 133, 282, 334
Robert of Bourbon-Parma, Duke, 19–20
Robeson, Paul, 320
Roller, Alfred: collaborations with Mahler, 34–35; costume designs for *Die Frau ohne Schatten*, 84, 85, 91, 93, 250, 252; stage and costume designs for *Der Rosenkavalier*, 30, 35, 344; stage designs for *Die Frau ohne Schatten*, 61, 94, 140, 232, 233, 235, 239, 241, 253, 257, 262, 263–64, 271; stage designs for *Jedermann*, 271; stage designs for *Parsifal*, 286, 310; stage designs for *Die Zauberflöte*, 271
Roman, Stella, 329
Romania, 175, 269
Roosevelt, Eleanor, 340, 341
Roosevelt, Franklin, 337, 339, 340, 341–42
Rosé, Arnold, 153, 208, 262
Der Rosenkavalier (Strauss and Hofmannsthal): *Arabella* comparison, 302, 303; critical reception, 30–31, 248, 346; cross-dressing in, 44; donation of autograph score, 292; *Die Frau ohne Schatten* comparison, 135, 136, 167, 172–73, 203, 244, 254; Hofmannsthal's criticism of, 170; as nostalgic, 136, 244, 320, 343; performances, 171, 186–87, 194, 209, 231, 273, 274, 277, 291, 296, 308, 310, 312, 320, 325–26, 328, 329, 343, 346, 350, 361; premiere, 1, 30, 46; Schalk as conductor, 90; sentimentality of, 172, 173; spirit of Maria Theresa and Vienna in, 6, 14, 15, 30, 31, 134, 301; stage and costume designs, 30, 35, 344; Strauss in 1945, 345
Rosenkavalier trio, 135, 136, 172, 173, 174, 203, 244, 303, 365
Roth, Joseph, "The Bust of the Emperor," 146
Royalston, Massachusetts, 334-35
Rudolf, Archduke of Austria (son of Karl and Zita), 242, 339
Rudolf, Crown Prince of Austria, 41–42, 83, 306, 356. *See also* Mayerling
Russia: declaration of war against (WWI), 114; eastern front developments (WWI), 116, 128, 144, 151, 170; as empire, 2, 64, 191; interest in Galician border, 50, 72; interest in southeastern Europe, 57, 59; Nicholas and Alexandra, 2, 7, 64, 141, 191, 201, 268, *313*; peace negotiations (WWI), 193; postwar blockade, 248; Revolution, 191, 201; Romanov tricentennial, 64; Soviet collapse, 358; Soviet occupations after WWII, 344, 348
Rysanek, Leonie, 349, 351, 353, 354, 356
Rysanek, Lotte, 354

Salazar, António, 330
Salome (Strauss): Downes on, 346; eroticism of, 60, 209; Jeritza in, 209, 236, 270, 286, 306, 349; performances, 292, 293; premiere, 5; Strauss in 1945, 345
Salzburg Festival, 271–72, 273, 292, 308, 311, 312, 320, 342, 353, 359
Salzburg and the Trapp family, *The Sound of Music*, 312, 313, 352
San Francisco Opera, 353, 354
Sarajevo, 41, 54, 96. *See also* Franz Ferdinand, Archduke of Austria: assassination of
Schalk, Franz: conducting *Die Frau ohne Schatten*, 90, 140, 241, 258, 291; as

conductor, 30, 90, 140, 175, 209, 241, 258, 275, 286, 291; fundraising concerts, 153; joint musical directorship of Vienna Opera with Strauss, 209, 212, 230, 294–95
Schiele, Egon, 217, 239
Schlesinger, Hans, 157
Schloss Frohsdorf, Austria, 20, 115
Schloss Hetzendorf, Austria, 82, 95, 114, 323
Schloss Schwarzau, Austria, 20, 27, 29, 45, 116
Schloss Wartholz, Austria, 45, 50, 58, 59, 96
Schnitzler, Arthur, 18, 100, 134, 242, 248; *Anatol*, 19; *Professor Bernhardi*, 58
Schoenberg, Arnold, 59–60, 149, 254, 326; *Pierrot Lunaire*, 205; "six little piano pieces," 35; on Strauss, 60
Schonberg, Harold, 351–52
Schönbrunn Palace, Austria, 115, 116, 117–19, 140, 168, 216–17
Schorske, Carl, 7, 18, 77, 164
Schuschnigg, Herma, 322
Schuschnigg, Kurt, 319, 322, 324–25
Second Balkan War (1912), 57, 76–77
Second Vienna School, 60. *See also* Berg, Alban; Schoenberg, Arnold; Webern, Anton
Seebach, Nikolaus von, 137
Serafin, Tullio, 273
Serbia: in Balkan Wars, 57, 76–77; declaration of war against (WWI), 113–14; eastern front developments (WWI), 128; militants in, 43, 54, 77; ultimatum to, 99, 100, 110, 113, 129
Sezession movement, 35, 164, 196, 239. *See also* Klimt, Gustav; Roller, Alfred
silver rose symbolism, 27, 326
Sixtus, Prince of Bourbon-Parma: as Adelheid's godfather, 82; death of, 322; peace negotiations (WWI), 185–86, 187, 189–90, 197; royalist perspective on WWI, 115–16
Slezak, Leo, 130, 189, 198, 236
Smetana, Bedřich, *Dalibor*, 209

socioeconomic class relations, in Vienna, 77, 119–20, 254–55, 256–57, 308, 323
Solomonic judgment, in *Die Frau ohne Schatten*, 32, 138, 143, 156, 176–77, 204–6
Solti, Georg, 365
Sophie, Duchess of Hohenberg (wife of Franz Ferdinand), 42, 58–59, 95–97, 124
The Sound of Music (Broadway musical and film), 312, 352. *See also* Trapp Family Singers
Sousa Mendes, Aristides de, 330
South America, 151, 272–74, 292, 337, 347
Spain, Zita's exile in, 288–89, 290, 304
Spanish Civil War, 290
Spanish flu, 217
Spanish Habsburgs, 25–26
spectacles: baroque opera, 25–27, 56, 63; *Die Frau ohne Schatten* as, 25, 56–57, 63, 296, 351; Hungarian coronation as, 183, *184*; imperial weddings, 27–29; *Turandot* as, 296, *297*
Stalin, Joseph, 344, 348
Starhemberg, Ernst Rüdiger, 324
St. Cecilia Benedictine convent, Solesmes, France, 291, 313, 336, 348
Steinberg, Michael, 7, 92, 272
Stephanie of Belgium, 41–42; *Ich sollte Kaiserin werden*, 42
Stevens, Risë, 326
St. Helena (island), 268–69, 282
Stier, Lucy (Erber), 49–50, 237, *238*, 308, 309, 326, *327*, 333, 335, 348, 354
Stier, Martin (Moses), *238*, 308–9, 326, *327*, 333
Stier, Renee, 308, 326, *327*, 333, 335, 352
St. Johannes-Stift, Zizers, Switzerland, 348
Strauss, Alice (Grab von Hermannswörth), 301, 311
Strauss, Franz (Bubi), 65, 200, 301
Strauss, Johann, I, "Radetzky March," 46
Strauss, Johann, II, 2, 31, 54, 153, 319, 320; "Blue Danube Waltz," 130, 195; *Die Fledermaus*, 57, 275, 346; *The Gypsy Baron*, 28; *Wiener Blut*, 167
Strauss, Pauline, 32, 64–66, 69, 110–11, 157, 173

Strauss, Richard, 47; birthday celebrations, 294, 308, 310, 328; collaboration dynamics with Hofmannsthal, 167–69, 259–60, 295; collaborations with Hofmannsthal, overview, 1–2, 6; as conductor, 65, 166, 221, 270, 271, 275, 284, 294; correspondence with Pauline, 32, 64–65, 66, 69; death and burial, 345, 364–65; on *Die Frau ohne Schatten* as "problem child," 6, 8, 166; left-handed piano concerto, 149; marriage to Pauline, 65-66; and modernism, 34, 35, 60, 307; musical directorship of Vienna Opera, 209, 212, 230, 262, 291, 294–95; under Nazi regime, 310–11, 323, 342–43, 345–46; patriotic compositions, 153, 195; presidency of Reichsmusikkammer, 310, 323; tours in South America, 272–74, 292
— works: "Aus Italien," 63; "Cäcilie," 130, 189, 236; *Capriccio*, 311; *Daphne*, 342; *Death and Transfiguration*, 1, 231; *Don Juan*, 1; *Don Quixote*, 1; *Festmusik der Stadt Wien*, 343; *Feuersnot*, 284; *Friedenstag*, 311, 328; *Ein Heldenleben*, 168; *Intermezzo*, 65, 66, 200; *Josephslegende* (with Hofmannsthal and Kessler), 55, 56, 76, 94, 130, 284; *Die Liebe der Danae*, 311; "Morgen," 189, 236; *Schlagobers*, 259, 294; *Die schweigsame Frau* (with Zweig), 311, 342; "September," 297, 356; *Thus Spoke Zarathustra*, 1. See also *Die ägyptische Helena*; *Arabella*; *Ariadne auf Naxos*; *Elektra*; *Die Frau ohne Schatten*; *Der Rosenkavalier*; *Salome*
Strauss-Hofmannsthal correspondence: publication of, 295; on *Die ägyptische Helena*, 292–93, 295–98, 300, 302; on *Arabella*, 299, 300, 301, 302, 303–4; on *Ariadne auf Naxos*, 43–44, 167, 171–72, 187, 288; on collaboration dynamics, 167–69; on *Der Rosenkavalier*, 170, 171, 172–73, 186–87; on *Die Frau ohne Schatten*, music in, 80, 90–92, 99, 101–2, 109–11, 124, 163–65, 171–74, 190, 204–5; on *Die Frau ohne Schatten*, production and performances of, 166–67, 191, 194, 230–31, 232, 233–34, 235–41, 242–43, 263–64, 270–71, 284–85; on *Die Frau ohne Schatten*, revisions to, 89, 90, 92, 97–100, 136–39; on *Die Frau ohne Schatten*, writing progress, 32–33, 46–48, 54, 55–56, 60, 63–64, 71–76, 79–80, 110, 121–22, 123, 128, 129, 133, 135–36, 154–56; on South America, 273–74; thoughts on relation of poetry to opera, 44–45, 61–62, 75, 298; on Vienna Opera and cultural revival, 209–12, 230, 231, 233; on wartime concerns, 105, 121, 122–23, 129, 130–32
Stravinsky, Igor: *Oedipus Rex*, 298; *Rite of Spring*, 60
Strutt, Edward Lisle, 229
St. Stephen's Cathedral, Vienna, 355, 360–61
Stürgkh, Karl von, 134
Stuttgart, Germany, 293, 296
submarine warfare (WWI), 132–33, 134, 186
Switzerland: Karl-Zita exile in, 7, 227–30, 282, 348; as neutral in wartime, 187, 192, 227
Szczepanowski, Stanisław, *Nędza Galicji w cyfrach* (*The Misery of Galicia in Statistics*), 48
Szell, George, 329

Taddei, Giuseppe, 328
Taglicht, Israel, 187, 325
Tchaikovsky, Pyotr Ilyich, *The Nutcracker*, 15
Thälmann, Ernst, 317
Theodora, Byzantine Empress, 268
Third Reich. *See* Nazi Germany
Thousand and One Nights, 15, 16, 53, 148
Tibbett, Lawrence, 320–21
Tietjen, Heinz, 349
Time Magazine, 312
Tisza, István, 114
Titanic (ship), 54
Tokyo, Japan, 354
Toscanini, Arturo, 296, 310, 312

totem animals, 81–82
Toulmin, Stephen, 33
Trakl, Georg, 149–50; "Evening," 150; "Grodek," 150
Trapp, Georg von, 312
Trapp, Maria von, 312, 313, 357
Trapp Family Singers, 312, 313, 326, 334, 339–40, 352
Treaty of Sèvres (1920), 280, 281
Treaty of Saint-Germain-en-Laye (1919), 241, 242, 261, 269, 270
Treaty of Trianon (1920), 269, 270, 276
Treaty of Versailles (1919), 239, 248, 282
Tuxedo Park, New York, 344, 347
Twain, Mark, 13–14

uncanny (*unheimlich*) effects, 258, 259, 260, 261
Unification or Death (Black Hand), 43, 54, 94
United States: Alien Registration Act (1940), 337, *338*, 339; declarations of war (WWI), 191, 193; Fourteen Points, 194–95; and *Lusitania*, 133, 135; neutrality in WWI, 134–35; press interest in Habsburg restoration, 316–17, 318, 319, 329, 331, 334; Zita's exile in, 331–33, *332*, 334–35, 337–38, *338*, 339, 344. *See also* New York
University of Vienna, 45, 58
Uribarren Palace, Lekeitio, Biscay, 290
Ursuleac, Viorica, 305–6, 307–8, 309, 311, 312, 328

Velázquez, Diego, *Las Meninas*, 25–26
Venice, Italy, 64, 76, 79, 309–10
Verdi, Giuseppe: *Aida*, 277; *La Forza del Destino*, 274
Verona, Italy, 64
Vetsera, Mary, Baroness, 42, 306
Victoria, Queen of England, 83
Vienna, Austria: anti-Semitism in, 77, 191–92; architecture in, 45; beauty of, 128–29; craftsmen, 119–20, 255, 306, crisis of language in, 33, 35; cult of aestheticism in, 18, 49, 164; cultural prestige, 120, 262, 263, 343; Galician refugees in, 152–54, 195; Hitler's view of, 16; postwar plundering, 217; representation in *Der Rosenkavalier*, 15, 30, 31; Ringstraße, 264–65; St. Stephen's Cathedral, 355, 360–61; socioeconomic class relations, 77, 119–20, 254–55, 256–57, 308, 323; Soviet occupation of, 344. *See also* Vienna Opera
Vienna, Congress of (1814–1815), 167
Vienna Opera: and Anschluss, 325; bombing of (WWII), 310, 344, 349; conditions after WWI, 209, 232–33; Jeritza's 1922 return to, 286–87; musical directorship, 34–35, 209–12, 230, 262, 291, 294–95, 328, 350; performances of *Die Frau ohne Schatten*, in 1920s, 270, 271, 276, 277, 287, 291, 293, 294, 299; performances of *Die Frau ohne Schatten*, in 1930s, 305–6, 307–8, 309–10, 316, 320, 328–29; performances of *Die Frau ohne Schatten*, during WWII, 310, 328–29, 342–43, 350; performances of *Die Frau ohne Schatten*, after WWII, 349–50, 354, 355; premiere of *Die Frau ohne Schatten*, 247–63; restoration and reopening after WWII, 348–49; and site selection for premiere of *Die Frau ohne Schatten*, 166–67, 191, 230–31, 232. *See also* Jeritza, Maria; Lehmann, Lotte; Mayr, Richard
Völkischer Beobachter (newspaper), 310
Vossische Zeitung (newspaper), 134, 193
Votivkirche, Vienna, 45, 315
Voyer, Giovanni, 328

Wagner, Cosima, 303
Wagner, Richard, 174, 211, 254; *The Flying Dutchman*, 46, 209; *Karfreitagszauber*, 286; *Lohengrin*, 83, 120, 139, 146, 153, 189, 270, 275, 286; *Mein Leben*, 32; *Die Meistersinger*, 103, 312; *Parsifal*, 87, 286, 310; *Rienzi*, 231; *Der Ring des Nibelungen*, 143; *Siegfried*, 125, 236; *Tannhäuser*, 65, 209, 286; *Tristan und Isolde*, 35, 75, 85, 231–32, 308, 351; *Die Walküre*, 286

Waldheim, Kurt, 357, 358, 360
Wallerstein, Lothar, 263, 306, 307, 328–29, 344
Walter, Bruno, 308, 312
waltzes: in *Arabella*, 303-04; in the Nurse's music in *Die Frau ohne Schatten*, 51, 86, 87; in *Der Rosenkavalier*, 30-31, 320; "Zita Waltz," 2, *3*, 28, 31, 59. See also Strauss, Johann, II
watchmen, in *Die Frau ohne Schatten*, trio, 90, 103-04, *104*, 328
Webern, Anton, 60
Weidt, Lucie: in *Die Frau ohne Schatten*, 240, 241, 258, 270, 291, 294, 299; fundraising concerts, 153, 195; in *Jenufa*, 195; in *Parsifal*, 286; in *Der Rosenkavalier*, 291; in *Salome*, 270
Weill, Kurt: *Mahagonny-Songspiel* (with Brecht), 298; *Threepenny Opera* (with Brecht), 301
Weinzierl, Ulrich, 8
Weiskirchner, Richard, 77
Wellesz, Egon, 253
wet nurses, 83, *84*, 85–86
Widows and Orphans Assistance Fund, 130
Wiener Abendpost (newspaper), 257–59
Wiener Allgemeine Zeitung (newspaper), 263
Wiener Werkstätte, 196
Wilde, Oscar, *Salome*, 5
Wilhelm II, Emperor of Germany, 2, 59, 122, 131, 198, 216
Wilson, Woodrow: declaration of war against Germany (WWI), 191; elected president, 58; Fourteen Points, 194–95; and Habsburg empire, 58, 194–95, 199, 342; and Mother's Day, 95; at Paris Peace Conference, 94; stroke, 248; and Wilhelm II, 122
witches and witchcraft, *84*, 85, 99, 102, 139
Wittgenstein, Ludwig, 148; *Tractatus Logico-Philosophicus*, 33
Wittgenstein, Paul, 148–49, 150
Wolf, Hugo, 257
Wolff, Gustav, 315

Wolff, Joseph, 120
World's Fair, New York (1940), 333–34
World War I: declarations of war, 113–14, 147, 175, 191; disillusionment with and condemnation of, 132, 161; eastern front developments, 50, 72, 116, 128, 144, 147, 151–52, 170, 175; food and supply shortages, 168, 232; Franz Ferdinand assassination, 4, 41, 42, 43, 77, 95–97, 364; Gallipoli campaign, 141; Hofmannsthal's propaganda writing, 119–21, 122–23, 128–29, 134, 136, 147–48, 150–52; humanitarian aid and fundraising events, 130, 153, 187–89, 193, 195–96, 201, 207–8, 286; Italian Front developments, 167, 191, 213, 216; musicians and poets in, 148–50; patriotism in Austria-Hungary, 114, 121, 122–23, 131–32, 136, 147–48, 151, 161, 162–63, 180, 187, 195, 198, 266; peace negotiations and treaties, 115, 183–86, 190, 193, 194–95, 197, 239, 242, 247–48, 261, 269, 270; refugees, 152–54, 195; royalist perspective on, 115–16; socioeconomic concerns, 119–20; submarine warfare, 132–33, 134, 186; ultimatum leading to, 99, 100, 110, 113–14, 129; western front developments, 122, 124, 132, 140, 175, 186, 191, 208–9
World War II: Holocaust, *309*, 311, 352; Nazi conquest of Belgium, 329–30; Phoney War, 329; postwar occupations, 344; refugees, 311, 326, 329, 331, 335, 339–40, 341, 343–44; Zita's political efforts in America during, 340-42
Wright brothers, 29

Xavier, Prince of Bourbon-Parma, 115–16, 185–86, 187
Xinhai Chinese Revolution (1911), 4

Yugoslavia, 199, 213, 269, 276

Zeppelin dirigible airships, 29, 59
Zimmer, Christiane (Hofmannsthal), 217, 218, 237, 253–54, 300–301, 302, 311, 312

Zimmer, Heinrich, 301, 311
Zita of Bourbon-Parma, Empress of Austria and Queen of Hungary: accession and coronation as Empress and Queen, 176, 180–83, *184*; birthday celebrations and Zita Children's Day initiative, 187–89, *188*, 198, 208, 223–24, 325; and birthday wishes for Hofmannsthal, 293–94; birth of children, 50, 58, 82, 130, 133, 168–69, 196–97, 224, 242, 275, 288; Bourbon-Parma family, 2, 19–20, 115, 197–98; childhood and youth, 20–21; in Constantinople, 199–200, 280–81; criticism of, 186, 198, 216; death and burial, 4, 358, 359–63, 364; and death of Franz Ferdinand, 95–96, 97; and death of Franz Joseph, 175–76; and death of Karl, 282–83; Easter Holy Thursday tradition, 285–86; in exile, Europe, 7, 227–30, 279–82, 288–89, 290, 304, *313*, 314–15, 329–30; in exile, North America, 331–33, *332*, 334–35, 337–38, *338*, 339, 340, 344; in exile, return to Europe, 348, 355; family background, 19–20, 115; future premonitions, 35–37, 43, 95–96, 114; in Galicia, 48, 49, 50–51, 115, 116; and Habsburg succession, 42–43, 59; honeymoon, 40–41; and July Crisis, 113–14; in Lekeitio, Spain, 290, 291, 294, *313*, 321; on Madeira, 281–82, 283–84, 288; motherhood experience, 83, 95; as oblate, 291, 313–14, 348; at Otto's wedding, 347–48; and Penfield, 134–35; postwar removal from power (1918), 216–18, 228–30, 284; postwar status as Queen of Hungary, 216, 270, 275–76, 278–79; proposed beatification of, 267, 285, 336–39; return to Austria, 355–56; at Steenokkerzeel, Belgium, 304, *313*, 314, 315, 316, 317, 318, 319, 321, 325, 329; support of Otto's restoration, 218, 284, 290, 315–19, 321, 322, 323–25, 340–42; titles, 182, 362; on treaties of Saint-Germain and Trianon, 269; wartime service and concerns (WWI), 116–17, 130, 154, 183, *185*, 186, 193, 201, 207–8, 216, 286, 360; wartime service and concerns (WWII), 340, 341–42, 344–45; wedding, 2, 27–29, *28*
Zweig, Stefan: death of, 273; on Franz Ferdinand assassination, 96–97; on Hofmannsthal's discovery as poetic genius, 17, 18; on Karl-Zita exile, 227–28; military service, 152; and Nazi Germany, 273, 310, 311; on Vienna Opera, 232–33; *Jeremiah*, 187, 257; *Die schweigsame Frau* (with Strauss), 311, 342

The authorized representative in the EU for product safety and compliance is:
Mare Nostrum Group
B.V Doelen 72
4831 GR Breda
The Netherlands

www.ingramcontent.com/pod-product-compliance
Lightning Source LLC
Chambersburg PA
CBHW020827160426
43192CB00007B/547